STP Caribbean Mathematics 3

Second Edition

C Layne MA Dip Ed

Former Headmaster, Harrison College, Barbados
Deputy Headmaster, The Lodge School, Barbados
Mathematics Master, Excelsior School, Jamaica
Mathematics Master, Dominica Grammar School, Dominica
Assistant Registrar, Measurement and Evaluation Department CXC

L Bostock BSc

S Chandler BSc

A Shepherd BSc

E Smith MSc

Stanley Thornes (Publishers) Ltd

First published 1989.
Second edition published in 1997 by
Stanley Thornes (Publishers) Ltd,
Ellenborough House,
Wellington Street,
CHELTENHAM,
GL50 1YW

A catalogue record for this book is available from the British Library.

ISBN 0 7487 3025 7

97 98 99 00 / 10 9 8 7 6 5 4 3 2 1

Illustrations by A & R Nelson, Guyana and Steve Ballinger
Typeset by Tech-Set Ltd, Gateshead, Tyne & Wear, UK
Printed and bound in Great Britain.

CONTENTS

INTRODUCTION

This book has been designed for those of you who are hoping to attempt the highest CXC General Proficiency papers in Mathematics. The book contains a good deal of revision of earlier work which makes it large. As is the case with earlier books there are plenty of straightforward questions and the exercises are divided into three types of question:

The first type, identified by plain numbers, e.g. **12.**, helps you to see if you understand the work. These questions are considered necessary for every chapter you attempt.

The second type, identified by a single underline, e.g. **12.**, are extra, but not harder, questions for quicker workers, for extra practice or for later revision.

The third type, identified by a double underline, e.g. **12.**, are for those of you who manage Type 1 questions fairly easily and therefore need to attempt questions that are a little harder.

Most chapters end with 'mixed exercises'. These will help you revise what you have done, either when you have finished the chapter or at a later date.

Finally a word of advice: when you are doing numerical work, whether with the help of a calculator or not, remember always to ask yourself 'Is my answer a reasonable one for the question that was asked?'

PREFACE

To the Teacher

The general aims of the series are:

(1) to help students to
- attain solid mathematical skills
- connect mathematics to their everyday lives and appreciate its role in the development of our contemporary society
- see the importance of thinking skills in everyday problems
- discover the fun of doing mathematics and reinforce their positive attitudes to it.

(2) to encourage teachers to include historical information about mathematics in their programme.

In writing this three book series the authors attempted to present topics in such a way that students will appreciate the connections in mathematics and be encouraged to see and use mathematics as a means to help make sense in the real world.

Topics from the history of mathematics have been incorporated to ensure that mathematics is not dissociated from its past. This should lead to an increase in the levels of enthusiasm, interest and fascination for mathematics, and should also enrich the teaching of it.

Careful grading of exercises makes the books approachable.

Some suggestions:

(1) Before each lesson give a brief outline of the topic to be covered in the lesson. As examples are given refer back to the outline to show how the example fits into it.

(2) List terms on the chalkboard that you consider new to the students.
Solicit additional words from the class and encourage students to read from the text and make their own vocabulary.
Remember that mathematics is a foreign language. The ability to communicate mathematically must involve the careful use of the correct terminology.

(3) When possible have students construct alternative ways to phrase questions. This ties in with seeing mathematics as a language. Students, especially in the junior classes, tend to concentrate on the numerical or 'maths' part of the question and pay little attention to the instructions which give the information that is required to solve the problem.

(4) When solving problems have students identify their own problem-solving strategies and listen to others. This practice should create an atmosphere of discussion in the class centred around different approaches to the same problem.
As the students try to solve problems on their own they will make mistakes. This is healthy, as this was the experience of the inventors of mathematics; they tried,

guessed, made many mistakes and worked for hours, days and sometimes years before reaching a solution.

There are enough problems in the exercises to allow the students to try and try again. The excitement, disappointment and struggle with a problem until a solution is found provide a healthy classroom atmosphere.

To the Student

These books are written for you. As you study:

Try to break up the material in a chapter into manageable bits.
Always have paper and pencil when you study mathematics.
When you meet a new word write it down together with its meaning.
Read your questions carefully and rephrase them in your own words.
The information which you need to solve your problem is given in the wording of the problem, not the number part only.
Your success in mathematics may be achieved through practice.
You are therefore advised to try to solve as many problems as you can.
Always try more problems than those set by your teacher for homework.
Remember that the greatest cricketer or netball player became great by practising for many hours.

We have provided enough problems in the books to allow you to practice. Above all don't be afraid to make mistakes as you are learning. The greatest mathematicians all made many mistakes as they tried to solve problems.

You are now on your way to success in mathematics. – GOOD LUCK!

1 ▸ BASIC ARITHMETIC

At the end of the chapter you should be able to:

1. Identify prime numbers.
2. List factors of a given number.
3. Write a number as a product of primes.
4. Write a set of multiples of a given number.
5. Identify square numbers.

PRIME NUMBERS

A number greater than 1 that can be divided exactly only by itself and 1 is called a prime number; for example, 7 is a prime number (as 7 can only be 7×1) but 6 is not a prime number (because $6 = 6 \times 1$ or 3×2).

The smallest prime number is 2.

The Greek mathematician Euclid (born about 300 BC) showed that the number of primes is infinite.

Exercise 1a

1. Write down the first four prime numbers, starting with 2.

2. Write down the prime numbers that are less than 10.

3. Write down the prime numbers that are between 10 and 20.

4. In the set $\{2, 3, 4, 5, 6, 7, 8\}$, which members are prime numbers?

5. In the set $\{5, 7, 9, 11, 13, 15\}$, which members are prime numbers?

6. In the set $\{12, 13, 14, 15, 16, 17\}$, which members are prime numbers?

7. In the set $\{20, 21, 22, 23, 24, 25\}$, which members are prime numbers?

8. Apart from 2, are there any even numbers that are prime numbers?

FACTORS

A factor of a number divides exactly into that number, for example, 2 is a factor of 10 because 2 divides into 10 exactly 5 times.

On the other hand 3 is not a factor of 10 because 3 does not divide exactly into 10.

1

Exercise 1b

1. Is 2 a factor of

   (a) 4 (b) 9 (c) 12 (d) 21 (e) 84?

2. How can you tell whether 2 is a factor of a number?

3. Is 5 a factor of

   (a) 8 (b) 10 (c) 15 (d) 25 (e) 32 (f) 85?

4. How can you tell whether 5 is a factor of a number?

5. Write down those members of the set { 8, 16, 40, 35, 41, 206, 515 } for which

   (a) 2 is a factor   (b) 5 is a factor.

6. Is 3 a factor of

   (a) 6 (b) 9 (c) 10 (d) 15 (e) 16?

7. The number 3 is a factor of 51. Add the digits of 51.

   Is 3 a factor of your answer?

8. The numbers 75 and 102 are each divisible by 3.

   (a) Add the digits of 75. Is your answer divisible by 3?

   (b) Add the digits of 102. Is your answer divisible by 3?

From the last exercise we see that

> any even number is divisible by 2
>
> any number ending in 0 or 5 is divisible by 5
>
> when the sum of the digits of a number is divisible by 3, the number itself is divisible by 3.

Exercise 1c

> Write down all the factors of 12.
>
> 1, 2, 3, 4, 6, 12 are all factors of 12.
>
> (Note that factors of a number are not always prime.)

Write down all the factors of:

1. 6
2. 8
3. 10
4. 4
5. 9
6. 18
7. 15
8. 16
9. 21
10. 26
11. 51
12. 19

PRIME FACTORS

Sometimes we need to know just the prime factors of a number and to be able to express the number as the product of its prime factors.

For example, the prime factors of 6 are 2 and 3

and $6 = 2 \times 3$

For larger numbers we need a more systematic approach.

Consider the number 84.

The lowest prime factor of 84 is 2,
so we divide 2 into 84 $84 \div 2 = 42$

We then repeat the process with 42 $42 \div 2 = 21$

We repeat the process again with 21
but 3 is the lowest prime factor of 21 $21 \div 3 = 7$

Repeating the process again $7 \div 7 = 1$

Therefore the prime factors of 84 are 2, 2, 3 and 7

i.e. $84 = 2 \times 2 \times 3 \times 7$

It is easier to keep track of the prime factors if the division is set out like this:

```
2 ) 84
2 ) 42
3 ) 21
7 )  7
     1
```

Exercise 1d

> Express 90 as the product of its prime factors.
>
> $$90 = 2 \times 3 \times 3 \times 5 \qquad \begin{array}{l} 2\,)\,90 \\ 3\,)\,45 \\ 3\,)\,15 \\ 5\,)\,\ 5 \\ 1 \end{array}$$

Express the following numbers as products of their prime factors.

1. 10	**4.** 12	**7.** 60	**10.** 66
2. 21	**5.** 8	**8.** 50	**11.** 126
3. 35	**6.** 28	**9.** 36	**12.** 108

MULTIPLES

If a number divides exactly into a second number, the second number is a multiple of the first.

For example, the first six multiples of 3 are 3, 6, 9, 12, 15, 18.

Exercise 1e

1. From the set

   { 2, 3, 5, 6, 8, 10, 12, 14, 15, 16, 18, 20 }

   write down the members that are

   (a) multiples of 2

   (b) multiples of 3

   (c) multiples of 4

   (d) multiples of 5

   (e) multiples of 6

   (f) multiples of 8

2. Write down the first four multiples of

   (a) 7 (b) 5 (c) 8 (d) 10 (e) 12 (f) 15

3. Write down the multiples of 9 between 50 and 100.

4. Write down the multiples of 7 between 10 and 50.

5. Write down the multiples of 11 between 10 and 100.

SQUARES

A square number, or a perfect square, can be written as the product of two equal numbers.

For example, 16 is a perfect square because $16 = 4 \times 4$.

Exercise 1f

1. Write down the perfect squares between 2 and 10.

2. Write down the perfect squares between 10 and 101.

3. In the set { 2, 4, 6, 8, 10, 12, 16, 18, 20 }, which members are perfect squares?

4. In the set { 2, 4, 8, 16, 32, 64, 128 }, which members are perfect squares?

5. In the set { 3, 9, 27, 81 }, which members are perfect squares?

6. A perfect cube is the product of three equal numbers, e.g. $27 = 3 \times 3 \times 3$.
   Find the prime factors of each number in the set { 6, 8, 25, 81, 125 }. Hence write down those members of the set that are perfect cubes.

MULTIPLYING A STRING OF NUMBERS

Consider $2 \times 3 \times 6$; this means multiply 2 by 3 and then multiply the result by 6,

therefore
$$2 \times 3 \times 6 = 6 \times 6$$
$$= 36$$

Similarly
$$2 \times 3 \times 4 \times 5 = 6 \times 4 \times 5 = 24 \times 5 = 120$$

Exercise 1g

Calculate:

1. $2 \times 4 \times 3$	**4.** $7 \times 2 \times 2$	**7.** $6 \times 2 \times 3$	**10.** $4 \times 2 \times 4 \times 3$
2. $3 \times 2 \times 5$	**5.** $3 \times 5 \times 2$	**8.** $3 \times 7 \times 2$	**11.** $3 \times 7 \times 1 \times 5$
3. $5 \times 4 \times 2$	**6.** $4 \times 5 \times 3$	**9.** $2 \times 5 \times 2 \times 3$	**12.** $5 \times 2 \times 3 \times 4$

MIXED OPERATIONS

When a calculation involves a mixture of addition, subtraction, multiplication and division, we do the multiplication and division first.

For example, $3 + 4 \times 2 = 3 + 8 = 11$

It helps if brackets are put round the parts that are to be done first.

Exercise 1h

Calculate $6 \div 2 + 4 \times 2 - 1$

$$6 \div 2 + 4 \times 2 - 1 = (6 \div 2) + (4 \times 2) - 1$$
$$= 3 + 8 - 1$$
$$= 10$$

Calculate:

1. $8 - 2 \times 2$	**4.** $5 + 2 \times 3$	**7.** $3 - 4 \div 2$	**10.** $5 \times 3 - 5$
2. $3 \times 4 - 6$	**5.** $3 \times 7 - 8$	**8.** $8 + 2 \times 2$	**11.** $7 + 12 \div 2$
3. $12 \div 4 + 3$	**6.** $10 \div 2 + 2$	**9.** $16 - 3 \times 2$	**12.** $24 \div 8 - 2$

13. $3 + 4 - 6 \div 3$ **16.** $7 - 10 \div 2 + 3$ **19.** $3 + 1 \times 3 - 2$ **22.** $10 - 15 \div 3 + 2$

14. $2 \times 7 + 8 \div 4$ **17.** $5 \times 2 - 3 + 1$ **20.** $12 \div 4 + 3 \times 2$ **23.** $7 \times 3 - 6 + 2$

15. $3 + 2 \times 4 - 5$ **18.** $18 \div 3 + 6 \div 2$ **21.** $6 + 3 \times 2 - 4$ **24.** $14 - 2 \times 4 + 7$

MIXED EXERCISES

Exercise 1i

1. From the set
   $\{\, 1, 2, 5, 9, 12, 18, 21, 36, 39, 41 \,\}$
   write down the numbers which are

   (a) prime
   (b) odd
   (c) even
   (d) multiples of 2
   (e) multiples of 3
   (f) factors of 36

2. Find the highest number which is a factor of

   (a) both 6 and 4
   (b) both 15 and 20
   (c) both 8 and 20

3. Find the lowest number that is a multiple of

   (a) both 2 and 3
   (b) both 4 and 5
   (c) both 3 and 4

4. Calculate:

   (a) $2 \times 4 \times 3$
   (b) $2 + 4 \times 3$
   (c) $2 \times 4 + 3$

5. Calculate:

   (a) $12 \div 6 + 4$
   (b) $3 + 4 \times 2$
   (c) $7 - 4 \div 2$

Exercise 1j

1. From the set
   $\{\, 4, 5, 6, 8, 12, 15, 20, 21, 23, 27, 29 \,\}$
   write down the numbers which are

   (a) odd
   (b) multiples of 5
   (c) factors of 40
   (d) prime
   (e) even
   (f) multiples of 4

2. Calculate:

   (a) $6 \times 2 \times 4$
   (b) $6 \times 2 - 4$
   (c) $16 - 2 \times 4$

3. Calculate:

   (a) $12 - 5 \times 2$
   (b) $4 \div 2 + 3$
   (c) $3 \times 2 \times 4 \times 3$

Exercise 1k

In this exercise you are given several alternative answers. Write down the letter that corresponds to the correct answer.

1. The prime numbers in the set $\{\, 1, 2, 4, 7, 11, 15 \,\}$ are

   A   1, 2, 7, 11   **B**   2, 4   **C**   2, 7, 11   **D**   2, 7, 11, 15

2. The value of $2 + 3 \times 2$ is

   A   7   **B**   10   **C**   6   **D**   8

3. The square numbers (perfect squares) in the set { 2, 4, 8, 9, 10, 16, 20 } are

   A   4, 9, 16   **B**   4, 8, 10, 16, 20   **C**   2, 4, 8, 9, 16

4. The highest number which is a factor of both 4 and 6 is

   A   2   **B**   4   **C**   1   **D**   12

5. The value of $3000 - 3$ is

   A   2007   **B**   2997   **C**   2907   **D**   2700

MATHS IS OUT THERE

Odd numbers – About 550 BC the Pythagoreans considered the odd numbers, except 13, to be masculine, heavenly and symbols for good luck. The luckiest odd number at that time was 3. Odd numbers were said to be 'strong numbers'.

Even numbers were considered to be feminine and earthly. The even numbers represented unlucky situations and were associated with poverty and sorrow. These were said to be 'weak numbers'.

Prime numbers were considered to be mysterious and divine. Two, the only even prime number, represented dissension – it takes two to argue.

2 ▷ MAKING SURE OF ARITHMETIC

At the end of the chapter you should be able to:

1. Write the reciprocal of a given number.
2. Change decimals to fractions and fractions to decimals.
3. Use the dot notation to write recurring decimals.
4. Multiply and divide decimals.
5. Write numbers using zero and negative indices.
6. Use standard form notation to write a given number.
7. Approximate a number to a given number of decimal places or significant figures.

NAMES FOR NUMBERS

As young children we start learning about numbers by counting objects: 1, 2, 3, ... 10, ...

The numbers that we use for counting are called the *natural numbers*.

We next learn that whole objects can be divided into parts, or fractions, for example, half an orange, one and a half bars of chocolate.

We use *common fractions*, e.g. $\frac{1}{2}$, $\frac{3}{4}$, $\frac{3}{2}$, ... to describe the size of the part. The *denominator* (bottom number) describes the number of equal parts of the object and the *numerator* (top number) tells us how many parts we have. For example, $\frac{3}{4}$ means that we have 3 of the 4 equal parts of the whole object.

A fraction such as $\frac{3}{2}$, where the numerator is bigger than the denominator, is called an *improper fraction*. The improper fraction $\frac{3}{2}$ can be written as $1\frac{1}{2}$ and in this form it is called a *mixed number*. Note that $1\frac{1}{2}$ means $1 + \frac{1}{2}$.

ADDITION AND SUBTRACTION OF FRACTIONS

We cannot add apples to oranges unless we reclassify them both as, say, fruit. In much the same way, we cannot add tenths to quarters unless we change them both into the same kind of fraction, i.e. change them so that both have the same, or common, denominator. To do this we use the following fact.

The value of a fraction is unaltered if both numerator and denominator are multiplied by the same number.

To find a common denominator for, say, $\frac{1}{4}$ and $\frac{3}{10}$, we look for the lowest number that both 4 and 10 divide into exactly. This number is called the *lowest common multiple* (LCM) of 4 and 10 and in this case it is 20.

Then, as $\qquad 20 = 4 \times 5 \quad$ we have $\quad \frac{1}{4} = \frac{1 \times 5}{4 \times 5} = \frac{5}{20}$

and as $\qquad 20 = 10 \times 2 \quad$ we have $\quad \frac{3}{10} = \frac{3 \times 2}{10 \times 2} = \frac{6}{20}$

Therefore $\qquad \frac{1}{4} + \frac{3}{10} = \frac{5}{20} + \frac{6}{20} = \frac{11}{20}$

Exercise 2a

Find the LCM of the following sets of numbers:

1. 3, 7	**3.** 2, 8, 10	**5.** 2, 6, 3	**7.** 4, 6	**9.** 2, 3, 7	**11.** 24, 8, 6
2. 2, 9	**4.** 3, 4, 6	**6.** 5, 4	**8.** 3, 5, 12	**10.** 18, 6, 9	**12.** 12, 36, 8

Find $\frac{5}{11} + \frac{2}{5} + \frac{7}{10}$

(110 is the LCM of 11, 5 and 10)

$$\frac{5}{11} + \frac{2}{5} + \frac{7}{10} = \frac{50 + 44 + 77}{110}$$

$$= \frac{171}{110}$$

$$= 1\frac{61}{110}$$

Find:

13. $\frac{2}{3} + \frac{7}{8}$	**16.** $\frac{2}{7} + \frac{1}{2} + \frac{3}{14}$	**19.** $\frac{1}{3} + \frac{5}{9}$	**22.** $\frac{2}{7} + \frac{1}{9} + \frac{1}{6}$
14. $\frac{3}{5} + \frac{3}{10}$	**17.** $\frac{3}{16} + \frac{3}{4} + \frac{5}{12}$	**20.** $\frac{5}{6} + \frac{2}{3} + \frac{1}{4}$	**23.** $\frac{5}{12} + \frac{3}{8} + \frac{3}{4}$
15. $\frac{3}{5} + \frac{5}{8} + \frac{1}{2}$	**18.** $\frac{1}{4} + \frac{2}{3}$	**21.** $\frac{3}{4} + \frac{13}{20} + \frac{4}{5}$	**24.** $\frac{8}{21} + \frac{1}{2} + \frac{2}{3}$

Find $\frac{7}{15} - \frac{5}{12}$

(60 is the LCM of 15 and 12)

$$\frac{7}{15} - \frac{5}{12} = \frac{28 - 25}{60}$$

$$= \frac{\cancel{3}^{1}}{\cancel{60}_{20}}$$

$$= \frac{1}{20}$$

25. $\frac{7}{9} - \frac{5}{12}$ $\qquad$ **27.** $\frac{3}{10} - \frac{1}{15}$ $\qquad$ <u>**29.**</u> $\frac{2}{5} - \frac{3}{8}$

26. $\frac{1}{4} - \frac{2}{9}$ $\qquad$ **28.** $\frac{1}{10} - \frac{1}{20}$ $\qquad$ <u>**30.**</u> $\frac{5}{6} - \frac{5}{9}$

Find $\quad$ (a) $1\frac{2}{3} + \frac{1}{6} + 2\frac{1}{2}$ $\qquad$ (b) $2\frac{1}{4} - \frac{3}{5}$

(a) $1\frac{2}{3} + \frac{1}{6} + 2\frac{1}{2} = 3 + \frac{2}{3} + \frac{1}{6} + \frac{1}{2}$ $\qquad$ (adding whole numbers)

$$= 3 + \frac{4+1+3}{6}$$

$$= 3 + \frac{\cancel{8}^{4}}{\cancel{6}_{3}}$$

$$= 3 + 1\frac{1}{3}$$

$$= 4\frac{1}{3}$$

(b) $2\frac{1}{4} - \frac{3}{5} = 2 + \frac{5 - 12}{20}$

$$= 1 + \frac{20 + 5 - 12}{20} \qquad \text{(changing 1 unit into } \tfrac{20}{20}\text{)}$$

$$= 1 + \frac{13}{20}$$

$$= 1\frac{13}{20}$$

Find:

31. $2\frac{3}{5} + 1\frac{1}{8}$ $\qquad$ **34.** $2\frac{3}{4} + 1\frac{1}{2} - \frac{1}{3}$ $\qquad$ <u>**37.**</u> $2\frac{3}{5} + 1\frac{8}{15}$

32. $4\frac{2}{9} - 3\frac{5}{6}$ $\qquad$ **35.** $3\frac{1}{8} - 2\frac{3}{4} + 4\frac{1}{2}$ $\qquad$ <u>**38.**</u> $1\frac{3}{8} + 1\frac{1}{4} - 2\frac{1}{2}$

33. $2\frac{1}{5} - 4\frac{1}{8} + 1\frac{7}{10}$ $\qquad$ **36.** $1\frac{3}{10} - \frac{9}{20}$ $\qquad$ <u>**39.**</u> $2\frac{1}{4} - 1\frac{5}{6} + \frac{2}{3}$

MULTIPLICATION OF FRACTIONS

Remember that $\frac{2}{3} \times \frac{1}{5}$ means $\frac{2}{3}$ of $\frac{1}{5}$.

Now $\frac{1}{3}$ of $\frac{1}{5}$ is $\frac{1}{15}$, so $\frac{2}{3}$ of $\frac{1}{5}$ is $\frac{2}{15}$,

i.e. $\qquad \frac{2}{3} \times \frac{1}{5} = \frac{2 \times 1}{3 \times 5} = \frac{2}{15}$

> To multiply fractions, multiply the numerators together and multiply the denominators together.

Any mixed numbers must be changed into improper fractions, and factors that are common to the numerator and denominator should be cancelled before multiplication.

Exercise 2b

Find $2\frac{1}{2} \times \frac{3}{15}$

$$2\frac{1}{2} \times \frac{3}{15} = \frac{5}{2} \times \frac{3}{15}$$
$$= \frac{\cancel{5}^1 \times \cancel{3}^1}{2 \times \cancel{15}_{\,3}}$$
$$= \frac{1}{2}$$

Find:

1. $\frac{2}{3} \times \frac{5}{6}$

2. $1\frac{1}{2} \times \frac{8}{9}$

3. $4 \times \frac{3}{8}$

4. $\frac{2}{3} \times \frac{1}{4} \times \frac{3}{5}$

5. $1\frac{1}{3} \times \frac{1}{2} \times \frac{5}{7}$

6. $\frac{3}{4} \times \frac{2}{5}$

7. $\frac{2}{5} \times 1\frac{3}{7}$

8. $\frac{3}{5} \times 10$

9. $\frac{2}{5} \times \frac{7}{8} \times \frac{10}{11}$

In questions 10 to 15 find the missing numbers:

10. $\frac{3}{4} \times \frac{}{6} = \frac{1}{4}$

11. $\frac{1}{3} \times \frac{}{2} = \frac{1}{2}$

12. $\frac{2}{} \times \frac{1}{4} = \frac{1}{6}$

13. $\frac{}{} - \times \frac{2}{3} = 1$

14. $\frac{3}{4} \times - = 1$

15. $- \times \frac{7}{8} = 1$

RECIPROCALS

If the product of two numbers is 1 then each number is called the reciprocal of the other.

We know that $\frac{1}{3} \times 3 = 1$ so

$\frac{1}{3}$ is the reciprocal of 3   and   3 is the reciprocal of $\frac{1}{3}$.

To find the reciprocal of $\frac{3}{4}$ we require the number which, when multiplied by $\frac{3}{4}$, gives 1

Now $\frac{4}{3} \times \frac{3}{4} = 1$

so $\frac{4}{3}$ is the reciprocal of $\frac{3}{4}$

In all cases the reciprocal of a fraction is obtained by turning the fraction upside down.

Any number can be written as a fraction, e.g. $3 = \frac{3}{1}$, $2.5 = \frac{2.5}{1}$, ...

so   the reciprocal of $\frac{3}{1}$ is $\frac{1}{3}$ or $1 \div 3$,
            the reciprocal of $\frac{2.5}{1}$ is $\frac{1}{2.5}$ or $1 \div 2.5$

The reciprocal of a number is 1 divided by that number.

DIVISION BY A FRACTION

Consider $\frac{2}{5} \div \frac{3}{7}$

This can be interpreted as $\frac{2}{5} \times 1 \div \frac{3}{7} = \frac{2}{5} \times \left(1 \div \frac{3}{7}\right)$

Now $1 \div \frac{3}{7}$ is the reciprocal of $\frac{3}{7}$, i.e. $\frac{7}{3}$.

Therefore $\quad \frac{2}{5} \div \frac{3}{7} = \frac{2}{5} \times \frac{7}{3} = \frac{14}{15}$

i.e. to divide by a fraction we multiply by its reciprocal.

Exercise 2c

Write down the reciprocals of the following numbers.

1. 4

2. $\frac{1}{2}$

3. $\frac{2}{5}$

4. 10

5. $\frac{1}{8}$

6. $\frac{3}{11}$

7. 100

8. $\frac{2}{9}$

9. $\frac{15}{4}$

Find $3\frac{1}{2} \div \frac{7}{8}$

(Before multiplying or dividing, mixed numbers must be changed into improper fractions.)

$$3\frac{1}{2} \div \frac{7}{8} = \frac{7}{2} \div \frac{7}{8}$$
$$= \frac{\cancel{7}^{1}}{\cancel{2}_{1}} \times \frac{\cancel{8}^{4}}{\cancel{7}_{1}}$$
$$= 4$$

Find:

10. $\frac{2}{3} \div \frac{1}{2}$

11. $1\frac{2}{3} \div \frac{5}{6}$

12. $2\frac{1}{2} \div 4$

13. $5 \div \frac{4}{5}$

14. $\frac{2}{9} \div 1\frac{2}{7}$

15. $\frac{1}{2} \div \frac{3}{4}$

16. $\frac{3}{7} \div 1\frac{3}{4}$

17. $\frac{5}{9} \div 10$

18. $3 \div \frac{2}{3}$

Find $2\frac{1}{2} + \frac{3}{5} \div 1\frac{1}{2} - \frac{1}{2}\left(\frac{3}{5} + \frac{1}{3}\right)$

(Remember that brackets are worked out first, then multiplication and division and lastly addition and subtraction.)

$$2\frac{1}{2} + \frac{3}{5} \div 1\frac{1}{2} - \frac{1}{2}\left(\frac{3}{5} + \frac{1}{3}\right) = 2\frac{1}{2} + \frac{3}{5} \div 1\frac{1}{2} - \frac{1}{2}\left(\frac{9+5}{15}\right)$$

$$= 2\frac{1}{2} + \frac{3}{5} \div \frac{3}{2} - \frac{1}{2} \times \frac{14}{15}$$

$$= 2\frac{1}{2} + \frac{3}{5} \times \frac{2}{3} - \frac{1}{2} \times \frac{14}{15}$$

$$= 2\frac{1}{2} + \frac{2}{5} - \frac{7}{15}$$

$$= 2 + \frac{15+12-14}{30}$$

$$= 2 + \frac{13}{30}$$

$$= 2\frac{13}{30}$$

19. $1\frac{2}{3} \times \frac{1}{2} - \frac{2}{5}$

20. $\frac{3}{7} + \frac{1}{4} \div 1\frac{1}{3}$

21. $\frac{2}{5} \div \left(\frac{1}{2} + \frac{3}{4}\right)$

22. $5\frac{1}{2} \div 3 + \frac{2}{9}$

23. $\frac{4}{5} \div \frac{1}{6} + \frac{1}{3} \times 1\frac{1}{2}$

24. $\frac{9}{11} - \frac{2}{5} \times \frac{3}{4}$

25. $2\frac{1}{2} \div \frac{7}{9} + 1\frac{1}{3}$

26. $\frac{3}{5}\left(1\frac{1}{4} - \frac{2}{3}\right)$

27. $3\frac{1}{2} - \frac{2}{3} \times 6$

28. $2\frac{1}{3} + \frac{1}{2}\left(2 \div \frac{4}{5}\right)$

29. $\frac{3}{4}\left(5\frac{1}{3} - 2\frac{1}{5}\right) \div \frac{7}{9}$

30. $\left(\frac{2}{3} - \frac{1}{2}\right) \div \left(\frac{3}{4} - \frac{1}{3}\right)$

31. $\frac{7}{9} - \frac{1}{3}$ of $1\frac{2}{7}$

32. $\frac{1}{2} + \left(\frac{3}{4} \div \frac{1}{6}\right)$ of 3

33. $\dfrac{\frac{1}{3} + \frac{1}{4}}{\frac{5}{6} - \frac{3}{4}}$

34. $\dfrac{1\frac{1}{5} - \frac{3}{4}}{2\frac{1}{2}}$

35. $\dfrac{\frac{9}{10}}{\frac{5}{6}}$

36. $\frac{2}{3} \times \frac{6}{7} - \frac{5}{8} \div 1\frac{1}{4}$

37. $\dfrac{\frac{7}{8}}{3\frac{1}{2} - \frac{2}{3}}$

38. $\dfrac{3\frac{1}{4}}{2\frac{3}{5}}$

39. $\dfrac{\frac{2}{3} \times \frac{3}{4}}{\frac{5}{6} \times \frac{3}{10}}$

DECIMAL FRACTIONS

Long after meeting common fractions, we learn that we can represent fractions of an object by placing a point after the units and continuing to add figures to the right. The first figure after the decimal point is the number of tenths, the next figure is the number of hundredths, and so on.

For example, 0.75 is 7 tenths plus 5 hundredths.

Fractions written this way are called *decimal fractions*.

Usually we refer to common fractions simply as fractions and to decimal fractions simply as decimals.

INTERCHANGING DECIMALS AND FRACTIONS

Exercise 2d

Express 0.705 as a fraction.

$$0.705 = \frac{7}{10} + \frac{5}{1000} \qquad \text{(this step is usually omitted)}$$

$$= \frac{\cancel{705}^{141}}{\cancel{1000}_{200}}$$

$$= \frac{141}{200}$$

Express the following decimals as fractions:

1. 0.35 **3.** 0.204 **5.** 0.03 **7.** 0.005 **9.** 0.11 **11.** 1.104

2. 0.216 **4.** 1.36 **6.** 0.012 **8.** 1.01 **10.** 2.05 **12.** 0.0001

Express $\frac{7}{8}$ as a decimal.

$$\frac{7}{8} = 0.875 \qquad\qquad \begin{array}{r} 0.875 \\ 8\overline{)7.000} \end{array}$$

Express the following fractions as decimals:

13. $\frac{3}{20}$ **16.** $\frac{6}{25}$ **19.** $1\frac{3}{4}$ **22.** $\frac{5}{16}$

14. $\frac{1}{8}$ **17.** $\frac{1}{16}$ **20.** $\frac{5}{32}$ **23.** $2\frac{3}{8}$

15. $\frac{3}{5}$ **18.** $\frac{27}{50}$ **21.** $\frac{4}{25}$ **24.** $\frac{1}{500}$

RECURRING DECIMALS

If we try to change $\frac{1}{6}$ to a decimal, i.e. $6\overline{)1.0000 \ldots}$ with quotient $0.1666\ldots$ we discover that

(a) we cannot write $\frac{1}{6}$ as an exact decimal

(b) from the second decimal place, the 6 recurs for as long as we have the patience to continue the division.

Similarly if we convert $\frac{2}{11}$ to a decimal by dividing 2 by 11, we get $0.18181818 \ldots$ and we see that

(a) $\frac{2}{11}$ cannot be expressed as an exact decimal

(b) the pair of figures '18' recurs indefinitely.

Decimals like these are called *recurring decimals*. To save time and space we place a dot over the figure that recurs. In the case of a group of figures recurring we place a dot over the first and last figure in the group.

Therefore	we write $0.166666 \ldots$	as $0.1\dot{6}$
and	we write $0.181818 \ldots$	as $0.\dot{1}\dot{8}$
Similarly	we write $0.316316316 \ldots$	as $0.\dot{3}1\dot{6}$

Exercise 2e

Use the dot notation to write the following fractions as decimals:

1. $\frac{1}{3}$ 3. $\frac{5}{6}$ 5. $\frac{1}{7}$ 7. $\frac{1}{11}$ 9. $\frac{5}{12}$ 11. $\frac{7}{30}$

2. $\frac{2}{9}$ 4. $\frac{1}{15}$ 6. $\frac{1}{12}$ 8. $\frac{1}{18}$ 10. $\frac{1}{14}$ 12. $\frac{1}{13}$

ADDITION AND SUBTRACTION OF DECIMALS

Decimals are added and subtracted in the same way as whole numbers. It is sensible to write them in a column so that the decimal points are in a vertical line. This ensures that units are added to units, tenths are added to tenths, and so on.

MULTIPLICATION OF DECIMALS

To multiply decimals we can first convert them to fractions.

For example,

$$\underset{\text{(2 d.p.)}}{0.05} \times \underset{\text{(2 d.p.)}}{1.04} = \frac{5}{100} \times \frac{104}{100}$$

$$= \frac{520}{10\,000}$$

$$= \underset{\text{(4 d.p.)}}{0.0520}$$

From such examples we deduce the following rule.

First ignore the decimal points and multiply the numbers together. Then the sum of the number of decimal places in the original numbers gives the number of decimal places in the answer (including any zeros at the end).

DIVISION BY DECIMALS

To divide a decimal by a whole number, proceed as with whole numbers, adding zeros after the point when necessary. For example, to find $3.14 \div 5$ we have

$$5\overline{)3.140}^{\,0.628}$$

(Make sure that the decimal points are in a vertical line.)

Therefore $3.14 \div 5 = 0.628$

To divide by a decimal we use the fact that the top and bottom of a fraction can be multiplied by the same number without altering the value of the fraction. Division by a decimal can therefore be converted to division by a whole number.

For example, $3.14 \div 0.5 = \frac{3.14}{0.5}$

$$= \frac{31.4}{5} \qquad \left(\frac{3.14 \times 10}{0.5 \times 10} \right)$$

$$= 6.28$$

Exercise 2f

Calculate, without using a calculator:

1. $1.26 + 3.75$
2. $12.4 + 6.7$
3. $5.82 + 0.35$
4. $0.04 + 8.76$
5. $1.8 + 0.02$
6. $25 + 1.36$
7. $4.002 + 0.83$
8. $0.016 + 1.09$
9. $0.000\,32 + 0.0017$

10. $5.3 - 2.1$
11. $8.2 - 4.9$
12. $0.16 - 0.08$
13. $1.3 - 0.09$
14. $1.07 - 0.58$
15. $24 - 0.98$
16. $0.37 - 0.009$
17. $2 - 0.17$
18. $0.0127 - 0.0059$

19. 1.2×0.8
20. 0.7×0.06
21. 0.4×0.02
22. 0.1×0.1
23. 0.5×0.5
24. 1.002×0.36
25. 42×0.08
26. 3.0501×1.1
27. 0.0012×0.32

28. $2.8 \div 0.4$
29. $0.36 \div 1.2$
30. $1.08 \div 0.4$
31. $0.02 \div 2.5$
32. $0.018 \div 1.2$
33. $5.31 \div 0.9$
34. $0.1 \div 0.1$
35. $0.01 \div 0.5$
36. $0.0013 \div 1.3$

Evaluate $3.7 + 0.2(1.3 - 0.27)$

$$3.7 + 0.2(1.3 - 0.27) = 3.7 + 0.2 \times 1.03 \qquad \text{(bracket)}$$

$$= 3.7 + 0.206 \qquad \text{(multiplication)}$$

$$= 3.906$$

Evaluate:

37. $2.6 - 1.4 \div 0.7$

38. $200 \times 0.04 - 0.2$

39. $(1.2 - 0.8) \div 0.8$

40. $4.3 \times 2.1 \div 0.07$

41. $3.2(0.6 - 0.09) + 10.25$

42. $2.73 \div 0.9 \times 1.02$

43. $(20 \times 0.06) \div (3.1 - 1.9)$

44. $(2.5 + 1.3) \div (2.06 - 0.16)$

45. $\dfrac{2.4 + 0.98}{1.78 + 0.22}$

46. $\dfrac{0.04 \times 1.02}{3.4 \times 0.06}$

47. $\dfrac{1.2 \times 0.05}{0.07 + 0.08}$

48. $\dfrac{4.02 + 12.09}{0.9 \times 2}$

RELATIVE SIZES

Before we can compare the sizes of a set of numbers we must either change them all into decimals or change them all into fractions with the same denominator. Choose whichever method is easier.

Exercise 2g

Place > or < between the two numbers $\frac{3}{5}$, 0.67

(Remember that > means 'is greater than' and < means 'is less than'.)

$$\frac{3}{5} = 0.6$$

Comparing 0.6 and 0.67 we see that $0.6 < 0.67$

$\therefore$
$$\frac{3}{5} < 0.67$$

Place > or < between each of the following pairs of numbers:

1. $\frac{5}{8}$, 0.63

2. 0.16, $\frac{3}{20}$

3. $\frac{9}{11}$, 0.9

4. $\frac{1}{16}$, 0.07

5. $\frac{2}{7}$, 0.16

6. 0.48, $\frac{4}{9}$

7. 0.33, $\frac{7}{25}$

8. $\frac{3}{11}$, 0.25

9. $\frac{2}{3}$, 0.66

Arrange the following numbers in ascending order (i.e. the smallest first): $\frac{1}{2}$, 0.52, $\frac{11}{20}$, 0.51

Writing them all as fractions with denominator 100 gives

$$\frac{1}{2} = \frac{50}{100}, \quad 0.52 = \frac{52}{100}, \quad \frac{11}{20} = \frac{55}{100}, \quad 0.51 = \frac{51}{100}$$

Therefore the required order is $\frac{1}{2}$, 0.51, 0.52, $\frac{11}{20}$.

In each of the following questions arrange the numbers in ascending order of size:

10. $\frac{2}{3}$, 0.6, $\frac{4}{5}$

12. $\frac{2}{7}$, 0.3, $\frac{1}{5}$

14. 0.16, $\frac{3}{20}$, 0.2, $\frac{6}{25}$

11. 0.85, $\frac{4}{5}$, 0.79

13. 0.75, $\frac{5}{7}$, 0.875, $\frac{7}{9}$

15. $1\frac{1}{5}$, 1.3, 1.24, $1\frac{1}{8}$

INDICES

In the number 2^3, the 3 is called the *index* or *power* and 2^3 means $2 \times 2 \times 2$. Thus, indices are a kind of shorthand notation. All other forms of indices are derived from this.

Exercise 2h

Find the value of (a) $2^2 \times 3^3$ (b) $(3^3)^2$

$$(a)\ 2^2 \times 3^3 = 4 \times 27 \qquad\qquad (b)\ (3^3)^2 = (27)^2$$
$$= 108 \qquad\qquad\qquad\qquad\qquad = 729$$

Find the value of:

1. 5^2

4. 5^3

7. $8^2 \times 5^2$

10. $7^3 \times 9^2$

13. 0.072×10^4

2. 3^4

5. 4^3

8. $6^3 \times 2^2$

11. 3.25×10^2

14. 1.102×10^3

3. 2^5

6. $2^4 \times 3^2$

9. $4^4 \times 2^3$

12. 8.01×10^3

15. 1.1×10^6

Remember that we can multiply one number to a power by the *same* number to another power by adding the powers.

Where possible write as a single number in index form
(a) $5^2 \times 5^4$ (b) $3^2 \times 2^3$

(a) $5^2 \times 5^4 = 5^6$

$$(5^2 \times 5^4 = 5 \times 5 \times 5 \times 5 \times 5 \times 5)$$

(b) $3^2 \times 2^3$ cannot be written as a single number in index form

$$(3^2 \times 2^3 = 3 \times 3 \times 2 \times 2 \times 2)$$

Write the following, where possible, as a single number in index form:

16. $2^3 \times 2^4$

19. $5^1 \times 5^3$

22. $4^2 \times 4^7$

17. $3^2 \times 3^5$

20. 2×2^4

23. $a^2 \times a^3$

18. $5^2 \times 3^5$

21. $7^2 \times 7^5$

24. $a^2 \times b^3$

We can also divide one number to a power by the *same* number to another power by subtracting the powers.

Where possible write as a single number in index form
(a) $2^5 \div 2^2$ (b) $3^3 \div 5^3$

(a) $2^5 \div 2^2 = 2^3$

$$\left(2^5 \div 2^2 = \frac{\cancel{2}^1 \times \cancel{2}^1 \times 2 \times 2 \times 2}{\cancel{2}_1 \times \cancel{2}_1} = 2^3 \right)$$

(b) $3^3 \div 5^3$ cannot be simplified.

$$\left(3^3 \div 5^3 = \frac{3 \times 3 \times 3}{5 \times 5 \times 5} \right)$$

Write the following, where possible, as a single number in index form:

25. $2^4 \div 2^2$ **28.** $4^5 \div 4^2$ **31.** $3^4 \div 3$ **34.** $(2^3)^2$

26. $7^3 \div 7^2$ **29.** $2^3 \div 3^2$ **32.** $a^8 \div a^4$ **35.** $(3^2)^2$

27. $5^3 \div 3^2$ **30.** $3^6 \div 3^2$ **33.** $a^3 \div b^2$ **36.** $(5^3)^2$

ZERO AND NEGATIVE INDICES

Consider $a^3 \div a^3$.
Subtracting indices gives $a^3 \div a^3 = a^0$
Dividing gives $a^3 \div a^3 = 1$

$$a^0 = 1$$
i.e. (any number)$^0 = 1$

Now consider $a^3 \div a^5$.
Subtracting indices gives $a^3 \div a^5 = a^{-2}$

Dividing gives $\dfrac{a^3}{a^5} = \dfrac{\cancel{a}^1 \times \cancel{a}^1 \times \cancel{a}^1}{\cancel{a}_1 \times \cancel{a}_1 \times \cancel{a}_1 \times a \times a} = \dfrac{1}{a^2}$

Therefore a^{-2} means $\dfrac{1}{a^2}$

A negative sign in front of the index means 'the reciprocal of'

i.e. $a^{-b} = \dfrac{1}{a^b}$

Exercise 2i

Find the value of 3^{-1}

$$3^{-1} = \frac{1}{3^1} = \frac{1}{3}$$

Find the value of:

1. 2^{-1} 3. 5^{-1} 5. 8^{-1} 7. a^{-1}

2. 10^{-1} 4. 7^{-1} 6. 4^{-1} 8. x^{-1}

Find the value of   (a) $\left(\frac{1}{2}\right)^{-1}$ (b) $\left(\frac{2}{5}\right)^{-1}$

(a) $\left(\frac{1}{2}\right)^{-1} = \left(\frac{2}{1}\right)^{1}$ (b) $\left(\frac{2}{5}\right)^{-1} = \left(\frac{5}{2}\right)^{1}$

$= 2$ $= 2\frac{1}{2}$

Find the value of:

9. $\left(\frac{1}{3}\right)^{-1}$ 11. $\left(\frac{1}{4}\right)^{-1}$ 13. $\left(\frac{1}{5}\right)^{-1}$ 15. $\left(\frac{1}{a}\right)^{-1}$

10. $\left(\frac{2}{3}\right)^{-1}$ 12. $\left(\frac{3}{4}\right)^{-1}$ 14. $\left(\frac{4}{5}\right)^{-1}$ 16. $\left(\frac{x}{y}\right)^{-1}$

Find the value of 3^{-2}

$$3^{-2} = \frac{1}{3^2}$$

$$= \frac{1}{9}$$

Find the value of:

17. 2^{-3} 19. 10^{-3} 21. 2^{-5} 23. 10^{-2}

18. 5^{-2} 20. 6^{-2} 22. 10^{-4} 24. 4^{-3}

Find the value of $\left(\frac{1}{3}\right)^{-2}$

$$\left(\frac{1}{3}\right)^{-2} = \left(\frac{3}{1}\right)^{2}$$

$$= 9$$

Find the value of:

25. $\left(\frac{1}{5}\right)^{-3}$ **27.** $\left(\frac{1}{2}\right)^{-5}$ **29.** $\left(\frac{1}{8}\right)^{-3}$ **31.** $\left(\frac{1}{2}\right)^{-3}$

26. $\left(\frac{1}{4}\right)^{-2}$ **28.** $\left(\frac{1}{3}\right)^{-4}$ **30.** $\left(\frac{1}{10}\right)^{-4}$ **32.** $\left(\frac{1}{6}\right)^{-2}$

Find the value of $\left(\frac{2}{5}\right)^{-3}$

$$\left(\frac{2}{5}\right)^{-3} = \left(\frac{5}{2}\right)^{3}$$

$$= \frac{125}{8}$$

$$= 15\frac{5}{8}$$

Find the value of:

33. $\left(\frac{3}{4}\right)^{-2}$ **35.** $\left(\frac{4}{9}\right)^{-2}$ **37.** $\left(\frac{2}{3}\right)^{-4}$ **39.** $\left(\frac{3}{10}\right)^{-4}$

34. $\left(\frac{2}{3}\right)^{-3}$ **36.** $\left(\frac{2}{7}\right)^{-2}$ **38.** $\left(\frac{3}{5}\right)^{-2}$ **40.** $\left(\frac{5}{8}\right)^{-2}$

Exercise 2j

Find the value of:

1. $\left(\frac{1}{8}\right)^{-1}$ **5** $\left(\frac{1}{2}\right)^{0}$ **9.** $\left(\frac{1}{2}\right)^{-4}$ **13.** 5^{0} **17.** 12^{-1}

2. $\left(\frac{2}{5}\right)^{-2}$ **6.** $\left(\frac{2}{3}\right)^{0}$ **10.** 6^{0} **14.** $\left(\frac{7}{10}\right)^{-3}$ **18.** 9^{3}

3. 4^{-2} **7.** 5^{3} **11.** $\left(\frac{3}{4}\right)^{-3}$ **15.** 2^{-2} **19.** $\left(\frac{1}{4}\right)^{-3}$

4. 8^{2} **8.** 9^{-1} **12.** $\left(\frac{2}{7}\right)^{-1}$ **16.** $\left(\frac{4}{5}\right)^{3}$ **20.** $\left(\frac{3}{7}\right)^{0}$

STANDARD FORM (SCIENTIFIC NOTATION)

Very large or very small numbers are more briefly written in standard form. It is easier to compare sizes of numbers written in standard form.

Standard form is a number between 1 and 10 multiplied by the appropriate power of 10.

Exercise 2k

The following numbers are given in standard form. Write them as ordinary numbers:

1. 3.45×10^2

2. 1.2×10^3

3. 5.01×10^{-2}

4. 4.7×10^{-3}

5. 2.8×10^2

6. 7.3×10^{-1}

7. 9.02×10^5

8. 6.37×10^{-4}

9. 8.72×10^6

Write the following numbers in standard form:
(a) 3840   (b) 0.0025

(First, write the given figures as a number between 1 and 10 and then decide what power of 10 to multiply by to bring it back to the correct size.)

$$(a) \quad 3840 = 3.84 \times 10^3$$
$$(b) \quad 0.0025 = 2.5 \times 10^{-3}$$

Write the following numbers in standard form:

10. 265

11. 0.18

12. 3020

13. 0.019

14. 76 700

15. 390 000

16. 0.000 85

17. 7000

18. 0.004

19. 58 700

20. 2600

21. 450 000

22. 0.000 007

23. 0.8

24. 0.000 56

25. 24 000

26. 39 000 000

27. 0.000 000 000 08

If you have a scientific calculator, it will display very large or very small numbers in scientific notation, but only the power of ten is given; 10 itself does not appear in the display.

Try this: enter 0.000 05, then press $\boxed{x^2}$.

The display will read $\boxed{2.5 \quad -09}$. This means 2.5×10^{-9}.

Now try entering 50 000 and then pressing $\boxed{x^2}$.

The display will read $\boxed{2.5 \quad 09}$. This means 2.5×10^9.

28. Use your calculator to find the value of
    (a) $(250\,000)^2$ (b) $(25\,700)^2$ (c) $(0.000\,08)^2$ (d) $(0.000\,007)^2$

APPROXIMATIONS (DECIMAL PLACES AND SIGNIFICANT FIGURES)

We have seen that it is sometimes unnecessary and often impossible to give exact values. In the case of measurements this is particularly true. However, we do need to know the degree of accuracy of an answer. For example, if a manufacturer is asked to make screws that are about $12\frac{1}{2}$ cm long, he does not know what is acceptable as being 'about $12\frac{1}{2}$ cm long'! But if he is asked to make them 12.5 cm long correct to one decimal place, he knows what tolerances to work to.

DECIMAL PLACES

To correct 0.078 22 to *two* decimal places (d.p.) we look at the *third* decimal place. If it is 5 or larger, we add 1 to the figure in the second decimal place. If it is less than 5, we do not alter the figure in the second decimal place.

In this example the figure in the third decimal place is 8,

so $0.07|822 = 0.08$ correct to 2 d.p.

SIGNIFICANT FIGURES

To determine the 1st, 2nd, 3rd, ... significant figure (s.f.) in a number we can change it into standard form. Then the figure to the left of the decimal point is the 1st s.f., the next figure is the 2nd s.f., ... and so on.

For example, $0.0\ 7\ 0\ 2\ 5 = 7.0\ 2\ 5 \times 10^{-2}$

(1st s.f., 2nd s.f., 3rd s.f. marked on the digits)

To correct 0.078 22 to two significant figures we look at the third significant figure; in this case it is 2.

Therefore $0.078\ 22 = 0.078$ correct to 2 s.f.

Exercise 2l

Give 0.070 25 correct to (a) 3 d.p.   (b) 3 s.f.

(a) $0.070|25 = 0.070$ correct to 3 d.p.

(We leave the zero at the end of the corrected answer to indicate that the third decimal place is zero.)

(b) $0.070\ 2|5 = 7.02|5 \times 10^{-2}$ (this step can be omitted)

$= 0.070\ 3$ correct to 3 s.f.

Give each of the following numbers correct to

(a) three decimal places   (b) three significant figures:

1. 2.7846   **4.** 0.073 25   **7.** 0.7801   **10.** 0.000 925 8

2. 0.1572   **5.** 0.150 76   **8.** 3.2994   **11.** 7.8196

3. 3.2094   **6.** 0.020 39   **9.** 254.1627   **12.** 0.009 638

Estimate a rough value for 0.826×38.3 by correcting each number to 1 significant figure. Then use your calculator to give the answer correct to 3 significant figures.

$$0.826 \times 38.3 \approx 0.8 \times 40 = 32 \approx 30$$

$0.826 \times 38.3 = 31.6$ correct to 3 s.f.

First estimate a rough value for each of the following calculations, then use your calculator to give the answer correct to three significant figures:

13. 0.035×1.098 **19.** $86.27 \div 39.8$ **25.** $(3.827)^3$

14. 258×184 **20.** $204 \div 942$ **26.** $\dfrac{3.257}{83.6}$

15. 0.0932×0.48 **21.** $0.827 \div 0.093$ **27.** $0.532 \times 3.621 \times 36$

16. 18.27×3.82 **22.** $0.0026 \div 0.0378$ **28.** $(0.32)^3$

17. 0.295×0.732 **23.** $16.97 \div 3.702$ **29.** $\dfrac{2.27 \times 3.84}{5.01}$

18. 1250×532 **24.** $3502 \div 651$ **30.** $\dfrac{0.016 \times 5.82}{2.31}$

31. $\dfrac{2.93 \times 0.037\,2}{1.84 \times 0.562}$

MIXED EXERCISES

Exercise 2m

1. Find the LCM of
(a) 2, 5 and 6   (b) 3, 7 and 14

2. Find the reciprocal of (a) $\frac{3}{4}$ (b) $\dfrac{x}{y}$

3. Calculate (a) $1\frac{1}{3} \div \frac{8}{9}$ (b) $1\frac{1}{3} - \frac{8}{9}$

4. Calculate $\left(3\frac{1}{4} + 2\frac{1}{2}\right) \times \frac{2}{5}$

5. Find, without using a calculator:

(a) $3.27 + 0.09$

(b) 3.27×0.09

(c) $3.27 \div 0.03$

6. Find the value of
(a) 2^4 (b) 2^0 (c) 2^{-4}

7. Write as a single number in index form

(a) $5^6 \div 5^4$ (b) $5^{10} \times 5^2$

8. Write the following numbers in standard form

(a) 2560   (b) 0.000 256

Exercise 2n

1. Find the LCM of

(a) 3, 8 and 24   (b) 2, 3 and 5

2. Find the reciprocal of

(a) $\frac{1}{5}$ (b) $1\frac{1}{2}$

3. Calculate (a) $\frac{3}{5} \times 1\frac{1}{4}$ (b) $\frac{3}{5} + 1\frac{1}{4}$

4. Calculate $2\frac{1}{2} \times \frac{7}{10} + 1\frac{1}{3}$

5. Find, without using a calculator:

(a) $2.5 - 1.05$

(b) 2.5×1.05

(c) $1.05 \div 2.5$

6. Find the value of

(a) $\left(\frac{1}{2}\right)^2$ (b) $\left(\frac{1}{2}\right)^0$ (c) $\left(\frac{1}{2}\right)^{-2}$

7. Write in standard form

(a) 570 000   (b) 0.057

MATHS IS OUT THERE

Pythagoras once defined a friend as 'One who is the other I, such as 220 and 284'.

These two numbers are AMICABLE, because the proper divisors of one number adds up to the other number.

Divisors of 284 are {1, 2, 4, 71, 142}. Their sum, $1 + 2 + 4 + 71 + 142 = 220$.
Divisors of 220 are {1, 2, 4, 5, 10, 11, 20, 22, 44, 55, 110}. Their sum is

$$1 + 2 + 4 + 5 + 10 + 11 + 20 + 22 + 44 + 55 + 110 = 284.$$

The Hebrews believed that such numbers were good omens.

Today more than 600 pairs of friendly numbers are known.

In 1866 a sixteen year old Italian boy, Nicole Paganini, discovered the amicable numbers 1184 and 1210. Can you discover any?

DIRECTED NUMBERS

At the end of the chapter you should be able to:

1. Show the positions of positive and negative numbers on a number line.
2. Perform operations of addition, subtraction, multiplication and division on directed numbers.
3. Illustrate on a number line the range of values for a given number to a stated number of decimal places.

POSITIVE AND NEGATIVE NUMBERS

We use numbers to describe quantities. For example, we may talk about $\frac{2}{3}$ of a cake, 10.5 cm of wire, 35 apples, and so on.

These numbers, $\frac{2}{3}$, 10.5 and 35, are examples of *positive numbers*.

We cannot however use positive numbers to describe temperatures below $0°$C (the freezing point of water), or any other quantity that can fall below a zero level.

To do this we need *negative numbers*.

Positive numbers are written, for example, as $+2$ or simply as 2.
Negative numbers are written, for example, as -2.

Positive numbers and negative numbers are together known as *directed numbers*.

USING A NUMBER LINE

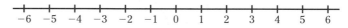

On the number line, positive numbers are in positions to the right of zero and negative numbers are in positions to the left of zero.

If a number a is to the *right* of a number b, then

$\qquad$ a is greater than b

e.g. $\qquad$ $3 > 1$ and $-1 > -3$

If a number c is to the *left* of a number d then

$\qquad$ c is less than d

e.g. $\qquad$ $2 < 6$ and $-6 < -4$

Exercise 3a

Insert $>$ or $<$ between each of the following pairs of numbers.

1.	4 2		**7.**	−5 −6
2.	3 5		**8.**	0 −4
3.	−1 −4		**9.**	5 −5
4.	−5 −2		**10.**	4 −2
5.	2 −1		**11.**	−3 0
6.	−4 3		**12.**	0 6

ADDING AND SUBTRACTING DIRECTED NUMBERS

Adding directed numbers can be interpreted as adding steps to the left or right,

e.g. $+(+2)$ can mean 'add 2 steps to the right'

therefore $+(+2) = +2$

Also $+(-2)$ can mean 'add 2 steps to the left'

therefore $+(-2) = -2$

Subtracting directed numbers can be interpreted as taking away steps to the left or right,

e.g. $-(+2)$ can mean 'take away 2 steps to the right'

i.e.   'go 2 steps to the left'

therefore $-(+2) = -2$

Also $-(-2)$ can mean 'take away 2 steps to the left'

i.e.   'go 2 steps to the right'

therefore $-(-2) = +2$

> i.e.   subtracting a negative number has the same effect as adding a positive number.

Exercise 3b

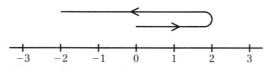

Find $+2+(-4)$

$$+2+(-4) = +2-4$$
$$= -2$$

($+2-4$ means 'go 2 steps to the right and then 4 steps to the left')

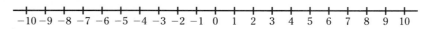

Use this number line, if it helps, to calculate:

1. $-2+(-3)$	**7.** $-5+(-4)$	**13.** $-3+(-2)$	**19.** $-4-(-8)$
2. $+4-(+6)$	**8.** $3-(-3)$	**14.** $+4-(-2)$	**20.** $+6+(-9)$
3. $-2+(-4)$	**9.** $-3-(+3)$	**15.** $-3-(+2)$	**21.** $-5-(+7)$
4. $-8+(+6)$	**10.** $+2-(-5)$	**16.** $+2-(+5)$	**22.** $+4+(-10)$
5. $-3-(-4)$	**11.** $-6+(-4)$	**17.** $+7+(-4)$	**23.** $-8-(-3)$
6. $+2-(-6)$	**12.** $-2+(+8)$	**18.** $+8-(+10)$	**24.** $+10-(+6)$

Remember that the $+$ sign is often left out, i.e. $2+8-4$ means $+2+(+8)-(+4)$

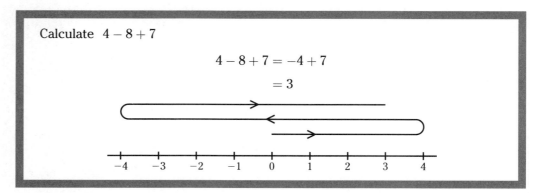

Calculate $4-8+7$

$$4-8+7 = -4+7$$
$$= 3$$

Calculate:

25. $3-4+6$	**28.** $-4+2-(-4)$	**31.** $-7+9-2$	**34.** $5+6-4$
26. $2+6-4$	**29.** $5-3+9$	**32.** $3+(-2)-3$	**35.** $-3-7+9$
27. $-3+2-4$	**30.** $3-(-2)+2$	**33.** $5-9+3$	**36.** $2-7-(-6)$

MULTIPLYING AND DIVIDING DIRECTED NUMBERS

$(+2) \times (+3)$ means 'add 2 lots of $+3$'

therefore $\quad (+2) \times (+3) = +(+6) = +6$

$(-2) \times (-3)$ means 'take away 2 lots of -3'

therefore $\quad\quad (-2) \times (-3) = -(-6) = +6$

In the same way $\;(+2) \times (-3) = +(-6) = -6$

and $\quad\quad\quad\quad (-2) \times (+3) = -(+6) = -6$

Dividing by, say, -2 is the same as multiplying by $-\frac{1}{2}$

e.g. $\quad\quad\quad 12 \div (-2) = 12 \times \left(-\frac{1}{2}\right) = -6$

From this we can deduce the general rule that

> when multiplying or dividing,
> like signs give a positive answer
> unlike signs give a negative answer

Exercise 3c

Find (a) $(-4)^2$ (b) $6 \div (-2)$

$$\text{(a) } (-4)^2 = (-4) \times (-4)$$
$$= +16$$
$$\text{(b) } 6 \div (-2) = 6 \times \left(-\tfrac{1}{2}\right)$$
$$= -3$$

Find:

1. $(3) \times (-2)$
2. $(-2) \times (-6)$
3. 7×8
4. $(-3) \times (-7)$
5. $(-2) \times (+4)$
6. 5×6

7. $(+3) \times (-4)$
8. $(-2) \times (-7)$
9. $(-2)^2$
10. $(-5) \times (+3)$
11. $(-3)^2$
12. $(+3) \times (-6)$

13. $(+6) \div (+3)$
14. $(+6) \div (-3)$
15. $(-6) \div (+3)$
16. $(-6) \div (-3)$
17. $(-8) \div (+4)$
18. $(+10) \div (-2)$

19. $(+9) \div (+3)$
20. $(-5) \div (-1)$
21. $4 \div 2$
22. $(-12) \div (+4)$
23. $(-3) \div 3$
24. $15 \div (-5)$

RANGE OF VALUES FOR A CORRECTED NUMBER

Suppose we are told that, correct to the nearest 10, 250 people boarded a particular train. People are counted in whole numbers only. Hence in this case, 245 is the lowest number that gives 250 when corrected to the nearest 10 and 254 is the highest number that can be corrected to 250. We can therefore say that the actual number of people who boarded the train is any whole number from 245 to 254.

Now suppose that we are given a nail and are told that its length is 25 mm correct to the nearest millimetre. The length may be a whole number of millimetres, but may also be any part of a millimetre.

Look at this magnified section of a measuring gauge:

The lowest number that can be rounded up to 25 is 24.5. The highest number that can be rounded down to 25 is not so easy to determine. All we can say is that any number up to, but not including, 25.5 can be rounded down to 25.

The length of the nail is therefore in the range from 24.5 mm up to, but not including, 25.5 mm.

If l mm is the length of the nail, we can therefore write

$$24.5 \leqslant l < 25.5$$

To illustrate this on the diagram we use a solid circle to show that 24.5 is included in the range and an open circle to show that 25.5 is not included in the range.

Exercise 3d

Illustrate on a number line the range of values of x given by $0.1 < x \leqslant 0.8$

Use a number line like this for questions 1 to 10:

In each case illustrate the range on your number line:

1. $5 \leqslant x \leqslant 10$ 3. $-2 \leqslant x \leqslant 6$ 5. $0 < x < 10$ **7.** $4 \leqslant x \leqslant 12$ **9.** $-5 < x < 8$

2. $0 < x \leqslant 15$ 4. $5 \leqslant x < 15$ **6.** $-5 < x \leqslant 5$ **8.** $3 < x \leqslant 18$ **10.** $-1 < x \leqslant 11$

Use a number line like this for questions 11 to 20. In each case illustrate the range on your number line:

11. $0 < x < 0.1$	**16.** $0.03 < x \leqslant 0.13$
12. $0.1 \leqslant x < 0.2$	**17.** $0.05 \leqslant x \leqslant 0.2$
13. $0.05 \leqslant x \leqslant 0.15$	**18.** $0.07 < x \leqslant 0.14$
14. $0.08 < x \leqslant 0.16$	**19.** $0.10 < x < 0.19$
15. $0.02 < x < 0.08$	**20.** $0.13 \leqslant x < 0.18$

A number is given as 3.15 correct to 2 d.p. Illustrate on a number line the range in which this number lies.

(3.15 is between 3.14 and 3.16 so we will use just that part of the number line.)

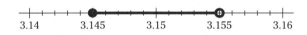

Illustrate on a number line the range of possible values for each of the following corrected numbers:

21. 1.5 correct to 1 d.p.	**31.** 0.25 correct to 2 d.p.
22. 0.2 correct to 1 d.p.	**32.** 1.15 correct to 2 d.p.
23. 0.1 correct to 1 d.p.	**33.** 12.26 correct to 2 d.p.
24. 4.8 correct to 1 d.p.	**34.** 0.05 correct to 2 d.p.
25. 2.0 correct to 1 d.p.	**35.** 3.10 correct to 2 d.p.
26. 0.6 correct to 1 d.p.	**36.** 0.52 correct to 2 d.p.
27. 1.3 correct to 1 d.p.	**37.** 6.89 correct to 2 d.p.
28. 6.2 correct to 1 d.p.	**38.** 26.35 correct to 2 d.p.
29. 8.0 correct to 1 d.p.	**39.** 8.50 correct to 2 d.p.
30. 12.9 correct to 1 d.p.	**40.** 0.70 correct to 2 d.p.

PROBLEMS

Exercise 3e

It is stated that a packet of pins contains 500 pins to the nearest 10. Find the range in which the actual number of pins lies.

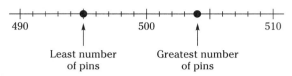

(There must be a whole number of pins in the packet.)
If n is the number of pins in the packet then n is a whole number such that $495 \leqslant n \leqslant 504$.

A copper tube is sold as having an internal bore (diameter) of 10 mm to the nearest millimetre. Find the range in which the actual bore lies.

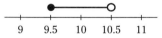

If d mm is the diameter of the tube then $9.5 \leqslant d < 10.5$

In some of the following questions you are asked to find a range of values for a quantity that can only have whole number values. When this is the case, it *must* be clearly stated in your answer:

1. The weight, w kg, of a bag of sand is given as 5.6 kg correct to 1 decimal place. Find the range of values in which the actual weight lies.

2. A shop is said to make a profit of $2500 a month. If this figure is given correct to the nearest $100, find the range in which the actual monthly figure, $x, lies.

3. Correct to one decimal place, the length of a room is given as 2.8 m. Find the range in which the actual length of the room, x m, lies.

4. On a certain model of bicycle, the brake pads have to be 12.5 mm thick to work efficiently. Find the range in which the thickness, x mm, can lie, if the figure given is correct to 1 decimal place.

5. Referring to a football match, a newspaper headline proclaimed '7000 watch Barbados win'. If this figure for the number of spectators is correct to the nearest 1000, find the range in which x, the number of people who actually attended the match, lies.

6. One of the component parts of a metal hinge is a pin. In order to work properly this pin must have a diameter of 1.25 mm correct to 2 decimal places. Find the range in which the diameter, d mm, must lie.

7. One hundred people were asked if they ate cornflakes for breakfast that morning. To the nearest 10, 40 people said they did. Of the 100 people interviewed, what is the largest possible number who did *not* eat cornflakes?

8. An advertisement says 'For about $250 you can buy this automatic watch'. If this price is correct to the nearest $10, what is the most that you would expect to have to pay for such a watch?

9. The length of a car is given as 255 cm. If this figure is correct to the nearest 5 cm, find the range in which the actual length lies.

10. Knitting yarn is sold by weight. It is found that 10 g of double knitting pure wool has a length of 20 m correct to the nearest metre. What is the minimum length of yarn you would expect in a 50 g ball of double knitting pure wool?

MIXED EXERCISE

Exercise 3f

Find:

1. $2 + 6 - 5$

2. $(+3) \times (-4)$

3. $(-5)^2$

4. $2 + 7 - 9 + 2$

5. $(-3) \div (-1)$

6. $2 \times (-6)$

7. $2 - (-3)$

8. $(-6)^2$

9. $3 - (-4) + 6$

10. $(-5) \times 6$

11. $12 \div (-3)$

12. $2 - (-5) - 4$

13. $8 - 7 - 3$

14. $(-4) \times 7$

15. $(-9)^2$

16. $8 \div (-2)$

17. $5 - 7 - (-4)$

18. 4×5

19. $(-10) \div 5$

20. $7 + (-3) - 4$

21. $(-2) + 6 - 3$

22. $15 \div (-3)$

23. $7 \times (-2)$

24. $(-14) \div (-2)$

25. The diameter of a ball bearing is given as 1.5 mm correct to 1 decimal place. Find the range in which the diameter lies.

26. To the nearest 10, 70 children brought a packed lunch to school. Find the range in which the actual number of children lies.

27. A box contains 450 tacks to the nearest 10. Find the range in which the actual number of tacks lies.

28. To fit properly, the diameter of a bicycle tyre has to be 0.75 m correct to 2 decimal places. Find the range in which the diameter can lie.

 MATHS IS OUT THERE

Look up the meaning of each of the following words and write it in your notebook:

(i) GEMATRIA   (ii) NUMEROLOGY   (iii) TRISKAIDEKAPHOBIA.

4 ▸ EQUATIONS, INEQUALITIES AND FORMULAE

At the end of the chapter you should be able to:

1. Simplify algebraic expressions.
2. Solve simple equations.
3. Solve inequalities and illustrate the solutions on a number line.
4. Construct formulae from data.
5. Substitute numbers into formulae.
6. Change the subject of a simple formula.

SIMPLIFYING ALGEBRAIC EXPRESSIONS

If an algebraic expression contains two terms each with the same letter then we can usually add them.

For example, $x + x$ can be written as $2x$

and $2x + 3x$ can be written as $5x$
$(2x + 3x = x + x + x + x + x)$

However, if the two terms contain different letters then, as we do not know what numbers the letters stand for, we cannot add them.

For example, $x + y$ cannot be simplified, neither can $x - x^2$.

Exercise 4a

Simplify where possible (a) $x - (-y)$ (b) $x + 2y - 3x$

(a) $x - (-y) = x + y$ (b) $x + 2y - 3x = 2y - 2x$
(We usually write the positive term first.)

Simplify where possible:

1. $p + q$
2. $a + a$
3. $2s + 3t$
4. $3v + 4v$
5. $5x - 3x$
6. $p - (-q)$
7. $x + 3x - 2y$
8. $3u - (-2u)$
9. $a + 3b - 2a$
10. $c + 2d - (-3c)$

34

When terms are multiplied together we can write them in a slightly shorter form by omitting the multiplication sign.

For example

$a \times b$ can be written as ab
$p \times p$ can be written as p^2 (using index notation)
$5a \times 2b$ can be written as $10ab$ (multiplication can be done in any order
so 5 can be multiplied by 2)

But we cannot simplify ab or $\dfrac{x}{y}$.

Exercise 4b

> Simplify (a) $4x \div (-2y)$ (b) $2p \times q$
>
> (a) $4x \div (-2y) = \dfrac{\overset{2}{\cancel{4}}x}{\underset{1}{\cancel{-2}}y}$ (b) $2p \times q = 2pq$
>
> $\qquad\qquad = -\dfrac{2x}{y}$

Simplify where possible:

1. $x \times y$

2. $a \times a$

3. $2s \times 3s$

4. $4x \times 3x$

5. $u \div v$

6. $a \div (-b)$

7. $a \div a$

8. $6b \div 2c$

9. $s + t$

10. $m - n$

11. $m \times (-n)$

12. $3s - 2t$

13. $a - 3a$

14. $p \times 4p^2$

15. $8u \div 4w$

16. $2z - 3y$

17. $3s \times 2t$

18. $p \times 2p$

19. $q - 5q$

20. $r - (-4s)$

21. $8p \div 2q$

22. $(-3s) \times (-2t)$

23. $(b) \times (-2b)$

24. $(-x) \div (-y)$

> Simplify $a(a - b) - (b - a)$
>
> (Remember that $-(b - a)$ means minus b *and* minus $(-a)$.)
>
> $$a(a - b) - (b - a) = a^2 - ab - b - (-a)$$
> $$= a^2 - ab - b + a$$

Simplify $3(a-b) - 2(a+b)$

$$3(a-b) - 2(a+b) = 3a - 3b - 2a - 2b$$
$$= a - 5b$$

Simplify:

25. $a - 3(a - b)$

26. $2a + a(a - 3)$

27. $2(a - b) - (b - a)$

28. $4(a - c) + 2(a - b)$

29. $y - 2(y - z)$

30. $4(x + y) + 2(x + z)$

31. $3(p + q) - 2(p + r)$

32. $2x - (x + y)$

33. $2(p + q) - 3(p - q)$

34. $a(a + b) - 2(a - b)$

35. $x(x - y) + y(y - x)$

36. $4(b - c) - 2(b + c)$

37. $4(p - q) + 2(q - p)$

38. $w(w + x) - x(w - x)$

39. $3(m + n) - 5(m - n)$

40. $5(b - c) - 3(b + c)$

SOLVING EQUATIONS

Consider the statement

$$3x + 6 = 2 - x$$

This is an equation. It means that the left hand side is *equal* to (i.e. has the same value as) the right hand side.

We can think of the two sides of an equation as the contents of the two pans on a pair of scales which are exactly balanced. The equality will remain true provided that we always do the same thing to both sides.

Solving an equation means finding the number that the letter stands for so that the two sides *are* equal.

When solving equations like these it is sensible to proceed in the following order:

1. remove any brackets
2. collect any like terms on each side
3. collect the letter terms on one side (choose the side with the greater number to start with remembering that, say, $-2x > -3x$)
4. collect the number terms on the other side.

Exercise 4c

Solve the equation $3x + 6 = 2 - x$

$$3x + 6 = 2 - x$$

Add x to each side $4x + 6 = 2$

Take 6 from each side $4x = -4$

Divide each side by 4 $x = -1$

Check: when $x = -1$,   LHS $= 3(-1) + 6 = -3 + 6 = 3$

RHS $= 2 - (-1) = 2 + 1 = 3$

$\therefore \qquad x = -1$

Solve the following equations:

1. $2p + 5 = 3 - p$

2. $3 - s = 4 - 3s$

3. $x + 5 = 3x - 2$

4. $2a + 3 = 4 - 3a$

5. $3 - 2x = 8x - 7$

6. $3y + 2 = 7 - 2y$

7. $4 - x = 8 - 3x$

8. $a + 7 = 4a - 5$

9. $2x + 5 = 7 - 2x$

10. $3 - 2x = 9 - 5x$

Solve the equation $3 - 2(4 + x) = x - 6$

$$3 - 2(4 + x) = x - 6$$

Expand bracket $3 - 8 - 2x = x - 6$

Collect like terms $-5 - 2x = x - 6$

Add $2x$ to both sides $-5 = 3x - 6$

Add 6 to both sides $1 = 3x$

Divide both sides by 3 $\frac{1}{3} = x$ or $x = \frac{1}{3}$

Solve:

11. $3 - 2(x - 2) = 8$

12. $x - 4(x + 3) = 3$

13. $4x = 2 - 3(x + 1)$

14. $2y = 8 - (y - 2)$

15. $3(2 - x) = 4(x - 3)$

16. $5 - 3(x - 4) = 6$

17. $a - 2(a + 3) = 5$

18. $3p - 2 = 4 - 3(p + 2)$

19. $4w = w - (w - 8)$

20. $7(5 - x) = 3(x - 5)$

21. $5(x - 2) - 3(x + 1) = 0$

22. $3 - 5(2x + 1) = 2x$

23. $3(2x + 1) - 2(4x - 1) = 0$

24. $4 - 2(3 - 2x) = 5$

25. $3x - 4(1 - 3x) = 2x - (x + 1)$

26. $7(b - 4) - 5(b + 2) = 0$

27. $12 - 3(4x - 1) = 5$

28. $5(3x - 1) - 4(3x - 2) = 0$

29. $8 - 5(2 - x) = 8$

30. $4x - 2(1 - 3x) = 3 - (2x - 1)$

INEQUALITIES

Consider the statement

$$x > 5$$

This is an *inequality* (as opposed to $x = 5$ which is an equality or equation).

This inequality is true when x stands for any number that is greater than 5. Thus there is a range of numbers that x can stand for and we can illustrate this range on a number line.

The circle at the left hand end of the range is 'open', because 5 is not included in the range.

Exercise 4d

Use a number line to illustrate the range of values of x for which $x < -1$

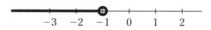

Use a number line to illustrate the range of values of x for which each of the following inequalities is true:

1. $x > 7$

2. $x < 4$

3. $x > -2$

4. $x > 0$

5. $x < -2$

6. $x > \frac{1}{2}$

7. $x < 5$

8. $x < 0$

9. $x < 1.5$

10. State which of the inequalities given in questions 1 to 9 are satisfied by a value of x equal to (a) 2 (b) −3 (c) 0 (d) 1.5 (e) 0.0005

11. For each of the questions 1 to 9 give a number that satisfies the inequality and is

(a) a whole number

(b) not a whole number

12. Consider the true inequality $3 > 1$

(a) Add 2 to each side.

(b) Add −2 to each side.

(c) Take 5 from each side.

(d) Take −4 from each side.

In each case state whether or not the inequality remains true.

13. Repeat question 12 with the inequality $-2 > -3$

14. Repeat question 12 with the inequality $-1 < 4$

15. Try adding and subtracting different numbers on both sides of a true inequality of your own choice.

SOLVING INEQUALITIES

From the last exercise we can see that

an inequality remains true when the *same* number is added to, or subtracted from, *both* sides.

Now consider the inequality $x - 2 < 3$

Solving this inequality means finding the range of values of x for which it is true. Adding 2 to each side gives $x < 5$

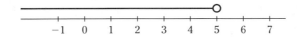

We have now solved the inequality.

Exercise 4e

Solve the following inequalities and illustrate your solutions on a number line:

1. $x - 4 < 8$

2. $x + 2 < 4$

3. $x - 2 > 3$

4. $x - 3 > -1$

5. $x + 4 < 2$

6. $x - 5 < -2$

7. $x - 3 < -6$

8. $x + 7 < 0$

9. $x + 2 < -3$

Solve the inequality $4 - x < 3$

$$4 - x < 3$$

Add x to each side $4 < 3 + x$

Take 3 from each side $1 < x$ or $x > 1$

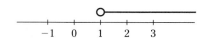

Solve the following inequalities and illustrate your solutions on a number line:

10. $4 - x > 6$

11. $2 < 3 + x$

12. $7 - x > 4$

13. $5 < x + 5$

14. $5 - x < 8$

15. $2 > 5 + x$

<u>16.</u> $3 - x > 2$

<u>17.</u> $6 < x + 8$

<u>18.</u> $2 + x < -3$

19. $2 > x - 3$

20. $4 < 5 - x$

21. $1 < -x$

22. $3 - x < 3$

23. $5 < x - 2$

24. $7 > 2 - x$

<u>25.</u> $3 > -x$

<u>26.</u> $4 - x > -9$

<u>27.</u> $5 - x < -7$

28. Consider the true inequality $12 < 36$

(a) Multiply each side by 2
(b) Divide each side by 4
(c) Multiply each side by 0.5
(d) Divide each side by 6
(e) Multiply each side by -2
(f) Divide each side by -3

In each case state whether or not the inequality remains true.

29. Repeat question 28 with the true inequality $36 > -12$

30. Repeat question 28 with the true inequality $-18 < -6$

31. Repeat question 28 with a true inequality of your own choice.

32. Can you multiply both sides of an inequality by any one number and be confident that the inequality remains true?

An inequality remains true when both sides are multiplied or divided by the same *positive* number.

Multiplication or division of an inequality by a negative number must be avoided, because it destroys the truth of the inequality.

Exercise 4f

Solve the inequality $2x - 4 > 5$ and illustrate the solution on a number line.

$$2x - 4 > 5$$

Add 4 to both sides $\qquad\qquad 2x > 9$

Divide both sides by 2 $\qquad\qquad x > 4\frac{1}{2}$

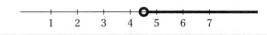

Solve the inequalities and illustrate the solutions on a number line:

1. $3x - 2 < 7$ **3.** $4x - 1 > 7$ **5.** $5 + 2x < 6$ **7.** $4x - 5 < 4$

2. $1 + 2x > 3$ **4.** $3 + 5x < 8$ **6.** $3x + 1 > 5$ **8.** $6x + 2 > 11$

Solve the inequality $3 - 2x \leqslant 5$ and illustrate the solution on a number line. ($\leqslant$ means 'less than or equal to')

(As with equations, we collect the letter term on the side with the greater number to start with. In this case we collect on the right.)

$$3 - 2x \leqslant 5$$

Add $2x$ to each side $\qquad\qquad 3 \leqslant 5 + 2x$

Take 5 from each side $\qquad\qquad -2 \leqslant 2x$

Divide each side by 2 $\qquad\qquad -1 \leqslant x$ i.e. $x \geqslant -1$

(A solid circle is used for the end of the range because -1 *is* included.)

Solve the inequalities and illustrate the solution on a number line:

9. $3 \leqslant 5 - 2x$ **12.** $4 \geqslant 9 - 5x$ **15.** $x - 1 > 2 - 2x$ **18.** $2x + 1 \leqslant 7 - 4x$

10. $5 \geqslant 2x - 3$ **13.** $10 < 3 - 7x$ **16.** $2x + 1 \geqslant 5 - x$ **19.** $1 - x > 2x - 2$

11. $4 - 3x \leqslant 10$ **14.** $8 - 3x \geqslant 2$ **17.** $3x + 2 \leqslant 5x + 2$ **20.** $2x - 5 > 3x - 2$

Find, where possible, the range of values of x which satisfy both of the inequalities (a) $x \geqslant 2$ and $x > -1$ (b) $x \leqslant 2$ and $x > -1$ (c) $x \geqslant 2$ and $x < -1$

(a)

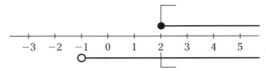

(Illustrating the ranges on a number line, we can see that both inequalities are satisfied for values on the number line where the ranges overlap.)

$\therefore$ $x \geqslant 2$ and $x > -1$ are both satisfied for $x \geqslant 2$

(b)

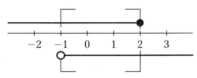

$x \leqslant 2$ and $x > -1$ are both satisfied for $-1 < x \leqslant 2$

(c)

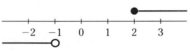

There are no values of x for which $x \geqslant 2$ and $x < -1$ are both satisfied. (The lines do not overlap.)

Find, where possible, the range of values of x for which the two inequalities are both true:

21. (a) $x > 2$ and $x > 3$
(b) $x \geqslant 2$ and $x \leqslant 3$
(c) $x < 2$ and $x > 3$

22. (a) $x \geqslant 0$ and $x \leqslant 1$
(b) $x \leqslant 0$ and $x \leqslant 1$
(c) $x < 0$ and $x > 1$

23. (a) $x \leqslant 4$ and $x > -2$
(b) $x \geqslant 4$ and $x < -2$
(c) $x \leqslant 4$ and $x < -2$

24. (a) $x < -1$ and $x > -3$
(b) $x < -1$ and $x < -3$
(c) $x > -1$ and $x < -3$

Solve each of the following pairs of inequalities and then find the range of values of x which satisfy both of them:

25. $x - 4 < 8$ and $x + 3 > 2$

26. $3 + x \leqslant 2$ and $4 - x \leqslant 1$

27. $x - 3 \leqslant 4$ and $x + 5 \geqslant 3$

28. $2x + 1 > 3$ and $3x - 4 < 2$

29. $5x - 6 > 4$ and $3x - 2 < 7$

30. $3 - x > 1$ and $2 + x > 1$

31. $1 - 2x \leqslant 3$ and $3 + 4x < 11$

32. $0 > 1 - 2x$ and $2x - 5 \leqslant 1$

Find the values of x for which $x - 2 < 2x + 1 < 3$

$(x - 2 < 2x + 1 < 3$ represents two inequalities,
i.e. $x - 2 < 2x + 1$ and $2x + 1 < 3)$

$$x - 2 < 2x + 1 \qquad\qquad 2x + 1 < 3$$
$$-2 < x + 1 \qquad\qquad 2x < 2$$
$$-3 < x \text{ i.e. } x > -3 \qquad\qquad x < 1$$

$$-3 < x < 1$$

Find the range of values of x for which the following inequalities are true:

33. $x + 4 > 2x - 1 > 3$

34. $x - 3 \leqslant 2x \leqslant 4$

35. $3x + 1 < x + 4 < 2$

36. $2 - x < 3x + 2 < 8$

37. $2 - 3x \leqslant 4 - x \leqslant 3$

38. $x - 3 < 2x + 1 < 5$

39. $2x < x - 3 < 4$

40. $4x - 1 < x - 4 < 2$

41. $4 - 3x < 2x - 5 < 1$

42. $x < 3x - 1 < x + 1$

CONSTRUCTING FORMULAE

Electricity bills are presented every quarter. They are made up of a fixed standing charge plus the cost of the number of units used in the quarter.

By using letters for the unknown quantities, we can construct a formula for a quarterly electricity bill.

If $\$C$ is the total bill, $\$R$ is the standing charge, the cost of one unit is x cents and N units are used, then

$$\text{the cost of the units is } Nx \text{ cents or } \$\frac{Nx}{100}$$

$$\text{therefore } C = R + \frac{Nx}{100}$$

Notice that the units are the same throughout, i.e. the cost of the units was converted from cents to dollars so that we added dollars to dollars, not dollars to cents.

Exercise 4g

A number p is equal to the sum of a number q and twice a number r. Write down a formula for p in terms of q and r.

$$p = q + 2r$$

In questions 1 to 12 write down a formula connecting the given letters:

1. A number a is equal to the sum of two numbers b and c.

2. A number m is equal to twice the sum of two numbers n and p.

3. A number z is equal to the product of two numbers x and y.

4. A number a is equal to twice the product of two numbers b and c.

5. A number v is equal to the square of a number n.

6. A number d is equal to the difference of two numbers e and f, where e is greater than f.

7. A number x is equal to half a number y.

8. A number a is equal to a number b divided by twice a number c.

9. A number k is equal to the sum of twice a number u and three times a number v.

10. A number x is equal to twice a number y, minus a number z.

11. A number n is equal to the sum of a number p and its square.

12. A number v is equal to the sum of a number u and the product of the numbers a and t.

13. Cloth is sold at $\$p$ per metre. The cost of N metres is $\$R$. Find a formula for R in terms of N and p.

14. Oranges are sold at x cents each. The cost of n oranges is y cents. Find a formula for y in terms of n and x.

15. A ship moving with constant speed takes x minutes to cover one nautical mile. It takes X minutes to cover y nautical miles. Find a formula for X in terms of x and y.

16. A shop sells two brands of baked beans. It has N tins of baked beans altogether; y of them are one brand and z of them are the other brand. Find a formula for N in terms of y and z.

17. A rectangle is x centimetres wide and y centimetres long and its perimeter is P metres. Find a formula for P in terms of x and y.

18. Fertiliser is applied at the rate of a grams per square metre. It takes b kilograms to cover a field of area c square metres. Find a formula for b in terms of a and c.

19. A money box contains l one-cent coins and m five-cent coins. The total value of money in the money box is n cents. Find a formula for n in terms of l and m.

20. A bag of coins contains x ten-cent coins and y five-cent coins. The total value of the coins is $\$R$. Find a formula for R in terms of x and y.

SUBSTITUTING NUMBERS INTO FORMULAE

Exercise 4h

Given that $s = ut - \frac{1}{2}gt^2$, find s when $u = 8$, $t = 6$ and $g = -10$

$$s = ut - \frac{1}{2}gt^2$$

When $u = 8$, $t = 6$ and $g = -10$

$$s = (8)(6) - (\tfrac{1}{2})(-10)(6)^2$$
$$= 48 - (-5)(36)$$
$$= 48 - (-180)$$
$$= 48 + 180$$
$$= 228$$

(Notice that we have put each number in brackets; this is particularly important in the case of negative numbers.)

1. Given that $p = r - nt$, find p when $r = 40$, $n = 8$ and $t = 4$

2. Given that $v = \dfrac{u-t}{3}$, find v when $u = 4$ and $t = -2$

3. Given that $z = \dfrac{1}{x} + \dfrac{1}{y}$, find z when $x = 2$ and $y = 4$

4. Given that $a = bc + d$, find a when $b = 3$, $c = 2$ and $d = -4$

5. If $x = y^2$, find x when $y = 5$

6. If $C = rt$, find C when $r = -3$ and $t = -10$

7. If $x = rt - v$, find x when $r = 2$, $t = 10$ and $v = -4$

8. If $p = x + x^2$, find p when $x = 2$

9. Given that $s = \frac{1}{2}(a+b+c)$, find s when $a = 6$, $b = 9$ and $c = 5$

10. Given that $v = ab + bc + cd$, find v when $a = 2$, $b = \frac{1}{2}$, $c = 4$ and $d = -2$

11. If $p = r(2t - s)$, find p when $r = \frac{1}{2}$, $t = 3$ and $s = -2$

12. If $a = (b+c)^2$, find a when $b = 8$ and $c = -5$

13. If $r = \dfrac{2}{s+t}$, find r when $s = \frac{1}{2}$ and $t = \frac{1}{4}$

14. If $n = \dfrac{r}{p-q}$, find n when $r = 4$, $p = 3$ and $q = -5$

15. Given that $a = bc - \frac{1}{2}dc$, find a when $b = 3$, $c = -4$ and $d = 7$

16. Given that $V = \frac{1}{2}(X - Y)^2$, find V when $X = 3$ and $Y = -5$

17. Given that $P = 2Q + 5RT$, find P when $Q = 8$, $R = -2$ and $T = -\frac{1}{2}$

18. Given that $a = (b-c)(c-d)$, find a when $b = 2$, $c = 4$ and $d = 7$

CHANGING THE SUBJECT OF A FORMULA

Consider the formula

$$A = B + C$$

Taking C from each side gives

$$A - C = B$$

i.e.

$$B = A - C$$

We have changed the subject of this formula from A to B. Changing the subject of a formula is very similar to solving equations.

Exercise 4i

Make the letter in brackets the subject of the formula:

1. $p = s + r$ (s)

6. $k = l + m$ (m)

11. $x = 2y$ (y)

16. $a = 3b$ (b)

2. $x = 3 + y$ (y)

7. $u = v - 5$ (v)

12. $v = \frac{1}{2}t$ (t)

17. $X = \frac{1}{10}N$ (N)

3. $a = b - c$ (b)

8. $z = x + y$ (y)

13. $a = bc$ (b)

18. $v = ut$ (u)

4. $X = Y - Z$ (Y)

9. $N = P - Q$ (P)

14. $t = \dfrac{u}{3}$ (u)

19. $z = \dfrac{w}{100}$ (w)

5. $r = s + 2t$ (s)

10. $v = u + 10t$ (u)

15. $l = \dfrac{m}{k}$ (m)

20. $n = \dfrac{p}{q}$ (p)

Make t the subject of the formula $v = u + 2t$

$$v = u + 2t$$

Take u from each side $v - u = 2t$

$\therefore$ $2t = v - u$

Divide each side by 2 $t = \dfrac{(v - u)}{2}$

Make the letter in brackets the subject of the formula:

21. $p = 2s + r$ (s)

25. $x = 2w - y$ (w)

29. $x = \dfrac{3y}{4}$ (y)

33. $V = \dfrac{2R}{I}$ (R)

22. $v = u - 3t$ (t)

26. $l = k + 4t$ (t)

30. $u = v + 5t$ (t)

34. $p = 2r - w$ (r)

23. $a = b - 4c$ (c)

27. $w = x - 6y$ (y)

31. $A = P + \frac{1}{10}I$ (I)

35. $a = b + \frac{1}{2}c$ (c)

24. $V = 2v + 3u$ (v)

28. $N = It - 2s$ (s)

32. $z = x - \dfrac{y}{3}$ (y)

36. $p = q - \dfrac{r}{5}$ (r)

37. Make u the subject of the formula
$v = u + at$
Find u when $v = 80$, $a = -10$ and $t = 6$

38. Make B the subject of the formula
$A = \dfrac{C}{100} + B$
Find B when $A = 20$ and $C = 250$

39. Make C the subject of the formula $P = \dfrac{C}{N}$
Find C when $N = 20$ and $P = \frac{1}{2}$

40. Make x the subject of the formula
$z = \frac{1}{2}x - 3t$
Find x when $z = 4$ and $t = -3$

41. A number a is equal to the sum of a number b and twice a number c

(a) Find a formula for a in terms of b and c

(b) Find a when $b = 8$ and $c = -2$

(c) Make b the subject of the formula.

42. A number x is equal to the product of a number z and twice a number y

(a) Find a formula for x in terms of z and y

(b) Find x when $z = 3$ and $y = 2$

(c) Make y the subject of the formula.

43. A number d is equal to the square of a number e plus twice a number f

(a) Find a formula for d in terms of e and f

(b) Make f the subject of the formula

(c) Find f when $d = 10$ and $e = 3$

44. A retailer sells bags of crisps at x cents each. The cost of n dozen bags of crisps is R.

(a) Find a formula for R in terms of x and n

(b) Find R when $x = 10$ and $n = 4$

MIXED EXERCISES

Exercise 4j

1. Evaluate (a) $8 \times (-\frac{1}{2})$ (b) $5 + 2 - 8$ (c) $8 \div (-4)$

2. Simplify (a) $x + 3x$ (b) $2b - (-4b)$ (c) $(x)(x)(-3x)$

3. Simplify (a) $2a - (a - b)$ (b) $3(a + b) - 2(a - b)$

4. Solve (a) $x - 3 = 2 - 3x$ (b) $3(x - 2) - 8 = 0$

5. Solve (a) $2x > 4$ (b) $2(x - 3) \leqslant 6$ (c) $x - 1 < 2 - x < 4$

6. Make r the subject of the formula (a) $v = 4r + u$ (b) $s = \dfrac{5r}{p}$

7. Find P, given that $P = \dfrac{100I}{RT}$, when

(a) $I = 3$, $R = 4$ and $T = 2$ (b) $I = 6$, $R = 5$, $T = 3$

Exercise 4k

1. Evaluate (a) $3 - (-10)$ (b) $(-\frac{1}{2}) \times (-4)$ (c) $(-20) \div (-5)$

2. Simplify (a) $4a - 3b + 6a$ (b) $x + x^2 + 3x$ (c) $3a \times 4b$

3. Simplify   (a) $x - 3(x - y)$ (b) $2(x + 3y) - 4(2x + y)$

4. Solve   (a) $4 - 3a = 5 - 2a$ (b) $2(x + 4) = 3(5 - 2x)$

5. Solve   (a) $2x > 3 - x$ (b) $3 - x < 4$ (c) $2x < 3 - x < 4$

6. Make d the subject of the formula   (a) $C = \pi d$ (b) $a = 7d - s$

7. Find u, given that $u = v - gt$,   when

    (a) $v = 16$, $g = -10$ and $t = 4$ (b) $v = -6$, $g = 10$ and $t = 8$

MATHS IS OUT THERE

Did you find the meaning of 'GEMATRIA'?

Gematria has been defined as a method of interpretation of the Hebrew scriptures based upon the numerical value of the letters in the words.

It was thought that a person whose numerical 'value' exceeded another's was superior.

Example: Assign the numbers 1 to 26 to the letters of the alphabet as follows:

$$A = 1, B = 2, C = 3, \text{ etc.}$$

Using the above, John's numerical value is $\;10 + 15 + 8 + 14 = 47$.
                     Jane's numerical value is $\;10 + 1 + 14 + 5 = 30$.

This shows that John is superior to Jane.

What is your numerical value?

In the Bible, the number 666 is referred to as the 'number of the beast'. Because 666 was associated with the Devil, any person with a gematria of 666 was thought to be the Antichrist. The enemies of Martin Luther, Pope Leo X, and Napoleon identified them as being 666's.

5 ▷ PERCENTAGES

At the end of the chapter you should be able to:

1. Convert fractions and decimals to percentages and vice versa.
2. Express one quantity as a percentage of another.
3. Calculate a given percentage increase or decrease of a quantity.
4. Express the gain or loss in a transaction as a percentage of the cost.
5. (a) Calculate the selling price, given the cost and profit (loss) percentage.
    (b) Calculate the CP given the SP and profit (loss) percentage.
6. Calculate the income tax on an income given the rate of taxation and allowances.
7. Calculate the price paid for an article, given the marked price and the rate of discount.
8. Solve problems involving percentage increase and decrease.
9. Calculate the simple interest or amount on a sum of money, given the rate, time and principal.
10. Calculate P, R or T from the formula

$$I = \frac{PRT}{100}$$

11. Calculate the compound interest or depreciation on a sum of money given the rate, time and principal.

MEANING OF PERCENTAGES

We first met percentages in Book 2, Chapter 2 and we begin this chapter by reminding ourselves of the work we did then:

65% means 65 out of 100

Therefore, as a fraction $65\% = \frac{65}{100} = \frac{13}{20}$

and as a decimal $65\% = \frac{65}{100} = 0.65$

Similarly the fraction $\frac{7}{20} = \frac{7}{20} \times 100\% = 35\%$

and $\frac{7}{20} = \frac{35}{100} = 0.35$

49

Exercise 5a

Complete the following tables:

	Fraction	Percentage	Decimal
1.	$\frac{3}{5}$		
2.		40%	
3.			0.55
4.	$\frac{17}{20}$		
5.		54%	

	Fraction	Percentage	Decimal
6.			0.24
7.			0.92
8.		84%	
9.	$\frac{37}{40}$		
10.	$\frac{2}{3}$		

If 20% of the children in a class play the violin, what percentage do not?

(All the children either do, or do not, play the violin.) The percentage who do play the violin is 20% and the percentage who do not play the violin is

$$100\% - 20\% = 80\%$$

---

11. Seventy-six per cent of the passengers on an aeroplane are British. What percentage of them are not?

12. Deductions from a man's wage were: income tax 21%, pension scheme 8%, other deductions 7%. What percentage did he keep?

13. In the third year at Stanley School, 35% take woodwork only, 25% take metalwork only and 20% take both subjects. What percentage of the third year pupils study neither?

Express 45 cm as a percentage of 2 m

(First express both lengths in the same unit. We will express 2 m in cm.)

$$2\,m = 2 \times 100\,cm = 200\,cm$$

Then 45 cm as a percentage of 2 m is

$$\frac{45}{200} \times 100\% = 22\frac{1}{2}\%$$

Express the first quantity as a percentage of the second:

14. 20 cm, 50 cm

15. $3\,cm^2$, $12\,cm^2$

16. $1.53, $4.50

17. 15 cm, 3 m

18. $210\,mm^2$, $84\,cm^2$

19. $200\,mm^3$, $10\,cm^3$

20. 54 mm, 20 cm

21. 800 g, 2 kg

22. $4500\,cm^3$, 2 litres

> Find 24% of 7.5 m
>
> $$24\% \text{ of } 7.5\,\text{m} = \tfrac{24}{100} \times 7.5\,\text{m}$$
> $$= 1.8\,\text{m}$$

Find the value of:

23. 30% of 250

25. $12\tfrac{1}{2}\%$ of 4.88 cm

27. 84% of 225 g

24. 5% of $18.40

26. 12% of 4.5 km

28. $33\tfrac{1}{3}\%$ of 126 m^2

> A pupil measures the length of a line as 8.2 cm. If its actual length is 8 cm find the percentage error.
>
> $$\text{Error} = 0.2\,\text{cm}$$
> $$\text{Percentage error} = \frac{\text{error}}{\text{actual value}} \times 100$$
> $$= \frac{0.2}{8} \times 100$$
> $$= 2.5$$
>
> Therefore the percentage error is 2.5%

Find the percentage error for each of the following values:

29. Measured length 12.3 m, actual length 12 m.

30. Measured area 147 cm^2, actual area 150 cm^2.

31. Measured volume 456.75 cm^3, actual volume 450 cm^3.

32. Measured weight 975 g, actual weight 1000 g.

33. Estimated cost $25.60, actual cost $25.

> In Treetown 1680 out of a workforce of 12 000 are unemployed. What percentage is this?
>
> $$\text{Percentage unemployed} = \frac{1680}{12\,000} \times 100\% = 14\%$$

34. Paul scored 27 out of a possible 45 in a science test. What percentage was this?

35. In a form of 30 pupils, 21 of them are boys. What percentage are girls?

36. A department store employs 250 female staff. If 26 of them have long hair, what percentage of the female staff do not have long hair?

If 72% of the 25 pupils in a class are good at mathematics how many are not good at it?

If 72% are good at mathematics
$(100 - 72)\% = 28\%$ are not good at it

$$28\% \text{ of class} = \frac{28}{100} \times 25 = 7$$

Therefore 7 pupils are not good at mathematics.

37. There are 1460 pupils in my school and 35% are non-swimmers. How many pupils can swim?

38. All the students at a college live either in hall or in lodgings. If 62% of the 2650 students live in lodgings, how many live in hall?

39. Sixty-two per cent of the audience of 1650 at a concert were females. How many males attended?

Increase 250 by 42%

The new value is 142% of the old value

i.e.   new value $= \frac{142}{100} \times 250$

$$= 355$$

40. Increase 300 by 27%

41. Increase 44 by 12%

42. Increase 240 by 45%

43. Increase 23.4 by 35%

44. Decrease 200 by 14%

45. Decrease 84 by 23%

46. Decrease 350 by 16%

47. Decrease 16.4 by 65%

48. John is 8% heavier now than he was two years ago. If he weighed 55 kg then, how much does he weigh now?

49. The price of a car that cost $18 000 last year was increased by 7.5% on 1st January this year. What is its present price?

50. A school employs 60 teachers. Next year they must reduce their teaching staff by 15%. How many teachers will there be next year?

PERCENTAGE INCREASE AND PERCENTAGE DECREASE

Percentage increase or decrease arises in many different areas of life today. We read that certain workers are to receive an increase in their wages of 8%; sales tax may be increased from 15% to 18%; that the basic rate of income tax should be reduced from 30% to 27%; or that all the items in a sale are offered at a discount of 20%.

Changes are expressed in percentage terms, because this makes it easier to calculate the actual change in a particular case and to compare one change with another.

If a wage of $100 per week is increased by 8% then the new wage is

$$\frac{108}{100} \times \$100 = \$108$$

If an article costs $55 plus sales tax at 15%, then the full cost is

$$\frac{115}{100} \times \$55 = \$63.25$$

If a woman earns $550 and has to pay tax on it at the rate of 30% she actually receives

$$\frac{70}{100} \times \$550 = \$385$$

If a discount of 25% is offered in a sale, a piece of furniture, originally marked at $760, will cost

$$\frac{75}{100} \times \$760 = \$570$$

Profit and loss are normally given as a percentage of the *original* price. If a store makes a profit of 50% on an article it buys for $100 (called the cost price, CP), its profit is

$$\frac{50}{100} \times \$100 = \$50$$

and the selling price (SP) is

$$\frac{150}{100} \times \$100 = \$150$$

Exercise 5b

> A second-hand car dealer bought a car for $3500 and sold it for $4340. Find his percentage profit.
>
> $$\text{Profit} = \text{SP} - \text{CP}$$
> $$= \$4340 - \$3500$$
> $$= \$840$$
>
> $$\% \text{ profit} = \frac{\text{profit}}{\text{CP}} \times 100$$
>
> $$= \frac{\overset{120}{\$840}}{\underset{5}{\$3500}} \times 100 = 24$$
>
> Therefore the profit is 24%

Find the percentage profit:

1. CP $12, profit $3

2. CP $28, profit $8.40

3. CP $16, profit $4

4. CP $55, profit $5.50

A retailer bought a leather chair for $375 and sold it for $285. Find his percentage loss.

$$\text{Loss} = \text{CP} - \text{SP}$$
$$= \$375 - \$285$$
$$= \$90$$

$$\% \text{ loss} = \frac{\text{loss}}{\text{CP}} \times 100$$

$$= \frac{\$\overset{6}{90}}{\underset{15}{\$375}} \times \overset{4}{100} = 24$$

Therefore the loss is 24%

Find the percentage loss:

5. CP $20, loss $4

6. CP $125, loss $25

7. CP $64, loss $9.60

8. CP $160, loss $38.40

An article costing $30 is sold at a profit of 25%. Find the selling price.

Method 1 $\text{Profit} = \frac{\overset{1}{25}}{\underset{4}{100}} \times \$30$

$$= \$7.50$$
$$\text{SP} = \$30 + \$7.50$$

Therefore the selling price is $37.50

Method 2 $\text{SP} = \frac{\overset{5}{125}}{\underset{4}{100}} \times \$30$

Therefore the selling price is $37.50

Find the selling price:

9. CP $50, profit 12%

10. CP $64, profit $12\frac{1}{2}$%

11. CP $29, profit 110%

12. CP $36, loss 50%

13. CP $75, loss 64%

14. CP $128, loss $37\frac{1}{2}$%

Find the weekly cash increase for each of the following employees:

15. Ian Dickenson earning $80 p.w. receives a rise of 10%

16. Nairn Williams earning $120 p.w. receives a rise of 12%

17. Sylvia Smith earning $150 p.w. receives a rise of 8%

18. Lyn Wyman earning $180 p.w. receives a rise of 9%

19. Joe Bright earning $200 p.w. receives a rise of 7%

Which is the better cash pay rise, and by how much?

20. (a) 12% on a weekly pay of $100, or
(b) 8% on a weekly pay of $250

21. (a) 7% on a weekly pay of $90, or
(b) $3\frac{1}{2}$% on a weekly pay of $200

22. (a) 4% on a weekly pay of $300, or
(b) 3% on a weekly pay of $400

Find the purchase price of the given object, assuming that the rate of sales tax is 15%:

23. An electric iron marked $120 plus sales tax.

24. A food mixed marked $320 plus sales tax.

25. A calculator marked $84 plus sales tax.

26. A car tyre costing $152 plus sales tax.

27. A living room suite costing $2400 plus sales tax.

28. A ticket for a concert costing $8 plus sales tax.

29. Two chisels each marked $20.80 plus sales tax.

30. Three metres of material costing $5 per metre plus sales tax.

INCOME TAX AND SALE REDUCTIONS

Exercise 5c

Peter Smith has a taxable income of $8000 per annum. How much tax will he pay if the basic rate is 30%?

$$\text{Tax due} = \tfrac{30}{100} \times \$8000$$
$$= \$2400$$

Assuming that the basic rate of income tax is 30%, find the yearly tax on the following taxable incomes:

1. $5000   **2.** $8000   **3.** $6500   **4.** $12 500   **5.** $6450   **6.** $8260

Find the yearly income tax due on a taxable income of:

7. $10 000 if the basic tax rate is 33%

8. $8000 if the basic tax rate is 28%

9. $16 000 if the basic tax rate is 25%

10. $24 000 if the basic tax rate is 32%

Edgar Brooks earns $30 000 each year. If his allowances amount to $14 520, how much tax will he pay when the basic rate is 30%?

$$\text{Taxable income} = \$30\,000 - \$14\,520$$

$$= \$15\,480$$

$$\text{Tax due} = \frac{30}{100} \times \$15\,480$$

$$= \$4644$$

Use the following details to find the income tax due in each case:

	Name	Gross Income	Allowances	Basic Tax Rate
11.	Miss Deats	$24 000	$6000	30%
12.	Mr Evans	$30 000	$9000	30%
13.	Mrs Khan	$45 000	$9600	30%
14.	Mr Amos	$27 000	$7800	33%
15.	Miss Eyles	$60 000	$14 250	28%

During the January sales, a department store offers a discount of 10% off marked prices. What is the purchase price of
(a) a dinner service marked $338.00
(b) a pair of jeans marked $65.20?

Method 1

(a) Discount of 10% on a marked price of $338.00 is

$$\frac{10}{100} \times \$338 = \$33.80$$

∴ $$\text{Purchase price} = \$338 - \$33.80$$

$$= \$304.20$$

(b) Discount of 10% on a marked price of $65.20 is

$$\frac{10}{100} \times \$65.20 = \$6.52$$

∴ Purchase price $= \$65.20 - \$6.52$

$$= \$58.68$$

Method 2

(a) If the discount is 10%, the cash price is 90% of the marked selling price
i.e. purchase price of dinner service is

$$\frac{90}{100} \times \$338 = \$304.20$$

(b) Similarly, purchase price of jeans is

$$\frac{90}{100} \times \$65.20 = \$58.68$$

In a sale, a shop offers a discount of 20%. What would be the cash price for each of the following articles?

16. A dress marked $105

17. A lawn mower marked $460

18. A pair of shoes marked $64

19. A set of garden tools priced $290.00

20. Light fittings marked $168 each

In a sale, a department store offers a discount of 50% on the following articles. Find their sale price:

21. A pair of curtains marked $153

22. A leather football marked $129.20

23. A boy's jacket marked $85.80

24. A girl's dress marked $64.50

25. In order to clear a large quantity of goods a shopkeeper puts them on sale at a discount of $33\frac{1}{3}$%. Find the cash price of

(a) a shirt marked $36.60
(b) a skirt marked $66.60

FINDING THE ORIGINAL QUANTITY

Sometimes we are given an increased or decreased quantity and we want to find the original quantity. For example, if the cost of a chair including sales tax at 15% is $172.50, we might wish to find the price of the chair before the tax was added.

Exercise 5d

An article is sold for $252. If this gives a profit of 5% find the cost price.

If there is a profit of 5% and the cost price is $x

then $\qquad SP = \frac{105}{100}$ of the CP

i.e. $\qquad 252 = \frac{105}{100} \times x$

$$100 \times 252 = \cancel{100} \times \frac{105}{\cancel{100}} \times x$$

$\therefore \qquad 252 \times \frac{100}{105} = x$

i.e. $\qquad x = 240$

Therefore the cost price is $240

Find the cost price:

1. SP $98, profit 40%

2. SP $64, profit 60%

3. SP $28, profit 75%

4. SP $12, profit 100%

5. SP $4.50, profit $66\frac{2}{3}$%

6. SP $40, profit 25%

7. SP $920, profit 15%

8. SP $1008, profit 12%

9. SP $888, profit 11%

10. SP $21.50, profit $7\frac{1}{2}$%

A book is sold for $12.60 at a loss of 30%. Find the cost price.

If there is a loss of 30% and the cost price is x cents

then $\qquad SP = \frac{70}{100}$ of the CP

i.e. $\qquad 1260 = \frac{70}{100}x$

$\therefore \qquad 1260 \times \frac{100}{70} = x$

i.e. $\qquad x = 1800$

The cost price of the book is 1800 c, or $18

Find the cost price:

11. SP $30, loss 25%

12. SP $56, loss 30%

13. SP $70, loss 65%

14. SP $12, loss $33\frac{1}{3}$%

15. SP $8.16, loss 40%

18. SP $8.50, loss 50%

16. SP $45, loss 10%

19. SP $64, loss 60%

17. SP $120, loss 25%

20. SP $1200, loss 40%

After a pay rise of 5%, Peter's weekly pay is $273. How much did he earn before the rise?

If Peter's original pay was x and he receives a 5% pay rise his new pay will be 105% of his original pay.
But his new pay is $273,

$\therefore$
$$273 = \frac{105}{100} \times x$$

i.e.
$$x = \frac{273 \times 100}{105}$$

$$= 260$$

Peter's original weekly pay was $260

The following table shows the weekly wage of a number of employees after percentage increases as shown. Find the original weekly wage of each employee:

	Name	% increase in pay	Weekly wage after increase
21.	George Black	10%	$264
22.	Anne Reed	8%	$270
23.	John Rowlands	15%	$598
24.	Beryl Lewis	7%	$196.88
25.	Enid Jones	4%	$191.36

The purchase price of a watch is $276. If this includes sales tax at 15%, find the price before sales tax was added.

If the cost of an article is C,
the cost including sales tax at 15% will be $\frac{115}{100} \times \$C$

i.e.
$$\frac{115}{100} \times C = 276$$

i.e.
$$C = 276 \times \frac{100}{115}$$

$$= 240$$

The price before sales tax was added was $240

26. The purchase price of a hairdryer is $82.80. If this includes sales tax at 15%, find the price before sales tax was added.

27. I paid $2242.50 for a dining table and four chairs. If the price includes sales tax at 15%, find the price before sales tax was added.

28. John's income last week was $224 after income tax had been deducted at 30%. Calculate his pay before the tax was deducted.

29. Water increases in volume by 4% when it is frozen. How much water is required to make $884 \, \text{cm}^3$ of ice?

30. The stretched length of an elastic string is 31 cm. If this is 24% more than its unstretched length, find its unstretched length.

PROBLEMS INVOLVING PERCENTAGE INCREASE AND DECREASE

Remember that a percentage increase or decrease is always calculated as a percentage of the original quantity.

Exercise 5e

1. A house is bought for $112 000 and sold at a profit of 14%. Find the selling price.

2. Carpets that had been bought for $55.50 per square metre were sold at a loss of 26%. Find the selling price per square metre.

3. Potatoes bought at $45 per 50 kg are sold at $1.20 per kg. Find the percentage profit.

4. A shopkeeper buys 80 articles for $600 and sells them for $10.50 each. Find his percentage profit.

5. An art dealer sold a picture for $1980 thus making a profit of 65%. What did she pay for it?

6. My present average weekly grocery bill is $121.50, which is 8% more than the same goods cost me, on average, each week last year. What was my average weekly grocery bill last year?

7. When water freezes, its volume increases by 4%. What volume of water is required to make $221 \, \text{cm}^3$ of ice?

8. What is Fred Proctor's monthly wage, if, after paying deductions of 35%, he is left with $2236?

9. Engine modifications were made to a particular model of car. As a result the number of kilometres it travels on one litre of petrol increases by 8%. If the new petrol consumption is 16.2 km/l what was the previous value?

10. Between two elections, the size of the electorate in a constituency fell by 16%. For the second election, 37 191 people were entitled to vote. How many could have voted at the first election?

11. When the rate of sales tax is 15% an LP record costs $13.80. What will it cost if the rate of sales tax is
(a) increased to 20%
(b) decreased to 10%?

12. The purchase price of a diamond ring increases by $60 when the rate of sales tax is increased from 12% to 20%. Find the original purchase price of the ring.

SIMPLE INTEREST

If you borrow money, you will normally have to pay for it, i.e. you must repay more than you borrow.

The difference between what you borrow and what you repay is called the *interest*. The sum of money borrowed (or lent) is called the *principal*. If the interest is an agreed percentage of this sum it is called *simple interest*.

In Book 2, we developed the formula

$$I = \frac{PRT}{100}$$

where I is the simple interest, P the principal, R the rate per cent each year, and T the time in years for which the principal is borrowed or invested.

Hence $\qquad 100I = PRT$

This formula enables us to find any one of four quantities, if the other three are known.

The sum of the principal (P) and the interest (I) is called the amount. This is denoted by A, i.e. $A = P + I$

Exercise 5f

Find the simple interest on:

1. $200 invested for 2 years at 8% p.a.

2. $160 invested for 5 years at 14% p.a.

3. $730 invested for 3 years at 13% p.a.

4. $337 invested for 7 years at 8% p.a.

5. $650 invested for 4 years at $6\frac{1}{4}$ p.a.

6. $420 invested for 3 years at 10% p.a.

7. $280 invested for 6 years at 12% p.a.

8. $834 invested for 5 years at 9% p.a.

9. $500 invested for 8 years at $12\frac{1}{2}$% p.a.

10. $726 invested for 3 years at $7\frac{3}{4}$% p.a.

11. What sum of money invested for 5 years at 12% p.a. gives $264 simple interest?

12. How long must $3700 be invested at 9% p.a. simple interest to give interest of $2331?

13. What annual rate of simple interest is necessary to give interest of $416 on a principal of $800 invested for 8 years?

14. What sum of money earns $312 simple interest if invested for 8 years at 13%?

15. Find the annual rate per cent that earns $234 simple interest when $900 is invested for $6\frac{1}{2}$ years.

> What will $780 amount to if invested for 6 years at 11% p.a. simple interest?
>
> Interest of $780 for 6 years at 11% is
>
> $$\$780 \times \frac{11}{100} \times 6 = \$514.80$$
>
> $$\text{Amount} = \text{Original sum} + \text{interest}$$
>
> $$= \$780 + \$514.80 = \$1294.80$$
>
> $\therefore$ $780 amounts to $1294.80 in 6 years at 11% p.a. simple interest.
>
> [For a method using the formula see Book 2.]

16. Find the amount if:

(a) $120 is invested for 3 years at 14% p.a. simple interest.

(b) $280 is invested for 5 years at 8% p.a. simple interest.

(c) $530 is invested for 6 years at 9% p.a. simple interest.

> What annual rate of simple interest enables $500 to amount to $900 in 10 years?
>
> $$(A = P + I \quad \text{i.e.} \quad I = A - P)$$
>
> $\therefore \qquad\qquad I = 900 - 500 = 400$
>
> but $\qquad\qquad 100I = PRT$
>
> $\therefore \qquad 100 \times 400 = 500 \times R \times 10$
>
> $\therefore \qquad\qquad R = \frac{100 \times 400}{500 \times 10}$
>
> $$= 8$$
>
> i.e. rate of simple interest is 8% p.a.

17. What sum of money amounts to:

(a) $254 if invested for 3 years at 9% p.a. simple interest?

(b) $210.80 if invested for 4 years at 6% p.a. simple interest?

(c) $473.40 if invested for 7 years at $4\frac{1}{2}$% p.a. simple interest?

18. What length of time is required if:

(a) $500 amounts to $635 when invested at 9% p.a. simple interest?

(b) $380 amounts to $570 when invested at 10% p.a. simple interest?

(c) $144 amounts to $192.96 when invested at $8\frac{1}{2}$% p.a. simple interest?

COMPOUND PERCENTAGE PROBLEMS

There are many occasions when a percentage increase or decrease happens more than once. Suppose that a plot of land is bought for $20 000 and increases in value (appreciates) by 10% of its value each year.

After one year, its value will be 110% of its initial value, i.e.

$$\frac{110}{100} \times \$20\,000 = \$22\,000$$

The next year it will increase by 10% of the $22 000 it was worth at the beginning of the year, i.e. its value after two years will be

$$\frac{110}{100} \times \$22\,000 = \$24\,200$$

While some things increase in value year after year, many things decrease in value (depreciate) each year. If you buy a car or a motorcycle it will probably depreciate in value more quickly than anything else you buy.

If you invest money in a Building Society or Savings Bank Account and do not spend the interest, your money will increase by larger amounts each year.
This kind of interest is called *compound interest*.

Exercise 5g

In this exercise give all answers that are not exact correct to the nearest cent.

Find the compound interest on $2600 invested for 2 years at 8% p.a.

$$\text{Simple interest for first year at 8\%} = \frac{8}{100} \times \$2600$$

$$= \$\,\frac{20\,800}{100}$$

$$= \$208$$

$$\text{New principal} = \text{original principal} + \text{interest}$$

$$= \$2600 + \$208$$

$$= \$2808$$

Simple interest for second year at 8%

$$= \frac{8}{100} \times \$2808$$

$$= \$224.64$$

∴ total of interest for the two years is

$$\$208 + \$224.64 = \$432.64$$

i.e. compound interest on $2600 for 2 years at 8% is $432.64

Find the compound interest on:

1. $200 for 2 years at 10% p.a.

2. $300 for 2 years at 12% p.a.

3. $400 for 3 years at 8% p.a.

4. $650 for 3 years at 9% p.a.

5. $520 for 2 years at 13% p.a.

6. $690 for 2 years at 14% p.a.

7. $624 for 3 years at 12% p.a.

8. A house is bought for $80 000 and appreciates at 10% each year. What will it be worth in 2 years' time?

9. A postage stamp increases in value by 15% each year. If it is bought for $50, what will it be worth in 3 years' time?

10. A motorcycle bought for $6000 depreciates in value by 10% each year. Find its value after 3 years.

11. A motor car bought for $20 000 depreciates in any one year by 20% of its value at the beginning of that year. Find its value after 2 years.

MATHS IS OUT THERE

Numerologists believe that events in our lives can be explained by using numbers.

Ask your history teacher to tell you about the following people: Churchill, Hitler, Mussolini, Roosevelt and Stalin. Some information on them is shown below:

Name	Year born	Age in 1944	Year he took office	No. of years in office	Total
Churchill	1874	70	1940	4	3888
Hitler	1889	55	1933	11	3888
Mussolini	1883	61	1921	23	3888
Roosevelt	1882	62	1933	11	3888
Stalin	1879	65	1924	20	3888

1944 was considered to be the year of the turning point of World War II.

$$1944 \times 2 = 3888\,!!$$

6 ▶ CONGRUENT TRIANGLES

At the end of the chapter you should be able to:

1. Identify congruent shapes.
2. Identify transformations under which shapes are congruent.
3. State the necessary and sufficient conditions for triangles to be congruent.
4. Use the properties in (3) to solve problems on congruent triangles.
5. Use conditions necessary for congruent triangles to prove properties of parallelograms.
6. Use conditions for congruence to investigate properties of special quadrilaterals.

THE BASIC FACTS

These facts were introduced in Book 1:

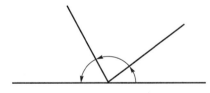

angles on a straight line add up to 180°;

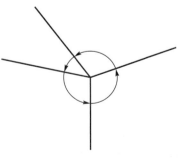

angles at a point add up to 360°;

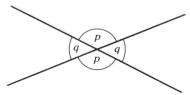

vertically opposite angles are equal.

When a transversal cuts a pair of parallel lines, various angles are formed and:

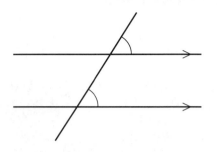

corresponding angles are equal;

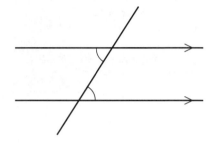

alternate angles are equal;

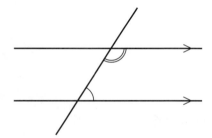

interior angles add up to 180°.

In *any* triangle, whatever its shape or size, the sum of the three angles is 180°,

e.g.

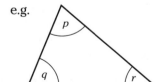

$$p + q + r = 180°$$

The exercise that follows will help you revise these facts. However, you must state which fact you have used as a reason for statements that you make. The facts do not have to be quoted in full but can be shortened using a number of standard abbreviations.

For example, if you state that $x = 60°$ and the reason is that x and $60°$ are vertically opposite angles then you could write

$$x = 60° \ (\text{vert. opp. } \angle s)$$

Exercise 6a

Find the size of the angle marked x, giving brief reasons to justify your statements.

(Fill in the size of any angles that you find.)

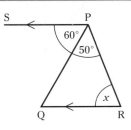

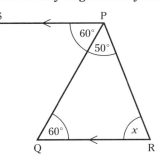

From the diagram

$$\widehat{PQR} = 60° \quad (\text{alt. } \angle s)$$

$$50° + 60° + x = 180° \quad (\angle \text{ sum of } \triangle PQR)$$

$$\therefore \qquad x = 70°$$

In each of the following diagrams find the size of the angle marked x, giving brief reasons for your answer:

1.

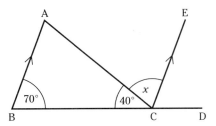

2.

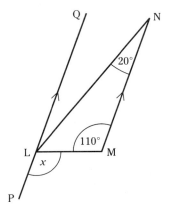

3.

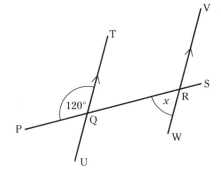

4.

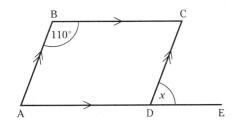

5.

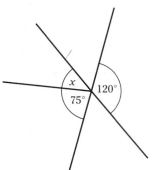

7.

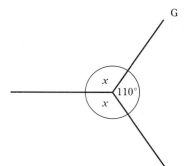

6.

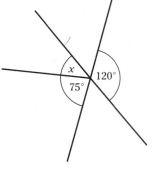

8.

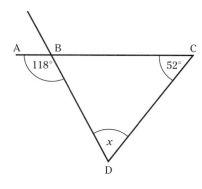

Prove that $\widehat{ABC} = \widehat{CDE}$

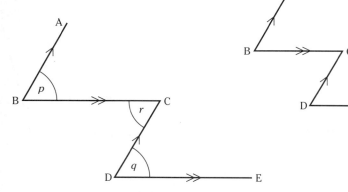

(Mark with a letter the angles you need to refer to.)

From the diagram

$$p = r \quad (\text{alt. } \angle s)$$

$$r = q \quad (\text{alt. } \angle s)$$

$\therefore$ $$p = q$$

i.e. $$\widehat{ABC} = \widehat{CDE}$$

9.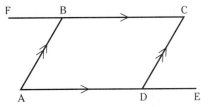

Prove that $\hat{ABF} = \hat{CDE}$

10.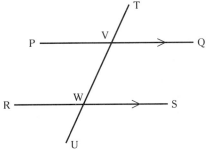

Prove that $\hat{TVQ} + \hat{RWV} = 180°$

11.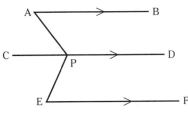

Prove that $\hat{APE} = \hat{BAP} + \hat{FEP}$

12.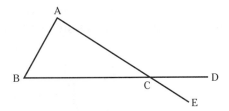

Prove that $\hat{DCE} + \hat{CAB} + \hat{CBA} = 180°$

13.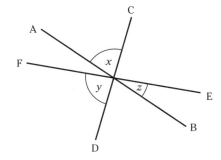

Prove that $x + y + z = 180°$

14.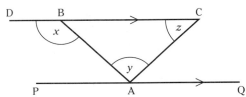

Prove that $x = y + z$

CONGRUENT SHAPES

Two shapes are *congruent* if they are exactly the same shape and size, i.e. one shape is an exact copy of the other shape, although not necessarily drawn in the same position.

In each of these diagrams the two figures are congruent:

In each case the second shape is an exact copy of the first shape although it may be turned round or turned over.

In each of these diagrams the two figures are not congruent (they may be similar; i.e. have the same shape but different sizes):

Exercise 6b

In the following questions state whether or not the two shapes are congruent. If you are not sure, trace one shape and see if it fits exactly over the other shape:

1.

6.
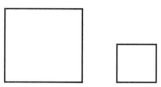

2.

7.
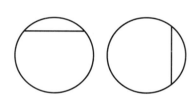

3.
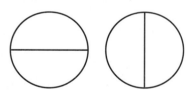

8.
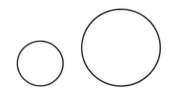

4.

9.
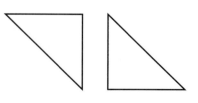

5.

10.
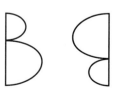

TRANSFORMATIONS AND CONGRUENT FIGURES

The shape and size of a figure are not altered by certain transformations. Reflection produces congruent shapes:

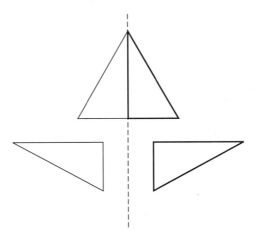

Rotation produces congruent shapes:

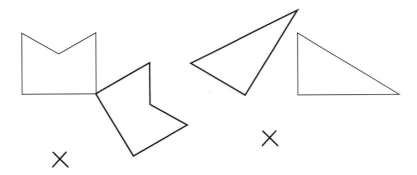

Translation produces congruent shapes:

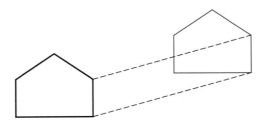

But enlargement does *not* produce congruent shapes, it produces similar shapes:

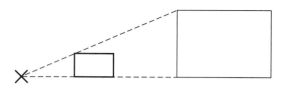

Exercise 6c

Describe the transformation in each of the following cases. The grey shape is the image. State whether the object and the image are congruent:

1.

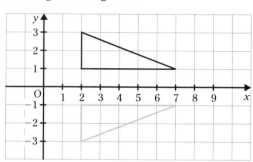

2.

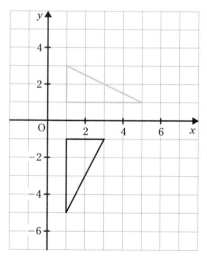

3.

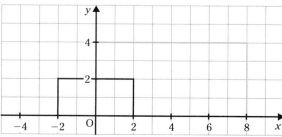

4.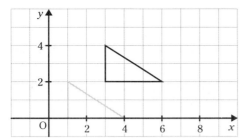

5.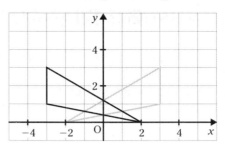

6.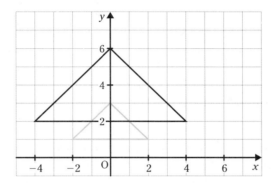

7.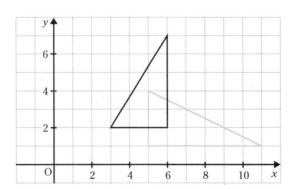

8.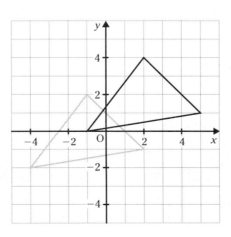

CONGRUENT TRIANGLES

It is not always practical or possible to use tracing paper to determine whether two shapes are congruent.

Triangles are simple figures and not very much information is needed to determine whether one triangle is an exact copy of another triangle.

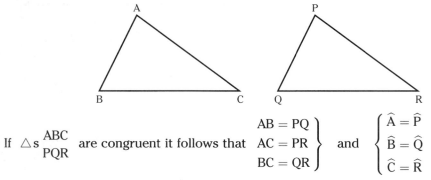

If $\triangle$s $\dfrac{\text{ABC}}{\text{PQR}}$ are congruent it follows that $\left.\begin{array}{l} \text{AB} = \text{PQ} \\ \text{AC} = \text{PR} \\ \text{BC} = \text{QR} \end{array}\right\}$ and $\left\{\begin{array}{l} \hat{\text{A}} = \hat{\text{P}} \\ \hat{\text{B}} = \hat{\text{Q}} \\ \hat{\text{C}} = \hat{\text{R}} \end{array}\right.$

To make an exact copy of these triangles we do not need to know the lengths of all three sides and the sizes of all three angles: three measurements are usually enough and we now investigate which three measurements are suitable.

Exercise 6d

In each of the following questions make a rough sketch of $\triangle$ABC. Construct a triangle with the same measurements as those given for $\triangle$ABC. Is your construction an exact copy of $\triangle$ABC? (Try to construct a different triangle with the given measurements.)

1. $\triangle$ABC, in which AB = 8 cm, BC = 5 cm, AC = 6 cm.

2. $\triangle$ABC, in which $\hat{\text{A}} = 40°$, $\hat{\text{B}} = 60°$, $\hat{\text{C}} = 80°$.

3. $\triangle$ABC, in which AB = 7 cm, BC = 12 cm, AC = 8 cm.

4. $\triangle$ABC, in which $\hat{\text{A}} = 20°$, $\hat{\text{B}} = 40°$, $\hat{\text{C}} = 120°$.

5. What extra information do you need about $\triangle$ABC in questions 2 and 4 in order to make an exact copy?

THREE PAIRS OF SIDES

From the last exercise you should be convinced that an exact copy of a triangle can be made if the lengths of the three sides are known. Therefore,

> two triangles are congruent if the three sides of one triangle are equal to the three sides of the other triangle.

However if the three angles of one triangle are equal to the three angles of another triangle they may not be congruent (but they are similar).

Exercise 6e

Decide whether the following pairs of triangles are congruent. Give brief reasons for your answers.

(a)

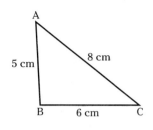 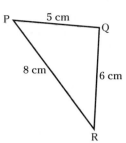

$$\left.\begin{array}{l} AB = PQ \\ BC = QR \\ AC = PR \end{array}\right\} \quad \therefore \quad \triangle s \begin{array}{l} ABC \\ PQR \end{array} \text{ are congruent (3 sides)}$$

(Notice that we write corresponding vertices one under the other.)

(b)

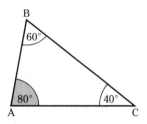 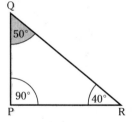

In $\triangle ABC$, $\widehat{A} = 80°$ (angles of $\triangle$)

In $\triangle PQR$, $\widehat{Q} = 50°$ (angles of $\triangle$)

$\therefore \triangle ABC$ and $\triangle PQR$ are not congruent.

(c)

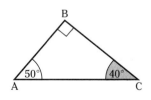 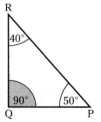

In $\triangle ABC$, $\widehat{C} = 40°$ (angles of $\triangle$)

In $\triangle PQR$, $\widehat{Q} = 90°$ (angles of $\triangle$)

$\therefore \quad \triangle s \begin{array}{l} ABC \\ PQR \end{array}$ are similar, but probably not congruent.

In questions 1 to 6 state whether or not the two triangles are congruent. Give a brief reason for your answers. All lengths are in centimetres:

1.

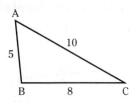

2.

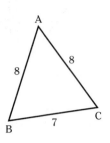

3.

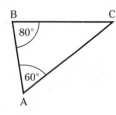   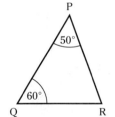

4.

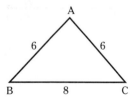   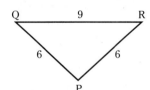

5.

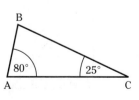   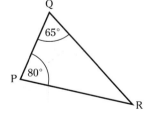

6.

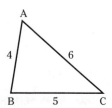   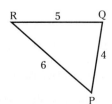

7.

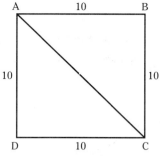

Are $\triangle$ADC and $\triangle$ABC congruent?

8.

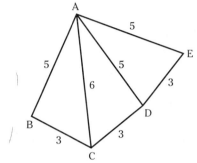

Which triangles are congruent?

9.

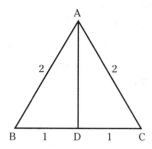

Are $\triangle$ABD and $\triangle$ACD congruent?

10.

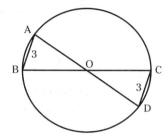

The point O is the centre of the circle and the radius is 5 cm. Are $\triangle$ABO and $\triangle$CDO congruent?

TWO ANGLES AND A SIDE

To make an exact copy of a triangle we need to know the length of at least one side.

Exercise 6f

1. Construct $\triangle$ABC, in which AB = 6 cm, $\widehat{A} = 30°$, $\widehat{B} = 60°$

2. Construct $\triangle$PQR, in which PR = 6 cm, $\widehat{P} = 30°$, $\widehat{Q} = 60°$

3. Construct $\triangle$LMN, in which LM = 6 cm, $\widehat{L} = 30°$, $\widehat{M} = 60°$

4. Construct $\triangle$XYZ, in which YZ = 6 cm, $\widehat{X} = 30°$, $\widehat{Y} = 60°$

5. How many of the triangles that you have constructed are congruent?

6. How many different triangles can you construct from the following information: one angle is 40°, another angle is 70° and the length of one side is 8 cm?

Now you can see that we are able to make an exact copy of a triangle if we know the sizes of two of its angles and the length of one side provided that we place the side in the same position relative to the angles in both triangles, i.e.

two triangles are congruent if two angles and one side of one triangle are equal to two angles and the *corresponding* side of the other triangle.

Exercise 6g

Decide whether these triangles are congruent. Give a brief reason for your answer.

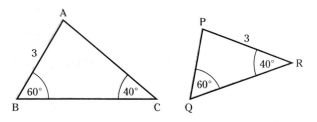

$\triangle s \begin{array}{l} \text{ABC} \\ \text{PQR} \end{array}$ are similar   (angles equal)

but not congruent   (AB and PQ are corr. sides and are *not* equal).

In questions 1 to 8 state whether or not the two triangles are congruent. Give brief reasons for your answers. All lengths are in centimetres:

1.

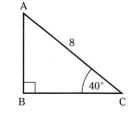

2.

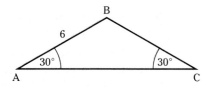

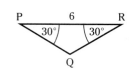

3.

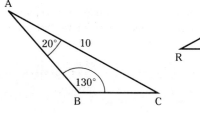

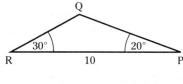

4.

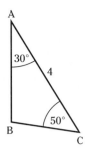

5.

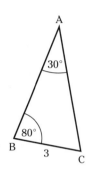

6.

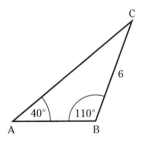
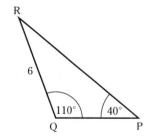

7.

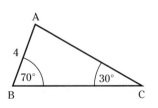
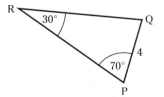

8.

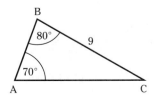
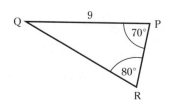

9.

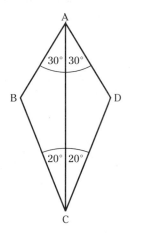

Are △ABC and △ADC congruent?

10.

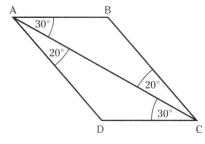

Are △ABC and △ADC congruent?

TWO SIDES AND AN ANGLE

We are now left with one more possible combination of three measurements: if we know the lengths of two sides and the size of one angle in a triangle, does this fix the size and shape of the triangle?

Exercise 6h

Can you make an exact copy of the following triangles from the information given about them? (Try to construct each triangle.)

1. △ABC, in which AB = 8 cm, BC = 5 cm, $\widehat{B} = 30°$

2. △XYZ, in which XY = 8 cm, XZ = 5 cm, $\widehat{Y} = 30°$

3. △PQR, in which $\widehat{Q} = 60°$, PQ = 6 cm, QR = 8 cm

4. △LMN, in which LM = 8 cm, $\widehat{M} = 20°$, LN = 4 cm

5. △DEF, in which DE = 5 cm, $\widehat{E} = 90°$, EF = 6 cm

Now it is possible to see that we can make an exact copy of a triangle if we know the lengths of two sides and the size of one angle, provided that the angle is between those two sides. Therefore,

> two triangles are congruent if two sides and the *included* angle of one triangle are equal to two sides and the *included* angle of the other triangle.

If the angle is not between the two known sides, then we cannot always be sure that we can make an exact copy of the triangle. We will now investigate this case further.

Exercise 6i

Can you make an exact copy of each of the following triangles from the information given about them?

1. $\triangle$ABC, in which AB = 6 cm, $\widehat{B} = 90°$, AC = 10 cm.

2. $\triangle$PQR, in which PQ = 8 cm, $\widehat{Q} = 40°$, PR = 6.5 cm.

3. $\triangle$XYZ, in which XY = 5 cm, $\widehat{Y} = 90°$, XZ = 13 cm.

4. $\triangle$LMN, in which LM = 5 cm, $\widehat{M} = 60°$, LN = 4.5 cm.

5. $\triangle$DEF, in which DE = 7 cm, $\widehat{E} = 90°$, DF = 10 cm.

6. $\triangle$RST, in which RS = 5 cm, $\widehat{S} = 120°$, RT = 8 cm.

7. Can you calculate any further information about any of the triangles in questions 1 to 6?

From question 7 you can see that, when the given angle is 90° the length of the remaining side of the triangle can be calculated.

Therefore, if we are told that one angle in a triangle is a right angle and we are also given the length of one side and the hypotenuse, then this information fixes the shape and size of the triangle since it is equivalent to knowing the lengths of the three sides.

> Two triangles are congruent if they both have a right angle, and the hypotenuse and a side of one triangle are equal to the hypotenuse and a side of the other triangle.

Exercise 6j

In questions 1 to 8 state whether or not the two triangles are congruent. Give brief reasons for your answers. All lengths are in centimetres:

1.

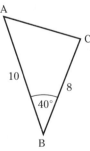 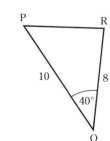

2.

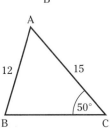 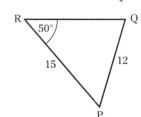

3.

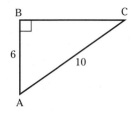

4.

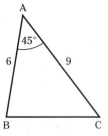   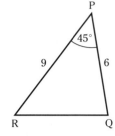

5.

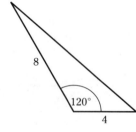

6.

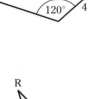

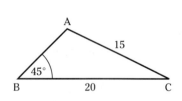

7.

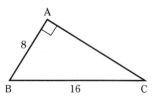   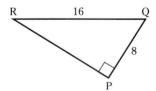

8.

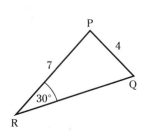   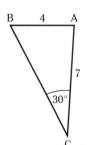

9.

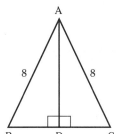

Are △ABD and △ACD congruent?

10.

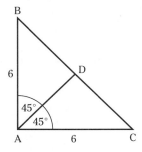

Are △ABD and △ACD congruent?

Summing up, two triangles are congruent if:

either   the three sides of one triangle are equal to the three sides of the other triangle (SSS)

or   two angles and a side of one triangle are equal to two angles and the corresponding side of the other triangle (AAS)

or   two sides and the included angle of one triangle are equal to two sides and the included angle of the other triangle (SAS)

or   two triangles each have a right angle, and the hypotenuse and a side of one triangle are equal to the hypotenuse and a side of the other triangle (RHS).

 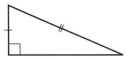

Exercise 6k

State whether or not each of the following pairs of triangles are congruent. Give brief reasons for your answers. All measurements are in centimetres:

1.

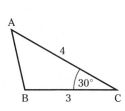

2.

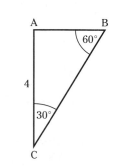

3.

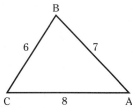

4.

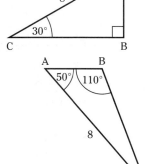

5.

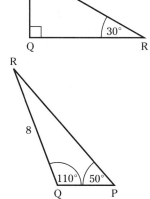

6.

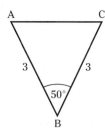

7.

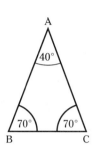   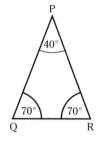

8.

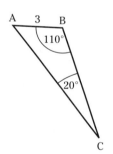   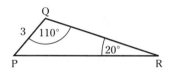

9.

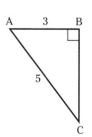   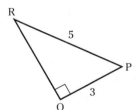

10.

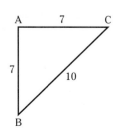   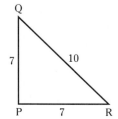

11.

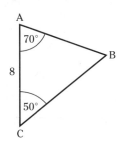

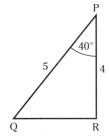

12.

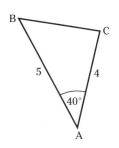

13.

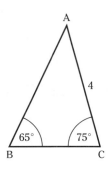

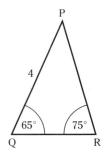

14.

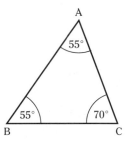

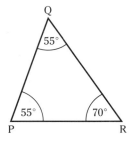

15.

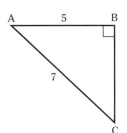

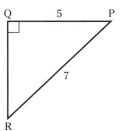

PROBLEMS

We do not need to know actual measurements to prove that triangles are congruent. If we can show that a correct combination of sides and angles are the same in both triangles, the triangles must be congruent.

Exercise 61

In a quadrilateral ABCD, AB = DC and AD = BC. The diagonal BD is drawn. Prove that △ABD and △CDB are congruent.

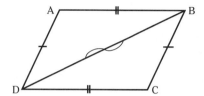

(Mark on your diagram all the information given and any further facts that you discover. The symbol ⁓ on BD indicates that it is common to both triangles.)

In △s ABD, CDB   AB = CD (given)

AD = CB (given)

DB is the same for both triangles

∴ △s ABD / CDB are congruent (SSS).

1.

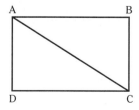

ABCD is a rectangle. Prove that △ABC and △CDA are congruent.

2.

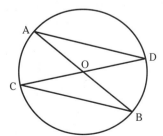

AB and CD are diameters of the circle and O is the centre. Prove that △AOD and △COB are congruent.

3.

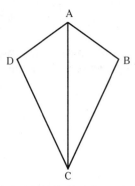

ABCD is a kite in which AD = AB and CD = BC. Prove that △ADC and △ABC are congruent.

4.

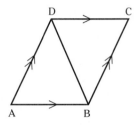

ABCD is a parallelogram. Prove that △ABD and △CDB are congruent.

5.

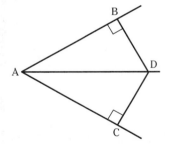

AD bisects BÂC, DB is perpendicular to AB and DC is perpendicular to AC. Prove that △ABD and △ACD are congruent.

6.

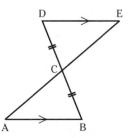

Prove that △ABC and △EDC are congruent.

7.

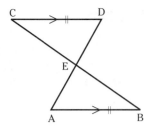

CD and AB are equal and parallel. Prove that △ABE and △DCE are congruent.

8.

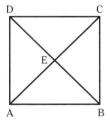

ABCD is a square. Show that △s ABE, BCE, CDE and DAE are all congruent.

9.

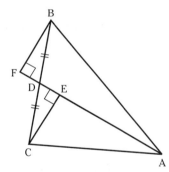

D is the midpoint of BC. CE and BF are perpendicular to AF. Find a pair of congruent triangles.

10.

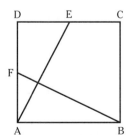

ABCD is a square. E is the midpoint of DC and F is the midpoint of AD. Show that △ADE and △BAF are congruent.

11.

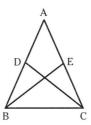

ABC is an isosceles triangle in which AB = AC. D is the midpoint of AB and E is the midpoint of AC. Prove that $\triangle$BDC is congruent with $\triangle$CEB.

12. ABCD is a rectangle and E is the midpoint of AB. Join DE and CE and show that $\triangle$ADE is congruent with $\triangle$BCE.

13. ABCD is a rectangle. E is the midpoint of AB and F is the midpoint of DC. Join DE and BF and show that $\triangle$ADE is congruent with $\triangle$CBF.

USING CONGRUENT TRIANGLES

Once two triangles have been shown to be congruent it follows that the other corresponding sides and angles are equal. This gives a good way of proving that certain angles are equal or that certain lines are the same length.

Exercise 6m

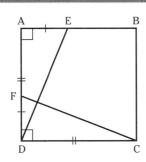

ABCD is a square and AE = DF.
Show that DE = CF.

In $\triangle$s DAE and CDF

$$AE = DF \quad (\text{given})$$

$$DA = CD \quad (\text{sides of a square})$$

$$\widehat{DAE} = \widehat{CDF} \quad (\text{angles of a square are } 90°)$$

$\therefore$ $\triangle$s $\begin{matrix} \text{DAE} \\ \text{CDF} \end{matrix}$ are congruent (SAS).

(We have written the triangles so that corresponding vertices are lined up. We can then see the remaining corresponding sides and angles.)

$\therefore$ $\qquad\qquad\qquad\qquad$ DE = CF

1.

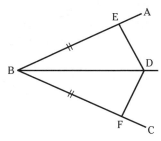

BD bisects A$\widehat{B}$C. BE and BF are equal. Show that triangles BED and BFD are congruent and hence prove that ED = FD.

2.

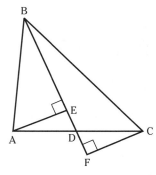

D is the midpoint of AC. AE and CF are both perpendicular to BF. Show that triangles AED and CFD are congruent and hence prove that AE = CF.

3.

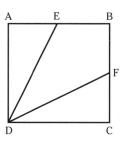

ABCD is a square and E and F are the midpoints of AB and BC. Show that $\triangle$ADE is congruent with $\triangle$CDF and hence prove that DE = DF.

4.

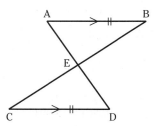

AB and CD are parallel and equal in length. Show that $\triangle$AEB and $\triangle$DEC are congruent and hence prove that E is the midpoint of both CB and AD.

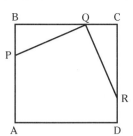

ABCD is a square and P, Q and R are points on AB, BC and CD respectively such that AP = BQ = CR. Show that $P\widehat{Q}R = 90°$

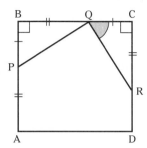

(We will first prove that $\triangle PBQ$ and $\triangle QCR$ are congruent.)

In $\triangle PBQ$ and $\triangle QCR$

$$BQ = CR \qquad\qquad \text{(given)}$$

$$P\widehat{B}Q = Q\widehat{C}R = 90° \qquad\qquad \text{(angles of a square)}$$

also $\quad PB = QC \begin{cases} AB = BC & \text{(sides of a square)} \\ AP = BQ & \text{(given)} \end{cases}$

$\therefore \; \triangle s \begin{matrix} PBQ \\ QCR \end{matrix}$ are congruent. $\qquad\qquad$ (SAS)

$\therefore \qquad\qquad B\widehat{Q}P = Q\widehat{R}C$

In $\triangle QRC \qquad Q\widehat{R}C + C\widehat{Q}R = 90° \qquad$ (angles of triangle)

$\therefore \qquad\qquad B\widehat{Q}P + C\widehat{Q}R = 90°$

But $\qquad B\widehat{Q}P + P\widehat{Q}R + C\widehat{Q}R = 180° \qquad$ (angles on st. line)

$\therefore \qquad\qquad P\widehat{Q}R = 90°$

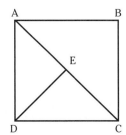

ABCD is a square and E is the midpoint of the diagonal AC. First show that triangles ADE and CDE are congruent and hence prove that DE is perpendicular to AC.

6.

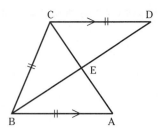

CD is parallel to BA and CD = CB = BA.

Show that △CDE is congruent with △BAE and hence that CA bisects BD.

7. Using the same diagram and the result from question 6, show that △BEC is congruent with △CED. Hence prove that CA and BD cut at right angles.

8.

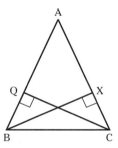

Triangle ABC is isosceles, with AB = AC. BX is perpendicular to AC and CQ is perpendicular to AB. Prove that BX = CQ.
(Find a pair of congruent triangles first.)

9.

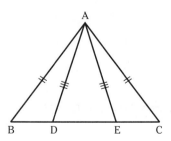

In the diagram, AB = AC and AD = AE. Prove that BD = EC.

(Consider triangles ABD and ACE.)

10. AB is a straight line. Draw a line AX perpendicular to AB. On the other side of AB, draw a line BY perpendicular to AB so that BY is equal to AX. Prove that $A\hat{X}Y = B\hat{Y}X$.

PROPERTIES OF PARALLELOGRAMS

In Book 1 we investigated the properties of parallelograms by observation and measurement of a few particular parallelograms. Now we can use congruent triangles to prove that these properties are true for all parallelograms.

A parallelogram is formed when two pairs of parallel lines cross each other.

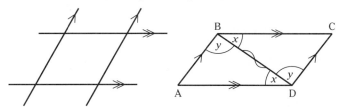

In the parallelogram ABCD, joining BD gives two triangles in which:

the angles marked x are equal (they are alternate angles with respect to parallels AD and BC);

the angles marked y are equal (they are alternate angles with respect to parallels AB and DC);

and BD is the same for both triangles.

$\therefore$ $\triangle$s $\begin{matrix} \text{BCD} \\ \text{DAB} \end{matrix}$ are congruent (AAS).

$\therefore$ BC = AD and AB = DC

i.e.   the opposite sides of a parallelogram are the same length.

Also from the congruent triangles

$\hat{A} = \hat{C}$

and $A\hat{B}C = C\hat{D}A$ $(x + y = y + x)$

i.e.   the opposite angles of a parallelogram are equal.

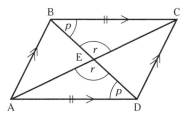

Drawing both diagonals of the parallelogram gives four triangles.

Considering the two triangles BEC, DEA

$\qquad$ BC = AD   (opp. sides of ||gram)

$\qquad$ $E\hat{B}C = E\hat{D}A$ (alt. $\angle$s)

$\qquad$ $B\hat{E}C = A\hat{E}D$ (vert. opp. $\angle$s)

$\therefore$ $\triangle$s $\begin{array}{c}\text{BEC}\\\text{DEA}\end{array}$ are congruent (AAS).

$\therefore$ BE = ED and AE = EC

i.e. | the diagonals of a parallelogram bisect each other. |

The diagrams below summarise these properties.

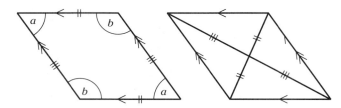

It is equally important to realise that, in general,

the diagonals are *not* the same length,

the diagonals do *not* bisect the angles of a parallelogram.

In the exercise that follows, you are asked to investigate the properties of some of the other special quadrilaterals.

Exercise 6n

1.

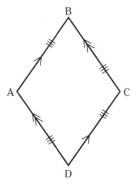

ABCD is a rhombus (a parallelogram in which all four sides are equal in length). Join AC and show that $\triangle$ABC and $\triangle$ADC are congruent. What does AC do to the angles of the rhombus at A and C? Does the diagonal BD do the same to the angles at B and D?

2.

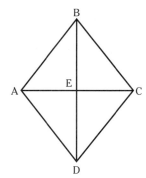

ABCD is a rhombus. Use the results from question 1 to show that $\triangle$s ABE and BCE are congruent. What can you now say about the angles AEB and BEC?

3.

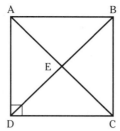

ABCD is a square (a rhombus with right-angled corners). Use the properties of the diagonals of a rhombus to show that △AEB is isosceles. Hence prove that the diagonals of a square are the same length.

Are the two diagonals of *every* rhombus the same length?

4.

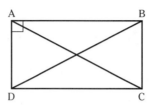

ABCD is a rectangle (a parallelogram with right-angled corners). Prove that △s ADB and DAC are congruent. What can you deduce about the lengths of AC and DB?

5.

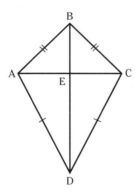

ABCD is a kite in which AB = BC and AD = DC.
Does the diagonal BD bisect the angles at B and D?
Does the diagonal AC bisect the angles at A and C?
Is E the midpoint of either diagonal?
What can you say about the angles at E?

6.

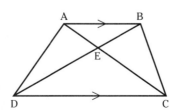

ABCD is a trapezium: it has just one pair of parallel sides. Are there any congruent triangles in this diagram?

7.

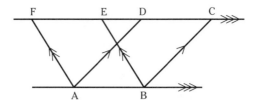

In the diagram, ABCD and ABEF are parallelograms. Show that △s ADF and BCE are congruent.

By considering the shape ABCF and then removing each of the triangles AFD and BEC in turn, what can you say about the areas of the two parallelograms?

USING PROPERTIES OF SPECIAL QUADRILATERALS

In question 7 you proved a property of two parallelograms.

> Two parallelograms with the same base and drawn between the same pair of parallel lines are equal in area.

The diagrams below summarise the other results from Exercise 6n:

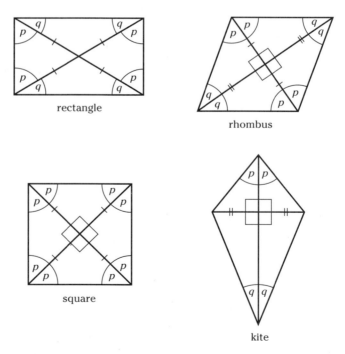

rectangle

rhombus

square

kite

You can now use any of these facts in the following exercise.

Exercise 6p

1.

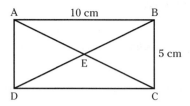

ABCD is a rectangle. The diagonals AC and DB cut at E. How far is E from BC?

2.

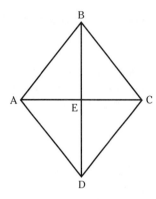

ABCD is a rhombus in which AC = 6 cm and BD = 8 cm. Find the length of AB.

3.

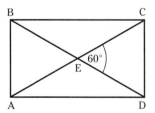

ABCD is a rectangle in which CÊD = 60°. Find EĈD.

4.

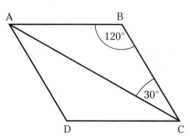

ABCD is a parallelogram in which AB̂C = 120° and BĈA = 30°. Show that ABCD is also a rhombus.

5. In a rectangle ABCD, AB = 6 cm and the diagonal BD is 10 cm. Make a rough sketch of the rectangle and then construct ABCD. Measure AD.

6. In a rhombus ABCD, the diagonal AC is 8 cm and the diagonal BD is 6 cm. Construct the rhombus and measure AB.
(Remember first to make a rough sketch.)

7. ABCD is a parallelogram in which the diagonal AC is 10 cm and the diagonal BD is 12 cm. AC and BD cut at E and $\hat{AEB} = 60°$. Make a rough sketch of the parallelogram and then construct ABCD. Measure BC.

8. Construct a rhombus ABCD in which the sides are 5 cm long and the diagonal AC is 8 cm long. Measure the diagonal BD.

9. Construct a square ABCD whose diagonal, AC, is 8 cm long. Measure the side AB.

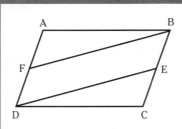

ABCD is a parallelogram. E is the midpoint of BC and F is the midpoint of AD.
Prove that   BF = DE.

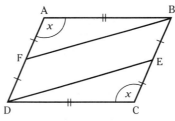

In △s ABF and CDE

$$AF = EC \quad (\tfrac{1}{2} \text{ opp. sides of parallelogram})$$

$$AB = DC \quad (\text{opp. sides of parallelogram})$$

$$\hat{FAB} = \hat{ECD} \quad (\text{opp. angles of parallelogram})$$

∴   △s ABF / CDE are congruent (SAS).

10.

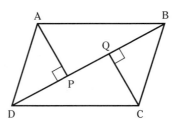

ABCD is a parallelogram. AP is perpendicular to BD and CQ is perpendicular to BD.
Prove that   AP = CQ.

11.

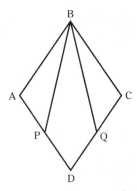

ABCD is a rhombus. P is the midpoint of AD and Q is the midpoint of CD.
Prove that   BP = BQ.

12.

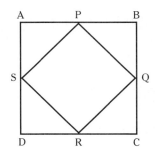

ABCD is a square and P, Q, R and S are the midpoints of AB, BC, CD and DA.
Prove that PQRS is a square.

13.

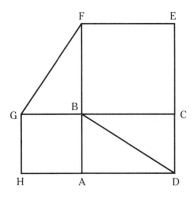

ABCD is a rectangle. ABGH and BCEF are squares. Show that GF = BD.

MATHS IS OUT THERE

Did you know that Cathleen Morawetz was the daughter of John Synge, an applied
mathematician? She is the first woman to head a mathematics institute – Courant
Institute of Mathematics.

SIMULTANEOUS EQUATIONS

At the end of the chapter you should be able to:

1. Solve a pair of simultaneous equations by
   (a) the method of elimination
   (b) a graphical method.
2. Solve problems using simultaneous equations.
3. Identify a pair of equations which have
   (a) no solution
   (b) an infinite number of solutions.

EQUATIONS WITH TWO UNKNOWN QUANTITIES

Up to now the equations we have solved have had only one unknown quantity, but there can be more.

Looking at the equation $2x + y = 8$, we can see that there are many possible values which will fit, for instance $x = 2$ and $y = 4$, or $x = 1$ and $y = 6$. We could also have $x = -1$ and $y = 10$ or even $x = 1.681$ and $y = 4.638$. Indeed, there is an infinite set of pairs of solutions.

If however we are *also* told that $x + y = 5$, then we shall find that not every pair of numbers which satisfies the first equation also satisfies the second. While $x = 2$, $y = 4$ satisfies the first equation, it does not satisfy $x + y = 5$. On the other hand $x = 3$, $y = 2$ satisfies both equations.

These two equations together form a pair of *simultaneous* equations. 'Simultaneous' means that the two equations are both satisfied by the same values of x and y; that is, when x has the same value in both equations then y has the same value in both.

There are several different methods for solving simultaneous equations. We start with the simplest.

ELIMINATION METHOD

Whenever we meet a new type of equation, we try to reorganise it so that it is similar to equations we have already met.

Previous equations have had only one unknown quantity, so we try to *eliminate* one of the two unknowns.

Consider the pair of equations

$$2x + y = 8 \qquad [1]$$
$$x + y = 5 \qquad [2]$$

In this case, if we try subtracting the second equation from the first we find that the y term disappears but the x term does not:

i.e. $\qquad [1] - [2]$ gives $\qquad x = 3$

Then, substituting 3 for x in equation [2], we see that $3 + y = 5$ so $y = 2$

We can check that $x = 3$ and $y = 2$ also satisfy equation [1].

Notice that it is essential to number the equations and to say that you are subtracting them.

Sometimes it is easier to subtract the first equation from the second rather than the second equation from the first. (In this case we would write equation [1] again, underneath equation [2].)
Sometimes we can eliminate x rather than y.

Exercise 7a

Solve the equations
$$x + y = 5$$
$$3x + y = 7$$

$$x + y = 5 \qquad [1]$$
$$3x + y = 7 \qquad [2]$$
$$x + y = 5 \qquad [1]$$

$[2] - [1]$ gives
$$2x = 2$$
$$x = 1$$

(To find y choose the simpler equation, i.e. the first.) Substituting in [1] gives
$$1 + y = 5$$
$$y = 4$$

(Check in the equation *not* used for finding y.)

Check in [2] $\qquad$ left-hand side $= 3 + 4$
$$= 7 = \text{right-hand side}$$

Therefore the solution is $x = 1$, $y = 4$

Solve the following pairs of equations:

1. $x + y = 5$
    $4x + y = 14$

4. $2x + 3y = 23$
    $x + 3y = 22$

7. $4p + 3q = -5$
    $7p + 3q = -11$

10. $9c + 2d = 54$
    $c + 2d = 6$

2. $5x + y = 14$
    $3x + y = 10$

5. $5x + 2y = 14$
    $7x + 2y = 22$

8. $12x + 5y = 65$
    $9x + 5y = 50$

11. $2x + 3y = -8$
    $2x + y = -4$

3. $2a + b = 11$
    $4a + b = 17$

6. $x + 2y = 12$
    $x + y = 7$

9. $3x + 4y = 15$
    $3x + 2y = 12$

12. $9x + 5y = 45$
    $4x + 5y = 45$

Not all pairs of simultaneous equations can be solved by subtracting one from the other.

Consider $4x + y = 6$ [1]

$2x - y = 0$ [2]

If we subtract we get $2x + 2y = 6$ which is no improvement.

On the other hand, if we add we get $6x = 6$ which eliminates y.

If the signs in front of the letter to be eliminated are the same we should *subtract*; if the signs are different we should *add*.

Exercise 7b

Solve the equations
$$x - 2y = 1$$
$$3x + 2y = 19$$

$$x - 2y = 1 \qquad [1]$$
$$3x + 2y = 19 \qquad [2]$$

$[1] + [2]$ gives
$$4x = 20$$
$$x = 5$$

(It is easier to use the equation with the $+$ sign to find y.)

Substitute 5 for x in [2] $15 + 2y = 19$

Take 15 from both sides $2y = 4$
$$y = 2$$

Check in [1]   left-hand side $= 5 - 4$
$$= 1 = \text{right-hand side}$$

Therefore the solution is $x = 5, \ y = 2$

Solve the following pairs of equations:

1. $x - y = 2$
$3x + y = 10$

2. $2x - y = 6$
$3x + y = 14$

3. $p + 2q = 11$
$3p - 2q = 1$

4. $3a - b = 10$
$a + b = 2$

5. $6x + 2y = 19$
$x - 2y = 2$

6. $4x + y = 37$
$2x - y = 17$

7. $x + y = 2$
$2x - y = 10$

8. $5p + 3q = 5$
$4p - 3q = 4$

9. $3x - 4y = -24$
$5x + 4y = 24$

10. $5x - 2y = 4$
$3x + 2y = 12$

To solve the following equations, first decide whether to add or subtract:

11. $3x + 2y = 12$
$x + 2y = 8$

12. $x - 2y = 6$
$4x + 2y = 14$

13. $x + 3y = 12$
$x + y = 8$

14. $9x + 2y = 48$
$x - 2y = 2$

15. $4x + y = 19$
$3x + y = 15$

16. $2x + 3y = 13$
$2x + 5y = 21$

17. $5x - 2y = 24$
$x + 2y = 0$

18. $x + 3y = 0$
$x - y = -4$

19. $5p - 3q = 9$
$4p + 3q = 9$

20. $6a - b = 20$
$6a + 5b = 8$

Solve the equations $\qquad 4x - y = 10$
$\qquad\qquad\qquad\qquad x - y = 1$

$$4x - y = 10 \qquad\qquad [1]$$
$$x - y = 1 \qquad\qquad [2]$$

(The signs in front of the y terms are the same so we subtract:
$-y - (-y) = -y + y = 0$)

$[1] - [2]$ gives $\qquad\qquad\qquad 3x = 9$
$$x = 3$$

Substitute 3 for x in [2] $\qquad 3 - y = 1$

Add y to both sides $\qquad\qquad 3 = 1 + y$

Take 1 from both sides $\qquad\quad 2 = y$

Check in [1] $\qquad$ left-hand side $= 12 - 2$
$$= 10 = \text{right-hand side}$$

Therefore the solution is $x = 3$, $y = 2$

Solve the following pairs of equations:

21. $2x - y = 4$
         $x - y = 1$

22. $2p - 3q = -7$
         $4p - 3q = 1$

23. $x - y = 3$
         $3x - y = 9$

24. $6x - y = 7$
         $2x - y = 1$

25. $5x - 2y = -19$
         $x - 2y = -7$

26. $2x - 3y = 14$
         $2x - y = 10$

27. $3x - 2y = 14$
         $x + 2y = 10$

28. $3p - 5q = -3$
         $4p - 5q = 1$

29. $3p + 5q = 17$
         $4p + 5q = 16$

30. $3p - 5q = 7$
         $4p + 5q = -14$

31. $3p + 5q = 35$
         $4p - 5q = 0$

32. $3x - y = 10$
         $x + y = -2$

HARDER ELIMINATION

Equations are not always as simple as the ones we have had so far.

Consider $2x + 3y = 4$ [1]

             $4x + y = -2$ [2]

Whether we add or subtract neither letter will disappear, so it is necessary to do something else first. If we multiply the second equation by 3 to give $12x + 3y = -6$, we have the same number of *y*s in each equation. Then we can use the same method as before:

[2] × 3 $12x + 3y = -6$ [3]

                           $2x + 3y = 4$ [1]

[3] − [1] gives $10x = -10$

                           $x = -1$

Substitute -1 for x in [2] $-4 + y = -2$

Add 4 to both sides $y = 2$

Therefore the solution is $x = -1, \; y = 2$

Exercise 7c

Solve the equations
$$3x - 2y = 1$$
$$4x + y = 5$$

	$3x - 2y = 1$ [1]
	$4x + y = 5$ [2]
$[2] \times 2$ gives	$8x + 2y = 10$ [3]
	$3x - 2y = 1$ [1]
$[1] + [3]$ gives	$11x = 11$
	$x = 1$
Substitute 1 for x in [2]	$4 + y = 5$
Take 4 from both sides	$y = 1$
Check in [1]	left-hand side $= 3 - 2$
	$= 1 =$ right-hand side

Therefore the solution is $x = 1$, $y = 1$

Solve the following pairs of equations:

1. $2x + y = 7$
     $3x + 2y = 11$

2. $5x - 4y = -3$
     $3x + y = 5$

3. $9x + 7y = 10$
     $3x + y = 2$

4. $5x + 3y = 21$
     $2x + y = 3$

5. $6x - 4y = -4$
     $5x + 2y = 2$

6. $4x + 3y = 25$
     $x + 5y = 19$

Solve the equations
$$5x + 3y = 7$$
$$10x + 4y = 16$$

	$5x + 3y = 7$ [1]
	$10x + 4y = 16$ [2]
$[1] \times 2$ gives	$10x + 6y = 14$ [3]
	$10x + 4y = 16$ [2]
$[3] - [2]$ gives	$2y = -2$
	$y = -1$
Substitute -1 for y in [1]	$5x - 3 = 7$
Add 3 to both sides	$5x = 10$
	$x = 2$
Check in [2]	left-hand side $= 20 + (-4) = 16 =$ right-hand side

Therefore the solution is $x = 2$, $y = -1$

Solve the following pairs of equations:

7. $5x + 3y = 11$
    $4x + 6y = 16$

8. $2x - 3y = 1$
    $5x + 9y = 19$

9. $2x + 5y = 1$
    $4x + 3y = 9$

10. $9x + 5y = 15$
    $3x - 2y = -6$

11. $4x + 3y = 1$
    $16x - 5y = 21$

12. $7p + 2q = 22$
    $3p + 4q = 11$

Sometimes we need to alter both equations before we add or subtract.

Exercise 7d

Solve the equations $3x + 5y = 6$
                         $2x + 3y = 5$

Method 1

$$3x + 5y = 6 \qquad [1]$$
$$2x + 3y = 5 \qquad [2]$$

$[1] \times 3$ gives $9x + 15y = 18 \qquad [3]$

$[2] \times 5$ gives $10x + 15y = 25 \qquad [4]$

$$9x + 15y = 18 \qquad [3]$$

$[4] - [3]$ gives $x = 7$

Substitute 7 for x in [2] $14 + 3y = 5$

Take 14 from both sides $3y = -9$

Divide both sides by 3 $y = -3$

Check in [1]   left-hand side $= 21 - 15$

$$= 6 = \text{right-hand side}$$

Therefore the solution is $x = 7,\ y = -3$

Method 2
Another method of solving linear equations is by *ratio and proportion*:

$$3x + 5y = 6 \qquad [1]$$
$$2x + 3y = 5 \qquad [2]$$

$$\frac{3x + 5y}{2x + 3y} = \frac{6}{5}$$

$\therefore$ $5(3x + 5y) = 6(2x + 3y)$

$\therefore$ $15x + 25y = 12x + 18y$

$\therefore$ $3x = -7y$

$\therefore$ $\dfrac{x}{y} = -\dfrac{7}{3}$

Therefore $x = -7K$ and $y = 3K$, where K is a constant

Substituting these values in [1], we have

$$3(-7K) + 5(3K) = 6$$

$$\therefore \qquad -21K + 15K = 6$$

$$-6K = 6$$

$$\therefore \qquad K = -1$$

$$\therefore \qquad x = -7(-1) = 7$$

$$y = 3(-1) = -3$$

Therefore the solution is $x = 7$, $y = -3$

Solve the following pairs of equations:

1. $2x + 3y = 12$
$5x + 4y = 23$

2. $3x - 2y = -7$
$4x + 3y = 19$

3. $2x - 5y = 1$
$5x + 3y = 18$

4. $6x + 5y = 9$
$4x + 3y = 6$

5. $14x - 3y = -18$
$6x + 2y = 12$

6. $6x - 7y = 25$
$7x + 6y = 15$

7. $5x + 4y = 21$
$3x + 6y = 27$

8. $9x + 8y = 17$
$2x - 6y = -4$

9. $9x - 2y = 14$
$7x + 3y = 20$

10. $5x + 4y = 11$
$2x + 3y = 3$

11. $4x + 5y = 26$
$5x + 4y = 28$

12. $2x - 6y = -6$
$5x + 4y = -15$

13. $5x - 6y = 6$
$2x + 9y = 10$

14. $3p + 4q = 5$
$2p + 10q = 18$

15. $6x + 5y = 8$
$3x + 4y = 1$

16. $7x - 3y = 20$
$2x + 4y = -4$

17. $10x + 3y = 12$
$3x + 5y = 20$

18. $6x - 5y = 4$
$4x + 2y = -8$

19. $5x + 3y = 8$
$3x + 5y = 8$

20. $7x + 2y = 23$
$3x - 5y = 4$

21. $6x - 5y = 17$
$5x + 4y = 6$

22. $3x + 8y = 56$
$5x - 6y = 16$

23. $7x + 3y = -9$
$2x + 5y = 14$

24. $7x + 6y = 0$
$5x - 8y = 43$

25. $2x + 6y = 30$
$3x + 10y = 49$

26. $4x - 3y = -7$
$3x + 2y = 16$

27. $17x - 2y = 47$
$5x - 3y = 9$

28. $8x + 3y = -17$
$7x - 4y = 5$

MIXED QUESTIONS

Exercise 7e

Solve the following pairs of equations:

1. $x + 2y = 9$
   $2x - y = -2$

2. $x + y = 4$
   $x + 2y = 9$

3. $2x + 3y = 0$
   $3x + 2y = 5$

4. $3x - y = -10$
   $4x - y = -4$

5. $5x + 2y = 16$
   $2x - 3y = -5$

6. $3x + 2y = -5$
   $3x - 4y = 1$

7. $x + y = 6$
   $x - y = 1$

8. $3x - 5y = 13$
   $2x + 5y = -8$

9. $7x + 3y = 35$
   $2x - 5y = 10$

10. $9x + 2y = 8$
    $7x + 3y = 12$

11. $2x - 5y = 1$
    $3x + 4y = 13$

12. $3x - 2y = -2$
    $5x - y = -15$

Sometimes the equations are arranged in an awkward fashion and need to be rearranged before solving them.

Exercise 7f

Solve the equations $x = 4 - 3y$
                       $2y - x = 1$

$$x = 4 - 3y \qquad [1]$$
$$2y - x = 1 \qquad [2]$$

(We must first arrange the letters in the same order in both equations. By adding $3y$ to both sides, equation [1] can be written $3y + x = 4$)

$$3y + x = 4 \qquad [3]$$
$$2y - x = 1 \qquad [2]$$

[3] + [2] gives $5y = 5$

                               $y = 1$

Substitute 1 for y in [1] $x = 4 - 3$

                               $x = 1$

Check in [2]   left-hand side $= 2 - 1 = 1 =$ right-hand side

Therefore the solution is $x = 1$, $y = 1$

Solve the following pairs of equations:

1. $y = 6 - x$
   $2x + y = 8$

2. $x - y = 2$
   $2y = x + 1$

3. $3 = 2x + y$
   $4x + 6 = 10y$

4. $9 + x = y$
   $x + 2y = 12$

5. $2y = 16 - x$
   $x - 2y = -8$

6. $3x + 4y = 7$
   $2x = 5 - 3y$

As long as the x and y and number terms are in corresponding positions in the two equations, they need not be in the order we have had so far.

Solve the equations
$$y = x + 5$$
$$y = 7 - x$$

$$y = x + 5 \qquad [1]$$
$$y = 7 - x \qquad [2]$$

Rewrite [1] as
$$y = 5 + x \qquad [3]$$

$[2] + [3]$ gives
$$2y = 12$$
$$y = 6$$

Substitute 6 for y in [1]
$$6 = x + 5$$
$$x = 1$$

Check in [2]

left-hand side $= 6$

right-hand side $= 7 - 1 = 6$

Therefore the solution is $x = 1$, $y = 6$

Solve the following pairs of equations:

7. $y = 9 + x$
  $y = 11 - x$

9. $y = 4 - x$
  $y = x + 6$

11. $x + 4 = y$
  $y = 10 - 2x$

8. $x = 3 + y$
  $2x = 4 - y$

10. $2y = 4 + x$
  $y = x + 8$

12. $x + y = 12$
  $y = 3 + x$

SPECIAL CASES

Some pairs of equations have no solution and some have an infinite number of solutions.

Exercise 7g

Try solving the following pairs of equations. Comment on why the method breaks down:

1. $x + 2y = 6$
  $x + 2y = 7$

3. $y = 4 + 2x$
  $y - 2x = 6$

2. $3x + 4y = 1$
  $6x + 8y = 2$

4. $9x = 3 - 6y$
  $3x + 2y = 1$

5. Make up other pairs of equations which either have no solution or have an infinite set of solutions.

PROBLEMS

I think of two numbers. If I add three times the smaller number to the bigger number I get 14. If I subtract the bigger number from twice the smaller number I get 1. Find the two numbers.

Let the smaller number be x and the bigger number be y.

$$3x + y = 14 \qquad [1]$$

$$2x - y = 1 \qquad [2]$$

$[1] + [2]$ gives $\qquad 5x = 15$

$$x = 3$$

Substitute 3 for x in [1] $\qquad 9 + y = 14$

Take 9 from both sides $\qquad y = 5$

Therefore, the two numbers are 3 and 5

(Check by reading the original statements to see if the numbers fit.)

Solve the following problems by forming a pair of simultaneous equations:

1. The sum of two numbers is 20 and their difference is 4. Find the numbers.

2. The sum of two numbers is 16 and they differ by 6. What are the numbers?

3. I think of two numbers. If I double the first and add the second I get 18. If I double the first and subtract the second I get 14. What are the numbers?

4. Three times a number added to a second number is 33. The first number added to three times the second number is 19. Find the two numbers.

5. Find two numbers such that twice the first added to the second is 26 and the first added to three times the second is 28.

6. Find the two numbers such that twice the first added to the second gives 27 and twice the second added to the first gives 21.

A shop sells bread rolls. If five brown rolls and six white rolls cost 98 c while three brown rolls and four white rolls cost 62 c, find the cost of each type of roll.

Let one brown roll cost x c and one white roll cost y c.

$$5x + 6y = 98 \qquad [1]$$
$$3x + 4y = 62 \qquad [2]$$

[1] × 2 gives
$$10x + 12y = 196 \qquad [3]$$

[2] × 3 gives
$$9x + 12y = 186 \qquad [4]$$

[3] − [4] gives
$$x = 10$$

Substitute 10 for x in [1]
$$50 + 6y = 98$$

Take 50 from both sides
$$6y = 48$$
$$y = 8$$

Therefore one brown roll costs 10 c and one white roll costs 8 c.

7. I buy x choc ices and y orange ices and spend $2.30. I buy ten ices altogether. The choc ices cost 30 c each and the orange ices cost 20 c each. How many of each do I buy?

8.

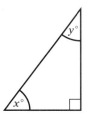

x is bigger than y. The difference between x and y is 18. Find x and y.

9. A cup and saucer cost $3.15 together. A cup and two saucers cost $4.50. Find the cost of a cup and of a saucer.

10. The cost of two Roti is the same as the cost of three Petties. One Roti and one Pettie together cost $3.50. What do they each cost?

11. In a test, the sum of Harry's marks and Adam's marks is 42. Sam has twice as many marks as Adam, and the sum of Harry's and Sam's marks is 52. What are the marks of each of the three boys?

12.

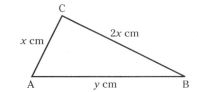

The perimeter of triangle ABC is 14 cm. AB is 2 cm longer than AC. Find x and y.

13.

The perimeter of the rectangle is 31 cm. The difference between the lengths of AB and BC is $3\frac{1}{2}$ cm. Find the lengths of AB and BC.

14. The equation of a straight line is $y = mx + c$. When $x = 1$, $y = 6$ and when $x = 3$, $y = 10$. Form two equations for m and c and hence find the equation of the line.

GRAPHICAL SOLUTIONS OF SIMULTANEOUS EQUATIONS

We saw in Book 2 that when we are given an equation we can draw a graph. Any of the equations which occur in this chapter give us a straight line. Two equations give us two straight lines which usually cross one another.

Consider the two equations $x + y = 4$

$$y = 1 + x$$

Suppose we know that the x coordinate of the point of intersection is in the range $0 \leqslant x \leqslant 5$:

$x + y = 4$

x	0	4	5
y	4	0	-1

$y = 1 + x$

x	0	2	5
y	1	3	6

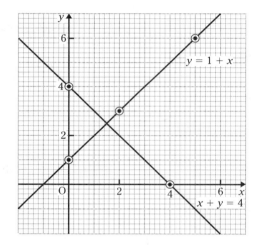

At the point where the two lines cross, the values of x and y are the same for both equations, so they are the solutions of the pair of equations.

From the graph we see that the solution is $x = 1\frac{1}{2}$, $y = 2\frac{1}{2}$.

Exercise 7i

Solve the following equations graphically. In each case draw axes for x and y and use values in the ranges indicated, taking 2 cm to 1 unit:

1. $x + y = 6$ $0 \leqslant x \leqslant 6,\ 0 \leqslant y \leqslant 6$
    $y = 3 + x$

2. $x + y = 5$ $0 \leqslant x \leqslant 6,\ 0 \leqslant y \leqslant 6$
    $y = 2x + 1$

3. $y = 4 + x$ $0 \leqslant x \leqslant 6,\ 0 \leqslant y \leqslant 6$
    $y = 1 + 3x$

4. $x + y = 1$ $-3 \leqslant x \leqslant 2,\ -2 \leqslant y \leqslant 4$
    $y = x + 2$

5. $2x + y = 3$ $\quad 0 \leqslant x \leqslant 3, \; -3 \leqslant y \leqslant 3$
$\quad\; x + y = 2\frac{1}{2}$

8. $2x + 3y = 4$ $\quad -2 \leqslant x \leqslant 2, \; 0 \leqslant y \leqslant 4$
$\quad\; y = x + 2$

6. $y = 5 - x$ $\quad 0 \leqslant x \leqslant 5, \; 0 \leqslant y \leqslant 7$
$\quad\; y = 2 + x$

9. $x + 3y = 6$ $\quad 0 \leqslant x \leqslant 5, \; 0 \leqslant y \leqslant 5$
$\quad\; 3x - y = 6$

7. $3x + 2y = 9$ $\quad 0 \leqslant x \leqslant 4, \; -2 \leqslant y \leqslant 5$
$\quad\; 2x - 2y = 3$

10. $x = 2y - 3$ $\quad -2 \leqslant x \leqslant 3, \; 0 \leqslant y \leqslant 4$
$\quad\;\; y = 2x + 1$

SPECIAL CASES

Exercise 7j

Try to solve the following equations graphically. Why do you think the method breaks down?

1. $x + y = 9$ $\quad 0 \leqslant x \leqslant 9$
$\quad x + y = 4$ $\quad 0 \leqslant y \leqslant 9$

3. $2x + y = 3$ $\quad 0 \leqslant x \leqslant 3$
$\quad 4x + 2y = 7$ $\quad -3 \leqslant y \leqslant 4$

2. $y = 2x + 3$ $\quad 0 \leqslant x \leqslant 4$
$\quad y = 2x - 1$ $\quad -1 \leqslant y \leqslant 11$

4. $y = 2x - 4$ $\quad 0 \leqslant x \leqslant 4$
$\quad 2x = y + 4$ $\quad -4 \leqslant y \leqslant 4$

MATHS IS OUT THERE

I think, therefore I am

Did you know that Rene Descartes was nicknamed 'The philosopher'? He was born into a rich French family. He was so small and sickly that nobody thought that he would live long, but he surprised everyone and lived fifty-three years. He studied law to please his father but law did not really interest him. He turned to gambling and was very lucky. He did serious thinking about life and mathematics. He is famous for his statement 'I think, therefore I am'. He is remembered for inventing a branch of mathematics known as analytical geometry.

8 ▷ MATRICES

At the end of the chapter you should be able to:

1. Arrange a set of data in a rectangular array called a matrix.
2. State the size of a given matrix.
3. Write down the entry in a matrix, given its row and column.
4. Add and subtract two or more matrices.
5. Multiply a matrix by a constant.
6. Multiply two matrices.
7. Determine if two matrices are compatible for multiplication.

SHOPPING LISTS

Mrs Smith and Mrs Jones go shopping for oranges, lemons and grapefruit. Mrs Smith buys six oranges, two lemons and three grapefruit while Mrs Jones buys five oranges, one lemon and two grapefruit. We can arrange this information in a table:

	Oranges	Lemons	Grapefruit
Mrs Smith	6	2	3
Mrs Jones	5	1	2

We can write this information more briefly in the form

$$\begin{pmatrix} 6 & 2 & 3 \\ 5 & 1 & 2 \end{pmatrix}$$

All the numerical information is given, though we have missed out the descriptions of what the various rows and columns mean.

A *rectangular array* of numbers is called a *matrix* (plural *matrices*). It is held together by curved brackets. Each item is called an *entry*. A matrix can have any number of *rows* and *columns*; rows go across and columns go down. If we had the shopping lists of three people buying four different sorts of fruit we would have a matrix with three rows and four columns.

e.g.
$$\begin{pmatrix} 4 & 3 & 1 & 2 \\ 1 & 2 & 0 & 4 \\ 9 & 0 & 1 & 1 \end{pmatrix}$$

We use the number of rows and the number of columns to describe the size of a matrix. This matrix is a 3×4 matrix (number of rows first, then the number of columns).

Exercise 8a

(a) Give the size of the matrix $\begin{pmatrix} 1 & 4 & 3 & 2 \\ 7 & 0 & 6 & 5 \end{pmatrix}$

(b) What is the entry in the second row, third column?

       (a) The matrix is a 2×4 matrix

       (b) The entry in the second row, third column is 6

Give the sizes of the matrices in questions 1 to 6:

1. $\begin{pmatrix} 2 & 4 \\ 1 & 2 \end{pmatrix}$

2. $\begin{pmatrix} 2 & 3 & 4 \\ 1 & 1 & 4 \end{pmatrix}$

3. $\begin{pmatrix} 1 \\ 2 \end{pmatrix}$

4. $(1 \quad 2 \quad 3)$

5. (2)

6. $\begin{pmatrix} 2 & 3 \\ 4 & 5 \\ 6 & 7 \end{pmatrix}$

7. In the matrix $\begin{pmatrix} 1 & 2 & 3 \\ 4 & 5 & 6 \\ 7 & 8 & 9 \end{pmatrix}$ give the entry in

(a) the second row, third column
(b) the third row, second column
(c) the first row, second column
(d) the third row, first column

8. Write down the second row and the third column of the matrix

$\begin{pmatrix} 5 & 2 & 4 \\ 3 & 1 & 7 \\ 9 & 6 & 2 \end{pmatrix}$

(a) Give the entry in the second row of the third column.
(b) Give the entry in the third row of the second column.
(c) Give the entry in the first row of the third column.

9. Write down the matrix with three rows and three columns in which the first row is a row of zeros, the second row is a row of ones and the third row is a row of twos.

10. Write down the 3×2 matrix in which the first column is a column of threes and the second column is a column of ones.

ADDITION OF MATRICES

Mrs Smith's and Mrs Jones' first shopping lists were represented by the matrix

$$\begin{pmatrix} 6 & 2 & 3 \\ 5 & 1 & 2 \end{pmatrix}$$

The next week, Mrs Smith buys three oranges, no lemons and one grapefruit and Mrs Jones buys four oranges, two lemons and one grapefruit. We can arrange this in a table:

	Oranges	Lemons	Grapefruit
Mrs Smith	3	0	1
Mrs Jones	4	2	1

and represent it by the matrix $\begin{pmatrix} 3 & 0 & 1 \\ 4 & 2 & 1 \end{pmatrix}$

We see that over the two weeks Mrs Smith buys nine oranges, two lemons and four grapefruit and Mrs Jones buys nine oranges, three lemons and three grapefruit. This information can be written briefly in the form

$$\begin{pmatrix} 6 & 2 & 3 \\ 5 & 1 & 2 \end{pmatrix} + \begin{pmatrix} 3 & 0 & 1 \\ 4 & 2 & 1 \end{pmatrix} = \begin{pmatrix} 9 & 2 & 4 \\ 9 & 3 & 3 \end{pmatrix}$$

Each of these matrices is a 2×3 matrix.

We have added the entries in corresponding positions, e.g. in the first row, third column, $3 + 1 = 4$

In the third week, Mrs Smith buys two oranges and one lemon and Mrs Jones buys four oranges and one lemon.

The matrix showing this information is $\begin{pmatrix} 2 & 1 \\ 4 & 1 \end{pmatrix}$

This is a 2×2 matrix.

We do not know how many grapefruit were bought in the third week. This makes it impossible to add the matrices for the second and third weeks

i.e. $\begin{pmatrix} 3 & 0 & 1 \\ 4 & 2 & 1 \end{pmatrix} + \begin{pmatrix} 2 & 1 \\ 4 & 1 \end{pmatrix}$ cannot be worked out.

We can add matrices if they are the same size, but not if they are of different sizes.

Exercise 8b

Find, where possible

(a) $\begin{pmatrix} 6 & 3 \\ 1 & 2 \end{pmatrix} + \begin{pmatrix} 4 & 1 \\ 3 & 2 \end{pmatrix}$ (b) $\begin{pmatrix} 1 \\ 2 \end{pmatrix} + \begin{pmatrix} 4 & 1 \\ 0 & 3 \end{pmatrix}$

(a) $\begin{pmatrix} 6 & 3 \\ 1 & 2 \end{pmatrix} + \begin{pmatrix} 4 & 1 \\ 3 & 2 \end{pmatrix} = \begin{pmatrix} 10 & 4 \\ 4 & 4 \end{pmatrix}$

(b) $\begin{pmatrix} 1 \\ 2 \end{pmatrix} + \begin{pmatrix} 4 & 1 \\ 0 & 3 \end{pmatrix}$ not possible

Find, where possible:

1. $\begin{pmatrix} 2 \\ 3 \end{pmatrix} + \begin{pmatrix} 10 \\ 12 \end{pmatrix}$

2. $\begin{pmatrix} 9 & 2 \\ 4 & 1 \end{pmatrix} + \begin{pmatrix} 6 & 2 \\ 3 & 0 \end{pmatrix}$

3. $\begin{pmatrix} 1 \\ 2 \\ 3 \end{pmatrix} + \begin{pmatrix} 3 & 6 \\ 4 & 7 \\ 5 & 8 \end{pmatrix}$

4. $(6 \quad 1) + (3 \quad 4)$

5. $\begin{pmatrix} 4 & 1 & 2 \\ 3 & 5 & 6 \end{pmatrix} + \begin{pmatrix} 7 & 1 & 0 \\ 3 & 2 & 1 \end{pmatrix}$

6. $\begin{pmatrix} 7 & 8 \\ 9 & 1 \end{pmatrix} + \begin{pmatrix} 4 & 3 \\ 2 & 4 \end{pmatrix}$

7. $(2 \quad 1 \quad 4) + (3 \quad 2 \quad 1)$

8. $\begin{pmatrix} 1 \\ 2 \end{pmatrix} + (3 \quad 4)$

9. $\begin{pmatrix} 1 & 2 \\ 3 & 4 \\ 5 & 6 \end{pmatrix} + \begin{pmatrix} 5 & 6 \\ 4 & 3 \\ 2 & 1 \end{pmatrix}$

10. $(6 \quad 3) + (4 \quad 5)$

Negative numbers can be used.

Find $\begin{pmatrix} 4 & -3 \\ 4 & -1 \end{pmatrix} + \begin{pmatrix} -3 & 2 \\ 1 & 4 \end{pmatrix}$

$$\begin{pmatrix} 4 & -3 \\ 4 & -1 \end{pmatrix} + \begin{pmatrix} -3 & 2 \\ 1 & 4 \end{pmatrix} = \begin{pmatrix} 1 & -1 \\ 5 & 3 \end{pmatrix}$$

Find, where possible:

11. $\begin{pmatrix} 2 & 4 \\ -1 & 4 \end{pmatrix} + \begin{pmatrix} -1 & 4 \\ -3 & 3 \end{pmatrix}$

12. $\begin{pmatrix} 1 \\ -4 \end{pmatrix} + \begin{pmatrix} -3 \\ 6 \end{pmatrix}$

13. $\begin{pmatrix} 4 & 3 \\ -2 & 1 \end{pmatrix} + \begin{pmatrix} -6 & 4 \\ -3 & 2 \end{pmatrix}$

14. $(1 \quad 2) + (3 \quad 4)$

15. $\begin{pmatrix} -2 \\ -3 \\ 4 \end{pmatrix} + \begin{pmatrix} -1 \\ 0 \\ 2 \end{pmatrix}$

16. $(1 \quad -6 \quad 1) + (-4 \quad 1)$

17. $\begin{pmatrix} 3 & 6 \\ 2 & -5 \end{pmatrix} + \begin{pmatrix} -1 & 4 \\ 3 & 2 \end{pmatrix}$

18. $\begin{pmatrix} 1 & -2 \\ -2 & 1 \end{pmatrix} + \begin{pmatrix} 4 & -3 \\ 5 & -1 \end{pmatrix}$

19. $\begin{pmatrix} 3 & 2 \\ -1 & -4 \end{pmatrix} + \begin{pmatrix} -3 & 6 \\ 9 & 2 \end{pmatrix}$

20. $\begin{pmatrix} 4 \\ -2 \end{pmatrix} + (4 \quad -2)$

21. $\begin{pmatrix} 3 & 2 & 0 \\ 1 & 4 & 3 \end{pmatrix} + \begin{pmatrix} 2 & 4 \\ -3 & 4 \\ 1 & 2 \end{pmatrix}$

22. $(1 \quad 4 \quad -3) + (0 \quad 2 \quad 0)$

23. $\begin{pmatrix} 3 & -1 & 1 \\ 5 & 6 & -7 \end{pmatrix} + \begin{pmatrix} -1 & 4 & 3 \\ 0 & -6 & -5 \end{pmatrix}$

MULTIPLES OF MATRICES

If Mrs Smith and Mrs Jones each have the same shopping list for three weeks running we can see that

$$\begin{pmatrix} 3 & 1 & 4 \\ 1 & 2 & 1 \end{pmatrix} + \begin{pmatrix} 3 & 1 & 4 \\ 1 & 2 & 1 \end{pmatrix} + \begin{pmatrix} 3 & 1 & 4 \\ 1 & 2 & 1 \end{pmatrix} = 3\begin{pmatrix} 3 & 1 & 4 \\ 1 & 2 & 1 \end{pmatrix} = \begin{pmatrix} 9 & 3 & 12 \\ 3 & 6 & 3 \end{pmatrix}$$

In the same way
$$5\begin{pmatrix} 1 & 4 \\ 3 & -2 \end{pmatrix} = \begin{pmatrix} 5 & 20 \\ 15 & -10 \end{pmatrix}$$

When we multiply a matrix by five, we multiply *every* entry by five.

SUBTRACTION OF MATRICES

We can subtract matrices if they are the same size.

Two weeks' shopping   First week's shopping   Second week's shopping
$$\begin{pmatrix} 7 & 9 & 2 \\ 6 & 4 & 1 \end{pmatrix} - \begin{pmatrix} 3 & 2 & 1 \\ 3 & 3 & 1 \end{pmatrix} = \begin{pmatrix} 4 & 7 & 1 \\ 3 & 1 & 0 \end{pmatrix}$$

Exercise 8c

Find, where possible

(a) $4\begin{pmatrix} 4 & 1 \\ 3 & -2 \end{pmatrix}$ (b) $\begin{pmatrix} 4 & 2 \\ 1 & 1 \end{pmatrix} - \begin{pmatrix} 3 & 4 \\ 0 & 1 \end{pmatrix}$

(a) $4\begin{pmatrix} 4 & 1 \\ 3 & -2 \end{pmatrix} = \begin{pmatrix} 16 & 4 \\ 12 & -8 \end{pmatrix}$

(b) $\begin{pmatrix} 4 & 2 \\ 1 & 1 \end{pmatrix} - \begin{pmatrix} 3 & 4 \\ 0 & 1 \end{pmatrix} = \begin{pmatrix} 1 & -2 \\ 1 & 0 \end{pmatrix}$

Find, where possible:

1. $3\begin{pmatrix} 1 \\ 2 \\ 4 \end{pmatrix}$

2. $2\begin{pmatrix} 1 & 4 & 0 \\ 2 & -1 & 3 \end{pmatrix}$

3. $\frac{1}{2}\begin{pmatrix} 2 & 4 \\ 1 & 6 \\ 3 & 8 \end{pmatrix}$

4. $6\begin{pmatrix} 1 & 4 \\ 3 & -2 \end{pmatrix}$

5. $6\begin{pmatrix} -1 & -5 \\ 1 & 2 \end{pmatrix}$

6. $\frac{2}{3}\begin{pmatrix} 6 & 0 \\ 1 & 2 \\ 3 & 5 \end{pmatrix}$

7. $\begin{pmatrix} 3 & 2 \\ 1 & 4 \end{pmatrix} - \begin{pmatrix} 1 & 4 \\ 0 & 1 \end{pmatrix}$

10. $\begin{pmatrix} 4 & 5 & 3 \\ 1 & -2 & 1 \end{pmatrix} - \begin{pmatrix} 2 & 1 & 1 \\ 4 & 1 & 2 \end{pmatrix}$

8. $\begin{pmatrix} 1 \\ 3 \end{pmatrix} - \begin{pmatrix} 2 & 3 \\ 4 & 1 \end{pmatrix}$

11. $(1 \quad 6 \quad 2) - (4 \quad 3)$

9. $\begin{pmatrix} 1 \\ 2 \\ 3 \end{pmatrix} - \begin{pmatrix} 4 \\ -1 \\ 3 \end{pmatrix}$

12. $\begin{pmatrix} 1 & 2 & 3 \\ 4 & 5 & 6 \\ 7 & 8 & 9 \end{pmatrix} - \begin{pmatrix} 4 & 3 & 1 \\ -5 & 0 & 2 \\ 6 & -3 & 4 \end{pmatrix}$

MIXED QUESTIONS

Exercise 8d

Find, where possible:

1. $\begin{pmatrix} 1 & 4 \\ 3 & 2 \end{pmatrix} + \begin{pmatrix} -2 & 4 \\ 3 & -1 \end{pmatrix}$

7. $2\begin{pmatrix} 1 & 4 \\ 3 & 2 \end{pmatrix}$

2. $\begin{pmatrix} 1 & 4 \\ 3 & 2 \end{pmatrix} - \begin{pmatrix} -2 & 4 \\ 3 & -1 \end{pmatrix}$

8. $\frac{1}{2}\begin{pmatrix} -2 & 4 \\ 3 & -1 \end{pmatrix}$

3. $(1 \quad 2 \quad 4) - (3 \quad 2)$

9. $\begin{pmatrix} 1 \\ 2 \\ 3 \end{pmatrix} + \begin{pmatrix} 4 \\ 5 \\ -1 \end{pmatrix} + \begin{pmatrix} 3 \\ 2 \\ 1 \end{pmatrix}$

4. $\begin{pmatrix} 3 & 2 \\ 4 & -1 \end{pmatrix} + \begin{pmatrix} 4 & -3 \\ 1 & 0 \end{pmatrix}$

10. $4\begin{pmatrix} 6 & 2 & -1 \\ 4 & 3 & 4 \end{pmatrix}$

5. $\frac{1}{3}\begin{pmatrix} 4 \\ 5 \\ -1 \end{pmatrix}$

11. $\begin{pmatrix} 6 & 2 & 1 \\ 4 & 3 & 4 \end{pmatrix} + \begin{pmatrix} -2 & 4 \\ 3 & -1 \end{pmatrix}$

6. $\begin{pmatrix} 1 \\ 2 \\ 3 \end{pmatrix} - \begin{pmatrix} 4 \\ 5 \\ 6 \end{pmatrix}$

12. $\begin{pmatrix} 6 & 2 & -1 \\ 4 & 3 & 4 \end{pmatrix} - \begin{pmatrix} -2 & 4 & 1 \\ 3 & -1 & 0 \end{pmatrix}$

USE OF LETTERS

In Book 1, we saw that we could use a single small letter in heavy type to denote a vector,

e.g. $\qquad \mathbf{a} = \begin{pmatrix} 1 \\ 2 \end{pmatrix}$

In the same way we can represent a matrix by giving it a capital letter in heavy type:

e.g. $\qquad \mathbf{A} = \begin{pmatrix} 1 & 2 \\ 4 & 1 \end{pmatrix}$ and $\mathbf{B} = \begin{pmatrix} 4 & 1 \\ 3 & 0 \end{pmatrix}$

then $A + B = \begin{pmatrix} 1 & 2 \\ 4 & 1 \end{pmatrix} + \begin{pmatrix} 4 & 1 \\ 3 & 0 \end{pmatrix} = \begin{pmatrix} 5 & 3 \\ 7 & 1 \end{pmatrix}$

and $2A = 2\begin{pmatrix} 1 & 2 \\ 4 & 1 \end{pmatrix} = \begin{pmatrix} 2 & 4 \\ 8 & 2 \end{pmatrix}$

We cannot *write* **A**, so we write $\underline{A}$.

Exercise 8e

The questions in this exercise refer to the following matrices:

$A = \begin{pmatrix} 4 & 3 & 1 \\ 1 & 2 & 3 \end{pmatrix}$ $B = \begin{pmatrix} 4 \\ 1 \end{pmatrix}$ $C = \begin{pmatrix} 2 & 3 \\ 1 & -2 \end{pmatrix}$ $D = \begin{pmatrix} 6 & 2 \\ 1 & 4 \end{pmatrix}$

$E = (6 \quad -1 \quad 2)$ $F = (3 \quad 2)$ $G = \begin{pmatrix} 5 & 1 & 3 \\ 6 & -1 & 4 \end{pmatrix}$

Give the size of **A**.

A is a 2×3 matrix

1. Give the sizes of the matrices **B** to **G**.

Find, where possible (a) **C** − **D**   (b) **B** + **F**.

(a) $C - D = \begin{pmatrix} 2 & 3 \\ 1 & -2 \end{pmatrix} - \begin{pmatrix} 6 & 2 \\ 1 & 4 \end{pmatrix} = \begin{pmatrix} -4 & 1 \\ 0 & -6 \end{pmatrix}$

(b) $B + F = \begin{pmatrix} 4 \\ 1 \end{pmatrix} + (3 \quad 2)$ not possible

Find, where possible:

2. **A** + **G**	5. 3**A**	8. **G** + **B**	11. $\frac{3}{4}$**D**
3. **B** + **C**	6. **E** + **F**	9. **G** − **A**	12. **C** + **D** + **G**
4. **D** − **C**	7. $\frac{1}{2}$**F**	10. 6**B**	13. **F** − **E**

MATRIX MULTIPLICATION

We can use the idea of shopping lists to find an operation that we call matrix multiplication.

Mrs Smith buys six bananas and one lemon and Mrs Jones buys four bananas and two lemons.

The matrix showing this information is $\begin{pmatrix} 6 & 1 \\ 4 & 2 \end{pmatrix}$

The bananas cost 12 c each and the lemons 8 c and this information can be written as $\begin{pmatrix} 12 \\ 8 \end{pmatrix}$

We can work out that Mrs Smith spends 80 c and Mrs Jones 64 c. This can be written in a table

	Amount spent in cents
Mrs Smith	80
Mrs Jones	64

or as a matrix $\begin{pmatrix} 80 \\ 64 \end{pmatrix}$

We can say $\begin{pmatrix} 6 & 1 \\ 4 & 2 \end{pmatrix}\begin{pmatrix} 12 \\ 8 \end{pmatrix} = \begin{pmatrix} 80 \\ 64 \end{pmatrix}$

This is a sort of multiplication, though different from any multiplication we have done so far.

It is called *matrix multiplication* or *row–column multiplication*.

Notice how the numbers have been paired:

$$\begin{pmatrix} 6 & 1 \end{pmatrix}\begin{pmatrix} 12 \\ 8 \end{pmatrix} = \begin{pmatrix} 80 \end{pmatrix} \quad 6 \times 12 + 1 \times 8 = 80$$

Exercise 8f

Find $\begin{pmatrix} 4 & 3 \\ 6 & 1 \end{pmatrix}\begin{pmatrix} 3 \\ 2 \end{pmatrix}$

$$\begin{pmatrix} 4 & 3 \\ 6 & 1 \end{pmatrix}\begin{pmatrix} 3 \\ 2 \end{pmatrix} = \begin{pmatrix} 18 \\ 20 \end{pmatrix} \qquad \begin{array}{l} 4 \times 3 + 3 \times 2 = 18 \\ 6 \times 3 + 1 \times 2 = 20 \end{array}$$

Find the following products:

1. $\begin{pmatrix} 1 & 4 \\ 3 & 2 \end{pmatrix}\begin{pmatrix} 5 \\ 6 \end{pmatrix}$

2. $\begin{pmatrix} 6 & 2 \\ 3 & 5 \end{pmatrix}\begin{pmatrix} 2 \\ 1 \end{pmatrix}$

3. $\begin{pmatrix} 3 & 2 \\ 4 & 3 \end{pmatrix}\begin{pmatrix} 1 \\ 1 \end{pmatrix}$

4. $\begin{pmatrix} 1 & 3 \\ 0 & 1 \end{pmatrix}\begin{pmatrix} 3 \\ 2 \end{pmatrix}$

5. $\begin{pmatrix} 5 & 2 \\ 1 & 2 \end{pmatrix} \begin{pmatrix} 1 \\ 2 \end{pmatrix}$

6. $\begin{pmatrix} 6 & 2 \\ 1 & 4 \end{pmatrix} \begin{pmatrix} 2 \\ 3 \end{pmatrix}$

7. $\begin{pmatrix} 5 & 4 \\ 3 & 1 \end{pmatrix} \begin{pmatrix} 2 \\ 4 \end{pmatrix}$

8. $\begin{pmatrix} 6 & 4 \\ 1 & 2 \end{pmatrix} \begin{pmatrix} 5 \\ 7 \end{pmatrix}$

9. $\begin{pmatrix} 11 & 12 \\ 10 & 9 \end{pmatrix} \begin{pmatrix} 4 \\ 1 \end{pmatrix}$

10. $\begin{pmatrix} 3 & 4 \\ 1 & 2 \end{pmatrix} \begin{pmatrix} 6 \\ 2 \end{pmatrix}$

Mrs Smith bought six bananas and one lemon and Mrs Jones bought four bananas and two lemons. Bananas cost 12 c each and lemons 8 c each.

This gives the matrix multiplication $\begin{pmatrix} 6 & 1 \\ 4 & 2 \end{pmatrix} \begin{pmatrix} 12 \\ 8 \end{pmatrix} = \begin{pmatrix} 80 \\ 64 \end{pmatrix}$

If they chose to do their shopping at a second shop where the bananas cost 11 c each and the lemons 9 c, the matrix multiplication would be $\begin{pmatrix} 6 & 1 \\ 4 & 2 \end{pmatrix} \begin{pmatrix} 11 \\ 9 \end{pmatrix} = \begin{pmatrix} 75 \\ 62 \end{pmatrix}$

The table for the bills is as follows:

	First shop	Second shop
Mrs Smith	80	75
Mrs Jones	64	62

This gives the 2×2 matrix $\begin{pmatrix} 80 & 75 \\ 64 & 62 \end{pmatrix}$

We can combine the previous two matrix multiplications into one:

$$\begin{matrix} \text{Mrs Smith} \\ \text{Mrs Jones} \end{matrix} \begin{pmatrix} 6 & 1 \\ 4 & 2 \end{pmatrix} \times \begin{matrix} \text{First} & \text{Second} \\ \text{shop} & \text{shop} \\ \begin{pmatrix} 12 & 11 \\ 8 & 9 \end{pmatrix} \end{matrix} = \begin{pmatrix} 80 & 75 \\ 64 & 62 \end{pmatrix}$$

Notice that we pair the entries in the *first row* of the first matrix with the entries in the *first column* of the second matrix to give the entry in the *first row, first column* of the final matrix.

$$\begin{pmatrix} 6 & 1 \end{pmatrix} \begin{pmatrix} 12 \\ 8 \end{pmatrix} = \begin{pmatrix} 80 \end{pmatrix} \qquad 6 \times 12 + 1 \times 8 = 80$$

Then the entries in the *first row* of the first matrix paired with the entries in the *second column* of the second matrix give the entry in the *first row, second column* of the final matrix.

$$\begin{pmatrix} 6 & 1 \end{pmatrix} \begin{pmatrix} 11 \\ 9 \end{pmatrix} = \begin{pmatrix} 75 \end{pmatrix} \qquad 6 \times 11 + 1 \times 9 = 75$$

Then we use the second row in the same way.

Exercise 8g

Find the missing entries in the matrix multiplication

$$\begin{pmatrix} 2 & 4 \\ 3 & 2 \end{pmatrix}\begin{pmatrix} 4 & 1 \\ 3 & 2 \end{pmatrix} = \begin{pmatrix} 20 & \\ & 7 \end{pmatrix}$$

$$\begin{pmatrix} 2 & 4 \\ 3 & 2 \end{pmatrix}\begin{pmatrix} 4 & 1 \\ 3 & 2 \end{pmatrix} = \begin{pmatrix} 20 & 10 \\ 18 & 7 \end{pmatrix}$$

(1st row, 2nd column
$2 \times 1 + 4 \times 2 = 10$)
(2nd row, 1st column
$3 \times 4 + 2 \times 3 = 18$)

Find the missing entries in the following matrix multiplications:

1. $\begin{pmatrix} 1 & 4 \\ 3 & 1 \end{pmatrix}\begin{pmatrix} 3 & 2 \\ 1 & 4 \end{pmatrix} = \begin{pmatrix} & 18 \\ & 10 \end{pmatrix}$

2. $\begin{pmatrix} 3 & 2 \\ 4 & 6 \end{pmatrix}\begin{pmatrix} 4 & 1 \\ 1 & 3 \end{pmatrix} = \begin{pmatrix} & 9 \\ 22 & \end{pmatrix}$

3. $\begin{pmatrix} 9 & 1 \\ 0 & 2 \end{pmatrix}\begin{pmatrix} 1 & 4 \\ 3 & 1 \end{pmatrix} = \begin{pmatrix} 12 & \\ 6 & \end{pmatrix}$

4. $\begin{pmatrix} 5 & 6 \\ 7 & 9 \end{pmatrix}\begin{pmatrix} 1 & 2 \\ 3 & 1 \end{pmatrix} = \begin{pmatrix} & \\ 34 & 23 \end{pmatrix}$

5. $\begin{pmatrix} 1 & 2 \\ 3 & 1 \end{pmatrix}\begin{pmatrix} 5 & 6 \\ 7 & 9 \end{pmatrix} = \begin{pmatrix} & 24 \\ & 27 \end{pmatrix}$

6. $\begin{pmatrix} 5 & 1 \\ 0 & 6 \end{pmatrix}\begin{pmatrix} 4 & 3 \\ 2 & 1 \end{pmatrix} = \begin{pmatrix} 22 & \\ & 6 \end{pmatrix}$

7. $\begin{pmatrix} 3 & 9 \\ 2 & 1 \end{pmatrix}\begin{pmatrix} 1 & 1 \\ 1 & 1 \end{pmatrix} = \begin{pmatrix} 12 & \\ 3 & \end{pmatrix}$

8. $\begin{pmatrix} 5 & 3 \\ 1 & 1 \end{pmatrix}\begin{pmatrix} 1 & 2 \\ 4 & 3 \end{pmatrix} = \begin{pmatrix} & \\ & 5 \end{pmatrix}$

Find the following products:

9. $\begin{pmatrix} 4 & 6 \\ 1 & 3 \end{pmatrix}\begin{pmatrix} 1 & 4 \\ 3 & 6 \end{pmatrix}$

10. $\begin{pmatrix} 4 & 8 \\ 1 & 1 \end{pmatrix}\begin{pmatrix} 5 & 6 \\ 3 & 1 \end{pmatrix}$

11. $\begin{pmatrix} 5 & 1 \\ 3 & 2 \end{pmatrix}\begin{pmatrix} 3 & 2 \\ 1 & 4 \end{pmatrix}$

12. $\begin{pmatrix} 1 & 4 \\ 3 & 6 \end{pmatrix}\begin{pmatrix} 4 & 6 \\ 1 & 3 \end{pmatrix}$

13. $\begin{pmatrix} 6 & 4 \\ 5 & 1 \end{pmatrix}\begin{pmatrix} 2 & 6 \\ 8 & 1 \end{pmatrix}$

14. $\begin{pmatrix} 3 & 2 \\ 1 & 4 \end{pmatrix}\begin{pmatrix} 5 & 1 \\ 3 & 2 \end{pmatrix}$

Sometimes the entries are negative.

Find $\begin{pmatrix} 1 & -2 \\ 2 & 1 \end{pmatrix}\begin{pmatrix} 2 & 4 \\ -3 & 1 \end{pmatrix}$

$$\begin{pmatrix} 1 & -2 \\ 2 & 1 \end{pmatrix}\begin{pmatrix} 2 & 4 \\ -3 & 1 \end{pmatrix} = \begin{pmatrix} 8 & 2 \\ 1 & 9 \end{pmatrix}$$ (1st row, 2nd column
$1 \times 4 + (-2) \times 1 = 4 - 2 = 2$)

Find the following products:

15. $\begin{pmatrix} 3 & 2 \\ 1 & 4 \end{pmatrix}\begin{pmatrix} -2 & 4 \\ 3 & 1 \end{pmatrix}$

16. $\begin{pmatrix} 3 & 4 \\ -1 & 2 \end{pmatrix}\begin{pmatrix} 1 & 4 \\ 3 & 2 \end{pmatrix}$

17. $\begin{pmatrix} 5 & 2 \\ 3 & 4 \end{pmatrix}\begin{pmatrix} -1 & -2 \\ 4 & 3 \end{pmatrix}$

18. $\begin{pmatrix} 5 & -2 \\ 4 & 3 \end{pmatrix}\begin{pmatrix} -4 & -3 \\ 2 & 1 \end{pmatrix}$

19. $\begin{pmatrix} 4 & 3 \\ -1 & 4 \end{pmatrix}\begin{pmatrix} 3 & 2 \\ 3 & 1 \end{pmatrix}$

20. $\begin{pmatrix} 4 & -3 \\ 2 & -1 \end{pmatrix}\begin{pmatrix} -1 & -2 \\ 4 & -3 \end{pmatrix}$

ORDER OF MULTIPLICATION

We can see from the answers to questions 4 and 5 and others in the previous exercise, that the order in which we write the matrices *does* matter when we multiply. For example,

if $\quad\quad \mathbf{A} = \begin{pmatrix} 3 & 1 \\ 2 & 4 \end{pmatrix}$ and $\mathbf{B} = \begin{pmatrix} 5 & 6 \\ 1 & 1 \end{pmatrix}$

then $\quad\quad \mathbf{AB} = \begin{pmatrix} 16 & 19 \\ 14 & 16 \end{pmatrix}$ but $\mathbf{BA} = \begin{pmatrix} 27 & 29 \\ 5 & 5 \end{pmatrix}.$

That is, $\quad \mathbf{AB} \neq \mathbf{BA}$.

Occasionally, with a few special matrices, the order does not affect the answer.

Exercise 8h

The questions in this exercise refer to the following matrices:

$$\mathbf{A} = \begin{pmatrix} 4 & 3 \\ 2 & 1 \end{pmatrix} \quad\quad \mathbf{B} = \begin{pmatrix} 2 & 1 \\ 4 & 3 \end{pmatrix} \quad\quad \mathbf{C} = \begin{pmatrix} 7 & 8 \\ 1 & 1 \end{pmatrix} \quad\quad \mathbf{D} = \begin{pmatrix} 2 & 0 \\ 0 & 2 \end{pmatrix}$$

Find:

1. **AB**

2. **BA**

3. **AC**

4. **CA**

5. **AD**

6. **DA**

7. **BC**

8. **CB**

9. **BD**

10. **DB**

11. **CD**

12. **DC**

13. In some cases in questions 1 to 12 the order mattered and in some cases it did not. What is special about the matrices for which the order did not matter?

14. Make up a set of matrices similar to the ones used in this exercise and see whether the same results occur when you multiply them together in pairs.

MULTIPLICATION OF MATRICES OF DIFFERENT SIZES

We can multiply matrices of sizes other than 2×2. If Mrs Smith and Mrs Jones are buying bananas, lemons and grapefruit then we might have the information in the following tables:

Shopping lists	Bananas	Lemons	Grapefruit
Mrs Smith	4	0	1
Mrs Jones	2	3	2

Costs in cents	First shop	Second shop
Bananas	12	11
Lemons	8	9
Grapefruit	15	12

Then we would have the matrix multiplication

$$\begin{pmatrix} 4 & 0 & 1 \\ 2 & 3 & 2 \end{pmatrix} \begin{pmatrix} 12 & 11 \\ 8 & 9 \\ 15 & 12 \end{pmatrix}$$

Again we pair entries in a row in the first matrix with the entries in a column in the second matrix:

$$\begin{pmatrix} 4 & 0 & 1 \end{pmatrix} \begin{pmatrix} 12 \\ 8 \\ 15 \end{pmatrix} = \begin{pmatrix} 63 \end{pmatrix} \qquad 4 \times 12 + 0 \times 8 + 1 \times 15 = 63$$

This gives us Mrs Smith's bill at the first shop; she would spend 63 c.

$$\begin{pmatrix} 4 & 0 & 1 \end{pmatrix} \begin{pmatrix} 11 \\ 9 \\ 12 \end{pmatrix} = \begin{pmatrix} 56 \end{pmatrix} \qquad 4 \times 11 + 0 \times 9 + 1 \times 12 = 56$$

Mrs Smith would spend 56 c at the second shop.

The complete multiplication is as follows:

$$\begin{pmatrix} 4 & 0 & 1 \\ 2 & 3 & 2 \end{pmatrix} \begin{pmatrix} 12 & 11 \\ 8 & 9 \\ 15 & 12 \end{pmatrix} = \begin{pmatrix} 63 & 56 \\ 78 & 73 \end{pmatrix}$$

For example, pairing the entries in the *second row* of the first matrix with the entries in the *first column* of the second matrix gives the entry in the *second row*, *first column* of the resulting matrix,

i.e. $\qquad 2 \times 12 + 3 \times 8 + 2 \times 15 = 78$

Exercise 8i

Find (a) $\begin{pmatrix} 3 & 1 & 4 \\ 4 & 0 & 3 \end{pmatrix} \begin{pmatrix} 1 \\ 2 \\ 3 \end{pmatrix}$ (b) $\begin{pmatrix} 1 & 2 \end{pmatrix} \begin{pmatrix} 1 & 3 \\ 4 & 2 \end{pmatrix}$

(a) $\begin{pmatrix} 3 & 1 & 4 \\ 4 & 0 & 3 \end{pmatrix} \begin{pmatrix} 1 \\ 2 \\ 3 \end{pmatrix} = \begin{pmatrix} 17 \\ 13 \end{pmatrix}$

(first row, first column
$3 \times 1 + 1 \times 2 + 4 \times 3 = 17$)

(second row, first column
$4 \times 1 + 0 \times 2 + 3 \times 3 = 13$)

(b) $\begin{pmatrix} 1 & 2 \end{pmatrix} \begin{pmatrix} 1 & 3 \\ 4 & 2 \end{pmatrix} = \begin{pmatrix} 9 & 7 \end{pmatrix}$

(first row, first column
$1 \times 1 + 2 \times 4 = 9$)

(first row, second column
$1 \times 3 + 2 \times 2 = 7$)

Find:

1. $\begin{pmatrix} 1 & 4 \\ 3 & 1 \end{pmatrix}\begin{pmatrix} 3 \\ 1 \end{pmatrix}$

2. $\begin{pmatrix} 1 & 4 & 1 \\ 3 & 2 & 4 \end{pmatrix}\begin{pmatrix} 6 \\ 1 \\ 3 \end{pmatrix}$

3. $\begin{pmatrix} 1 & 2 \end{pmatrix}\begin{pmatrix} 4 \\ 3 \end{pmatrix}$

4. $\begin{pmatrix} 3 & 2 & 1 \\ 3 & 4 & 8 \end{pmatrix}\begin{pmatrix} 2 & 1 \\ 4 & 3 \\ 6 & 1 \end{pmatrix}$

5. $\begin{pmatrix} 4 & 2 \\ 3 & 1 \end{pmatrix}\begin{pmatrix} 4 & 6 & 3 \\ 8 & 1 & 2 \end{pmatrix}$

6. $\begin{pmatrix} 1 & 4 \\ 2 & 5 \\ 3 & 6 \end{pmatrix}\begin{pmatrix} 4 \\ 5 \end{pmatrix}$

7. $\begin{pmatrix} 7 & 3 \end{pmatrix}\begin{pmatrix} 1 & 4 & 3 \\ 2 & 1 & 2 \end{pmatrix}$

8. $\begin{pmatrix} 4 & 1 & 2 \\ 3 & 8 & 1 \\ 5 & 6 & 2 \end{pmatrix}\begin{pmatrix} 1 & 2 \\ 4 & 3 \\ 1 & 0 \end{pmatrix}$

9. $\begin{pmatrix} 1 & 4 & 1 \\ 2 & 3 & 0 \end{pmatrix}\begin{pmatrix} 4 & 1 & 2 \\ 3 & 8 & 1 \\ 5 & 6 & 2 \end{pmatrix}$

10. $\begin{pmatrix} 1 & 2 & 3 \end{pmatrix}\begin{pmatrix} 4 \\ 1 \\ 3 \end{pmatrix}$

COMPATIBILITY FOR MULTIPLICATION

It was possible to find all the matrix products in the last exercise but, just as there are pairs of matrices that cannot be added together, there are pairs of matrices that we cannot multiply together.

Consider $\begin{pmatrix} 1 & 2 \\ 3 & 4 \end{pmatrix}\begin{pmatrix} 1 & 4 \\ 2 & 5 \\ 3 & 6 \end{pmatrix}$

If we try to multiply the entries in the first row of the first matrix with entries in the first column of the second matrix,

i.e. $\begin{pmatrix} 1 & 2 \end{pmatrix}\begin{pmatrix} 1 \\ 2 \\ 3 \end{pmatrix}$

we find that the entries do not fit together in pairs.

We need to make sure that the number of entries in the row we use is the same as the number of entries in the column that goes with it. The easiest way to check this is to write the size below each matrix:

$$\underset{2 \times 3}{\begin{pmatrix} 3 & 1 & 4 \\ 4 & 0 & 3 \end{pmatrix}}\underset{3 \times 1}{\begin{pmatrix} 1 \\ 2 \\ 3 \end{pmatrix}} = \underset{2 \times 1}{\begin{pmatrix} 17 \\ 3 \end{pmatrix}}$$

There are three columns in the first matrix and three rows in the second, so these two matrices are compatible for multiplication. The two outer numbers give us the size of the resulting matrix.

Exercise 8j

Under each matrix write its size and find the product

$$(1 \quad 2)\begin{pmatrix} 1 & 2 & 3 \\ 3 & 4 & 6 \end{pmatrix}$$

Give the size of this product.

$$(1 \quad 2)\begin{pmatrix} 1 & 2 & 3 \\ 3 & 4 & 6 \end{pmatrix} = (7 \quad 10 \quad 15) \qquad \begin{array}{l} 1 \times 1 + 2 \times 3 = 7 \\ 1 \times 2 + 2 \times 4 = 10 \\ 1 \times 3 + 2 \times 6 = 15 \end{array}$$

$$1 \times 2 \qquad 2 \times 3 \qquad 1 \times 3$$

In questions 1 to 8, under each matrix write its size and give the size of the product. Find the product. (The pairs of matrices in these questions are all compatible for multiplication.)

1. $\begin{pmatrix} 3 & 2 \\ 4 & 1 \end{pmatrix}\begin{pmatrix} 1 \\ 2 \end{pmatrix}$

2. $\begin{pmatrix} 1 & 4 & 5 \\ 3 & 2 & 1 \end{pmatrix}\begin{pmatrix} 1 \\ 4 \\ 1 \end{pmatrix}$

3. $(1 \quad 2)\begin{pmatrix} 4 \\ 3 \end{pmatrix}$

4. $\begin{pmatrix} 3 & 2 & 1 \\ 3 & 4 & 8 \end{pmatrix}\begin{pmatrix} 2 & 1 \\ 4 & 3 \\ 6 & 1 \end{pmatrix}$

5. $\begin{pmatrix} 3 & 2 \\ 4 & 5 \end{pmatrix}\begin{pmatrix} 1 & 2 \\ 4 & 7 \end{pmatrix}$

6. $\begin{pmatrix} 1 \\ 2 \end{pmatrix}(3 \quad 4)$

7. $(9 \quad 4)\begin{pmatrix} 1 & 4 \\ 3 & 0 \end{pmatrix}$

8. $\begin{pmatrix} 1 \\ 2 \\ 3 \end{pmatrix}(4 \quad 5 \quad 6)$

Find, if possible, $\begin{pmatrix} 4 & 3 \\ 1 & 2 \end{pmatrix}(3 \quad 1 \quad 4)$

$$\begin{pmatrix} 4 & 3 \\ 1 & 2 \end{pmatrix}(3 \quad 1 \quad 4)$$
$$2 \times 2 \qquad 1 \times 3$$

It is not possible.

Find, where possible, the following products. Some of the matrices are not compatible for multiplication; in these cases, write 'not possible':

9. $\begin{pmatrix} 3 & 4 \\ 1 & 2 \end{pmatrix}\begin{pmatrix} 4 \\ 1 \end{pmatrix}$

10. $\begin{pmatrix} 2 & 4 \\ 1 & 0 \end{pmatrix}\begin{pmatrix} 2 & 3 \\ 1 & 4 \\ 1 & 5 \end{pmatrix}$

11. $\begin{pmatrix} 3 & 2 \\ 4 & 5 \end{pmatrix}\begin{pmatrix} 1 & 2 \\ 4 & 7 \end{pmatrix}$

12. $\begin{pmatrix} 7 & 2 & 3 \\ 4 & 1 & 0 \end{pmatrix}\begin{pmatrix} 1 & 2 \\ 4 & 5 \end{pmatrix}$

13. $\begin{pmatrix} 1 & 2 \\ 4 & 5 \end{pmatrix} \begin{pmatrix} 7 & 2 & 3 \\ 4 & 1 & 0 \end{pmatrix}$

14. $\begin{pmatrix} 1 & 4 \\ 0 & 6 \end{pmatrix} \begin{pmatrix} 3 & 2 \end{pmatrix}$

15. $\begin{pmatrix} 2 & 5 & 4 \end{pmatrix} \begin{pmatrix} 3 \\ 4 \\ 1 \end{pmatrix}$

16. $\begin{pmatrix} 1 \\ 2 \end{pmatrix} \begin{pmatrix} 3 & 2 \\ 4 & 1 \end{pmatrix}$

17. $\begin{pmatrix} 3 & 2 \end{pmatrix} \begin{pmatrix} 1 & 4 \\ 0 & 6 \end{pmatrix}$

18. $\begin{pmatrix} 3 \\ 4 \\ 1 \end{pmatrix} \begin{pmatrix} 2 & 4 & 5 \end{pmatrix}$

MATRICES CONTAINING NEGATIVE NUMBERS

Exercise 8k

Find $\begin{pmatrix} 1 & -2 \\ -4 & 3 \end{pmatrix} \begin{pmatrix} 4 \\ -2 \end{pmatrix}$

$$\begin{pmatrix} 1 & -2 \\ -4 & 3 \end{pmatrix} \begin{pmatrix} 4 \\ -2 \end{pmatrix} = \begin{pmatrix} 8 \\ -22 \end{pmatrix} \quad \begin{matrix} 1 \times 4 + (-2) \times (-2) = 8 \\ (-4) \times 4 + 3 \times (-2) = -22 \end{matrix}$$

$$2 \times 2 \quad 2 \times 1 \qquad 2 \times 1$$

Find the following matrix products:

1. $\begin{pmatrix} 4 & -2 \\ 2 & -3 \end{pmatrix} \begin{pmatrix} 1 \\ -1 \end{pmatrix}$

2. $\begin{pmatrix} 4 & -3 & 0 \\ 1 & 4 & -3 \end{pmatrix} \begin{pmatrix} 1 \\ -2 \\ 4 \end{pmatrix}$

3. $\begin{pmatrix} 2 & -1 & 4 \end{pmatrix} \begin{pmatrix} 1 & 2 \\ 0 & -2 \\ -1 & -3 \end{pmatrix}$

4. $\begin{pmatrix} 1 & -2 & 3 \\ -4 & 1 & 4 \\ 5 & 2 & 6 \end{pmatrix} \begin{pmatrix} -2 \\ -3 \\ -1 \end{pmatrix}$

5. $\begin{pmatrix} -4 & 2 \\ 2 & 5 \end{pmatrix} \begin{pmatrix} -3 & 4 \\ -2 & -5 \end{pmatrix}$

6. $\begin{pmatrix} -6 & -2 \end{pmatrix} \begin{pmatrix} 5 & -1 \\ 4 & -3 \end{pmatrix}$

7. $\begin{pmatrix} 6 & 1 & -3 \end{pmatrix} \begin{pmatrix} -4 \\ 1 \\ 1 \end{pmatrix}$

8. $\begin{pmatrix} -4 \\ 1 \\ 1 \end{pmatrix} \begin{pmatrix} 6 & 1 & -3 \end{pmatrix}$

9. $\begin{pmatrix} 2 & 3 \\ -2 & -3 \end{pmatrix} \begin{pmatrix} 5 & 6 & -2 \\ -1 & 2 & 1 \end{pmatrix}$

10. $\begin{pmatrix} 5 & -1 \\ 6 & 2 \\ -2 & 1 \end{pmatrix} \begin{pmatrix} 2 & 3 \\ -2 & -3 \end{pmatrix}$

Exercise 8l

The questions in this exercise refer to the following matrices:

$$A = \begin{pmatrix} 4 & 3 \\ 1 & 2 \end{pmatrix} \qquad B = \begin{pmatrix} 1 & -2 \\ 3 & 0 \end{pmatrix} \qquad C = \begin{pmatrix} 6 & 2 \\ -1 & 0 \end{pmatrix} \qquad D = \begin{pmatrix} 1 \\ 2 \end{pmatrix}$$

$$E = (3 \quad 4) \qquad F = \begin{pmatrix} 6 \\ 1 \\ -4 \end{pmatrix} \qquad G = \begin{pmatrix} 1 & 2 & 3 \\ 4 & -5 & 1 \\ 3 & 2 & 4 \end{pmatrix} \qquad H = (3)$$

Find, where possible, the following products:

1. **AB**	4. **AG**	7. **AF**	10. **ED**	13. **EH**
2. **BA**	5. **DE**	8. **GA**	11. **EC**	14. **HE**
3. **AD**	6. **AE**	9. **AH**	12. **EF**	15. **HD**

<u>**16.**</u> Find the other possible products of pairs of matrices chosen from **A** to **G**.

ADDITION, SUBTRACTION AND MULTIPLICATION

Exercise 8m

The questions in this exercise refer to the following matrices:

$$A = \begin{pmatrix} 1 & 2 \\ -4 & 3 \end{pmatrix} \quad B = \begin{pmatrix} 6 & 2 \\ 1 & 0 \end{pmatrix} \quad C = \begin{pmatrix} 1 & -1 & 3 \\ 2 & 2 & 0 \end{pmatrix} \quad D = \begin{pmatrix} 1 & 2 \\ 3 & 4 \\ 0 & 1 \end{pmatrix} \quad E = (1 \quad -2) \quad F = (3 \quad 1)$$

Find, where possible:

1. **AB**	4. **B − A**	7. **E − F**	10. **C − D**
2. **A + B**	5. **A + C**	8. **CD**	11. **BE**
3. **A − B**	6. **EF**	9. **DC**	12. **EB**

MULTIPLYING MORE THAN TWO MATRICES TOGETHER

Consider $\quad A = \begin{pmatrix} 1 & 4 \\ -1 & 0 \end{pmatrix} \qquad B = \begin{pmatrix} 6 & 2 \\ 0 & 3 \end{pmatrix} \qquad$ and $\qquad C = \begin{pmatrix} 1 & 2 \\ 3 & 4 \end{pmatrix}$

If we wish to find **ABC** we do this in two steps.
We can think of **ABC** either as (**AB**)**C** or as **A**(**BC**)

either $\qquad AB = \begin{pmatrix} 1 & 4 \\ -1 & 0 \end{pmatrix}\begin{pmatrix} 6 & 2 \\ 0 & 3 \end{pmatrix} = \begin{pmatrix} 6 & 14 \\ -6 & -2 \end{pmatrix}$

so $\qquad \mathbf{ABC} = \begin{pmatrix} 6 & 14 \\ -6 & -2 \end{pmatrix} \begin{pmatrix} 1 & 2 \\ 3 & 4 \end{pmatrix} = \begin{pmatrix} 48 & 68 \\ -12 & -20 \end{pmatrix}$

or $\qquad \mathbf{BC} = \begin{pmatrix} 6 & 2 \\ 0 & 3 \end{pmatrix} \begin{pmatrix} 1 & 2 \\ 3 & 4 \end{pmatrix} = \begin{pmatrix} 12 & 20 \\ 9 & 12 \end{pmatrix}$

so $\qquad \mathbf{ABC} = \begin{pmatrix} 1 & 4 \\ -1 & 0 \end{pmatrix} \begin{pmatrix} 12 & 20 \\ 9 & 12 \end{pmatrix} = \begin{pmatrix} 48 & 68 \\ -12 & -20 \end{pmatrix}$

We must pay careful attention to the order of the matrices. For example, if we found **AC** and then multiplied by **B**, the result would *not* be **ABC**.

POWERS OF MATRICES

$\mathbf{A}^2$ means $\mathbf{A} \times \mathbf{A}$, $\qquad \mathbf{A}^3$ means $\mathbf{A} \times \mathbf{A} \times \mathbf{A}$.

Exercise 8n

The questions in this exercise refer to the following matrices:

$$\mathbf{A} = \begin{pmatrix} 4 & -1 \\ 3 & 2 \end{pmatrix} \qquad \mathbf{B} = \begin{pmatrix} 2 & 3 \\ -4 & 2 \end{pmatrix} \qquad \mathbf{C} = \begin{pmatrix} 4 & 0 \\ 3 & -1 \end{pmatrix}$$

Find the following products. Make use of the answers and working from one question to help you with another:

1. **AB**
2. **ABC**
3. $\mathbf{A}^2$
4. **CBA**
5. **CAB**
6. $\mathbf{A}^3$
7. **ABA**
8. $\mathbf{A}^2\mathbf{B}$
9. **ACA**
10. $\mathbf{AB}^2$
11. $\mathbf{B}^3$
12. **CBC**

Where possible, check your answers by finding them in two different ways. For instance, in question 2, **ABC** can be found by thinking of it as (**AB**)**C** or as **A**(**BC**).

MIXED EXERCISES

Exercise 8p

The questions in this exercise refer to the following matrices:

$$\mathbf{A} = \begin{pmatrix} 5 & 2 \\ 1 & 4 \end{pmatrix} \qquad \mathbf{B} = \begin{pmatrix} 3 & -1 \\ 4 & -3 \end{pmatrix} \qquad \mathbf{C} = \begin{pmatrix} 1 \\ 4 \end{pmatrix}$$

1. What are the sizes of **A** and **C**?
2. Are **A** and **B** compatible for multiplication?
3. Are **A** and **C** compatible for multiplication?
4. Find **AB** if it is possible.

5. Find A^2 and C^2 if it is possible.

6. Find $A - C$ if it is possible.

7. Find 3**B**.

8. Find $2A + B$ if it is possible.

9. What is the entry in the second row of the first column of **C**?

10. Which is possible to find, **BC** or **CB**?

Exercise 8q

The questions in this exercise refer to the following matrices:

$$P = \begin{pmatrix} 2 & 1 & -1 \\ 4 & 3 & 1 \end{pmatrix} \qquad Q = \begin{pmatrix} 3 & 2 \\ -1 & 4 \end{pmatrix} \qquad R = \begin{pmatrix} 3 \\ 4 \end{pmatrix}$$

1. Find 2**P**.

2. Find $2P + Q$ if it is possible.

3. Find $Q + 2R$ if it is possible.

4. What are the sizes of **P** and **Q**?

5. Are **P** and **R** compatible for multiplication?

6. What is the entry in the first row of the first column of **R**?

7. What is the entry in the second row of the third column of **P**?

8. Which is it possible to find, **PQ** or **QP**?

9. Find **QR** if it is possible.

10. Find Q^2 and P^2 if it is possible.

MATHS IS OUT THERE

Consider the matrix $\begin{pmatrix} 5 & -2 & 3 \\ 0 & 2 & 4 \\ 1 & 6 & -1 \end{pmatrix}$

Find the sum of the terms in each row, column and diagonal.

For example, sum in column 1 is $5 + 0 + 1 = 6$.

What do you notice about the sum in each case?

Now consider another matrix whose terms are 2^x, where x is the entry in the matrix above.

For example, the element corresponding to 5 above is $2^5 = 32$.

Now complete the matrix

$$\begin{pmatrix} 32 & - & 8 \\ - & - & - \\ 2 & - & \frac{1}{2} \end{pmatrix}$$

Now find the product of the terms in each row, in each column, in each diagonal.

What do you notice about the products?

If we call our first matrix an 'additive magic square', we may refer to this matrix as a 'multiplicative magic square'.

Do you notice any relationship between the sum of entries in the 'additive square' and the product of entries in the 'multiplicative square'?

Try to form other multiplicative magic squares using bases other than 2.

9 INVERSE AND SQUARE MATRICES

At the end of the chapter you should be able to:

1. Identify a square matrix.
2. Identify unit and zero matrices.
3. Calculate the determinant of a square matrix.
4. Find the inverse of a square matrix.
5. Identify a given matrix which has no inverse.
6. Write a pair of simultaneous equations in matrix form.
7. Solve a pair of simultaneous equations using matrix theory.
8. Solve matrix equations of the form $\mathbf{A} + \mathbf{X} = \mathbf{B}$, where $\mathbf{A}$, $\mathbf{X}$ and $\mathbf{B}$ are matrices.

SQUARE MATRICES

A square matrix has the same number of rows and columns.

$$\begin{pmatrix} 1 & 2 \\ 3 & -1 \end{pmatrix} \text{ and } \begin{pmatrix} 1 & 6 & 3 \\ 1 & 0 & 1 \\ 4 & 4 & 3 \end{pmatrix} \text{ are square matrices.}$$

A square matrix has two diagonals:

$$\begin{pmatrix} 1 & 3 & 4 \\ 0 & 1 & 2 \\ 3 & 1 & 2 \end{pmatrix}$$

The diagonal that goes from top left to bottom right is the *leading diagonal*:

$$\begin{pmatrix} 1 & 2 \\ 3 & 4 \end{pmatrix}$$

Exercise 9a

State which of the two matrices $\begin{pmatrix} 1 \\ 2 \end{pmatrix}$ and $\begin{pmatrix} 4 & 1 \\ 3 & 2 \end{pmatrix}$ is a square matrix. Give its size and mark its leading diagonal.

$\begin{pmatrix} 4 & 1 \\ 3 & 2 \end{pmatrix}$ is a 2×2 square matrix.

State whether or not each of the following matrices is a square matrix. If it is, give its size and mark its leading diagonal:

1. $\begin{pmatrix} 3 & 6 & 1 \\ 4 & 0 & 1 \\ 3 & 2 & 1 \end{pmatrix}$

3. $\begin{pmatrix} 2 & 1 \\ 4 & 3 \end{pmatrix}$

5. $\begin{pmatrix} -1 & 4 \\ 4 & -1 \end{pmatrix}$

2. $\begin{pmatrix} 4 & 3 & 2 \\ 1 & 3 & 1 \end{pmatrix}$

4. $\begin{pmatrix} 2 & 3 \\ 6 & 2 \\ 1 & 4 \end{pmatrix}$

6. $\begin{pmatrix} 6 & 1 & -3 \\ 4 & 1 & 2 \\ 6 & 8 & 1 \end{pmatrix}$

REMINDER OF MATRIX MULTIPLICATION

Exercise 9b

Find, where possible

(a) $\begin{pmatrix} 2 & 3 \\ 1 & -3 \\ 4 & -2 \end{pmatrix}\begin{pmatrix} 2 & 3 \\ 1 & 4 \end{pmatrix}$ (b) $(1 \quad 2)(3 \quad 4)$

(a) $\begin{pmatrix} 2 & 3 \\ 1 & -3 \\ 4 & -2 \end{pmatrix}\begin{pmatrix} 2 & 3 \\ 1 & 4 \end{pmatrix} = \begin{pmatrix} 7 & 18 \\ -1 & -9 \\ 6 & 4 \end{pmatrix}$

$\qquad 3 \times 2 \qquad 2 \times 2 \qquad\qquad 3 \times 2$

(b) $(1 \quad 2)(3 \quad 4)$ not possible
$\qquad 1 \times 2 \quad 1 \times 2$

Find where possible:

1. $\begin{pmatrix} 3 & 1 \\ 4 & 3 \end{pmatrix}\begin{pmatrix} 1 & 2 \\ 1 & 1 \end{pmatrix}$

2. $(1 \quad 0 \quad 1)\begin{pmatrix} 4 & -1 \\ 2 & 4 \\ 3 & -5 \end{pmatrix}$

3. $\begin{pmatrix} 1 & 2 \\ 3 & 4 \end{pmatrix}\begin{pmatrix} 1 & 6 & -1 \\ 3 & 2 & 1 \end{pmatrix}$

4. $\begin{pmatrix} 1 & 6 & -1 \\ 3 & 2 & 1 \end{pmatrix}\begin{pmatrix} 1 & 2 \\ 3 & 4 \end{pmatrix}$

5. $\begin{pmatrix} 4 & -1 \\ 2 & 4 \\ 3 & -5 \end{pmatrix}(1 \quad 0 \quad 1)$

6. $\begin{pmatrix} 3 & 5 \\ 4 & -3 \end{pmatrix}\begin{pmatrix} 2 & 1 \\ 4 & 2 \end{pmatrix}$

7. $\begin{pmatrix} 1 & 2 \\ 1 & 1 \end{pmatrix}\begin{pmatrix} 3 & 1 \\ 4 & 3 \end{pmatrix}$

8. $\begin{pmatrix} 4 \\ 3 \\ 2 \end{pmatrix}\begin{pmatrix} 1 \\ 6 \\ 1 \end{pmatrix}$

9. $\begin{pmatrix} 4 \\ 3 \\ 2 \end{pmatrix}(1 \quad 6 \quad 1)$

10. $(1 \quad 6 \quad 1)\begin{pmatrix} 4 \\ 3 \\ 2 \end{pmatrix}$

11. $\begin{pmatrix} 1 & -1 \\ -1 & 1 \end{pmatrix}\begin{pmatrix} 4 \\ 3 \end{pmatrix}$

12. $(2 \quad 6)\begin{pmatrix} 5 & -3 \\ 4 & 2 \end{pmatrix}$

THE UNIT MATRIX AND THE ZERO MATRIX

Exercise 9c

Find:

1. $\begin{pmatrix} 4 & 2 \\ 3 & 4 \end{pmatrix}\begin{pmatrix} 1 & 0 \\ 0 & 1 \end{pmatrix}$

3. $(6 \quad 2)\begin{pmatrix} 0 & 0 \\ 0 & 0 \end{pmatrix}$

5. $(3 \quad 2)\begin{pmatrix} 1 & 0 \\ 0 & 1 \end{pmatrix}$

2. $\begin{pmatrix} 1 & 0 \\ 0 & 1 \end{pmatrix}\begin{pmatrix} 4 \\ 5 \end{pmatrix}$

4. $\begin{pmatrix} 0 & 0 \\ 0 & 0 \end{pmatrix}\begin{pmatrix} 2 & 3 \\ 4 & 1 \end{pmatrix}$

6. $\begin{pmatrix} 1 & 0 \\ 0 & 1 \end{pmatrix}\begin{pmatrix} 3 & 2 & -1 \\ 4 & 3 & 1 \end{pmatrix}$

The *unit matrix* $\begin{pmatrix} 1 & 0 \\ 0 & 1 \end{pmatrix}$ does not alter the matrix it multiplies or is multiplied by, e.g.:

$$\begin{pmatrix} 1 & 2 \\ 4 & 5 \end{pmatrix}\begin{pmatrix} 1 & 0 \\ 0 & 1 \end{pmatrix} = \begin{pmatrix} 1 & 2 \\ 4 & 5 \end{pmatrix} \text{ and } \begin{pmatrix} 1 & 0 \\ 0 & 1 \end{pmatrix}\begin{pmatrix} 1 & 2 \\ 4 & 5 \end{pmatrix} = \begin{pmatrix} 1 & 2 \\ 4 & 5 \end{pmatrix}$$

This is similar to multiplying by 1 in ordinary number multiplication.
A unit matrix is usually represented by **I**.

The *zero matrix* $\begin{pmatrix} 0 & 0 \\ 0 & 0 \end{pmatrix}$, when multiplied by any compatible matrix, gives the zero matrix:

$$\begin{pmatrix} 1 & 2 \\ 4 & 5 \end{pmatrix}\begin{pmatrix} 0 & 0 \\ 0 & 0 \end{pmatrix} = \begin{pmatrix} 0 & 0 \\ 0 & 0 \end{pmatrix} \text{ and } \begin{pmatrix} 0 & 0 \\ 0 & 0 \end{pmatrix}\begin{pmatrix} 1 & 2 \\ 4 & 5 \end{pmatrix} = \begin{pmatrix} 0 & 0 \\ 0 & 0 \end{pmatrix}$$

This is similar to multiplying by zero in ordinary number multiplication.
A zero matrix is usually represented by **0**.

There are other unit and zero matrices, e.g.

$$\begin{pmatrix} 1 & 0 & 0 \\ 0 & 1 & 0 \\ 0 & 0 & 1 \end{pmatrix} \text{ and } \begin{pmatrix} 0 & 0 & 0 \\ 0 & 0 & 0 \\ 0 & 0 & 0 \end{pmatrix}$$

but we are concerned mainly with 2×2 square matrices in this chapter.

Exercise 9d

Find:

1. $\begin{pmatrix} 1 & 1 \\ 2 & 3 \end{pmatrix}\begin{pmatrix} 3 & -1 \\ -2 & 1 \end{pmatrix}$

3. $\begin{pmatrix} 2 & -1 \\ -3 & 4 \end{pmatrix}\begin{pmatrix} 4 & 1 \\ 3 & 2 \end{pmatrix}$

2. $\begin{pmatrix} 4 & 1 \\ 3 & 2 \end{pmatrix}\begin{pmatrix} 2 & -1 \\ -3 & 4 \end{pmatrix}$

4. $\begin{pmatrix} 9 & 4 \\ 4 & 2 \end{pmatrix}\begin{pmatrix} 2 & -4 \\ -4 & 9 \end{pmatrix}$

5. $\begin{pmatrix} 6 & -3 \\ -3 & 2 \end{pmatrix}\begin{pmatrix} 2 & 3 \\ 3 & 6 \end{pmatrix}$

7. $\begin{pmatrix} 9 & 7 \\ 4 & 3 \end{pmatrix}\begin{pmatrix} 3 & -7 \\ -4 & 9 \end{pmatrix}$

6. $\begin{pmatrix} 2 & 3 \\ 3 & 6 \end{pmatrix}\begin{pmatrix} 6 & -3 \\ -3 & 2 \end{pmatrix}$

8. $\begin{pmatrix} 3 & -2 \\ -4 & 3 \end{pmatrix}\begin{pmatrix} 3 & 2 \\ 4 & 3 \end{pmatrix}$

9. What do you notice about the arrangement of the numbers and signs in each pair of matrices? What do you notice about the answers?

In questions 10 to 19, find a second matrix **B** such that **B** × **A** is of the form $\begin{pmatrix} k & 0 \\ 0 & k \end{pmatrix}$, i.e. like the answers to questions 1 to 8.

10. $\mathbf{A} = \begin{pmatrix} 3 & 2 \\ 8 & 6 \end{pmatrix}$

15. $\mathbf{A} = \begin{pmatrix} 5 & 3 \\ 9 & 6 \end{pmatrix}$

11. $\mathbf{A} = \begin{pmatrix} 2 & 1 \\ 2 & 3 \end{pmatrix}$

16. $\mathbf{A} = \begin{pmatrix} 5 & 4 \\ 9 & 8 \end{pmatrix}$

12. $\mathbf{A} = \begin{pmatrix} 6 & -1 \\ -20 & 3 \end{pmatrix}$

17. $\mathbf{A} = \begin{pmatrix} 6 & 2 \\ 14 & 4 \end{pmatrix}$

13. $\mathbf{A} = \begin{pmatrix} 1 & -3 \\ 1 & 5 \end{pmatrix}$

18. $\mathbf{A} = \begin{pmatrix} 1 & 2 \\ 2 & 1 \end{pmatrix}$

14. $\mathbf{A} = \begin{pmatrix} 5 & 7 \\ 3 & 4 \end{pmatrix}$

19. $\mathbf{A} = \begin{pmatrix} 4 & -3 \\ 3 & -2 \end{pmatrix}$

If we are given a 2×2 matrix **A** and we want a matrix **B** such that $\mathbf{A} \times \mathbf{B}$ is of the form $\begin{pmatrix} k & 0 \\ 0 & k \end{pmatrix}$ we

(a) interchange the numbers in the leading diagonal of **A**

(b) leave the other two numbers of **A** where they are, but change their signs.

For example, if $\mathbf{A} = \begin{pmatrix} 4 & 2 \\ 5 & 3 \end{pmatrix}$, to get **B**

we change $\begin{pmatrix} 4 & \\ & 3 \end{pmatrix}$ to $\begin{pmatrix} 3 & \\ & 4 \end{pmatrix}$ and $\begin{pmatrix} & 2 \\ 5 & \end{pmatrix}$ to $\begin{pmatrix} & -2 \\ -5 & \end{pmatrix}$

then $\begin{pmatrix} 4 & 2 \\ 5 & 3 \end{pmatrix}\begin{pmatrix} 3 & -2 \\ -5 & 4 \end{pmatrix} = \begin{pmatrix} 2 & 0 \\ 0 & 2 \end{pmatrix}$

This matrix is called a *diagonal matrix*.

THE INVERSE OF A MATRIX

In ordinary numbers we say $\frac{1}{7}$ is the inverse of 7 because $7 \times \frac{1}{7} = 1$
Similarly $\frac{2}{5}$ is the inverse of $\frac{5}{2}$ because $\frac{5}{2} \times \frac{2}{5} = 1$

In the same way $\begin{pmatrix} 3 & 5 \\ 1 & 2 \end{pmatrix} \times \begin{pmatrix} 2 & -5 \\ -1 & 3 \end{pmatrix} = \begin{pmatrix} 1 & 0 \\ 0 & 1 \end{pmatrix}$

so $\begin{pmatrix} 2 & -5 \\ -1 & 3 \end{pmatrix}$ is the inverse of $\begin{pmatrix} 3 & 5 \\ 1 & 2 \end{pmatrix}$

and $\begin{pmatrix} 3 & 5 \\ 1 & 2 \end{pmatrix}$ is the inverse of $\begin{pmatrix} 2 & -5 \\ -1 & 3 \end{pmatrix}$

Exercise 9e

Find the inverse of $\begin{pmatrix} 5 & 3 \\ 3 & 2 \end{pmatrix}$

Try $\begin{pmatrix} 2 & -3 \\ -3 & 5 \end{pmatrix}$

$$\begin{pmatrix} 5 & 3 \\ 3 & 2 \end{pmatrix}\begin{pmatrix} 2 & -3 \\ -3 & 5 \end{pmatrix} = \begin{pmatrix} 1 & 0 \\ 0 & 1 \end{pmatrix}$$

So $\begin{pmatrix} 2 & -3 \\ -3 & 5 \end{pmatrix}$ is the inverse of $\begin{pmatrix} 5 & 3 \\ 3 & 2 \end{pmatrix}$

Find the inverses of the following matrices:

1. $\begin{pmatrix} 4 & 1 \\ 7 & 2 \end{pmatrix}$ **3.** $\begin{pmatrix} 10 & -3 \\ 7 & -2 \end{pmatrix}$ **5.** $\begin{pmatrix} 7 & 4 \\ 12 & 7 \end{pmatrix}$

2. $\begin{pmatrix} 11 & 3 \\ 7 & 2 \end{pmatrix}$ **4.** $\begin{pmatrix} 3 & 5 \\ 4 & 7 \end{pmatrix}$ **6.** $\begin{pmatrix} 1 & 1 \\ 1 & 2 \end{pmatrix}$

Not all inverses can be produced in this way, e.g.

$$\begin{pmatrix} 5 & 4 \\ 3 & 3 \end{pmatrix} \times \begin{pmatrix} 3 & -4 \\ -3 & 5 \end{pmatrix} = \begin{pmatrix} 3 & 0 \\ 0 & 3 \end{pmatrix} \text{ and not } \begin{pmatrix} 1 & 0 \\ 0 & 1 \end{pmatrix}$$

But $\begin{pmatrix} 3 & 0 \\ 0 & 3 \end{pmatrix} = 3\begin{pmatrix} 1 & 0 \\ 0 & 1 \end{pmatrix}$ so our attempt at the inverse is three times too big.

We therefore divide our attempt at the inverse by 3.

The inverse of $\begin{pmatrix} 5 & 4 \\ 3 & 3 \end{pmatrix}$ is $\begin{pmatrix} 1 & -\frac{4}{3} \\ -1 & \frac{5}{3} \end{pmatrix}$

The number 3 is called the *determinant* of $\begin{pmatrix} 5 & 4 \\ 3 & 3 \end{pmatrix}$

In Exercise 9e, questions 1 to 6 the determinant in each case is 1.

Exercise 9f

Find the inverse of $\begin{pmatrix} 5 & 8 \\ 1 & 2 \end{pmatrix}$

Try $\begin{pmatrix} 2 & -8 \\ -1 & 5 \end{pmatrix}$

$$\begin{pmatrix} 5 & 8 \\ 1 & 2 \end{pmatrix}\begin{pmatrix} 2 & -8 \\ -1 & 5 \end{pmatrix} = \begin{pmatrix} 2 & 0 \\ 0 & 2 \end{pmatrix}$$

The determinant of $\begin{pmatrix} 5 & 8 \\ 1 & 2 \end{pmatrix}$ is 2,

so the inverse of $\begin{pmatrix} 5 & 8 \\ 1 & 2 \end{pmatrix}$ is $\begin{pmatrix} \frac{2}{2} & \frac{-8}{2} \\ \frac{-1}{2} & \frac{5}{2} \end{pmatrix} = \begin{pmatrix} 1 & -4 \\ -\frac{1}{2} & 2\frac{1}{2} \end{pmatrix}$

Note that this inverse can be written as $\frac{1}{2}\begin{pmatrix} 2 & -8 \\ -1 & 5 \end{pmatrix}$

Find the inverses of the following matrices:

1. $\begin{pmatrix} 6 & 2 \\ 8 & 3 \end{pmatrix}$ **4.** $\begin{pmatrix} 1 & -2 \\ 1 & 1 \end{pmatrix}$ **7.** $\begin{pmatrix} 4 & -3 \\ -5 & 4 \end{pmatrix}$

2. $\begin{pmatrix} 9 & 2 \\ 3 & 1 \end{pmatrix}$ **5.** $\begin{pmatrix} 2 & 0 \\ 0 & 3 \end{pmatrix}$ **8.** $\begin{pmatrix} 4 & 3 \\ 5 & 4 \end{pmatrix}$

3. $\begin{pmatrix} 4 & 2 \\ 10 & 6 \end{pmatrix}$ **6.** $\begin{pmatrix} 3 & 2 \\ 11 & 8 \end{pmatrix}$ **9.** $\begin{pmatrix} 3 & -4 \\ -2 & 4 \end{pmatrix}$

Sometimes the determinant is negative.

Find the inverse of $\begin{pmatrix} 1 & 5 \\ 1 & 2 \end{pmatrix}$

Try $\begin{pmatrix} 2 & -5 \\ -1 & 1 \end{pmatrix}$

$$\begin{pmatrix} 1 & 5 \\ 1 & 2 \end{pmatrix}\begin{pmatrix} 2 & -5 \\ -1 & 1 \end{pmatrix} = \begin{pmatrix} -3 & 0 \\ 0 & -3 \end{pmatrix}$$

The determinant of $\begin{pmatrix} 1 & 5 \\ 1 & 2 \end{pmatrix}$ is -3,

so the inverse of $\begin{pmatrix} 1 & 5 \\ 1 & 2 \end{pmatrix}$ is $\begin{pmatrix} \frac{2}{-3} & \frac{-5}{-3} \\ \frac{-1}{-3} & \frac{1}{-3} \end{pmatrix} = \begin{pmatrix} -\frac{2}{3} & \frac{5}{3} \\ \frac{1}{3} & -\frac{1}{3} \end{pmatrix}$

i.e. $-\frac{1}{3}\begin{pmatrix} 2 & -5 \\ -1 & 1 \end{pmatrix}$

Find the inverses of the following matrices:

10. $\begin{pmatrix} 6 & 2 \\ 7 & 2 \end{pmatrix}$
    12. $\begin{pmatrix} -4 & 1 \\ 1 & 1 \end{pmatrix}$
    14. $\begin{pmatrix} 3 & -4 \\ -3 & 3 \end{pmatrix}$

11. $\begin{pmatrix} 9 & 4 \\ 5 & 2 \end{pmatrix}$
    13. $\begin{pmatrix} 3 & 2 \\ 4 & 2 \end{pmatrix}$
    15. $\begin{pmatrix} 5 & 4 \\ 8 & 6 \end{pmatrix}$

Sometimes the determinant is zero. In this case, as we cannot divide by zero, we cannot produce an inverse.

16. State whether the given matrix has a zero determinant and hence no inverse:

(a) $\begin{pmatrix} 6 & 4 \\ 3 & 2 \end{pmatrix}$
    (b) $\begin{pmatrix} 11 & 3 \\ 4 & 1 \end{pmatrix}$
    (c) $\begin{pmatrix} 8 & 6 \\ 4 & 3 \end{pmatrix}$

17. Which of the following matrices are their own inverses?

(a) $\begin{pmatrix} 1 & 0 \\ 0 & -1 \end{pmatrix}$
    (b) $\begin{pmatrix} 0 & 1 \\ 1 & 0 \end{pmatrix}$
    (c) $\begin{pmatrix} -1 & 0 \\ 0 & -1 \end{pmatrix}$

Find, where possible, the inverses of the following matrices:

18. $\begin{pmatrix} 6 & 5 \\ 5 & 5 \end{pmatrix}$
    20. $\begin{pmatrix} 5 & 0 \\ 0 & 5 \end{pmatrix}$
    22. $\begin{pmatrix} 5 & 3 \\ 9 & 6 \end{pmatrix}$

19. $\begin{pmatrix} 6 & 4 \\ 6 & 4 \end{pmatrix}$
    21. $\begin{pmatrix} 5 & 7 \\ 3 & 4 \end{pmatrix}$
    23. $\begin{pmatrix} 8 & 3 \\ 16 & 6 \end{pmatrix}$

NOTATION

With ordinary numbers, $\frac{1}{3}$ is the inverse of 3 under multiplication.
$\frac{1}{3}$ can be written as 3^{-1}, so 3^{-1} is the inverse of 3.
In the same way, the inverse of **A** is written $\mathbf{A}^{-1}$.

If $\mathbf{A} = \begin{pmatrix} 4 & 7 \\ 1 & 2 \end{pmatrix}$, then $\mathbf{A}^{-1} = \begin{pmatrix} 2 & -7 \\ -1 & 4 \end{pmatrix}$

$$\begin{pmatrix} 4 & 7 \\ 1 & 2 \end{pmatrix}\begin{pmatrix} 2 & -7 \\ -1 & 4 \end{pmatrix} = \begin{pmatrix} 1 & 0 \\ 0 & 1 \end{pmatrix}$$

and $\mathbf{AA}^{-1} = \mathbf{I}$

The determinant of **A** is written $|\mathbf{A}|$. In this case $|\mathbf{A}| = 1$

Exercise 9g

The questions in this exercise refer to the following matrices:

$$\mathbf{A} = \begin{pmatrix} 5 & 3 \\ 3 & 2 \end{pmatrix} \quad \mathbf{B} = \begin{pmatrix} 4 & 4 \\ 2 & 3 \end{pmatrix} \quad \mathbf{C} = \begin{pmatrix} 6 & 2 \\ 5 & 2 \end{pmatrix} \quad \mathbf{D} = \begin{pmatrix} 7 & 3 \\ 2 & 1 \end{pmatrix} \quad \mathbf{I} = \begin{pmatrix} 1 & 0 \\ 0 & 1 \end{pmatrix}$$

Find (a) $|\mathbf{D}|$ (b) $\mathbf{D}^{-1}$ (c) $|\mathbf{C}|$ (d) $\mathbf{C}^{-1}$ (e) $\mathbf{D}^{-1}\mathbf{C}$

(a) Try $\begin{pmatrix} 1 & -3 \\ -2 & 7 \end{pmatrix}$

$$\begin{pmatrix} 7 & 3 \\ 2 & 1 \end{pmatrix}\begin{pmatrix} 1 & -3 \\ -2 & 7 \end{pmatrix} = \begin{pmatrix} 1 & 0 \\ 0 & 1 \end{pmatrix}$$
$$|\mathbf{D}| = 1$$

(b) $\mathbf{D}^{-1} = \begin{pmatrix} 1 & -3 \\ -2 & 7 \end{pmatrix}$

(c) Try $\begin{pmatrix} 2 & -2 \\ -5 & 6 \end{pmatrix}$

$$\begin{pmatrix} 6 & 2 \\ 5 & 2 \end{pmatrix}\begin{pmatrix} 2 & -2 \\ -5 & 6 \end{pmatrix} = \begin{pmatrix} 2 & 0 \\ 0 & 2 \end{pmatrix}$$
$$|\mathbf{C}| = 2$$

(d) $\mathbf{C}^{-1} = \frac{1}{2}\begin{pmatrix} 2 & -2 \\ -5 & 6 \end{pmatrix} = \begin{pmatrix} 1 & -1 \\ -2\frac{1}{2} & 3 \end{pmatrix}$

(e) $\mathbf{D}^{-1}\mathbf{C} = \begin{pmatrix} 1 & -3 \\ -2 & 7 \end{pmatrix}\begin{pmatrix} 6 & 2 \\ 5 & 2 \end{pmatrix} = \begin{pmatrix} -9 & -4 \\ 23 & 10 \end{pmatrix}$

Write out the matrices **A, B, C, D** and **I** and hence find:

1. $|\mathbf{A}|$ and $\mathbf{A}^{-1}$ **4.** $\mathbf{AB}$ **7.** $\mathbf{B}^{-1}\mathbf{A}^{-1}$ **10.** $(\mathbf{A}^{-1})^2$

2. $|\mathbf{B}|$ and $\mathbf{B}^{-1}$ **5.** $(\mathbf{AB})^{-1}$ **8.** $\mathbf{A}^2$ **11.** $\mathbf{C}^{-1}\mathbf{A}$

3. $\mathbf{I}^{-1}$ **6.** $\mathbf{A}^{-1}\mathbf{B}^{-1}$ **9.** $(\mathbf{A}^2)^{-1}$ **12.** $\mathbf{AC}^{-1}$

FINDING THE DETERMINANT

The determinant can be found without trying to find the inverse.

The determinant of the matrix $\begin{pmatrix} a & b \\ c & d \end{pmatrix}$ is $ad - bc$.

We find the product of the entries in the leading diagonal, ad, and then we subtract the product of the entries in the other diagonal, bc.

For example, the determinant of $\begin{pmatrix} 3 & 1 \\ 4 & 2 \end{pmatrix}$ is $3 \times 2 - 1 \times 4 = 2$

Exercise 9h

Find the determinant of $\begin{pmatrix} 3 & -1 \\ 5 & 2 \end{pmatrix}$

The determinant of $\begin{pmatrix} 3 & -1 \\ 5 & 2 \end{pmatrix} = 3 \times 2 - (-1) \times 5$

$$= 6 - (-5)$$

$$= 11$$

Find the determinants of the following matrices:

1. $\begin{pmatrix} 6 & 1 \\ 3 & 2 \end{pmatrix}$ **4.** $\begin{pmatrix} 4 & -3 \\ 1 & 4 \end{pmatrix}$ **7.** $\begin{pmatrix} 3 & 4 \\ 1 & 1 \end{pmatrix}$ **<u>10.</u>** $\begin{pmatrix} -2 & -3 \\ -1 & -4 \end{pmatrix}$

2. $\begin{pmatrix} 4 & 1 \\ 3 & 5 \end{pmatrix}$ **5.** $\begin{pmatrix} 5 & 1 \\ 4 & -2 \end{pmatrix}$ **8.** $\begin{pmatrix} 6 & -7 \\ -2 & 1 \end{pmatrix}$ **<u>11.</u>** $\begin{pmatrix} 2 & 3 \\ 1 & 4 \end{pmatrix}$

3. $\begin{pmatrix} 6 & 2 \\ 6 & 2 \end{pmatrix}$ **6.** $\begin{pmatrix} 6 & -2 \\ 2 & 1 \end{pmatrix}$ **<u>9.</u>** $\begin{pmatrix} 1 & 4 \\ -1 & 5 \end{pmatrix}$ **<u>12.</u>** $\begin{pmatrix} 6 & 1 \\ 3 & -1 \end{pmatrix}$

SOLUTION OF SIMULTANEOUS EQUATIONS USING MATRICES

A pair of simultaneous equations is sometimes given in matrix form.

Consider the matrix equation

$$\begin{pmatrix} 5 & 2 \\ 3 & 5 \end{pmatrix} \begin{pmatrix} x \\ y \end{pmatrix} = \begin{pmatrix} 1 \\ -7 \end{pmatrix}$$

Multiply the left-hand side

$$\begin{pmatrix} 5x + 2y \\ 3x + 5y \end{pmatrix} = \begin{pmatrix} 1 \\ -7 \end{pmatrix}$$

This represents the pair of equations

$$5x + 2y = 1$$
$$3x + 5y = -7$$

Similarly, a pair of given equations can be written in matrix form.

For example, $\begin{aligned} 4x + 2y &= 7 \\ x + 3y &= 8 \end{aligned}$ gives $\begin{pmatrix} 4x + 2y \\ x + 3y \end{pmatrix} = \begin{pmatrix} 7 \\ 8 \end{pmatrix}$

i.e. $\begin{pmatrix} 4 & 2 \\ 1 & 3 \end{pmatrix} \begin{pmatrix} x \\ y \end{pmatrix} = \begin{pmatrix} 7 \\ 8 \end{pmatrix}$

Exercise 9i

Find the pair of simultaneous equations which are equivalent to the matrix
equation $\begin{pmatrix} 1 & 2 \\ 3 & 1 \end{pmatrix}\begin{pmatrix} x \\ y \end{pmatrix} = \begin{pmatrix} 7 \\ 5 \end{pmatrix}$

$$\begin{pmatrix} 1 & 2 \\ 3 & 1 \end{pmatrix}\begin{pmatrix} x \\ y \end{pmatrix} = \begin{pmatrix} 7 \\ 5 \end{pmatrix}$$

(Multiply the left-hand side)

$$\begin{pmatrix} 1x + 2y \\ 3x + 1y \end{pmatrix} = \begin{pmatrix} 7 \\ 5 \end{pmatrix}$$

∴ the pair of equations is $\begin{array}{l} x + 2y = 7 \\ 3x + y = 5 \end{array}$

Find the pairs of simultaneous equations which are equivalent to the following matrix equations:

1. $\begin{pmatrix} 1 & 2 \\ 3 & 2 \end{pmatrix}\begin{pmatrix} x \\ y \end{pmatrix} = \begin{pmatrix} 3 \\ 5 \end{pmatrix}$

3. $\begin{pmatrix} 9 & 2 \\ 4 & 1 \end{pmatrix}\begin{pmatrix} x \\ y \end{pmatrix} = \begin{pmatrix} 24 \\ 11 \end{pmatrix}$

2. $\begin{pmatrix} 4 & 2 \\ 5 & 3 \end{pmatrix}\begin{pmatrix} x \\ y \end{pmatrix} = \begin{pmatrix} 12 \\ 15 \end{pmatrix}$

4. $\begin{pmatrix} 6 & -1 \\ 2 & 1 \end{pmatrix}\begin{pmatrix} p \\ q \end{pmatrix} = \begin{pmatrix} -8 \\ 0 \end{pmatrix}$

Find the matrix equation which is equivalent to the pair of equations
$$2x - 4y = 0$$
$$9x + y = 19$$

$$2x - 4y = 0$$
$$9x + y = 19$$

$$\begin{pmatrix} 2 & -4 \\ 9 & 1 \end{pmatrix}\begin{pmatrix} x \\ y \end{pmatrix} = \begin{pmatrix} 0 \\ 19 \end{pmatrix}$$

Find the matrix equations which are equivalent to the following pairs of equations:

5. $3x + 2y = 8$
     $x + y = 3$

7. $4x + 3y = 5$
     $5x + 4y = 6$

9. $7x - 2y = 3$
     $3x + 4y = 11$

6. $4x - 3y = 1$
     $2x + y = 3$

8. $3x - 2y = 1$
     $x - y = 0$

10. $5x + y = -8$
      $4x - 3y = -14$

Consider the equation $2x = 6$

If we multiply both sides by $\frac{1}{2}$, we get $\frac{1}{2} \times 2x = \frac{1}{2} \times 6$

i.e. $\qquad\qquad\qquad\qquad x = 3$

$\frac{1}{2}$ is the reciprocal of 2, i.e. $\frac{1}{2}$ is the inverse of 2 under multiplication.

In the same way, we can simplify a matrix equation if we multiply both sides by the inverse of the first matrix.

Exercise 9j

Solve the matrix equation $\begin{pmatrix} 3 & 1 \\ 1 & 2 \end{pmatrix}\begin{pmatrix} x \\ y \end{pmatrix} = \begin{pmatrix} 7 \\ 4 \end{pmatrix}$

(Find the inverse first.)

The determinant of $\begin{pmatrix} 3 & 1 \\ 1 & 2 \end{pmatrix} = 3 \times 2 - 1 \times 1 = 5$

∴ the inverse is $\frac{1}{5}\begin{pmatrix} 2 & -1 \\ -1 & 3 \end{pmatrix}$

Multiply both sides of the equation by $\frac{1}{5}\begin{pmatrix} 2 & -1 \\ -1 & 3 \end{pmatrix}$

(The order matters now. *The inverse must go in front on both sides.*)

$$\frac{1}{5}\begin{pmatrix} 2 & -1 \\ -1 & 3 \end{pmatrix}\begin{pmatrix} 3 & 1 \\ 1 & 2 \end{pmatrix}\begin{pmatrix} x \\ y \end{pmatrix} = \frac{1}{5}\begin{pmatrix} 2 & -1 \\ -1 & 3 \end{pmatrix}\begin{pmatrix} 7 \\ 4 \end{pmatrix}$$

$$\begin{pmatrix} 1 & 0 \\ 0 & 1 \end{pmatrix}\begin{pmatrix} x \\ y \end{pmatrix} = \frac{1}{5}\begin{pmatrix} 10 \\ 5 \end{pmatrix}$$

i.e. $$\begin{pmatrix} x \\ y \end{pmatrix} = \begin{pmatrix} 2 \\ 1 \end{pmatrix}$$

∴ $x = 2$ and $y = 1$

Solve the following matrix equations:

1. $\begin{pmatrix} 4 & 1 \\ 3 & 1 \end{pmatrix}\begin{pmatrix} x \\ y \end{pmatrix} = \begin{pmatrix} 6 \\ 5 \end{pmatrix}$

2. $\begin{pmatrix} 2 & 1 \\ 5 & 3 \end{pmatrix}\begin{pmatrix} x \\ y \end{pmatrix} = \begin{pmatrix} 7 \\ 19 \end{pmatrix}$

3. $\begin{pmatrix} 4 & 3 \\ 2 & 2 \end{pmatrix}\begin{pmatrix} x \\ y \end{pmatrix} = \begin{pmatrix} 1 \\ 0 \end{pmatrix}$

4. $\begin{pmatrix} 3 & -1 \\ 4 & 1 \end{pmatrix}\begin{pmatrix} x \\ y \end{pmatrix} = \begin{pmatrix} 7 \\ 7 \end{pmatrix}$

5. $\begin{pmatrix} 2 & 1 \\ 1 & 2 \end{pmatrix}\begin{pmatrix} x \\ y \end{pmatrix} = \begin{pmatrix} 6 \\ 3 \end{pmatrix}$

6. $\begin{pmatrix} 7 & -2 \\ 3 & 4 \end{pmatrix}\begin{pmatrix} x \\ y \end{pmatrix} = \begin{pmatrix} 3 \\ 11 \end{pmatrix}$

7. $\begin{pmatrix} 1 & -1 \\ 1 & 3 \end{pmatrix}\begin{pmatrix} x \\ y \end{pmatrix} = \begin{pmatrix} 2 \\ 10 \end{pmatrix}$

8. $\begin{pmatrix} 5 & 2 \\ 2 & 1 \end{pmatrix}\begin{pmatrix} x \\ y \end{pmatrix} = \begin{pmatrix} 1 \\ 0 \end{pmatrix}$

9. $\begin{pmatrix} 3 & 2 \\ 3 & 3 \end{pmatrix}\begin{pmatrix} x \\ y \end{pmatrix} = \begin{pmatrix} 16 \\ 18 \end{pmatrix}$

10. $\begin{pmatrix} 4 & -2 \\ -3 & 1 \end{pmatrix}\begin{pmatrix} p \\ q \end{pmatrix} = \begin{pmatrix} 2 \\ -2 \end{pmatrix}$

11. $\begin{pmatrix} -5 & 1 \\ 9 & -2 \end{pmatrix}\begin{pmatrix} s \\ t \end{pmatrix} = \begin{pmatrix} 13 \\ -24 \end{pmatrix}$

Give the following pairs of simultaneous equations in matrix form and hence solve them:

12. $x + y = 2$
$x + 2y = 3$

14. $5x + 4y = 1$
$x + y = 0$

16. $9x + 2y = 11$
$3x + y = 5$

18. $5x + 2y = 16$
$3x - y = 3$

13. $4x - y = 5$
$x + y = 5$

15. $2x + 3y = 15$
$3x + 5y = 23$

17. $2x + 3y = 7$
$3x + 2y = 8$

19. $x + 4y = 11$
$2x + 3y = 7$

20. Try using matrices to solve the equations $\begin{aligned} x + 2y = 3 \\ x + 2y = 6 \end{aligned}$

Comment on why the method breaks down.

21. Repeat question 20 with $\begin{aligned} 3x + 2y = 1 \\ 9x + 6y = 5 \end{aligned}$

MATRIX EQUATIONS

Exercise 9k

The questions in this exercise refer to the following matrices:

$$A = \begin{pmatrix} 4 & 3 \\ 2 & 1 \end{pmatrix} \qquad B = \begin{pmatrix} 1 & -2 \\ 0 & 1 \end{pmatrix} \qquad C = \begin{pmatrix} 6 & 4 \\ -3 & 1 \end{pmatrix}$$

Find **X** if **A** + **X** = **B**

$$\mathbf{A} + \mathbf{X} = \mathbf{B}$$

$$\mathbf{X} = \mathbf{B} - \mathbf{A} \quad (\text{taking } \mathbf{A} \text{ from each side})$$

$$\mathbf{X} = \begin{pmatrix} 1 & -2 \\ 0 & 1 \end{pmatrix} - \begin{pmatrix} 4 & 3 \\ 2 & 1 \end{pmatrix}$$

$$= \begin{pmatrix} -3 & -5 \\ -2 & 0 \end{pmatrix}$$

Find **X** in the following equations:

1. $\mathbf{B} + \mathbf{X} = \mathbf{C}$

3. $\mathbf{X} = \mathbf{AC}$

5. $2\mathbf{X} = \mathbf{A}$

7. $\mathbf{A} + \mathbf{X} = \mathbf{B} + \mathbf{C}$

2. $\mathbf{X} - \mathbf{C} = \mathbf{B}$

4. $\mathbf{B} - \mathbf{X} = \mathbf{C}$

6. $\frac{1}{3}\mathbf{X} = \mathbf{B}$

8. $\mathbf{AX} = \mathbf{I}$

MIXED EXERCISES

Exercise 9l

1. Find $\begin{pmatrix} 2 & 3 & -1 \\ 4 & 1 & 2 \end{pmatrix} + \begin{pmatrix} 3 & 1 & 4 \\ 6 & -9 & 2 \end{pmatrix}$

2. Find $\frac{1}{2}\begin{pmatrix} 2 & 7 \\ 3 & -1 \end{pmatrix}$

3. Find the determinant of $\begin{pmatrix} 16 & 3 \\ 8 & 3 \end{pmatrix}$

4. Find the inverse of $\begin{pmatrix} 4 & 3 \\ 3 & 4 \end{pmatrix}$

5. Find $\begin{pmatrix} 1 & 3 & -1 \end{pmatrix} \begin{pmatrix} 1 \\ -3 \\ 1 \end{pmatrix}$

6. Find $\begin{pmatrix} 1 & 4 \\ 3 & 1 \end{pmatrix} \begin{pmatrix} 2 & -1 \\ 2 & 1 \end{pmatrix} \begin{pmatrix} 1 & 3 \\ 1 & 1 \end{pmatrix}$

Exercise 9m

The questions in this exercise refer to the following matrices:

$$\mathbf{A} = \begin{pmatrix} 2 & 4 \\ 1 & 3 \end{pmatrix} \quad \mathbf{B} = \begin{pmatrix} 3 & -1 \\ -2 & 1 \end{pmatrix} \quad \mathbf{C} = \begin{pmatrix} 2 \\ 3 \end{pmatrix} \quad \mathbf{D} = \begin{pmatrix} 4 & -2 \end{pmatrix}$$

1. Find $\mathbf{A} + \mathbf{B}$.

2. Find the determinant of $\mathbf{A}$.

3. Find the inverse of $\mathbf{B}$.

4. Find $\mathbf{BC}$.

5. Find $\mathbf{DA}$.

6. Find $\frac{3}{4}\mathbf{D}$.

MATHS IS OUT THERE

Maria Agnesi (1718–1799) was born into a rich Italian family. By the age of nine she was able to speak five languages. As a teenager she argued about mathematics with teachers who visited her home. It is said that the queen sent her a diamond ring, the Pope sent her a letter of praise and a school in Italy was named after her. She was a kind and smart woman. In one of her books however she gave a Latin name to a curve. In a translation the word 'versoria' meaning 'free to move in every direction' was read as 'versiera' meaning 'a witch'. She became known as 'The witch of Agnesi'.

10 STRAIGHT LINE GRAPHS

At the end of the chapter you should be able to:

1. State the equations of lines drawn parallel to the coordinate axes.
2. Draw lines of the form $y = k$ and $x = h$ where h and k are constants.
3. Draw a line with equation $y = mx + c$, by finding points on the line.
4. Use the equation of a line to calculate the value of y for a given x.
5. Determine if a given point lies on a line whose equation is given.
6. Find the gradient of a line by drawing.
7. Calculate the gradient of a line, given the coordinates of two points on the line.
8. State the gradient of a line whose equation is given.
9. Determine if two lines whose equations are given are parallel.
10. Write the equation of a line given its gradient and intercept on the y-axis.
11. Write the equation of a line through two given points.

STRAIGHT LINES

Straight lines can lie anywhere and at any angle to the x-axis.

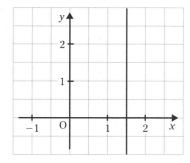
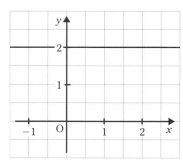

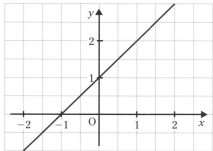

The lines go on for ever in both directions. We draw just part of the line.

146

LINES PARALLEL TO THE AXES

If we consider any point on the line given in the diagram we find that, no matter what the y coordinate is, the x coordinate is always 2.

We say that the equation of this line is $x = 2$.

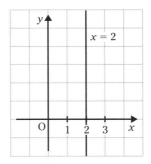

Notice that y is not mentioned because there is no restriction on the value it can take.

In the same way, any point on the line given in this diagram has a y coordinate of 3, while the x coordinate can take any value. The equation of this line is $y = 3$.

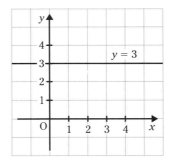

Exercise 10a

Give the equations of the lines in questions 1 to 4:

1.

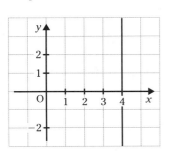

2.

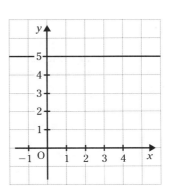

3.

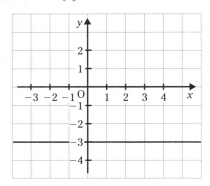

4.

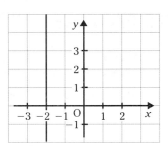

Draw similar diagrams to show the lines with the following equations:

5. $x = 1$

6. $x = -4$

7. $y = 4$

8. $y = -3$

SLANT LINES

If we take any point on the line shown, say $(2, 4)$ or $(3\frac{1}{2}, 5\frac{1}{2})$ or $(-1, 1)$ or $(0, 2)$, we find that the y coordinate is always 2 units more than the x coordinate.

The equation of the line is therefore $y = x + 2$.

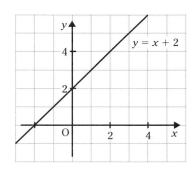

Conversely, if we are given the equation of a line we can draw the line by finding points on it. Two points are enough to draw a straight line but a third is useful as a check. If the three points do not lie in a straight line, at least one point is incorrect. Check all three points.

Suppose that we want to draw the line whose equation is $y = 2x + 1$. Think of this as an instruction for finding the y coordinate to go with a chosen x coordinate.

If $x = 1$, $y = 2 + 1 = 3$ so $(1, 3)$ is a point on the line.
If $x = 3$, $y = 2 \times 3 + 1 = 7$ so $(3, 7)$ is on the line.
If $x = -3$, $y = 2 \times (-3) + 1 = -5$ so $(-3, -5)$ is on the line.

It is simpler to list this information in a table.

x	-3	1	3
y	-5	3	7

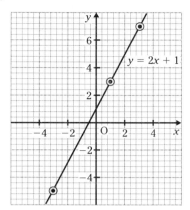

Exercise 10b

In all questions in this exercise use 1 cm to 1 unit.

In each of questions 1 to 4, copy and complete the table. On graph paper, draw x and y axes for the ranges indicated in the brackets. Mark the points and, if they are in a straight line, draw that line:

1. $y = x + 4$ $(-2 \leqslant x \leqslant 4, 0 \leqslant y \leqslant 8)$

x	-2	0	4
y			

2. $y = 2x + 1$ $(-2 \leqslant x \leqslant 3, -4 \leqslant y \leqslant 8)$

x	-2	0	3
y			

3. $y = 4 - x$ $(-3 \leqslant x \leqslant 3, 0 \leqslant y \leqslant 8)$

x	-3	0	3
y			

4. $y = 2 - 3x$ $(-1 \leqslant x \leqslant 3, -7 \leqslant y \leqslant 5)$

x	-1	0	3
y			

In each of questions 5 to 8, make a table, choosing your own values of x within the given range. (Choose one low value, one high value and one in between, such as zero.) Draw x and y axes for the ranges of values indicated. Draw the line.

5. $y = x - 3$ $(-2 \leqslant x \leqslant 5, -5 \leqslant y \leqslant 2)$

6. $y = \frac{1}{2}x + 4$ $(-2 \leqslant x \leqslant 4, 0 \leqslant y \leqslant 6)$

7. $y = 3 - 2x$ $(-2 \leqslant x \leqslant 4, -5 \leqslant y \leqslant 7)$

8. $y = 3x - 4$ $(0 \leqslant x \leqslant 6, -5 \leqslant y \leqslant 14)$

Make a table which can be used for drawing the graph of $y = 6 + 2x$, taking values of x in the range $-3 \leqslant x \leqslant 3$. Decide from the table what range of values of y is suitable.

$y = 6 + 2x$

x	-3	0	3
y	0	6	12

The range for y must be $0 \leqslant y \leqslant 12$

For each of questions 9 to 12, make a table, choosing your own values of x within the given range. Decide on a suitable range of values of y after completing the table.

Draw x and y axes using the given range for the x-axis and the range you have chosen for the y-axis. Draw the line:

9. $y = 3 - x \qquad (-3 \leqslant x \leqslant 3)$

10. $y = \frac{1}{2}x - 1 \qquad (-3 \leqslant x \leqslant 3)$

11. $y = 2x + 2 \qquad (-2 \leqslant x \leqslant 4)$

12. $y = 5 - 3x \qquad (-1 \leqslant x \leqslant 3)$

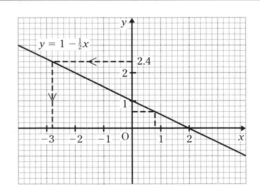

You are given the graph of the line with equation $y = 1 - \frac{1}{2}x$.
From the graph, find

(a) the value of y, if x is 0.8
(b) the value of x, if y is 2.4

(a) From the graph, if $x = 0.8$, $y = 0.6$
(b) From the graph, if $y = 2.4$, $x = -2.8$

13. You are given the graph of the line with equation $y = x + 1$.
From the graph, find

(a) y if $x = \frac{1}{2}$ (b) x if $y = 1.4$ (c) x if $y = -0.6$

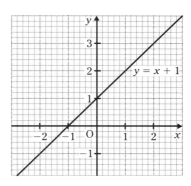

14. You are given the graph of the line with equation $y = 2x - 1$.
From the graph, find

(a) y if $x = \frac{1}{2}$ (b) x if $y = -2.6$ (c) y if $x = -1.2$

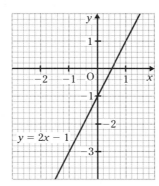

15. You are given the graph of the line with equation $y = -x - 1$.
From the graph, find

(a) y if $x = 1.6$ (b) x if $y = 0.8$ (c) x if $y = -2.2$

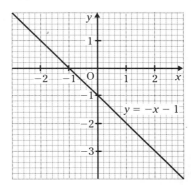

16. You are given the graph of the line with equation $y = 3 - 3x$.
From the graph, find

(a) y if $x = -0.2$ (b) x if $y = 1.2$ (c) x if $y = -0.6$

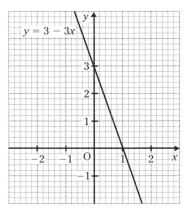

17. Using the graph you drew for question 5, find

(a) y if $x = \frac{1}{2}$
(b) x if $y = 1.4$
(c) x if $y = -0.6$

18. Using the graph you drew for question 6, find

(a) y if $x = 1.6$
(b) x if $y = 4.6$
(c) x if $y = -1.6$

19. Using the graph you drew for question 7, find

(a) y if $x = 2.2$
(b) x if $y = 0.2$
(c) x if $y = -4$

20. Using the graph you drew for question 8, find

(a) y if $x = 4.2$
(b) x if $y = 4.4$
(c) x if $y = 5$

POINTS ON A LINE

Exercise 10c

Do the points $(3, 6)$ and $(-2, -10)$ lie on the line whose equation is $y = 3x - 4$?

$$y = 3x - 4$$

When $x = 3$ $y = 3 \times 3 - 4 = 5$

$\therefore (3, 6)$ does not lie on the line.

When $x = -2$ $y = 3 \times (-2) - 4 = -10$

$\therefore (-2, -10)$ lies on the line.

Find whether the given points lie on the line whose equation is given:

1. $y = 2x - 1$; $(5, 9), (1, 2)$

4. $y = \frac{1}{2}x + 4$; $(4, 5), (3, 5\frac{1}{2})$

2. $y = 3 + 3x$; $(2, 9), (-4, -9)$

5. $y = 5 + 4x$; $(\frac{1}{2}, 7), (-2, -3)$

3. $y = 6 - 2x$; $(3, 1), (4, -1)$

6. $y = 6 - \frac{1}{2}x$; $(-2, 5), (-2, 7)$

COMPARING SLOPES

Exercise 10d

1. Draw, on the same pair of axes, the graphs of the lines

(a) $y = 2x - 3$
(b) $y = 2x$
(c) $y = 2x - 2$

for $-3 \leqslant x \leqslant 3$ and $-7 \leqslant y \leqslant 9$ using 1 cm to 1 unit.
Label each line with its equation.
What can you say about the lines?
What do the equations have in common?

2. Draw a pair of axes using $-2 \leqslant x \leqslant 2$ and $-7 \leqslant y \leqslant 9$. On these axes draw the three lines with the following equations

(a) $y = -3x - 1$
(b) $y = -3x$
(c) $y = -3x + 3$

What can you say about the lines?
What do the equations have in common?

3. Draw a pair of axes using $-4 \leqslant x \leqslant 4$, $-7 \leqslant y \leqslant 6$. On these axes draw the three lines with the following equations

(a) $y = \frac{1}{2}x - 4$
(b) $y = \frac{1}{2}x + 1$
(c) $y = \frac{1}{2}x + 3$

Comment on the three lines and their equations.

4. Draw x and y axes, marking values from -5 to 5 on each axis. Draw the three lines with the equations

(a) $y = x$
(b) $y = x - 3$
(c) $y = x + 2$

What do you notice?

5. Draw x and y axes, using $-3 \leqslant x \leqslant 3$, $-3 \leqslant y \leqslant 5$. Draw the three lines with the following equations

(a) $y = 2x + 2$
(b) $y = -2x + 1$
(c) $y = 2x$

Which two lines are parallel?

6. Draw x and y axes, marking values from -5 to 5 on each axis. Draw the lines with the equations

(a) $y = 4 - x$
(b) $y = -x$
(c) $y = -3 - x$

What do you notice?

GRADIENTS

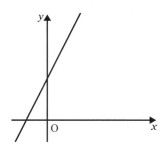

Different lines have different gradients or slopes. Some lines point steeply up to the right; they have large *positive* gradients.

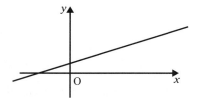

Some have a shallow slope up to the right; they have small *positive* gradients.

Some lines slope the other way; they have *negative* gradients.

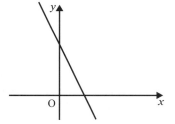

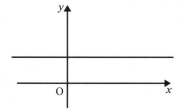

Some have zero gradient and are parallel to the *x*-axis.

Some are parallel to the *y*-axis.

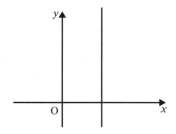

We can see from the questions in the last exercise that the *coefficient* of x (2 in question 1, -3 in question 2 and $\frac{1}{2}$ in question 3) has something to do with gradient.

CALCULATING THE GRADIENT OF A LINE

First method

The gradient is found by comparing the amount you move up as you go from A to B, with the amount you move across. In this case the gradient is $\frac{4}{3}$.

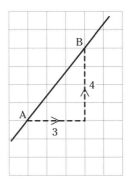

In the second case the distance moved is downwards so we take this distance as negative.

The gradient is $\frac{-3}{5}$, i.e. $-\frac{3}{5}$.

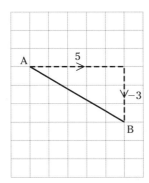

Second method

The distance moved up is given by the difference in the y coordinates and the distance moved across is given by the difference in the x coordinates, so the gradient is

$$\frac{\text{the difference in the } y \text{ coordinates}}{\text{the difference in the } x \text{ coordinates}}$$

If A is the point $(3, 5)$ and B is $(2, 7)$ then the gradient is

$$\frac{5-7}{3-2} = \frac{-2}{1} = -2$$

Notice that the coordinates of B are taken from the coordinates of A for both x and y. We may change the order as long as we change it for both x and y, i.e. the gradient is also $\frac{7-5}{2-3} = -2$

Exercise 10e

Find the gradients of the lines joining the points

(a) $(4, 2)$ and $(6, 7)$ (b) $(2, 3)$ and $(4, -3)$

(a)

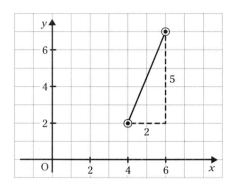

Either: from the diagram the gradient is $\frac{5}{2}$

Or: gradient $= \dfrac{\text{difference in the } y \text{ coordinates}}{\text{difference in the } x \text{ coordinates}}$

$= \frac{7-2}{6-4} = \frac{5}{2}$

(b)

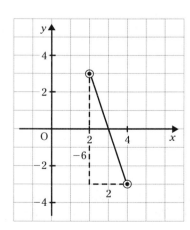

Either: from the diagram the gradient is $\frac{-6}{2} = -3$

Or: gradient $= \frac{-3-3}{4-2} = \frac{-6}{2} = -3$

(Notice that we could also say

gradient $= \frac{3-(-3)}{2-4} = \frac{6}{-2} = -3$)

Find the gradients of the lines joining the following pairs of points:

1. $(5, 1)$ and $(7, 9)$

2. $(3, 6)$ and $(5, 2)$

3. $(3, 4)$ and $(6, 7)$

4. $(-2, 4)$ and $(2, 1)$

5. $(1, 2)$ and $(6, -7)$

6. $(-3, 4)$ and $(-6, 2)$

7. Find the gradient of the line joining the points $(4, 3)$ and $(7, 3)$.

8. Which axis is parallel to the line joining the points $(4, 3)$ and $(4, 6)$?
What happens when you try to work out the gradient?

9. If lines are drawn joining the following pairs of points, state which lines have zero gradient and which are parallel to the *y*-axis:

(a) $(0, 4)$ and $(0, -2)$
(b) $(3, 0)$ and $(-10, 0)$
(c) $(-6, 0)$ and $(-2, 0)$
(d) $(0, 6)$ and $(0, 12)$

10. If $(2, 1)$ is a point on a line and its gradient is 3, draw the line and find the coordinates of two other points on it.

Exercise 10f

Find the gradient of the line $y = -2x + 3$

Choose two points on the line, e.g. $(-2, 7)$ and $(2, -1)$.

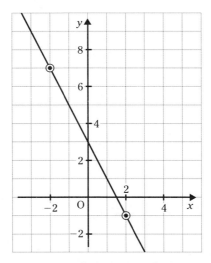

$$\text{Gradient} = \frac{-1-7}{2-(-2)} = \frac{-8}{4} = -2$$

(This is the same as the coefficient of *x* in the equation of the line.)

Choose two points on each line and hence find the gradient of the line. In each case compare your answer with the coefficient of x:

1. $y = 2x + 3$

2. $y = x + 4$

3. $y = 2x - 1$

4. $y = 3 - 2x$

5. State the gradient of the line $y = 4x + 1$, without calculation if possible.

6. Give the gradients of the lines with equations

   (a) $y = 4x + 4$ (c) $y = x - 3$
   (b) $y = 2 - 3x$ (d) $y = \frac{1}{2}x + 1$

7. Sketch a line with a gradient of

   (a) 3   (b) -1

8. Sketch a line with a gradient of

   (a) 4   (b) $\frac{1}{2}$

9. Sketch a line with a gradient of

   (a) -2 (b) 1

THE INTERCEPT ON THE *y*-AXIS

Consider the line with equation $y = x + 3$.
When $x = 0$, $y = 3$, so the line crosses the y-axis where $y = 3$.

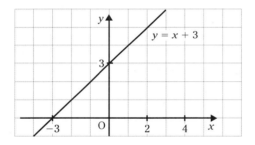

If the equation is $y = 2x - 3$ then, when $x = 0$, $y = -3$, i.e. the line cuts the y-axis where $y = -3$.

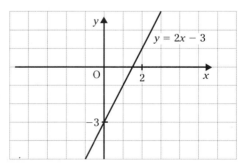

As long as the equation is of the form $y = mx + c$, i.e. like $y = 2x + 3$ or $y = -5x + 1$ then

> the number term c tells us where the line cuts the y-axis and m, the coefficient of x, tells us the gradient.

If the equation is $y = 3x$ then the number term is 0, i.e. the intercept is 0. Therefore, the line goes through the origin.

Exercise 10g

> Give the gradient and the intercept on the *y*-axis of the line with equation $y = x + 5$. Sketch the line.
>
> The gradient is 1
>
> The intercept on the *y*-axis is 5
>
>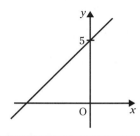

Give the gradients and the intercepts on the *y*-axis of the lines with the following equations. *Sketch* each line:

1. $y = 2x + 4$ **2.** $y = 5x + 3$ **3.** $y = 3x - 4$ **4.** $y = x - 6$

> Give the gradient and the intercept on the *y*-axis of the line with equation $y = 4 - 2x$. Sketch the line.
>
> Rewrite the equation as $y = -2x + 4$
>
> The gradient is -2. The intercept on the *y*-axis is 4.
>
>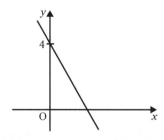

Give the gradients and the intercepts on the *y*-axis of the lines with the following equations. *Sketch* each line:

5. $y = 3 - 2x$

6. $y = -4x + 2$

7. $y = 2 + 5x$

8. $y = \frac{1}{2}x - 1$

9. $y = -\frac{1}{3}x + 4$

10. $y = 3x - 7$

11. $y = 7 - 3x$

12. $y = \frac{1}{3}x + 7$

13. $y = 9 - 0.4x$

14. $y = 4 + 5x$

Give the gradient and the intercept on the *y*-axis of the line with equation $2y = 3x - 1$. Sketch the line.

$$2y = 3x - 1$$

Divide both sides by 2 $y = \frac{3}{2}x - \frac{1}{2}$

The gradient is $\frac{3}{2}$

The intercept on the *y*-axis is $-\frac{1}{2}$

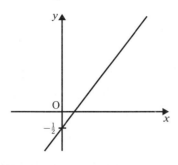

Give the gradients and the intercepts on the *y*-axis of the lines with the following equations. *Sketch* each line:

15. $2y = 4x + 5$

16. $3y = x - 6$

17. $5y = 5 + 2x$

18. $4y = 8 - 3x$

A line has a gradient of -2 and the intercept on the *y*-axis is 4. Find the equation of the line.

The equation is $y = -2x + 4$

Write down the equations of the lines with the given gradients and intercepts on the *y*-axis (*y* intercepts):

	Gradient	*y* intercept
19.	2	7
20.	3	1
21.	1	3
22.	2	−5

	Gradient	*y* intercept
23.	$\frac{1}{2}$	6
24.	−2	1
25.	1	−2
26.	$-\frac{1}{2}$	4

PARALLEL LINES

Exercise 10h

Which of the lines with the following equations are parallel:

$y = 2x + 3$, $y = 4 - 2x$, $y = 4 + 2x$, $2y = x + 1$, $y = x + 3$?

The gradients of the lines are 2, -2, 2, $\frac{1}{2}$ and 1, so the first and third lines are parallel.

In questions 1 to 4, state which of the lines with the given equations are parallel.

1. $y = 3x + 1$, $y = \frac{1}{3}x - 4$, $y = x + 1$,
   $y = 4 - 3x$, $y = 5 + 3x$, $y = 3x - 4$

2. $y = 2 - x$, $y = x + 2$, $y = 4 - x$,
   $2y = 3 - 2x$, $y = -x + 1$, $y = -x$

3. $3y = x$, $y = \frac{1}{3}x + 2$, $y = \frac{1}{3} + x$,
   $y = \frac{1}{3} + \frac{1}{3}x$, $y = \frac{1}{3}x - 4$

4. $y = \frac{1}{2}x + 2$, $y = 2 - \frac{1}{2}x$, $y = -x - 4$,
   $y = \frac{1}{2}x - 1$, $2y = 3 - x$

5. What is the gradient of the line with equation $y = 2x + 1$? Give the equation of the line that is parallel to the first line and which cuts the *y*-axis at the point $(0, 3)$.

6. What is the gradient of the line with equation $y = 6 - 3x$?
   If a parallel line goes through the point $(0, 1)$, what is its equation?

7. Give the equation of the line through the origin that is parallel to the line with equation $y = 4x + 2$.

8. Give the equations of any three lines that are parallel to the line with equation $y = 4 - x$.

9. Give the equations of the lines through the point $(0, 4)$ that are parallel to the lines with equations

   (a) $y = 4x + 1$
   (b) $y = 6 - 3x$
   (c) $y = \frac{1}{2}x + 1$

10. Give the equations of the lines, parallel to the line with equation $y = \frac{1}{3}x + 1$, that pass through the points

   (a) $(0, 6)$ (b) $(0, 0)$ (c) $(0, -3)$

11. Give the equations of the lines with gradient 2 which pass through the points

   (a) $(0, 2)$ (b) $(0, 10)$ (c) $(0, -4)$

12. Which two of the lines with the following equations are parallel?
   $y = 3 + 2x$, $y = 3 - 2x$, $y = 2x - 3$

13. Find the gradients and the intercepts on the *y*-axis of the lines with equations $y = 4 - 3x$ and $y = 4x - 3$. Give the equation of the line that is parallel to the first line and cuts the *y*-axis at the same point as the second line.

14. A line of gradient -4 passes through the origin.

   (a) Give its equation
   (b) Give the equation of the line that is parallel to the first line and that passes through the point $(0, -7)$

DIFFERENT FORMS OF THE EQUATION OF A STRAIGHT LINE

The terms in the equation of a straight line can only be x terms, y terms or number terms.

An equation containing terms like x^2, y^2, $\dfrac{1}{x}$, $\dfrac{1}{x^2}$ is not the equation of a straight line.

Sometimes the equation of a straight line is not given exactly in the form $y = mx + c$.

It could be $2x + y = 6$ or $\dfrac{x}{4} + \dfrac{y}{2} = 1$

An easy way to draw a line when its equation is in one of these forms is to start by finding the points where it cuts each axis.

Exercise 10i

Draw on graph paper the line with equation

$$3x - 4y = 12 \quad (\text{use } 0 \leqslant x \leqslant 5)$$

Find the gradient of the line.

$$3x - 4y = 12$$

When $x = 0$, $-4y = 12$, i.e. $y = -3$
When $y = 0$, $3x = 12$, i.e. $x = 4$
(Draw the line using these two points only. Choose a point on the line, e.g. $(2, -1\frac{1}{2})$, to check.)

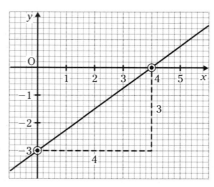

Check: when $x = 2$, $y = -1\frac{1}{2}$,
$3x - 4y = 6 - 4 \times (-1\frac{1}{2}) = 6 + 6 = 12$, which is correct.

From the graph, the gradient $= \frac{3}{4}$

Draw on graph paper the lines with the following equations. Use 1 cm to 1 unit.
Find the gradient of each line:

1. $3x + 5y = 15$ $0 \leqslant x \leqslant 6$

6. $x + 3y = 5$ $0 \leqslant x \leqslant 5$

2. $2x + 6y = 12$ $0 \leqslant x \leqslant 6$

7. $x - 3y = 6$ $0 \leqslant x \leqslant 6$

3. $x - 4y = 8$ $0 \leqslant x \leqslant 8$

8. $2x - y = 3$ $-2 \leqslant x \leqslant 2$

4. $x + y = 6$ $0 \leqslant x \leqslant 7$

9. On the same axes ($-6 \leqslant x \leqslant 6$ and $-6 \leqslant y \leqslant 6$) draw the lines $x + y = 1$, $x + y = 4$, $x + y = 6$, $x + y = -4$. Find their gradients.

5. $2x + y = 5$ $-2 \leqslant x \leqslant 4$

Exercise 10j

Draw on graph paper the line with equation

$$\frac{x}{3} + \frac{y}{2} = 1 \quad (-1 \leqslant x \leqslant 4)$$

Find its gradient.

When $x = 0$, $\dfrac{y}{2} = 1$, so $y = 2$

When $y = 0$, $\dfrac{x}{3} = 1$, so $x = 3$

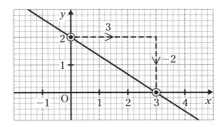

Check: from the graph, when $x = 1\frac{1}{2}$, $y = 1$

Therefore $\dfrac{x}{3} + \dfrac{y}{2} = \dfrac{1\frac{1}{2}}{3} + \dfrac{1}{2} = \dfrac{1}{2} + \dfrac{1}{2} = 1$ which is correct.

The gradient is $-\frac{2}{3}$

Draw on graph paper the lines whose equations are given below. Find the gradient of each line:

1. $\dfrac{x}{4} + \dfrac{y}{3} = 1$

3. $\dfrac{x}{4} - \dfrac{y}{2} = 1$

5. $\dfrac{x}{1} - \dfrac{y}{2} = 1$

2. $\dfrac{x}{5} + \dfrac{y}{3} = 1$

4. $\dfrac{x}{3} + \dfrac{y}{6} = 1$

6. $\dfrac{y}{3} - \dfrac{x}{4} = 1$

7. Without drawing a diagram, state where the lines with the following equations cut the axes

(a) $\dfrac{x}{2} + \dfrac{y}{4} = 1$ (b) $\dfrac{x}{12} - \dfrac{y}{9} = 1$

8. Form the equations of the lines which cut the axes at

(a) $(0, 5)$ and $(6, 0)$

(b) $(0, -3)$ and $(4, 0)$

9. Sketch the line with equation $\dfrac{x}{6} + \dfrac{y}{2} = 1$ and find its gradient.

GETTING INFORMATION FROM THE EQUATION OF A LINE

From the last exercise, we can see that if the equation of a line is in the form

$$\frac{x}{a} + \frac{y}{b} = 1 \quad \text{(i.e. like questions 1 to 6),}$$

then the line cuts the x-axis at $x = a$

     and the y-axis at $y = b$.

Then if we sketch the line we can work out the gradient.

If the equation is in the form $ax + by = c$, like those in Exercise 10i, we need to rearrange the equation so that it is in the form $y = mx + c$. Then the gradient and the intercept on the y-axis can be seen.

Exercise 10k

Find the gradient and the intercept on the y-axis of the line with equation $2x + 3y = 6$.

Take $2x$ from both sides $3y = 6 - 2x$

Divide both sides by 3 $y = 2 - \frac{2}{3}x$

i.e. $y = -\frac{2}{3}x + 2$

The gradient is $-\frac{2}{3}$ and the intercept on the y-axis is 2

Find the gradient and the intercept on the y-axis of each of the following lines:

1. $3x + 5y = 15$ **3.** $x - 4y = 8$ **5.** $y - 3x = 6$

2. $2x + 6y = 12$ **4.** $x - 3y = 6$ **6.** $x + 3y = 6$

Find the gradient and the intercept on the *y*-axis of the line with equation

$$\frac{x}{2} + \frac{y}{5} = 1$$

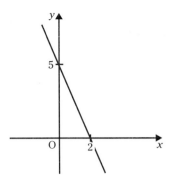

Either

This line cuts the axes at $(2, 0)$ and $(0, 5)$, hence the gradient is $-\frac{5}{2}$ and the intercept on the *y*-axis is 5

Or

$$\frac{x}{2} + \frac{y}{5} = 1$$

Multiply both sides by 5

$$\frac{5x}{2} + y = 5$$

Take $\frac{5x}{2}$ from both sides

$$y = 5 - \frac{5x}{2}$$

i.e.

$$y = -\tfrac{5}{2}x + 5$$

Then the gradient is $-\frac{5}{2}$ and the intercept is 5

Find the gradient and the intercept on the *y*-axis of each of the following lines:

7. $\dfrac{x}{4} + \dfrac{y}{3} = 1$

8. $\dfrac{x}{5} + \dfrac{y}{3} = 1$

9. $\dfrac{x}{4} - \dfrac{y}{2} = 1$

10. $\dfrac{x}{2} + \dfrac{y}{6} = 1$

11. $\dfrac{x}{3} + \dfrac{y}{4} = 1$

12. $\dfrac{x}{3} - \dfrac{y}{4} = 1$

13. $y = 4x + 2$

14. $x + y = 4$

15. $\dfrac{x}{2} + \dfrac{y}{4} = 1$

16. $2x + 5y = 15$

17. $y = 5 - \tfrac{1}{2}x$

18. $2y = 4x + 5$

19. $\dfrac{x}{2} - \dfrac{y}{4} = 1$

20. $x + y = -3$

21. $3x + 4y = 12$

THE EQUATION OF A LINE THROUGH TWO GIVEN POINTS

Exercise 10I

Find the gradient and the intercept on the *y*-axis of the line through the points $(4, 2)$ and $(0, 4)$. Hence give the equation of the line.

(A sketch only is needed.)

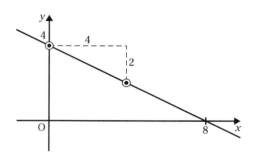

$$\text{Gradient} = \frac{2-4}{4-0} = \frac{-2}{4} = -\frac{1}{2}$$

$$\text{Intercept} = 4$$

∴ the equation is $y = -\frac{1}{2}x + 4$

(Multiplying by 2 and rearranging, allows this equation to be written in the form $2y = 8 - x$ or $2y + x = 8$.)

Find the gradient and the intercept on the *y*-axis of the line through the given points. Hence give the equation of the line:

1. $(0, 4)$ and $(3, 0)$

2. $(0, 7)$ and $(2, 3)$

3. $(5, 4)$ and $(0, 1)$

4. $(0, 2)$ and $(3, -2)$

5. $(0, -4)$ and $(2, 3)$

6. $(-6, -3)$ and $(0, -1)$

7. $(6, 2)$ and $(0, 1)$

8. $(5, 1)$ and $(0, -3)$

9. $(0, -4)$ and $(3, 1)$

10. $(-5, 0)$ and $(0, -5)$

11. $(0, 12)$ and $(-6, 0)$

12. $(-6, 1)$ and $(0, 6)$

13. A, B and C are the points $(0, 4)$, $(5, 6)$ and $(3, -1)$. Find the equations of lines AB and AC.

Find the gradient and the equation of the line through $(6, 2)$ and $(4, 8)$.

The gradient is $\qquad\qquad \frac{2-8}{6-4} = \frac{-6}{2} = -3$

(We do not know the intercept on the y-axis.)

Let the equation be $y = -3x + c$.

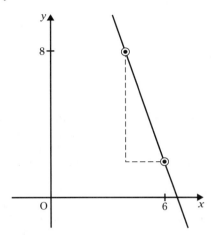

When $x = 6$, $y = 2$ so $\qquad\qquad 2 = -18 + c$

$\therefore \qquad\qquad\qquad\qquad\qquad c = 20$

$\therefore$ the equation is $y = -3x + 20$

(Check: when $x = 4$, the equation gives $y = -12 + 20$, i.e. $y = 8$, which is correct.)

In questions 14 to 35, find the gradient and the equation of the line through the given pair of points:

14. $(4, 1)$ and $(7, 10)$

15. $(1, 4)$ and $(2, 1)$

16. $(3, 7)$ and $(5, 12)$.

17. $(-2, 3)$ and $(-1, 5)$

18. $(4, -1)$ and $(3, -6)$

19. $(5, -2)$ and $(-4, 7)$

20. $(-6, 7)$ and $(1, 0)$

21. $(4, -3)$ and $(2, -7)$

22. $(-9, -3)$ and $(6, 0)$

23. $(3, 2)$ and $(1, 7)$

Questions 24 to 35 can be done by using either the method of questions 1 to 6 or the method and ideas of Exercise 10j:

24. $(4, 0)$ and $(0, 5)$

25. $(3, 0)$ and $(0, 2)$

26. $(3, 0)$ and $(0, -2)$

27. $(2, 0)$ and $(0, 6)$

28. $(4, 2)$ and $(6, 8)$

29. $(0, 4)$ and $(3, 1)$

30. $(2, 1)$ and $(0, -6)$

31. $(-1, 4)$ and $(5, -2)$

32. $(0, 5)$ and $(-2, 0)$

33. $(-6, 3)$ and $(5, 5)$

34. $(-1, -2)$ and $(-5, -6)$

35. $(3, 2)$ and $(7, 1)$

PROBLEMS

Exercise 10m

1. Find the equation of the line through the point $(6, 2)$, which is parallel to the line $y = 3x - 1$.

2. On the same pair of axes, for $-8 \leqslant x \leqslant 8$ and $-12 \leqslant y \leqslant 4$, using 1 cm to 1 unit, draw the four lines $y = 2x - 4, y = 2x + 6$, $x + 2y + 10 = 0$ and $2y + x = 0$. What type of quadrilateral is formed by the four lines?

3. On the same pair of axes, for $-4 \leqslant x \leqslant 10$ and $-6 \leqslant y \leqslant 10$ using 1 cm to 1 unit, draw the four lines $y = 3x + 4$, $y = 3x - 6$, $y = -3x$ and $y = 10 - 3x$. Name the type of quadrilateral formed by the lines.

4. Find the point where the lines $y = 2x + 2$ and $y = 4 - 2x$ meet.

5. Find the equation of the line with gradient -2 that passes through the midpoint of the line joining the points $(3, 2)$ and $(7, 4)$. (The midpoint can be found either from a drawing on squared paper or from a rough sketch.)

6. Find the equation of the line that is parallel to the line joining $(-1, 4)$ and $(3, 2)$ and which passes through the point $(4, 0)$.

7. On the same pair of axes, for $-2 \leqslant x \leqslant 5$ and $-5 \leqslant y \leqslant 2$, using 1 cm to 1 unit, draw the four lines $4y = x + 1$, $4y = x - 16$, $4x + y - 13 = 0$ and $4x + y + 4 = 0$.
Name the type of quadrilateral formed by the lines.

MIXED EXERCISES

Exercise 10n

1. What is the gradient of the line with equation $y = 2x + 1$?

2. At what point does the line with equation $y = 4 - 2x$ cut the y-axis?

3. At what point does the line with equation $\dfrac{x}{4} - \dfrac{y}{3} = 1$ cut the x-axis?

4. On the line with equation $y = 6 - 2x$, if $x = -3$, what is y?

5. What is the equation of the line whose gradient is 5 and which passes through the origin?

6. At what point does the line with equation $2x + 3y = 24$ cut the x-axis?

7. Does the point $(2, 4)$ lie on the line with equation $y = 6x - 8$?

8. Find the gradient of the line joining the points $(6, 4)$ and $(1, 1)$.

Exercise 10p

1. What is the gradient of the line with equation $y = 4 - 3x$?

2. Does the point $(6, -1)$ lie on the line $3x + 11y = 8$?

3. What is the equation of the line that passes through the origin and has a gradient of -4?

4. At what point does the line with equation $y = 4 - x$ cut the y-axis?

5. At what points does the line with equation $x + y = 6$ cut the two axes?

6. Find the gradient of the line through the points $(3, 1)$ and $(5, -2)$.

7. Give the equation of the line that is parallel to the line with equation $y = 4 + \frac{1}{2}x$ and which passes through the origin.

8. At what points does the line $\frac{x}{2} + \frac{y}{3} = 1$ cut the two axes?

GRAPHS

At the end of the chapter you should be able to:

1. Draw a graph when corresponding values of two variables are given.
2. Construct a table of values when a formula connecting two variables is given.
3. Use a graph to find the value of one quantity, given the corresponding value of another.
4. Use a graph to find the least or greatest value of a quadratic function.

GRAPHS FROM TABLES

Graphs are used to give a visual representation of information about two, related, varying quantities.

You can see examples of graphs in many newspapers and periodicals. The best of them give a clear visual impression of the way in which the related quantities vary and allow us to get more information from the graph. The worst graphs are misleading, often because the axes are incorrectly labelled or because the scales are distorted.

Before we can draw a graph we have to know how the quantities vary. Sometimes we are given this information in a table, while at other times we are told that the two quantities are connected by a formula. The following example shows how to draw a clear, informative graph.

The Agricultural Department collected data for a particular type of tree. This data is given in the following table:

Age of tree in years (A)	0.8	1.4	2.2	3.5	5.4	6.7	7.8
Girth of tree in cm (G)	15.8	20.9	26.5	33.2	41.2	45.9	49.5

To draw a graph to represent this data we must:

(a) draw axes that intersect at right angles in the bottom left-hand corner of the graph paper

(b) state the scale used on each axis

(c) name the axes
(We put time along the horizontal axis and the distance around the tree, or *girth*, along the vertical axis.)

(d) plot carefully the points representing the data given in the table
   (We shall use a dot for each point.)

(e) draw a smooth curve to pass through the points

(f) give the graph a title.

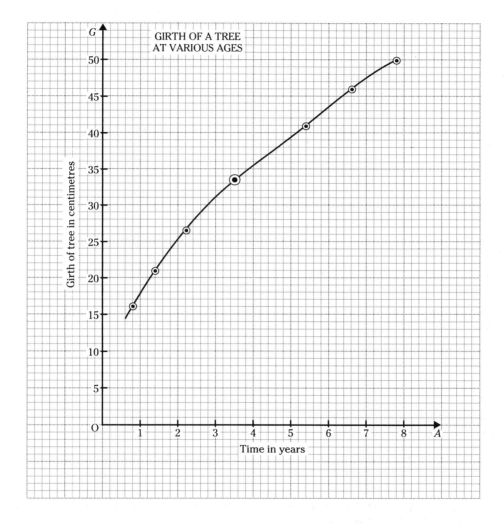

We can use this graph to find the girth of the tree at any given age, or the age of the tree when it has a particular girth, provided that we keep within the range of values on our axes.

From the graph:

(a) when the tree is four years old its girth is 35.5 cm

(b) when the girth is 40 cm the tree is five years old.

Exercise 11a

1. The table shows the weight (W) in tonnes which a chain of diameter (D) centimetres will support before breaking.

D	1.2	1.8	2.2	2.6	2.8	3	3.4	3.8
W	72	162	242	338	392	450	578	722

Draw a graph for values of D from 0 to 4. Take 4 cm as 1 unit for D and 1 cm as 50 units for W. Use your graph to find

(a) the greatest weight that a chain of diameter 2 cm will support

(b) the smallest diameter of chain that will support a load of 500 tonnes.

2. When a sum of money is invested, the interest added to the original value gives an increased value called the amount. The table shows the amount (V) of $100 when it has been invested for T years at 10% compound interest.

T	0	1	2	3	4	5	6	7	8	9
V	100	110	121	133	146	161	177	195	214	236

Draw the graph connecting T and V. Take 2 cm as 1 unit for T and 4 cm as 50 units for V. From your graph find

(a) the amount of $100 after $5\frac{1}{2}$ years

(b) the time, in years, in which $100 will double in value.

3. The table shows the connection between two quantities X and Y as X takes different values from 1 to 8

X	1	1.5	2	3	4	5	6	8
Y	14	10	8	6	5	4.4	4	3.5

Draw a graph connecting X and Y taking 2 cm as 1 unit for X and 1 cm as 1 unit for Y. Start at 0 for each scale. From your graph find

(a) the value of Y when X is 7.2

(b) the value of X when Y is 7.2

4. The table gives values for the surface area, A cm^2, of a closed rectangular box of fixed volume, which has square ends of side x cm.

x (cm)	1	1.5	2	3	4	5	6
A (cm^2)	110	76.5	62	54	59	71.6	90

Draw a graph connecting A and x taking 4 cm to represent 1 unit on the x-axis and 1 cm to represent 5 units on the A-axis. Let 40 be the lowest value on the A-axis. Use your graph to find

(a) the value of x that gives the lowest value of A

(b) the value of A when x is 1.8

5. The table shows the capacity (C), in litres, for jugs that are mathematically similar, but of different heights (H cm).

Height of jug in cm (H)	4	5.25	7.5	10.25	12.75	15.5	18.25
Capacity of jug in litres (C)	0.05	0.11	0.33	0.84	1.67	2.90	4.74

Draw a graph to represent this data using 4 cm to represent 5 units on the *H*-axis and 1 unit on the *C*-axis. Use your graph to find

(a) the height of a similar jug with a capacity of 3.5 litres

(b) the capacity of a similar jug that is 14 cm high.

CONSTRUCTING A TABLE FROM A FORMULA

In the exercise we have just completed, all the data was given in tables. However, in many questions we are given a formula and have to construct our own table for given values of the variables.

Consider a car that starts from rest and travels a distance D metres in T seconds. Suppose that the formula connecting D and T for the first 10 seconds of the journey is

$$D = 50\sqrt{T}$$

and that we wish to draw a graph to show this relationship. Before we can draw the graph, we must work our some corresponding values of D and T.

If we take the whole number values of T from 0 to 10 we get:

when
$$T = 1 \qquad D = 50\sqrt{1} \ = 50 \times 1 = 50$$
$$T = 2 \qquad D = 50\sqrt{2} \ = 50 \times 1.414 = 71$$
$$T = 3 \qquad D = 50\sqrt{3} \ = 50 \times 1.732 = 87$$
$$T = 4 \qquad D = 50\sqrt{4} \ = 50 \times 2 = 100$$
$$T = 5 \qquad D = 50\sqrt{5} \ = 50 \times 2.236 = 112$$
$$T = 6 \qquad D = 50\sqrt{6} \ = 50 \times 2.449 = 122$$
$$T = 7 \qquad D = 50\sqrt{7} \ = 50 \times 2.646 = 132$$
$$T = 8 \qquad D = 50\sqrt{8} \ = 50 \times 2.828 = 141$$
$$T = 9 \qquad D = 50\sqrt{9} \ = 50 \times 3 = 150$$
$$T = 10 \qquad D = 50\sqrt{10} = 50 \times 3.162 = 158$$

Each value of D is calculated correct to the nearest whole number.
These values of T in seconds and D in metres can be set out in table form:

T	0	1	2	3	4	5	6	7	8	9	10
D	0	50	71	87	100	112	122	132	141	150	158

We plot time (T) along the horizontal axis and distance (D) along the vertical axis.

When all the points have been plotted, draw a smooth curve to pass through them. The resulting graph is shown in the diagram overleaf. From this graph we can find D for any given value of T from 0 to 10, e.g. the distance travelled in 4.4 s is 105 m. Similarly, the time to travel 146 m is 8.5 s.

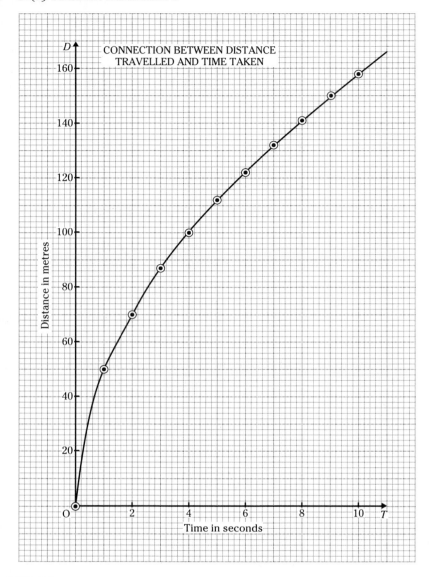

Exercise 11b

1. A stone is dropped from the top of a cliff. After t seconds it has fallen s metres, where $s = 5t^2$. Construct a table to show the relation between s and t, for values of t from 0 to 6, at half-unit intervals.
   Use these values to draw a graph, and use your graph to find

   (a) how far the stone has fallen in 3.4 s

   (b) how long the stone takes to fall 100 m.

2. Two quantities P and Q are connected by the formula
   $$P = \frac{36}{Q}$$
   Construct a table to show the relation between P and Q for values of Q from 1 to 8. Plot these points on a graph and from this graph find

   (a) the value of P when Q is 7.5

   (b) the value of Q when P is 4.8

3. Draw the graph of $y = \dfrac{6}{x}$ for values of x from 1 to 6 inclusive, plotting points at whole number values of x and at $x = 1\frac{1}{2}$. Take 2 cm as 1 unit on each axis. Use your graph to find

(a) the value of x when $y = 3.6$

(b) the value of y when $x = 5.5$

4. Taking 2 cm as the unit on both axes, draw the graph of $y = x + \dfrac{7}{x}$ for values of x between 1 and 7 at unit intervals. Use your graph to find the lowest value of y and the corresponding value of x.

5. Draw the graph of $xy = 8$ for values of x from -8 to -1 and from 1 to 8. (We cannot take $x = 0$ since there is no value of y which enables the product xy to be 8.) Let each axis range from -8 to 8, and take 1 cm as 1 unit on both axes. Use your graph to find

(a) the value of y when x is 2.4

(b) the value of x when y is -5.6

POINTS TO REMEMBER WHEN DRAWING GRAPHS OF CURVES

1. Do not take too few points. About ten are usually necessary.

2. To decide where you need to draw the y-axis, look at the range of x-values.

3. To decide where to draw the x-axis, look at the range of y-values.

4. In some questions you will be given most of the y-values but you may have to calculate a few more for yourself. In this case always plot first those points that you were given and, from these, get an idea of the shape of the curve. Then you can plot the points you calculated and see if they fit on to the curve you have in mind. If they do not, go back and check your calculations.

5. When you draw a smooth curve to pass through the points, always turn the page into a position where your wrist is on the inside of the curve.

QUADRATIC GRAPHS

The most important family of curves we consider give what are called *quadratic graphs*. The simplest of these is the graph of $y = x^2$.

We will draw the graph of $y = x^2$ for values of x ranging from -3 to $+3$ at half-unit intervals. The corresponding values for x and y are given in the table below:

x	-3	-2.5	-2	-1.5	-1	-0.5	0	0.5	1	1.5	2	2.5	3
$y\,(=x^2)$	9	6.25	4	2.25	1	0.25	0	0.25	1	2.25	4	6.25	9

A suitable scale for you to take is 2 cm to represent 1 unit on both axes but we have taken 1 cm to represent 1 unit on both axes.

We draw the *y*-axis vertically in the centre of the page, since the *x*-values range from −3 to +3, i.e. they are symmetrical about **0**.

The *x*-axis is drawn along the bottom of the page since all the *y*-values are positive.

The table gives us thirteen points. In drawing any quadratic graph, aim for at least ten points. It is especially important to have plenty of points where the graph is changing direction most quickly. For quadratic graphs this means around the lowest (or highest) point.

From the graph we can find the value of *y* that corresponds to any value of *x* within the range −3 to +3. For any value of *y* between 0 and 9 we can find the two corresponding values of *x*.

For example: (a) if $x = 1.8$, $y = 3.2$

(b) if $x = -2.3$, $y = 5.3$

(c) if $y = 2$, $x = 1.4$ or -1.4

(There are two values of *x* for which $y = 2$)

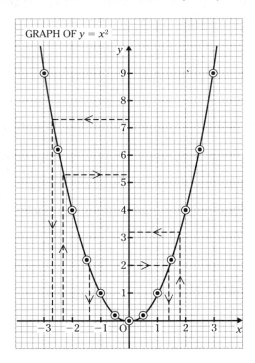

GRAPH OF $y = x^2$

Exercise 11c

1. Draw on the same axes the graphs of $y = x^2$, $y = 2x^2$ and $y = 3x^2$, taking half-unit intervals for *x* in the range −2 to +2. Take 4 cm as the unit on the *x*-axis and 2 cm as the unit on the *y*-axis for values of *y* from 0 to 12.
What can you deduce about the graph of $y = ax^2$ for any positive value of *a*?

2. Draw the graph of $y = x^2 + 3$ for values of x in the range -3 to 3. Take 4 cm as the unit for x and 1 cm as the unit for y.

   (a) Use your graph to find the values of x when $y = 6$.

   (b) Are there any values of x for which y has the value 0?

3. Draw the graph of $y = -x^2 + 4$ for values of x in the range -3 to 3. Take 2 cm as the unit for both x and y. Use your graph to find the value of x when (a) $y = 0$ (b) $y = 3$.
   Is the graph upside down compared with the graphs you drew in questions 1 and 2?

4. Draw on the same axes the graphs of $y = x^2$, $y = x^2 + 4$ and $y = x^2 - 4$. Use values of x from -3 to $+3$ at unit intervals, taking 2 cm as 1 unit on the x-axis and 1 cm as 1 unit on the y-axis. Let the scale on the y-axis range from -5 to $+14$.
   What can you say about the shapes of the three graphs?
   What can you deduce about the graph of $y = x^2 + C$ for different positive or negative values of C?

5. Complete the following table which gives values of $x(x - 3)$ for values of x in the range -1 to 4 at half-unit intervals.

x	-1	-0.5	0	0.5	1	1.5	2	2.5	3	3.5	4
$x - 3$	-4			-2.5		-1.5					1
$x(x - 3)$	4			-1.25		-2.25					4

   Hence draw the graph of $y = x(x - 3)$ within the given range taking 2 cm as the unit on both axes.
   Use your graph to write down

   (a) the values of x where the graph crosses the x-axis

   (b) the values of x when $x(x - 3) = 3$ (i.e. when $y = 3$).

6. Draw the graph of $y = x(2x - 3)$ for values of x in the range -2 to 3 taking values of x at half-unit intervals. Use a scale of 2 cm for 1 unit on the x-axis and 1 cm for 1 unit on the y-axis. Use your graph to find

   (a) the values of x where the graph crosses the x-axis

   (b) the lowest value of $x(2x - 3)$, i.e. the lowest value of y and the corresponding value of x.

7. Draw the graph of $y = 2x(2 + x)$ for values of x in the range -5 to 3. Take values of x at unit intervals, with extra values where you think they are needed. Let the scale on your y-axis range from -4 to $+32$. Let 1 cm represent 2 units. Use your graph to find

   (a) the smallest value of $2x(2 + x)$ and the value of x for which it occurs

   (b) the value of $2x(2 + x)$ when $x = -3.5$

   (c) the values of x when $2x(2 + x) = 0$

Draw the graph of $y = x^2 + x - 6$ for whole number values of x from -4 to $+4$. Take $1\,\text{cm}$ as 1 unit on the x-axis and $1\,\text{cm}$ as 2 units on the y-axis. Use your graph to find

(a) the lowest value of $x^2 + x - 6$ and the corresponding value of x

(b) the values of x when $x^2 + x - 6$ is 4.

x	-4	-3	-2	-1	0	1	2	3	4
x^2	16	9	4	1	0	1	4	9	16
x	-4	-3	-2	-1	0	1	2	3	4
-6	-6	-6	-6	-6	-6	-6	-6	-6	-6
$x^2 + x - 6$	6	0	-4	-6	-6	-4	0	6	14

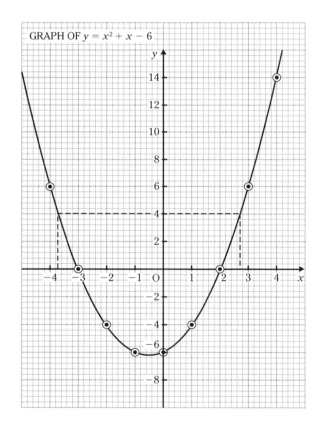

GRAPH OF $y = x^2 + x - 6$

(a) From the graph, the lowest value of $x^2 + x - 6$ is $-6\frac{1}{4}$.
This occurs when $x = -\frac{1}{2}$.

(b) The values of x when $x^2 + x - 6$ is 4 are -3.70 and 2.70

8. Draw the graph of $y = x^2 - 2x - 3$ for whole number values of x in the range -3 to 5. Take 2 cm as 1 unit for x and 1 cm as 1 unit for y. Use your graph to find

(a) the lowest value of $x^2 - 2x - 3$ and the corresponding value of x

(b) the values of x when $x^2 - 2x - 3$ has a value of
(i) 1   (ii) 8

9. Draw the graph of $y = 6 + x - x^2$ for whole number values of x from -3 to 4. Take 2 cm as 1 unit on both axes. Use your graph to find

(a) the highest value of $6 + x - x^2$ and the corresponding value of x

(b) the values of x when $6 + x - x^2$ has a value of
(i) -2 (ii) 4

REVIEW TEST 1: CHAPTERS 1–11

In questions 1–10, choose the letter for the correct answer.

1. What is the value of $\left(\frac{4}{5}\right)^{-2}$?

   (A) $\frac{25}{16}$ (B) $\frac{16}{25}$ (C) $-\frac{8}{10}$ (D) $-\frac{4}{10}$

2. The solution of $-3x > 6$, is

   (A) $x > 2$ (B) $x > -2$ (C) $x < 2$ (D) $x < -2$

3. What number when decreased by 25% is equal to 48?

   (A) 75   (B) 73   (C) 64   (D) 60

4. For which one of the following transformations will the figure and its image NOT be congruent?

   (A) Translation   (B) Enlargement   (C) Rotaticn   (D) Reflection

5. Given $\mathbf{X} = \begin{pmatrix} 2 & 3 \\ -4 & 5 \end{pmatrix}$, then $2\mathbf{X} =$

   (A) $\begin{pmatrix} 4 & 3 \\ -8 & 5 \end{pmatrix}$ (B) $\begin{pmatrix} 2 & 6 \\ -4 & 10 \end{pmatrix}$ (C) $\begin{pmatrix} 4 & 6 \\ -8 & 10 \end{pmatrix}$ (D) $\begin{pmatrix} 4 & 6 \\ -4 & 5 \end{pmatrix}$

6. The determinant of $\begin{pmatrix} 2 & 5 \\ 7 & -3 \end{pmatrix} =$

   (A) -41 (B) -29 (C) 29   (D) 41

7. Which of the points lie on the line $y = 2x + 3$?
   (i) $(-2, 1)$ (ii) $(1, 5)$ (iii) $(-1, 1)$

   (A) i and ii only   (B) i and iii only   (C) ii and iii only   (D) i, ii and iii

8. What is the gradient of $3x + 4y = 9$?

   (A) -3 (B) $-\frac{3}{4}$ (C) $\frac{3}{4}$ (D) 3

9. To make a skeleton model of a cube, 48 cm of wire was used. What is the length of one side?

   (A) 4 cm   (B) 6 cm   (C) 8 cm   (D) 12 cm

10. Which of the following is the solution to the pair of equations $3x + y = 5$ and $x + y = 1$?
    (i) $(2, -1)$ (ii) $(0, 1)$ (iii) $(1, 2)$ (iv) $(1, 0)$

    (A) i only   (B) ii only   (C) iii only   (D) iv only

11. (a) If $3x - 7y = 8$ and $4x + 5y = 8$, find the ratio of $x : y$.

   (b) Solve the equation $\dfrac{(x+1)}{2} + \dfrac{(x-2)}{3} = \dfrac{(x+4)}{4}$

12. (a) A commission agent received a commission of $980 on a sale for $28\,000$. At what rate per cent was the commission paid to the agent?

   (b) A car is bought for $50\,000$ and depreciates at 10% each year. What is its value at the end of two years?

13. (a) Without using a set-square or a protractor, construct a triangle ABC in which $AB = 8$ cm, $\widehat{A} = 45°$, $\widehat{B} = 60°$. Measure the length of BC.

   (b) In the figure, $PT = TQ$ and $\widehat{S} = \widehat{R}$, $P\widehat{T}Q = 90°$.

   If the angle marked x measures $60°$, what is the measure of y? Name two congruent triangles, giving reasons for your answer.

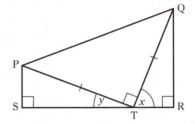

14. (a) If $x = 9$, $y = 3$, $p = \frac{1}{2}$, $q = 2$, find the value of $x^p + q^y$

   (b) If x is an integer, find the values of x which satisfy $x - 5 < 3x + 2 < 7$

15. (a) Write the equations $2x + 3y = 7$ and $3x - y = 5$ in matrix form and hence solve them.

   (b) Find the equation of the line through the point $(5, -2)$ which is parallel to $y = 4x + 1$

12 AREAS

At the end of the chapter you should be able to:

1. Calculate the areas of triangles, rectangles and parallelograms.
2. Calculate the area of a polygon by subdividing it into triangles, rectangles or parallelograms.
3. Calculate the area of a trapezium given the lengths of its parallel sides and height.
4. Identify triangles or parallelograms which have equal area.
5. State the ratio of the areas of two triangles which have equal heights (bases) but different bases (heights).
6. Solve problems using the fact that triangles with equal heights (bases) have areas proportional to their bases (heights).

AREAS OF FAMILIAR SHAPES

Rectangle 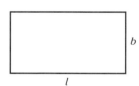 $A = lb$

Parallelogram 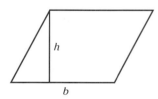 $A = bh$

Triangle 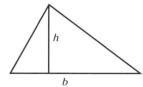 $A = \frac{1}{2} bh$

Remember that when we talk about the height of a figure we mean the *perpendicular height*, not the slant height.

Remember also that both the lengths we use must be measured in the *same* unit.

Exercise 12a

Find the areas of the following figures:

1.

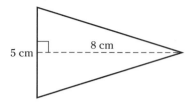

3.

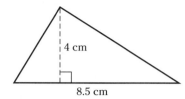

2.

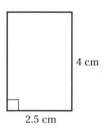

4.

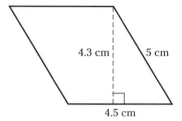

In questions 5 to 9 use squared paper and draw axes for x and y in the ranges $-6 \leqslant x \leqslant 6$, $-6 \leqslant y \leqslant 6$ using 1 square to 1 unit. Draw the figure and find its area in square units:

5. Triangle ABC with $A(0, 6)$, $B(6, 6)$ and $C(5, 2)$.

6. Parallelogram ABCD with $A(0, 1)$, $B(0, 6)$, $C(6, 4)$ and $D(6, -1)$.

7. Rectangle ABCD with $A(-4, 2)$, $B(0, 2)$ and $C(0, -1)$.

8. Square ABCD with $A(0, 0)$, $B(0, 4)$ and $C(4, 4)$.

9. Triangle ABC with $A(-5, -4)$, $B(2, -4)$, $C(-2, 3)$.

For each of the following figures, find the missing measurement. Draw a diagram in each case:

	Figure	Base	Height	Area
10.	Triangle	8 cm		16 cm^2
11.	Rectangle	3 cm	15 mm	
12.	Parallelogram	4 cm		20 cm^2
13.	Square	5 m		
14.	Triangle	70 mm		14 cm^2

In questions 15 to 18 give answers correct to three significant figures where necessary.

15.

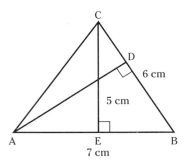

In △ABC, AB = 7 cm, CB = 6 cm and CE = 5 cm.
Find

(a) the area of △ABC

(b) the length of AD.

16.

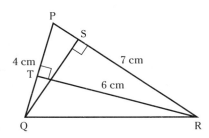

In △PQR, PQ = 4 cm, PR = 7 cm and RT = 6 cm.
Find

(a) the area of △PQR

(b) the length of QS.

17.

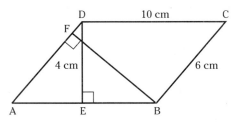

In parallelogram ABCD, DC = 10 cm, BC = 6 cm and DE = 4 cm.
Find

(a) the area of ABCD

(b) the length of BF.

18.

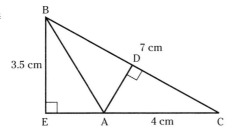

In △ABC, AC = 4 cm, BC = 7 cm and BE = 3.5 cm.

Find

(a) the area of △ABC
(b) the length of AD.

AREAS OF COMPOUND SHAPES

Exercise 12b

ABCD is a rhombus. AC = 8 cm and BD = 12 cm.
Find the area of ABCD.

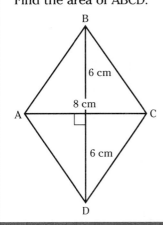

(The diagonals of a rhombus bisect each other at right angles.)

Area △ABC = $\frac{1}{2}$ base × height

$\qquad = \frac{1}{2} \times 8 \times 6 \text{ cm}^2$

$\qquad = 24 \text{ cm}^2$

Area △ACD = area △ABC

(AC is an axis of symmetry)

∴ total area = 48 cm²

Find the area of each of the following shapes. Draw a diagram for each question and mark in all the measurements:

1.

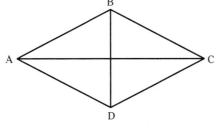

ABCD is a rhombus.
AC = 15 cm and BD = 8 cm

2.

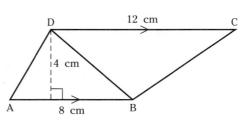

3.

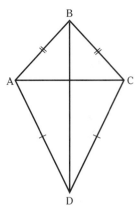

ABCD is a kite.
AC = 6 cm and BD = 10 cm

4.

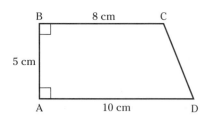

In questions 5 and 6, find the area of the shaded figure (find the area of the complete figure, then subtract the areas of the unshaded parts).

5.

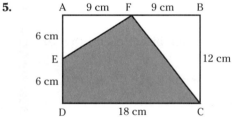

ABCD is a rectangle.

6.

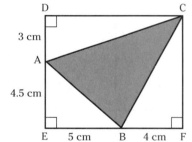

AREA OF A TRAPEZIUM

In the last exercise we found the areas of several trapeziums. A trapezium is a shape that occurs often enough to justify finding a formula for its area.

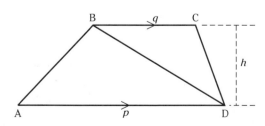

Area of $\triangle$ABD $= \frac{1}{2}$ base $\times$ height $= \frac{1}{2}p \times h$

Area of $\triangle$BCD $= \frac{1}{2}$ base $\times$ height $= \frac{1}{2}q \times h$

The heights of both triangles are the same, as each is the distance between the parallel sides of the trapezium.

$\therefore$ total area of ABCD $= \frac{1}{2}ph + \frac{1}{2}qh = \frac{1}{2}(p + q) \times h$

i.e.   the area of a trapezium is equal to

$\frac{1}{2}$ (sum of parallel sides) × (distance between them)

Exercise 12c

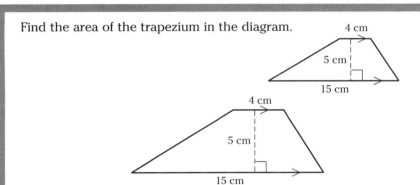

Find the area of the trapezium in the diagram.

Area $= \frac{1}{2}$ (sum of parallel sides) × (distance between them)

$= \frac{1}{2}(4 + 15) \times 5 \, \text{cm}^2$

$= \frac{1}{2} \times 19 \times 5 \, \text{cm}^2$

$= 47.5 \, \text{cm}^2$

Find the area of each of the following trapeziums:

1.

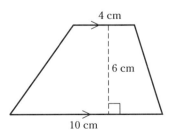

2.

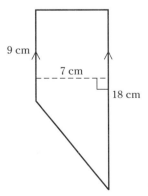

3.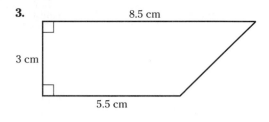

4.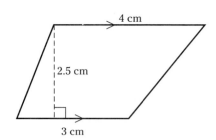

For questions 5 to 10 use squared paper and draw axes for x and y using ranges $-6 \leqslant x \leqslant 6$ and $-6 \leqslant y \leqslant 6$ and a scale of one square to 1 unit. Plot the points and join them up in alphabetical order. Find, in square units, the area of the resulting shape:

5. A$(6, 1)$, B$(4, -3)$, C$(-2, -3)$, D$(-3, 1)$

6. A$(4, 4)$, B$(-2, 2)$, C$(-2, -2)$, D$(4, -3)$

7. A$(3, 5)$, B$(-4, 4)$, C$(-4, -2)$, D$(3, -5)$

8. A$(1, 0)$, B$(5, 0)$, C$(5, 3)$, D$(3, 5)$, E$(1, 3)$

9. A$(6, -4)$, B$(6, 1)$, C$(2, 5)$, D$(-5, 3)$, E$(-5, -4)$

10. A$(2, 0)$, B$(6, 4)$, C$(-4, 4)$, D$(-4, -2)$, E$(5, -2)$

SHAPES THAT HAVE EQUAL AREAS

Exercise 12d

1.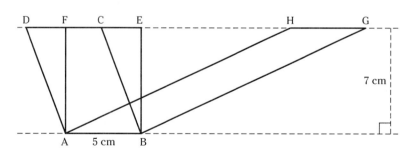

There are three parallelograms in the diagram. Write down the area of each one.

2.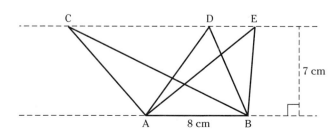

Write down the area of each of the three triangles ABC, ABD and ABE.

In questions 3 and 4, take the side of a square as the unit of length.

3.

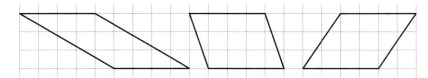

What is the length of the base and the height of each of these parallelograms? What can you conclude about the areas of the three parallelograms?

4.

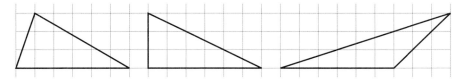

What is the length of the base and the height of each of these triangles? What can you conclude about the areas of the three triangles?

5. Using squared paper draw x and y axes for $-8 \leqslant x \leqslant 8$ and $-4 \leqslant y \leqslant 12$. Draw parallelogram ABCD where A(2, 2), B(2, 7), C(7, 4), D(7, −1). Using AB as the base in each case, draw three other parallelograms whose areas are equal to the area of ABCD.

6. Use the same set of axes as you used for question 5. Draw the triangle LMN where L(−6, 1), M(−1, 1), N(−5, 5). Using LM as the base draw two other triangles whose areas are equal to the area of triangle LMN.

7. Draw again the diagram that you used for question 6. Draw a triangle which is equal in area to triangle LMN and which has LN for one of its sides.

8. There are four triangles in the diagram all with the same base AB.
Find, in ascending order, the ratio of their heights.
Find, in ascending order, the ratio of their areas.
Comment on your results.

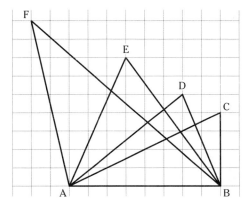

9. Using squared paper draw x and y axes for $0 \leqslant x \leqslant 10$ and $0 \leqslant y \leqslant 12$. Plot the points A$(2, 1)$, B$(10, 1)$ and C$(8, 5)$. Draw a triangle ABD whose area is twice that of triangle ABC. Give the y coordinate of D.

10. Using the same set of axes as in question 9, draw a triangle ABE whose area is half the area of △ABC. Give the y coordinate of E.

11. The triangles XAB, YBD, ZBC and ZCE all have equal heights of 5 units.

(a) Find the ratio of their bases.

(b) Find the ratio of their areas.

Comment on your results.

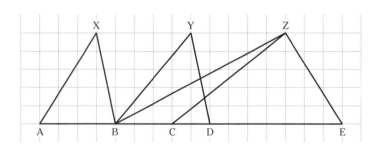

From the last exercise we see that:

> parallelograms with equal bases and equal heights have the same area.

> triangles with equal bases and equal heights have the same area.

> triangles on equal bases but with different heights have areas proportional to their heights.

> triangles with equal heights but different bases have areas proportional to their bases.

Exercise 12e

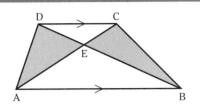

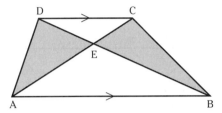

ABCD is a trapezium. Show that the shaded triangles have the same area.

Area △ADB = area △ACB

(Same base AB and same height, as DC ∥ AB)

Area △AEB is common to both △ADB and △ACB. Removing it from each triangle in turn leaves the shaded areas.

∴   area △AED = area △BEC

1.

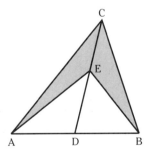

D is the midpoint of AB. Show that the shaded triangles have the same area.

2.

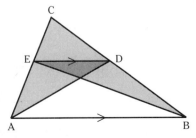

ED is parallel to AB. Show that area △ACD = area △BCE.

3.

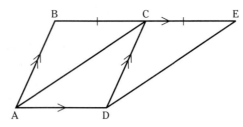

BC = CE, AB is parallel to DC and AD is parallel to BE. Show that area △ADC = area △DCE.

4.

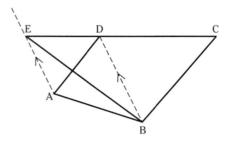

AE is parallel to BD. Show that the area of △BCE is equal to the area of the quadrilateral ABCD.

5.

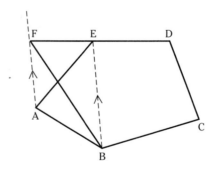

AF is parallel to BE. Show that the area of the pentagon ABCDE is equal to the area of the quadrilateral BCDF.

6.

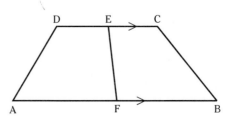

ABCD is a trapezium. E is the midpoint of DC and F is the midpoint of AB. Show that EF divides the area of ABCD into two equal parts.

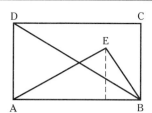

ABCD is a rectangle.
The height of △ABE (i.e. the distance of E above AB) is two thirds of the height, AD, of the rectangle.
The area of ABCD is $12\,\text{cm}^2$.
Find the area of △AEB.

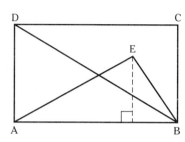

Area of △ADB $= 6\,\text{cm}^2$ (half area of ABCD)

△s ABD, ABE are on the same base AB, so their areas are in the same ratio as their heights.

∴

$$\frac{\text{area }\triangle\text{ABE}}{\text{area }\triangle\text{ADB}} = \frac{2}{3}$$

$$\frac{\text{area }\triangle\text{ABE}}{6} = \frac{2}{3}$$

$$\require{cancel}\cancel{6}\times\frac{\text{area }\triangle\text{ABE}}{\cancel{6}} = \cancel{6}\times\frac{2}{\cancel{3}}$$

∴

$$\text{area }\triangle\text{ABE} = 4\,\text{cm}^2$$

7.

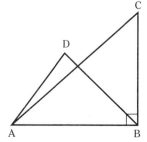

The area of △ABD is $\frac{3}{5}$ of the area of △ABC. BC $= 20\,\text{cm}$. Find the height of D above AB.

8.

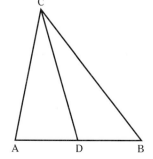

D is the midpoint of AB. Find the ratio of the area of △ABC to the area of △ADC.

9.

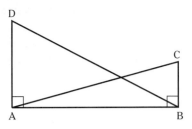

The area of △ABC $= \frac{7}{12}$ of the area of △ADB. AD $= 24$ cm.
Find the length of BC.

10.

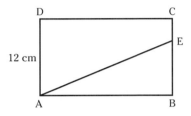

In the rectangle ABCD, E is a point on BC such that area of △ABE is $\frac{1}{3}$ of the area of the rectangle ABCD.

Find the length of BE.

11.

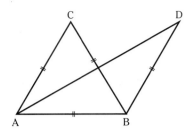

AB $=$ AC $=$ CB $=$ BD.
Area △ABC $=$ area △ABD.
Find the size of $A\hat{D}B$.

12.

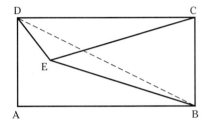

E is a point inside the rectangle ABCD such that the distance of E from BC is $\frac{3}{4}$ of the distance of A from BC and the distance of E from DC is $\frac{1}{3}$ of the distance of A from DC. The area of the rectangle ABCD is 72 cm^2.

Find the areas of △BEC and △DEC.

In questions 13 and 14, before beginning the construction draw a rough sketch and on it mark any extra lines that you will need:

13. Construct a parallelogram ABCD with AB $= 4$ cm, BC $= 6$ cm and $A\hat{B}C = 60°$. Construct a parallelogram ABEF that is equal in area to ABCD such that BE $= 7$ cm, and such that E and D are on opposite sides of BC. Measure $A\hat{B}E$.

14. Construct △ABC with AB $= 12$ cm, $\hat{A} = 30°$ and $\hat{B} = 30°$. On AC as base, construct a triangle ADC that is equal in area to △ABC, such that $C\hat{A}D = 90°$. Measure AD.

15. In the △ABC, D is the midpoint of BC. E is a point on AD so that AE $= \frac{1}{4}$AD. If BC$= 16$ cm and the area of △ABC $= 96$ cm^2, find the area of △DEC.

13 ▷ AVERAGES

At the end of the chapter you should be able to:

1. Calculate the arithmetic mean of a given set of numbers.
2. Solve problems using the mean of a set of data.
3. Calculate the average speed of a body given the time and distance travelled.
4. Solve problems involving distance, speed and time.

ARITHMETIC AVERAGE

The arithmetic average or mean of a set of numbers is their sum divided by the number of numbers in the set.

For example, the mean of the six numbers 5, 10, 15, 21, 25 and 32 is

$$\frac{5 + 10 + 15 + 21 + 25 + 32}{6} = \frac{108}{6} = 18$$

Exercise 13a

Find the arithmetic average or mean of the following sets of numbers:

1. 40, 48, 44, 63, 35

2. 6, 36, 21, 59, 47, 80, 34, 14, 63

3. 9.3, 26.5, 14.2, 18.7, 32.4, 18.2, 20.7

4. 47.4, 40.6, 53.8, 41.1, 29.9, 35.6

Peter's marks in his eight examination subjects were: 43, 62, 37, 82, 54, 47, 56 and 35. How many marks did he score altogether? What was his average mark?

$$\text{Total marks scored} = 43 + 62 + 37 + 82 + 54 + 47 + 56 + 35$$

$$= 416$$

$$\text{Average mark} = \frac{416}{8}$$

$$= 52$$

5. In five frames of snooker, Ray scored 76, 12, 43, 83 and 41.

(a) How many did he score altogether?

(b) What was his average score per frame?

6. Janet's marks in six consecutive geography examinations were 72, 54, 58, 73, 47 and 62.

(a) Find the total marks she scored.

(b) What was her average mark?

7. The heights of five girls were 147 cm, 151 cm, 149 cm, 160 cm and 158 cm. Find the total of the heights of the five girls, and hence find their average height.

8. Jennifer's average mark for nine examination papers was 62. How many marks did she score altogether?

9. During a certain week in June, the midday temperatures in degrees Celsius at a holiday resort were 30°, 29°, 22°, 31°, 32°, 26° and 33°. What was the average midday temperature for the week?

I bought six apples at $1.00 each and nine apples at 75 c each. Find the average price of the apples I bought.

6 apples at $1.00 each cost $6 \times 100\,c = \$6.00$

9 apples at 75 c each cost $9 \times 75\,c = \$6.75$

$\therefore$ 15 apples cost $\$6.00 + \$6.75 = \$12.75$

$$\text{Average price of an apple} = \frac{\text{total cost}}{\text{total number}}$$

$$= \frac{\$12.75}{15}$$

$$= 85\,c$$

---

10. I bought four white loaves at 98 c each and three brown loaves at $1.12 each. Find the average price I paid for a loaf of bread.

11. Andrew buys seven books at $6.20 each and three books at $4.70 each. What is the average amount that Andrew pays for a book?

12. Betty buys eight bottles of Cola each containing 70 cl and four bottles of Cola each containing 1 litre. Find, in centilitres, the average amount in the bottles she buys.

13. A shipping company owns three ships of average gross tonnage 18 400 t, eight ships of average gross tonnage 11 500 t and 12 ships of average gross tonnage 4600 t. Calculate the average gross tonnage of the company's ships.

The average height of the ten boys in a class is 160 cm and the average height of the 15 girls is 154 cm. Find the average height of the class. As a result of a new boy joining the class, the average height of the class increases by 0.1 cm. How tall is he?

$$\text{Total height of the 10 boys} = 160 \times 10 \text{ cm} = 1600 \text{ cm}$$

$$\text{Total height of the 15 girls} = 154 \times 15 \text{ cm} = 2310 \text{ cm}$$

$$\therefore \quad \text{Total height of the 25 pupils in the class} = 3910 \text{ cm}$$

$$\text{Average height of the class} = \frac{3910}{25} \text{ cm}$$

$$= 156.4 \text{ cm}$$

When a new boy joins, the average height increases by 0.1 cm to 156.5 cm.

Then the total height of the 26 pupils in the class

$$= 156.5 \times 26 \text{ cm}$$

$$= 4069 \text{ cm}$$

But, total height of the original 25 pupils $= 3910$ cm

Therefore, the height of the boy who joins is

$$(4069 - 3910) \text{ cm} = 159 \text{ cm}$$

14. The average daily 'takings' in the corner shop from Monday to Friday of a certain week was $120.50, while the average daily 'takings' from Monday to Saturday of the same week was $132.40.

(a) How much was taken over the five days Monday to Friday?

(b) How much was taken over the six days Monday to Saturday?

(c) How much was taken on the Saturday?

15. The average number of birthday cards sold by a newsagent from Monday to Friday during a certain week was 26, while the average number sold from Monday to Saturday of the same week was 32.

(a) How many cards were sold over the five days Monday to Friday?

(b) How many cards were sold over the six days Monday to Saturday?

(c) How many birthday cards were sold on the Saturday?

16. In the first year of Stanley School, the average size of forms 1E, 1L, 1M and 1W is 30; the average size of forms 1P, 1D and 1B is 23; and the average size of 1L and 1K is 18.

(a) How many pupils are there in the first year?

(b) What is the average size of a first year form?

17. The average age of a family of five is 28 years 11 months. If the average age of the parents is 46 years 2 months, find the average age of the children. If the father's age is 48 years 7 months, how old is the mother?

Susan's average mark for her first five examinations was 54. What must she score in her sixth examination to raise her average mark to 60?

Total marks scored in her first five examinations is

$$54 \times 5 = 270$$

Total marks scored in the six examinations is

$$60 \times 6 = 360$$

$\therefore$ the mark scored in sixth examination must be $360 - 270 = 90$

18. In a boat race the average weight of the eight oarsmen was 63.2 kg and the average weight of the crew was 60.9 kg. How heavy was the cox?

19. The average weight of the eleven players in a school football team was 55.6 kg, while the average weight of the team plus a travelling reserve was 56.5 kg. How heavy was the reserve?

20. In twelve completed innings, a batsman's average score was 47.5. After a further innings his average fell to 44. How many runs did he score in his thirteenth innings?

AVERAGE SPEEDS

If a car travels 180 km in three hours, we say that the average distance it travels in each hour is $\dfrac{180}{3}$ km $= 60$ km

i.e. its average speed is 60 km/h.

The general result was given in Book 2, Chapter 20:

$$\text{average speed} = \frac{\text{total distance travelled}}{\text{total time taken}}$$

or $$S = \frac{D}{T}$$

It follows that $$D = ST$$

i.e. $$\text{distance} = \text{average speed} \times \text{time}$$

and $$T = \frac{D}{S}$$

i.e. $$\text{time} = \frac{\text{distance}}{\text{average speed}}$$

Exercise 13b

> Find the average speed, in km/h, for a journey of 24 kilometres in 36 minutes.
>
> The distance travelled is 24 km.
>
> The time taken is 36 minutes $= \frac{36}{60}$ h $= \frac{3}{5}$ h
>
> $$\text{Average speed} = \frac{\text{distance}}{\text{time}}$$
>
> $$= \frac{24 \text{ km}}{\frac{3}{5} \text{ h}}$$
>
> $$= 24 \times \frac{5}{3} \text{ km/h}$$
>
> i.e.   average speed $= 40$ km/h

Find the average speed, in km/h, for a journey of:

1. 180 km in 3 hours

2. 75 km in $2\frac{1}{2}$ hours

3. 12 km in 20 minutes

4. 99 km in 66 minutes

5. 27 km in $1\frac{1}{2}$ hours

6. 175 km in 40 minutes

Find the average speed, in m.p.h., for a journey of:

7. 200 miles in 4 hours

8. 12 miles in $1\frac{1}{2}$ hours

9. 30 miles in 40 minutes

10. 90 miles in 100 minutes

> How far will a car travel in 45 minutes at an average speed of 56 m.p.h.?
>
> Average speed is 56 m.p.h.
>
> Time taken is 45 minutes $= \frac{45}{60}$ h $= \frac{3}{4}$ h
>
> $$\text{Distance travelled} = \text{average speed} \times \text{time}$$
>
> $$= 56 \times \frac{3}{4} \text{ miles}$$
>
> $$= 42 \text{ miles}$$

How far will a car travel:

11. In 4 hours at an average speed of 65 m.p.h.?

12. In $2\frac{1}{2}$ hours at an average speed of 32 m.p.h.?

13. In 50 minutes at an average speed of 186 km/h?

14. In 15 minutes at an average speed of 324 m.p.h.?

How long will it take to travel 77 km at 140 km/h?

$$\text{Time taken} = \frac{\text{distance travelled}}{\text{average speed}}$$

$$= \frac{77}{140} \text{ hours}$$

$$= 0.55 \text{ hours}$$

$$= 0.55 \times 60 \text{ minutes}$$

$$= 33 \text{ minutes}$$

How long will it take to travel:

15. 96 km at an average speed of 32 km/h?

16. 135 miles at an average speed of 27 m.p.h.?

17. 4 km at an average speed of 12 km/h?

18. 27 miles at an average speed of 36 m.p.h.?

PROBLEMS

Exercise 13c

Adrian lives on a farm. To go to school he walks one kilometre to the bus stop at an average speed of 6 km/h and immediately gets on the bus. He spends 20 minutes on the bus, which is travelling at an average speed of 39 km/h, before he arrives at school.

(a) How far does he travel on the bus?

(b) How long, in hours, does he take to go from home to school?

(c) What is his average speed for the whole journey?

(We must work in the same units throughout and we will use kilometres and hours.)

(a) Time spent on the bus is 20 minutes $= \frac{20}{60}$ h $= \frac{1}{3}$ h

Distance travelled on bus = average speed × time

$$= 39 \times \frac{1}{3} \text{ km}$$

$$= 13 \text{ km}$$

(b) Time spent walking $= \dfrac{\text{distance walked}}{\text{average walking speed}}$

$$= \dfrac{1\,\text{km}}{6\,\text{km/h}}$$

$$= \tfrac{1}{6}\,\text{h}$$

Total journey time $=$ time walking $+$ time on bus

$$= \left(\tfrac{1}{6} + \tfrac{1}{3}\right)\text{h}$$

$$= \tfrac{1}{2}\,\text{h}$$

(c) Average speed for the journey $= \dfrac{\text{total distance}}{\text{total time}}$

$$= \dfrac{(1 + 13)\,\text{km}}{\tfrac{1}{2}\,\text{h}}$$

$$= 14 \times \tfrac{2}{1}\,\text{km/h}$$

$$= 28\,\text{km/h}$$

When solving problems it is particularly important to remember that you should never add or subtract average speeds. Always consider total distances and total times.

1. A cyclist travels the 20 kilometres from St Peter to St Michael at an average speed of 30 km/h and immediately continues the journey to St Andrew, which is a further 40 kilometres away, at an average speed of 20 km/h. Find the average speed for the whole journey.

2. A motorist travels for one hour at an average speed of 80 km/h and then for two hours at an average speed of 110 km/h. Find his average speed for the whole journey.

3. For the first 50 km of its journey a train travels at an average speed of 100 km/h, for the next 50 km at an average speed of 200 km/h and for the last 40 km at an average speed of 160 km/h. Find its average speed for the whole journey.

4. Jean jogs $\tfrac{2}{3}$ km at 12 km/h and then walks $1\tfrac{1}{3}$ km at 8 km/h. Find her average speed for the whole journey.

In New York a train is scheduled to make a 120 km journey at an average speed of 150 km/h. It leaves three minutes late and its average speed is increased so that it arrives on time. What is the increased average speed?

Time taken if train leaves on time $= \dfrac{\text{distance travelled}}{\text{average speed}}$

$$= \tfrac{120}{150}\ \text{hours}$$

$$= \tfrac{4}{5} \times 60\ \text{minutes}$$

$$= 48\ \text{minutes}$$

If the train leaves three minutes late it must complete the journey in 45 minutes, i.e. $\frac{45}{60}$ hours $= \frac{3}{4}$ hour

$$\text{Average speed} = \frac{\text{distance travelled}}{\text{time taken}}$$

$$= \frac{120 \text{ km}}{\frac{3}{4} \text{ hours}}$$

$$= 120 \times \frac{4}{3} \text{ km/h}$$

$$= 160 \text{ km/h}$$

5. A coach is scheduled to make a 60 km journey at an average speed of 80 km/h. If it leaves five minutes late, what must its average speed be increased to, so that it arrives on time?

6. The distance from Georgetown to New Amsterdam is 110 km. A bus is due to leave Georgetown at 08.20 and to arrive in New Amsterdam at 10.26. If it leaves Georgetown six minutes late, find its average speed if it is to arrive on time.

7. I normally drive the 20 km to school at an average speed of 60 km/h. If I am five minutes late leaving home, calculate my average speed if I am to arrive on time.

8. A continental holiday maker is motoring at a steady 20 m/s oblivious to the world. When he is 500 m from an unmanned railway crossing an express train, 100 m long, is travelling towards the crossing at a steady 45 m/s, and is 1 km from it. Which of the following happens?

 (a) The car crosses safely before the train arrives.

 (b) There is an unfortunate accident.

 (c) The train passes through the crossing before the car reaches it.

MATHS IS OUT THERE

Did you ever find the meaning of TRISKAIDEKAPHOBIA? We have come to the end of Chapter 13. If the number 13 did not cause you any fear, then you do not suffer from triskaidekaphobia, which means 'the fear of the number 13'.

'Thirteen' is usually associated with awkwardness and bad luck. For this reason many buildings do not have a 13th floor.

ALGEBRAIC PRODUCTS

At the end of the chapter you should be able to:

1. Calculate the product of expressions in two brackets each of which contains two terms.
2. Square an expression of the form $(ax + b)$.

BRACKETS

Remember that $\quad 5(x + 1) = 5x + 5$

and that $\qquad 4x(y + z) = 4xy + 4xz$

Exercise 14a

Expand:

1. $2(x + 1)$

2. $3(x - 1)$

3. $4(x + 3)$

4. $5(a + 4)$

5. $3(b + 7)$

6. $3(1 - a)$

7. $5(1 - b)$

8. $2(3a - 1)$

9. $4(2 + 3b)$

10. $5a(b - c)$

11. $4a(b - 2c)$

12. $3a(2a + b)$

13. $5x(3y + z)$

14. $4y(4x + 3z)$

15. $2n(3p - 5q)$

16. $8r(2t - s)$

17. $3a(b - 5c)$

18. $4x(3y + 2z)$

THE PRODUCT OF TWO BRACKETS

Frequently, we wish to find the product of two brackets, each of which contains two terms, e.g. $(a + b)(c + d)$. The meaning of this product is that each term in the first bracket has to be multiplied by each term in the second bracket.

Always multiply the brackets together in the following order:

1. the first terms in the brackets
2. the outside terms
3. the inside terms
4. the second terms in the brackets.

Thus

$$(a+b)(c+d) = ac + ad + bc + bd$$

Exercise 14b

Expand $(x+2y)(2y-z)$

$$(x+2y)(2y-z) = 2xy - xz + 4y^2 - 2yz$$

Expand:

1. $(a+b)(c+d)$

2. $(p+q)(s+t)$

3. $(2a+b)(c+2d)$

4. $(5x+2y)(z+3)$

5. $(x+y)(z-4)$

6. $(a-b)(c+d)$

7. $(x+y)(y+z)$

8. $(2a+b)(3c+d)$

9. $(5x+4y)(z+2)$

10. $(3x-2y)(5-z)$

11. $(p+q)(2s-3t)$

12. $(a-2b)(c-d)$

13. $(6u-5v)(w-5r)$

14. $(3a+4b)(2c-3d)$

15. $(3x+2y)(3z+2)$

16. $(3p-q)(4r-3s)$

17. $(3a-4b)(3c+4d)$

18. $(7x-2y)(3-2z)$

19. $(2a+b)(5c-2)$

20. $(5a-4b)(3-2d)$

We get a slightly simpler form when we find the product of two brackets such as $(x+2)$ and $(x+3)$,
i.e. using the order we chose earlier

$$(x+2)(x+3) = x^2 + 3x + 2x + 6$$

$$= x^2 + 5x + 6 \quad (\text{since } ② \text{ and } ③ \text{ are like terms})$$

i.e. $\qquad (x+2)(x+3) = x^2 + 5x + 6$

Exercise 14c

Expand:

1. $(x+3)(x+4)$

2. $(x+2)(x+4)$

3. $(x+1)(x+6)$

4. $(x+5)(x+2)$

5. $(x+8)(x+3)$

<u>6.</u> $(a+4)(a+5)$

<u>7.</u> $(b+2)(b+7)$

<u>8.</u> $(c+4)(c+6)$

<u>9.</u> $(p+3)(p+12)$

<u>10.</u> $(q+7)(q+10)$

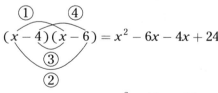

Expand $(x-4)(x-6)$

$$(x-4)(x-6) = x^2 - 6x - 4x + 24$$

$$= x^2 - 10x + 24$$

Expand:

11. $(x-2)(x-3)$

12. $(x-5)(x-7)$

13. $(a-2)(a-8)$

14. $(x-10)(x-3)$

15. $(b-5)(b-5)$

<u>16.</u> $(x-3)(x-4)$

<u>17.</u> $(x-4)(x-8)$

<u>18.</u> $(b-4)(b-2)$

<u>19.</u> $(a-4)(a-4)$

<u>20.</u> $(p-7)(p-8)$

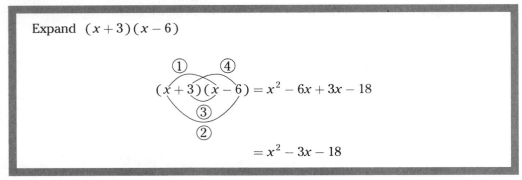

Expand $(x+3)(x-6)$

$$(x+3)(x-6) = x^2 - 6x + 3x - 18$$

$$= x^2 - 3x - 18$$

Expand:

21. $(x+3)(x-2)$

22. $(x-4)(x+5)$

23. $(x-7)(x+4)$

24. $(a+3)(a-10)$

25. $(p+5)(p-5)$

26. $(x+7)(x-2)$

27. $(x-5)(x+6)$

28. $(x+10)(x-1)$

29. $(b-8)(b-7)$

30. $(z-1)(z-12)$

FINDING THE PATTERN

You may have noticed in the previous exercise, that when you expanded the brackets and simplified the answers, there was a definite pattern,

e.g.
$$(x+5)(x+9) = x^2 + 9x + 5x + 45$$
$$= x^2 + 14x + 45$$

We could have written it
$$(x+5)(x+9) = x^2 + (9+5)x + (5) \times (9)$$
$$= x^2 + 14x + 45$$

Similarly
$$(x+4)(x-7) = x^2 + (-7+4)x + (4) \times (-7)$$
$$= x^2 - 3x - 28$$

and
$$(x-3)(x-8) = x^2 + (-8-3)x + (-3) \times (-8)$$
$$= x^2 - 11x + 24$$

In each case there is a pattern:
the *product* of the two numbers in the brackets gives the number term in the expansion, while *collecting* them gives the number of *x*s.

Exercise 14d

Use the pattern given above to expand the following products:

1. $(x+4)(x+5)$

2. $(a+2)(a+5)$

3. $(x-4)(x-5)$

4. $(a-2)(a-5)$

5. $(x+8)(x+6)$

6. $(a+10)(a+7)$

7. $(x-8)(x-6)$

8. $(a-10)(a-7)$

9. $(a+2)(a-5)$

10. $(y-6)(y+3)$

11. $(z+4)(z-10)$

12. $(p+5)(p-8)$

13. $(a-10)(a+7)$

14. $(y+10)(y-2)$

15. $(z-12)(z+1)$

16. $(p+2)(p-13)$

17. $(x-5)(x-1)$

18. $(b+9)(b+7)$

19. $(a+4)(a-4)$

20. $(r-14)(r+2)$

21. $(p+12)(p+2)$

22. $(t+5)(t-12)$

23. $(c-5)(c+8)$

24. $(x+5)(x-5)$

The pattern is similar when the brackets are slightly more complicated.

Exercise 14e

Expand the product $(2x+3)(x+2)$

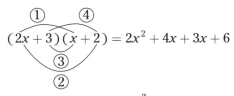

$$= 2x^2 + 7x + 6$$

Expand the following products:

1. $(2x+1)(x+1)$

2. $(x+2)(5x+2)$

3. $(5x+2)(x+3)$

4. $(3x+4)(x+5)$

5. $(3x+2)(x+1)$

6. $(x+3)(3x+2)$

7. $(4x+3)(x+1)$

8. $(7x+2)(x+3)$

Expand the product $(3x - 2)(2x + 5)$

$$(3x - 2)(2x + 5) = 6x^2 + 15x - 4x - 10$$

$$= 6x^2 + 11x - 10$$

Expand:

9. $(3x + 2)(2x + 3)$

10. $(4x - 3)(3x - 4)$

11. $(5x + 6)(2x - 3)$

12. $(7a - 3)(3a - 7)$

13. $(5x + 3)(2x + 5)$

14. $(7x - 2)(3x - 2)$

15. $(3x - 2)(4x + 1)$

16. $(3b + 5)(2b - 5)$

17. $(2a + 3)(2a - 3)$

18. $(3b - 7)(3b + 7)$

19. $(7y - 5)(7y + 5)$

20. $(5a + 4)(4a - 3)$

21. $(4x + 3)(4x - 3)$

22. $(5y - 2)(5y + 2)$

23. $(3x - 1)(3x + 1)$

24. $(4x - 7)(4x + 5)$

Expand $(3x - 2)(5 - 2x)$

$$(3x - 2)(5 - 2x) = 15x - 6x^2 - 10 + 4x$$

$$= 19x - 6x^2 - 10$$

$$= -6x^2 + 19x - 10$$

Expand:

25. $(2x + 1)(1 + 3x)$

26. $(5x + 2)(2 - x)$

27. $(6x - 1)(3 - x)$

28. $(5a - 2)(3 - 7a)$

29. $(3x + 2)(4 - x)$

30. $(4x - 5)(3 + x)$

31. $(5x + 2)(4 + 3x)$

32. $(7x + 4)(3 - 2x)$

33. $(4x - 3)(3 - 5x)$

34. $(3 - p)(4 + p)$

35. $(x - 5)(2 + x)$

36. $(4x - 3)(3 + x)$

IMPORTANT PRODUCTS

Three very important products are:

$$(x+a)^2 = (x+a)(x+a)$$
$$= x^2 + xa + ax + a^2$$
$$= x^2 + 2ax + a^2 \quad (\text{since } xa \text{ is the same as } ax)$$

i.e. $\quad (x+a)^2 = x^2 + 2ax + a^2$

so $\quad (x+3)^2 = x^2 + 6x + 9$

$$(x-a)^2 = (x-a)(x-a)$$
$$= x^2 - xa - ax + a^2$$

i.e. $\quad (x-a)^2 = x^2 - 2ax + a^2$

so $\quad (x-4)^2 = x^2 - 8x + 16$

$$(x+a)(x-a) = x^2 - xa + ax - a^2$$
$$= x^2 - a^2$$

i.e. $\quad (x+a)(x-a) = x^2 - a^2$

and $\quad (x-a)(x+a) = x^2 - a^2$

so $\quad (x+5)(x-5) = x^2 - 25$

and $\quad (x-3)(x+3) = x^2 - 9$

You should learn these three results thoroughly, for they will appear time and time again. Given the left-hand side you should know the right-hand side and vice versa.

Exercise 14f

Expand $(x+5)^2$

$$(x+5)^2 = x^2 + 10x + 25$$

Expand:

1. $(x+1)^2$ **3.** $(a+3)^2$ **5.** $(t+10)^2$ **7.** $(x+8)^2$

2. $(x+2)^2$ **4.** $(b+4)^2$ **6.** $(x+12)^2$ **8.** $(p+7)^2$

9. $(x+y)^2$ **11.** $(c+d)^2$ **13.** $(p+q)^2$ **15.** $(e+f)^2$

10. $(y+z)^2$ **12.** $(m+n)^2$ **14.** $(a+b)^2$ **16.** $(u+v)^2$

Expand $(2x+3)^2$

$$(2x+3)^2 = (2x)^2 + 2(2x)(3) + (3)^2$$

i.e. $$(2x+3)^2 = 4x^2 + 12x + 9$$

Expand:

17. $(2x+1)^2$ **19.** $(5x+2)^2$ **21.** $(3a+1)^2$ **23.** $(3a+4)^2$

18. $(4b+1)^2$ **20.** $(6c+1)^2$ **22.** $(2x+5)^2$ **24.** $(4y+3)^2$

Expand $(2x+3y)^2$

$$(2x+3y)^2 = (2x)^2 + 2(2x)(3y) + (3y)^2$$

i.e. $$(2x+3y)^2 = 4x^2 + 12xy + 9y^2$$

Expand:

25. $(x+2y)^2$ **27.** $(2x+5y)^2$ **29.** $(3a+b)^2$ **31.** $(7x+2y)^2$

26. $(3x+y)^2$ **28.** $(3a+2b)^2$ **30.** $(p+4q)^2$ **32.** $(3s+4t)^2$

Expand $(x-5)^2$

$$(x-5)^2 = x^2 - 10x + 25$$

Expand:

33. $(x-2)^2$ **35.** $(a-10)^2$ **37.** $(x-3)^2$ **39.** $(a-b)^2$

34. $(x-6)^2$ **36.** $(x-y)^2$ **38.** $(x-7)^2$ **40.** $(u-v)^2$

Expand $(2x-7)^2$

$$(2x-7)^2 = (2x)^2 + 2(2x)(-7) + (-7)^2$$

i.e. $$(2x-7)^2 = 4x^2 - 28x + 49$$

Expand:

41. $(3x-1)^2$ **43.** $(10a-9)^2$ **45.** $(2a-1)^2$ **47.** $(7b-2)^2$

42. $(5z-1)^2$ **44.** $(4x-3)^2$ **46.** $(4y-1)^2$ **48.** $(5x-3)^2$

Expand $(7a-4b)^2$

$$(7a-4b)^2 = (7a)^2 + 2(7a)(-4b) + (-4b)^2$$

i.e. $$(7a-4b)^2 = 49a^2 - 56ab + 16b^2$$

Expand:

49. $(2y-x)^2$ **51.** $(3m-2n)^2$ **53.** $(a-3b)^2$ **55.** $(5a-2b)^2$

50. $(5x-y)^2$ **52.** $(7x-3y)^2$ **54.** $(m-8n)^2$ **56.** $(3p-5q)^2$

THE DIFFERENCE BETWEEN TWO SQUARES

Exercise 14g

Expand (a) $(a+2)(a-2)$ (b) $(2x+3)(2x-3)$

(a) $(a+2)(a-2) = a^2 - 4$
(b) $(2x+3)(2x-3) = 4x^2 - 9$

Expand:

1. $(x+4)(x-4)$ **9.** $(2x-1)(2x+1)$

2. $(b+6)(b-6)$ **10.** $(3x+1)(3x-1)$

3. $(c-3)(c+3)$ **11.** $(7a+2)(7a-2)$

4. $(x+12)(x-12)$ **12.** $(5a-4)(5a+4)$

5. $(x+5)(x-5)$ **13.** $(5x+1)(5x-1)$

6. $(a-7)(a+7)$ **14.** $(2a-3)(2a+3)$

7. $(q+10)(q-10)$ **15.** $(10m-1)(10m+1)$

8. $(x-8)(x+8)$ **16.** $(6a+5)(6a-5)$

Expand $(3x + 2y)(3x - 2y)$

$$(3x + 2y)(3x - 2y) = (3x)^2 - (2y)^2$$
$$= 9x^2 - 4y^2$$

Expand:

17. $(3x + 4y)(3x - 4y)$

18. $(2a - 5b)(2a + 5b)$

19. $(1 - 2a)(1 + 2a)$

20. $(7y + 3z)(7y - 3z)$

21. $(10a - 9b)(10a + 9b)$

22. $(5a - 4b)(5a + 4b)$

23. $(1 + 3x)(1 - 3x)$

24. $(3 - 5x)(3 + 5x)$

25. $(5m + 8n)(5m - 8n)$

26. $(6p - 7q)(6p + 7q)$

The results from this exercise are very important when written the other way around,

i.e. $a^2 - b^2 = (a + b)(a - b)$

We refer to this as 'factorising the difference between two squares' and we will deal with it in detail in the next chapter.

HARDER EXPANSIONS

Exercise 14h

Simplify $(x + 2)(x + 5) + 2x(x + 7)$

$$(x + 2)(x + 5) + 2x(x + 7) = x^2 + 5x + 2x + 10 + 2x^2 + 14x$$
$$= 3x^2 + 21x + 10$$

Simplify:

1. $(x + 3)(x + 4) + x(x + 2)$

2. $x(x + 6) + (x + 1)(x + 2)$

3. $(x + 4)(x + 5) + 6(x + 2)$

4. $(a - 6)(a - 5) + 2(a + 3)$

5. $(a - 5)(2a + 3) - 3(a - 4)$

6. $(x + 3)(x + 5) + 5(x + 2)$

7. $(x - 3)(x + 4) - 3(x + 3)$

8. $(x + 7)(x - 5) - 4(x - 3)$

9. $(2x + 1)(3x - 4) + (2x + 3)(5x - 2)$

10. $(5x - 2)(3x + 5) - (3x + 5)(x + 2)$

Expand $(xy - z)^2$

$$(xy - z)^2 = (xy)^2 - 2(xy)(z) + z^2$$

i.e. $$(xy - z)^2 = x^2 y^2 - 2xyz + z^2$$

Expand:

11. $(xy - 3)^2$ **14.** $(3pq + 8)^2$ **17.** $(6 - pq)^2$

12. $(5 - yz)^2$ **15.** $(a - bc)^2$ **18.** $(mn + 3)^2$

13. $(xy + 4)^2$ **16.** $(ab - 2)^2$ **19.** $(uv - 2w)^2$

SUMMARY

The following is a summary of the most important types of examples considered in this chapter that will be required in future work.

1. $2(3x + 4) = 6x + 8$

2. $(x + 2)(x + 3) = x^2 + 5x + 6$

3. $(x - 2)(x - 3) = x^2 - 5x + 6$

4. $(x - 2)(x + 3) = x^2 + x - 6$

5. $(2x + 1)(3x + 2) = 6x^2 + 7x + 2$

6. $(2x - 1)(3x - 2) = 6x^2 - 7x + 2$

7. $(2x + 1)(3x - 2) = 6x^2 - x - 2$

Note that   (a) if the signs in the brackets are the same, i.e. both + or both −, then the number term is +
(numbers **2, 3, 5** and **6**)

whereas   (b) if the signs in the brackets are different, i.e. one + and one −, then the number term is −
(numbers **4** and **7**)

(c) the middle term is given by collecting the product of the outside terms in the brackets and the product of the inside terms in the brackets,

i.e.   in **2** the middle term is $3x + 2x$ or $5x$

in **3** the middle term is $-3x - 2x$ or $-5x$

in **4** the middle term is $3x - 2x$ or x

in **5** the middle term is $4x + 3x$ or $7x$

in **6** the middle term is $-4x - 3x$ or $-7x$

in **7** the middle term is $-4x + 3x$ or $-x$.

Most important of all we must remember the general expansions:

$$(x+a)^2 = x^2 + 2ax + a^2$$
$$(x-a)^2 = x^2 - 2ax + a^2$$
$$(x+a)(x-a) = x^2 - a^2$$

MIXED EXERCISES

Exercise 14i

Expand:

1. $5(x+2)$

2. $8p(3q-2r)$

3. $(3a+b)(2a-5b)$

4. $(4x+1)(3x-5)$

5. $(x+6)(x+10)$

6. $(x-8)(x-12)$

7. $(4y+3)(4y-7)$

8. $(4y-9)(4y+9)$

9. $(5x+2)^2$

10. $(2a-7b)^2$

Exercise 14j

Expand:

1. $4(2-5x)$

2. $8a(2-3a)$

3. $(4a+3)(3a-11)$

4. $(x+11)(x-9)$

5. $(2x+5)(1-10x)$

6. $(y+2z)^2$

7. $(6y-z)(6y+5z)$

8. $(4a+1)^2$

9. $(5a-7)^2$

10. $(6z-13y)^2$

Exercise 14k

Expand:

1. $3(2-a)$

2. $4a(2b+c)$

3. $(5a+2b)(2c+5d)$

4. $(x-7)(x-12)$

5. $(a+7)(a+9)$

6. $(a+4)(a-5)$

7. $(3x+1)(2x+3)$

8. $(5x-2)(5x+2)$

9. $(3x-7)^2$

10. $(5x+2y)(5x-2y)$

Exercise 14I

Expand:

1. $5(3-x)$

2. $12x(3x-2)$

3. $3x(2y-5z)$

4. $(a-b)(c+d)$

5. $(x+7)(x-4)$

6. $(x-9)(x-2)$

7. $(4x+1)(3x+2)$

8. $(x-4y)^2$

9. $(2x+7z)^2$

10. $(1-5a)(1+5a)$

MATHS IS OUT THERE

What do you call two students who cheat on mathematics tests?
Co-efficients!

How would you wake up twenty mathematics students living on a farm?
By roster.

First exponent. Will you give me a loan?
Second exponent. If it's within my power.

ALGEBRAIC FACTORS

At the end of the chapter you should be able to factorise expressions of the form:

1. $ax + ab$
2. $ax^2 - bx$
3. $ax^2 + bx + c$
4. $a^2x^2 - b^2y^2$
5. $ax + ay + bx + by$

FINDING FACTORS

In a previous chapter we removed brackets and expanded expressions. Frequently we need to be able to do the reverse, i.e. to find the factors of an expression. This is called *factorising*.

COMMON FACTORS

In the expression $7a + 14b$ we could write the first term as $7 \times a$ and the second term as $7 \times 2b$,

i.e. $\qquad 7a + 14b = 7 \times a + 7 \times 2b$

The 7 is a common factor.
However we already know that $7(a + 2b) = 7 \times a + 7 \times 2b$

$\therefore \qquad 7a + 14b = 7 \times a + 7 \times 2b = 7(a + 2b)$

Exercise 15a

Factorise $3x - 12$

$$3x - 12 = 3(x - 4)$$

Factorise:

1. $4x + 4$

2. $12x - 3$

3. $6a + 2$

4. $5a - 10b$ **6.** $10a - 5$ **8.** $2a + 4b$

5. $3t - 9$ **7.** $12a + 4$ **9.** $14x - 7$

Factorise $x^2 - 7x$

$$x^2 - 7x = x \times x - 7 \times x$$
$$= x(x - 7)$$

Factorise:

10. $x^2 + 2x$ **13.** $2x^2 + x$ **16.** $x^2 - 4x$

11. $x^2 - 7x$ **14.** $4t - 2t^2$ **17.** $b^2 + 4b$

12. $a^2 + 6a$ **15.** $x^2 + 5x$ **18.** $4a^2 - a$

Factorise $9ab + 12bc$

$$9ab + 12bc = 3b \times 3a + 3b \times 4c$$
$$= 3b(3a + 4c)$$

Factorise:

19. $2x^2 - 6x$ **22.** $12x^2 + 16x$ **25.** $2a^2 - 12a$

20. $2z^3 + 4z$ **23.** $5ab - 10bc$ **26.** $6p^2 + 2p$

21. $25a^2 - 5a$ **24.** $3y^2 + 27y$ **27.** $9y^2 - 6y$

Factorise $ab + 2bc + bd$

$$ab + 2bc + bd = b(a + 2c + d)$$

Factorise:

28. $2x^2 + 4x + 6$ **33.** $3x^2 - 6x + 9$

29. $10a^2 - 5a + 20$ **34.** $4a^2 + 8a - 4$

30. $ab + 4bc - 3bd$ **35.** $5xy + 4xz + 3x$

31. $8x - 4y + 12z$ **36.** $5ab + 10bc + 5bd$

32. $9ab - 6ac - 3ad$ **37.** $2xy - 4yz + 8yw$

Factorise $8x^3 - 4x^2$

$$8x^3 - 4x^2 = 4x^2(2x - 1)$$

Factorise:

38. $x^3 + x^2$ **40.** $20a^2 - 5a^3$ **42.** $4x^4 + 12x^2$ **44.** $b^3 - b^2$ **46.** $27a^2 - 18a^3$

39. $x^2 - x^3$ **41.** $12x^3 - 16x^2$ **43.** $a^2 + a^3$ **45.** $4x^3 - 2x^2$ **47.** $10x^2 - 15x^4$

Factorise:

48. $12x + 8$

49. $8x^2 + 12x$

50. $9x^2 - 6x + 12$

51. $5x^3 - 10x$

52. $8pq + 4qr$

53. $x^2 - 8x$

54. $12 + 9y^2$

55. $12xy + 16xz + 8x$

56. $4x^3 + 6x$

57. $12abc - 8bcd$

Factorise (a) $2\pi r^2 + 2\pi rh$ (b) $\frac{1}{2}Mu^2 - \frac{1}{2}mu^2$

(a) $2\pi r^2 + 2\pi rh = 2\pi r(r + h)$

(b) $\frac{1}{2}Mu^2 - \frac{1}{2}mu^2 = \frac{1}{2}u^2(M - m)$

Factorise:

58. $\frac{1}{2}ah + \frac{1}{2}bh$

59. $mg - ma$

60. $\frac{1}{2}mv^2 + \frac{1}{2}mu^2$

61. $P + \dfrac{PRT}{100}$

62. $2\pi r^2 + \pi rh$

63. $\pi R^2 + \pi r^2$

64. $2gh_1 - 2gh_2$

65. $\frac{1}{2}mv^2 - mgh$

66. $\frac{4}{3}\pi r^3 - \frac{1}{3}\pi r^2 h$

67. $3\pi r^2 + 2\pi rh$

68. $\frac{1}{2}mu^2 + \frac{1}{2}mu$

69. $\frac{1}{2}bc - \frac{1}{4}ca$

FACTORISING BY GROUPING

The expression $ax + ay + bx + by$ can be factorised by grouping the terms in pairs. If we group the first two terms followed by the remaining two terms, we have a common factor for the first two terms and a different common factor for the remaining two terms

i.e. $\overbrace{ax + ay} + \overbrace{bx + by} = a(x+y) + b(x+y)$

We can think of this as $aB + bB$, where B stands for $(x+y)$.

We have reduced the original four terms to two terms and these two terms now have the bracket B as a common factor.

Therefore $\overbrace{ax + ay} + \overbrace{bx + by} = a(x+y) + b(x+y)$

$$= aB + bB$$

$$= B(a+b)$$

$$= (x+y)(a+b)$$

If, on the other hand, we pair the first and third terms followed by the remaining terms we have

$$ax + ay + bx + by = x(a+b) + y(a+b)$$

$$= (a+b)(x+y)$$

This shows that, while it is often possible to pair the terms with a common factor in more than one way, the result is the same. Always check your factors by multiplying out.

Exercise 15b

Factorise $xy + 2x + 3y + 6$

$$\overbrace{xy + 2x} + \overbrace{3y + 6} = xy + 2x \quad (\text{common factor } x)$$

$$+ 3y + 6 \quad (\text{common factor } 3)$$

$$= x(y+2) + 3(y+2)$$

$$\qquad\qquad (\text{common factor } y+2)$$

$$= (y+2)(x+3)$$

Alternatively

$$xy + 2x + 3y + 6 = y(x+3) + 2(x+3)$$

$$= (x+3)(y+2)$$

Factorise the following expressions by grouping:

1. $xy + 3x + 3y + 9$

2. $a + ab + 2b + 2b^2$

3. $a^2 + ab + ac + bc$

4. $xy - 3y + 2x - 6$

5. $xz + z + xy + y$

6. $xy + 4x + 2y + 8$

7. $ac + 4a + bc + 4b$

8. $xy - 2x + 4y - 8$

9. $pr + ps + qr + qs$

10. $xy - 3y + 4x - 12$

11. $xy - 5x + 2y - 10$

12. $pr - ps + qr - qs$

13. $ab - 3a + 2b - 6$

14. $pr - qr + ps - qs$

15. $2p + pq + 4q + 8$

16. $6 + 2b + 3a + ab$

Factorise $2x - 2xy - y + y^2$

$$2x - \overgroup{2xy - y} + y^2 = 2x(1 - y) - y(1 - y)$$
$$= (1 - y)(2x - y)$$

Factorise:

17. $pr - ps - qr + qs$

18. $9a - 3b - 3ab + b^2$

19. $2a - b - 2ab + b^2$

20. $a^2 + 2ab - 2a - 4b$

21. $6 - 3x - 2y + xy$

22. $4a^2 - ab - 8a + 2b$

23. $6a^2 - 9a - 2ab + 3b$

24. $2m - 3n - 2mn + 3n^2$

25. $t^2 + tr + st + sr$

26. $x^2 - x + xy - y$

27. $4a - 4a^2 + 2b - 2ab$

28. $x - xy + y - y^2$

29. $4a + 6b - 6a^2 - 9ab$

30. $2a^2 + 2ab + bc + ac$

31. $4x - 4xy + 2y - 2y^2$

32. $xy + xz + y^2 + yz$

Factorise $ac - ad + bd - bc$

$$\overgroup{ac - ad} + \overgroup{bd - bc} = a(c - d) + b(d - c)$$
$$= a(c - d) - b(c - d)$$
$$= (c - d)(a - b)$$

Factorise:

33. $5x - xy + 2y - 10$　　　**35.** $xy - xz - 3z + 3y$　　　**37.** $6 - 2b + ab - 3a$

34. $ab - 3a - 12 + 4b$　　　**36.** $2p - pq + 4q - 8$　　　**38.** $3a - ab + 4b - 12$

Factorise $a^2 - ab + a - b$

$$a^2 \overset{\frown}{-ab} + a \overset{\frown}{- b} = a(a - b) + 1(a - b)$$
$$= (a - b)(a + 1)$$

Factorise:

39. $m^2 + mn + m + n$　　　**41.** $2p^2 - 4pq + p - 2q$　　　**43.** $a^2 + ab + a + b$

40. $a^2 - ab + a - b$　　　**42.** $x - xy + 1 - y$　　　**44.** $a^2 - ab + a - b$

Factorise $a^2 + ab - a - b$

$$a^2 \overset{\frown}{+ ab} - a \overset{\frown}{- b} = a(a + b) - 1(a + b)$$
$$= (a + b)(a - 1)$$

Factorise:

45. $x^2 + xy - x - y$　　　　　　**49.** $3x^2 + xy - 3x - y$

46. $2a^2 + ab - 2a - b$　　　　　**50.** $2p^2 + 4pq - p - 2q$

47. $5x^2 + 10xy - x - 2y$　　　　**51.** $3a + b - 3a^2 - ab$

48. $mn - m - n + 1$　　　　　　**52.** $2x + y - 2xz - yz$

FACTORISING QUADRATIC EXPRESSIONS

The type of expression we are most likely to want to factorise is one of the form $ax^2 + bx + c$ where a, b and c are numbers.

To factorise such an expression we look for two brackets whose product is the original expression.

When we expanded $(x + 2)(x + 4)$ we had

$$(x + 2)(x + 4) = x^2 + 6x + 8$$

If we write $x^2 + 6x + 8 = (x + 2)(x + 4)$ we say we have factorised $x^2 + 6x + 8$,

i.e. just as $\quad 10$ is 2×5 so $x^2 + 6x + 8$ is $(x + 2) \times (x + 4)$.

To factorise an expression of the form $x^2 + 7x + 10$, i.e. where all the terms are positive, we remind ourselves of the patterns we observed in the previous chapter and summarised on pages 213–14.

We found when expanding brackets that:

(a) if the sign in each bracket is $+$ then the number term in the expansion is $+$

(b) the x^2 term comes from $x \times x$

(c) the number term in the expansion comes from multiplying the numbers in the brackets together

(d) the middle term, or x term in the expansion, comes from collecting the product of the outside terms in the brackets and the product of the inside terms in the brackets.

Using these ideas in reverse order

$$x^2 + 7x + 10 = (x +)(x +)$$
$$= (x + 2)(x + 5)$$

(choosing two numbers whose product is 10 and whose sum is 7).

Exercise 15c

> Factorise $x^2 + 8x + 15$
>
> $$x^2 + 8x + 15 = (x + 3)(x + 5) \text{ or } (x + 5)(x + 3)$$
>
> (The product of 3 and 5 is 15, and their sum is 8.)

Factorise:

1. $x^2 + 3x + 2$	6. $x^2 + 8x + 7$	11. $x^2 + 8x + 16$	16. $x^2 + 6x + 9$
2. $x^2 + 6x + 5$	7. $x^2 + 8x + 12$	12. $x^2 + 15x + 36$	17. $x^2 + 20x + 36$
3. $x^2 + 7x + 12$	8. $x^2 + 13x + 12$	13. $x^2 + 19x + 18$	18. $x^2 + 9x + 18$
4. $x^2 + 8x + 15$	9. $x^2 + 16x + 15$	14. $x^2 + 22x + 40$	19. $x^2 + 11x + 30$
5. $x^2 + 21x + 20$	10. $x^2 + 12x + 20$	15. $x^2 + 9x + 8$	20. $x^2 + 14x + 40$

To factorise an expression of the form $x^2 - 6x + 8$ remember the pattern:

(a) the numbers in the brackets must multiply to give $+8$, i.e. they must have the same sign. Since the middle term in the expression is $-$ they must both be $-$

(b) the x^2 term comes from $x \times x$

(c) the middle term, or x term, comes from collecting the product of the outside terms and the product of the inside terms.

Thus $\qquad x^2 - 6x + 8 = (x - 2)(x - 4)$

Since $\qquad (-2) \times (-4) = +8$

and $\qquad x \times (-4) + (-2) \times x = -4x - 2x = -6x$

Exercise 15d

> Factorise $x^2 - 7x + 12$
>
> $$x^2 - 7x + 12 = (x - 3)(x - 4)$$
>
> (The product of -3 and -4 is $+12$.
> The outside product is $-4x$ and the inside product is $-3x$.
> Collecting these gives $-7x$.)

Factorise:

1. $x^2 - 9x + 8$

2. $x^2 - 7x + 12$

3. $x^2 - 17x + 30$

4. $x^2 - 11x + 28$

5. $x^2 - 13x + 42$

6. $x^2 - 5x + 6$

7. $x^2 - 16x + 15$

8. $x^2 - 6x + 9$

9. $x^2 - 18x + 32$

10. $x^2 - 16x + 63$

Similarly $\qquad x^2 + x - 12 = (x + 4)(x - 3)$

If the number term in the expansion is negative the signs in the brackets are different.

Thus $\qquad (+4) \times (-3) = -12$

Working as before, the product of the outside terms is $-3x$
and the product of the inside terms is $+4x$

Therefore the total is $+x$.

Similarly $\qquad x^2 + 2x - 15 = (x + 5)(x - 3)$

or $\qquad x^2 + 2x - 15 = (x - 3)(x + 5)$

Exercise 15e

Factorise:

1. $x^2 - x - 6$

2. $x^2 + x - 20$

3. $x^2 - x - 12$

4. $x^2 + 3x - 28$

5. $x^2 + 2x - 15$

6. $x^2 - 2x - 24$

7. $x^2 + 6x - 27$

8. $x^2 - 9x - 22$

9. $x^2 - 2x - 35$

10. $x^2 - 8x - 20$

Most of the values in the previous three exercises have been easy to spot. Should you have difficulty, set out all possible pairs of numbers, as shown below, until you find the pair that gives the original expression when you multiply back.

Factorise

(a) $x^2 - 11x + 24$

(Because the number term is $+$ the two numbers in the brackets must have the same sign.)

Possible numbers		Sum
-1	-24	-25
-2	-12	-14
-3	-8	-11

$\therefore \qquad x^2 - 11x + 24 = (x - 3)(x - 8)$

(b) $x^2 + 5x - 24$

(Because the number term is $-$ the two numbers in the brackets have different signs)

Possible numbers		Sum
-1	$+24$	$+23$
-2	$+12$	$+10$
-3	$+8$	$+5$

$\therefore \qquad x^2 + 5x - 24 = (x - 3)(x + 8)$

Remember that a $+$ before the number term means that the signs in the brackets are the same, whereas a $-$ before the number term means that they are different.

Exercise 15f

Factorise:

1. $x^2 + 9x + 14$

2. $x^2 - 10x + 21$

3. $x^2 + 5x - 14$

4. $x^2 + x - 30$

5. $x^2 + 9x + 8$

6. $x^2 - 10x + 25$

7. $x^2 + 8x - 9$

8. $x^2 - 15x + 26$

9. $x^2 + x - 56$

10. $x^2 + 32x + 60$

11. $x^2 - 6x - 27$

12. $x^2 + 16x - 80$

13. $x^2 + 14x + 13$

14. $x^2 + 12x - 28$

15. $x^2 + 2x - 80$

16. $x^2 - 11x + 30$

17. $x^2 + 8x - 48$

18. $x^2 + 18x + 72$

19. $x^2 + 17x + 52$

20. $x^2 - 12x - 28$

21. $x^2 + 11x + 24$

22. $x^2 - 11x - 42$

23. $x^2 - 18x + 32$

24. $x^2 + 7x - 60$

Sometimes the terms need rearranging before we try to factorise.

Exercise 15g

Factorise $6 + x^2 - 5x$

$$6 + x^2 - 5x = x^2 - 5x + 6$$
$$= (x - 2)(x - 3)$$

Factorise:

1. $8 + x^2 + 9x$

2. $9 + x^2 - 6x$

3. $11x + 28 + x^2$

4. $20 - x^2 - x$

5. $9 + x^2 + 6x$

6. $8 + x^2 - 9x$

7. $17x + 30 + x^2$

8. $27 - 6x - x^2$

9. $x^2 + 22 + 13x$

10. $x^2 - 11x - 26$

11. $7 + x^2 - 8x$

12. $x + x^2 - 42$

13. $x^2 - 5x - 24$

14. $14 + x^2 - 9x$

15. $28x + 27 + x^2$

16. $2x - 63 + x^2$

Factorise $x^2 + 6x + 9$

$$x^2 + 6x + 9 = (x + 3)(x + 3)$$
$$= (x + 3)^2$$

Factorise:

17. $x^2 + 10x + 25$

18. $x^2 - 10x + 25$

19. $x^2 + 4x + 4$

20. $x^2 - 14x + 49$

21. $x^2 + 12x + 36$

22. $x^2 - 12x + 36$

23. $x^2 - 4x + 4$

24. $x^2 + 16x + 64$

Exercise 15h

Factorise $6 - 5x - x^2$

$$6 - 5x - x^2 = (6 + x)(1 - x)$$

Factorise:

1. $2 - x - x^2$

2. $6 + x - x^2$

3. $4 - 3x - x^2$

4. $8 + 2x - x^2$

5. $6 - x - x^2$

6. $2 + x - x^2$

7. $8 - 2x - x^2$

8. $5 - 4x - x^2$

9. $10 - 3x - x^2$

10. $12 + 4x - x^2$

11. $5 + 4x - x^2$

12. $14 - 5x - x^2$

13. $6 + 5x - x^2$

14. $20 - x - x^2$

15. $15 - 2x - x^2$

16. $12 + x - x^2$

THE DIFFERENCE BETWEEN TWO SQUARES

In the last chapter, one of the expansions we listed was

$$(x + a)(x - a) = x^2 - a^2$$

If we reverse this we have

$$x^2 - a^2 = (x + a)(x - a)$$
$$\text{or} \quad x^2 - a^2 = (x - a)(x + a)$$

(the order of multiplication of two brackets makes no difference to the result).

This result is known as *factorising the difference between two squares* and is *very important*.

When factorising do not confuse $x^2 - 4$ with $x^2 - 4x$.

$$x^2 - 4 = (x + 2)(x - 2)$$
whereas $\quad x^2 - 4x = x(x - 4)$ $\quad (4x$ is *not* a square)

Exercise 15i

Factorise $x^2 - 9$

$$x^2 - 9 = x^2 - 3^2$$
$$= (x + 3)(x - 3) \quad \text{or} \quad (x - 3)(x + 3)$$

Factorise:

1. $x^2 - 25$

2. $x^2 - 4$

3. $x^2 - 100$

4. $x^2 - 1$

5. $x^2 - 64$

6. $x^2 - 16$

7. $x^2 - 36$

8. $x^2 - 81$

9. $x^2 - 49$

Factorise $4 - x^2$

$$4 - x^2 = 2^2 - x^2$$
$$= (2 + x)(2 - x) \quad \text{or} \quad (2 - x)(2 + x)$$

Factorise:

10. $9 - x^2$

11. $36 - x^2$

12. $100 - x^2$

13. $a^2 - b^2$

14. $9y^2 - z^2$

15. $16 - x^2$

16. $25 - x^2$

17. $81 - x^2$

18. $x^2 - y^2$

We began this chapter by considering common factors. A little revision is now necessary followed by expressions of the form $ax^2 + bx + c$ where a is a common factor.

Exercise 15j

Factorise $12x - 6$

$$12x - 6 = 6(2x - 1)$$

Factorise:

1. $3x + 12$

2. $25x^2 + 10x$

3. $12x^2 - 8$

4. $14x + 21$

5. $4x^2 + 2$

6. $21x - 7$

7. $9x^2 - 18x$

8. $20x + 12$

9. $4x - 14$

10. $8x^2 - 4x$

Factorise $3x^2 + 9x + 6$

$$3x^2 + 9x + 6 = 3(x^2 + 3x + 2)$$
$$= 3(x + 1)(x + 2)$$

Factorise:

11. $2x^2 + 14x + 24$

12. $3x^2 - 27x + 24$

13. $7x^2 + 14x + 7$

14. $4x^2 - 4x - 48$

15. $5x^2 + 40x + 35$

16. $3x^2 + 24x + 36$

17. $4x^2 - 24x + 36$

18. $5x^2 - 5x - 30$

19. $2x^2 - 18x - 44$

20. $3x^2 + 9x - 120$

In the previous exercises we considered the factors of the expression $ax^2 + bx + c$ when either a was 1 or a was a common factor. We must now consider other values of a which mean that the two brackets do not both start with x.

When the coefficient of x^2 was 1 as in $x^2 + 7x + 10$, we chose two numbers whose product was $(1)(10)$ and whose sum was 7.

It can be shown that this condition is also required when the coefficient of x^2 is not 1. In order to factorise $ax^2 + bx + c$ we find two numbers whose product is ac and sum is b, for example, to factorise $6x^2 + 19x + 10$ we find two numbers whose product is $(6)(10) = 60$ and sum equals 19. These are 15 and 4. We then write

$$6x^2 + 19x + 10 = 6x^2 + 15x + 4x + 10$$
$$= (6x^2 + 15x) + (4x + 10)$$
$$= 3x(2x + 5) + 2(2x + 5)$$
$$= (2x + 5)(3x + 2)$$

Exercise 15k

Factorise:

1. $2x^2 + 3x + 1$
2. $3x^2 - 5x + 2$
3. $4x^2 + 7x + 3$
4. $2x^2 - 7x + 3$
5. $3x^2 + 13x + 4$

6. $3x^2 - 8x + 4$
7. $2x^2 + 9x + 4$
8. $5x^2 - 17x + 6$
9. $2x^2 + 11x + 12$
10. $7x^2 - 29x + 4$

11. $2x^2 - 3x - 2$
12. $3x^2 + x - 4$
13. $5x^2 - 13x - 6$
14. $4x^2 + 5x - 6$
15. $3x^2 + 10x - 8$

16. $7x^2 - 19x - 6$
17. $6x^2 - 7x - 10$
18. $5x^2 - 19x + 12$
19. $3x^2 - 11x - 20$
20. $4x^2 + 17x - 15$

After a little practice, you should be able to find the factors without going into too much detail.

Exercise 15l

Factorise:

1. $6x^2 + 7x + 2$
2. $6x^2 + 19x + 15$
3. $15x^2 + 11x + 2$
4. $12x^2 + 28x + 15$
5. $35x^2 + 24x + 4$

6. $6x^2 - 11x + 3$
7. $9x^2 - 18x + 8$
8. $16x^2 - 10x + 1$
9. $15x^2 - 44x + 21$
10. $20x^2 - 23x + 6$

11. $8x^2 - 10x - 3$
12. $15x^2 - x - 2$
13. $21x^2 + 2x - 8$
14. $80x^2 - 6x - 9$
15. $24x^2 + 17x - 20$

16. $6a^2 - a - 15$
17. $6t^2 - t - 2$
18. $9b^2 - 12b + 4$
19. $5x^2 - 7xy - 6y^2$
20. $4x^2 - 11x + 6$

Exercise 15m

Factorise $4x^2 - 9$

$$4x^2 - 9 = (2x)^2 - 3^2$$
$$= (2x + 3)(2x - 3)$$

Factorise:

1. $4x^2 - 25$

2. $9x^2 - 4$

3. $36a^2 - 1$

4. $16a^2 - b^2$

5. $9x^2 - 25$

6. $4a^2 - 1$

Factorise $4x^2 - 9y^2$

$$4x^2 - 9y^2 = (2x)^2 - (3y)^2$$
$$= (2x + 3y)(2x - 3y)$$

Factorise:

7. $16a^2 - 9b^2$

8. $25s^2 - 9t^2$

9. $100x^2 - 49y^2$

10. $9y^2 - 16z^2$

11. $4x^2 - 49y^2$

12. $81x^2 - 100y^2$

13. $9a^2 - 4b^2$

14. $64p^2 - 81q^2$

Factorise $2 - 18a^2$

$$2 - 18a^2 = 2(1 - 9a^2)$$
$$= 2(1^2 - (3a)^2)$$
$$= 2(1 + 3a)(1 - 3a)$$

Factorise:

15. $3a^2 - 27b^2$

16. $18t^2 - 50s^2$

17. $27x^2 - 3y^2$

18. $45x^2 - 20$

19. $5a^2 - 20$

20. $45 - 5b^2$

21. $\frac{1}{2}a^2 - 2b^2$

22. $\dfrac{a^2}{4} - \dfrac{b^2}{9}$

23. $27x^2 - \frac{1}{3}y^2$

24. $\dfrac{x^2}{16} - \dfrac{y^2}{25}$

CALCULATIONS USING FACTORISING

Exercise 15n

Find $1.7^2 + 0.3 \times 1.7$

$$1.7^2 + 0.3 \times 1.7 = 1.7(1.7 + 0.3)$$
$$= 1.7 \times 2$$
$$= 3.4$$

Find, without using a calculator:

1. $2.5^2 + 0.5 \times 2.5$

2. $1.3 \times 3.7 + 3.7^2$

3. $5.9^2 - 2.9 \times 5.9$

4. $8.76^2 - 4.76 \times 8.76$

5. $5.2^2 + 0.8 \times 5.2$

6. $2.6 \times 3.4 + 3.4^2$

7. $4.3^2 - 1.3 \times 4.3$

8. $16.27^2 - 5.27 \times 16.27$

Find $100^2 - 98^2$

$$100^2 - 98^2 = (100 + 98)(100 - 98)$$
$$= 198 \times 2$$
$$= 396$$

9. $55^2 - 45^2$

10. $20.6^2 - 9.4^2$

11. $7.82^2 - 2.82^2$

12. $2.667^2 - 1.333^2$

13. $10.2^2 - 9.8^2$

14. $13.5^2 - 6.5^2$

15. $8.79^2 - 1.21^2$

16. $0.763^2 - 0.237^2$

Finally in this chapter we take out a common factor that does not leave the first term as x^2; and factorise expressions that do not begin with the x^2 term.

Exercise 15p

Factorise $8x^2 + 28x + 12$

$$8x^2 + 28x + 12 = 4(2x^2 + 7x + 3)$$
$$= 4(2x + 1)(x + 3)$$

Factorise:

1. $15x^2 + 25x + 10$ **5.** $8x^2 + 34x - 30$ **9.** $6x^2 + 26x + 8$ **13.** $12x^2 + 14x + 4$

2. $4x^2 - 6x - 4$ **6.** $8x^2 + 14x + 6$ **10.** $15x^2 + 50x - 40$ **14.** $100x^2 - 115x + 30$

3. $6x^2 + 9x + 3$ **7.** $25x^2 - 65x - 30$ **11.** $18x^2 - 36x + 16$ **15.** $24x^2 - 4x - 8$

4. $18x^2 - 21x - 30$ **8.** $9x^2 + 3x - 12$ **12.** $48x^2 - 30x + 3$ **16.** $21x^2 + 70x - 56$

Factorise $12 + 7x - 10x^2$

$$12 + 7x - 10x^2 = (3 - 2x)(4 + 5x)$$

Factorise:

17. $4 - 5x - 6x^2$ **22.** $9 + 8x - x^2$

18. $12 + 7x - 12x^2$ **23.** $12 - 11x - x^2$

19. $21 + 25x - 4x^2$ **24.** $8 + 24x + 18x^2$

20. $24 - 16x + 2x^2$ **25.** $45 - 30x + 5x^2$

21. $16 - 20x - 6x^2$ **26.** $20 + 40x + 15x^2$

MIXED QUESTIONS

Some quadratic expressions such as $x^2 + 9$ and $x^2 + 3x + 1$ will not factorise. The next exercise in this chapter includes some expressions that will not factorise.

Exercise 15q

Factorise where possible:

1. $x^2 + 13x + 40$ **7.** $x^2 + 6x - 7$

2. $6x^2 + 5x + 1$ **8.** $5x^2 + 3x - 2$

3. $x^2 - 36$ **9.** $x^2 - 11x + 24$

4. $x^2 + 4$ **10.** $3x^2 + 11x + 6$

5. $x^2 - 8x + 12$ **11.** $x^2 + 14x - 15$

6. $2x^2 + 7x - 15$ **12.** $12x^2 - 7x + 1$

13. $x^2 + 8x + 12$

14. $8x^2 - 2x - 1$

15. $x^2 - 49$

16. $x^2 - 7x + 2$

17. $6x^2 - 11x - 10$

18. $x^2 + 13x + 42$

19. $4x^2 - 9y^2$

20. $15x^2 - 22x + 8$

21. $6x^2 - 5x - 6$

22. $x^2 + 11x - 26$

23. $30x^2 - 2x - 4$

24. $28 + 3x - x^2$

25. $6x^2 + 5x - 4$

26. $30x^2 + 35x + 10$

27. $x^2 + 11x + 18$

28. $x^2 - 10x + 24$

29. $4x^2 - 16y^2$

30. $x^2 - 11x - 10$

31. $12x^2 - 22x - 20$

32. $x^2 + 13x - 30$

33. $28 - 12x - x^2$

34. $a^2 - 16a + 63$

35. $6 - 16x + 8x^2$

36. $1 + 2x + 4x^2 + 8x^3$

37. $x^2 + 13x - 68$

38. $2x^4 - x^3 + 4x - 2$

39. $6x^2 - 9x - 6$

40. $p^3 + p^2 + p + 1$

41. $(a+b)^2 - c^2$

42. $116x^2 - 25x - 1$

43. $a^2 + 23a + 112$

44. $x^4 - y^2 - 2y - 1$

45. $3a^2 + 56 - 31a$

46. $2x^2 - 8x - 154$

47. $4x^2 - (y-z)^2$

48. $a^2b^2 - ab - 342$

The quadratic expression $ax^2 + bx + c$ will factorise only if we can find two numbers whose product is ac and whose sum is b.

MIXED EXERCISES

Exercise 15r

1. Expand

(a) $7(a+3)$ (b) $3(x-2y)$

2. Expand

(a) $(x+4)(x+10)$

(b) $(2x-3)(3x-5)$

3. Expand

(a) $(5+x)^2$

(b) $(5-x)^2$

(c) $(5+x)(5-x)$

4. Factorise

(a) $10a + 20$

(b) $15p^2 - 10p$

5. Factorise

(a) $a^3 + a^2 + a + 1$

(b) $2km - kn + 2lm - ln$

6. Factorise

(a) $x^2 + 6x - 27$

(b) $5x^2 - 42x + 49$

(c) $a^2 - \dfrac{b^2}{4}$

7. Factorise

(a) $10x^2 - 11x - 6$

(b) $100a^2 - 81b^2$

Exercise 15s

1. Expand

(a) $5a(a + 3)$ (b) $4x(3x - 2y)$

2. Expand

(a) $(y - 4)(y - 5)$

(b) $(3x - 4y)(5x + 2y)$

3. Expand

(a) $(2p + 3q)^2$

(b) $(2p - 3q)^2$

(c) $(2p + 3q)(2p - 3q)$

4. Factorise

(a) $8z^3 - 4z^2$ (b) $5xy - 20yz$

5. Factorise

(a) $2m + 3mn + 3n + 2$

(b) $ac - 2ad + 2bc - 4bd$

6. Factorise

(a) $x^2 - 6x - 27$

(b) $4x^2 + 27x - 7$

(c) $4m^2 - 81n^2$

7. Factorise

(a) $15x^2 - 54x + 27$

(b) $15 + 25x - 20x^2$

Exercise 15t

1. Expand

(a) $4(a + 7)$ (b) $3x(2x - 3y)$

2. Expand

(a) $(x + 3)(x + 9)$

(b) $(5x - 2)(3x + 1)$

3. Expand

(a) $(5x + 2)^2$

(b) $(5x - 2)^2$

(c) $(5x + 2)(5x - 2)$

4. Factorise

(a) $12z^2 - 6z$

(b) $8xy - 12yz$

5. Factorise

(a) $z^3 + 2z^2 + z + 2$

(b) $3ac + bc + 6a + 2b$

6. Factorise

(a) $x^2 - 2x - 24$

(b) $4a^2 + 4a - 15$

(c) $9m^2 - \dfrac{n^2}{9}$

7. Factorise

(a) $15x^2 + x - 6$

(b) $6 + x - 15x^2$

8. If n is a three-digit number whose hundreds digit is a, tens digit is b and units digit is c, then $n = 100a + 10b + c$.

(a) Prove that if $a + b = 7$ and $b + c = 7$ then n is divisible by 7.

(b) Prove that if $a + b = 13$ and $b + c = 13$ then n is divisible by 13.

16 ▶ QUADRATIC EQUATIONS AND INEQUATIONS

At the end of the chapter you should be able to:

1. Solve quadratic equations of the form $(ax + b)(cx + d) = 0$.
2. Solve quadratic equations by factorisation.
3. Solve equations of the form $ax^3 + bx^2 + cx = 0$.
4. Form quadratic equations to solve given problems.
5. Solve quadratic equations by the method of completing the square.
6. Solve a pair of equations – one linear and one quadratic.
7. Find the maximum or minimum value of a given quadratic function.
8. Solve a given quadratic inequation.

MULTIPLICATION BY ZERO

Exercise 16a

Find the value of $(x - 3)(x - 7)$ if

(a) $x = 8$ (b) $x = 7$ (c) $x = 3$

(a) If $x = 8$ $(x - 3)(x - 7) = (8 - 3)(8 - 7)$
$$= (5)(1)$$
$$= 5$$

(b) If $x = 7$ $(x - 3)(x - 7) = (4)(0)$
$$= 0$$

(c) If $x = 3$ $(x - 3)(x - 7) = (0)(-4)$
$$= 0$$

1. Find the value of $(x - 4)(x - 2)$ if

(a) $x = 6$ (b) $x = 4$ (c) $x = 2$

2. Find the value of $(x - 5)(x - 9)$ if

(a) $x = 5$ (b) $x = 10$ (c) $x = 9$

3. Find the value of $(x - 7)(x - 1)$ if

(a) $x = 1$ (b) $x = 8$ (c) $x = 7$

4. Find the value of $(x - 4)(x - 6)$ if

(a) $x = 4$ (b) $x = 6$ (c) $x = 3$

5. Find the value of $(x - 6)(x - 7)$ if

(a) $x = 2$ (b) $x = 6$ (c) $x = 9$

Find the value of $(x-2)(x+4)$ if

(a) $x=2$ (b) $x=4$ (c) $x=-4$

(a) If $x=2$ $(x-2)(x+4)=(0)(6)$
$$= 0$$

(b) If $x=4$ $(x-2)(x+4)=(2)(8)$
$$= 16$$

(c) If $x=-4$ $(x-2)(x+4)=(-6)(0)$
$$= 0$$

6. Find the value of $(x-3)(x+5)$ if

(a) $x=6$ (b) $x=3$ (c) $x=-5$

7. Find the value of $(x-4)(x+6)$ if

(a) $x=0$ (b) $x=-6$ (c) $x=4$

8. Find the value of $(x-7)(x+2)$ if

(a) $x=-7$ (b) $x=-2$ (c) $x=7$

9. Find the value of $(x+4)(x+5)$ if

(a) $x=-4$ (b) $x=-5$ (c) $x=0$

10. Find the value of $(x+7)(x+1)$ if

(a) $x=-4$ (b) $x=-1$ (c) $x=-7$

The results of this exercise show that if the product of two factors is 0, then either one or both of these factors must be 0

In general we can say

if $A \times B = 0$
then either $A = 0$ or/and $B = 0$

Exercise 16b

In questions 1 to 12 find, if possible, the value or values of A. Note that if $A \times 0 = 0$ then A can have any value.

1. $A \times 6 = 0$ **4.** $A \times 0 = 0$ **7.** $A \times 10 = 0$ **10.** $A \times 3 = 21$

2. $A \times 7 = 0$ **5.** $3 \times A = 12$ **8.** $A \times 9 = 18$ **11.** $0 \times A = 0$

3. $A \times 4 = 0$ **6.** $8 \times A = 8$ **9.** $A \times 20 = 0$ **12.** $4 \times A = 0$

13. If $AB = 0$ find

(a) A if $B = 2$ (b) B if $A = 10$

14. If $AB = 0$ find

(a) A if $B = 5$ (b) B if $A = 5$

15. If $AB = 0$ find

(a) A if $B = 10$ (b) B if $A = 3$

16. If $AB = 0$ find

(a) B if $A = 6$ (b) A if $B = 0$

Find a and b if $a(b-3)=0$

Either $\qquad\qquad a=0 \quad$ or/and $\quad b-3=0$

i.e., either $\qquad\qquad a=0 \quad$ or/and $\quad b=3$

Find a and b if:

17. $a(b-1)=0$

18. $a(b-5)=0$

19. $a(b-2)=0$

20. $(a-3)b=0$

21. $(a-9)b=0$

22. $a(b-4)=0$

23. $a(b-10)=0$

24. $(a-1)b=0$

25. $(a-7)b=0$

26. $(a-12)b=0$

QUADRATIC EQUATIONS

Previously we have considered equations such as $x-1=0$ and $3x+2=0$. These are examples of *linear equations*. The first equation is true only for $x=1$ and the second only for $x=-\frac{2}{3}$.

If, however, we consider the equation

$$(x-1)(x-2)=0$$

we find that it is true either when $x-1=0$ or when $x-2=0$, i.e. either when $x=1$ or when $x=2$.

There are, therefore, two values of x that satisfy the equation $(x-1)(x-2)=0$

Expanding the left-hand side gives

$$x^2-3x+2=0$$

Equations like this, which contain an x^2 term, are called *quadratic equations*.

When we are given a quadratic equation we can often factorise the left-hand side into two linear factors,

e.g. $\qquad\qquad x^2-5x+4=0$

gives $\qquad\qquad (x-4)(x-1)=0$

It is this technique that concerns us in the present chapter.

Exercise 16c

What values of x satisfy the equation $x(x-9)=0$?

$$x(x-9)=0$$

Either $x=0$ or $x-9=0$

i.e., either $x=0$ or $x=9$

What values of x satisfy the following equations?

1. $x(x-3)=0$

2. $x(x-5)=0$

3. $(x-3)x=0$

4. $x(x+4)=0$

5. $(x+5)x=0$

6. $x(x-6)=0$

7. $x(x-10)=0$

8. $(x-7)x=0$

9. $x(x+7)=0$

10. $(x+9)x=0$

What values of x satisfy the equation $(x-3)(x+5)=0$?

$$(x-3)(x+5)=0$$

Either $x-3=0$ or $x+5=0$

i.e., either $x=3$ or $x=-5$

What values of x satisfy the following equations?

11. $(x-1)(x-2)=0$

12. $(x-5)(x-9)=0$

13. $(x-10)(x-7)=0$

14. $(x-4)(x-7)=0$

15. $(x-6)(x-1)=0$

16. $(x-8)(x+11)=0$

17. $(x-3)(x+5)=0$

18. $(x+7)(x-2)=0$

19. $(x+2)(x+3)=0$

20. $(x+4)(x+9)=0$

21. $(x+1)(x+8)=0$

22. $(x-p)(x-q)=0$

23. $(x+a)(x+b)=0$

24. $(x-4)(x+1)=0$

25. $(x+9)(x-8)=0$

26. $(x+6)(x+7)=0$

27. $(x+10)(x+11)=0$

28. $(x-a)(x-b)=0$

29. $(x+a)(x-b)=0$

30. $(x-c)(x+d)=0$

Exercise 16d

Solve the equation $(2x - 3)(3x + 1) = 0$

$$(2x - 3)(3x + 1) = 0$$

Either $2x - 3 = 0$ or $3x + 1 = 0$

i.e., either $2x = 3$ or $3x = -1$

i.e., either $x = \frac{3}{2} = 1\frac{1}{2}$ or $x = -\frac{1}{3}$

Solve the following equations:

1. $(2x - 5)(x - 1) = 0$

2. $(x - 4)(3x - 2) = 0$

3. $(5x - 4)(4x - 3) = 0$

4. $x(4x - 5) = 0$

5. $x(10x - 3) = 0$

6. $(5x + 2)(x - 7) = 0$

7. $(6x + 5)(3x - 2) = 0$

8. $(8x - 3)(2x + 5) = 0$

9. $(7x - 8)(4x + 15) = 0$

10. $(4x + 3)(2x + 3) = 0$

11. $(3x - 7)(x - 2) = 0$

12. $(3x - 5)(2x - 1) = 0$

13. $x(3x - 1) = 0$

14. $x(7x - 3) = 0$

15. $(2x + 3)(x - 3) = 0$

16. $(4x + 3)(2x - 5) = 0$

17. $(10x + 9)(5x - 4) = 0$

18. $(3x - 2)(4x + 9) = 0$

19. $(5x - 12)(2x + 7) = 0$

20. $(5x + 8)(4x + 3) = 0$

SOLUTION BY FACTORISATION

The previous two exercises suggest that if the left-hand side of a quadratic equation can be expressed as two linear factors, we can use these factors to solve the equation.

Exercise 16e

Solve the equation $x^2 - 10x + 9 = 0$

If $x^2 - 10x + 9 = 0$

then $(x - 1)(x - 9) = 0$

$\therefore$ either $x - 1 = 0$ or $x - 9 = 0$

i.e. $x = 1$ or 9

Solve the equations:

1. $x^2 - 3x + 2 = 0$

2. $x^2 - 8x + 7 = 0$

3. $x^2 - 5x + 6 = 0$

4. $x^2 - 7x + 10 = 0$

5. $x^2 - 7x + 12 = 0$

6. $x^2 - 6x + 5 = 0$

7. $x^2 - 12x + 11 = 0$

8. $x^2 - 6x + 8 = 0$

9. $x^2 - 8x + 12 = 0$

10. $x^2 - 13x + 12 = 0$

Solve the equation $x^2 + 2x - 8 = 0$

$$x^2 + 2x - 8 = 0$$
$$(x + 4)(x - 2) = 0$$

$\therefore$ either $x + 4 = 0$ or $x - 2 = 0$

i.e. $x = -4$ or 2

Solve the equations:

11. $x^2 + 6x - 7 = 0$

12. $x^2 - 2x - 8 = 0$

13. $x^2 + x - 12 = 0$

14. $x^2 - 2x - 15 = 0$

15. $x^2 + 7x - 18 = 0$

16. $x^2 - 12x - 13 = 0$

17. $x^2 + x - 6 = 0$

18. $x^2 - 4x - 12 = 0$

19. $x^2 + x - 20 = 0$

20. $x^2 - 5x - 24 = 0$

Solve the equation $x^2 + 9x + 8 = 0$

$$x^2 + 9x + 8 = 0$$
$$(x + 1)(x + 8) = 0$$

Either $x + 1 = 0$ or $x + 8 = 0$

i.e. $x = -1$ or -8

Solve the equations:

21. $x^2 + 3x + 2 = 0$

22. $x^2 + 8x + 7 = 0$

23. $x^2 + 8x + 15 = 0$

24. $x^2 + 8x + 12 = 0$

25. $x^2 + 11x + 18 = 0$

26. $x^2 + 7x + 6 = 0$

27. $x^2 + 7x + 10 = 0$

28. $x^2 + 14x + 13 = 0$

29. $x^2 + 16x + 15 = 0$

30. $x^2 + 9x + 18 = 0$

Solve the equation $x^2 - 49 = 0$

$$x^2 - 49 = 0$$
$$(x + 7)(x - 7) = 0$$

Either $\qquad\qquad x + 7 = 0 \quad$ or $\quad x - 7 = 0$

i.e. $\qquad\qquad\qquad\qquad x = -7 \quad$ or $\quad 7$

Solve the equations:

31. $x^2 - 1 = 0$

32. $x^2 - 9 = 0$

33. $x^2 - 16 = 0$

34. $x^2 - 81 = 0$

35. $x^2 - 169 = 0$

36. $x^2 - 4 = 0$

37. $x^2 - 25 = 0$

38. $x^2 - 100 = 0$

39. $x^2 - 144 = 0$

40. $x^2 - 36 = 0$

The equations we have solved by factorising have all been examples of the equation $ax^2 + bx + c = 0$ when $a = 1$. We consider next the case when $c = 0$,

e.g. solve the equation $3x^2 + 2x = 0$

Since x is common to both terms on the left-hand side we can rewrite this equation

$$x(3x + 2) = 0$$

Then, either $x = 0$ or $3x + 2 = 0$

i.e. $\qquad\qquad x = 0$ or $3x = -2$

i.e. $\qquad\qquad x = 0$ or $-\frac{2}{3}$

Exercise 16f

Solve the equations:

1. $x^2 - 2x = 0$

2. $x^2 - 10x = 0$

3. $x^2 + 8x = 0$

4. $2x^2 - x = 0$

5. $4x^2 - 5x = 0$

6. $x^2 - 5x = 0$

7. $x^2 + 3x = 0$

8. $x^2 + x = 0$

9. $3x^2 - 5x = 0$

10. $5x^2 - 7x = 0$

11. $2x^2 + 3x = 0$

12. $8x^2 + 5x = 0$

13. $x^2 - 7x = 0$

14. $3x^2 + 5x = 0$

15. $7x^2 - 12x = 0$

16. $6x^2 + 7x = 0$

17. $12x^2 + 7x = 0$

18. $x^2 + 4x = 0$

19. $7x^2 - 2x = 0$

20. $14x^2 + 3x = 0$

Sometimes a quadratic equation has two answers, or *roots*, that are exactly the same.

Consider $x^2 - 4x + 4 = 0$

then $(x - 2)(x - 2) = 0$

i.e., either $x - 2 = 0$ or $x - 2 = 0$

i.e. $x = 2$ or $x = 2$

i.e. $x = 2$ (twice)

Such an equation involves a *perfect square*. As with any quadratic equation, it has two answers, or roots, but they are equal. We say that such an equation has a repeated root.

Exercise 16g

> Solve the equation $x^2 + 14x + 49 = 0$
>
> $$x^2 + 14x + 49 = 0$$
> $$(x + 7)(x + 7) = 0$$
>
> Either $x + 7 = 0$ or $x + 7 = 0$
>
> i.e. $x = -7$ (twice)

Solve the equations:

1. $x^2 - 2x + 1 = 0$

2. $x^2 - 10x + 25 = 0$

3. $x^2 - 20x + 100 = 0$

4. $x^2 + 8x + 16 = 0$

5. $x^2 + 6x + 9 = 0$

6. $x^2 - 6x + 9 = 0$

7. $x^2 - 8x + 16 = 0$

8. $x^2 - 18x + 81 = 0$

9. $x^2 + 2x + 1 = 0$

10. $x^2 + 20x + 100 = 0$

11. $x^2 + 18x + 81 = 0$

12. $x^2 - 14x + 49 = 0$

13. $x^2 - 22x + 121 = 0$

14. $x^2 + 12x + 36 = 0$

15. $x^2 - x + \frac{1}{4} = 0$

16. $x^2 + 10x + 25 = 0$

17. $x^2 - 12x + 36 = 0$

18. $x^2 - 40x + 400 = 0$

19. $x^2 - 16x + 64 = 0$

20. $x^2 + \frac{4}{3}x + \frac{4}{9} = 0$

Frequently $a \neq 1$ in the equation $ax^2 + bx + c = 0$. The next exercise considers quadratic equations for values of a other than 1.

Exercise 16h

Solve the equation $5x^2 - 13x - 6 = 0$

$$5x^2 - 13x - 6 = 0$$
$$(5x + 2)(x - 3) = 0$$

Either $\qquad\qquad 5x - 2 = 0 \quad$ or $\quad x + 3 = 0$

i.e $\qquad\qquad\qquad 5x = 2 \quad$ or $\quad x = -3$

i.e. $\qquad\qquad\qquad x = \frac{2}{5} \quad$ or $\quad -3$

Solve the equations:

1. $2x^2 - 5x + 2 = 0$

2. $2x^2 - 11x + 12 = 0$

3. $2x^2 - 13x + 20 = 0$

4. $3x^2 + 5x + 2 = 0$

5. $2x^2 + 9x - 35 = 0$

6. $3x^2 - 11x + 6 = 0$

7. $3x^2 - 7x + 2 = 0$

8. $2x^2 + 5x - 12 = 0$

9. $3x^2 + 11x + 6 = 0$

10. $5x^2 + 27x + 10 = 0$

11. $6x^2 - x - 2 = 0$

12. $15x^2 + 14x - 8 = 0$

13. $12x^2 - 7x + 1 = 0$

14. $6x^2 - 13x - 5 = 0$

15. $20x^2 + 19x + 3 = 0$

16. $8x^2 - 18x + 9 = 0$

17. $12x^2 - 20x - 25 = 0$

18. $4x^2 + 8x + 3 = 0$

19. $12x^2 + 17x + 6 = 0$

20. $10x^2 - 29x - 21 = 0$

Solve the equation $4x^2 - 9 = 0$

$$4x^2 - 9 = 0$$
$$(2x - 3)(2x + 3) = 0$$

Either $\qquad\qquad 2x - 3 = 0 \quad$ or $\quad 2x + 3 = 0$

i.e. $\qquad\qquad\quad 2x = 3 \quad$ or $\quad 2x = -3$

i.e. $\qquad\qquad\qquad x = \frac{3}{2} \quad$ or $\quad -\frac{3}{2}$

Solve the equations:

21. $16x^2 - 25 = 0$	**26.** $9x^2 - 4 = 0$
22. $100x^2 - 81 = 0$	**27.** $81x^2 - 25 = 0$
23. $4x^2 - 25 = 0$	**28.** $25x^2 - 4 = 0$
24. $9x^2 - 16 = 0$	**29.** $36x^2 - 25 = 0$
25. $25x^2 - 144 = 0$	**30.** $4x^2 - 81 = 0$

Exercise 16i

Solve the equation $x^2 - x = 12$

$$x^2 - x = 12$$

Subtracting 12 from each side gives

$$x^2 - x - 12 = 0$$
$$(x - 4)(x + 3) = 0$$

Either $\qquad x - 4 = 0 \quad$ or $\quad x + 3 = 0$

i.e. $\qquad\qquad x = 4 \quad$ or $\quad -3$

Solve the equations:

1. $x^2 - x = 30$ **3.** $x^2 + 9x = 36$ **5.** $x^2 - x = 6$ **7.** $2x^2 + 5x = 3$

2. $x^2 - 6x = 16$ **4.** $3x^2 + 4x = 4$ **6.** $x^2 + 6x = 7$ **8.** $5x^2 - 12x = 9$

Solve the equations $x^2 = 2x + 3$

$$x^2 = 2x + 3$$

Subtract $2x$ and 3 from each side:

$$x^2 - 2x - 3 = 0$$
$$(x - 3)(x + 1) = 0$$

Either $\qquad x - 3 = 0 \quad$ or $\quad x + 1 = 0$

i.e. $\qquad\qquad x = 3 \quad$ or $\quad -1$

Solve the equations:

9. $x^2 = 2x + 3$

13. $x^2 = 3x + 10$

17. $10 = 7x - x^2$

21. $12 = 8x - x^2$

10. $x^2 = 2x + 24$

14. $x^2 = 6x - 8$

18. $7 = 8x - x^2$

22. $20 = 9x - x^2$

11. $x^2 = 12x - 35$

15. $6x^2 = x + 1$

19. $8 = 6x - x^2$

23. $35 = 12x - x^2$

12. $10x^2 = 13x + 3$

16. $3x^2 = 13x - 4$

20. $21 = 10x - x^2$

24. $15 = 8x - x^2$

Solve the equation $12x^2 + 10x - 12 = 0$

$$12x^2 + 10x - 12 = 0$$

Taking out the common factor 2 gives

$$(2)(6x^2 + 5x - 6) = 0$$

Since 2 is not zero, $6x^2 + 5x - 6$ must be zero

$\therefore$ $\qquad\qquad 6x^2 + 5x - 6 = 0$

i.e. $\qquad\qquad (3x - 2)(2x + 3) = 0$

Either $\qquad\qquad 3x - 2 = 0 \quad$ or $\quad 2x + 3 = 0$

i.e. $\qquad\qquad 3x = 2 \quad$ or $\quad 2x = -3$

i.e. $\qquad\qquad x = \frac{2}{3} \quad$ or $\quad -\frac{3}{2}$

Solve the equations:

25. $8x^2 - 4x = 0$

30. $3x^2 - 9x = 0$

26. $2x^2 - 10x + 12 = 0$

31. $5x^2 - 15x + 10 = 0$

27. $3x^2 - 24x + 36 = 0$

32. $6x^2 + 18x + 12 = 0$

28. $12x^2 + 20x + 8 = 0$

33. $15x^2 - 35x + 10 = 0$

29. $8x^2 + 20x = 12$

34. $30x^2 = 39x + 9$

SUMMARY

To solve a quadratic equation by factorising:

(a) collect all terms on one side of the equation, i.e. arrange it in the form $ax^2 + bx + c = 0$

(b) take out any common factors (these may or may not include x)

(c) factorise.

Exercise 16j

Solve the equations:

1. $x^2 - x - 20 = 0$

2. $x^2 = 4x - 4$

3. $9x^2 - 1 = 0$

4. $2x^2 + 7x = 0$

5. $x^2 + 13x + 12 = 0$

6. $1 - 16x^2 = 0$

7. $x^2 - 6x = 0$

8. $x^2 = 2x + 35$

9. $2x^2 + 3x - 14 = 0$

10. $2x^2 + 12x + 18 = 0$

11. $x^2 = 7 - 6x$

12. $4 = 25x^2$

13. $4x^2 = 25$

14. $x^2 + 11x + 18 = 0$

15. $2 - x = 6x^2$

16. $5x - 2x^2 = 0$

17. $5x = 3x^2 - 2$

18. $4 + 11x + 6x^2 = 0$

19. $7x = 4x^2$

20. $14x - 2 = 24x^2$

21. $6x^2 + 13x - 5 = 0$

22. $5x + 2 = 3x^2$

23. $3 + 8x + 4x^2 = 0$

24. $3 - 12x^2 = 0$

Solve the equation $x(x - 2) = 15$

$$x(x - 2) = 15$$
$$x^2 - 2x = 15$$
$$x^2 - 2x - 15 = 0$$
$$(x - 5)(x + 3) = 0$$

Either $\qquad x - 5 = 0 \quad$ or $\quad x + 3 = 0$

i.e. $\qquad x = 5 \quad$ or $\quad -3$

Solve the equations:

25. $x(x + 1) = 12$

26. $x(x - 1) = x + 3$

27. $3x(2x + 1) = 4x + 1$

28. $5x(x - 1) = 4x^2 - 4$

29. $x(x - 5) = 24$

30. $x(x + 3) = 5(3x - 7)$

31. $3x(x + 3) = 5x + 4$

32. $2x(2x - 1) = x^2 + 3x + 2$

Solve the equation $(x-3)(x+2)=6$

$$(x-3)(x+2)=6$$
$$x^2-x-6=6$$
$$x^2-x-12=0$$
$$(x-4)(x+3)=0$$

Either $\qquad\qquad x-4=0 \quad$ or $\quad x+3=0$

i.e. $\qquad\qquad\qquad x=4 \quad$ or $\quad -3$

Solve the equations:

33. $(x+2)(x+3)=56$

34. $(x+9)(x-6)=34$

35. $(x-2)(x+6)=33$

36. $(x+3)(x-8)+10=0$

37. $(x-5)(x+2)=18$

38. $(x+8)(x-2)=39$

39. $(x+1)(x+8)+12=0$

40. $(x-1)(x+10)+30=0$

Solve the equation $x(x-3)(x-7)=0$

$$x(x-3)(x-7)=0$$

Either $\qquad x=0 \quad$ or $\quad x-3=0 \quad$ or $\quad x-7=0$

i.e. $\qquad\qquad x=0 \quad$ or $\quad 3 \quad$ or $\quad 7$

Solve the equations:

41. $x(x-1)(x-2)=0$

42. $x(x-3)(x+4)=0$

43. $x(2x-5)(x-2)=0$

44. $x^3-2x^2+x=0$

45. $2x^3+9x^2+4x=0$

46. $x(x-6)(x-7)=0$

47. $x(x+2)(x-5)=0$

48. $x(3x+7)(x-5)=0$

49. $4x^3-9x=0$

50. $8x=6x^2-x^3$

PROBLEMS

Exercise 16k

I think of a positive number x, square it and then add three times the number I first thought of. If the answer is 54, form an equation in x and solve it to find the number I first thought of.

If the given number is x, its square is x^2 and three times the number is $3x$

i.e.
$$x^2 + 3x = 54$$
$$x^2 + 3x - 54 = 0$$
$$(x - 6)(x + 9) = 0$$

Either
$$x - 6 = 0 \quad \text{or} \quad x + 9 = 0$$

i.e.
$$x = 6 \quad \text{or} \quad -9$$

The number I first thought of was therefore 6

---

1. The square of a number x is 16 more than six times the number. Form an equation in x and solve it.

2. When five times a number x is subtracted from the square of the same number, the answer is 14. Form an equation in x and solve it.

3. I think of a number x. If I square it and add it to the number I first thought of the total is 42. Find the number I first thought of.

4. Peter had x marbles. The number of marbles Fred had was six fewer than the square of the number Peter had. Together they had 66 marbles. Form an equation in x and solve it. How many marbles did Fred have?

5. Ahmed is x years old and his father is x^2 years old. If the sum of their ages is 56 years, form an equation in x and solve it to find the age of each.

6. Kathryn is x years old. If her mother's age is two years more than the square of Kathryn's age, and the sum of their ages is 44 years, form an equation in x and solve it to find the ages of Kathryn and her mother.

7. Peter is x years old and his sister is 5 years older. If the product of their ages is 84, form an equation in x and solve it to find Peter's age.

8. Sally is x years old and her sister Ann is 4 years younger. If the product of their ages is 140, form an equation in x and solve it to find Ann's age.

A rectangle is $4\,$cm longer than it is wide. If it is $x\,$cm wide and has an area of $77\,$cm^2, form an equation in x and solve it to find the dimensions of the rectangle.

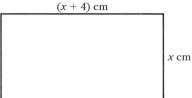

$(x + 4)\,$cm

$x\,$cm

The area of a rectangle is length $\times$ breadth.

$$\text{Area} = (x + 4) \times x \,\text{cm}^2$$

But the area is $77\,$cm^2,

$\therefore$ $(x + 4)x = 77$

i.e. $x^2 + 4x = 77$

$$x^2 + 4x - 77 = 0$$
$$(x - 7)(x + 11) = 0$$

Either $x - 7 = 0$ or $x + 11 = 0$

i.e. $x = 7$ or -11

The breadth of a rectangle cannot be negative, so we use $x = 7$.
Therefore, the rectangle measures $(7 + 4)\,$cm by $7\,$cm, i.e. $11\,$cm by $7\,$cm.

9. A rectangle is $x\,$cm long and is $3\,$cm longer than it is wide. If its area is $28\,$cm^2, form an equation in x and solve it to find the dimensions of the rectangle.

10. A rectangle is $5\,$cm longer than it is wide. If its width is $x\,$cm and its area is $66\,$cm^2 form an equation in x and solve it. Hence find the dimensions of the rectangle.

11. The base of a triangle is $x\,$cm long and its perpendicular height is half the length of its base. If the triangle has an area of $25\,$cm^2, form an equation in x and solve it. What is the height of the triangle?

12. A rectangular lawn measuring $30\,$m by $20\,$m is bordered on two adjacent sides by a uniform path of width $x\,$m as shown in the diagram.

(a) Express in terms of x each of the areas denoted by the letters A, B and C.

(b) If the area of the path is $104\,$m^2 form an equation in x and solve it to find the width of the path.

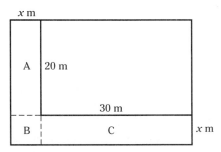

$x\,$m

A $20\,$m

$30\,$m

B   C $x\,$m

SOLUTION BY COMPLETING SQUARES

It was stated in Chapter 15 that the quadratic expression $ax^2 + bx + c$ will factorise only if we can find two numbers whose product is ac and whose sum is b.

When the expression cannot be factorised we may solve the equation $ax^2 + bx + c = 0$ in the following way.

$$ax^2 + bx + c = 0$$

multiply by $4a$

$$4a^2x^2 + 4abx + 4ac = 0$$

$$4a^2x^2 + 4abx = -4ac$$

completing the square

$$4a^2x^2 + 4abx + b^2 = b^2 - 4ac$$

$$(2ax + b)^2 = b^2 - 4ac$$

$$2ax + b = \pm\sqrt{b^2 - 4ac}$$

$$2ax = -b \pm \sqrt{b^2 - 4ac}$$

Therefore the solution is

$$x = \frac{-b \pm \sqrt{b^2 - 4ac}}{2a}$$

This is called the *method of completing squares* and the result is usually referred to as the *quadratic formula*.

Exercise 16I

(a) Solve the equation $3x^2 + 2x - 4 = 0$
(b) Solve the equation $4x^2 + x - 2 = 0$

(a)
$$3x^2 + 2x - 4 = 0$$

Multiply by $4(3) = 12$
$$36x^2 + 24x - 48 = 0$$

$$36x^2 + 24x = 48$$

Completing the square
$$36x^2 + 24x + 4 = 48 + 4$$

$$(6x + 2)^2 = 52$$

$$6x + 2 = \pm\sqrt{52} = \pm 7.21$$

$\therefore$
$$6x + 2 = 7.21 \quad \text{or} \quad 6x + 2 = -7.21$$

$\therefore$
$$6x = 5.21 \quad \text{or} \quad 6x = -9.21$$

$$x = \frac{5.21}{6} \quad \text{or} \quad x = \frac{-9.21}{6}$$

Therefore the solution is $x = 0.87$ or $x = -1.54$

(b) $$4x^2 + x - 2 = 0$$

In this equation $a = 4$, $b = 1$, $c = -2$

Using the quadratic formula $x = \dfrac{-b \pm \sqrt{b^2 - 4ac}}{2a}$

$$x = \frac{-1 \pm \sqrt{1 + 32}}{8}$$

$$= \frac{-1 \pm \sqrt{33}}{8}$$

$$= \frac{-1 \pm 5.74}{8}$$

$$x = \frac{-1 + 5.74}{8} \quad \text{or} \quad x = \frac{-1 - 5.74}{8}$$

Therefore the solution is $x = \dfrac{4.74}{8} \quad \text{or} \quad x = \dfrac{-6.74}{8}$

Therefore $x = 0.59$ or -0.84

Solve the following equations, giving your answers correct to three significant figures:

1. $2x^2 + 4x - 1 = 0$

2. $5x^2 - 3x - 1 = 0$

3. $4x^2 - 16x + 15 = 0$

4. $4x^2 + 6x + 1 = 0$

5. $2x^2 - 8x + 3 = 0$

6. $3y^2 = 7y + 1$

7. $2x^2 + 8x + 4 = 1 - x$

8. $\dfrac{x^2}{3} - 2x = 5$

SOLUTION OF TWO SIMULTANEOUS EQUATIONS— ONE FIRST DEGREE (LINEAR) AND ONE SECOND DEGREE (QUADRATIC)

The method of substitution may be used to eliminate one of the variables in the second degree equation.

The first degree equation can be solved for one of the variables in terms of the other, and the expression obtained then substituted for that variable in the second degree equation.

Exercise 16m

Solve the equations $\qquad\qquad x - y = 7$ [1]

$$x^2 - xy - y^2 = 19 \qquad\qquad [2]$$

From [1] $\qquad\qquad\qquad\qquad\qquad x = 7 + y$

Substituting into [2] $\qquad (y + 7)^2 - y(y + 7) - y^2 = 19$

$$y^2 + 14y + 49 - y^2 - 7y - y^2 = 19$$

$$-y^2 + 7y + 30 = 0$$

$$y^2 - 7y - 30 = 0$$

$$(y - 10)(y + 3) = 0$$

Either $\qquad\qquad\qquad\qquad y = 10 \qquad$ or $\quad y = -3$

i.e. $\qquad\qquad\qquad\qquad x = 10 + 7 \quad$ or $\quad x = -3 + 7$

i.e. $\qquad\qquad\qquad\qquad x = 17 \qquad$ or $\quad x = 4$

Solve algebraically each of the following systems of equations:

1. $x^2 + y^2 = 25$
$y = 2x + 5$

2. $x = 2y + 4$
$x^2 + y^2 = 5$

3. $x = 3y - 5$
$x^2 + 2y^2 = 6$

4. $y = 10 - 3x$
$2x^2 + y^2 = 19$

5. $y = 3x - 1$
$4x^2 - xy = 2$

6. $3x - y = 3$
$9x^2 - y^2 = 45$

7. $x + 2y = 1$
$x + 12y + 3y^2 = -6$

8. $5x - 2y = 2$
$25x^2 - 4y^2 = 36$

9. $3x - 4y = 2$
$9x^2 + 16y^2 = 52$

10. $2x - 3y = 12$
$x^2 - xy = 15$

11. $x - y = 10$
$$\dfrac{12}{y} - \dfrac{12}{x} = 5$$

12. $2x + y = 3$
$$\dfrac{1}{x} + \dfrac{1}{y} + \dfrac{1}{2} = 0$$

MAXIMUM AND MINIMUM VALUES OF THE QUADRATIC FUNCTION

When $f(x) = ax^2 + bx + c$ is written in the form $f(x) = a(x - h)^2 + k$, it can be shown that $f(x)$ has a minimum value K at $x = h$ if $a > 0$ or a maximum value K when $x = h$ if $a < 0$.

This is clearly seen since

$$a(x-h)^2 + K > K \quad \text{if } a > 0$$

and

$$a(x-h)^2 + K < K \quad \text{if } a < 0$$

Exercise 16n

(a) Find the maximum or minimum value of

$$f(x) = 2x^2 + 6x - 5$$

$$
\begin{aligned}
f(x) &= 2x^2 + 6x - 5 \\
&= 2\left(x^2 + 3x - \tfrac{5}{2}\right) \\
&= 2\left(x^2 + 3x + \tfrac{9}{4} - \tfrac{9}{4} - \tfrac{5}{2}\right) \\
&= 2\left(x^2 + 3x + \tfrac{9}{4}\right) - 2\left(\tfrac{9}{4} + \tfrac{5}{2}\right) \\
&= 2\left(x + \tfrac{3}{2}\right)^2 - \tfrac{19}{2} \\
&\geqslant -\tfrac{19}{2} \quad \text{since } 2\left(x + \tfrac{3}{2}\right)^2 \geqslant 0
\end{aligned}
$$

Therefore $f(x)$ has a minimum of $-\tfrac{19}{2}$ when $\left(x + \tfrac{3}{2}\right) = 0$

i.e. when $x = -\tfrac{3}{2}$.

(b) In a triangle PQR, the sum of the length of the side PR and the altitude from Q to PR is 12 cm. Find the length of PR and the altitude from Q so that the triangle has maximum area.

Let the length of PR be x cm and the altitude by y cm.

$$\therefore \qquad\qquad x + y = 12$$

$$
\begin{aligned}
\text{Area, } A &= \tfrac{1}{2}xy \\
&= \tfrac{1}{2}x(12 - x) \\
&= 6x - \tfrac{1}{2}x^2 \\
&= -\tfrac{1}{2}(x^2 - 12x) \\
&= -\tfrac{1}{2}(x^2 - 12x + 36 - 36) \\
&= -\tfrac{1}{2}(x - 6)^2 + 18
\end{aligned}
$$

A is maximum when $(x - 6)^2 = 0$

i.e. $\qquad\qquad x = 6 \quad \therefore \quad y = 6$

Therefore PR $= 6$ cm and altitude $= 6$ cm

Find the maximum or minimum values for the following expressions:

1. $x^2 + 8x + 3$

3. $-x^2 + 6x - 5$

5. $-6x^2 + 3x - 2$

2. $x^2 - 3x - 10$

4. $2x^2 + 6x - 5$

6. $4 - 5x - 10x^2$

7. A fence of length 300 m is to be used to enclose a rectangular area.

Calculate:

(a) the maximum area of the enclosure,

(b) the dimensions of the rectangle of maximum area.

8. The sum of two real numbers is 18.

Find their value if their product is a maximum.

9. A farmer needs to enclose a rectangular field which has a stream on one side and therefore needs no fence. Calculate the dimensions of the field of maximum area that can be enclosed with 150 m of fence.

10. A bullet is shot directly upwards with a velocity of 500 metres per second. Its distance above the ground, y, at the time, t, in seconds is given by the formula $y = 500t - 5t^2$. Calculate the maximum height of the bullet and after how many seconds it reaches this height.

SOLVING QUADRATIC INEQUATIONS

In this section we shall consider the solution of the inequality $ax^2 + bx + c \geqslant 0$ in which $ax^2 + bx + c$ can be factorised.

Exercise 16p

Solve the inequation $x^2 + 3x - 10 > 0$

Factorising we get $(x + 5)(x - 2) > 0$

Since the product of the two factors is positive, the two factors must be of the same sign:

$$x + 5 > 0 \quad \text{and} \quad x - 2 > 0$$

or
$$x + 5 < 0 \quad \text{and} \quad x - 2 < 0$$

$\therefore$
$$x > -5 \quad \text{and} \quad x > 2$$

or
$$x < -5 \quad \text{and} \quad x < 2$$

The solution set is then

$$\{x : x > -5\} \cap \{x : x > 2\} \cup \{x : x < -5\} \cap \{x : x < 2\}$$

Consider first the set $\{x : x > -5\} \cap \{x : x > 2\}$

The diagram below shows that this set contains all real numbers x greater than 2.

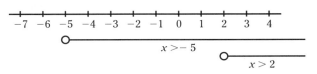

$$\{x : x > -5\} \cap \{x : x > 2\} = \{x : x > 2\}$$

Now consider $\{x : x < -5\} \cap \{x : x < 2\}$

The diagram below shows that this set contains all real numbers x less than -5.

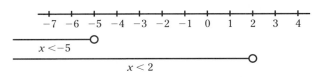

$$\{x : x < -5\} \cap \{x : x < 2\} = \{x : x < -5\}$$

Therefore the solution set of $x^2 + 3x - 10 > 0$ is $\{x : x > 2\} \cup \{x : x < -5\}$

The above diagram shows that this set contains all real numbers excluding those from -5 to 2 inclusive.

Therefore the solution set of $x^2 + 3x - 10 > 0$ is $\{x : -5 \leqslant x \leqslant 2\}'$

Solve the following quadratic inequations:

1. $x^2 - 5x - 6 < 0$

2. $x^2 + 3x - 40 > 0$

3. $x^2 + 5x + 6 > 0$

4. $x^2 - 7x + 12 < 0$

5. $x^2 - 3x < 0$

6. $x^2 + 4x < -3$

7. $3x^2 + 2x > 5$

8. $(x + 1)(x - 2) < (x + 1)^2$

9. $3x^2 + 8x - 3 \geqslant 0$

10. $(2x - 3)(3x + 1) \leqslant x(2x - 11)$

MIXED EXERCISES

Exercise 16q

1. Find the value of $(x + 4)(x - 3)$ if

(a) $x = 1$ (b) $x = 3$ (c) $x = 4$

2. Solve

(a) $x(x + 7) = 0$ (b) $4x(2x - 1) = 0$

3. Solve

    (a) $(x-3)(x-8)=0$

    (b) $(x-2)(5x+3)=0$

4. Solve

    (a) $x^2-2x-35=0$

    (b) $x^2-13x+40=0$

5. Solve

    (a) $10x^2-13x+4=0$

    (b) $15x^2-x-2=0$

    (c) $9x^2-4=0$

6. Solve

    (a) $7x^2-14x=0$

    (b) $4x^2-3x=0$

7. Solve

    (a) $9x^2-3x=2$

    (b) $6x^2=17x-7$

8. Solve

    (a) $x(x+4)=45$

    (b) $x(x+2)=x+30$

9. Find, to one decimal place, the roots of

    (a) $2x^2+2x-1=0$

    (b) $4x^2-8x=21$

Exercise 16r

1. Find the value of $(2x-1)(x+2)$ if

    (a) $x=0$

    (b) $x=\frac{1}{2}$

    (c) $x=2$

    (d) $x=-2$

2. Solve

    (a) $3x(x-2)=0$

    (b) $x(7x+3)=0$

3. Solve

    (a) $(x-2)(x+5)=0$

    (b) $(3x-4)(x+2)=0$

    (c) $(2x+3)(2x-3)=0$

4. Solve

    (a) $x^2+x-6=0$

    (b) $x^2+11x+30=0$

5. Solve

    (a) $20x^2+11x-3=0$

    (b) $15x^2+41x+14=0$

6. Solve

    (a) $15x^2+10x=0$

    (b) $7x^2+3x=0$

7. Solve

    (a) $4x^2-17x-15=0$

    (b) $6x^2=11x+7$

8. Solve

    (a) $x(x-4)=32$

    (b) $x(2x-1)=3x+16$

9. Solve, by completing the square

    (a) $2(3x^2-1)=x$

    (b) $x(4x-3)=3-2x$

Exercise 16s

1. Find the value of $(5x+1)(x-3)$ if

(a) $x=2$

(b) $x=3$

(c) $x=-\frac{1}{5}$

2. Solve

(a) $5x(x+7)=0$

(b) $3x(4x-3)=0$

3. Solve

(a) $(x+4)(x-5)=0$

(b) $(4x-7)(x+3)=0$

(c) $(5x-3)(5x+3)=0$

4. Solve

(a) $x^2-2x-15=0$

(b) $x^2+12x+32=0$

5. Solve

(a) $20x^2+19x+3=0$

(b) $28x^2+x-2=0$

6. Solve

(a) $12x^2+16x=0$

(b) $3x^2+5x=0$

7. Solve

(a) $7x^2+5x=2$

(b) $6x^2=7x+5$

8. Solve

(a) $x(x+6)=3x+10$

(b) $x(x+8)=x+30$

9. Find the solution set of each of the following

(a) $6x^2-54>0$

(b) $3x^2+x-2\leqslant 0$

(c) $x+2<3x^2$

MATHS IS OUT THERE

Do you know that Emmy Noether (1882–1935) was the daughter of the outstanding nineteenth century mathematician Max Noether. She was the only woman in a class of over 900 at her father's university. She was a mentor for several female mathematicians including Olga Taussky-Todd, Ruth Stauffer McKee, Marie Weiss and Grace Shover-Quinn.

17 ▷ INEQUALITIES AND REGIONS

At the end of the chapter you should be able to:

1. Represent inequalities involving two variables in the x–y plane.
2. Draw diagrams to represent regions in the x–y plane defined by a set of inequalities.
3. Find, in a given region, the coordinates of a point where $ax + by$ is greatest or least.
4. Solve problems using linear programming.

USING TWO-DIMENSIONAL SPACE

In a previous chapter, we discussed inequalities in a purely algebraic way. In this chapter, we will be looking at them in a more visual way, using graphs.

If we have the inequality $x \geqslant 2$, x can take any value greater than or equal to 2. This can be represented by the following diagram.

On this number line, x can take any value on the heavy part of the line including 2 itself, as indicated by the solid circle at 2.

If $x > 2$ then the diagram is as shown below.

In this case, x cannot take the value 2 and this is shown by the open circle at 2.

It is sometimes more useful to use two-dimensional space with x and y axes, rather than a one-dimensional line. We represent $x \geqslant 2$ by the set of points whose x coordinates are greater than or equal to 2. (y is not mentioned in the inequality so y can take any value.)

The boundary line represents all the points for which $x = 2$ and the region to the right contains all points with x coordinates greater than 2.

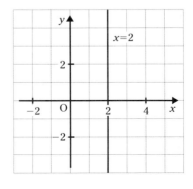

To indicate this, and to make future work easier, we use a continuous line for the boundary when it is included and we shade the region we do *not* want.

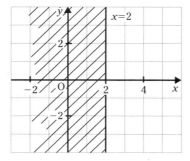

The inequality $x > 2$ tells us that x may not take the value 2. In this case we use a broken line for the boundary.

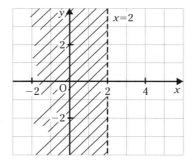

We can draw a similar diagram for $y > -1$

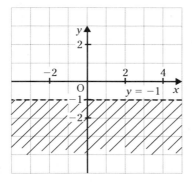

Exercise 17a

Draw diagrams to represent the inequalities

(a) $x \leqslant 1$ (b) $2 < y$

(a) $x \leqslant 1$

The boundary line is $x = 1$ (included).

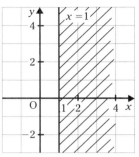

The unshaded region represents $x \leqslant 1$

(b) $2 < y$

The boundary line is $y = 2$
(not included).

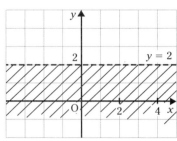

The unshaded region represents $2 < y$

Draw diagrams to represent the following inequalities:

1. $x \geqslant 2$ **4.** $y < 4$ **7.** $x \leqslant -4$

2. $y \leqslant 3$ **5.** $x \geqslant 0$ **8.** $y > -3$

3. $x > -1$ **6.** $0 > y$ **9.** $2 < x$

Draw a diagram to represent $-3 < x < 2$ and state whether or not the points $(1, 1)$ and $(-4, 2)$ lie in the given region.

($-3 < x < 2$ gives two inequalities, $-3 < x$ and $x < 2$)

Boundary lines are $x = -3$
and $x = 2$ (neither included)

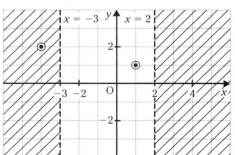

The unshaded region represents
$-3 < x < 2$
$(-4, 2)$ does not lie in the given region.
$(1, 1)$ lies in the given region.

Draw diagrams to represent the following pairs of inequalities:

10. $2 \leqslant x \leqslant 4$ **13.** $4 < y < 5$ **16.** $-\frac{1}{2} \leqslant x \leqslant 1\frac{1}{2}$

11. $-3 < x < 1$ **14.** $0 \leqslant x < 4$ **17.** $-2 \leqslant y < -1$

12. $-1 \leqslant y \leqslant 2$ **15.** $-2 < y \leqslant 3$ **18.** $3 \leqslant x < 5$

19. In each of the questions 10 to 12, state whether or not the point $(1, 4)$ lies in the unshaded region.

Give the inequality that defines the unshaded region

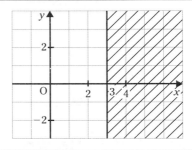

Boundary line $x = 3$ (included)

Inequality $x \leqslant 3$

Give the inequalities that define the unshaded region

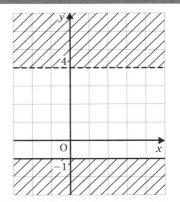

Boundary lines $y = 4$ (not included)

and $y = -1$ (included)

Inequalities $-1 \leqslant y < 4$

Give the inequalities that define the unshaded regions:

20.

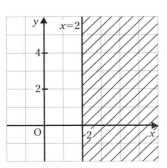

21.

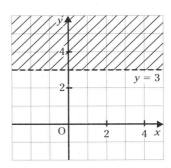

22.

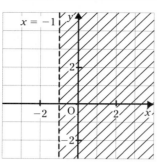

24.

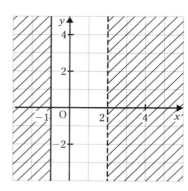

23.

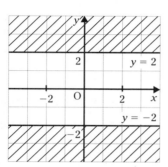

25.

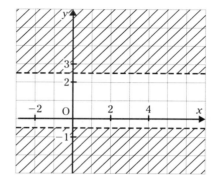

26. In each of the questions 20 to 25 state whether or not the point $(2, -1)$ is in the unshaded region.

Give the inequalities that define the *shaded* regions:

27.

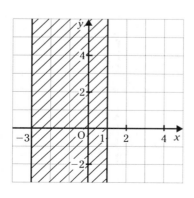

28.

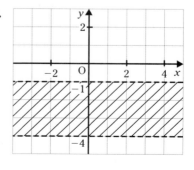

29.

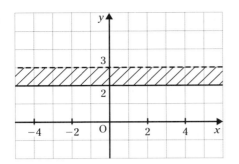

30.

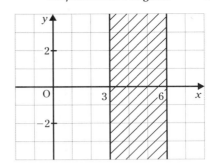

31. In each of the questions 27 to 30 state whether or not the point $(0, 2)$ is in the shaded region.

Exercise 17b

Draw a diagram to represent the region defined by the set of inequalities
$-1 \leqslant x \leqslant 2$ and $-5 \leqslant y \leqslant 0$

The boundary lines are

$x = -1$

$x = 2$

$y = -5$

$y = 0$

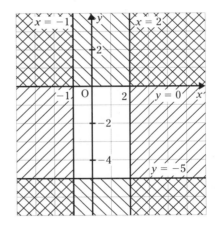

The unshaded region represents the inequalities.

Draw diagrams to represent the regions described by the following sets of inequalities. In each case, draw axes for values of x and y from -5 to 5.

1. $2 \leqslant x \leqslant 4, -1 \leqslant y \leqslant 3$

2. $-2 < x < 2, -2 < y < 2$

3. $-3 < x \leqslant 2, -1 \leqslant y$

4. $0 \leqslant x \leqslant 4, 0 \leqslant y \leqslant 3$

5. $-4 < x < 0, -2 < y < 2$

6. $-1 < x < 1, -3 < y < 1$

7. $x \geqslant 0, y \geqslant 0$

8. $x \geqslant 1, -1 \leqslant y \leqslant 2$

Give the sets of inequalities that describe the unshaded regions:

9.

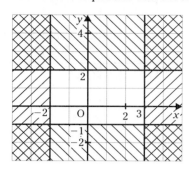

10.

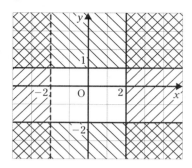

11. Is the point $(2\frac{1}{2}, 0)$ in either of the unshaded regions in questions 9 and 10?

Give the sets of inequalities that describe the unshaded regions:

12.

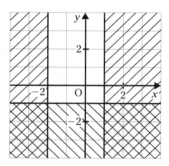

15.

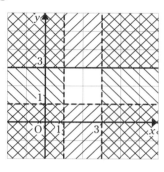

13.

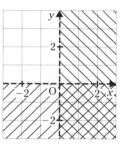

16.

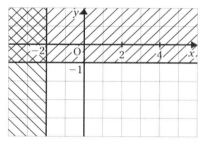

14.

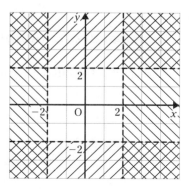

17.

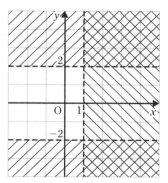

18. Is the point $(2, -1)$ in either of the unshaded regions in questions 16 and 17?

INEQUALITIES INVOLVING TWO VARIABLES

The boundary lines for inequalities are parallel to the x or y axis when the equalities contain either x or y, but not both.

Now we will consider some inequalities involving *both x and y* and we will find that the boundary lines are no longer parallel to an axis.

Consider $x + y \geqslant 4$.
In this case the boundary line is $x + y = 4$; as it is included in the region it is drawn as a solid line.

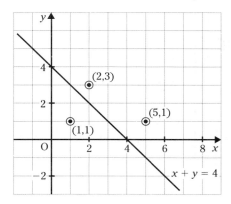

The boundary line divides the space into two regions, one on each side of the line. We need to decide which of the two regions is the one that we want.

Test a point such as $(2, 3)$.
When $x = 2$ and $y = 3$, $x + y = 5$ which is greater than 4, so the point $(2, 3)$ is in the required region.
The point $(5, 1)$ is also in the region, but the point $(1, 1)$ is not.
We can now see which region is required.

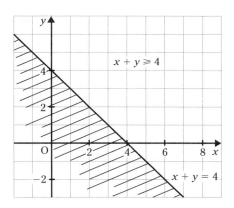

Exercise 17c

Leave unshaded the region defined by the inequality $2x + 3y < 12$

The boundary line is $2x + 3y = 12$ (not included in the inequality).

x	0	6	3
y	4	0	2

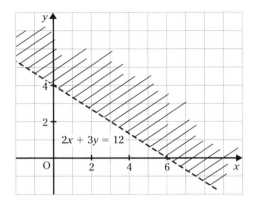

(To decide which of the two regions is wanted, we test an easy point such as $(0, 0)$.)

When $x = 0$ and $y = 0$, $2x + 3y = 0$ which is less than 12

Therefore $(0, 0)$ is in the required region. (Shade the region on the other side of the line.)

The unshaded region represents the inequality $2x + 3y < 12$

Find the regions defined by the following inequalities (draw axes for values of x and y from -6 to 6).

1. $x + y \leqslant 3$

2. $x + 4y \leqslant 8$

3. $x + y > 1$

4. $x + y \leqslant 2$

5. $2x + 5y \geqslant -6$

6. $3x + 4y \geqslant 12$

7. $4x + y < 4$

8. $2x + 5y > 10$

9. $2x + y \leqslant 6$

10. $3x + 2y > 5$

Sometimes the x and y terms are not on the same side of the inequality.

Leave unshaded the region defined by the inequality $y \geqslant 2x + 1$

The boundary line is $y = 2x + 1$

x	-2	0	2
y	-3	1	5

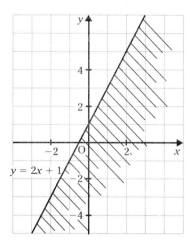

Test $(0, 0)$ $y = 0$

$$2x + 1 = 1$$

$0 < 1$ so $(0, 0)$ is not in the required region.

The unshaded region represents the inequality $y \geqslant 2x + 1$

Find the regions defined by the following inequalities:

11. $y \leqslant x + 1$

12. $y > 2x - 1$

13. $y \geqslant \frac{1}{2}x + 1$

14. $y < 2 - 2x$

15. $y < 4 - x$

16. $y \geqslant 2x - 2$

<u>17.</u> $y < 2x + 3$

<u>18.</u> $y < 5 + 3x$

<u>19.</u> $y > 3 + x$

<u>20.</u> $y \leqslant 5 - 2x$

<u>21.</u> $y \leqslant x - 4$

<u>22.</u> $y \geqslant 1 - x$

Exercise 17d

Find the inequality defining the unshaded region.

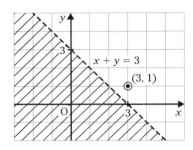

The boundary line is $x + y = 3$ and is not included.

Test the point $(3, 1)$, which is in the required region.

When $x = 3$ and $y = 1$, $x + y = 4$

$4 > 3$, so the inequality is $x + y > 3$

Find the inequalities that define the unshaded regions:

1.

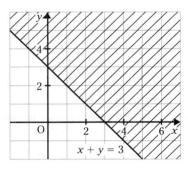

2.

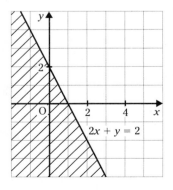

3.

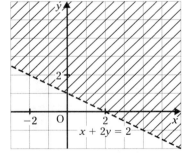

4.

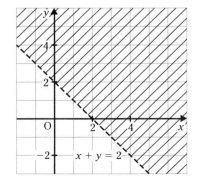

5.

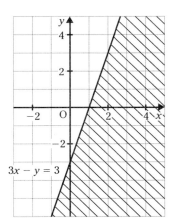

6.

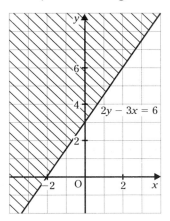

Find the inequality that defines the unshaded region

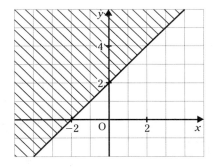

The gradient of the boundary line is

$$\frac{2-0}{0-(-2)} = \frac{2}{2} = 1$$

The line cuts the *y*-axis when $y = 2$ so the equation of the boundary line is $y = x + 2$

The boundary line is included in the region.

Test the point $(0, 0)$, which is in the required region.
At $(0, 0)$, $y = 0$ and $x + 2 = 2$
$0 < 2$, so the inequality is $y \leqslant x + 2$

Find the inequalities that define the unshaded regions:

7.

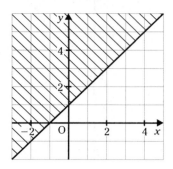

8.

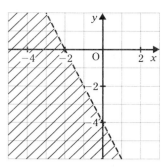

9.

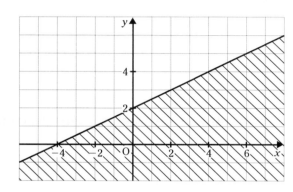

10.

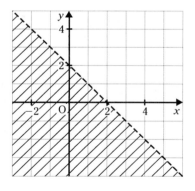

12.

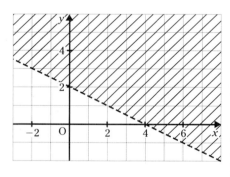

11.

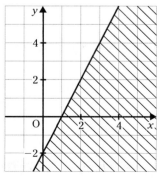

13.

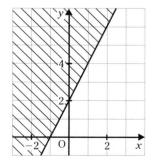

Exercise 17e

Leave unshaded the region defined by the set of inequalities
$x+y<4$, $x \geqslant 0$ and $x+2y \geqslant 2$

1st boundary line (not included) $x+y=4$

x	4	0	2
y	0	4	2

2nd boundary line (included) $x=0$

3rd boundary line (included) $x+2y=2$

x	0	2	4
y	1	0	-1

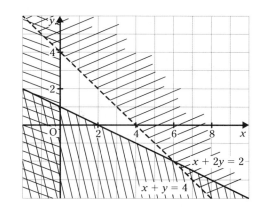

The unshaded region is defined by the given inequalities.

Leave unshaded the regions defined by the following sets of inequalities:

1. $x \geqslant -3$, $y \geqslant -2$, $x+y \leqslant 3$

2. $x > -1$, $-2 < y < 4$, $x+y < 4$

3. $y > 0$, $y \leqslant \frac{1}{2}x$, $x+y \geqslant 1$, $x+y \leqslant 5$

4. $y < 3$, $2x+3y \geqslant 6$, $y > x-2$

5. $y \leqslant 0$, $x \leqslant 0$, $x+y \geqslant -4$

6. $y > x$, $y < 4x$, $x+y < 5$

7. $y \geqslant 1$, $x \leqslant 0$, $y \leqslant x+2$

8. $x+y \leqslant 6$, $3x+y \geqslant 3$, $y \geqslant -1$, $x \geqslant -1$

9. $x \geqslant 0$, $y \geqslant x-1$, $2y+x < 4$

10. $x > 0$, $y \geqslant \frac{1}{2}x$, $x+y \geqslant 1$, $x+y \leqslant 5$

11. $y \geqslant 0$, $x \geqslant 0$, $x+y \leqslant 1$

12. What can you say about the region defined by $x+y>4$, $x+y<1$, $x>0$ and $y>0$?

13. Do the regions defined by the following sets of inequalities exist?

(a) $x+y \geqslant 3$, $y \leqslant 2$, $y \geqslant 2x$

(b) $x+y > 3$, $y < 2$, $y > 2x$

SHADING THE REQUIRED REGION

In some simple cases you might be asked to shade the region defined by the inequality, instead of leaving it unshaded.

Occasionally, you may be asked to shade the required region when it is defined by several inequalities. If you try to do it by shading the required side of each boundary line, you will find yourself with overlapping shadings, resulting in a confused diagram.

For instance, if $y \geqslant 0$, $x \geqslant 0$ and $x + y \leqslant 3$, the diagram looks like this and the required region disappears in a muddle.

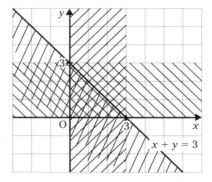

A better method is to do the shading as before so that the required region is left unshaded, then draw a second diagram on which you shade the required area.

1st diagram   2nd diagram

The required region is shaded

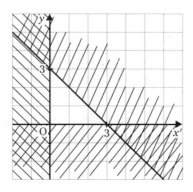 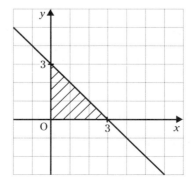

Exercise 17f

Shade the region defined by the set of inequalities $x < 3$, $y < 4$, $x + y > 0$

Boundary lines are $x = 3$, $y = 4$ and $x + y = 0$

1st diagram

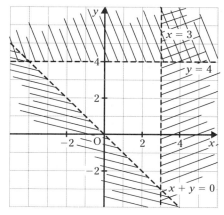

2nd diagram
The required
region is shaded.

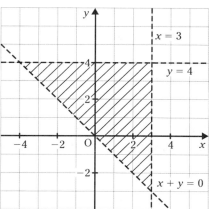

Shade the regions defined by the sets of inequalities:

1. $x \geqslant 0$, $y \geqslant 0$, $x + y \leqslant 3$

2. $x > -2$, $y \geqslant 2x$, $x + y < 4$

3. $x \leqslant 4$, $y \leqslant 3$, $x + y \geqslant 0$

4. $2x + y \geqslant 4$, $y \leqslant 0$, $x \leqslant 4$

5. $y > \frac{1}{2}x$, $0 < x < 2$, $x + y < 4$, $y < 3$

6. $\dfrac{x}{2} + \dfrac{y}{3} \geqslant 1$, $\dfrac{x}{2} - \dfrac{y}{3} \geqslant 1$, $x \leqslant 8$

7. $3x + 4y \leqslant 12$, $y \leqslant 2x + 1$, $y \geqslant -1$

8. $5x + 2y \leqslant -10$, $y \geqslant -1$, $x \geqslant -6$

9. $\dfrac{x}{5} + \dfrac{y}{4} \leqslant 1$, $y \leqslant 3x$, $y \geqslant \frac{1}{2}x$

10. $3x + 2y \geqslant -6$, $y \geqslant -3$, $x \geqslant -1$

If you wish to use diagrams for solving problems, it is best to leave the required regions unshaded.

Exercise 17g

Give the inequalities that define the unshaded region

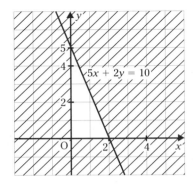

The first two inequalities are $x \geqslant 0, \ y \geqslant 0$

The 3rd boundary line is $5x + 2y = 10$

Test the point $(1, 1)$

When $x = 1$ and $y = 1, \ 5x + 2y = 7$

$7 < 10$ so the 3rd inequality is $5x + 2y \leqslant 10$

Give the sets of inequalities that define the unshaded regions:

1.

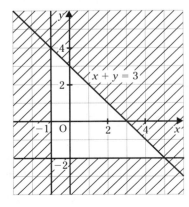

2.

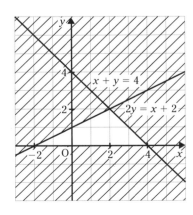

3.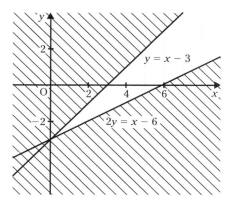

4.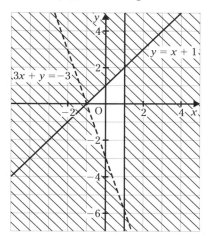

In the next four questions it is necessary to find the equations of the boundary lines first:

5.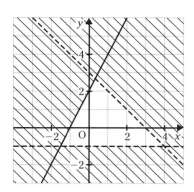

6.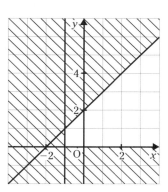

7.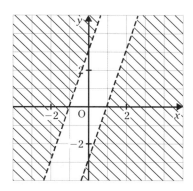

8.

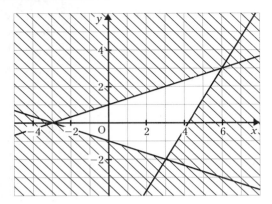

9. Use inequalities to describe the regions:

(a) A   (b) B   (c) C   (d) D   (e) E   (f) A + F

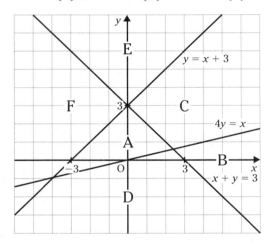

10. Use inequalities to describe the regions:

(a) A   (b) B   (c) C   (d) D   (e) E   (f) A + B

(The axes are not boundary lines.)

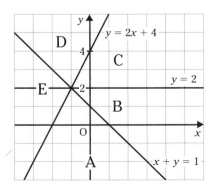

11. In the diagram, which region (A, B or C) does each of the following sets of inequalities refer to?

(a) $x + y < 2$, $x < -2$, $y > -2$

(b) $x + y < 2$, $x > -2$, $y > -2$

(c) $x + y < 2$, $x > -2$, $y < -2$

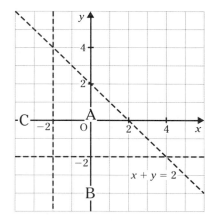

COORDINATES OF POINTS IN A REGION

Exercise 17h

From the given diagram read off the coordinates of the vertices of the unshaded region

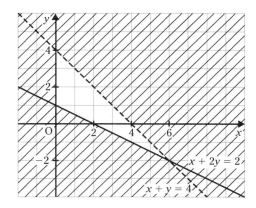

The vertices are $(0, 1)$, $(0, 4)$ and $(6, -2)$

From the diagrams, give the coordinates of the vertices of the unshaded regions in questions 1 to 4:

1.

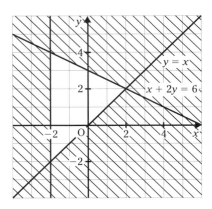

2.

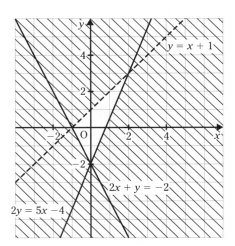

3.

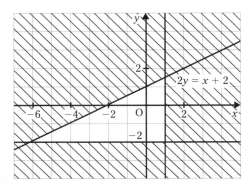

4.

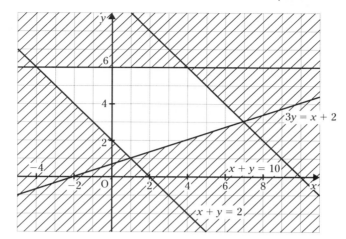

5. Draw a diagram and find the coordinates of the vertices of the region defined by the inequalities $x \geqslant -2$, $y \geqslant 2x$ and $y \leqslant x$

6. Draw a diagram and give the vertices of the region defined by the inequalities $y \geqslant 1$, $x \leqslant 0$ and $y \leqslant x + 2$

Give the points whose coordinates are integers and that lie in the region given in the worked example at the beginning of the exercise.

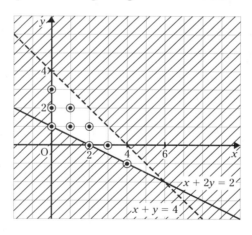

(Notice that points on the broken line are *not* in the region.)

Points are $(0, 1)$, $(0, 2)$, $(0, 3)$, $(1, 1)$, $(1, 2)$, $(2, 0)$, $(2, 1)$, $(3, 0)$ and $(4, -1)$.

7. Give the points whose coordinates are integers and that lie in the regions in questions 1 to 3.

8. Draw a diagram and give the coordinates of the points whose coordinates are integers and that lie in the region defined by the inequalities $y \leqslant 3x + 6$, $y > x - 2$, $x + y > -2$ and $x + y \leqslant 3$

9. Draw a diagram and give the points whose coordinates are integers and that lie in the region defined by the inequalities $y > 0$, $x > 0$, $3x + 4y < 12$ and $4x + 3y < 12$

10. Draw a diagram and give the points with coordinates that are integers, on the boundaries of the region defined by the inequalities $x \geqslant 2$, $y \geqslant -1$ and $x + y \leqslant 4$

GREATEST AND LEAST VALUES

Exercise 17i

Find the value of $x - 2y$ at the points $(4, 1)$, $(3, 0)$ and $(2, -1)$. At which point is the value greatest?

At $(4, 1)$ $\qquad\qquad$ $x - 2y = 4 - 2 = 2$

At $(3, 0)$ $\qquad\qquad$ $x - 2y = 3 - 0 = 3$

At $(2, -1)$ $\qquad\qquad$ $x - 2y = 2 - (-2) = 4$

$x - 2y$ has its greatest value at $(2, -1)$.

1. Find the value of $x + y$ at the points $(2, 3)$, $(4, -2)$ and $(-3, -1)$.

2. Find the value of $x - y$ at the points $(6, 2)$, $(1, 4)$ and $(4, -3)$.

3. Find the value of $2x + y$ at the points $(5, 1)$, $(-6, -2)$ and $(-1, 2)$.

4. Find the value of $3x - 2y$ at the points $(5, 5)$ and $(2, -8)$. At which point is the value greatest?

5. Find the value of $y - 3x$ at the points $(-6, -8)$ and $(3, 8)$. At which point is the value least?

From the diagram give the coordinates of the vertices of the unshaded region. At which vertex is the value of $x + 2y$ least?

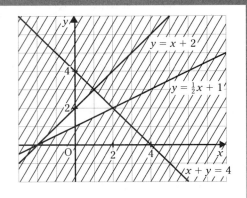

The three vertices are $(1, 3)$, $(2, 2)$ and $(-2, 0)$.

At $(1, 3)$ $\qquad\qquad$ $x + 2y = 1 + 6 = 7$

At $(2, 2)$ $\qquad\qquad$ $x + 2y = 2 + 4 = 6$

At $(-2, 0)$ $\qquad\qquad$ $x + 2y = -2 + 0 = -2$

$\therefore$ $x + 2y$ is least at point $(-2, 0)$.

6.

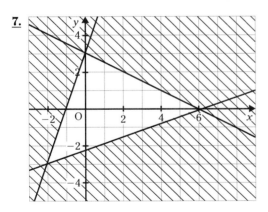

(a) Find from the diagram the coordinates of the vertices of the unshaded region.

(b) Find the vertex at which the value of $x + y$ is greatest.

(c) Find the vertex at which the value of $x + y$ is least.

(d) Mark the other points in the unshaded region whose coordinates are integers. How many are there?

(e) Is there a point in the region where the value of $x + y$ is greater than its value at the vertex chosen in (b)?

7.

(a) Find from the diagram the coordinates of the vertices of the region.

(b) Find the vertex at which the value of $2x - y$ is greatest.

8.

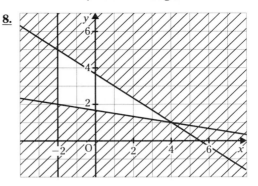

(a) From the diagram find the coordinates of the vertices of the unshaded region.

(b) Find the vertex at which the value of $3x - 2y$ is
(i) greatest   (ii) least.

(c) List the other points in the unshaded region whose coordinates are integers.

(d) Is there a point in the region where the value of $3x - 2y$ is less than its value at the vertex chosen in (b)(ii)?

9. (a) Draw axes for the values of x and y from -5 to 5 and leave unshaded the region defined by the set of inequalities $x \geqslant -2$, $y \geqslant -3$ and $x + y \leqslant 2$.

(b) Find the coordinates of the vertices of the region.

(c) Mark the other points in the region with integer coordinates. How many are there?

(d) At which of these points in the region is the value of $x - y$ greatest and at which point is it least?

As we see from the answers to questions 7 to 9, the greatest and least values of any expression such as $2x + 3y$ occur at or near the vertices of a region and not at points between the vertices or in the middle of the region. Therefore to find the greatest or least values, we need to test points at or near the vertices only.

Exercise 17j

For the region defined by the set of inequalities $x \geqslant -1$, $y \geqslant -2$ and $x + y < 3$, draw a diagram and find the points with coordinates that are integers, where the value of $2x - y$ is (a) greatest (b) least.

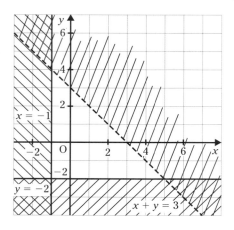

At $(-1, 3)$ $2x - y = -2 - 3 = -5$

At $(-1, -2)$ $2x - y = -2 + 2 = 0$

At $(4, -2)$ $2x - y = 8 + 2 = 10$

(a) $(2x - y)$ is greatest at $(4, -2)$.

(b) $(2x - y)$ is least at $(-1, 3)$.

1. In the region defined by $x \geqslant -3$, $y \leqslant x + 1$ and $y \geqslant 2x$, find the point with integer coordinates where the value of $3x - y$ is greatest.

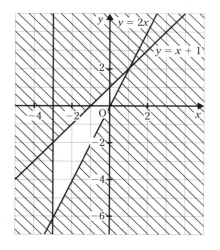

2. In the region defined by $x + y > -1$, $x < 3$ and $y \leqslant 2$, find the point with integer coordinates where the value of $x + 2y$ is least.

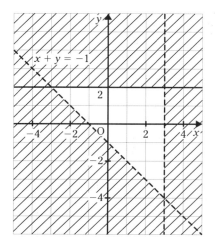

3. In the region defined by $y < x + 3$, $3x + y < 6$ and $y \geqslant -1$, find the point with integer coordinates where the value of $3x - 2y$ is greatest.

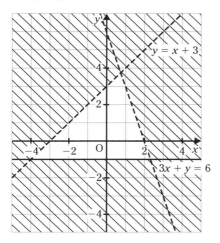

4. In the region defined by $y \leqslant 4 - 2x$, $y \geqslant -2$ and $x \geqslant 0$, by drawing a diagram, find the points or point with integer coordinates at which the value of $2x + y$ is greatest.

5. In the region defined by $x + y < 4$, $x > -1$ and $y > 1$, by drawing a diagram, find the point with integer coordinates at which the value of $2x - y$ is least.

6. In the region defined by $4x + y \leqslant 4$, $y \leqslant 3$ and $x \leqslant 1$, by drawing a diagram, find the point with integer coordinates at which the value of $x + y$ is greatest. Is there a point at which the value of $x + y$ is least?

LINEAR PROGRAMMING

A branch of mathematics known as linear programming is an essential tool in business planning. It provides a useful application for systems of linear inequations similar to those solved above.

The following exercise will illustrate this.

Exercise 17k

1. A factory produces two grades of a product, grade A and grade B. Each unit of grade A requires 2 hours work on a machine and each unit of grade B requires 3 hours work on the machine. The factory can only afford a maximum of 40 working hours per week on the machine. Denoting the number of units of grade A product produced weekly by x and the number of units of grade B product by y, graph the relation which shows the combinations of the two products that the factory is capable of producing weekly.

If grade A units are sold at $150 per unit and grade B units are sold at $200 per unit, what is the maximum value of sales which the factory can make in one week?

2. The Ministry of Housing has 2 hectares of land on which to build houses. It plans to build type A houses which cost $80 000 and type B houses which cost $60 000. The former will occupy one-quarter of a hectare, the latter only one-eighth. The Ministry cannot spend more than $600 000 on this project.

If they decide to build x type A houses and y type B houses, write down two inequalities to express the above information.

If the Ministry makes $12 000 on a type A house and $6 000 on a type B house, find how many of each type of house they should build in order to make the maximum profit on the project.

3. A building contractor can employ no more than 5 carpenters; also, he can employ at least 7 masons but no more than 10.

He must have at least 1 carpenter and the total number of carpenters and masons must not exceed 12.

Using x to represent the number of carpenters and y to represent the number of masons, write a system of inequalities to show the permissible combinations he can employ.

4. A recommended animal feed is to be a mixture of two foodstuffs, each unit of which contains protein, fat and carbohydrate in the number of grams shown in the table below.

	Foodstuff 1	2
Protein (g)	10	5
Fat (g)	0.1	0.9
Carbohydrate (g)	10	30

Each bag of the resulting mixture is to contain at least 40 g of protein, 1.8 g of fat and 120 g of carbohydrate. Denoting the number of units of foodstuff 1 in the mixture by x and the number of units of foodstuff 2 by y, write and graph the system of inequalities which shows the mixtures that meet these requirements.

18 ▷ ALGEBRAIC FRACTIONS

At the end of the chapter you should be able to:

1. Reduce a given algebraic fraction to its lowest form.
2. Multiply or divide two algebraic expressions.
3. Find the LCM of a set of algebraic expressions.
4. Add or subtract two algebraic fractions.
5. Solve simple equations containing algebraic fractions.
6. Solve quadratic equations containing algebraic fractions.

SIMPLIFYING FRACTIONS

We simplify a fraction such as $\frac{10}{50}$ by recognising that 10 is a common factor of the numerator and denominator and then cancelling that common factor,

i.e. $\qquad \frac{10}{50} = \frac{\cancel{10}^1}{5 \times \cancel{10}_1} = \frac{1}{5}$

To simplify an algebraic fraction, we do exactly the same: we find and then cancel the common factors of the numerator and denominator.

Note that we do not have to write the number 50 as 5×10 but that when the factors are letters it helps at this stage to put in the multiplication sign.

For example $\qquad xy$ can be written as $x \times y$

and $\qquad 2(a+b)$ can be written as $2 \times (a+b)$

Exercise 18a

Simplify (a) $\dfrac{2xy}{6y}$ (b) $\dfrac{2a}{a^2b}$

(a) $\dfrac{2xy}{6y} = \dfrac{\cancel{2}^1 \times x \times \cancel{y}^1}{\cancel{6}_3 \times \cancel{y}_1}$

$\qquad = \dfrac{x}{3}$

(b) $\dfrac{2a}{a^2b} = \dfrac{2 \times \cancel{a}^1}{\cancel{a}_1 \times a \times b}$

$\qquad = \dfrac{2}{ab}$

Simplify:

1. $\dfrac{2x}{8}$

2. $\dfrac{ab}{2b}$

3. $\dfrac{p^2}{pq}$

4. $\dfrac{a^2}{ab}$

5. $\dfrac{xy}{y^2}$

6. $\dfrac{3}{6a}$

7. $\dfrac{2ab}{4bc}$

8. $\dfrac{6p}{3pq}$

9. $\dfrac{5p^2q}{10p}$

10. $\dfrac{a^2b}{abc}$

11. $\dfrac{7a}{14}$

12. $\dfrac{yz}{2x}$

13. $\dfrac{b^2}{bd}$

14. $\dfrac{4}{12x}$

15. $\dfrac{3pq}{6p}$

16. $\dfrac{10x}{15xy}$

17. $\dfrac{m^2n}{kmn}$

18. $\dfrac{5s^2}{20st}$

FACTORS

We know that $3 \times 2 = 6$ but neither $3 + 2$ nor $3 - 2$ is equal to 6.

We can write a number as the product of its factors but, in general, we cannot write a number as the sum or difference of its factors.

Thus $\qquad \begin{cases} p \text{ and } q \text{ are factors of } pq \\ a \text{ and } (a - b) \text{ are factors of } a(a - b) \end{cases}$

but in general $\begin{cases} p \text{ is } not \text{ a factor of } p + q \\ b \text{ is } not \text{ a factor of } a - b \end{cases}$

This means that in the fraction $\dfrac{p + q}{pq}$ we *cannot* cancel q because q is not a factor of the numerator.

Sometimes the common factors in a fraction are not very obvious.

Consider $\qquad \dfrac{x - 2}{y(x - 2)}$

Placing the numerator in brackets and using the multiplication sign gives $\dfrac{(x - 2)}{y \times (x - 2)}$

Now we can see clearly that $(x - 2)$ is a common factor, so

$$\frac{\cancel{(x - 2)}}{y \times \cancel{(x - 2)}} = \frac{1}{y}$$

Exercise 18b

Simplify where possible (a) $\dfrac{2a(a-b)}{a-b}$ (b) $\dfrac{pq}{p-q}$

(a) $\dfrac{2a(a-b)}{a-b} = \dfrac{2 \times a \times \cancel{(a-b)}}{\cancel{(a-b)}}$

$$= 2a$$

(b) $\dfrac{pq}{p-q} = \dfrac{p \times q}{(p-q)}$ which cannot be simplified.

Simplify where possible:

1. $\dfrac{x-y}{x(x-y)}$

2. $\dfrac{st}{s(s-t)}$

3. $\dfrac{2a}{a-b}$

4. $\dfrac{p+q}{2p}$

5. $\dfrac{4x}{8(x-y)}$

6. $\dfrac{3(a+b)}{6ab}$

7. $\dfrac{(p-q)(p+q)}{p+q}$

8. $\dfrac{(4+a)}{(4+a)(4-a)}$

9. $\dfrac{(a-b)}{3(a+b)}$

10. $\dfrac{u-v}{v(u-v)}$

11. $\dfrac{xy}{x(x+y)}$

12. $\dfrac{s-t}{2(s-t)}$

13. $\dfrac{10a}{15(a-b)}$

14. $\dfrac{8(x-y)}{12xy}$

15. $\dfrac{s-t}{3s}$

16. $\dfrac{(u+v)(u-v)}{u+v}$

17. $\dfrac{x+y}{2(x-y)}$

18. $\dfrac{s+6}{(s+6)(s-6)}$

Sometimes we have to factorise the numerator and/or the denominator before we look for common factors.

Consider for example $\dfrac{12a-4b}{3a-b}$

In the numerator there is a common factor of 4, so

$$12a - 4b = 4(3a - b)$$

The fraction becomes $\dfrac{4(3a-b)}{(3a-b)}$

It is now clear that 4 and $(3a-b)$ are factors of $12a-4b$ so we can cancel $(3a-b)$, i.e. $\dfrac{4\cancel{(3a-b)}}{\cancel{(3a-b)}} = 4$

We have been writing expressions such as $4(3a-b)$ in the form $4 \times (3a-b)$, but the multiplication sign is not necessary and we will no longer put it in. If, however, you find that the multiplication sign makes it easier to see individual factors then continue to use it.

Exercise 18c

Simplify $\dfrac{xy - y^2}{3y}$

$$\frac{xy - y^2}{3y} = \frac{\cancel{y}(x - y)}{3\cancel{y}_1}$$

$$= \frac{x - y}{3}$$

Simplify:

1. $\dfrac{4a}{8a - 2b}$

2. $\dfrac{2pq}{p^2 - pq}$

3. $\dfrac{a - b}{a^2 - ab}$

4. $\dfrac{3a - 6b}{5a - 10b}$

5. $\dfrac{2x - x^2}{3xy}$

6. $\dfrac{a^2}{3a - ab}$

7. $\dfrac{2a - 3b}{6a^2 - 9ab}$

8. $\dfrac{2s^2 - st}{2s - t}$

9. $\dfrac{3a - 6b}{a^2 - 2ab}$

10. $\dfrac{6x}{9x - 3y}$

11. $\dfrac{3ab}{ab + b^2}$

12. $\dfrac{p^2 + pq}{5p}$

13. $\dfrac{2p - 4q}{6p - 12q}$

14. $\dfrac{3a + a^2}{4ab}$

15. $\dfrac{2x - xy}{x^2}$

16. $\dfrac{2x + y}{6xy + 3y^2}$

17. $\dfrac{a^2b - ac}{ab - c}$

18. $\dfrac{p^2 + 2pq}{2p + 4q}$

Simplify $\dfrac{pq - 3q}{p^2 - 6p + 9}$

$$\frac{pq - 3q}{p^2 - 6p + 9} = \frac{q\cancel{(p - 3)}}{(p - 3)\cancel{(p - 3)}}$$

$$= \frac{q}{p - 3}$$

Simplify:

19. $\dfrac{a - 4}{a^2 - 6a + 8}$

20. $\dfrac{x - 2}{x^2 - 6x + 8}$

21. $\dfrac{y + 3}{y^2 + 5y + 6}$

22. $\dfrac{2a - 8}{a^2 - a - 12}$

23. $\dfrac{3x + 12}{x^2 + 7x + 12}$

24. $\dfrac{9y - 36}{y^2 - 2y - 8}$

25. $\dfrac{xy - 2y}{x^2 - 4x + 4}$

26. $\dfrac{pq + 5q}{p^2 + 7p + 10}$

27. $\dfrac{st - t}{s^2 - 8s + 7}$

28. $\dfrac{p+3}{p^2+6p+9}$

30. $\dfrac{2x+6}{x^2-x-12}$

32. $\dfrac{uv+6v}{u^2+12u+36}$

29. $\dfrac{x-5}{x^2+x-30}$

31. $\dfrac{3x-15}{x^2-9x+20}$

33. $\dfrac{xy-7y}{x^2-9x+14}$

FURTHER SIMPLIFYING

The next exercise contains slightly more complicated factorising.

Remember that $a^2 - b^2 = (a-b)(a+b)$

It sometimes happens that the numerator has a factor $(a-b)$
and the denominator has a factor $(b-a)$

Now $\qquad (a-b) = (-1)(b-a)$

therefore a fraction such as $\dfrac{a-b}{b-a}$ can be simplified,

i.e. $\qquad \dfrac{a-b}{b-a} = \dfrac{(-1)\cancel{(b-a)}'}{\cancel{(b-a)},} = -1$

Exercise 18d

Simplify (a) $\dfrac{2x^2+5x-3}{4x^2-1}$ (b) $\dfrac{a^2-2ab+b^2}{b^2-ab}$

(a) $\dfrac{2x^2+5x-3}{4x^2-1} = \dfrac{\cancel{(2x-1)}'(x+3)}{\cancel{(2x-1)}_{,}(2x+1)}$

$\qquad\qquad = \dfrac{(x+3)}{(2x+1)}$

(b) $\dfrac{a^2-2ab+b^2}{b^2-ab} = \dfrac{(a-b)(a-b)}{b(b-a)}$

$\qquad\qquad = \dfrac{(-1)\cancel{(b-a)}'(a-b)}{b\cancel{(b-a)}_{,}}$

$\qquad\qquad = \dfrac{(-1)(a-b)}{b}$

$\qquad\qquad = \dfrac{b-a}{b}$

Simplify:

1. $\dfrac{x^2 - 9}{2x^2 - 7x + 3}$

2. $\dfrac{4x - 8}{x^2 - 4}$

3. $\dfrac{4x^2 - 1}{2x^2 - 3x - 2}$

4. $\dfrac{2 - x}{x^2 - 4x + 4}$

5. $\dfrac{a^2 - b^2}{b^2 - 2ab + a^2}$

6. $\dfrac{2a^2 + ab - b^2}{4a^2 - b^2}$

7. $\dfrac{3x^2 - xy - 2y^2}{9x^2 - 4y^2}$

8. $\dfrac{x^2 - 5x + 6}{3y - xy}$

9. $\dfrac{a - a^2}{a - 1}$

10. $\dfrac{2y^2 + 5y - 3}{4y^2 - 1}$

11. $\dfrac{x^2 - 6xy + 9y^2}{x^2 - 3xy}$

12. $\dfrac{4x^2 - 7x - 2}{4x^2 - 8x}$

13. $\dfrac{2x^2 - 13x + 15}{x^2 - 10x + 25}$

14. $\dfrac{a - 1}{1 - a^2}$

15. $\dfrac{ac + bc - ad - bd}{c - d}$

16. $\dfrac{2x^2 + 3x - 35}{7 + 5x - 2x^2}$

17. $\dfrac{4x^2 + 6x - 4}{x^2 - x - 6}$

18. $\dfrac{x^2 - xy - 2y^2}{y^2 + xy}$

19. $\dfrac{1 - x^2}{3x^2 + 9x + 6}$

20. $\dfrac{y + x + xy + y^2}{x^2 + 2xy + y^2}$

MULTIPLYING AND DIVIDING FRACTIONS

Reminder: The product of two fractions is found by multiplying the numerators and multiplying the denominators,

e.g.
$$\frac{2}{3} \times \frac{4}{5} = \frac{2 \times 4}{3 \times 5} = \frac{8}{15}$$

and
$$\frac{p}{q} \times \frac{(a - b)}{(a + b)} = \frac{p(a - b)}{q(a + b)}$$

To divide by a fraction, we multiply by its reciprocal,

e.g.
$$\frac{2}{3} \div \frac{3}{4} = \frac{2}{3} \times \frac{4}{3} = \frac{8}{9}$$

$$\frac{p}{q} \div r = \frac{p}{q} \times \frac{1}{r} = \frac{p}{qr}$$

and
$$\frac{p}{q} \div \frac{a}{(a - b)} = \frac{p}{q} \times \frac{(a - b)}{a} = \frac{p(a - b)}{qa}$$

Exercise 18e

Find:

1. $\dfrac{a}{b} \times \dfrac{c}{d}$

2. $\dfrac{a}{b} \div \dfrac{c}{d}$

3. $\dfrac{x - y}{2} \times \dfrac{5}{x}$

4. $\dfrac{x - y}{2} \div \dfrac{5}{x}$

5. $\dfrac{a}{b} \div c$

6. $\dfrac{a}{b} \times c$

7. $\dfrac{(a-b)}{4} \div \dfrac{(a+b)}{3}$

9. $\dfrac{(x-2)}{3} \div (x+3)$

8. $\dfrac{(x-2)}{3} \times (x+3)$

10. $\dfrac{p}{q} \div \dfrac{1}{r}$

As is the case in number fractions, it is sometimes possible to simplify before multiplying.

Simplify $\dfrac{ab}{4} \times \dfrac{8}{a^2}$

$$\dfrac{ab}{4} \times \dfrac{8}{a^2} = \dfrac{\overset{1}{ab}}{\underset{1}{4}} \times \dfrac{\overset{2}{8}}{\underset{a}{a^2}}$$

$$= \dfrac{2b}{a}$$

Simplify:

11. $\dfrac{2a}{b} \div \dfrac{a^2}{3b^2}$

16. $\dfrac{x^2}{4} \div \dfrac{xy}{2}$

12. $\dfrac{pq}{6} \times \dfrac{3}{p^2}$

17. $\dfrac{1}{b^2} \div \dfrac{2}{b}$

13. $\dfrac{4xy}{3} \times \dfrac{9}{x^2}$

18. $\dfrac{7p}{5q} \times \dfrac{10q}{21p^2}$

14. $\dfrac{2ab}{5} \div \dfrac{a}{b}$

19. $\dfrac{a^2}{2b} \div 2a$

15. $\dfrac{2p^2}{3} \times \dfrac{q}{4p}$

20. $\dfrac{a}{b} \times \dfrac{2a}{3b} \div \dfrac{2b}{3a}$

Simplify $\dfrac{(a^2-b^2)}{a} \times \dfrac{b}{(a+b)}$

$$\dfrac{(a^2-b^2)}{a} \times \dfrac{b}{(a+b)} = \dfrac{(a-b)\overset{1}{(a+b)}b}{a\underset{1}{(a+b)}}$$

$$= \dfrac{b(a-b)}{a}$$

(Notice that we leave the answer in factor form.)

Simplify $(x^2 - 3x - 4) \div (x - 4)$

$\left(\text{Remember that } 7 \div 4 \text{ can be written } \frac{7}{4}; \text{ similarly } (x^2 - 3x - 4) \div (x - 4) \right.$

$\left. \text{can be written } \dfrac{x^2 - 3x - 4}{x - 4} \right)$

$$(x^2 - 3x - 4) \div (x - 4) = \frac{x^2 - 3x - 4}{x - 4}$$

$$= \frac{(x - 4)(x + 1)}{(x - 4)}$$

$$= x + 1$$

Simplify:

21. $\dfrac{(b - 2)}{4} \times \dfrac{1}{(b^2 - 4b + 4)}$

22. $\dfrac{(x^2 - 4)}{3} \times \dfrac{6}{(x + 2)}$

23. $\dfrac{(a^2 - 9)}{2} \div \dfrac{(a - 3)}{4}$

24. $\dfrac{(3b - 6)}{5} \div \dfrac{(b - 2)}{10}$

25. $(x^2 - 6x + 9) \div (x - 3)$

26. $\dfrac{1}{(x - 2)} \times (x^2 - 5x + 6)$

27. $(x - 4) \div (x^2 - 6x + 8)$

28. $(2x - 4) \times \dfrac{1}{(x^2 + 2x - 8)}$

29. $\dfrac{(x^2 - 4)}{5} \times \dfrac{3}{(x^2 + 8x + 12)}$

30. $\dfrac{(4x^2 - 9)}{3} \div \dfrac{(6x + 9)}{2}$

31. $(3x - 6) \div (3x^2 - 4x - 4)$

32. $\dfrac{(2x^2 - 5x + 3)}{2} \times \dfrac{(x - 1)}{(x^2 - 2x + 1)}$

33. $(4x^2 - 1) \div (12x^2 + 8x + 1)$

34. $\dfrac{(ab + a^2)}{b} \times \dfrac{b}{a + b}$

35. $\dfrac{a^2 - b^2}{c} \div \dfrac{b^2 - ab}{c^2}$

36. $\dfrac{(x^2 - 5x + 4)}{(x + 2)} \times \dfrac{(x^2 - 4)}{(x - 1)}$

LOWEST COMMON MULTIPLE

Before we can simplify $\frac{2}{3} + \frac{1}{5}$ we must change both $\frac{2}{3}$ and $\frac{1}{5}$ into equivalent fractions with the same denominator. This common denominator must contain both 3 and 5 as factors; there are many numbers we could choose but 15 is the lowest such number, i.e. 15 is the *lowest common multiple* (LCM) of 3 and 5.

To simplify $\dfrac{3}{x} + \dfrac{2}{y}$ we follow the same pattern. We need a common denominator with both x and y as factors. Again there are many we could use, but the simplest is xy; this is the LCM of x and y.

Exercise 18f

Find the LCM of ab and c

The LCM is abc

Find the LCM of:

1. p, q

2. r, st

3. $2, 3, 5$

4. a, b, c

5. x, y, wz

6. a, d

7. v, uw

8. $3, 7, 8$

9. p, q, r

Find the LCM of (a) 4, 10   (b) ab, a^2 (c) $2x, 6x$

(a) $4 = 2 \times 2$ and $10 = 2 \times 5$

(The LCM is the *lowest* number that 4 and 10 divide into exactly, so the factors it must include are

2×2 from 4 and 5 from 10

The factor of 2 from 10 is not needed as 2 is already included.)

∴ the LCM of 4 and 10 is $2 \times 2 \times 5 = 20$

(b) $ab = a \times b$ and $a^2 = a \times a$

∴ the LCM is $a \times b \times a = a^2b$

(c) $2x = 2 \times x$ and $6x = 2 \times 3 \times x$

∴ the LCM is $2 \times 3 \times x = 6x$

Find the LCM of:

10. x, xy

11. $x^2, 2x$

12. $pq, 3p$

13. $x^2, 2xy$

14. ab, bc

15. s, st

16. $3p, p^2$

17. $5a, ab$

18. $3pq, q^2$

19. $2x, 3x$

20. $4x, 8x$

21. $6a, 9a$

22. $6, 4, 10$

23. a, ab, a^2

24. $10x, 15x$

25. $4x, 6x$

26. $3y, 5y$

27. $2x, 3x, 4x$

ADDITION AND SUBTRACTION OF FRACTIONS

To add or subtract fractions we first have to change them into equivalent fractions with a common denominator.

Thus to find $\frac{2}{3} + \frac{1}{5}$, we choose a common denominator of 15 which is the LCM of 3 and 5.

Now
$$\frac{2}{3} = \frac{2 \times 5}{3 \times 5} = \frac{10}{15} \quad \text{and} \quad \frac{1}{5} = \frac{1 \times 3}{5 \times 3} = \frac{3}{15}$$

Therefore
$$\frac{2}{3} + \frac{1}{5} = \frac{10 + 3}{15} = \frac{13}{15}$$

To simplify $\frac{3}{x} + \frac{2}{y}$ we follow the same pattern:

xy is the LCM of x and y.

$$\frac{3}{x} = \frac{3 \times y}{x \times y} = \frac{3y}{xy} \quad \text{and} \quad \frac{2}{y} = \frac{2 \times x}{y \times x} = \frac{2x}{xy}$$

$$\therefore \qquad \frac{3}{x} + \frac{2}{y} = \frac{3y + 2x}{xy}$$

Exercise 18g

Simplify $\dfrac{1}{2a} + \dfrac{1}{b}$

($2ab$ is the LCM of $2a$ and b)

$$\frac{1}{2a} + \frac{1}{b} = \frac{(1) \times (b) + (1) \times (2a)}{2ab}$$

$$= \frac{b + 2a}{2ab}$$

Simplify $\dfrac{3}{4x} - \dfrac{1}{6x}$

($12x$ is the LCM of $4x$ and $6x$)

$$\frac{3}{4x} - \frac{1}{6x} = \frac{(3) \times (3) - (1) \times (2)}{12x}$$

$$= \frac{7}{12x}$$

Simplify:

1. $\dfrac{1}{x} + \dfrac{1}{y}$

2. $\dfrac{3}{p} + \dfrac{2}{q}$

3. $\dfrac{2}{s} - \dfrac{1}{t}$

4. $\dfrac{3}{a} + \dfrac{1}{2b}$

5. $\dfrac{1}{3x} - \dfrac{2}{5y}$

6. $\dfrac{1}{a} + \dfrac{5}{2b}$

7. $\dfrac{2}{x} - \dfrac{3}{y}$

8. $\dfrac{4}{3p} + \dfrac{2}{q}$

9. $\dfrac{3}{x} - \dfrac{2}{y}$

10. $\dfrac{5}{7a} + \dfrac{3}{4b}$

11. $\dfrac{1}{2x} + \dfrac{1}{3x}$

12. $\dfrac{2}{5x} - \dfrac{3}{7x}$

13. $\dfrac{2}{y} - \dfrac{3}{4y}$

14. $\dfrac{3}{8p} - \dfrac{1}{4p}$

15. $\dfrac{1}{a} + \dfrac{5}{8a}$

16. $\dfrac{1}{3x} - \dfrac{1}{7x}$

17. $\dfrac{4}{7x} - \dfrac{2}{5x}$

18. $\dfrac{1}{y} - \dfrac{2}{3y}$

Simplify $\dfrac{4a}{3b} - \dfrac{b}{6a}$

$(3b = 3 \times b \ \text{ and } \ 6a = 2 \times 3 \times a, \ \therefore \ \text{LCM} = 6ab)$

$$\dfrac{4a}{3b} - \dfrac{b}{6a} = \dfrac{(4a) \times (2a) - (b) \times (b)}{6ab}$$

$$= \dfrac{8a^2 - b^2}{6ab}$$

Simplify:

19. $\dfrac{1}{2a} + \dfrac{3}{4b}$

20. $\dfrac{a}{2b} - \dfrac{a^2}{b^2}$

21. $\dfrac{3}{x} - \dfrac{4}{xy}$

22. $\dfrac{2}{p^2} - \dfrac{3}{2p}$

23. $\dfrac{3a}{4b} + \dfrac{b}{6a}$

24. $\dfrac{5}{2p} - \dfrac{3}{4q}$

25. $\dfrac{s}{t^2} + \dfrac{s^2}{2t}$

26. $\dfrac{5}{2a} + \dfrac{2}{3ab}$

27. $\dfrac{1}{x^2} + \dfrac{2}{3x}$

28. $\dfrac{2y}{3x} - \dfrac{3x}{2y}$

29. $\dfrac{5}{8x} + \dfrac{2}{4y}$

30. $\dfrac{p}{3q} + \dfrac{p^2}{q^2}$

31. $\dfrac{5}{7x} - \dfrac{3}{14xy}$

32. $\dfrac{9}{a^2} - \dfrac{3}{2ab}$

33. $\dfrac{3x}{2y} - \dfrac{3y}{2x}$

34. $\dfrac{7}{9p} - \dfrac{5}{6q}$

35. $\dfrac{a^2}{b^2} + \dfrac{4a}{5b}$

36. $\dfrac{7}{5pq} + \dfrac{8}{15q}$

Exercise 18h

Simplify $\dfrac{x-2}{3} - \dfrac{x-4}{2}$

$$\dfrac{(x-2)}{3} - \dfrac{(x-4)}{2} = \dfrac{2(x-2) - 3(x-4)}{6}$$

$$= \dfrac{2x - 4 - 3x + 12}{6}$$

$$= \dfrac{-x + 8}{6}$$

$$= \dfrac{8 - x}{6}$$

(Notice that we placed brackets round the numerators *before* putting the fractions over a common denominator. This ensured that each numerator was kept together and that the signs were not confused.)

Simplify:

1. $\dfrac{x+2}{5} + \dfrac{x-1}{4}$

2. $\dfrac{x+3}{4} - \dfrac{x+1}{3}$

3. $\dfrac{2x-1}{3} + \dfrac{x+2}{5}$

4. $\dfrac{2x+3}{4} - \dfrac{x-2}{6}$

5. $\dfrac{x+3}{7} - \dfrac{x+2}{5}$

6. $\dfrac{x+4}{5} + \dfrac{x-1}{2}$

7. $\dfrac{2x-1}{7} - \dfrac{x-2}{5}$

8. $\dfrac{3x+1}{14} - \dfrac{2x+3}{21}$

Remember that $\frac{1}{5}(x-2) = \dfrac{(x-2)}{5}$

9. $\frac{1}{7}(2x-3) - \frac{1}{3}(4x-2)$

10. $\frac{1}{4}(5x-1) - \frac{1}{3}(2x-3)$

11. $\dfrac{5-2x}{3} + \dfrac{4-3x}{2}$

12. $\frac{1}{4}(3-x) + \frac{1}{6}(1-2x)$

13. $\frac{1}{8}(5x+4) - \frac{1}{3}(4x-1)$

14. $\dfrac{2x+3}{5} - \dfrac{3x-2}{4}$

15. $\dfrac{3-x}{2} + \dfrac{1-2x}{6}$

16. $\dfrac{2+5x}{8} - \dfrac{3-4x}{6}$

17. $\frac{1}{5}(4-3x) + \frac{1}{10}(3-x)$

18. $\frac{1}{9}(4-x) - \frac{1}{6}(2+3x)$

Simplify $\dfrac{2(x+1)}{3} - \dfrac{3(x-2)}{5}$

$$\dfrac{2(x+1)}{3} - \dfrac{3(x-2)}{5} = \dfrac{5 \times 2(x+1) - 3 \times 3(x-2)}{15}$$

$$= \dfrac{10(x+1) - 9(x-2)}{15}$$

$$= \dfrac{10x + 10 - 9x + 18}{15}$$

$$= \dfrac{x + 28}{15}$$

Simplify:

19. $\dfrac{4(x+2)}{3} + \dfrac{2(x-1)}{5}$

20. $\dfrac{3(x-1)}{4} + \dfrac{2(x+1)}{3}$

21. $\dfrac{2(x-2)}{3} - \dfrac{3(x-1)}{7}$

22. $\dfrac{5(2x-1)}{2} - \dfrac{4(x+3)}{5}$

23. $\dfrac{3(x-1)}{2} + \dfrac{3(x+4)}{7}$

24. $\dfrac{7(x-3)}{3} - \dfrac{2(x+5)}{9}$

25. $\dfrac{2(3x-1)}{5} + \dfrac{4(2x-3)}{15}$

26. $\dfrac{3(x-2)}{5} - \dfrac{7(x-4)}{6}$

Simplify $\dfrac{2}{x} - \dfrac{1}{x+2}$

$$\dfrac{2}{x} - \dfrac{1}{(x+2)} = \dfrac{(2)(x+2) - (1)(x)}{x(x+2)}$$

$$= \dfrac{2x + 4 - x}{x(x+2)}$$

$$= \dfrac{x + 4}{x(x+2)}$$

(Notice that we placed the two-term denominator in brackets. Notice also that we left the common denominator in factorised form.)

Simplify:

27. $\dfrac{2}{a} + \dfrac{1}{a+3}$

28. $\dfrac{4}{x+2} + \dfrac{2}{x}$

29. $\dfrac{3}{x-4}+\dfrac{1}{2x}$

30. $\dfrac{2}{2x+1}-\dfrac{3}{4x}$

31. $\dfrac{3}{a}+\dfrac{2}{a+4}$

32. $\dfrac{3}{x-1}+\dfrac{4}{x}$

33. $\dfrac{3}{2x+1}+\dfrac{1}{3x}$

34. $\dfrac{5}{2x+3}-\dfrac{2}{5x}$

MIXED QUESTIONS

Exercise 18i

Simplify:

1. $\dfrac{2}{a}-\dfrac{b}{c}$

2. $\dfrac{pq}{r}\times\dfrac{r^3}{p^2}$

3. $\dfrac{x+2}{4}+\dfrac{x-5}{3}$

4. $\dfrac{a^2+ab}{a^2-b^2}$

5. $\dfrac{3}{4x}-\dfrac{2}{3x}$

6. $\dfrac{x+3}{x^2+5x+6}$

7. $\dfrac{p^2-pq}{q^2-p^2}$

8. $\dfrac{4}{x^2}-\dfrac{2}{3x}$

9. $\dfrac{1}{x}-\dfrac{3}{x+1}$

10. $\dfrac{a^2}{bc}\div\dfrac{a}{b^2}$

11. $\dfrac{2}{5x}\div\dfrac{3}{4x}$

12. $\dfrac{2}{5x}+\dfrac{3}{4x}$

13. $\dfrac{2}{5x}\times\dfrac{3}{4x}$

14. $\dfrac{x+4}{5}+\dfrac{2x-1}{10}$

15. $\dfrac{x+4}{5}\times\dfrac{2x-1}{10}$

16. $\dfrac{5}{4x}+\dfrac{5}{6x}$

17. $\dfrac{5}{4x}\times\dfrac{5}{6x}$

18. $\dfrac{5}{4x}\div\dfrac{5}{6x}$

19. $\dfrac{1}{3x}+\dfrac{6}{x-1}$

20. $\dfrac{1}{3x}\times\dfrac{6}{x-1}$

21. $\dfrac{3}{2a}-\dfrac{2}{a-1}$

22. $\dfrac{3}{2a}\times\dfrac{2}{a-1}$

23. $\dfrac{3}{4y-3}\div\dfrac{y}{4y-3}$

24. $\dfrac{3}{4y-3}-\dfrac{4y}{4y-3}$

SOLVING EQUATIONS WITH FRACTIONS

Remember that when solving an equation we *must* keep the equality true. This means that if we alter the size of one side of the equation then we must alter the other side in the same way.

Consider the equation $\dfrac{1}{x} + \dfrac{1}{2x} = \dfrac{5}{6}$

If we choose to multiply each side by the LCM of the denominators, we can remove all fractions from the equation.

The LCM of x, $2x$ and 6 is $6x$.

Multiplying each side by $6x$ gives

$$6x\left(\frac{1}{x} + \frac{1}{2x}\right) = 6x \times \frac{5}{6}$$

$$\therefore \quad \frac{\cancel{6x}^{\,\prime}}{1} \times \frac{1}{\cancel{x}_{\prime}} + \frac{\cancel{6x}^{\,3}}{1} \times \frac{1}{\cancel{2x}_{\prime}} = \frac{\cancel{6x}^{\,\prime}}{1} \times \frac{5}{\cancel{6}_{\prime}}$$

$$\therefore \quad 6 + 3 = 5x$$

$$9 = 5x$$

$$\tfrac{9}{5} = x \quad \text{i.e.} \quad x = 1\tfrac{4}{5}$$

Exercise 18j

Solve the following equations:

1. $\dfrac{1}{2} + \dfrac{4}{x} = 1$

2. $\dfrac{2}{3} - \dfrac{1}{x} = \dfrac{13}{15}$

3. $\dfrac{3}{4} - \dfrac{2}{x} = \dfrac{5}{12}$

4. $\dfrac{1}{x} - \dfrac{1}{3x} = \dfrac{1}{2}$

5. $\dfrac{1}{2x} + \dfrac{2}{x} = \dfrac{1}{4}$

6. $\dfrac{3}{x} + \dfrac{3}{10} = \dfrac{9}{10}$

7. $\dfrac{3}{8} - \dfrac{2}{x} = \dfrac{1}{6}$

8. $\dfrac{3}{2x} + \dfrac{1}{4x} = \dfrac{1}{3}$

9. $\dfrac{1}{x} - \dfrac{1}{2} = \dfrac{3}{2x}$

10. $\dfrac{3}{2x} + \dfrac{2}{5} = \dfrac{5}{x}$

Solve the equation $\dfrac{x-2}{4} - \dfrac{x-3}{6} = 2$

$$\frac{(x-2)}{4} - \frac{(x-3)}{6} = 2$$

Multiply each side by 12

$$12\left[\frac{(x-2)}{4} - \frac{(x-3)}{6}\right] = 12 \times 2$$

$$\therefore \quad \frac{\overset{3}{\cancel{12}}}{1} \times \frac{(x-2)}{\cancel{4}_{1}} - \overset{2}{\cancel{12}} \times \frac{(x-3)}{\cancel{6}_{1}} = 24$$

$$\therefore \quad 3(x-2) - 2(x-3) = 24$$

$$3x - 6 - 2x + 6 = 24$$

$$x = 24$$

Solve the following equations:

11. $\dfrac{x+2}{4} + \dfrac{x-3}{2} = \dfrac{1}{2}$

12. $\dfrac{x}{4} - \dfrac{x+3}{3} = \dfrac{1}{2}$

13. $\dfrac{x}{5} + \dfrac{x+1}{4} = \dfrac{8}{5}$

14. $\dfrac{2x}{5} - \dfrac{x-3}{8} = \dfrac{1}{10}$

15. $\dfrac{x-4}{3} - \dfrac{x+1}{4} = \dfrac{1}{6}$

16. $\dfrac{x+3}{5} + \dfrac{x-2}{4} = \dfrac{3}{10}$

17. $\dfrac{2}{3} - \dfrac{x+1}{9} = \dfrac{5}{6}$

18. $\dfrac{x+3}{4} - \dfrac{x}{2} = 5$

19. $\dfrac{3x}{20} + \dfrac{x-2}{8} = \dfrac{3}{10}$

20. $\dfrac{x+3}{7} - \dfrac{x-4}{3} = 1$

21. $\dfrac{2x-1}{7} + \dfrac{3x-3}{4} = \dfrac{1}{7}$

22. $\dfrac{2x}{9} - \dfrac{3x+2}{4} = \dfrac{7}{12}$

Sometimes a fractional equation is a quadratic equation in disguise.

Solve the equation $\dfrac{x-4}{2} + \dfrac{4}{x} = 1$

$$\frac{(x-4)}{2} + \frac{4}{x} = 1$$

Multiply each side by $2x$ $2x\left[\dfrac{(x-4)}{2} + \dfrac{4}{x}\right] = 2x \times 1$

$$\frac{\cancel{2x}^{1}}{1} \times \frac{(x-4)}{\cancel{2}} + \frac{\cancel{2x}^{1}}{1} \times \frac{4}{\cancel{x}} = 2x$$

$$x(x-4)+8 = 2x$$

$$x^2 - 4x + 8 = 2x$$

(This contains an x^2 term so it is a quadratic equation. Therefore we collect all terms on one side.)

Take $2x$ from each side $\qquad\qquad x^2 - 6x + 8 = 0$

$\therefore \qquad\qquad\qquad\qquad\qquad (x-2)(x-4) = 0$

$\therefore \qquad\qquad$ either $x - 2 = 0$ or $x - 4 = 0$

$\therefore \qquad\qquad\qquad\qquad x = 2$ or $\qquad x = 4$

Solve the equations in questions 23 to 42:

23. $\dfrac{x+5}{2} + \dfrac{1}{x} = 1$

24. $\dfrac{2}{x} + \dfrac{x+1}{3} = 2$

25. $\dfrac{x+2}{2} + \dfrac{2}{x} + 1 = 0$

26. $\dfrac{x+12}{3} + \dfrac{3}{x} = 2$

27. $\dfrac{x+9}{2} - \dfrac{2}{x} = 3$

28. $x + 8 + \dfrac{9}{x} = 2$

29. $\dfrac{2-x}{4} + \dfrac{1}{2x} = \dfrac{3}{4x}$

30. $\dfrac{1}{x} - \dfrac{2}{x-2} = 3$

31. $\dfrac{1}{3x} - \dfrac{x-2}{4} = \dfrac{1}{6}$

32. $\dfrac{2}{x+3} + x = 0$

Not all of the following questions give quadratic equations:

33. $\dfrac{1}{2x} + \dfrac{1}{4x} = \dfrac{1}{6}$

34. $\dfrac{x+2}{3} - \dfrac{3x}{2} = \dfrac{1}{5}$

35. $\dfrac{x-1}{2} + \dfrac{1}{x} = 1$

36. $\dfrac{2x-1}{3} - \dfrac{3x}{2} = 2$

37. $\dfrac{x+4}{3} + 2 = \dfrac{x}{4}$

38. $\dfrac{x+1}{x} + \dfrac{1}{2} = 4$

39. $\dfrac{x}{5} + \dfrac{1}{x+1} = 1$

40. $\dfrac{1}{2}(x-1) + \dfrac{1}{3}(2x-3) = 2$

41. $\dfrac{4x+1}{2} - \dfrac{1}{2x} = \dfrac{1}{2}$

42. $\dfrac{x-3}{x} = 0$

MIXED EXERCISES

Exercise 18k

1. Simplify:

(a) $\dfrac{ab^2}{2ab}$

(c) $\dfrac{a^2 - b^2}{a + b}$

(b) $\dfrac{a(a+b)}{a+b}$

2. Simplify:

(a) $\dfrac{1}{x} + \dfrac{1}{3x}$

(c) $\dfrac{1}{x} \div \dfrac{1}{3x}$

(b) $\dfrac{1}{x} \times \dfrac{1}{3x}$

3. Solve the equations:

(a) $\dfrac{x+1}{3} - \dfrac{x-1}{2} = 3$

(b) $\dfrac{x+1}{3} - \dfrac{1}{x} = 1$

4. (a) Simplify $\dfrac{1}{2}(x-1) + \dfrac{1}{3}(x-2)$

(b) Solve the equation

$$\dfrac{1}{2}(x-1) + \dfrac{1}{3}(x-2) = \dfrac{1}{4}$$

Exercise 18l

1. Simplify:

(a) $\dfrac{6xy}{3y^2}$

(c) $\dfrac{x^2 + 4x + 3}{x + 1}$

(b) $\dfrac{2x(x-y)}{4x^2}$

2. Simplify:

(a) $\dfrac{1}{2p} - \dfrac{1}{3p}$

(c) $\dfrac{2y^2}{3} \times \dfrac{9}{4xy}$

(b) $(x^2 - 2x) \div x$

3. Solve the equations:

(a) $\dfrac{x}{4} + \dfrac{3x-2}{6} = \dfrac{1}{3}$

(b) $\dfrac{x-5}{4} + \dfrac{1}{2x} = \dfrac{4}{x}$

4. (a) Simplify $\dfrac{x-2}{4} + \dfrac{3}{x}$

(b) Solve the equation $\dfrac{x}{2} - \dfrac{2x-4}{3} = \dfrac{1}{4}$

Exercise 18m

1. Simplify:

(a) $\dfrac{uv^2}{wu^2v}$

(c) $\dfrac{x^2}{3x - x^2}$

(b) $\dfrac{a-b}{(b-a)(b-2a)}$

2. Simplify:

(a) $\dfrac{3s}{t} \div \dfrac{1}{6st}$

(c) $\dfrac{3}{4x-1} - \dfrac{2}{x}$

(b) $\dfrac{x^2 - 4}{3} \times \dfrac{6}{x+2}$

3. Solve the equations:

(a) $\dfrac{x-2}{4} - \dfrac{x-3}{5} = \dfrac{3}{10}$

(b) $\dfrac{x-2}{4} + \dfrac{1}{2x} = \dfrac{1}{4}$

4. (a) Simplify $\frac{1}{2}(x-2) - \frac{1}{3}(x-3)$

(b) Solve the equation

$$\frac{1}{2}(x-2) - \frac{1}{3}(x-3) = 5$$

5. Solve the equations:

(a) $\dfrac{x}{5} - \dfrac{x}{8} = 3$ (c) $\dfrac{x}{6} - \dfrac{x}{11} = 5$

(b) $\dfrac{x}{3} - \dfrac{x}{7} = 4$

What pattern do you notice in the above?

6. Solve for x:

$$\dfrac{x}{a} - \dfrac{x}{b} = b - a$$

MATHS IS OUT THERE

On what day of the week were you born? Can you answer this question? There is a formula which you may use to help you.

If $d = $ day of the month, $y = $ year, and $m = $ month,

$$w = d + 2m + [3(m+1)/5] + y + [y/4] - [y/100] + [y/400] + 2$$

January is taken as the 13th month of the previous year, and February as the 14th month. All other months are given their regular number.

The numbers in the 'square' brackets denote 'the greatest whole number less than the number'

e.g. $[7.6] = 7;\ [18.39] = 18.$

When you have a value for w, divide it by 7. Your remainder is the day of the week. Sunday is the first day and Saturday is day 0.

On what day of the week did New Year's Day fall in 1982?

$d = 1,\ m = 13,\ y = 1981$ (using the previous year for January) we have,

$$w = 1 + 2(13) + [3(14)/5] + 1981 + [1981/4] - [1981/100] + [1981/400] + 2$$
$$= 1 + 26 + [8.4] + 1981 + [495.25] - [19.81] + [4.95] + 2$$
$$= 1 + 26 + 8 + 1981 + 495 - 19 + 4 + 2 = 2498$$

$2498/7 = 356$ remainder 6. The day of the week is therefore Friday.

Try the following exercises:

1. Find the day of the week on which you were born.
2. On what day of the week will your birthday fall in the year 2010?

At the end of the chapter you should be able to:

1. Give the position vector of a point (x, y).
2. Illustrate with a sketch the position vector of a point (x, y).
3. Give the coordinates of a point whose position vector is given.
4. Find the image of a position vector under a given transformation.
5. Use a transformation matrix to find the image of a given point.
6. Classify a given transformation as a reflection, a rotation, an enlargement or some other transformation.
7. Recognise the identity transformation.
8. Find the inverse of a given transformation.
9. Find the inverse matrix of a given transformation matrix.
10. Identify the following as transformations which cannot be described by matrices:

   (a) a rotation about a point other than the origin
   (b) a reflection in a line not passing through the origin
   (c) a sheer with an invariant line through the origin
   (d) an enlargement whose centre is not the origin
   (e) a translation.

Matrices can be used for several different purposes; in a previous chapter they were used for solving simultaneous equations. Now we will see how they can be used for defining some transformations.

THE POSITION VECTOR OF A POINT

If a point has coordinates $(2, 4)$, then the vector $\overrightarrow{OA}$ is $\begin{pmatrix} 2 \\ 4 \end{pmatrix}$ and this is called the *position vector* of A relative to the original O.

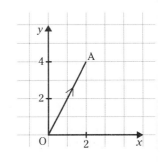

Exercise 19a

Give the position vector of the point A(6, −1). Illustrate with a sketch.

A is the point (6, −1)

$$\overrightarrow{OA} = \begin{pmatrix} 6 \\ -1 \end{pmatrix}$$

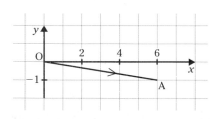

Give the position vectors of the points in questions 1 to 6. Illustrate each with a sketch:

1. (4, 5)   **2.** (3, −2)   **3.** (−7, 5)   **4.** (−3, −5)   <u>**5.**</u> (5, 3)   <u>**6.**</u> (−5, 2)

Give the coordinates of the points whose position vectors are given in questions 7 to 12. Illustrate each with a sketch:

7. $\begin{pmatrix} 5 \\ 2 \end{pmatrix}$ **8.** $\begin{pmatrix} 1 \\ -3 \end{pmatrix}$ **9.** $\begin{pmatrix} -2 \\ -4 \end{pmatrix}$ **10.** $\begin{pmatrix} 2 \\ -3 \end{pmatrix}$ <u>**11.**</u> $\begin{pmatrix} -6 \\ 2 \end{pmatrix}$ <u>**12.**</u> $\begin{pmatrix} 2 \\ -6 \end{pmatrix}$

THE IMAGE OF A POSITION VECTOR

Exercise 19b

Find the image of the position vector $\begin{pmatrix} 3 \\ 5 \end{pmatrix}$ under a reflection in the *y*-axis.

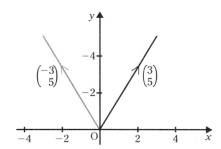

The image is the vector $\begin{pmatrix} -3 \\ 5 \end{pmatrix}$

For each of the following questions, draw x and y axes, marking values from -5 to 5 on each axis:

1. Find the image of the position vector $\begin{pmatrix} 5 \\ 2 \end{pmatrix}$ under a rotation of 90° clockwise about the origin.

2. Find the image of the position vector $\begin{pmatrix} -4 \\ 3 \end{pmatrix}$ under a reflection in the x-axis.

3. Find the image of the position vector $\begin{pmatrix} 4 \\ -2 \end{pmatrix}$ under a rotation of 180° about the origin.

4. Find the image of the position vector $\begin{pmatrix} 3 \\ -5 \end{pmatrix}$ under a rotation of 90° anticlockwise about the origin.

<u>5.</u> Find the image of the position vector $\begin{pmatrix} 5 \\ 3 \end{pmatrix}$ under a reflection in the line $y = x$.

<u>6.</u> Find the image of the position vector $\begin{pmatrix} 2 \\ 1 \end{pmatrix}$ under an enlargement with scale factor 2, centre the origin.

TRANSFORMATION MATRIX

Consider the transformation which is a reflection in the x-axis. If the object is the position vector $\begin{pmatrix} 3 \\ 2 \end{pmatrix}$, the image is $\begin{pmatrix} 3 \\ -2 \end{pmatrix}$.

We can say that this transformation changes $\begin{pmatrix} 3 \\ 2 \end{pmatrix}$ to $\begin{pmatrix} 3 \\ -2 \end{pmatrix}$.

This transformation changes any position vector in the same way: it leaves the x coordinate alone but it changes the sign of the y coordinate,

i.e., it changes $\begin{pmatrix} a \\ b \end{pmatrix}$ to $\begin{pmatrix} a \\ -b \end{pmatrix}$.

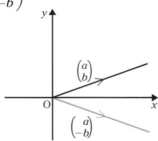

We also know that premultiplying by a matrix changes a vector,

e.g. $\begin{pmatrix} 1 & 0 \\ 0 & -1 \end{pmatrix}\begin{pmatrix} 4 \\ 3 \end{pmatrix} = \begin{pmatrix} 4 \\ -3 \end{pmatrix}$ and $\begin{pmatrix} 1 & 0 \\ 0 & -1 \end{pmatrix}\begin{pmatrix} a \\ b \end{pmatrix} = \begin{pmatrix} a \\ -b \end{pmatrix}$

So we can use the matrix $\begin{pmatrix} 1 & 0 \\ 0 & -1 \end{pmatrix}$ to define the transformation 'reflection in the x-axis'. We call $\begin{pmatrix} 1 & 0 \\ 0 & -1 \end{pmatrix}$ a *transformation matrix*.

FINDING THE IMAGE

If we are given a transformation matrix $\begin{pmatrix} 2 & 1 \\ 1 & 1 \end{pmatrix}$ and a point $A(2, 3)$, then we can find the image A' under this transformation, by multiplying the position vector of A by the transformation matrix.

i.e.
$$\begin{matrix} & A & & A' \\ \begin{pmatrix} 2 & 1 \\ 1 & 1 \end{pmatrix} & \begin{pmatrix} 2 \\ 3 \end{pmatrix} & = & \begin{pmatrix} 7 \\ 5 \end{pmatrix} \end{matrix}$$

Note that the transformation matrix *must* come first.

The position vector of A' is then $\begin{pmatrix} 7 \\ 5 \end{pmatrix}$ and A' is the point $(7, 5)$.

Exercise 19c

Find the image, A', of the point $A(1, 2)$ under the transformation defined by the matrix $\begin{pmatrix} 3 & 1 \\ 1 & 1 \end{pmatrix}$. Illustrate with a sketch.

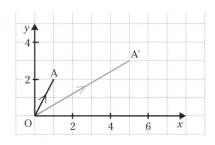

The position vector of A is $\begin{pmatrix} 1 \\ 2 \end{pmatrix}$

$$\begin{matrix} & & A & & A' \\ \begin{pmatrix} 3 & 1 \\ 1 & 1 \end{pmatrix} & & \begin{pmatrix} 1 \\ 2 \end{pmatrix} & = & \begin{pmatrix} 5 \\ 3 \end{pmatrix} \end{matrix}$$

The position vector of A' is $\begin{pmatrix} 5 \\ 3 \end{pmatrix}$, i.e. A' is the point $(5, 3)$.

Find the image, A′, of the given point A under the transformation defined by the given matrix. Illustrate with a diagram:

1. The point A is $(1, 2)$ and the transformation matrix is $\begin{pmatrix} 1 & 2 \\ 3 & 4 \end{pmatrix}$

2. The point A is $(4, 1)$ and the transformation matrix is $\begin{pmatrix} 2 & 1 \\ 1 & 2 \end{pmatrix}$

3. The point A is $(-2, 3)$ and the transformation matrix is $\begin{pmatrix} 1 & 2 \\ 1 & 1 \end{pmatrix}$

4. The point A is $(-1, -3)$ and the transformation matrix is $\begin{pmatrix} -1 & 1 \\ 2 & 1 \end{pmatrix}$

5. The point A is $(2, 3)$ and the transformation matrix is $\begin{pmatrix} 4 & -1 \\ -1 & 2 \end{pmatrix}$

6. The point A is $(2, -1)$ and the transformation matrix is $\begin{pmatrix} 1 & 3 \\ 0 & 1 \end{pmatrix}$

Sometimes, there are several object and image points on one diagram. If so, then it is clearer to mark only the points and to leave out the lines representing the position vectors.

Find the images, A′ and B′, of the points A$(3, 1)$ and B$(1, 4)$ under the transformation defined by the matrix $\begin{pmatrix} 0 & 1 \\ 1 & 0 \end{pmatrix}$. Mark the points on a sketch. Join AB and A′B′.

$$\begin{pmatrix} 0 & 1 \\ 1 & 0 \end{pmatrix}\begin{matrix}A\\\begin{pmatrix} 3 \\ 1 \end{pmatrix}\end{matrix} = \begin{matrix}A'\\\begin{pmatrix} 1 \\ 3 \end{pmatrix}\end{matrix}$$

$$\begin{pmatrix} 0 & 1 \\ 1 & 0 \end{pmatrix}\begin{matrix}B\\\begin{pmatrix} 1 \\ 4 \end{pmatrix}\end{matrix} = \begin{matrix}B'\\\begin{pmatrix} 4 \\ 1 \end{pmatrix}\end{matrix}$$

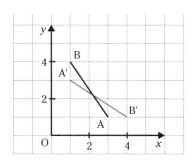

A′ is the point $(1, 3)$ and B′ is the point $(4, 1)$.

In questions 7 to 12 you are given the coordinates of two points A and B and a transformation matrix. Find the coordinates of the images, A′ and B′, of A and B under the transformation defined by the matrix. Mark all the points on a diagram, but do not draw the position vectors. In each case join AB and A′B′:

7. A is the point $(1, 1)$, B is the point $(3, 2)$ and the transformation matrix is $\begin{pmatrix} -1 & 0 \\ 0 & 1 \end{pmatrix}$

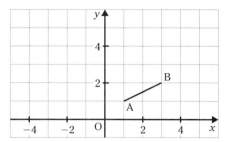

8. A is the point $(1, -1)$, B is the point $(2, 0)$ and the transformation matrix is $\begin{pmatrix} 1 & 2 \\ 2 & 3 \end{pmatrix}$

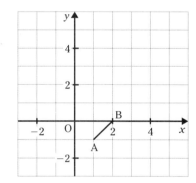

9. A is the point $(1, 3)$, B is the point $(1, -2)$ and the transformation matrix is $\begin{pmatrix} 1 & 3 \\ 0 & 1 \end{pmatrix}$

10. A is the point $(1, 1)$, B is the point $(-2, 0)$ and the transformation matrix is $\begin{pmatrix} 3 & 0 \\ 0 & 3 \end{pmatrix}$

11. A is the point $(1, 4)$, B is the point $(4, 1)$ and the transformation matrix is $\begin{pmatrix} 1 & -1 \\ -2 & 1 \end{pmatrix}$

12. A is the point $(3, 2)$, B is the point $(-3, 2)$ and the transformation matrix is $\begin{pmatrix} 1 & 2 \\ 2 & -1 \end{pmatrix}$

IDENTIFYING A TRANSFORMATION

To find out whether a transformation is a reflection, a rotation, an enlargement or some other transformation, we need a simple object to which the transformation can be applied.

A rectangle or a triangle is usually the most convenient.

REFLECTIONS

Exercise 19d

A, B, C and D are the points $(1, 0)$, $(3, 0)$, $(3, 3)$ and $(1, 3)$. Draw a diagram, mark the given points and join them up.

Find the image of each point under the transformation defined by the matrix $\begin{pmatrix} -1 & 0 \\ 0 & 1 \end{pmatrix}$, marking the points on the diagram. Join up the image points in order. What is the transformation?

$$\begin{pmatrix} -1 & 0 \\ 0 & 1 \end{pmatrix} \overset{A}{\begin{pmatrix} 1 \\ 0 \end{pmatrix}} = \overset{A'}{\begin{pmatrix} -1 \\ 0 \end{pmatrix}}$$

$$\begin{pmatrix} -1 & 0 \\ 0 & 1 \end{pmatrix} \overset{B}{\begin{pmatrix} 3 \\ 0 \end{pmatrix}} = \overset{B'}{\begin{pmatrix} -3 \\ 0 \end{pmatrix}}$$

$$\begin{pmatrix} -1 & 0 \\ 0 & 1 \end{pmatrix} \overset{C}{\begin{pmatrix} 3 \\ 3 \end{pmatrix}} = \overset{C'}{\begin{pmatrix} -3 \\ 3 \end{pmatrix}}$$

$$\begin{pmatrix} -1 & 0 \\ 0 & 1 \end{pmatrix} \overset{D}{\begin{pmatrix} 1 \\ 3 \end{pmatrix}} = \overset{D'}{\begin{pmatrix} -1 \\ 3 \end{pmatrix}}$$

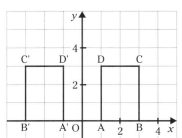

The transformation is a reflection. The mirror line is the y-axis.

Draw x and y axes, each using a scale from -4 to 4. Mark the given points and join them up in order. Find the image of each point under the transformation defined by the given matrix and join up the image points in order. You will see that the transformation is a reflection. What is the mirror line?

1. The given points are A$(-2, 1)$, B$(2, 1)$, C$(3, 2)$ and D$(-1, 2)$. The transformation matrix is $\begin{pmatrix} 1 & 0 \\ 0 & -1 \end{pmatrix}$

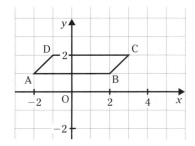

2. The given points are A$(1, 1)$, B$(4, 1)$ and C$(4, 2)$. The transformation matrix is $\begin{pmatrix} 0 & 1 \\ 1 & 0 \end{pmatrix}$

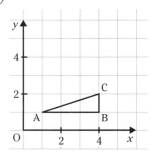

3. The given points are A(2, −3), B(5, −3) and C(3, 2). The transformation matrix is
$$\begin{pmatrix} -1 & 0 \\ 0 & 1 \end{pmatrix}$$

4. The given points are A(4, 1), B(3, 3) and C(2, 0). The transformation matrix is
$$\begin{pmatrix} 0 & -1 \\ -1 & 0 \end{pmatrix}$$

To save writing so many matrices, we can combine two or three or more position vectors into one matrix.

Find the images of A(2, 0), B(3, 3) and C(−1, 1) under the transformation defined by the matrix $\begin{pmatrix} -1 & 0 \\ 0 & 1 \end{pmatrix}$. Mark the object and the image points on a diagram. What is the transformation?

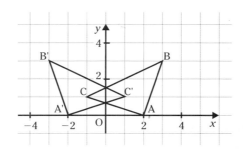

$$\begin{pmatrix} -1 & 0 \\ 0 & 1 \end{pmatrix} \overset{\text{A} \quad \text{B} \quad \text{C}}{\begin{pmatrix} 2 & 3 & -1 \\ 0 & 3 & 1 \end{pmatrix}} = \overset{\text{A}' \quad \text{B}' \quad \text{C}'}{\begin{pmatrix} -2 & -3 & 1 \\ 0 & 3 & 1 \end{pmatrix}}$$

The transformation is a reflection.
The mirror line is the *y*-axis.

---

5. The given points are A(1, 1), B(3, 1), C(3, 2) and D(1, 2). The transformation matrix is $\begin{pmatrix} 0 & 1 \\ 1 & 0 \end{pmatrix}$

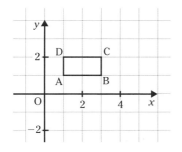

6. The given points are A(2, 0), B(4, 0), C(4, 2) and D(2, 2). The transformation matrix is $\begin{pmatrix} 0 & 1 \\ 1 & 0 \end{pmatrix}$

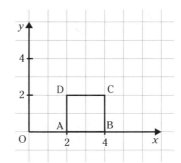

7. The given points are A(1, 1), B(2, 1), C(2, 2) and D(1, 2). The transformation matrix is $\begin{pmatrix} 0 & -1 \\ -1 & 0 \end{pmatrix}$

8. The given points are A(1, 0), B(4, 0) and C(4, 2). The transformation matrix is $\begin{pmatrix} -1 & 0 \\ 0 & 1 \end{pmatrix}$

9. The given points are A(2, 1), B(3, 1), C(3, 4) and D(2, 4). The transformation matrix is $\begin{pmatrix} 1 & 0 \\ 0 & -1 \end{pmatrix}$

10. The given points are A(1, 1), B(3, 1), C(4, 3) and D(3, 3). The transformation matrix is $\begin{pmatrix} 0 & 1 \\ 1 & 0 \end{pmatrix}$

11. The given points are A(2, 4), B(4, 5) and C(3, 2). The transformation matrix is $\begin{pmatrix} -1 & 0 \\ 0 & 1 \end{pmatrix}$

ROTATIONS

Exercise 19e

A, B and C are the points (1, 0), (3, 0) and (3, 1). Draw a diagram, mark the points and join them up. Find the image of each point under the transformation defined by the matrix $\begin{pmatrix} 0 & -1 \\ 1 & 0 \end{pmatrix}$. Mark the image points on the diagram and join them up. What is the transformation?

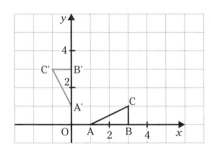

$$\begin{pmatrix} 0 & -1 \\ 1 & 0 \end{pmatrix} \overset{\text{A B C}}{\begin{pmatrix} 1 & 3 & 3 \\ 0 & 0 & 1 \end{pmatrix}} = \overset{\text{A' B' C'}}{\begin{pmatrix} 0 & 0 & -1 \\ 1 & 3 & 3 \end{pmatrix}}$$

The transformation is a rotation.
Its centre is O. The angle of rotation is 90° anticlockwise.

Draw x and y axes, marking values from -4 to 4 on each axis. Mark the given points and join them up in order. Find the image of each point under the transformation defined by the given matrix and join up the image points. You will see that the transformation is a rotation. Describe the rotation:

1. The given points are A$(1, 1)$, B$(4, 1)$, C$(4, 3)$ and D$(1, 3)$. The transformation matrix is $\begin{pmatrix} 0 & 1 \\ -1 & 0 \end{pmatrix}$

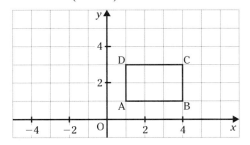

2. The given points are A$(1, 1)$, B$(4, 1)$, C$(4, 2)$ and D$(1, 2)$. The transformation matrix is $\begin{pmatrix} -1 & 0 \\ 0 & -1 \end{pmatrix}$

3. The given points are A$(1, 0)$, B$(3, 0)$ and C$(4, 4)$. The transformation matrix is $\begin{pmatrix} 0 & -1 \\ 1 & 0 \end{pmatrix}$

4. The given points are A$(1, 1)$, B$(4, 1)$ and C$(4, 4)$. The transformation matrix is $\begin{pmatrix} 0 & 1 \\ -1 & 0 \end{pmatrix}$

5. The given points are A$(3, 2)$, B$(4, 3)$ and C$(1, 4)$. The transformation matrix is $\begin{pmatrix} -1 & 0 \\ 0 & -1 \end{pmatrix}$

ENLARGEMENTS

Exercise 19f

A, B, C and D are the points $(1, 0)$, $(3, 0)$, $(3, 3)$ and $(1, 3)$. Draw a diagram, mark the points and join them up in order.

Find the image of each point under the transformation defined by the matrix $\begin{pmatrix} 2 & 0 \\ 0 & 2 \end{pmatrix}$ and mark each point on the diagram. Join up the image points. What is the transformation?

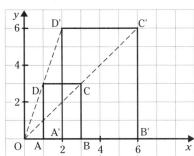

$$\begin{pmatrix} 2 & 0 \\ 0 & 2 \end{pmatrix} \begin{array}{cccc} A & B & C & D \\ \begin{pmatrix} 1 & 3 & 3 & 1 \\ 0 & 0 & 3 & 3 \end{pmatrix} \end{array} = \begin{array}{cccc} A' & B' & C' & D' \\ \begin{pmatrix} 2 & 6 & 6 & 2 \\ 0 & 0 & 6 & 6 \end{pmatrix} \end{array}$$

The transformation is an enlargement, centre O, with scale factor 2.

Draw x and y axes, marking values from 0 to 10 on each. Mark the given points and join them up in order. Find the image of each of the given points under the transformation defined by the given matrix. Mark the image points and join them up in order. Describe the enlargement.

1. The given points are A$(1, 0)$, B$(3, 0)$ and C$(3, 3)$. The transformation matrix is $\begin{pmatrix} 2 & 0 \\ 0 & 2 \end{pmatrix}$

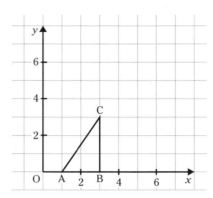

2. The given points are A$(0, 1)$, B$(-2, 1)$, C$(-2, 0)$ and O$(0, 0)$.

   The transformation matrix is $\begin{pmatrix} 3 & 0 \\ 0 & 3 \end{pmatrix}$

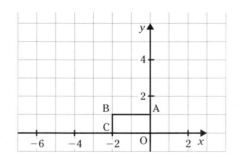

3. The given points are A$(2, 2)$, B$(2, 4)$, C$(4, 4)$ and D$(4, 2)$. The transformation matrix is $\begin{pmatrix} 1\frac{1}{2} & 0 \\ 0 & 1\frac{1}{2} \end{pmatrix}$

4. The given points are A$(4, 2)$, B$(4, 4)$ and C$(-4, 4)$. The transformation matrix is $\begin{pmatrix} 2\frac{1}{2} & 0 \\ 0 & 2\frac{1}{2} \end{pmatrix}$

For questions 5 and 6, mark the axes with values from -5 to 5.

5. The given points are O$(0, 0)$, A$(0, 1)$, B$(-1, 1)$ and C$(-1, 0)$. The transformation matrix is $\begin{pmatrix} -2 & 0 \\ 0 & -2 \end{pmatrix}$

6. The given points are A$(0, 2)$, B$(3, 2)$, C$(3, 5)$ and D$(0, 5)$. The transformation matrix is $\begin{pmatrix} -1 & 0 \\ 0 & -1 \end{pmatrix}$

   Is there another transformation which produces the same image?

OTHER TRANSFORMATIONS – ONE-WAY STRETCH

Exercise 19g

A, B, C and D are the points $(0, 1)$, $(0, 3)$, $(2, 3)$ and $(2, 1)$. Draw a diagram, mark the points and join them up. Find the images of the given points under the transformation defined by the matrix $\begin{pmatrix} 4 & 0 \\ 0 & 1 \end{pmatrix}$. Mark the points and join them up. What is the transformation?

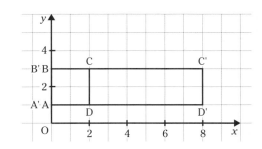

$$\begin{pmatrix} 4 & 0 \\ 0 & 1 \end{pmatrix} \overset{\text{A B C D}}{\begin{pmatrix} 0 & 0 & 2 & 2 \\ 1 & 3 & 3 & 1 \end{pmatrix}} = \overset{\text{A}' \ \text{B}' \ \text{C}' \ \text{D}'}{\begin{pmatrix} 0 & 0 & 8 & 8 \\ 1 & 3 & 3 & 1 \end{pmatrix}}$$

The transformation is a stretch parallel to the *x*-axis, with scale factor 4.

Draw *x* and *y* axes marking the values indicated on each. Mark the given points and join them up. Find the image of each of the given points under the transformation defined by the given matrix. Mark in the points and join them up. You will see that each transformation is a one-way stretch. Describe the transformation:

1. $0 \leqslant x \leqslant 10$, $-3 \leqslant y \leqslant 4$. The given points are A$(1, 0)$, B$(3, 0)$, C$(3, 2)$ and D$(1, 2)$.

   The transformation matrix is $\begin{pmatrix} 3 & 0 \\ 0 & 1 \end{pmatrix}$

2. $0 \leqslant x \leqslant 5$, $0 \leqslant y \leqslant 5$. The given points are A$(1, 0)$, B$(3, 0)$, C$(3, 2)$ and D$(1, 2)$.

   The transformation matrix is $\begin{pmatrix} 1 & 0 \\ 0 & 2 \end{pmatrix}$

3. $0 \leqslant x \leqslant 7$, $0 \leqslant y \leqslant 3$. The given points are A$(1, 1)$, B$(4, 1)$, C$(4, 2)$ and D$(1, 2)$.

   The transformation matrix is $\begin{pmatrix} 1\frac{1}{2} & 0 \\ 0 & 1 \end{pmatrix}$

4. $-3 \leqslant x \leqslant 3$, $0 \leqslant y \leqslant 7$. The given points are A$(-2, 1)$, B$(1, 1)$, C$(1, 2)$ and D$(-2, 2)$. The transformation matrix is $\begin{pmatrix} 1 & 0 \\ 0 & 3 \end{pmatrix}$

SHEARS

Imagine a stack of paper. This can be pushed sideways with the top layer moving further than the middle layer and the bottom layer not moving at all.

The side view, which is a rectangle to start with, becomes a parallelogram. The base line is unchanged and this is called the *invariant* line.

This type of transformation is called a *shear*.

To describe it, we need to give the invariant line and an indication of how much the object is sheared by showing how far one point has moved.

Exercise 19h

A, B, C and D are the points $(1, 0)$, $(3, 0)$, $(3, 2)$ and $(1, 2)$. Draw a diagram, mark the points and join them up in order. Find the images of the points under the transformation defined by the matrix $\begin{pmatrix} 1 & 2 \\ 0 & 1 \end{pmatrix}$. Mark the image points and join them up. Describe the transformation.

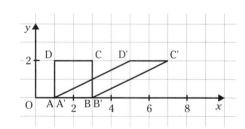

$$\begin{pmatrix} 1 & 2 \\ 0 & 1 \end{pmatrix} \overset{\text{A B C D}}{\begin{pmatrix} 1 & 3 & 3 & 1 \\ 0 & 0 & 2 & 2 \end{pmatrix}} = \overset{\text{A}'\ \text{B}'\ \text{C}'\ \text{D}'}{\begin{pmatrix} 1 & 3 & 7 & 5 \\ 0 & 0 & 2 & 2 \end{pmatrix}}$$

The transformation is a shear. The invariant line is the *x*-axis and $(3, 2)$ is mapped to $(7, 2)$.

Draw *x* and *y* axes, marking values from −6 to 6 on each axis. Mark the given points and join them up. Find the image of each point under the transformation defined by the given matrix. Mark the image points and join them up. You will see that the transformation is a shear. Describe the shear by giving the invariant line and indicating how one point has been transformed:

1. The given points are A(−2, 0), B(2, 0), C(2, 2) and D(−2, 2).

    The transformation matrix is $\begin{pmatrix} 1 & 1 \\ 0 & 1 \end{pmatrix}$

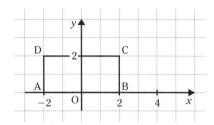

2. The given points are A(0, 1), B(2, 1), C(2, 2) and D(0, 2).

    The transformation matrix is $\begin{pmatrix} 1 & 0 \\ 2 & 1 \end{pmatrix}$

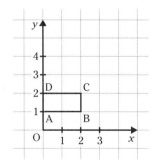

3. The given points are A(1, 0), B(3, 0) and C(2, 2). The transformation matrix is $\begin{pmatrix} 1 & 2 \\ 0 & 1 \end{pmatrix}$

4. The given points are A(−2, 0), B(2, 0), C(2, 2) and D(−2, 2). The transformation matrix is $\begin{pmatrix} 1 & -2 \\ 0 & 1 \end{pmatrix}$

5. The given points are A(0, 1), B(3, 1), C(3, 2) and D(0, 2). The transformation matrix is $\begin{pmatrix} 1 & 0 \\ 1 & 1 \end{pmatrix}$

6. The given points are A(−1, 1), B(2, 1), C(2, 4) and D(−1, 4). The transformation matrix is $\begin{pmatrix} 1 & 0 \\ -1 & 1 \end{pmatrix}$

7. The given points are A(−1, −1), B(2, −1) and C(0, 2). The transformation matrix is $\begin{pmatrix} 1 & 1 \\ 0 & 1 \end{pmatrix}$

8. Make up a transformation matrix which will give a shear. Test it on the object square OPQR, where O is (0, 0), P is (2, 0), Q is (2, 2) and R is (0, 2).

Sometimes the invariant line is not a line of the object and is more difficult to spot.

Draw x and y axes. Mark and join up the points $A(1, 1)$, $B(3, 1)$, $C(3, 3)$ and $D(1, 3)$. Find the image of each point under the transformation defined by the matrix $\begin{pmatrix} 1 & 1 \\ 0 & 1 \end{pmatrix}$ and mark and join up the image points. Describe the transformation.

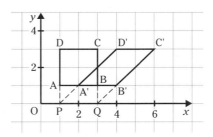

$$\begin{pmatrix} 1 & 1 \\ 0 & 1 \end{pmatrix} \overset{\text{A B C D}}{\begin{pmatrix} 1 & 3 & 3 & 1 \\ 1 & 1 & 3 & 3 \end{pmatrix}} = \overset{\text{A' B' C' D'}}{\begin{pmatrix} 2 & 4 & 6 & 4 \\ 1 & 1 & 3 & 3 \end{pmatrix}}$$

(Extend DA and D′A′ until they meet at P, and CB and C′B′ until they meet at Q. Then the dotted lines have become parts of the object and image and we can see that P and Q are on the invariant line.)

The transformation is a shear. The invariant line is the x-axis and $(1, 3)$ is mapped to $(4, 3)$.

9. The given points are $A(-1, 1)$, $B(3, 1)$, $C(3, 4)$ and $D(-1, 4)$.

The transformation matrix is $\begin{pmatrix} 1 & -1 \\ 0 & 1 \end{pmatrix}$

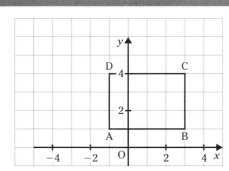

10. The given points are $A(-3, 1)$, $B(-1, 1)$, $C(-1, 3)$ and $D(-3, 3)$.

The transformation matrix is $\begin{pmatrix} 1 & 2 \\ 0 & 1 \end{pmatrix}$

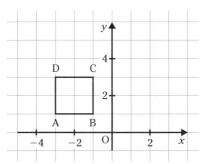

11. The given points are $A(-1, -1)$, $B(-1, 2)$, $C(-3, 2)$ and $D(-3, 1)$.

The transformation matrix is $\begin{pmatrix} 1 & 0 \\ 2 & 1 \end{pmatrix}$

12. The given points are $A(0, 2)$, $B(3, 2)$, $C(3, 4)$ and $D(0, 4)$.

The transformation matrix is $\begin{pmatrix} 1 & -2 \\ 0 & 1 \end{pmatrix}$

13. Make up two shear matrices, one with invariant line the x-axis and one with invariant line the y-axis. Test them on the object ABCD where A is $(1, 1)$, $B(2, 1)$, $C(2, 2)$ and $D(1, 2)$.

TRANSFORMATIONS THAT CANNOT BE DESCRIBED SIMPLY

Some transformation matrices define transformations which are different from any of the previous transformations and which sometimes cannot be described adequately. The next exercise gives some examples of these.

Exercise 19i

Draw x and y axes, marking values from -8 to 8 on each. Mark the given points and join them up. Find the image of each point under the transformation defined by the given matrix. Mark the image points and join them up. Do *not* try to describe the transformation.

1. The given points are $A(-1, 0)$, $B(1, 0)$, $C(1, 2)$ and $D(-1, 2)$. The transformation matrix is $\begin{pmatrix} 1 & 2 \\ 3 & 1 \end{pmatrix}$

2. The given points are $A(-1, 0)$, $B(1, 0)$, $C(1, 2)$ and $D(-1, 2)$. The transformation matrix is $\begin{pmatrix} 1 & -2 \\ -3 & 1 \end{pmatrix}$

3. The given points are $A(-2, -1)$, $B(1, -1)$, $C(1, 2)$ and $D(-2, 2)$. The transformation matrix is $\begin{pmatrix} 2 & 0 \\ 0 & 3 \end{pmatrix}$

4. The given points are $A(-2, -1)$, $B(1, -1)$, $C(1, 1)$ and $D(-2, 1)$. The transformation matrix is $\begin{pmatrix} 2 & 4 \\ 1 & 2 \end{pmatrix}$

5. The given points are $A(-2, -1)$, $B(2, -1)$, $C(2, 1)$ and $D(-2, 1)$. The transformation matrix is $\begin{pmatrix} -1 & 1 \\ 2 & -2 \end{pmatrix}$

6. The given points are $A(-2, -2)$, $B(1, -1)$, $C(1, 2)$ and $D(-2, 2)$. The transformation matrix is $\begin{pmatrix} 0 & 0 \\ 0 & 0 \end{pmatrix}$

MIXED TRANSFORMATIONS

Exercise 19j

In each of the questions 1 to 12, O is point $(0, 0)$, A is $(2, 0)$, B is $(2, 1)$ and C is $(0, 1)$. The rectangle OABC is the object. Draw x and y axes, marking values from -8 to 8 on each axis. Find the image of OABC under the transformation defined by the given matrix and (where possible) describe the transformation:

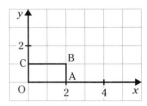

1. $\begin{pmatrix} 1 & 0 \\ 0 & -1 \end{pmatrix}$

2. $\begin{pmatrix} 1 & 1\frac{1}{2} \\ 0 & 1 \end{pmatrix}$

3. $\begin{pmatrix} 0 & -1 \\ -1 & 0 \end{pmatrix}$

4. $\begin{pmatrix} -3 & 0 \\ 0 & 3 \end{pmatrix}$

5. $\begin{pmatrix} 2 & -3 \\ 3 & 2 \end{pmatrix}$

6. $\begin{pmatrix} 2 & 0 \\ 0 & 1 \end{pmatrix}$

7. $\begin{pmatrix} 4 & 0 \\ 0 & 4 \end{pmatrix}$

8. $\begin{pmatrix} 1 & 2 \\ 1 & 4 \end{pmatrix}$

9. $\begin{pmatrix} 1 & 0 \\ 0 & 3 \end{pmatrix}$

10. $\begin{pmatrix} \frac{1}{2} & 0 \\ 0 & \frac{1}{2} \end{pmatrix}$

11. $\begin{pmatrix} 2 & 2 \\ 1 & 3 \end{pmatrix}$

12. $\begin{pmatrix} 1 & 0 \\ 2 & 1 \end{pmatrix}$

13. What are the simplest objects you could use to identify a transformation?

Find and describe the transformation given by $\begin{pmatrix} 1 & -3 \\ 0 & 1 \end{pmatrix}$, using as simple an object as you can.

14. Draw x and y axes, marking values from -5 to 5 on each axis. Use $1\,\text{cm}$ to 1 unit.
The object is the quadrilateral OABC where O is $(0, 0)$, A is $(3, 0)$, B is $(5, 2)$ and C is $(2, 2)$.
Find and draw the eight images of OABC under the transformations defined by the following eight matrices:

(a) $\begin{pmatrix} 1 & 0 \\ 0 & -1 \end{pmatrix}$

(b) $\begin{pmatrix} -1 & 0 \\ 0 & -1 \end{pmatrix}$

(c) $\begin{pmatrix} -1 & 0 \\ 0 & 1 \end{pmatrix}$

(d) $\begin{pmatrix} 0 & 1 \\ 1 & 0 \end{pmatrix}$

(e) $\begin{pmatrix} 0 & -1 \\ 1 & 0 \end{pmatrix}$

(f) $\begin{pmatrix} 0 & 1 \\ -1 & 0 \end{pmatrix}$

(g) $\begin{pmatrix} 0 & -1 \\ -1 & 0 \end{pmatrix}$

(h) $\begin{pmatrix} 1 & 0 \\ 0 & 1 \end{pmatrix}$

15. Find the images of the following objects under the transformations defined by the matrix $\begin{pmatrix} 1 & 0 \\ 0 & 1 \end{pmatrix}$

(a) OABC: O $(0, 0)$, A $(2, 0)$, B $(2, 2)$ and C $(0, 2)$

(b) $\triangle$ PQR: P $(-1, 1)$, Q $(-3, 1)$ and R $(-3, 4)$

(c) Parallelogram WXYZ: W $(1, -1)$, X $(0, -3)$, Y $(-3, -3)$ and Z $(-2, -1)$.

What do you notice about the results?

16. A is the point with position vector $\begin{pmatrix} 1 \\ 0 \end{pmatrix}$ and B is the point with position vector $\begin{pmatrix} 0 \\ 1 \end{pmatrix}$

A$'$ and B$'$ are the images of A and B under the transformations defined by the following matrices:

(a) $\begin{pmatrix} 1 & 0 \\ 0 & -1 \end{pmatrix}$ (b) $\begin{pmatrix} 2 & 0 \\ 0 & 2 \end{pmatrix}$ (c) $\begin{pmatrix} 1 & 2 \\ 0 & 1 \end{pmatrix}$ (d) $\begin{pmatrix} 2 & 5 \\ 4 & -1 \end{pmatrix}$

In each case write down the position vectors of A$'$ and B$'$ and illustrate with a diagram. What do you notice about the position vectors of A$'$ and B$'$ and the columns of the matrix which produced them?

THE IDENTITY TRANSFORMATION

We saw in questions 14 and 15 in the last exercise that, under the transformation defined by the unit matrix $\begin{pmatrix} 1 & 0 \\ 0 & 1 \end{pmatrix}$ the image is the same as the object.

If the image is identical to the object the transformation is called an *identity* transformation.

A rotation of 360° about the origin is an example of an identity transformation.

TRANSFORMATIONS AND IMAGES

Remember that a transformation is the *operation* or *process* that changes an object into its image; it is *not* the resulting image. If we use the same matrix to transform several different objects, we will obtain different images but the *transformation* is the same in each case.

A transformation transforms the whole space we are using and carries the object with it to become the image.

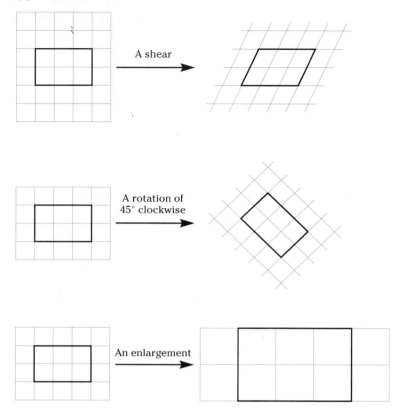

A shear

A rotation of
45° clockwise

An enlargement

INVERSE TRANSFORMATIONS

An inverse transformation is one that will map an image back to its object.

Suppose, for example, that we start with an enlargement of scale factor 2. An enlargement of scale factor $\frac{1}{2}$ will then shrink the image down to the size of the object again.

If we produce an image by rotating an object through 60° anticlockwise about a point P, then a rotation of 60° clockwise will return it to its original position.

Exercise 19k

1. What is the inverse of a rotation of 90° clockwise about the origin?

2. What is the inverse of an enlargement of scale factor 3 and centre the origin?

3. What is the inverse of a reflection in the *x*-axis?

4. What is the inverse of a rotation of 45° anticlockwise about the origin?

INVERSE MATRIX TRANSFORMATIONS

Exercise 19l

1.

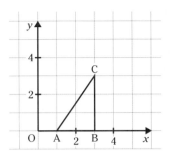

Draw x and y axes, marking values from -4 to 4 on each axis.
A is the point $(1, 0)$, B is $(3, 0)$ and C is $(3, 3)$.

M is the matrix $\begin{pmatrix} 0 & -1 \\ 1 & 0 \end{pmatrix}$

(a) Transform $\triangle ABC$ using the matrix **M** and label the image $A'B'C'$.

(b) Describe the transformation.

(c) Find the inverse of the matrix **M**.

(d) Use the inverse matrix to transform $\triangle A'B'C'$. What happens?

(e) Describe the transformation defined by the inverse matrix.

2.

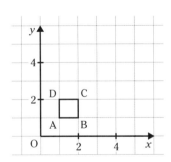

Draw x and y axes, marking values from 0 to 6 on each axis.
A is the point $(1, 1)$, B is $(2, 1)$, C is $(2, 2)$ and D is $(1, 2)$.

M is the matrix $\begin{pmatrix} 3 & 0 \\ 0 & 3 \end{pmatrix}$

(a) Transform the square ABCD using the matrix M and label the image $A'B'C'D'$.

(b) Describe the transformation.

(c) Find the inverse of the matrix **M**.

(d) Use the inverse matrix to transform $A'B'C'D'$. What happens?

(e) Describe the transformation defined by the inverse matrix. Is this the inverse of the transformation described in (b)?

3. Draw x and y axes, marking values from -4 to 4 on each axis. Mark the points $A(1, 0)$, $B(3, 1)$, $C(3, 2)$ and $D(1, 1)$:

(a) Transform the parallelogram using the matrix $\begin{pmatrix} 0 & 1 \\ -1 & 0 \end{pmatrix}$ and label the image $A'B'C'D'$.

(b) Describe the transformation.

(c) Find the inverse of the matrix $\begin{pmatrix} 0 & 1 \\ -1 & 0 \end{pmatrix}$

(d) Use the inverse matrix to transform $A'B'C'D'$. What happens?

(e) Describe the transformation defined by the inverse matrix. Is this the inverse of the transformation defined by $\begin{pmatrix} 0 & 1 \\ -1 & 0 \end{pmatrix}$?

4. Draw x and y axes, marking values from 0 to 9 on each axis. Mark the points $A(1, 1)$, $B(3, 3)$ and $C(1, 3)$:

(a) Transform $\triangle ABC$ using the matrix $\begin{pmatrix} 1 & 2 \\ 0 & 1 \end{pmatrix}$. Label the image $A'B'C'$.

(b) Describe the transformation.

(c) Find the inverse of the matrix $\begin{pmatrix} 1 & 2 \\ 0 & 1 \end{pmatrix}$

(d) Use the inverse matrix to transform $\triangle A'B'C'$. What happens?

(e) Describe the transformation defined by the inverse matrix. Is this the inverse of the transformation defined by $\begin{pmatrix} 1 & 2 \\ 0 & 1 \end{pmatrix}$?

5. Draw x and y axes, marking values from 0 to 13 on each. Mark the points $A(1, 0)$, $B(3, 0)$, $C(3, 2)$ and $D(1, 2)$:

(a) Transform the square ABCD using the matrix $\begin{pmatrix} 1 & 1 \\ 3 & 2 \end{pmatrix}$

(b) Find the inverse of the matrix $\begin{pmatrix} 1 & 1 \\ 3 & 2 \end{pmatrix}$

(c) Use the inverse matrix to transform $A'B'C'D'$. What happens?

6. Draw x and y axes, marking values from 0 to 10 on each. Mark the points $O(0, 0)$, $A(1, 0)$, $B(1, 2)$ and $C(0, 2)$:

(a) Find the image of rectangle OABC under the transformation defined by the matrix $\begin{pmatrix} 2 & 4 \\ 1 & 2 \end{pmatrix}$. What happens?

(b) Find, if possible, the inverse of the matrix $\begin{pmatrix} 2 & 4 \\ 1 & 2 \end{pmatrix}$

(c) Comment on your answers to (a) and (b). Does the transformation in (a) have an inverse?

INVERSE MATRICES AND INVERSE TRANSFORMATIONS

We conclude that if a transformation is defined by a matrix **M**, the inverse transformation is defined by the inverse matrix $\mathbf{M}^{-1}$.

If $\mathbf{M}^{-1}$ does not exist then the transformation does not have an inverse.

AN INVARIANT POINT

There is one point which is invariant under every transformation defined by a matrix. This is found in the next exercise.

Exercise 19m

For each question draw x and y axes, marking values from -5 to 5 on each axis. Mark the points $O\,(0, 0)$, $A\,(2, 0)$, $B\,(2, 2)$ and $C\,(0, 2)$ and use the square OABC as the object:

1. Find the image of OABC under the transformation defined by the matrix $\begin{pmatrix} 1 & 2 \\ 0 & 1 \end{pmatrix}$. Which of the four points are invariant?

2. Find the image of OABC under the transformation defined by the matrix $\begin{pmatrix} 2 & 0 \\ 0 & 2 \end{pmatrix}$. Which of the four points are invariant?

3. Find the image of OABC under the transformation defined by the matrix $\begin{pmatrix} 1 & 0 \\ 0 & -1 \end{pmatrix}$. Which of the four points are invariant?

4. Find the image of OABC under the transformation defined by the matrix $\begin{pmatrix} 2 & 1 \\ 1 & 2 \end{pmatrix}$. Which point is invariant?

5. Which one point is always invariant whichever transformation is used? Find the image of this point under a transformation defined by a matrix of your choice. Is it still invariant?

We see from the last exercise that, for any transformation defined by a 2×2 matrix, *the origin is invariant.*

TRANSFORMATIONS NOT USING MATRICES

Some of the transformations that can be defined by matrices are:

    rotations with centres at the origin
    reflections whose mirror lines pass through the origin
    shears with invariant lines which pass through the origin
    enlargements whose centres are at the origin.

There is no transformation matrix that will produce a rotation about $(1, 1)$ or a reflection in the line $x = 2$ or an enlargement with centre $(0, 6)$, because in each of these cases, the origin changes.

In a translation in particular, the origin is not an invariant point and therefore a translation cannot be produced by a matrix. We can describe a translation only by stating what the movement or *displacement* is. The easiest way to do this is to give the vector that describes the displacement.

Exercise 19n

Describe the transformation that maps ABCD to A'B'C'D'.

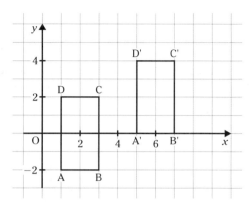

(Consider the displacement from D to D').

The transformation is a translation given by the vector $\begin{pmatrix} 4 \\ 2 \end{pmatrix}$

Describe the transformations in questions 1 to 4:

1.

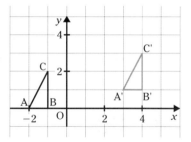

2.

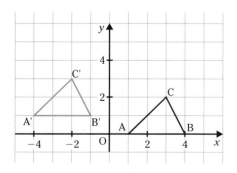

3.

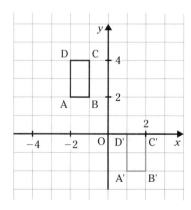

4.

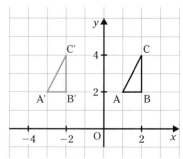

In questions 5 to 8, find the image of the given object under a translation defined by the given vector:

5.

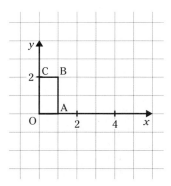

The vector is $\begin{pmatrix} 3 \\ 1 \end{pmatrix}$

6.

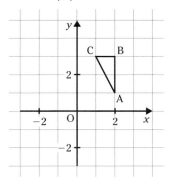

The vector is $\begin{pmatrix} -3 \\ -3 \end{pmatrix}$

7.

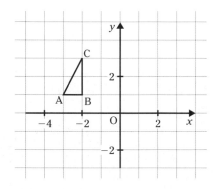

The vector is $\begin{pmatrix} 4 \\ -2 \end{pmatrix}$

8.

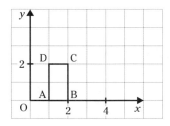

The vector is $\begin{pmatrix} -1 \\ 1 \end{pmatrix}$

9. Describe the inverse of the transformations given in questions 1 to 8.

MATHS IS OUT THERE

Teacher: Where do mathematicians who want to reflect or to enlarge their figure sleep ?
Student: On matrices.

20 ▷ POLYGONS

At the end of the chapter you should be able to:

1. Classify polygons in terms of their number of sides.
2. Identify regular polygons.
3. State the sum of the exterior or interior angles of a given polygon with n sides as $360°$ or $(n-2)180°$ respectively.
4. Calculate the size of an exterior or interior angle of a regular polygon.
5. Use the formula for the sum of the exterior angles of a polygon and that for interior to solve problems.
6. Make patterns using regular polygons that tessellate.

POLYGONS

A polygon is a plane (flat) figure bounded by straight lines.

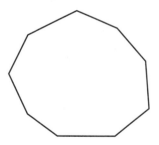

This is a nine-sided polygon.

Some polygons have names which you already know:

a three-sided polygon is a triangle

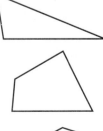

a four-sided polygon is a quadrilateral

a five-sided polygon is a pentagon

a six-sided polygon is a hexagon

an eight-sided polygon is an octagon

REGULAR POLYGONS

A polygon is called regular when all its sides are the same length *and* all its angles are the same size. The polygons below are all regular:

Exercise 20a

State which of the following figures are regular polygons. Give a brief reason for your answer:

1. Rhombus

2. Square

3. Rectangle

4. Parallelogram

5. Isosceles triangle

6. Right-angled triangle

7. Equilateral triangle

8. Circle

Make a rough sketch of each of the following polygons. (Unless you are told that a polygon is regular, you must assume that it is *not* regular.)

9. A regular quadrilateral

10. A hexagon

11. A triangle

12. A regular triangle

13. A regular hexagon

14. A pentagon

15. A quadrilateral

16. A ten-sided polygon

When the vertices of a polygon all point outwards, the polygon is convex.

Sometimes one or more of the vertices point inwards, in which case the polygon is concave.

convex polygon   concave polygon

In this chapter we consider only convex polygons.

INTERIOR ANGLES

The angles enclosed by the sides of a polygon are the *interior angles*. For example,

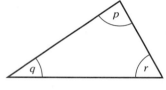

p, q and r are the interior angles of the triangle,

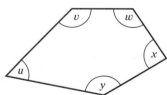

u, v, w, x and y are the interior angles of the pentagon.

THE EXTERIOR ANGLES

If we produce (extend) one side of a polygon, an angle is formed outside the polygon. It is called an *exterior angle*.

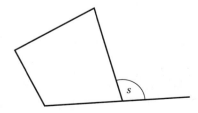

For example, s is an exterior angle of the quadrilateral.

If we produce all the sides in order we have all the exterior angles.

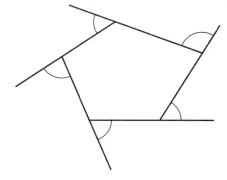

Exercise 20b

1. What is the sum of the interior angles of any triangle?

2. What is the sum of the interior angles of any quadrilateral?

3. In triangle ABC, find

   (a) the size of each marked angle
   (b) the sum of the exterior angles.

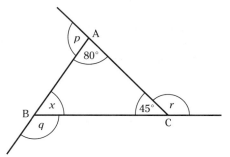

4. ABCD is a parallelogram. Find

   (a) the size of each marked angle
   (b) the sum of the exterior angles.

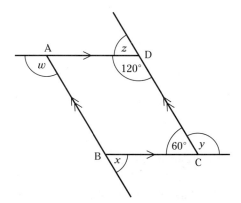

5. In a triangle ABC, write down the value of

(a) $x + q$

(b) the sum of all six marked angles

(c) the sum of the interior angles

(d) the sum of the exterior angles.

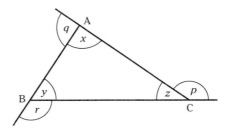

6. Draw a pentagon. Produce the sides in order to form the five exterior angles. Measure each exterior angle and then find their sum.

7. Construct a regular hexagon of side 5 cm. (Start with a circle of radius 5 cm and then with your compasses still open to a radius of 5 cm, mark off points on the circumference in turn.) Produce each side of the hexagon in turn to form the six exterior angles.

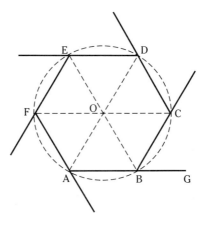

If O is the centre of the circle, joining O to each vertex forms six triangles:

(a) What kind of triangle is each of these triangles?

(b) What is the size of each interior angle in these triangles?

(c) Write down the value of $A\hat{B}C$.

(d) Write down the value of $C\hat{B}G$.

(e) Write down the value of the sum of the six exterior angles of the hexagon.

THE SUM OF THE EXTERIOR ANGLES OF A POLYGON

In the last exercise, we found that the sum of the exterior angles is 360° in each case. This is true of any polygon, whatever its shape or size.

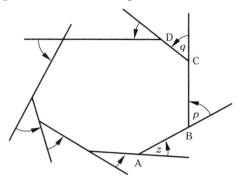

Consider walking round this polygon. Start at A and walk along AB. When you get to B you have to turn through angle p to walk along BC. When you get to C you have to turn through angle q to walk along CD, ... and so on until you return to A. If you then turn through angle z you are facing in the direction AB again. You have now turned through each exterior angle and have made just one complete turn, i.e.

the sum of the exterior angles of a polygon is 360°.

Exercise 20c

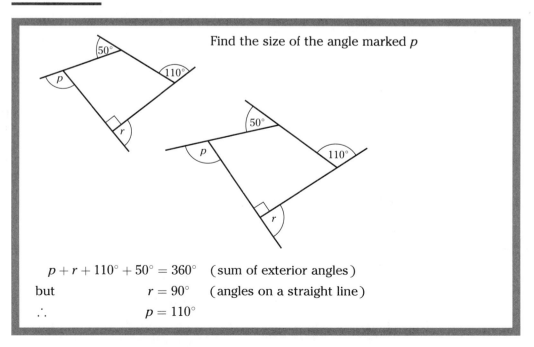

Find the size of the angle marked p

$$p + r + 110° + 50° = 360° \quad \text{(sum of exterior angles)}$$
$$\text{but} \qquad\qquad\qquad r = 90° \quad \text{(angles on a straight line)}$$
$$\therefore \qquad\qquad\qquad p = 110°$$

In each case find the size of the angle marked *p*:

1.

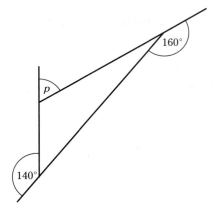

4.

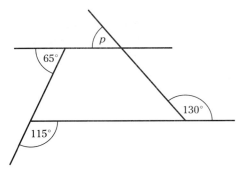

2.

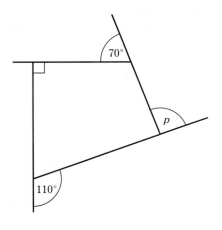

5.

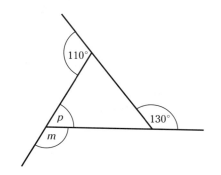

6.

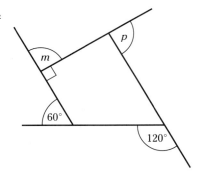

3.

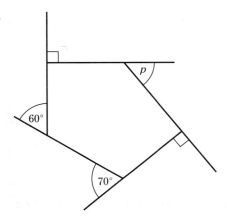

7.

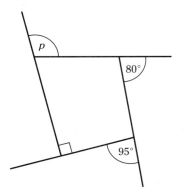

8.

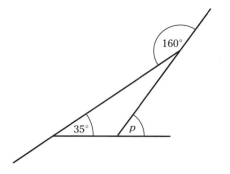

9.

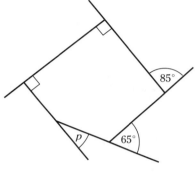

10.

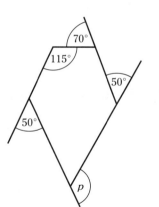

In questions 11 and 12 find the value of *x*.

11.

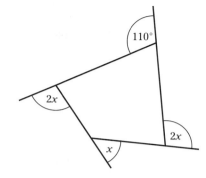

12.

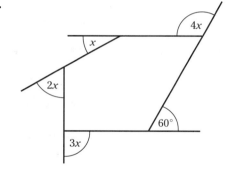

13. The exterior angles of a hexagon are *x*, 2*x*, 3*x*, 4*x*, 3*x* and 2*x*. Find the value of *x*.

14. Find the number of sides of a polygon if each exterior angle is (a) 72° (b) 45°.

THE EXTERIOR ANGLE OF A REGULAR POLYGON

If a polygon is regular, all its exterior angles are the same size. We know that the sum of th exterior angles is 360°, so the size of one exterior angle is easily found; we just divide 360° by the number of sides of the polygon, i.e.

> in a *regular* polygon with *n* sides, the size of an exterior angle is $\dfrac{360°}{n}$

Exercise 20d

Find the size of each exterior angle of a 24-sided regular polygon.

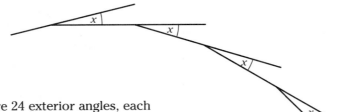

(There are 24 exterior angles, each of the same size.)

Each exterior angle $= \dfrac{360°}{24} = 15°$.

Find the size of each exterior angle of a regular polygon with:

1. 10 sides   **4.** 6 sides   **7.** 9 sides

2. 8 sides   **5.** 15 sides   **8.** 16 sides

3. 12 sides   **6.** 18 sides   **9.** 20 sides

THE SUM OF THE INTERIOR ANGLES OF A POLYGON

Consider an octagon:

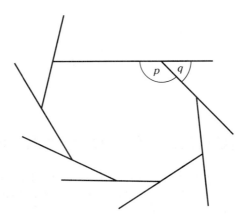

At each vertex there is an interior angle and an exterior angle and the sum of these two angles is 180° (angles on a straight line), i.e. $p + q = 180°$ at each one of the eight vertices.

Therefore, the sum of the interior angles and exterior angles together is

$$8 \times 180° = 1440°$$

The sum of the eight exterior angles is $360°$.

Therefore, the sum of the interior angles is

$$1440° - 360° = 1080°$$

Exercise 20e

Find the sum of the interior angles of a 14-sided polygon.

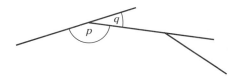

At each vertex $\qquad p + q = 180°$

∴ sum of interior angles and exterior angles is

$$14 \times 180° = 2520°$$

∴ sum of interior angles

$$= 2520° - 360°$$

$$= 2160°$$

Find the sum of the interior angles of a polygon with:

1. 6 sides

2. 5 sides

3. 10 sides

4. 4 sides

5. 7 sides

6. 12 sides

7. 18 sides

8. 9 sides

9. 15 sides

FORMULA FOR THE SUM OF THE INTERIOR ANGLES

If a polygon has n sides, then the sum of the interior and exterior angles together is $n \times 180° = 180n°$ so the sum of the interior angles only is $180n° - 360°$ which, as $360° = 180° \times 2$, can be written as $180°(n-2)$,

i.e.

in a polygon with n sides, the sum of the interior angles is

$$(180n - 360)° \quad \text{or} \quad (n-2)\,180°$$

Exercise 20f

1. Find the sum of the interior angles of a polygon with
   (a) 20 sides   (b) 16 sides   (c) 11 sides.

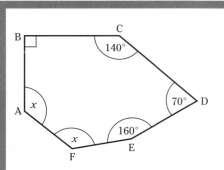

In the hexagon ABCDEF, the angles marked x are equal. Find the value of x.

The sum of the interior angles is $180° \times 6 - 360° = 720°$

$$\therefore 90° + 140° + 70° + 160° + 2x = 720°$$
$$460° + 2x = 720°$$
$$2x = 260°$$
$$x = 130°$$

In each of the following questions find the size of the angle(s) marked x:

2.

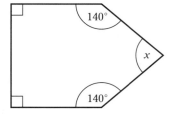

4.

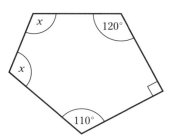

3.

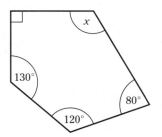

5.

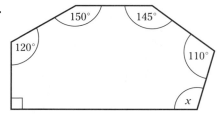

6.

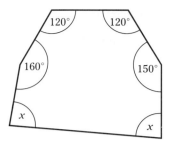

7.

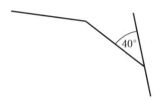

Find the size of each interior angle of a regular nine-sided polygon.

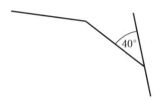

(As the polygon is regular, all the exterior angles are equal and all the interior angles are equal.)

Method 1   Sum of exterior angles $= 360°$

$\therefore$ each exterior angle $= 360° \div 9 = 40°$

$\therefore$ each interior angle $= 180° - 40° = 140°$

Method 2   Sum of interior angles $= 180° \times 9 - 360° = 1260°$

$\therefore$ each interior angle $= 1260° \div 9 = 140°$

Find the size of each interior angle of:

8. A regular pentagon.

9. A regular hexagon.

10. A regular octagon.

11. A regular ten-sided polygon.

12. A regular 12-sided polygon.

13. A regular 20-sided polygon.

14. How many sides has a regular polygon if each exterior angle is

(a) $20°$ (b) $15°$?

15. How many sides has a regular polygon if each interior angle is

(a) $150°$ (b) $162°$

(Find the exterior angle first.)

16. Is it possible for each exterior angle of a regular polygon to be

(a) $30°$ (d) $60°$

(b) $40°$ (e) $70°$

(c) $50°$ (f) $90°$?

In those cases where it is possible, give the number of sides.

17. Is it possible for each interior angle of a regular polygon to be

(a) 90°   (c) 180°   (e) 170°

(b) 120°   (d) 175°   (f) 135°?

In those cases where it is possible, give the number of sides.

18. Construct a regular pentagon with sides 5 cm long. (Find the size of each interior angle using your protractor.)

19. Construct a regular octagon of side 5 cm.

MIXED PROBLEMS

Exercise 20g

ABCDE is a pentagon, in which the interior angles at A and D are each $3x°$, the interior angles at B, C and E are each $4x°$. AB and DC are produced until they meet at F.
Find $B\widehat{F}C$.

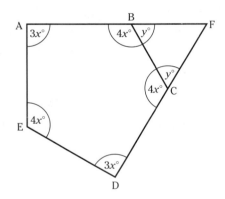

Sum of the interior angles of a pentagon $= 180° \times 5 - 360°$

$$= 540°$$

$\therefore$ $3x + 4x + 3x + 4x + 4x = 540$

$$18x = 540$$

$$x = 30$$

$\therefore$ $A\widehat{B}C = 120°$ and $B\widehat{C}D = 120°$

$\therefore$ $y = 60°$

$\therefore$ $B\widehat{F}C = 180° - 2 \times 60°$ (angle sum of $\triangle BFC$)

$$= 60°$$

In questions 1 to 10 find the value of *x*:

1.

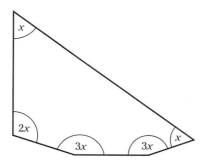

6.

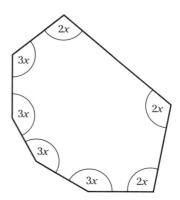

2.

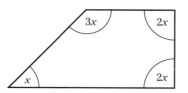

7.

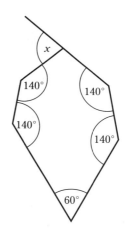

3.

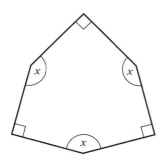

8.

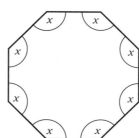

4.

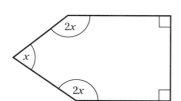

9.

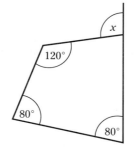

<u>**5.**</u>

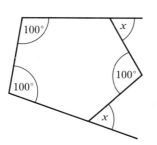

10.

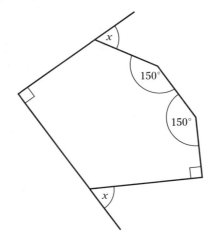

11. ABCDE is a regular pentagon.

OA = OB = OC = OD = OE.

Find the size of each angle at O.

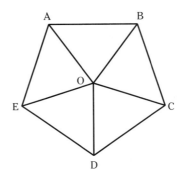

12. ABCDEFGH is a regular octagon. O is a point in the middle of the octagon such that O is the same distance from each vertex. Find $A\widehat{O}B$.

13. ABCDEF is a regular hexagon. AB and DC are produced until they meet at G. Find $B\widehat{G}C$.

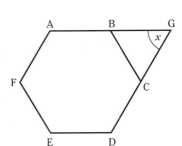

14. ABCDE is a regular pentagon. AB and DC are produced until they meet at F. Find $B\widehat{F}C$.

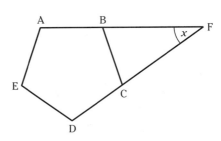

ABCDEF is a regular hexagon.
Find AD̂B.

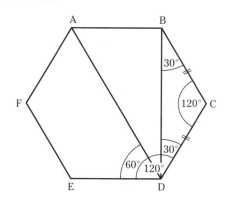

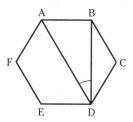

As ABCDEF is regular, the exterior angles are all equal.

$$\text{Each exterior angle} = 360° \div 6$$
$$= 60°$$
$$\therefore \quad \text{each interior angle} = 180° - 60°$$
$$= 120°$$

△BCD is isosceles (BC = DC).

$$\therefore \quad \text{CB̂D} = \text{BD̂C} = 30° \quad (\text{angle sum of } \triangle \text{BCD})$$

AD is a line of symmetry.

$$\therefore \qquad \qquad \text{ED̂A} = \text{CD̂A} = 60°$$
$$\therefore \qquad \qquad \text{AD̂B} = 60° - 30°$$
$$= 30°$$

In questions 15 to 20, each polygon is regular. Give answers correct to one decimal place where necessary:

15.

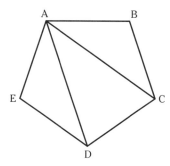

Find (a) AĈB   (b) DÂC

16.

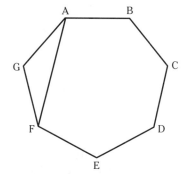

Find (a) AĜF   (b) GÂF

17.

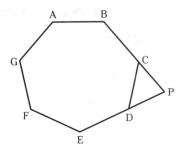

Find CP̂D

18.

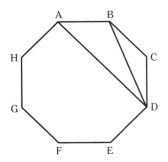

Find (a) CB̂D (b) BD̂A

19.

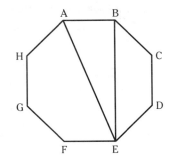

Find AÊB

20.

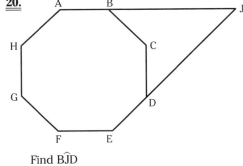

Find BĴD

PATTERN MAKING WITH REGULAR POLYHEDRA

Regular hexagons fit together without leaving gaps, to form a flat surface. We say that they *tessellate*.

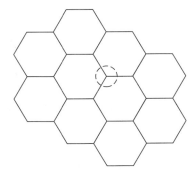

The hexagons tessellate because each interior angle of a regular hexagon is 120°, so three vertices fit together to make 360°.

Exercise 20h

1.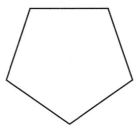

This is a pattern using regular octagons. They do not tessellate:

(a) Explain why they do not tessellate.

(b) What shape is left between the four octagons?

(c) Continue the pattern. (Trace one of the shapes above, cut it out and use it as a template.)

2. Trace this regular pentagon and use it to cut out a template:

(a) Will pentagons tessellate?

(b)

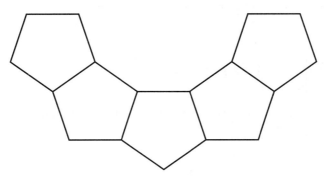

Use your template to copy and continue this pattern until you have a complete circle of pentagons. What shape is left in the middle?

(c) Make up a pattern using pentagons.

3.

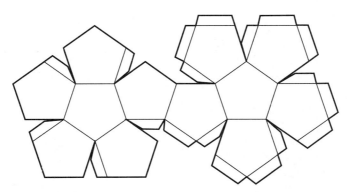

Use your template from question 2 to copy this net on to thick paper. Cut it out and fold along the lines. Stick the edges together using the flaps. You have made a regular dodecahedron.

4. Apart from the hexagon, there are two other regular polygons that tessellate. Which are they, and why?

5. Regular hexagons, squares and equilateral triangles can be combined to make interesting patterns. Some examples are given below:

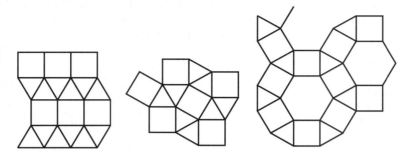

Copy these patterns and extend them. (If you make templates to help you, make each shape of side 2 cm.)

6. Make some patterns of your own using the shapes in question 5.

MATHS IS OUT THERE

What did the trapezium say to the rhombus when the rhombus straightened up?
Why, you're such a square!

21 > CIRCLES

At the end of the chapter you should be able to:

1. Identify centre, radius, diameter, chord, arc, segment and sector of a circle.
2. Identify angles subtended by the same arc of a circle and state the relationship between them.
3. Identify a cyclic quadrilateral and state its properties.
4. State the relationship between an angle at the centre and an angle at the circumference subtended by the same arc.
5. State the size of an angle in a semicircle.
6. Use ruler and a pair of compasses to construct the circumcircle of a given triangle.

THE BASIC FACTS

First we will revise some of the facts we already know about the circle

Every point on a circle is the same distance from its centre. This distance is called the *radius* of the circle.

Sometimes we use the word 'circle' to include the space inside the curve. When we do this we call the curve itself the *circumference* of the circle.

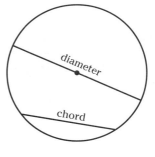

A straight line joining any two points on the circumference is called a *chord*.

Any chord passing through the centre of a circle is called a *diameter*.

We will now learn some new facts and definitions.

Any part of the circumference is called an arc. If the arc is less than half the circumference it is called a *minor arc*; if it is greater than half the circumference it is called a *major arc*.

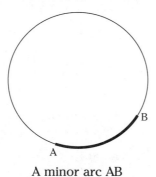

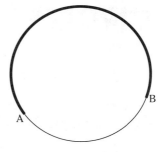

A minor arc AB   A major arc AB

The shaded area is enclosed by two radii and an arc. It looks like a slice of cake and is called a *sector*.

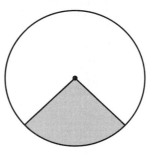

A chord divides a circle into two regions called segments. The larger region is called a *major segment* and the smaller region is called a *minor segment*.

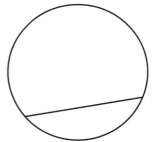

Exercise 21a

1. Name six chords in this diagram. Is any one of these chords a diameter? If so, name it.

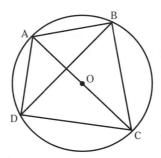

Copy the following diagrams. They do not have to be identical:

2. DC divides the circle into two segments. Shade the minor segment.

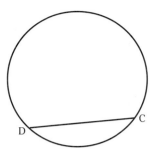

4. AB divides the circle into two segments. Shade the major segment.

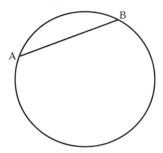

3. BC divides the circle into two segments. Shade the major segment.

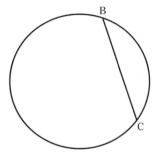

5. AD divides the circle into two segments. Shade the minor segment.

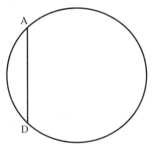

THE ANGLE SUBTENDED BY AN ARC

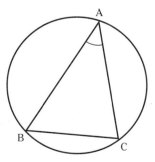

Consider a triangle ABC whose vertices A, B and C lie on a circle. The angle BAC is said to stand on the minor arc BC. We say that BC *subtends* an angle BAC at A which is on the circumference.

Similarly the angle ABC stands on the arc AC, or AC subtends an angle ABC at B, and the angle ACB stands on the arc AB, or AB subtends an angle ACB at C.

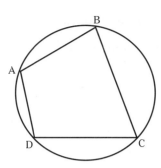

If the four vertices of a quadrilateral ABCD all lie on a circle, we say that the quadrilateral is *cyclic*, i.e. ABCD is a *cyclic quadrilateral*.

Exercise 21b

Questions 1 to 6 refer to the following diagram:

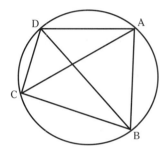

1. What arc does $D\hat{B}C$ stand on?

2. What arc does $B\hat{D}C$ stand on?

3. Name the two angles at the circumference standing on arc AB.

4. Name the two angles at the circumference standing on the arc BC.

5. What arc subtends $D\hat{B}A$?

6. What arc subtends $A\hat{C}B$?

Questions 7 to 12 refer to the following diagram:

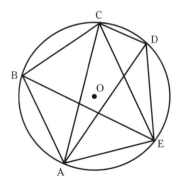

7. What arc does $B\hat{C}E$ stand on?

8. What arc does $C\hat{A}D$ stand on?

9. What arc subtends $C\hat{A}E$?

10. What arc subtends $D\hat{A}B$?

11. What angles stand on

   (a) the arc AB   (b) the arc BC?

12. What angles stand on

   (a) the arc AE   (b) the arc CE?

DISCOVERING RELATIONSHIPS BETWEEN ANGLES

Exercise 21c

Copy the following diagrams making them at least twice as large. For each diagram measure the angles denoted by the letters:

1.

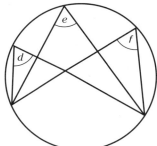

3.

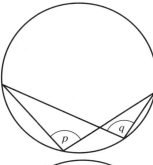

2.

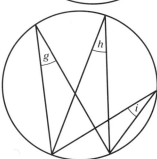

4.

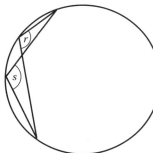

First Fact

The results for questions 1 to 4 show that

angles standing on the same arc of a circle and in the same segment are equal.

Exercise 21d

Find the angle denoted by the letter *x*.

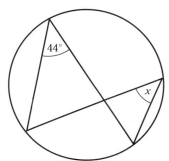

$$x = 44°$$
(angles in the same segment of a circle)

Find the angles denoted by the letters:

1.

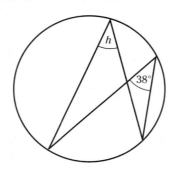

3.

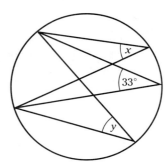

2.

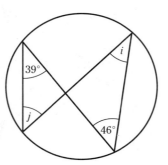

4.

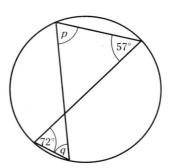

Find the angle denoted by the letter *k*.

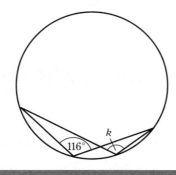

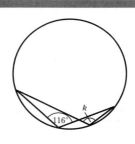

$$k = 116°$$
(angles in the same segment)

5.

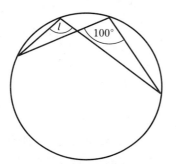

6.

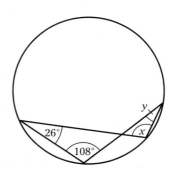

7.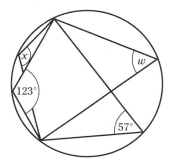

8.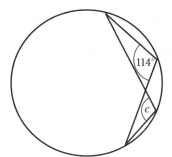

Exercise 21e

Copy the following diagrams making them at least twice as large. They need not be identical. For each diagram measure the angles denoted by the letters. Hence find a relationship between x and y:

1.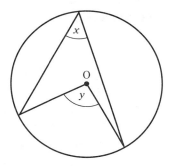

3.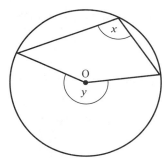

2.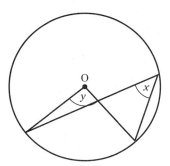

4.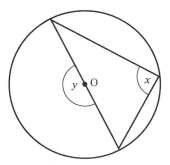

Second Fact
These results show that

> the angle which the arc of a circle subtends at the centre is equal to twice the angle it subtends at any point on the remaining circumference

Exercise 21f

Find the angle denoted by the letter *d*.

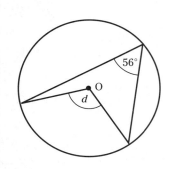

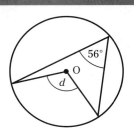

$$d = 2 \times 56°$$
$$= 112°$$

($\angle$ at centre $= 2 \times \angle$ at circumference)

Find the angles denoted by the letters. O denotes the centre of the circle:

1.

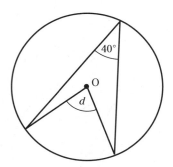

3.

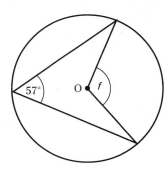

2.

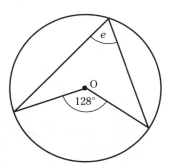

4.

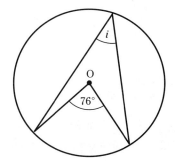

Find the angle denoted by the letter *f*.

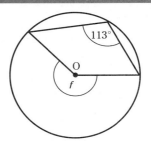

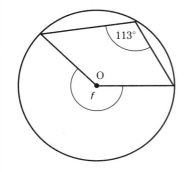

$$f = 2 \times 113°$$
$$= 226°$$
$$(\angle \text{ at centre} = 2 \times \angle \text{ at circumference})$$

5.

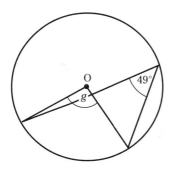

7.

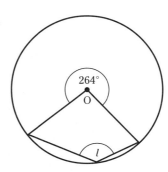

6.

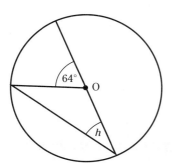

8.

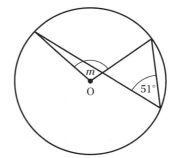

Exercise 21g

Copy the following diagrams making them at least twice as large. For each diagram measure the angles denoted by *p* and *q*. What do you notice about their sum?

1.

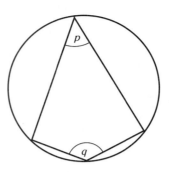

2.

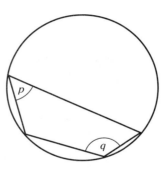

3.

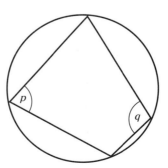

Third Fact
These results show that

the opposite angles of a cyclic quadrilateral are supplementary.

Exercise 21h

Find the angle denoted by the letter *p*.

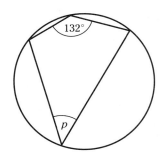
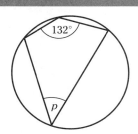

$$p + 132° = 180° \quad \text{(opp. } \angle\text{s cyclic quad. supplementary)}$$
$$\therefore \quad p = 180° - 132°$$
$$= 48°$$

Find the angles denoted by the letters.

1.

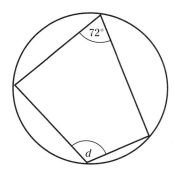

2.

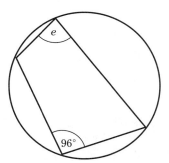

3.

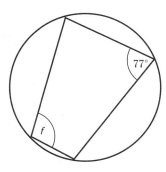

4.

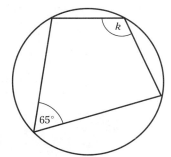

5.

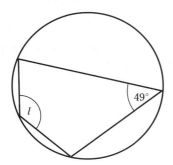

7.

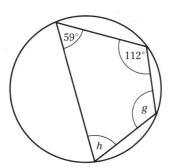

6.

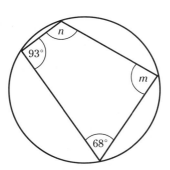

8.

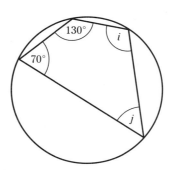

Fourth Fact

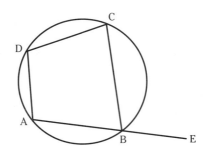

If the side AB of the cyclic quadrilateral ABCD is produced to E, the angle $C\hat{B}E$ is called an exterior angle of quadrilateral ABCD.

Then	$A\hat{B}C + C\hat{B}E = 180°$	($\angle$s on a str. line)
and	$A\hat{B}C + A\hat{D}C = 180°$	(opp. $\angle$s cyclic quadrilateral)
Hence	$C\hat{B}E = A\hat{D}C$	

i.e.   any exterior angle of a cyclic quadrilateral is equal to the opposite interior angle.

Exercise 21i

Copy each of the following diagrams making them at least twice as large. For each diagram measure the angles denoted by the letters. What result do they confirm?

1.

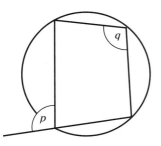

3.

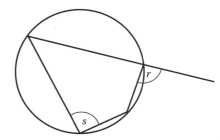

2.

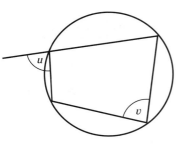

4.

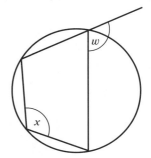

In questions 5 to 8 find the angles denoted by the letters:

5.

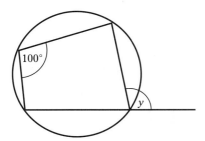

7.

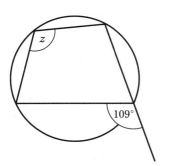

6.

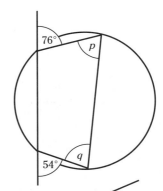

8.

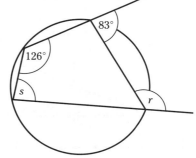

Exercise 21j

This exercise brings together the results used in the last few exercises. In some questions more than one of those results is required. It begins by revising some of the results for 'angles in a triangle' and 'parallel lines'.

Find the angles denoted by the letters:

1.

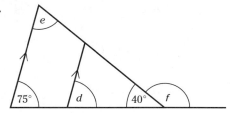

2.

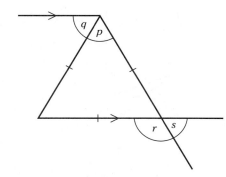

3.

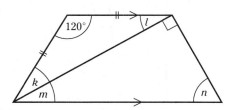

4.

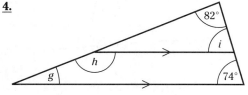

5.

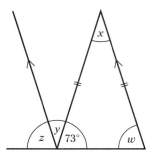

6.

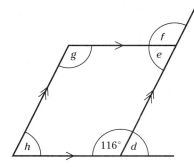

7.

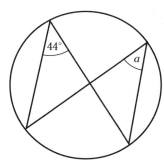

8.

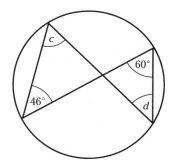

9.

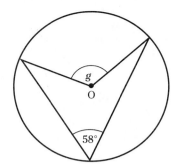

10.

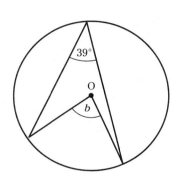

11.

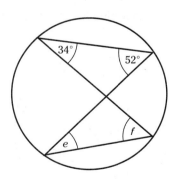

12.

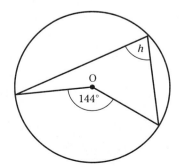

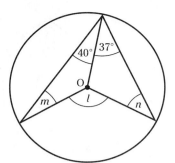

14.

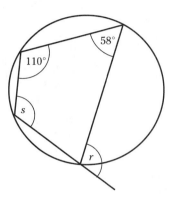

15.

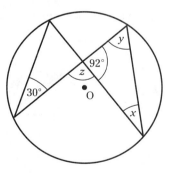

16.

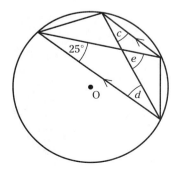

17.

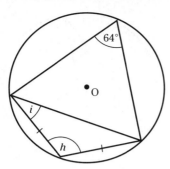

18.

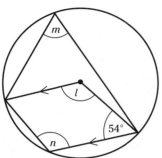

19.

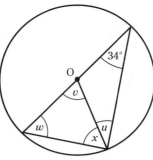

20.

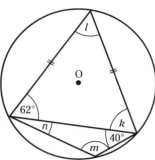

Exercise 21k

Copy the following diagrams making yours at least twice as big. Measure the angles denoted by the letters. What result do these values show?

1.

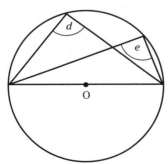

2.

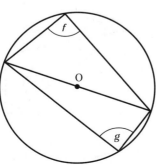

3.

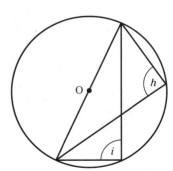

Fifth Fact

The angle in a semicircle is a right angle.

Exercise 21I

Find the angles denoted by the letters. The centre of the circle is marked O.

1.

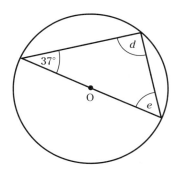

4.

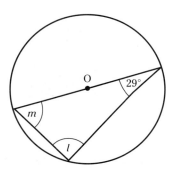

2.

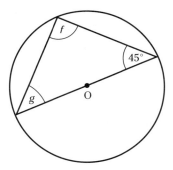

5.

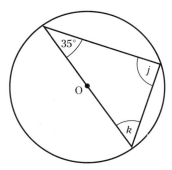

3.

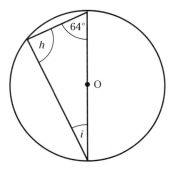

6.

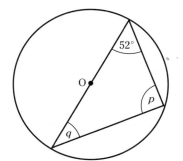

Find the angles denoted by the letters.

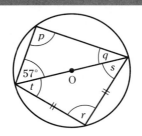

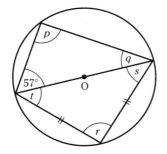

$$p = 90° \quad (\angle \text{ in a semicircle})$$
$$q = 33° \quad (\angle \text{s of a triangle})$$
$$r = 90° \quad (\angle \text{ in a semicircle})$$
$$s + t = 90° \quad (\angle \text{s of a triangle})$$

But $\quad s = t \quad$ (isosceles triangle)

$$\therefore \quad s = t = 45°$$

7.

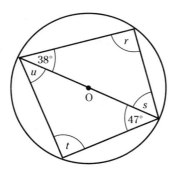

9.

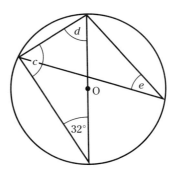

8.

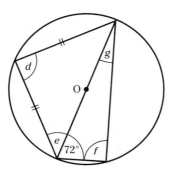

10.

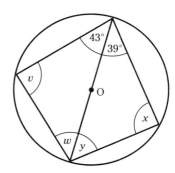

11.

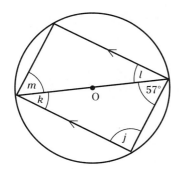

12.

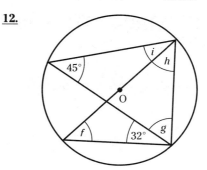

CONSTRUCTION OF THE PERPENDICULAR BISECTOR

Reminder

Any point on the perpendicular bisector of the line joining two points A and B is equidistant from those two points.

LMN is the perpendicular bisector of the line joining AB. For any point P on this line PA = PB.

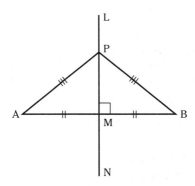

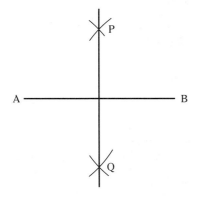

Use the following method to construct the perpendicular bisector of the line joining two points A and B.

With centre A and radius more than half AB, draw arcs above and below AB. *Keeping the radius the same*, move the point of your compasses to B and draw arcs above and below AB so that they intersect the first two arcs at P and Q. Join P to Q. PQ is the perpendicular bisector of AB. Any point on PQ is equidistant from A and B.

TO CONSTRUCT THE CIRCUMCIRCLE OF A GIVEN TRIANGLE

The circumcircle of a given triangle is the circle that passes through its vertices.

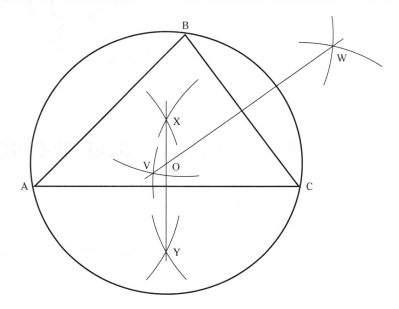

Draw a triangle ABC similar in size and shape to the triangle shown in the diagram. Use the method given above to construct the perpendicular bisector of AC and mark it XY. Next turn the page round so that BC is at the bottom and use the same method to construct the perpendicular bisector of BC. Mark this line VW. Any point on XY is equidistant from A and C and any point on VW is equidistant from B and C.

Mark O, the point of intersection of XY and VW. The point O is equidistant from all three vertices A, B and C.

With centre O and radius OA, draw a circle. If you have done your constructions carefully, you will find that this circle passes through A, B and C. This circle is called the circumcircle of triangle ABC and its centre O is called the circumcentre.

Now that you know exactly what to do, draw another triangle of a similar size and repeat this construction. When you have finished, the triangle and the circumcircle should stand out clearly from all construction lines.

Exercise 21m

1. Draw a triangle of any size and construct its circumcircle.

2. Construct a triangle PQR in which PQ = 11 cm, PR = 10 cm and QR = 9 cm. Construct the circumcircle of this triangle. Measure its radius.

3. Construct a triangle XYZ in which XY = 12.5 cm, YZ = 7.5 cm and XŶZ = 60°. Construct the circumcircle to this triangle. Measure

(a) the length of XZ

(b) the radius of the circumcircle.

4. Construct a triangle ABC in which AB = 12.5 cm, BC = 7.5 cm and AC = 10 cm. Find the position of the circumcentre O and hence draw the circumcircle. What do you notice about the position of O? What value would you now expect AĈB to have? Give reasons. Check you result by measuring AĈB with a protractor.

5. Construct a triangle DEF in which EF = 8.8 cm, DÊF = 30° and DF̂E = 45°. Construct the perpendicular bisectors of all three sides and hence draw the circumcircle. What do you notice

(a) about the three perpendicular bisectors

(b) about the circumcentre of an obtuse angled triangle?

6. Construct a trapezium ABCD in which AB = 10.2 cm, BC = AD = 5.2 cm, AB̂C = 60°, DÂB = 60°, AD̂C = 120° and BĈD = 120°. Construct the circumcircle to triangle ABC. Does this circle pass through any particular point? Can you give a reason for what has happened? Will this happen for every trapezium?

MIXED EXERCISE

Exercise 21n

Find the angles denoted by the letters:

1.

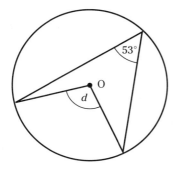

2.

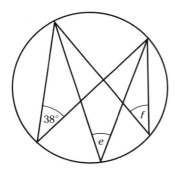

3.

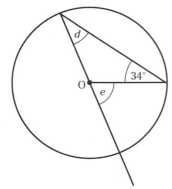

4.

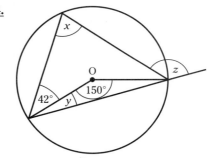

5.

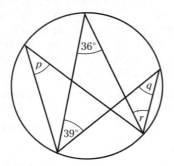

6.

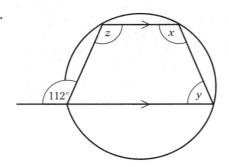

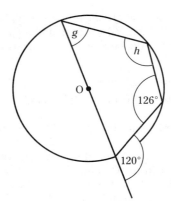

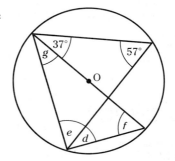

At the end of the chapter you should be able to:

1. Define a radian in terms of radius and arc length.
2. State a relationship between radians and degrees.
3. Calculate the length of an arc of a circle given the radius and angle at the centre in radians.
4. Calculate the area of a sector given the radius and angle at the centre.
5. Express in radians (degrees) an angle given in degrees (radians).
6. Calculate the area of a sector given the radius and length of the sector.

A *radian* is the measure of the angle subtended at the centre of a circle by an arc equal in length to the radius of the circle.

In this circle if the radius of the circle is r and the length of arc AB $= r$, then $A\widehat{O}B$ measures 1 radian.

Angles may therefore be measured either in degrees or radians. It can be shown that

$$\pi \text{ radians} = 180 \text{ degrees}$$

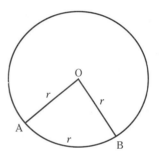

LENGTH OF AN ARC OF A CIRCLE

In this circle, arc length AB $= s$, radius of circle $= r$ and $A\widehat{O}B = \theta$ radians, then

$$s = r\theta \qquad [1]$$

If θ is given in degrees, then

since $\qquad 180° = \pi \text{ radians}$

$$\theta° = \frac{\pi}{180}\theta \text{ radians}$$

$\therefore \qquad s = \frac{\pi r\theta}{180} \qquad [2]$

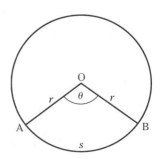

Formula [1] for arc length is clearly simpler than formula [2].

AREA OF SECTOR OF A CIRCLE

If the measure of the sector angle is given in radians, it is easy to calculate the area.

If $A\widehat{O}B$ in this circle were 2π radians, the sector would be the whole interior of the circle.

If the measure of $A\widehat{O}B = \theta$ radians then

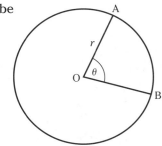

$$\frac{\text{area of sector}}{\text{area of circle}} = \frac{\theta}{2\pi}$$

$\therefore$ area of sector $= \dfrac{\theta}{2\pi} \times$ area of circle

$$= \frac{\theta}{2\pi} \times \pi r^2$$

$\therefore$ $\qquad\qquad = \frac{1}{2}r^2\theta$

Again, if θ is measured in degrees and A is the measure of the area of the sector,

then
$$A = \frac{\pi r^2\theta}{360}$$

Since $\theta° = \dfrac{\pi}{180}\ \theta$ radians, $A = \frac{1}{2}r^2\theta$ and arc length, $s = r\theta$

$$A = \tfrac{1}{2}r^2\theta$$

$$= \tfrac{1}{2}r \times r\theta$$

$\therefore$ $\qquad A = \tfrac{1}{2}rs$

This enables us to calculate the area of the sector given the length of the sector arc and the radius.

Exercise 22a

Calculate the length of the sector arc and the area of the sector in a circle of radius 5 cm, if the sector angle if 60°.

$$\theta = 60° = \frac{\pi \times 60}{180}\ \text{radians} = \frac{\pi}{3}\ \text{radians}$$

$$\text{arc length, } s = r\theta$$

$$= 5 \times \frac{\pi}{3}$$

$$\therefore \qquad \text{arc length} = \frac{5\pi}{3} \text{ cm}$$

$$\text{Area, } A = \tfrac{1}{2}r^2\theta$$

$$= \tfrac{1}{2} \times 25 \times \frac{\pi}{3}$$

$$= \frac{25\pi}{6}$$

$$\therefore \qquad \text{area of sector} = \frac{25\pi}{6} \text{ cm}^2$$

Use $\pi = 3.14$.

1. Calculate the length of the arc of a circle whose radius is $10\,$cm, if the sector angle is $20°$.

2. The measure of the angle at the centre of a circle of radius $4\,$cm is $30°$. Calculate the length of the arc which subtends this angle.

3. Calculate the radius of the circle, if the length of the arc subtending an angle of $72°$ at the centre is $25.12\,$cm.

4. Calculate, in radians, the angle at the centre subtended by an arc of length $31.4\,$cm, if the radius of the circle is $15\,$cm.

5. Calculate the area of a circular sector if the measure of the angle at the centre is $45°$ and the radius of the circle is $5\,$cm.

6. In a circle whose radius is $8\,$cm, calculate the area of a sector if the measure of its arc is $15.7\,$cm.

7. In a circle of radius $2\,$cm, a sector has an area of $5\pi\,$cm. Calculate, in terms of π, the length of the arc of the sector.

8. A sector of a circle, radius $35\,$cm, has an area of $588\,$cm^2. Find the size of the sector angle in

   (a) radians
   (b) degrees (to the nearest degree).

9. A sector of a circle has an area of $6.55\,$cm^2 and the sector angle is $30°$. Find the radius of the circle.

10. Answers to the following may be left in terms of π:

    (a) Express, in degrees, an angle of $\dfrac{3\pi}{2}$ radians.

    (b) Express, in radians, an angle of $600°$.

    (c) A wheel rotates at the rate of 165 rotations per minute. Express, in radians, the angle through which it rotates in one second.

MATHS IS OUT THERE

Erastothenes who lived in the third century B.C. wanted to calculate the circumference of the earth. He knew that the sun was directly overhead at a place in Egypt called Syene (now called Aswan) at noon on 21 June. Alexandria was 5000 stadia north of Syene (stadia were the units of length used by Egyptians at the time to measure long distances). Erastothenes found that on 21 June a tall pole at Alexandria cast a shadow on the ground. By using similar figures and measuring the similar angles he was able to find the circumference of the earth to a degree of accuracy close to the modern measurement.

REVIEW TEST 2: CHAPTERS 12–22

In questions 1–10, choose the letter for the correct answer.

1. The mean of six scores is 12 and the mean of four other scores is 17. What is the mean of the ten scores?

    (A) 13.5 (B) 14 (C) 14.5 (D) 29

2. $(3x+4)(2x-5) =$

    (A) $6x^2 - 20$ (B) $6x^2 - 15x - 20$ (C) $6x^2 - 7x - 20$ (D) $6x^2 + 8x - 20$

3. The solution of $(2x+5)(3x-4) = 0$ is $x =$

    (A) -5 (B) $-\frac{5}{2}$ (C) $\frac{3}{4}$ (D) 4

4. The minimum value of $7 + (x+3)^2$ is

    (A) -3 (B) 0 (C) 3 (D) 7

5. The image of $(2, 3)$ under the transformation given by the matrix $\begin{pmatrix} 1 & 2 \\ 0 & -1 \end{pmatrix}$ is

    (A) $(8, -3)$ (B) $(3, 5)$ (C) $(2, 2)$ (D) $(3, 3)$

6. An enlargement with centre O and scale factor 3 is given by the matrix

    (A) $\begin{pmatrix} 3 & 3 \\ 3 & 3 \end{pmatrix}$ (B) $\begin{pmatrix} 3 & 0 \\ 0 & 3 \end{pmatrix}$ (C) $\begin{pmatrix} 3 & 3 \\ 0 & 0 \end{pmatrix}$ (D) $\begin{pmatrix} 0 & 3 \\ 3 & 0 \end{pmatrix}$

7. Each interior angle of a regular 5-sided polygon measures

    (A) $144°$ (B) $108°$ (C) $72°$ (D) $36°$

8. In a cyclic quadrilateral PQRS, the angle at P measures 70 degrees. What is the measure of the angle at R in degrees?

    (A) 20 (B) $70°$ (C) $110°$ (D) 140

9. The area of a sector of a circle of radius 7 cm and sector arc of measure 8 cm is

    (A) $28\,\text{cm}^2$ (B) $44\,\text{cm}^2$ (C) $56\,\text{cm}^2$ (D) $154\,\text{cm}^2$

10. In terms of π, an angle of 50 degrees, expressed in radians is

    (A) $\dfrac{\pi}{50}$ (B) $\dfrac{5\pi}{18}$ (C) $\dfrac{\pi}{2}$ (D) 50π

11. For the first $2\frac{1}{2}$ hours of a 182 km journey the average speed was 60 km per hour. The average speed for the remainder of the journey was 64 km per hour. Calculate the average speed for the entire journey.

12. (a) A piece of cardboard is in the shape of a quarter of a circle of radius 14 cm bounded by perpendicular radii OX and OY. Points A and B are taken on OX and OY respectively such that OA = 6 cm and OB = 8 cm. The triangular part OAB is removed. Calculate the area and perimeter of the remaining piece. Take π to be $3\frac{1}{7}$.

(b)

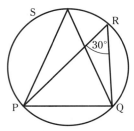

In the above diagram PR is the diameter of the circle. Given $Q\widehat{R}P = 30°$ and SP = SQ, find, giving reasons for your answers, (i) $P\widehat{S}Q$ (ii) $Q\widehat{S}R$ (iii) $S\widehat{Q}P$.

13. (a) Factorise completely (i) $2x^3 - 72xy^2$ (ii) $a^2 - 2ab - 2bc + ac$ (iii) $6x^2 - 5x - 4$

(b) Solve by the method of completing the squares, $2x^2 + 7x + 1 = 0$. Give your answers to two decimal places.

14. (a) Find the matrix of the transformation which maps $(1, 2)$ onto $(-4, 2)$ and $(0, 1)$ onto $(-2, 0)$.

(b) Find the matrix product $\begin{pmatrix} 2 & -1 \\ -3 & 4 \end{pmatrix} \begin{pmatrix} 4 & 1 \\ 3 & 2 \end{pmatrix}$

Hence solve the simultaneous equations $4x + y = 5$ and $3x + 2y = -1$

15. A region R is the set of integers (x, y) such that

$x > 0, \ y > 0, \ y - x < 10$ and $y > 2x$

Using a scale of 1 cm to represent 1 unit on each axis, construct accurately on graph paper, and shade the region R.
Find the values of x and y for which $2x + y$ is a maximum.

23 ▷ RATIO AND PROPORTION

At the end of the chapter you should be able to:

1. Reduce a given ratio to its simplest form.
2. Compare two ratios in terms of size.
3. Express a given ratio in the form $n:1$, where n is written correct to a stated number of significant figures.
4. Find the ratio of two quantities measured in different units.
5. Calculate the missing quantity, given two equivalent ratios.
6. Use ratios to solve problems in sharing.
7. Express quantities which are in direct or inverse proportion in terms of ratio.
8. Solve problems involving direct or inverse proportion.
9. Use the unitary method to solve problems.

The first few exercises are to remind you about ratios. Remember that ratios compare the sizes of related quantities.

SIMPLIFYING RATIOS

A ratio can be divided or multiplied throughout by the same number.

Exercise 23a

Give the ratios

(a) $225:105$ (b) $\frac{4}{5}:\frac{7}{8}:\frac{1}{2}$ in their simplest forms

(a) $225:105 = 45:21$ (dividing by 5)
$ = 15:7$ (dividing by 3)

(b) $\frac{4}{5}:\frac{7}{8}:\frac{1}{2} = \overset{8}{\cancel{40}} \times \frac{4}{\cancel{5}_1} : \overset{5}{\cancel{40}} \times \frac{7}{\cancel{8}_1} : \overset{20}{\cancel{40}} \times \frac{1}{\cancel{2}_1}$
$\phantom{\frac{4}{5}:\frac{7}{8}:\frac{1}{2}} = 32:35:20$

Give the following ratios in their simplest form:

1. 12:18

4. 320:480

7. 3.2:7.2

2. 3:6:9

5. 288:128:144

8. $\frac{1}{2} : \frac{5}{6} : \frac{2}{3}$

3. 3.5:2.5

6. $\frac{1}{2} : \frac{3}{4} : \frac{1}{4}$

9. 36:54:18

Which ratio is larger, 3:2 or 14:9?

(To compare the sizes of the ratios, we write them as fractions and then convert them to equivalent fractions with a common denominator.)

$$\frac{3}{2} = \frac{27}{18} \quad \text{and} \quad \frac{14}{9} = \frac{28}{18}$$

The second ratio is the larger.

Which ratio is the larger?

10. 6:11 or 2:5

12. 20:3 or 31:4

11. 15:4 or 11:3

13. 2:7 or 5:16

Express the ratio 7:5 in the form $n:1$

$$7:5 = \frac{7}{5} : 1$$
$$= 1.4 : 1$$

Express the following ratios in the form $n:1$, giving n correct to three significant figures where necessary:

14. 3:2

17. 30:11

20. 4:3

15. 12:5

18. 3:5

21. 3:4

16. 6:7

19. 21:8

22. 10:7

MIXED UNITS AND PROBLEMS

If we are asked to compare two quantities expressed in different units, we need to change one or both so that the two quantities are in the same unit. It is easier to change to smaller units (where multiplication is required) rather than to larger units (where division is required).

Exercise 23b

Simplify the ratio 63 cm : 0.72 m

$$63 \text{ cm} : 0.72 \text{ cm} = 63 \text{ cm} : 72 \text{ cm}$$
$$= 7 : 8$$

Simplify the following ratios:

1. 45 cm : 0.1 m   **3.** 340 m : 1.2 km   **5.** 450 mg : 1 g

2. 42 c : $1.05   **4.** 32 g : 2 kg   **6.** 2.2 t : 132 kg

Find the ratio of 14 c per gram to $120 per kilogram.

(In order to compare we will use both prices in $ per kg.)

$$14 \text{ c per g} = 14\,000 \text{ c per kg}$$
$$= \$140 \text{ per kg}$$
$$14 \text{ c per g} : \$120 \text{ per kg} = \$140 \text{ per kg} : \$120 \text{ per kg}$$
$$= 140 : 120$$
$$= 7 : 6$$

Find the ratios of the following prices:

7. 4 c per kilogram to $38 per tonne. (First express 4 c per kg as a price per tonne.)

8. 6 c each to 70 c per dozen. (First find the cost per dozen.)

9. $16.20 per metre to 15 c per centimetre.

10. 72 c for twenty to 4 c each.

Give the ratio of the cost of 6 m of material at $2.40 per metre to the cost of 8 m at $2.20 per metre.

$$\text{First cost} = \$6 \times 2.40$$
$$= \$14.40$$
$$\text{Second cost} = \$8 \times 2.20$$
$$= \$17.60$$
$$\text{Ratio of costs} = \$14.40 : \$17.60$$
$$= 144 : 176$$
$$= 18 : 22 = 9 : 11$$

11. In a school of 1029 pupils, 504 are girls. What is the ratio of the number of boys to the number of girls?

12. I spend $3.60 on groceries and $2.40 on vegetables. What is the ratio of the cost of

(a) groceries to vegetables

(b) vegetables to groceries

(c) groceries to the total?

13. One rectangle has a length of 6 cm and a width of $4\frac{1}{2}$ cm. A second rectangle has a length of 9 cm and a width of $2\frac{1}{2}$ cm. Find the ratios of

(a) their lengths

(b) their widths

(c) their perimeters

(d) their areas.

14. Find the ratio of the cost of $12\,\text{m}^2$ of carpet at $7.20 per m^2 to the cost of 50 carpet tiles at $2.40 per tile.

15. Find the ratios of the following areas

(a) $B : A$

(b) $C : B$

(c) $E : A + B$

(d) $E : D$

(e) $E : C + D$

(f) $C :$ whole square

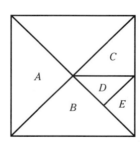

16. The areas of the small triangles are equal. Find the ratios of the following areas:

(a) $A :$ whole figure

(b) $A : A + B + C + D$

(c) $B + E + F + G :$ whole figure

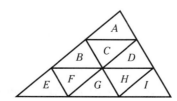

FINDING MISSING QUANTITIES

If we are given the ratio $x : 6 = 3 : 5$ we may write this as $\frac{x}{6} = \frac{3}{5}$ and solve the equation for x.

It does not matter in which order we compare the two quantities as long as we are consistent. If the ratio is $4 : x = 5 : 3$ we may rewrite it as $x : 4 = 3 : 5$.

Exercise 23c

Find x if (a) $x : 6 = 13 : 15$ (b) $4 : x = 3 : 2$

(a) $\dfrac{x}{6} = \dfrac{13}{15}$

$\cancel{6}^{1} \times \dfrac{x}{\cancel{6}_{1}} = \cancel{6}^{2} \times \dfrac{13}{\cancel{15}_{5}}$

$x = \dfrac{26}{5}$

$= 5.2$

(b) $x : 4 = 2 : 3$ (rearrange the ratio so that x comes first)

$\dfrac{x}{4} = \dfrac{2}{3}$

$4 \times \dfrac{x}{4} = 4 \times \dfrac{2}{3}$

$x = \dfrac{8}{3}$

$= 2\frac{2}{3}$

Find x in questions 1 to 6:

1. $x : 5 = 2 : 9$

2. $x : 3 = 1 : 7$

3. $x : 6 = 5 : 4$

4. $5 : x = 7 : 2$

5. $3 : 8 = 9 : x$

6. $15 : 2 = x : 3$

Complete the following ratios:

7. $4 : \quad = 3 : 7$

8. $\quad : 5 = 6 : 11$

9. $3 : \quad = 5 : 2$

10. $9 : 5 = \quad : 4$

11. $6 : 5 = 4 :$

12. $\quad : 12 = 5 : 7$

In a town, the ratio of the number of males to the number of females is $80:81$. There are 9680 males. How many females are there? What is the total population?

Suppose there are x females,

then $x : 9680 = 81 : 80$ (Notice the change of order.)

$$\frac{x}{9680} = \frac{81}{80}$$

$$\cancel{9680}^{\,1} \times \frac{x}{\cancel{9680}_{\,1}} = \cancel{9680}^{\,121} \times \frac{81}{\cancel{80}_{\,1}}$$

$$x = 9801$$

There are 9801 females and the total population is 19 481.

---

13. The numbers of Mr and Mrs James' grandsons and granddaughters are in the ratio $4 : 3$. There are nine granddaughters. How many grandsons are there? What is the ratio of the number of granddaughters to the number of grandchildren?

14. The ratio of the number of cats to the number of dogs owned by the children in one year group in a school is $5 : 3$. There are 95 cats. How many cats and dogs are there altogether?

15. The ratio of the lengths of two rectangles is $6 : 5$. The length of the second is 8.4 cm. What is the length of the first?

16. The ratio of the numbers of orange flowers to white flowers in a garden is $6 : 11$. There are 144 orange flowers. How many white flowers are there?

DIVISION IN A GIVEN RATIO

Exercise 23d

Share 72 c amongst three people so that their shares are in the ratio $3 : 4 : 5$.

There are 12 portions (i.e. $3 + 4 + 5$).

$$\text{First share} = \frac{3}{12} \times 72\,c = 18\,c$$

$$\text{Second share} = \frac{4}{12} \times 72\,c = 24\,c$$

$$\text{Third share} = \frac{5}{12} \times 72\,c = 30\,c$$

Check: $18\,c + 24\,c + 30\,c = 72\,c$

1. Divide $45 into two parts in the ratio 4 : 5

2. Divide 96 m into two parts in the ratio 9 : 7

3. Divide 5 kg into three parts in the ratio 1 : 2 : 5

4. Divide seven hours into three parts in the ratio 1 : 5 : 8

5. There are 32 children in a class. The ratio of the number of boys to the number of girls is 9 : 7. How many boys and how many girls are there?

6. The angles of a triangle are in the ratio 6 : 5 : 7. Find the sizes of the three angles.

7. Share the contents of a box containing 30 chocolates amongst Anne, Mary and Sue in the ratio 3 : 4 : 3. How many chocolates will each get?

8. A marksman fires at a target and the ratio of hits to misses is 11 : 4. He fires 90 times. How many hits does he score and how many times does he miss?

MIXED QUESTIONS

Exercise 23e

1. Simplify the ratio 324 : 252

2. Divide 72 m into two parts in the ratio 5 : 7

3. Complete the ratio 4 : 7 = 3 :

4. Find x if 4 : x = 9 : 5

5. The ratio of two lengths is 4 : 5. If the first length is 22 cm what is the second?

6. If $p : q = 2 : 3$, what is $5p : 2q$?

7. Find the ratio of 2 c per gram to $2.12 per kilogram.

8. Simplify $4\frac{2}{3} : 3\frac{1}{2}$

9. In a block of flats, 24 have two bedrooms and 32 have one bedroom. Give the ratio of the number of two-bedroomed flats to the number of one-bedroomed flats.

10. Simplify the ratio 3.2 : 4.8

SIMPLE DIRECT PROPORTION

If we know the cost of *one* article, we can easily find the cost of ten similar articles, or if we know that someone is paid for *one* hour's work, we can find what the pay is for five hours.

Exercise 23f

If 1 cm^3 of lead weighs 11.3 g, what is the weight of (a) 6 cm^3 (b) 0.8 cm^3?

$$1 \, \text{cm}^3 \text{ weighs } 11.3 \, \text{g}$$

(a)   6 cm^3 weigh 11.3×6 g $= 67.8$ g

(b)   0.8 cm^3 weigh 11.3×0.8 g $= 9.04$ g

1. The cost of 1 kg of sugar is 60 c. What is the cost of

   (a) 3 kg   (b) 12 kg?

2. In one hour an electric fire uses $1\frac{1}{2}$ units. Find how much it uses in

   (a) four hours   (b) $\frac{1}{2}$ hour.

3. One litre of petrol takes a car 18 km. At the same rate, how far does it travel on

   (a) four litres   (b) 6.6 litres?

4. A knitting pattern states that, at the correct tension, five rows measure 1 cm. How many rows must be knitted to measure

   (a) 7 cm   (b) 8.4 cm?

5. The cost of 1 kg of tomatoes is $2.25. Find the cost of

   (a) $\frac{1}{2}$ kg   (b) 2.4 kg.

We can reverse the process and, for instance, find the cost of *one* article if we know the cost of three similar articles.

Exercise 23g

---

18 cm^3 of copper weigh 162 g. What is the weight of 1 cm^3?

18 cm^3 weigh 162 g

1 cm^3 weighs $\dfrac{162}{18}$ g $= 9$ g

---

1. Six pens cost $7.20. What is the cost of one pen?

2. A car uses eight litres of petrol to travel 124 km. At the same rate, how far can it travel on one litre?

3. A man walks steadily for three hours and covers 13 km. How far does he walk in one hour?

4. Dress material costs $2.60 for 4 m. What is the cost of 1 m?

5. A carpet costs $92.40. Its area is 12 m^2. What is the cost of 1 m^2?

We can use the same process even if the quantities are not a whole number of units.

The mass of 0.6 cm^3 of a metal is 3 g. What is the mass of 1 cm^3?

The mass of 0.6 cm^3 is 3 g

The mass of 1 cm^3 is $\dfrac{3}{0.6}$ g $= 5$ g

---

6. The cost of 2.8 m of material is $11.76. What is the cost of 1 m?

7. 8.6 m^2 of carpet cost $71.38. What is the cost of 1 m^2?

8. The cost of running a refrigerator for 3.2 hours is 4.8 c. What is the cost of running the refrigerator for one hour?

9. A bricklayer takes 0.8 hour to build a wall 1.2 m high. How high a wall (of the same length) could he build in one hour?

10. A piece of webbing is 12.4 cm long and its area is 68.2 cm^2. What is the area of a piece of this webbing that is 1 cm long?

DIRECT PROPORTION

If two varying quantities are always in the same ratio, they are said to be *directly proportional* to one another (or sometimes simply *proportional*).

For example, when buying pens which each cost the same amount, the total cost is proportional to the number of pens. The ratio of the cost of 11 pens to the cost of 14 pens is 11 : 14, and if we know the cost of 11 pens, we can find the cost of 14 pens.

One method for solving problems involving direct proportion uses ratio, another uses the ideas in the last two exercises. This method is called the *unitary* method because it makes use of the cost of *one* article or the time taken by *one* man to complete a piece of work.

Exercise 23h

If the mass of 16 cm^3 of a metal is 24 g, what is the mass of 20 cm^3?

First Method (using ratios)

Let the mass of 20 cm^3 be x grams

Then $x : 24 = 20 : 16$ (The ratio of the masses = the ratio of the volumes)

$$\frac{x}{24} = \frac{20}{16}$$

$$\overset{1}{24} \times \frac{x}{24_{,1}} = \overset{3}{24} \times \frac{\overset{10}{20}}{16_{2}}{}_{1}$$

$$x = 30$$

The mass of 20 cm^3 is 30 g.

Second Method (unitary method)

(Write the first sentence so that it ends with the quantity you want, i.e. the mass.)

16 cm^3 has a mass of 24 g.

1 cm^3 has a mass of $\dfrac{24}{16}$ g. (There is no need to work out the value of $\dfrac{24}{16}$ yet.)

20 cm^3 has a mass of $\overset{10}{20} \times \dfrac{\overset{3}{24}}{16_{2}}{}_{1}$ g $= 30$ g

1. At a steady speed a car uses four litres of petrol to travel 75 km. At the same speed how much petrol is needed to travel 60 km?

2. A hiker walked steadily for four hours, covering 16 km. How long did he take to cover 12 km?

3. An electric fire uses $7\frac{1}{2}$ units in three hours. How many units does it use in five hours?

4. How long does the same electric fire take to use 9 units?

5. A taxi journey of 30 km costs $36. At the same rate per kilometre

   (a) what would be the cost of travelling 25 km

   (b) how far could you travel for $42?

6. It costs $108 to turf a lawn of area 63 m². How much would it cost to turf a lawn of area 56 m²?

7. A machine in a soft drinks factory fills 840 bottles in six hours. How many could it fill in five hours?

8. A 6 kg bag of beans costs 198 c. At the same rate, what would an 8 kg bag cost?

9. A knitting pattern states that the correct tension is such that 55 rows measure 10 cm. How many rows should be knitted to give 12 cm?

10. A scale model of a ship is such that the mast is 9 cm high and the mast of the original ship is 12 m high. The length of the original ship is 27 m. How long is the model ship?

Either method will work, whether the numbers are complicated or simple. Even if the question is about something unfamiliar, it is sufficient to know that the quantities are proportional.

In a spring balance, the extension in the spring is proportional to the load. If the extension is 2.5 cm when the load is 8 newtons, what is the extension when the load is 3.6 newtons?

Ratio Method

Let the extension be x cm. $x : 2.5 = 3.6 : 8$

$$\frac{x}{2.5} = \frac{3.6}{8}$$

$$2.5 \times \frac{x}{2.5} = 2.5 \times \frac{3.6}{8}$$

$$x = 1.125$$

The extension is 1.125 cm.

Unitary Method

If a load of 8 newtons gives an extension of 2.5 cm, then a load of 1 newton gives an extension of $\frac{2.5}{8}$ cm.

$\therefore$ a load of 3.6 newtons gives an extension of

$$3.6 \times \frac{2.5}{8} \text{ cm} = 1.125 \text{ cm}$$

11. It costs $196 to hire scaffolding for 42 days. How much would it cost to hire the same scaffolding for 36 days at the same rate per day?

12. The rates of currency exchange published in the newspapers on a certain day showed that 14 pounds could be exchanged for 49 dollars. How many dollars could be obtained for 112 pounds?

13. At a steady speed, a car uses 15 litres of petrol to travel 164 km. At the same speed, what distance could be travelled if six litres were used?

14. If a 2 kg bag of sugar contains 9×10^6 crystals, how many crystals are there in

    (a) 5 kg   (c) 0.03 kg?
    (b) 1.8 kg

15. The current flowing through a lamp is proportional to the voltage across the lamp. If the voltage across the lamp is ten volts the current is 0.6 amp. What voltage is required to make a current of 0.9 amp flow?

16. The amount of energy carried by an electric current is proportional to the number of coulombs. If five coulombs carry 19 joules of energy, how many joules are carried by 6.5 coulombs?

17. A recipe for date squares uses the following quantities:

Ingredients	Costs
125 g of brown sugar	500 g cost $1.52
75 g of oats	750 g cost $2.04
75 g of flour	$1\frac{1}{2}$ kg cost $1.76
100 g of margarine	250 g cost 72 c
100 g of dates	250 g cost $1.68
Pinch of bicarbonate of soda	–
Squeeze of lemon juice	4 c

Find the cost of making these date squares as accurately as possible, then give your answer correct to the nearest cent.

18. A do-it-yourself enthusiast makes a base for a table.

Materials	Costs
4 legs each 30 cm long	2 m cost $9.60
4 stretchers each 70 cm long	3 m cost $6.30
4 stretchers each 35 cm long	2 m cost $4.50
3 pieces each 80 cm long	3 m cost $18.90
$\frac{3}{4}$ litre of varnish	1 litre costs $14.40
12 screws	20 screws cost $2.40

What is the total cost of the materials that are actually used?

INVERSE PROPORTION

Some quantities are not directly proportional to one another, although there is a connection between them. As one increases in size, the other may decrease, so that the reciprocal, or inverse, of the second is proportional to the first.

Suppose, for example, that a certain amount of food is available for several days. If each person eats the same amount each day, the more people there are, the shorter is the time that the food will last. The number of days the food will last is *inversely proportional* to the number of people eating it.

Exercise 23i

In this exercise, assume that the rates are constant.

Four bricklayers can build a certain wall in ten days. How long would it take five bricklayers to build it?

Radio Method
Suppose it takes five bricklayers x days to build it.

(Five bricklayers will take a shorter time so we use the inverse ratio.)

$$\frac{x}{10} = \frac{4}{5}$$

$$\overset{\prime}{10} \times \frac{x}{10_{\prime}} = \overset{2}{10} \times \frac{4}{5_{\prime}}$$

$$x = 8$$

It would take them 8 days.

Unitary Method

Four bricklayers take 10 days.

One bricklayer would take 40 days.

Five bricklayers would take $\dfrac{40}{5}$ days

$$= 8 \text{ days}$$

1. Eleven taps fill a tank in three hours. How long would it take to fill the tank if only six taps are working?

2. Nine children share out equally the chocolates in a large tin and get eight each. If there were only six children, how many would each get?

3. The length of an essay is 174 lines with an average of 14 words per line. If it is rewritten with an average of 12 words per line, how many lines will be needed?

4. A field of grass feeds 24 cows for six days. How long would the same field feed 18 cows?

5. The dimensions of a block of stamps are 30 cm wide by 20 cm high. The same number of stamps could also have been arranged in a block 24 cm wide. How high would this second block be?

6. A batch of bottles was packed in 25 boxes taking 12 bottles each. If the same batch had been packed in boxes taking 15 each, how many boxes would be filled?

7. When knitting a scarf 48 stitches wide, one ball of wool will give a length of 18 cm. If there had been 54 stitches instead, how long a piece would the same ball give?

8. In a school, 33 classrooms are required if each class has 32 pupils. How many classrooms would be required if the class size was reduced to 22?

9. A factory requires 42 machines to produce a given number of articles in 63 days. How many machines would be required to produce the same number of articles in 54 days?

MIXED QUESTIONS

Exercise 23j

Some of the following questions cannot be answered because the quantities are neither in direct nor in inverse proportion. In these cases write 'There is no answer'. For those questions that can be solved, give answers correct to three significant figures where necessary:

1. The list of exchange rates states that US $1 = 126 yen and US $1 = TT $6.

   (a) How many TT dollars can 315 yen be exchanged for?

   (b) How many yen are 100 TT dollars worth?

2. A man earned $41.20 for an eight-hour day. How much would he earn at the same time for a 38-hour week?

3. A typist typed 3690 words in $4\frac{1}{2}$ hours. How long would it take to type 2870 words at the same rate?

4. At the age of twelve, a boy is 1.6 m tall. How tall will he be at the age of eighteen?

5. A ream of paper (500 sheets) is 6.2 cm thick. How thick is a pile of 360 sheets of the same paper?

6. If I buy balloons at 14 c each, I can buy 63 of them. If the price of a balloon increases to 18 c, how many can I buy for the same amount of money?

7. A boy's mark for a test is 18 out of a total of 30 marks. If the test had been marked out of 40 what would the boy's mark have been?

8. Twenty-four identical mathematics text books occupy 60 cm of shelf space. How many books will fit into 85 cm?

9. A lamp post 4 m high has a shadow 3.2 m long cast by the sun. A man 1.8 m high is standing by the lamp post. At the same moment, what is the length of his shadow?

10. A contractor decides that he can build a barn in nine weeks using four men. If he employs two more men, how long will the job take? Assume that all the men work at the same rate.

11. A girl twelve years old gained 27 marks in a competition. How many marks did her six-year-old sister gain?

12. For a given voltage, the current flowing is inversely proportional to the resistance. When the current flowing is 2.5 amps the resistance is 0.9 ohm. What is the current when the resistance is 1.5 ohms?

MIXED EXERCISES

Exercise 23k

1. Simplify the ratio 7.35 : 2.45

2. Complete the ratio   : 9 = 2 : 5

3. Divide 56 m into three parts in the ratio 1 : 2 : 4

4. A car uses seven litres of petrol for a 100 km journey. At the same rate, how far could it go on eight litres?

5. Eight typists together could complete a task in five hours. If all the typists work at the same rate, how long would six typists take?

6. Simplify the ratio $7\frac{1}{2} : 2\frac{1}{2} : 1\frac{1}{4}$

7. The ratio of the numbers of eleven-year-olds to twelve-year-olds in a class is 8 : 3. There are 24 eleven-year-olds. How many twelve-year-olds are there?

8. Give the ratio 6 : 5 in the form $n : 1$

Exercise 23l

1. Simplify the ratio 1024 : 768

2. Share 40 sweets amongst three people so that their shares are in the ratio 3 : 2 : 5

3. Find x if 3 : 5 = x : 11

4. Simplify the ratio $9\frac{1}{7} : 8$

5. Express the ratio 3 : 5 in the form $n : 1$

6. The ratio of two sums of money is 4 : 5. The first sum is £6. What is the second?

7. Mrs Jones buys 19 apples and five oranges. Mrs Brown buys five apples and three oranges. Find the ratio of the total numbers of oranges to apples.

8. A typist charges $75 for work which took her six hours. How much would she charge for nine hours' work at the same rate?

24 ▷ PYTHAGORAS' THEOREM

At the end of the chapter you should be able to:

1. State the relationship between the hypotenuse and the other sides of a right-angled triangle.
2. Calculate the length of one side of a right-angled triangle, given the other two sides.
3. Determine whether or not a triangle is right-angled, given the lengths of the sides.
4. Use Pythagoras' theorem to solve problems on three-dimensional figures.

SQUARES AND SQUARE ROOTS

The following exercise revises the finding of squares and square roots. Remember that you need a rough estimate first if you are using tables.

Exercise 24a

Use tables or a calculator to find the squares of

(a) 2.3   (b) 23   (c) 2300   (d) 0.023

(a) $$2.3^2 \approx 2 \times 2 = 4$$
$$2.3^2 = 5.29$$

(b) $$23^2 \approx 20 \times 20 = 400$$
$$23^2 = 529$$

(c) $$2300^2 \approx 2000 \times 2000 = 4\,000\,000$$
$$2300^2 = 5\,290\,000$$

(d) $$0.023^2 \approx 0.02 \times 0.02 = 0.0004$$
$$0.023^2 = 0.000\,529$$

Use tables or a calculator to find the squares of the following numbers, giving your answers correct to four significant figures where necessary:

1. 6.2	**5.** 0.71	**9.** 3.12	**13.** 5210
2. 13.7	**6.** 0.059	**10.** 0.0312	**14.** 52.1
3. 242	**7.** 0.0017	**11.** 9.2	**15.** 0.521
4. 2780	**8.** 312	**12.** 92	**16.** 0.0521

Use tables or a calculator to find, correct to four significant figures, the square root of

(a) 6.23   (b) 62.3   (c) 623 000   (d) 0.0623

(a) $\sqrt{6.23} = 2.496$ to 4 s.f.
(b) $\sqrt{62.3} = 7.893$ to 4 s.f.
(c) $\sqrt{623\,000} = 789.3$ to 4 s.f.
(d) $\sqrt{0.0623} = 0.2496$ to 4 s.f.

Use tables or a calculator to find the square roots of the following numbers, giving your answers correct to four significant figures:

17. 9.87	**21.** 0.0482	**25.** 2.62	**29.** 0.461
18. 19.9	**22.** 0.004 82	**26.** 0.062	**30.** 4.61
19. 124	**23.** 96	**27.** 0.000 78	**31.** 461
20. 96 800	**24.** 321	**28.** 0.5	**32.** 0.000 461

PYTHAGORAS' THEOREM

Pythagoras was a native of Samos who travelled frequently to Egypt for the purpose of education. The Egyptians are believed to have known this theorem many years before Pythagoras was born. It is very likely that the Egyptian priests explained this theorem to Pythagoras. Indeed it is claimed that Pythagoras offered a sacrifice to the Muses when the Egyptian priests explained to him the properties of the right-angled triangle.

Pythagoras' theorem states that, in a right-angled triangle, the square of the hypotenuse is equal to the sum of the squares of the other two sides,

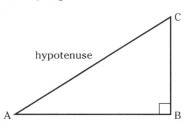

i.e. $\qquad AC^2 = AB^2 + BC^2$

If we are given any two sides of a right-angled triangle we can find the third side.

Exercise 24b

In $\triangle ABC$, $\hat{B} = 90°$, $AB = 62\,\text{cm}$ and $BC = 41\,\text{cm}$. Find AC.

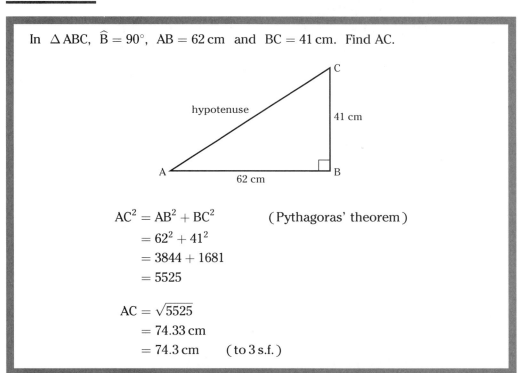

$$AC^2 = AB^2 + BC^2 \qquad (\text{Pythagoras' theorem})$$
$$= 62^2 + 41^2$$
$$= 3844 + 1681$$
$$= 5525$$

$$AC = \sqrt{5525}$$
$$= 74.33\,\text{cm}$$
$$= 74.3\,\text{cm} \qquad (\text{to 3 s.f.})$$

Use the information given in the diagrams to find the required lengths, giving your answers correct to three significant figures.

1. Find AC.

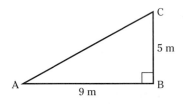

2. Find RQ.

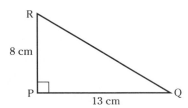

3. Find ZY.

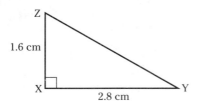

4. Find LN.

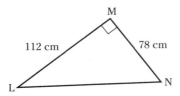

5. Find DF.

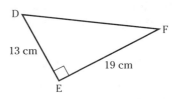

6. Find LN.

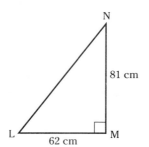

In $\triangle ABC$, $\widehat{B} = 90°$, $AC = 3.24\,\text{cm}$
and $BC = 1.6\,\text{cm}$.
Find AB.

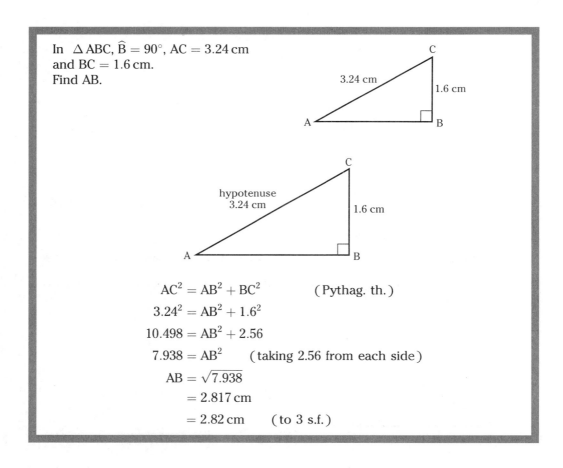

$$AC^2 = AB^2 + BC^2 \qquad (\text{Pythag. th.})$$
$$3.24^2 = AB^2 + 1.6^2$$
$$10.498 = AB^2 + 2.56$$
$$7.938 = AB^2 \qquad (\text{taking 2.56 from each side})$$
$$AB = \sqrt{7.938}$$
$$= 2.817\,\text{cm}$$
$$= 2.82\,\text{cm} \qquad (\text{to 3 s.f.})$$

Use the information in the diagrams to find the required lengths, giving your answers to three significant figures where necessary:

7. Find AB.

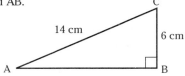

8. Find PQ.

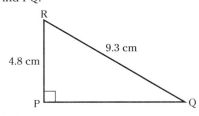

9. Find LM.

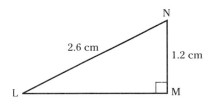

10. Find XY.

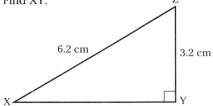

11. Find DE.

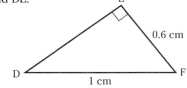

12. Find LN.

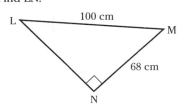

Some right-angled triangles are similar to triangles with sides of 3, 4 and 5 units or 5, 12 and 13 units.

In triangle ABC, $\widehat{B} = 90°$, AB = 16 cm and BC = 12 cm. Find AC.

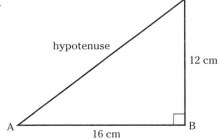

$$12 = 4 \times 3, \quad 16 = 4 \times 4$$

∴   △ ABC is similar to a 3, 4, 5 triangle

∴ $$AC = 4 \times 5 \text{ cm}$$

$$= 20 \text{ cm}$$

Find the missing lengths in the following triangles, using a 3, 4, 5 triangle or a 5, 12, 13 triangle:

13.

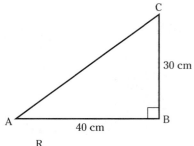

16.

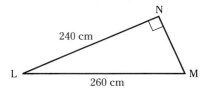

14.

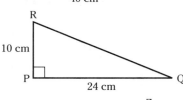

17.

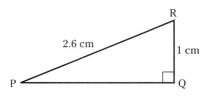

15.

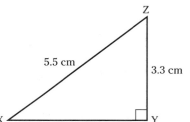

18.

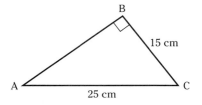

THE CONVERSE OF PYTHAGORAS' THEOREM

If we are given three sides of a triangle, we can tell whether or not the triangle contains a right angle. Bear in mind that, *if* there is a right angle the longest side will be the hypotenuse.

Exercise 24c

Are the following triangles right-angled?

(a) $\triangle$ABC: AB $= 17$ cm, BC $= 8$ cm, CA $= 15$ cm

(b) $\triangle$PQR: PQ $= 15$ cm, PR $= 7$ cm, RQ $= 12$ cm

(a)

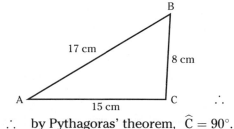

$$AB^2 = 17^2 = 289$$
$$AC^2 + BC^2 = 15^2 + 8^2$$
$$= 225 + 64$$
$$= 289$$
$$\therefore \quad AC^2 + BC^2 = AB^2$$

$\therefore$ by Pythagoras' theorem, $\widehat{C} = 90°$.

(b)

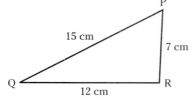

$$PQ^2 = 15^2 = 225$$
$$PR^2 + RQ^2 = 12^2 + 7^2$$
$$= 144 + 49$$
$$= 193$$
$$\therefore \quad PR^2 + RQ^2 \neq PQ^2$$

$\therefore$ the triangle is not right-angled.

Are the following triangles right-angled?

1. Triangle ABC: AB = 48 cm, BC = 64 cm and CA = 80 cm.

2. Triangle PQR: PQ = 2.1 cm, QR = 2.8 cm and RP = 3.5 cm.

3. Triangle LMN: LM = 6 cm, MN = 7.2 cm and NL = 9 cm.

4. Triangle ABC: AB = 9.2 cm, BC = 6.3 cm and CA = 4.6 cm.

5. Triangle DEF: DE = 6.4 cm, EF = 12 cm and DF = 13.6 cm.

6. Triangle XYZ: XY = 32 cm, YZ = 40 cm and ZX = 48 cm.

Exercise 24d

Find the missing lengths in the following triangles:

1.

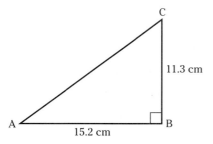

2.

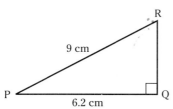

3.

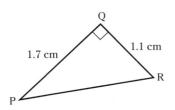

4.

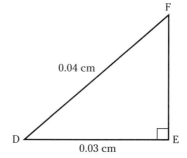

5.

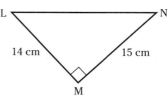

6.

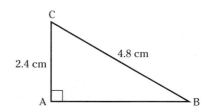

7.

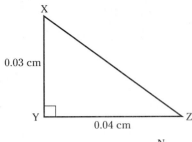

8.

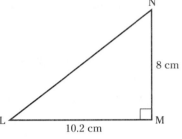

9. In triangle ABC, $\widehat{A} = 90°$, AB = 3.2 cm and BC = 4.8 cm. Find AC.

10. In triangle PQR, $\widehat{Q} = 90°$, PQ = 56 cm and QR = 32 cm. Find PR.

11. In triangle ABC, AB = 1 cm, BC = 2.4 cm and CA = 2.6 cm. Is $\widehat{B}$ a right angle?

12. In triangle DEF, $\widehat{F} = 90°$, DF = 2.8 cm and DE = 4.2 cm. Find EF.

13. In triangle XYZ, $\widehat{Y} = 90°$, XY = 17 cm and YZ = 20 cm. Find XZ.

14. In triangle LMN, NL = 25 cm, LM = 24 cm and MN = 7 cm. Is the triangle right-angled? If it is, which angle is 90°?

PROBLEMS

If you find one length first and use it to find a second length, or an angle, the first length should be given correct to four significant figures. Whenever you can, use at least four significant figures, rather than three significant figures. Your answer will be more accurate.

Exercise 24e

In a circle with centre O and radius 7 cm, there is a chord 11 cm long. How far is the chord from the centre?

(We need the *perpendicular* distance from O to the chord.)

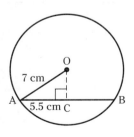

From symmetry,
$$AC = \tfrac{1}{2} \times 11 \text{ cm} = 5.5 \text{ cm}$$
$$AO^2 = AC^2 + OC^2 \text{ (Pythag. th.)}$$
$$7^2 = 5.5^2 + OC^2$$
$$49 = 30.25 + OC^2$$
$$18.75 = OC^2$$
$$OC = \sqrt{18.75}$$
$$= 4.330$$

The distance of the chord from the centre is 4.33 cm (to 3 s.f.)

1. A is the point $(3, 1)$ and B is the point $(7, 9)$. Find the length of AB.

2. A ship sails 32 nautical miles due north then 22 nautical miles due east. How far is it from its starting point?

3. A pole 4.5 m high stands on level ground. It is supported in a vertical position by two wires attached to its top and to points on opposite sides of the pole each 3.2 m from the foot of the pole.

   (a) How long is each wire?

   (b) What is the angle between each wire and the pole?

4. The diagonal AC of a rectangle ABCD is 0.67 m long and side AB is 0.32 m long. How long is side BC?

5. Find the length of the diagonal of a square of side 15 cm.

6. ABCD is a kite and AC is its line of symmetry. $\widehat{B} = \widehat{D} = 90°$, AB = 36 cm and BC = 16 cm.
   Find

   (a) AC

   (b) $B\widehat{A}D$

7.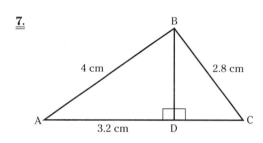

   In the figure, $A\widehat{D}B = 90°$
   AB = 4 cm, AD = 3.2 cm and BC = 2.8 cm.
   Find (a) BD (b) AC.
   Is $A\widehat{B}C$ a right angle?
   Give a reason for your answer.

8.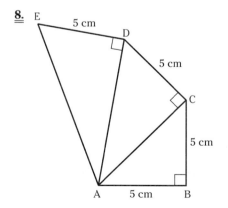

   (a) *Construct* the figure in the diagram, starting with △ABC then adding △ADC and △ADE.

   (b) Measure AC, AD and EA.

   (c) *Calculate* AC, AD and AE and check the accuracy of your drawing.

9. Construct a right-angled triangle, choosing whole numbers of centimetres for the lengths of the two shorter sides, such that the hypotenuse will be $\sqrt{65}$ cm long. Check the accuracy of your drawing by measuring the hypotenuse and by calculating $\sqrt{65}$.

THREE-DIMENSIONAL PROBLEMS

We can use Pythagoras' theorem and the trigonometry of right-angled triangles to find lengths and angles of various solids.

CUBOIDS

Exercise 24f

1.

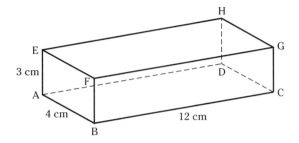

The solid above is a cuboid. Each face is a rectangle.

(a) Copy the diagram, noticing that, in the drawing, some faces look like parallelograms.
Which edges are equal in length to EA?
Which edges are equal in length to AB?
Which edges are equal in length to BC?
How many right angles are there?

(b) Join B to E on your diagram and draw triangle ABE (notice that $\widehat{EAB} = 90°$ and should now be drawn as a right angle).

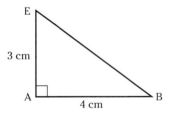

Find EB by using Pythagoras' theorem, and $\widehat{EBA}$ by using its tangent.

(c) Join F and C on your drawing of the cuboid. Draw triangle FBC, marking in all the information you know about it. Find FC and $\widehat{FCB}$.

2. (a) Copy the picture of the cuboid again. Join A and C. Draw triangle ABC (notice $\widehat{ABC} = 90°$) and find AC.

(b) Join E and C. What is the size of $\widehat{EAC}$? Draw triangle EAC and mark in the sizes of any sides and angles you know. Find EC and $\widehat{ECA}$.

3. Draw a picture of a cuboid like the first one but such that AB = 5 cm, EA = 2 cm and BC = 8 cm.

   (a) Draw the appropriate triangle and find FC.

   (b) Find AF and FÂB.

   (c) Find EG and the angle between FG and EG.

When dealing with solids like cuboids and the other types in this chapter, remember always to make a separate drawing of the triangle you are using.

Exercise 24g

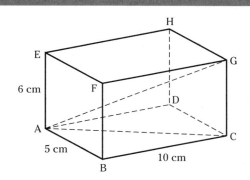

In the cuboid, EA = 6 cm, AB = 5 cm and BC = 10 cm. Find AG.

(To find AG, we use triangle AGC so we need to calculate AC^2 first.)

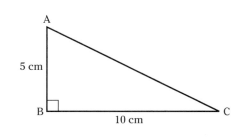

$$AC^2 = AB^2 + BC^2 \qquad \text{(Pythag. th.)}$$
$$= 25 + 100$$
$$= 125$$

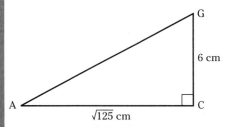

$$AG^2 = AC^2 + GC^2 \qquad \text{(Pythag. th.)}$$
$$= 125 + 36$$
$$= 161$$
$$AG = \sqrt{161}$$
$$= 12.7 \text{ cm} \qquad \text{(to 3 s.f.)}$$

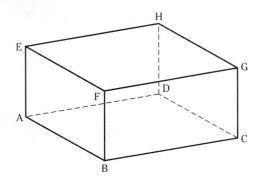

1. In the cuboid above, $AB = 8$ cm, $BC = 12$ cm and $CG = 5$ cm. Find

   (a) AC   (b) EC   (c) $E\widehat{C}A$

2. In the cuboid above, $EF = 3$ cm, $EA = 2$ cm and $AD = 6$ cm. Find

   (a) EB

   (b) the angle between AB and EB

   (c) EG

3. In the cuboid above, $HG = 6$ cm, $GC = 8$ cm and $BC = 12$ cm. Find

   (a) HC   (b) HB   (c) $H\widehat{B}C$

4. In the cuboid above, $AD = 11$ cm, $AB = 10$ cm and $EA = 12$ cm. Find

   (a) AC   (d) $G\widehat{B}C$

   (b) EC   (e) $E\widehat{G}H$

   (c) BH

5. In the cuboid above, $BC = 20$ cm, $CG = 8$ cm and $DC = 12$ cm. Find EC.

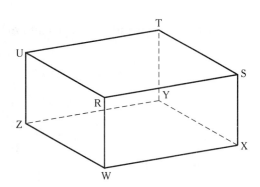

6. In the cuboid above, $RS = 12$ cm, $SX = 7$ cm and $XY = 9$ cm. Find

   (a) WY   (b) WT   (c) $T\widehat{W}Y$

7. In the cuboid above, $TX = 10$ cm, $T\widehat{X}Y = 45°$ and $UT = 12$ cm. Find

   (a) XY

   (b) TY

   (c) the volume of the cuboid.

8. In the cuboid above, $SX = 6$ cm, $WX = 9$ cm and $XY = 4$ cm. Find

   (a) $S\widehat{W}X$ (b) $S\widehat{Y}X$ (c) $S\widehat{Z}X$

9. In the cuboid above, $WX = 11$ cm, $XY = 5$ cm and $WT = 14$ cm. Find

   (a) TY

   (b) the surface area of the cuboid.

WEDGES

Exercise 24h

1.

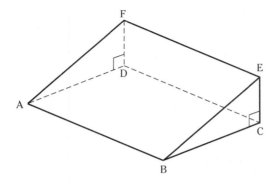

The solid above is a *wedge*. Two faces are right-angled triangles and three faces are rectangles.

(a) Copy the diagram. (Notice that, in the drawing, each rectangular face looks like a parallelogram.)

AB = 10 cm, BC = 6 cm and CE = 4 cm.

Which edges are equal to AB?

Which edges are equal to BC?

Which edges are equal to EC?

How many right angles are there?

(b) Draw triangle EBC. Find $E\hat{B}C$ and BE.

(c) Join A to C. Draw triangle ABC. Find AC and $C\hat{A}B$. Is AC at right angles to EC?

(d) Join A to E. Draw triangle AEC. Find AE. What other length (not yet drawn in) is equal to AE?

2. Draw a wedge similar to the wedge in question 1 but such that AB = BE = 8 m and $E\hat{B}C = 22°$. Find

(a) EC
(b) BC
(c) AC
(d) $E\hat{A}C$

3. Draw a wedge similar to the wedge in question 1 but such that EF = 40 m, EC = 10 m and $B\hat{E}C = 70°$. Find

(a) BC
(b) AC
(c) BE
(d) AE
(e) $E\hat{A}C$
(f) $E\hat{A}F$

4. Draw a wedge similar to the wedge in question 1, but such that BC = 4.4 m, AB = 6.8 m and EC = 2 m. Find

(a) $E\hat{B}C$
(b) $E\hat{A}C$

5. Draw a wedge similar to the wedge in question 1, but such that AE = 7 cm, $E\hat{A}C = 22°$ and AD = 3 cm. Find

(a) EC
(b) BE
(c) AB

PYRAMIDS

Exercise 24i

1.

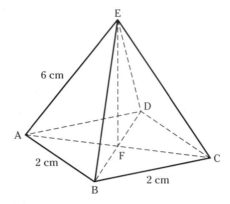

The solid above is called a square pyramid because its base is a square. Its vertex, E, is directly above the centre, F, of its base.

(a) Copy the diagram. (Start by drawing the base as a parallelogram. Draw the diagonals of the base, to cut at F, and then mark E directly above F.) Name as many right angles as you can find. Which edges are equal to AE?

(b) Draw the base ABCD as a square. Find AC and FC.

(c) Draw triangle EFC. Find EF and $E\widehat{C}F$.

2. Draw a square pyramid similar to the pyramid in question 1, but such that AB = 4 cm and EF = 5 cm.

(a) Find AC and AF.

(b) Find AE and $E\widehat{A}F$.

(c) G is the midpoint of AB. Draw triangle EFG and find EG and $E\widehat{G}F$.

3.

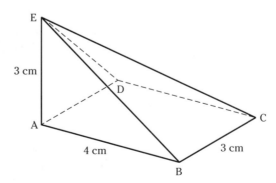

The base of the given pyramid is a rectangle and E is directly above A. AB = 4 cm, EA = BC = 3 cm. Find

(a) $E\widehat{B}A$ and $E\widehat{D}A$ (b) AC   (c) EC.

4.

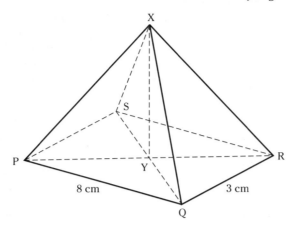

The base of the pyramid above is a rectangle. $PQ = 8\,cm$ and $QR = 3\,cm$. Its vertex, X, is directly above the centre, Y, of the base. $XY = 6\,cm$. Find

(a) PR   (b) PY   (c) $X\widehat{P}Y$ (d) XR

MIXED QUESTIONS

Exercise 24j

1.

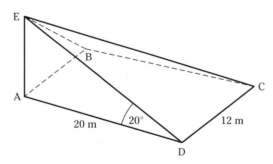

EA is a pole standing at the corner of a rectangular plot of level ground. $AD = 20\,m$ and $DC = 12\,m$. The angle of elevation of the top of the pole from D is $20°$.

(a) Find EA.

(b) Find the angle of elevation of E from B (i.e. $A\widehat{B}E$).

(c) Find AC and hence find the angle of elevation of E from C.

2. ABCD is the base of a cube of side $4\,cm$. A′, B′, C′ and D′ are the four vertices of the cube directly above A, B, C and D respectively.

(a) Find AC, CD′ and AD′. What sort of triangle is △ACD′?

(b) What sort of quadrilateral is ACC′A′? Find AC′. What other lengths are equal to AC′?

3.

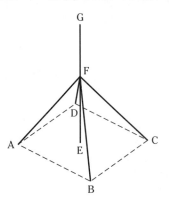

A pole, GE, is held upright by four equal guy ropes fastened to its midpoint, F. The other ends of the ropes are fastened to the four corners of a square, ABCD, on the level ground. AB = 6 m. Each rope is 6 m long.

(a) Find BD and BE.

(b) Find EF and the height of the pole.

(c) Find the angle that each rope makes with the pole.

4.

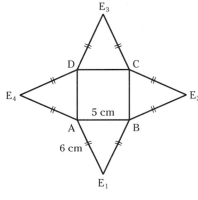

This is the net of a square pyramid with base ABCD and vertex E. AB = 5 cm. AE = 6 cm.

(a) Find AC.

(b) Draw a picture of the pyramid.

(c) Find the height of the pyramid.

5.

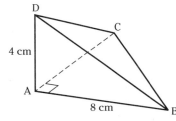

This is a triangular pyramid. The base is triangle ABC. $C\hat{A}B = 90°$ and AB = AC = 8 cm. D is directly above A and AD = 4 cm.

Find (a) BD (b) $D\hat{B}A$ (c) BC (d) DC (e) $D\hat{C}A$

MATHS IS OUT THERE

The integral triples (40, 42, 58), (24, 70, 74), and (15, 112, 113) are Pythagorean triples. Calculate the areas of triangles having these triples as the lengths of their sides.

TRIGONOMETRY

At the end of the chapter you should be able to:

1. Define sine, cosine and tangent of an angle in a right-angled triangle.
2. Use tables or a calculator to find the sine, cosine or tangent of a given angle.
3. Use tables or a calculator to find an angle given its sine, cosine or tangent.
4. Calculate the size of an angle in a right-angled triangle, given the lengths of the sides of the triangle.
5. Calculate the length of a side of a right-angled triangle, given one side and another angle.
6. Draw diagrams to show angles of elevation or depression.
7. Use trigonometric ratios to solve problems on angles of elevation and depression.
8. Use the sine and cosine rules for triangles to solve problems.

TANGENT OF AN ANGLE

In Book 2, we worked with right-angled triangles. This chapter is either a reminder of the work you did then or, if it is new to you, an introduction.

In triangle ABC, AC is the *hypotenuse*, opposite to the right angle.

BC is the *opposite side* to angle A.

AB is the *adjacent side* (or neighbouring side) to angle A.

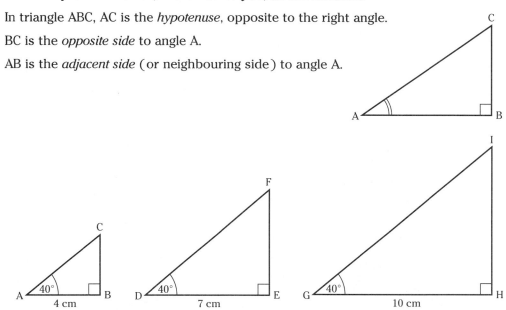

The three triangles above are similar, so their sides are proportional.

In particular, the opposite side and the adjacent side are in the same ratio in all three triangles and also in any other right-angled triangle containing an angle of 40°.

This ratio is called the *tangent* of 40° or, in shortened form, tan 40°. Its size is stored, together with the tangents of other angles, in natural tangent tables and in some calculators.

$$\tan \widehat{A} = \frac{\text{opposite side}}{\text{adjacent side}}$$

Exercise 25a

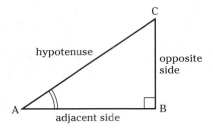

In questions 1 to 6, copy the diagram. Identify the hypotenuse and the sides opposite and adjacent to the marked angle:

1.

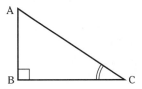

4.

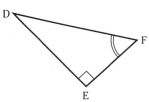

2.

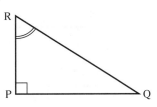

5.

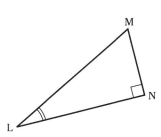

3.

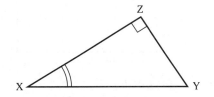

6.

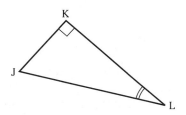

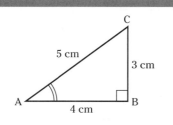

In $\triangle ABC$, $\widehat{B} = 90°$, $AB = 4\,cm$, $BC = 3\,cm$ and $AC = 5\,cm$.

Write down $\tan \widehat{A}$ as a fraction and as a decimal.

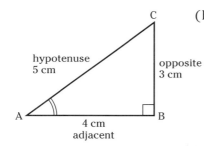

(First identify the sides.)

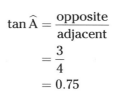

$$\tan \widehat{A} = \frac{\text{opposite}}{\text{adjacent}}$$
$$= \frac{3}{4}$$
$$= 0.75$$

In each of the following questions write down the tangent of the marked angle as a fraction and as a decimal (correct to four decimal places where necessary):

7.

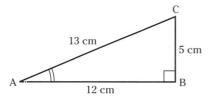

10.

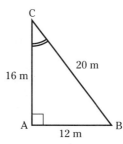

8.

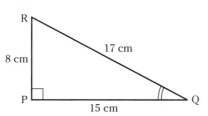

11.

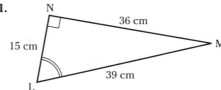

9.

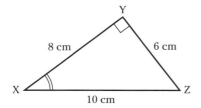

12.

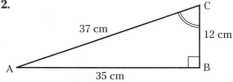

USING A CALCULATOR

To find the tangent of an angle, enter the size of the angle, then press the 'tan' button. Write the answer correct to four decimal places.

$$\tan 42.4° = 0.9131$$

To find an angle given its tangent, enter the value of the tangent and then press the inverse button followed by the tangent button. Write down the size of the angle correct to one decimal place.

Exercise 25b

Find $\tan 38.2°$ and $\tan 80°$

$$\tan 38.2° = 0.7869$$
$$\tan 80° = 5.671$$

Find the tangents of the following angles:

1. 62°	**5.** 4.6°	**9.** 30°
2. 14°	**6.** 72°	**10.** 48.2°
3. 30.5°	**7.** 78.4°	**11.** 3°
4. 16.8°	**8.** 45°	**12.** 29.4°

Find the angle whose tangent is 0.628

$$\tan \widehat{A} = 0.628$$
$$\widehat{A} = 32.1°$$

Find the angles whose tangents are given in questions 13 to 24:

13. 0.179	**17.** 1.362	**21.** 0.3214
14. 0.356	**18.** 0.632	**22.** 2.683
15. 1.43	**19.** 0.9213	**23.** 0.924
16. 0.4326	**20.** 0.8	**24.** 0.0024

FINDING AN ANGLE

Exercise 25c

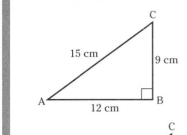

In triangle ABC, $\widehat{B} = 90°$, AB = 12 cm, BC = 9 cm and AC = 15 cm. Find $\widehat{A}$.

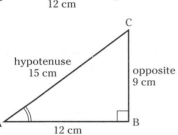

$$\tan \widehat{A} = \frac{\text{opp}}{\text{adj}} = \frac{9}{12}$$

$$= 0.75$$

$$\widehat{A} = 36.9°$$

Use the information given on the diagrams to find $\widehat{A}$:

1.

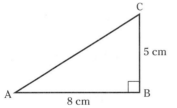

2.

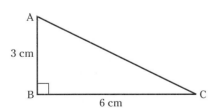

3.

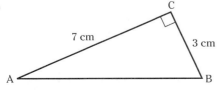

4.

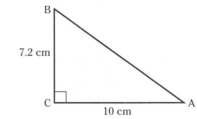

5.

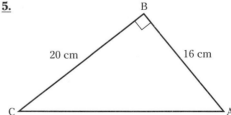

6.

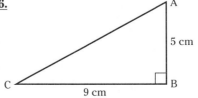

7. In triangle PQR, $\widehat{P} = 90°$, QP = 6 cm and PR = 10 cm. Find $\widehat{R}$.

8. In triangle XYZ, $\widehat{Y} = 90°$, XY = 4 cm and YZ = 5 cm. Find $\widehat{X}$.

9. In triangle LMN, $\widehat{L} = 90°$, LM = 7.2 cm and LN = 6.4 cm. Find $\widehat{N}$.

10. In triangle DEF, $\widehat{D} = 90°$, DE = 210 cm and DF = 231 cm. Find $\widehat{E}$.

11. In $\triangle$ABC, $\widehat{C} = 90°$,   AC = 3.2 m   and BC = 4.7 m. Find $\widehat{B}$.

FINDING A SIDE

Exercise 25d

In triangle ABC, $\widehat{B} = 90°$, AB = 4 cm and $\widehat{A} = 32°$. Find BC.

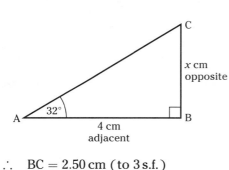

$$\frac{x}{4} = \frac{\text{opp}}{\text{adj}} = \tan 32°$$

$$\frac{x}{4} = 0.6249$$

$$\cancel{4} \times \frac{x}{\cancel{4}} = 4 \times 0.6249$$

$$x = 2.4996$$

∴   BC = 2.50 cm (to 3 s.f.)

Use the information given in the diagram to find the required side:

1. Find RQ.

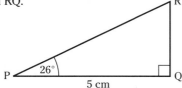

3. 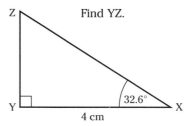 Find YZ.

2. Find BC.

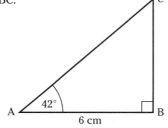

4. 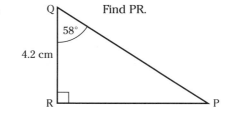 Find PR.

5. Find AB.

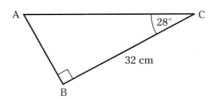

6. Find LN.

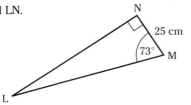

7. In triangle ABC, $\widehat{B} = 90°$, $\widehat{A} = 32°$ and AB = 9 cm. Find BC.

8. In triangle DEF, $\widehat{D} = 90°$, $\widehat{E} = 48°$ and DE = 20 cm. Find DF.

9. In triangle PQR, $\widehat{R} = 90°$, $\widehat{Q} = 10°$ and RQ = 16 cm. Find PR.

10. In triangle XYZ, $\widehat{Z} = 90°$, $\widehat{Y} = 67°$ and ZY = 3.2 cm. Find XZ.

In $\triangle ABC$, $\widehat{B} = 90°$, $\widehat{A} = 24°$ and BC = 6 cm. Find AB.

(AB is opposite to $\widehat{C}$, so find $\widehat{C}$ first.)

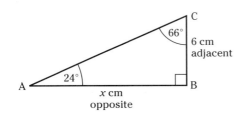

$\widehat{C} = 66°$ ($\angle$s of a triangle)

$$\frac{x}{6} = \frac{\text{opp}}{\text{adj}} = \tan 66°$$

$$\frac{x}{6} = 2.246$$

$$\not{6} \times \frac{x}{\not{6}} = 6 \times 2.246$$

$$x = 13.476$$

∴   AB is 13.5 cm   (to 3 s.f.)

Use the information given in the diagram to find the required side. It may be necessary to find the third angle of the triangle first.

11. Find AB.

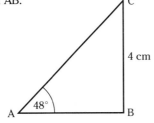

12. Find PQ.

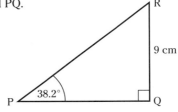

13. Find NL.

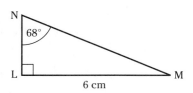

14. Find ZY.

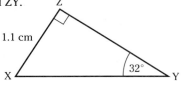

15. Find DE.

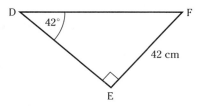

16. Find AC.

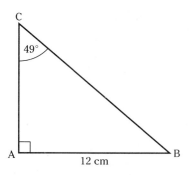

17. In triangle PQR, $\hat{P} = 90°$, $\hat{Q} = 52°$ and PR $= 6$ cm. Find QP.

18. In triangle ABC, $\hat{A} = 90°$, $\hat{B} = 31°$ and AC $= 220$ cm. Find AB.

19. In triangle XYZ, $\hat{Z} = 90°$, $\hat{X} = 67°$ and YZ $= 2.3$ cm. Find XZ.

20. In triangle LMN, $\hat{L} = 90°$, $\hat{M} = 9°$ and LN $= 11$ m. Find LM.

USING THE HYPOTENUSE

So far, we have used only the opposite and adjacent sides. If we wish to use the hypotenuse we need different ratios.

THE SINE OF AN ANGLE

For an angle in a right-angled triangle, the name given to the ratio $\dfrac{\text{opposite side}}{\text{hypotenuse}}$ is the *sine* of the angle.

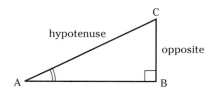

In triangle ABC $\dfrac{BC}{AC} = \sin \hat{A}$

The use of sines is similar to the use of tangents.

Exercise 25e

Find the sine of 32.6°

$$\sin 32.6° = 0.5388$$

Find the sines of the following angles:

1. 62.4°

2. 70°

3. 14.3°

4. 9°

5. 15.2°

6. 37.5°

7. 59.6°

8. 30°

9. 82°

10. 27.8°

11. 15.8°

12. 87.2°

Find the angle whose sine is 0.6284

Let the angle be $\widehat{A}$ $\sin \widehat{A} = 0.6284$
$$\widehat{A} = 38.9°$$

Find the angles whose sines are given:

13. 0.271

14. 0.442

15. 0.524

16. 0.909

17. 0.6664

18. 0.3720

19. 0.614

20. 0.7283

21. 0.1232

Exercise 25f

In triangle ABC, $\widehat{B} = 90°$, $BC = 3\,cm$ and $AC = 7\,cm$. Find $\widehat{A}$.

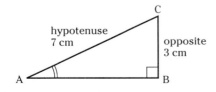

$$\sin \widehat{A} = \frac{opp}{hyp} = \frac{3}{7}$$
$$= 0.4286$$
$$\widehat{A} = 25.4°$$

Use the information given in the diagram to find the marked angle:

1.

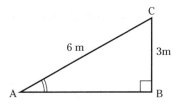

2..

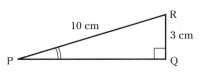

3.

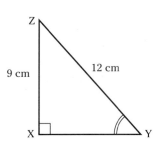

4.

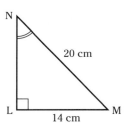

5.

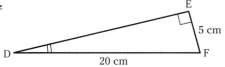

6.

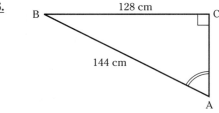

7. In triangle ABC, $\widehat{C} = 90°$, BC $= 7$ cm and AB $= 10$ cm. Find $\widehat{A}$.

8. In triangle PQR, $\widehat{Q} = 90°$, PQ $= 30$ cm and PR $= 45$ cm. Find $\widehat{R}$.

9. In triangle LMN, $\widehat{M} = 90°$, MN $= 3.2$ cm and LN $= 8$ cm. Find $\widehat{L}$.

10. In triangle DEF, $\widehat{E} = 90°$, EF $= 36$ cm and DF $= 108$ cm. Find $\widehat{D}$.

In triangle PQR, $\widehat{P} = 90°$, $\widehat{Q} = 32.4°$ and RQ $= 4$ cm. Find PR.

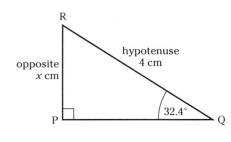

$$\frac{x}{4} = \frac{\text{opp}}{\text{hyp}} = \sin 32.4°$$

$$\cancel{4} \times \frac{x}{\cancel{4}} = 4 \times 0.5358$$

$$x = 2.1432$$

$\therefore$ PR $= 2.14$ cm (to 3 s.f.)

Use the information given in the diagram to find the required length:

11. Find AC.

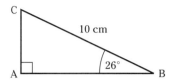

12. Find XY.

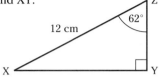

13. Find EF.

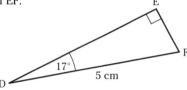

14. Find PR.

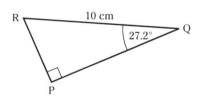

15. Find BC.

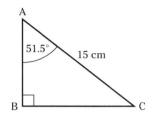

16. Find PR.

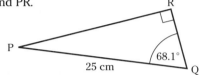

17. In triangle ABC, $\hat{A} = 90°$, BC = 11 cm and $\hat{C} = 35°$. Find AB.

18. In triangle PQR, $\hat{P} = 90°$, QR = 120 m and $\hat{Q} = 10.5°$. Find PR.

19. In triangle XYZ, $\hat{X} = 90°$, YZ = 3.6 cm and $\hat{Y} = 68°$. Find XZ.

20. In triangle DEF, $\hat{F} = 90°$, DE = 48 m and $\hat{D} = 72°$. Find EF.

THE COSINE OF AN ANGLE

For an angle in a right-angled triangle, the name given to the ratio $\dfrac{\text{adjacent side}}{\text{hypotenuse}}$ is the *cosine* of the angle.

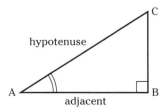

In triangle ABC $\dfrac{\text{AB}}{\text{AC}} = \cos \hat{A}$

Exercise 25g

> Find the cosine of 51.6°
>
> $$\cos 51.6° = 0.6211$$

Find the cosines of the following angles:

1. 32°

2. 41.8°

3. 82°

4. 47.8°

5. 60°

6. 15.6°

7. 52.1°

8. 49°

9. 72.3°

> Find the angle whose cosine is 0.862
>
> $$\cos \widehat{A} = 0.862$$
> $$\widehat{A} = 30.5°$$

Find the angles whose cosines are given:

10. 0.347

11. 0.936

12. 0.719

13. 0.349

14. 0.6281

15. 0.3149

16. 0.865

17. 0.014

18. 0.0732

Exercise 25h

> In triangle ABC, $\widehat{B} = 90°$, $AC = 20$ cm and $AB = 15$ cm. Find $\widehat{A}$.
>
>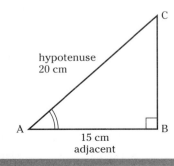
> hypotenuse
> 20 cm
>
> A
> 15 cm
> adjacent
> B
> C
>
> $$\cos \widehat{A} = \frac{\text{adj}}{\text{hyp}} = \frac{15}{20}$$
> $$= 0.75$$
> $$\widehat{A} = 41.4°$$

Find the marked angles in the following triangles:

1.

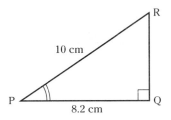

2.

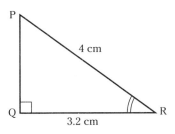

3.

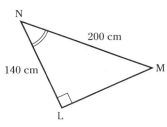

4.

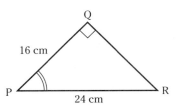

5.

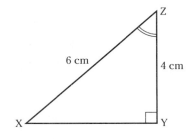

6.

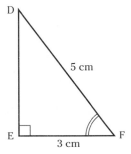

7. In triangle ABC, $\widehat{B} = 90°$, AB = 3.2 cm and AC = 5 cm. Find $\widehat{A}$.

8. In triangle PQR, $\widehat{P} = 90°$, QR = 12 cm and PQ = 4.8 cm. Find $\widehat{Q}$.

9. In triangle LMN, $\widehat{L} = 90°$, MN = 20 cm and ML = 3 cm. Find $\widehat{M}$.

10. In triangle DEF, $\widehat{F} = 90°$, DE = 18 cm and DF = 16.2 cm. Find $\widehat{D}$.

11. In triangle XYZ, $\widehat{Z} = 90°$, XY = 14 m and YZ = 11.6 m. Find $\widehat{Y}$.

In triangle XYZ, $\widehat{X} = 90°$, $\widehat{Y} = 27°$ and ZY = 3.2 cm. Find XY.

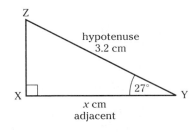

$$\frac{x}{3.2} = \frac{\text{adj}}{\text{hyp}} = \cos 27°$$

$$\frac{x}{3.2} = 0.8910$$

$$\cancel{3.2} \times \frac{x}{\cancel{3.2}} = 0.8910 \times 3.2$$

$$x = 2.8512$$

∴ XY = 2.85 cm   (to 3 s.f.)

Use the information given in the diagrams to find the required lengths:

12. Find AB.

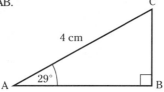

13. Find XY.

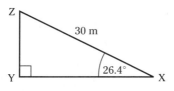

14. Find ED.

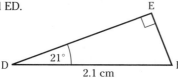

15. Find MN.

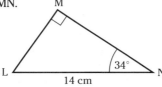

16. Find PQ.

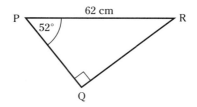

17. Find YZ.

18. In triangle PQR, $\widehat{Q} = 90°$, $\widehat{P} = 31°$ and PR = 20 cm. Find PQ.

19. In triangle LMN, $\widehat{N} = 90°$, $\widehat{L} = 42°$ and LM = 3 cm. Find LN.

20. In triangle DEF, $\widehat{D} = 90°$, $\widehat{E} = 68°$ and EF = 11 cm. Find DE.

21. In triangle XYZ, $\widehat{Z} = 90°$, $\widehat{Y} = 15°$ and YX = 14 cm. Find ZY.

SUMMARY

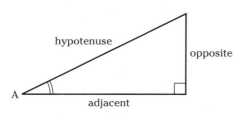

$$\text{Sin } \widehat{A} = \frac{\text{Opposite}}{\text{Hypotenuse}} \quad (\text{SOH})$$

$$\text{Cos } \widehat{A} = \frac{\text{Adjacent}}{\text{Hypotenuse}} \quad (\text{CAH})$$

$$\text{Tan } \widehat{A} = \frac{\text{Opposite}}{\text{Adjacent}} \quad (\text{TOA})$$

Some people remember by using the word 'SOHCAHTOA' or a sentence like 'Some Old Hangars Can Almost Hold Two Old Aeroplanes'.

SINES, COSINES AND TANGENTS

Exercise 25i

In questions 1 to 8, find the marked angles. Remember to label the given sides first and then decide which ratio you will have to use:

1.

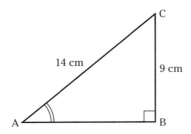

2.

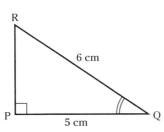

3.

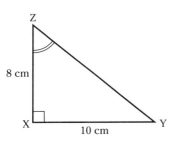

4.

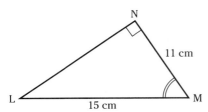

5.

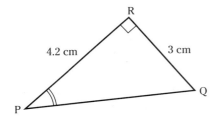

6.

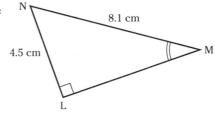

7.

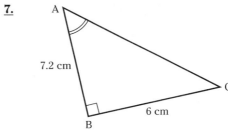

8.

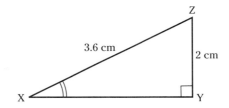

9.

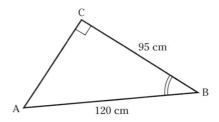

10.

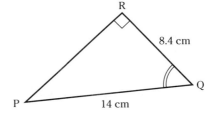

11. In triangle ABC, $\widehat{B} = 90°$, AC = 60 cm and BC = 22 cm. Find $\widehat{C}$.

12. In triangle PQR, $\widehat{R} = 90°$, PQ = 24 cm and QR = 6 cm. Find $\widehat{P}$.

13. In triangle ABC, $\widehat{B} = 90°$, AC = 1.5 cm and BC = 0.82 cm. Find $\widehat{C}$.

14. In triangle PQR, $\widehat{R} = 90°$, RQ = 8 cm and RP = 6.2 cm. Find $\widehat{Q}$.

15. In triangle DEF, $\widehat{F} = 90°$, DF = 16.2 cm and EF = 19.8 cm. Find $\widehat{E}$.

16. In triangle XYZ, $\widehat{X} = 90°$, YZ = 1.6 m and XY = 1.32 m. Find $\widehat{Z}$.

17. In triangle DEF, $\widehat{E} = 90°$, DE = 1.9 m and EF = 2.1 m. Find $\widehat{F}$.

18. In triangle GHI, $\widehat{H} = 90°$, GI = 52 cm and IH = 21 cm. Find $\widehat{I}$.

Use the information given in the diagram to find the required length:

19. Find BC.

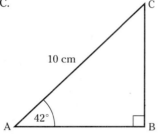

20. Find PQ.

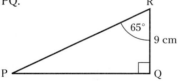

21. Find ZY.

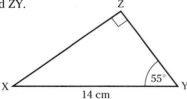

22. Find AB.

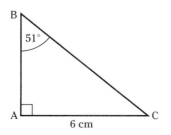

23. Find MN.

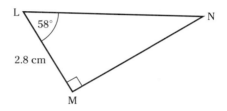

24. Find DE.

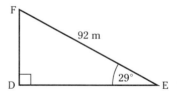

25. Find YZ.

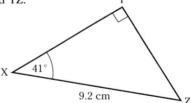

26. Find AB.

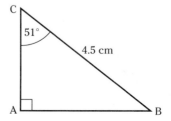

27. Find BC.

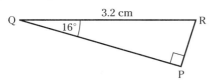

28. Find PQ.

29. In triangle ABC, $\widehat{C} = 90°$, $\widehat{A} = 78°$ and AC = 24 cm. Find BC.

30. In triangle PQR, $\widehat{P} = 90°$, $\widehat{Q} = 36°$ and QR = 3.2 cm. Find PQ.

31. In triangle XYZ, $\widehat{X} = 90°$, $\widehat{Y} = 36°$ and YZ = 17 cm. Find XZ.

32. In triangle DEF, $\widehat{F} = 90°$, $\widehat{E} = 51°$ and DF = 9.2 cm. Find EF.

33. In triangle LMN, $\widehat{M} = 90°$, $\widehat{N} = 25°$ and LN = 16 cm. Find MN.

34. In triangle LMN, $\widehat{L} = 90°$, $\widehat{M} = 56.2°$ and LN = 32 cm. Find ML.

35. In triangle ABC, $\widehat{C} = 90°$, $\widehat{B} = 72.8°$ and AB = 78 cm. Find AC.

36. In triangle PQR, $\widehat{R} = 90°$, $\widehat{P} = 31.2°$ and PQ = 117 cm. Find QR.

FINDING THE HYPOTENUSE

Up to now, when finding the length of a side, we have been able to form an equation in which our unknown length is on the top of the fraction. If we wish to find the hypotenuse, this is not possible and the equation we form takes slightly longer to solve.

Exercise 25j

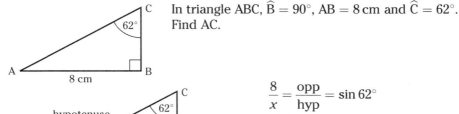

In triangle ABC, $\widehat{B} = 90°$, AB = 8 cm and $\widehat{C} = 62°$. Find AC.

$$\frac{8}{x} = \frac{\text{opp}}{\text{hyp}} = \sin 62°$$

$$\frac{8}{x} = 0.8829$$

Multiply both sides by x

$$x \times \frac{8}{x} = 0.8829 \times x$$

Divide both sides by 0.8829

$$\frac{8}{0.8829} = x$$

$$x = 9.061$$

∴ AC = 9.06 cm (to 3 s.f.)

Use the information given in the diagram to find the hypotenuse:

1.

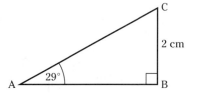

2.

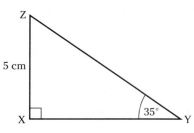

3.

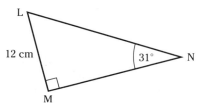

4.

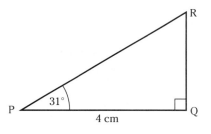

5.

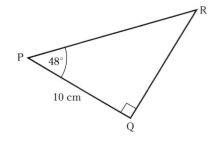

6.

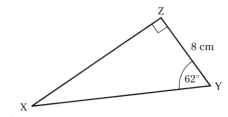

7. In triangle ABC, $\widehat{B} = 90°$, $\widehat{A} = 43°$ and BC = 3 cm. Find AC.

8. In triangle PQR, $\widehat{P} = 90°$, $\widehat{Q} = 28°$ and PR = 7 cm. Find QR.

9. In triangle LMN, $\widehat{L} = 90°$, $\widehat{M} = 14°$ and LN = 8 cm. Find MN.

10. In triangle XYZ, $\widehat{Z} = 90°$, $\widehat{Y} = 62°$ and ZY = 20 cm. Find XY.

ANGLES OF ELEVATION AND DEPRESSION

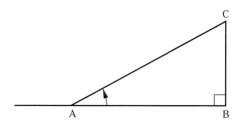

Imagine that you are at A, a point on level ground some distance from a cliff BC. You look horizontally at B, then *elevate* your line of view until you are looking at C.

$B\widehat{A}C$ is the *angle of elevation* of C from A.

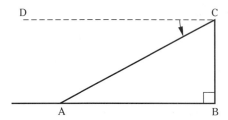

Now imagine you are on top of the cliff, at C. You look out horizontally to D, then *depress* your line of view until you are looking at A.

DĈA is the *angle of depression* of A from C.

PROBLEMS

Exercise 25k

A flagpole stands on level ground. From a point on the ground 30 m away from its foot, the angle of elevation of the top of the pole is 22°. Find the height of the pole.

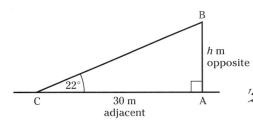

$$\frac{h}{30} = \frac{\text{opp}}{\text{adj}} = \tan 22°$$

$$\frac{h}{30} = 0.4040$$

$$\cancel{30} \times \frac{h}{\cancel{30}} = 0.4040 \times 30$$

$$h = 12.12$$

The pole is 12.1 m high   (to 3 s.f.)

1.

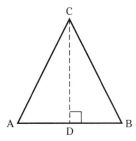

In triangle ABC, $AC = CB = 10\,\text{m}$ and $\widehat{A} = 64°$. Find the height of the triangle.

2. From a point on level ground 40 m from the base of a pine tree, the angle of elevation of the top of the tree is 50°. Find the height of the tree.

3. The angle of elevation of the top of a church tower, from a point of level ground 500 m away, is 16°. Find the height of the tower.

4. A is the point (2, 0), B is (8, 0) and C is (8, 5). Calculate the angle between AC and the *x*-axis.

5. ABCD is a rectangle with AB = 26 cm and BC = 48 cm. Find the angle between the diagonal AC and side AB.

6. A is the point (1, 2), B (3, 2) and C (1, 5). Find AB̂C.

7. ABCD is a rhombus of side 15 cm. The diagonal AC is of length 20 cm. Find the angle between AC and the side CD.

8.

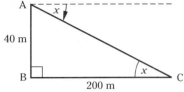

A boat C is 200 m from the foot B of a vertical cliff, which is 40 m high. What is the angle of depression of the boat from the top of the cliff?

9.

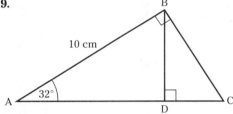

In the figure, AB = 10 cm, Â = 32° and AB̂C = BD̂C = 90°. Copy the figure and then mark in the sizes of the remaining angles. Find

(a) BD   (b) BC

10. Triangle ABC is an equilateral triangle of side 6 cm.
Find

(a) its height

(b) its area.

11. A lamp post stands on level ground. From a point which is 10 m from its foot, the angle of elevation of the top is 25°. How high is the lamp post?

12.

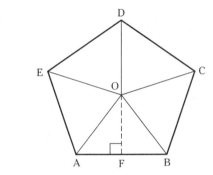

ABCDE is a regular pentagon of side 10 cm. Find

(a) AÔB and OÂB

(b) OF

(c) the area of triangle AOB and hence find the area of the pentagon.

We have considered the solution of right-angled triangles. We shall now seek a method of solving any triangle, given three of its parts.

SINE RULE FOR TRIANGLES

In a △ABC

$$\frac{a}{\sin A} = \frac{b}{\sin B} = \frac{c}{\sin C}$$

where a, b and c are the lengths of the sides facing angles A, B and C respectively.

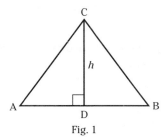

Fig. 1

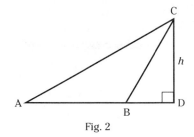

Fig. 2

Proof

Draw CD perpendicular to AB (Fig. 1) or AB produced (Fig. 2).

In right-angled triangle CAD

$$\frac{h}{b} = \sin A$$

$\therefore$ $h = b \sin A$ [1]

In right-angled triangle CDB

In Fig. 1, $$\frac{h}{a} = \sin B$$

$\therefore$ $h = a \sin B$

In Fig. 2, $$\frac{h}{a} = \sin CBD = \sin B$$

$\therefore$ $h = a \sin B$ [2]

$\therefore$ From [1] and [2] $b \sin A = a \sin B$

$\therefore$ $$\frac{b}{\sin B} = \frac{a}{\sin A}$$

Similarly, by drawing the perpendicular from A to BC in Fig. 1 or A to BC produced (Fig. 2) it may be proved that

$$\frac{b}{\sin B} = \frac{c}{\sin C}$$

$\therefore$ $$\frac{a}{\sin A} = \frac{b}{\sin B} = \frac{c}{\sin C}$$

The above rule is used when one side and two angles of a triangle are given.

Exercise 25i

In a triangle ABC, $\widehat{B} = 60°$, $\widehat{C} = 45°$, $a = 6$ cm. Find b.

Since
$$\widehat{A} + \widehat{B} + \widehat{C} = 180°$$
$$\widehat{A} = 180° - 105° = 75°$$

Using,
$$\frac{a}{\sin A} = \frac{b}{\sin B}$$
$$\frac{6}{\sin 75°} = \frac{b}{\sin 60°}$$

∴
$$b = \frac{6 \sin 60°}{\sin 75°} = \frac{6 \times 0.866}{0.966} = 5.4$$

1. In $\triangle ABC$, sin A = 0.3, sin B = 0.5, $b = 10$ cm. Find a.

2. In $\triangle ABC$, sin A = $\frac{1}{4}$, sin C = $\frac{2}{5}$, $a = 22.5$ cm. Find c.

3. In $\triangle ABC$, $\widehat{A} = 30°$, $\widehat{B} = 45°$, $a = 6$ cm. Find b.

4. In $\triangle ABC$, find a and c given $\widehat{B} = 60°$, $\widehat{A} = 40°$, $b = 10$ cm.

5. In $\triangle ABC$, $a = 24$ cm, sin A = $\frac{2}{3}$ and $b = 9$ cm. Find sin B.

6. In $\triangle PQR$, $\widehat{P} = 135°$, $\widehat{Q} = 30°$, find the ratio QR : PR.

7. In $\triangle ABC$, $a = 13$ cm, $\widehat{A} = 39°$, $b = 19$ cm. Find $\widehat{B}$.

COSINE RULE FOR TRIANGLES

When two sides and the included angle or three sides of a triangle are given we use one of the following formulae:

In a $\triangle ABC$,

$$a^2 = b^2 + c^2 - 2bc \cos A$$
$$b^2 = c^2 + a^2 - 2ca \cos B$$
$$c^2 = a^2 + b^2 - 2ab \cos C$$

Exercise 25m

(a) In a triangle ABC, $\widehat{A} = 60°$, $b = 6$ cm, $c = 9$ cm. Find a.

$$a^2 = b^2 + c^2 - 2bc \cos A$$
$$= 36 + 81 - 2(6 \times 9) \times 0.5$$
$$= 117 - 54$$
$$= 63$$
$$\therefore \qquad a = \sqrt{63} = 7.94 \text{ cm}$$

(b) Given ABC in which $a = 9$, $b = 12$, $c = 10$. Find $\widehat{A}$.

Using $$a^2 = b^2 + c^2 - 2bc \cos A$$

$$\cos A = \frac{b^2 + c^2 - a^2}{2bc}$$

$$= \frac{144 + 100 - 81}{2 \times 12 \times 10}$$

$$= \frac{163}{240}$$

$$= 0.6792$$

$$\therefore \qquad \widehat{A} = 47.22°$$

1. In $\triangle ABC$, $\widehat{C} = 30°$, $b = 10$ cm, $a = 11$ cm. Find c.

2. In $\triangle ABC$, $\widehat{B} = 45°$, $a = 15$ cm, $c = 25$ cm. Find b.

3. In $\triangle ABC$, $b = 20$ cm, $a = 8$ cm, $\widehat{C} = 32°$. Find c.

4. Find the remaining side and angles of $\triangle ABC$ in which $c = 16$ cm, $a = 10$ cm, $\widehat{B} = 43°$.

5. Solve $\triangle ABC$, given that $a = 12$ cm, $b = 8$ cm, $\widehat{C} = 37°$.

6. Given $\triangle ABC$ in which $a = 6$ cm, $b = 8$ cm, $c = 12$ cm. Find the largest angle.

7. Find the smallest angle in $\triangle ABC$ in which $a = 8$ cm, $b = 10$ cm, $c = 12$ cm.

In the following questions, give answers to two significant figures:

8. A ship sails due west from a harbour for 40 nautical miles. It then sails on a bearing of 115° for 30 nautical miles. How far is it then from the harbour?

9. From the top of a cliff 108 metres high, the angle of depression of the top of a tower on level horizontal ground below is 56°. From the foot of the cliff the angle of elevation of the top of the tower is 36°. Find the height of the tower.

MATHS IS OUT THERE

(i) Choose any odd number n, greater than 1, and calculate:

$$\frac{n^2 - 1}{2}, \ \frac{n^2 + 1}{2}$$

What do you notice about the values of n, $\dfrac{n^2 - 1}{2}$ and $\dfrac{n^2 + 1}{2}$?

(ii) Choose any number n, greater than 1, and calculate $2n$, $n^2 - 1$ and $n^2 + 1$.

What do you notice about these numbers?

At the end of the chapter you should be able to:

1. Give the bearings of one point relative to another using three figures.
2. Draw diagrams to show the bearing of a point relative to another point.
3. Solve problems involving distances and bearings.

If we wish to describe a direction in which one point lies relative to another, we need some sort of reference line. On paper, we can use axes. On the surface of the earth we use a line pointing north.

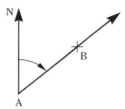

We start by standing at the first point A looking north, then turn clockwise until we are looking at the second point B.

The angle we have turned through gives the *bearing* of B from A.

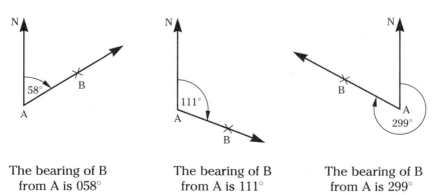

| The bearing of B from A is 058° | The bearing of B from A is 111° | The bearing of B from A is 299° |

Notice that we write 0 in front of the two-figure number to make it into a three-figure number.

A bearing gives a *line*. If a point is on a given bearing, it lies on that line.

Exercise 26a

Mark a point P, then mark point Q, so that the bearing of Q from P is 212°

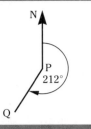

In questions 1 to 9, mark point A, then mark point B so that the bearing of B from A is:

1. 042°   4. 082°   **7.** 108°

2. 140°   5. 222°   **8.** 355°

3. 320°   6. 008°   **9.** 092°

Use the information in the diagram to find the bearing of Q from P.

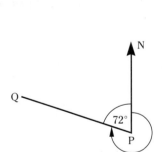

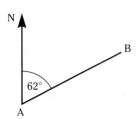

The reflex angle at P = 360° − 72°

                        = 288°

The bearing of Q from P is 288°.

Use the information given in each diagram to find the bearing of B from A:

10.

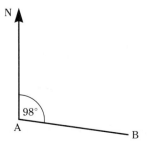

11.

12.

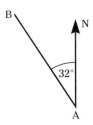

13.

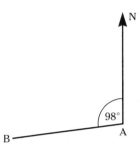

14.

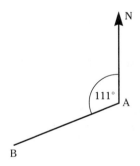

15.

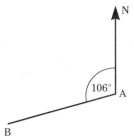

16.

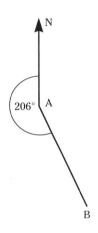

17.

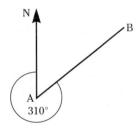

A man starts from point A and walks 4 km on a bearing of 036° to point B. Draw a diagram to represent this information.

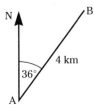

Draw diagrams to represent the information given in questions 18 to 27:

18. A car is driven 30 km on a bearing of 168°. It starts at point P and finishes at point Q.

20. A town X is 260 km from town Y. The bearing of X from Y is 282°.

19. A boy starts from C and cycles for 12 km, on a bearing of 213°, to D.

21. A man walks from A on a bearing of 027° to B. B is 11 km from A.

A car starts from A and is driven 50 km to B on a bearing of 072°. It is then driven 30 km to C on a bearing of 326°. Draw a diagram to represent this information.

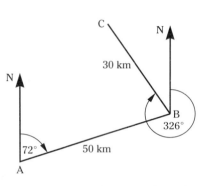

22. A ship sails 10 km from A, on a bearing of 100°, to point B. It then sails 12 km to C on a bearing of 070°.

25. From town P, town Q is 45 km away on a bearing of 098°. Town R is 60 km from P on a bearing of 003°.

23. Ship X is 5 km from ship Y on a bearing of 080°. Ship Z is 6 km from Y on a bearing of 300°.

26. ABC is a triangular field. B is 100 m from A on a bearing of 127° and C is 130 m from B on a bearing of 330°.

24. A man walks 7 km from A, on a bearing of 285°, to B. Then he walks 3 km due east to C.

27. Ship L is 10 km due east of ship M. The bearing of ship N from L is 343° and the bearing of N from M is 044°.

FINDING BEARINGS

If we are given the bearing of P from Q, we can draw a diagram in order to find the bearing of Q from P.

Exercise 26b

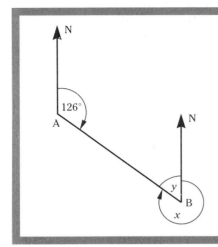

The bearing of B from A is 126°. What is the bearing of A from B?

(Draw a line pointing north at B. The bearing of A from B is x.)

$$y = 180° - 126° \text{ (interior angles)}$$
$$= 54°$$
$$x = 360° - 54° \text{ (angles at a point)}$$
$$= 306°$$

The bearing of A from B is 306°.

1. The bearing of P from Q is 060°. What is the bearing of Q from P?

2. The bearing of C from D is 292°. What is the bearing of D from C?

3. The bearing of Y from X is 162°. What is the bearing of X from Y?

4. The bearing of A from B is 212°. What is the bearing of B from A?

5. The bearing of D from C is 352°. What is the bearing of C from D?

6. The bearing of Z from Y is 125°. What is the bearing of Y from Z?

ANGLE CALCULATIONS

Exercise 26c

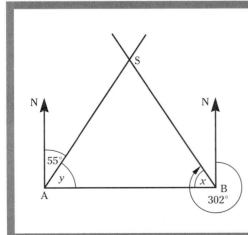

The bearing of a ship S from a lighthouse A is 055°. A second lighthouse B is due east of A. The bearing of S from B is 302°. Find $A\widehat{S}B$.

$$x = 302° - 270°$$
$$= 32°$$
$$y = 90° - 55°$$
$$= 35°$$
$$A\widehat{S}B = 180° - 32° - 35°$$
$$\text{(angles of a triangle)}$$
$$= 113°$$

1. A car starts from C and is driven for 10 km on a bearing of 278°, to D. The car is then driven for 15 km due north to E. Find EĈD.

2. The bearing of a town P from a town Q is 031°. The bearing of a town R from a town Q is 300°. Find PQ̂R.

3. A man starts from A and walks 5 km to B on a bearing of 112°. He then walks 3 km to C on a bearing of 260°. Find AB̂C.

4. A yacht starts from L and sails 12 km due east to M. It then sails 9 km on a bearing of 142° to K. Find LM̂K.

5. Point B is 60 km from A, on a bearing of 062°. C is 60 km from B on a bearing of 182°. Find AB̂C and BĈA.

6. The bearing of a ship X from a lighthouse Y is 101°. Ship Z is due west of X. The bearing of Z is 230°. Find the angles of triangle XYZ.

7. A ship sails 10 km from point A, on a bearing of 005°, to B. Then it sails another 10 km from B, on a bearing of 095°, to C. Find CÂB.

8. From a church tower P, the bearing of a bridge Q is 340° and the bearing of a crossroads R is 111°. Find QP̂R.

PROBLEMS

These problems use Pythagoras' theorem and trigonometry.

Exercise 26d

P is 12 km due east of Q. R is 8 km due north of Q. Find

(a) the distance of R from P   (b) the bearing of P from R.

(a)

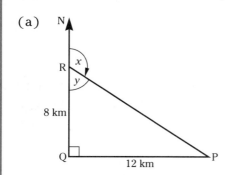

$$RP^2 = RQ^2 + PQ^2 \quad \text{(Pythag. th.)}$$
$$= 64 + 144$$
$$= 208$$
$$RP = \sqrt{208}$$
$$= 14.4$$

R is 14.4 km from P (to 3 s.f.)

(b) $\tan y = \dfrac{\text{opp}}{\text{adj}} = \dfrac{12}{8}$

$= 1.5$

$y = 56.3°$

$x = 180° - 56.3°$ (angles on a straight line)

$= 123.7°$

The bearing of P from R is 124° (to the nearest degree).

Give bearings correct to the nearest degree:

1. From a point P, a man walks 9 km north to Q, then 5 km east to R. What is the bearing of R from P?

2. Three towns P, Q and R, lie in such positions that the bearing of P from R is 027°, the bearing of Q from R is 297° and PR = QR = 21 km. Find $P\hat{R}Q$. How far is P from Q?

3. A ship sails 4 km on a bearing of 032° then 5 km on a bearing of 122°. How far is it from its starting point?

4.

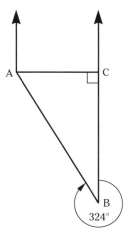

The bearing of a ship A from a ship B is 324°. Ship C is 8 km due north of B and is due east of A.

(a) How far is C from A?

(b) What is the bearing of B from A?

5. A is 20 km due west of B. The bearing of C from A is 044° and the bearing of C from B is 314°. Find

(a) the angles of triangle ABC

(b) the distance BC.

6. P is 16 km due north of Q. The bearing of R from P is 152°. The bearing of R from Q is 062°. Find

(a) RQ

(b) the bearing of P from R.

7. X is 25 km due west of Y. The bearing of Z from X is 052°. $X\hat{Y}Z = 90°$. Find the distances of Z from X and Y.

8. L is 5 km from M on a bearing of 241°. K is 7 km from M on a bearing of 331°. Find

(a) $M\hat{L}K$

(b) the bearing of L from K

(c) the bearing of K from L.

HOUSEHOLD BILLS

At the end of the chapter you should be able to:

1. Calculate the number of units of electricity or gas used from appropriate meter readings.
2. Calculate gas and electricity bills given the unit cost.
3. Calculate the income, given the rate and rateable value.
4. Calculate the rate, given the rateable value and the amount paid.
5. Calculate the rateable value given the rate and the amount paid.

ELECTRICITY BILLS

In Book 2 we considered the cost of using various electrical appliances for different periods of time. We also found the cost of buying a given number of units of electricity.

The unit of electricity is the kilowatt hour (kWh). It is the amount of electricity used in one hour by an appliance with a rating of 1 kilowatt. A 3 kW electric fire would use one unit in 20 minutes, whereas a 100 W bulb ($1 \text{ kW} = 1000 \text{ W}$) would burn for 10 hours on the same amount of electricity. Every consumer has a meter which shows the total number of units used since the meter was installed. The number of units used in any given quarter, or thirteen-week period, is the difference between the readings at the end and beginning of that quarter.

A quarterly electricity bill is calculated in much the same way as a telephone bill. There is a fixed, or standing charge, in addition to a charge for each unit.

Exercise 27a

If the meter reading at the beginning of a quarter was 13 205 and at the end of the quarter the reading was 13 524, find the number of units used in the quarter.

Number of units used was $13\,524 - 13\,205 = 319$

Copy and complete the following table which shows the meter readings at the beginning and end of a quarter:

	Reading at beginning	Reading at end	Number of units used in the quarter
1.	18 723	18 946	
2.	16 249	16 531	
3.	12 245	12 719	
4.	19 547	28 804	
5.	13 087	13 542	

6. Complete the following table which shows the meter readings in the Thorburn household for a year:

Date	Meter reading	Number of units used
2 January	13 274	
4 April	14 116	First quarter:
1 July	14 592	Second quarter:
8 October	14 945	Third quarter:
3 January	16 081	Fourth quarter:

<u>7.</u> Complete the following table which shows the meter readings in the Brown household for a year:

Date	Meter reading	Number of units used
5 January	24 136	
3 April	24 874	First quarter:
7 July	25 175	Second quarter:
5 October	25 349	Third quarter:
2 January	26 155	Fourth quarter:

8. Complete the following table which refers to meter readings in the Rahman household for a year:

Date	Meter reading	Number of units used in the specified quarter
10 February	28 194	
7 May		First: 847
9 August		Second: 346
12 November	29 689	Third:
11 February		Fourth: 1015

9. Complete the following table which refers to meter readings in the Evans household for a year:

Date	Meter reading	Number of units used in the specified quarter
13 March 8 June 14 September 9 December 10 March	34 275 35 987	First: 527 Second: 359 Third: Fourth: 943

The Davis household used 945 units of electricity during the second quarter of the year. If electricity costs 6.4 c per unit and there is a standing charge of $11.40, find the cost of electricity for the quarter.

$$\text{Cost of 945 units at } 6.4\,\text{c per unit} = 945 \times 6.4\,\text{c}$$
$$= 6048\,\text{c}$$
$$= \$60.48$$

$$\text{Total cost} = \text{standing charge} + \$60.48$$
$$= \$11.40 + \$60.48$$
$$= \$71.88$$

Find the quarterly electricity bill for each of the following households:

	Name	At beginning of quarter	At end of quarter	Number of units used	Standing charge	Cost per unit
		Meter reading				
10.	Mr Holmes	37 249	38 004		$12.50	6 c
11.	Mrs Shaw	58 146	61 285		$13.75	8 c
12.	Mr Kehoe	12 673	13 549		$15.00	9.5 c
13.	Mrs Yates	22 926	23 792		$18.20	7.55 c
14.	Mr Beale	35 446	36 314		$20.00	11.5 c
15.	Mr George	18 926	19 658		$16.60	8.4 c

GAS BILLS

Many households in the Caribbean and elsewhere use gas for cooking and heating. The amount of gas used is measured by volume and recorded by a meter in units, each of which is 100 cubic feet of gas.

The Gas Boards or Gas Corporation in Caribbean territories charge for their gas by the cubic foot or cubic metre.

In countries such as Britain, however, the Gas Boards charge for their gas in units of heat called therms. Therefore the volume of gas indicated by the meter has to be changed into therms. This is done by using the following formula which includes a conversion factor called the calorific value, which typically has the value $1032 \, \text{Btu/ft}^3$.

$$\text{Number of therms} = \frac{\text{number of} \atop \text{cubic feet} \times {\text{calorific value} \atop \text{in Btu/ft}^3}}{100\,000}$$

(A Btu is a much smaller unit of heat than a therm, in fact $1 \, \text{therm} = 10^5 \, \text{Btu}$.)

Now one unit of gas is $100 \, \text{ft}^3$, so if 260 units of gas, with a calorific value of $1032 \, \text{Btu/ft}^3$, have been used, the equivalent number of therms is

$$\frac{260 \times 100 \times 1032}{100\,000} = 268.32$$

Various quarterly tariffs are available, each of them consisting of a fixed or standard charge together with a charge for each therm used.

Exercise 27b

Copy and complete the following table which shows gas meter readings at the beginning and end of a quarter:

	Meter reading		Number of units used in the quarter
	At beginning of quarter	At end of quarter	
1.	008 867	009 242	
2.	000 627	000 836	
3.	005 249	007 364	
4.	014 387	017 255	

5. Copy and complete the following table which shows the gas meter readings in the Baxter household for a year:

Date	Meter reading	Number of units used in the quarter
10 January 8 April 14 July 6 October 12 January	007 849 008 253 008 437 008 640 009 036	First: Second: Third: Fourth:

Mrs Miles who emigrated to the UK used 720 units of gas during the winter quarter. If the calorific value of this gas is 1032 Btu/ft^3, how many therms were used? Give your answer correct to one decimal place.

$$\text{Number of therms} = \frac{720 \times 100 \times 1032}{100\,000}$$

$$= 743.0$$

How many cubic feet of gas did each of the following householders use during the quarter?

	Householder	Number of units used
6.	Mrs Thomas	170
7.	Miss Jacob	264
8.	Mr Kagan	624

How many therms, correct to one decimal place, did each of the following British householders use during the given quarter?

	Householder	Number of units used	Calorific value of gas in Btu/ft^3
9.	Mr Box	310	1035
10.	Mrs Gilbertson	454	1037
11.	Miss Selby	647	1032

Mr Scott used 250 therms of gas during the last quarter. Apart from a standing charge of $14.30, each therm was charged at 35 c. How much did his gas cost for the quarter?

$$\text{Standing charge} = \$14.30$$

$$250\,\text{c therms at 35 c per therm} = 250 \times 35\,\text{c} = \$87.50$$

$$\text{Total cost} = \$101.80$$

Calculate the quarterly gas bill for each of the following British householders:

	Name	Number of therms used	Standing charge	Cost of gas per therm
12.	Miss Brown	100	£10	30 p
13.	Mr Smith	450	£17	34 p
14.	Mrs Green	175	£12.50	38 p

Joan Whitehouse uses 464 units of gas in a quarter. If the standing charge is $11.50, the calorific value of gas is 1032 Btu/ft^3 and each unit costs 37.5 c, find

(a) the number of therms used, correct to the nearest whole number

(b) the total bill for the quarter.

(a)
$$\text{Number of therms used} = \frac{464 \times 100 \times 1032}{100\,000}$$

$$= 479$$

(b)
$$\text{Standing charge} = \$11.50$$

$$479 \text{ therms at 37.5 c per therm} = 479 \times 37.5\,\text{c}$$

$$= \$179.63$$

$$\text{Quarterly bill} = \$191.13$$

Calculate the quarterly gas bill for each of the following householders in the UK. Find the number of therms used, correct to the nearest whole number.

	Name	Units used	Calorific value of gas in Btu/ft^3	Standing charge	Cost of gas per therm in pence
15.	Mr Sadig	721	1032	£14	48
16.	Mr Coe	413	1037	£12.50	42
17.	Mrs Angel	859	1036	£18	52.3
18.	Miss De Roi	273	519	£20.50	25.4
19.	Mrs Green	672	517	£19.50	23.7

20. Mrs Edmonds' gas bill gives the following information:
   previous meter reading   039 254
   present meter reading   040 064
   calorific value of gas   1032 Btu/ft^3
   standing charge $30.25
   cost of gas per therm   36 c
Calculate the cost of Mrs Edmonds' gas for the quarter.

21. Mr Turner's gas bill gives the following information:
   previous meter reading   009 265
   present meter reading   010 040
   calorific value of gas   1039 Btu/ft^3
   standing charge $12.90
   cost of gas per therm   41.2 c
How much does Mr Turner pay for his gas for the quarter?

Mr Potter uses on average 300 therms each quarter.
He can pay for this gas using
either a CREDIT Tariff which charges 32 c per therm plus a standing charge of $10
or the DOMESTIC PREPAYMENT Tariff which charges
   50 c per therm for the first 50 therms
   plus 32 c per therm for additional therms
   plus a standing charge of $4.

Which method of payment should he use?

(a) If he uses the credit tariff

$$\text{cost of 300 therms at 32 c per therm} = 300 \times 32 \text{ c}$$
$$= \$96$$
$$\text{Standing charge} = \$10$$
$$\therefore \qquad \text{total cost} = \$106$$

(b) If he uses the domestic prepayment tariff

cost of first 50 therms at 50 c per therm $= 50 \times 50$ c
$$= \$25$$

Cost of remaining 250 therms at 32 c per therm
$$= 250 \times 32 \text{ c} = \$80$$

Standing charge $= \$4$

total cost $= \$109$

∴

Method (a) costs \$3 less than Method (b). It would therefore be cheaper to pay using the credit tariff.

For each of the following West Indian customers living in the UK calculate which tariff is the cheaper and by how much:

		Credit Tariff			Domestic Prepayment Tariff		
Customer	Number of therms used	Standing charge	Cost per therm	Standing charge	Price per therm for initial therms	Price per therm for further therms
22. Mr Wheat	400	\$12	30 p	£4	50 p for first 50 therms	32 p
23. Miss Evans	500	\$14	35 p	£5	55 p for first 50 therms	37 p
24. Mrs Khan	350	\$16	40 p	£6	58 p for first 40 therms	42 p

RATES

Many of the services provided by local councils are taken for granted, but all of them must be paid for. Local authorities are responsible for providing such things as education, the police force, libraries, refuse collection, street lighting, leisure facilities, housing, roads and public transport, cemeteries and crematoria.

Roughly half the cost of providing these services comes from central government, but the other half is paid for out of local taxes in the form of rates. The rating system, though in certain respects very unfair, is an easy and relatively efficient way of collecting the required money.

RATEABLE VALUE

Every house, shop, factory or office, is given what is called a *rateable value*. For every $1 of the rateable value the owner of any property has to pay a levy of so many cents in the dollar. If all the properties in a city have a total RV (rateable value) of $1 000 000 and the city needs to collect $500 000 to cover its expenditure it must collect 50 c for every $1 of the rateable value. Thus

$$\text{cash collected} = \text{RV} \times \text{rate in the dollar}$$
$$\text{(in cents)} \qquad\qquad \text{(in cents)}$$

Although the rateable value is always preceded by the $ sign, in all calculations it should be considered simply as a number.

Exercise 27c

Find the income from a rate of 1 c in the dollar in Edgecliff where the total rateable value is $4 000 000

Income from a rateable value of $1 is 1 c.

∴ income from a rateable value of $4 000 000 is

$$4\,000\,000 \times 1\,\text{c} = \$40\,000$$

Calculate the income from a cent rate (i.e. a rate of 1 c in the dollar) for each of the following councils:

	Parish Council	Rateable value
1.	St James	$1 400 000
2.	St Andrew	$7 600 000
3.	St Augustine	$34 500 000

	Parish Council	Rateable value in $1000s
4.	St George	15 000
5.	St Margaret's	1 625
6.	St Helena	7 347

> The rateable value of Kenton is $1 500 000. Find the income from a rate of 63 c in the dollar.
>
> Income from a rate of 63 c in the dollar is
>
> $$1\,500\,000 \times 63\,c = \$945\,000$$

Find the income for each of the following councils:

	Parish Council	RV of area	Rate in $
7.	St David's	$4 000 000	80 c
8.	Garvey Heights	$1 700 000	92 c
9.	St Bartholomew	$52 000 000	154 c

> The income from a cent rate in St Victoria is $46 700. Find the rateable value of St Victoria.
>
> To provide an income of $1 a 1 c rate must be charged on a rateable value of $100.
>
> The rateable value of St Victoria is $46 700 \times 100 = \$4\,670\,000$

Find the total rateable value for each of the following districts where the income from a cent is as given:

	Parish Council	Income from a cent rate
10.	Belleville	$72 420
11.	Southport	$5 925
12.	Belleplain	$37 470

> If the rateable value of Riverside is $450 000 and the council decides that it must collect $270 000, what rate in the dollar should they levy?
>
> $$\text{Cash collected} = \text{RV} \times \text{rate in the dollar}$$
> $$(\text{in cents}) \qquad\qquad (\text{in cents})$$
> $$27\,000\,000 = 450\,000 \times \text{rate in the dollar (in cents)}$$
>
> i.e. rate in the dollar is $\dfrac{27\,000\,000}{450\,000}\,c$
>
> $$= 60\,c$$

In each of the following questions find the rate in the dollar that the council should levy to collect the required amount of money:

	Parish Council	Rateable value of the area	Amount of cash required
13.	Grantstown	$5 000 000	$4 000 000
14.	Bayville	$3 700 000	$2 775 000
15.	Hillaby	$2 600 000	$3 484 000

Mr Appleyard lives in a house with rateable value $340. If the rate in the dollar is 78 c, how much must he pay in rates?

$$\text{Rates due} = 340 \times 78\,\text{c}$$
$$= 26\,520\,\text{c}$$
$$= \$265.20$$

Find the rates due to be paid by each of the following householders:

	Householder	Rateable value (RV)	Rate in the dollar
16.	Mrs Brown	$200	50 c
17.	Mr Capstick	$500	70 c
18.	Miss Deare	$600	120 c
19.	Miss Godfrey	$314	94 c
20.	Mr Hawkins	$830	68 c
21.	Mr Chin	$418	105 c
22.	Mrs Emery	$450	85 c
23.	Mrs Fox	$175	112 c
24.	Mrs James	$273	168 c
25.	Mr Knight	$516	84 c

Exercise 27d

Miss Lehman lives in a flat with a rateable value of $216 and pays $200.88 for a year in rates. Find the rate in the dollar.

$$\text{Rates paid} = \text{rateable value} \times \text{rate in the dollar}$$
$$\text{(in cents)} \qquad\qquad\qquad \text{(in cents)}$$

$$\text{i.e. } 20\,088 = 216 \times \text{rate in the dollar}$$
$$\text{(in cents)}$$

$$\therefore \qquad \text{rate in the dollar} = \frac{20\,088}{216}\,c$$

$$= 93\,c$$

Find the rate in the dollar for each of the following householders:

	Name	Rates paid	Rateable value
1.	Mr Newbold	$216	$240
2.	Mrs Osborne	$372	$310
3.	Miss Purley	$611	$470
4.	Mrs Rutter	$201.16	$214
5.	Mr Thomas	$810.54	$513
6.	Mr Underwood	$397.72	$244

Mrs Anthony pays $167.20 in rates when the rate in the dollar is 76 c. What is the rateable value of her home?

$$\text{Rates paid} = \text{rateable value} \times \text{rate in the dollar}$$
$$\text{(in cents)} \qquad\qquad\qquad \text{(in cents)}$$

$$\therefore \qquad 16\,720 = \text{rateable value} \times 76$$

$$\therefore \qquad \text{rateable value} = \frac{16\,720}{76}$$

$$= 220$$

Since the rateable value is always in dollars, the rateable value of Mrs Anthony's home is $220.

The rates paid and the rate in the dollar is given for various householders. Find the rateable value of each of their properties.

	Householder	Rates paid	Rate in the dollar
7.	Mr Burrows	$360	120 c
8.	Miss Campbell	$375	150 c
9.	Mrs Dunnock	$382.50	85 c
10.	Mr Gummer	$1189	145 c
11.	Miss Howells	$710.64	126 c
12.	Mr Ingram	$598.08	168 c

Exercise 27e

1. Find the income from a rate of 1 c in the dollar in Hoxton where the total rateable value is $7 550 000.

2. The rateable value of Hillside is $2 400 000. Find the income from a rate of 87 c in the dollar.

3. The income from a cent rate at Grand Bay is $3445. What is the rateable value of Grand Bay?

4. If the rateable value of Norman Heights is $7 570 000 and the council must collect $5 828 900 in rates, what rate in the dollar must be levied?

5. How much must Miss Donat pay in rates if she lives in a bungalow with a rateable value of $327 and the council levy a rate of 121 c in the dollar?

6. John Smith pays $366.24 in rates. If his house has a rateable value of $436, what rate in the dollar has the council levied?

7. When the council levied a rate of 73 c Mr McVitie paid $280.32 in rates. What is the rateable value of his property?

Exercise 27f

1. Mrs White lives in a house of rateable value $250, while her neighbour's house has a rateable value of $275. How much does each pay in rates when the rate in the dollar is 86 c?

2. Mr Peters lives in a house that has a rateable value of $310, while Mr John's house has a rateable value of $378. How much does each pay in rates when the rate in the dollar is 126 c?

3. Miss Smith pays $369.60 in rates on a flat with a rateable value of $330. If Mr Edwards lives in a house with a rateable value of $470, how much can he expect to pay in rates?

4. Mr Caton and Mr Weinberg live in properties with respective rateable values of $294 and $352. If the *difference* in the amount they pay in rates is $53.94, find the rate in the dollar and the amount paid by each in rates.

5. The Chard family pay $546.10 in rates when the rate in the dollar is 127 c. As a result of improvements to their home, its rateable value is increased by $23. How much will they pay in rates when the rate in the dollar is increased to 144 c?

6. Mr and Mrs Espley pay $227.90 in rates when the rate in the dollar is 86 c. They improve their flat and this results in its rateable value being increased by $54. How much will they pay in rates when the rate in the dollar is increased by 23 c?

7. The rateable value of my house is $444. When the rate is 96 cents in the dollar, 2.5 c is required for the library service and 48 c towards education. How much do I contribute to each service?

8. Miss Taylor lives in a cottage with a rateable value of $264. If the council levy a rate of 92 c in the dollar and the water board in addition levy a rate of 37 c in the dollar how much will she pay in rates?

MIXED EXERCISE

Exercise 27g

1. Mrs Florence used 1207 units of electricity between 12 April and 10 July. If each unit costs 7.2 c and there is a standing charge of $12.30 find the cost of electricity for the quarter.

2. How many therms is 777 units of gas when the calorific value is 506 Btu/ft^3? How much will this cost if gas is charged at 17.5 c per unit and there is a standing charge of $12.80?

3. Mr Higgins' gas bill gives the following details:
   previous meter reading   001 372
   present meter reading   001 579
   calorific value of gas   1037 Btu/ft^3
   standing charge $25.80
   cost of gas per therm   39.4 c
Calculate, correct to the nearest cent, the cost of Mr Higgins' gas for the quarter.

4. The rateable value of my house is $576. How much must I pay in rates when the rate in the dollar is 108 c?

5. The income from a cent rate in Fleetwood is $53 720. What is the rateable value of Fleetwood?

STATISTICS AND PROBABILITY

At the end of the chapter you should be able to:

1. Organise data in a frequency table.
2. Draw bar charts from data in a frequency table.
3. Draw histograms to represent data in a frequency table.
4. Find the mean, mode or median from a set of data.
5. Find the range and quartiles from a set of data.
6. Calculate the standard deviation from a frequency table of grouped or ungrouped data.
7. Determine if individual events of a given set are mutually exclusive.
8. Calculate the probability of a set of mutually exclusive events.
9. Determine if given events are independent.
10. Calculate the probability of a set of independent events.

COLLECTING INFORMATION

'Information Technology' is the name used for modern methods of dealing with information. Before information can be distributed, it has to be collected and organised.

The local health authority wanted some information about the heights of five-year-old children in its area. At their first school medical examination, the height of each child was recorded. The following figures are the recorded heights (in cm to the nearest cm) of ninety five-year-olds from one infant school:

99	107	102	98	115	95	106	110	108	105
118	102	114	108	94	104	113	102	105	95
105	110	109	101	106	108	107	107	101	109
108	105	116	109	114	110	97	110	113	116
112	101	92	105	104	115	111	103	110	99
93	104	103	113	107	94	102	117	116	104
99	114	106	114	98	109	107	114	106	107
109	113	112	100	109	113	118	104	94	114
107	96	108	103	112	106	115	111	115	101

This set of figures was written down in the same order as the children came into the medical examination, so the heights are listed in a random order. Disorganised figures like these are called *raw data*. They need organising before we can make sense of them.

FREQUENCY TABLES

The heights in the table above range from 92 cm to 118 cm and there are 18 different values. It is tedious to count the number of times each individual height occurs. It is better to organise them into groups. About five to ten groups is sensible. We will group them as follows:

90–94 cm, 95–99 cm, 100–104 cm, 105–109 cm, 110–114 cm, 115–119 cm.

Counting the number of heights in each group gives the following table which is called a frequency table:

Group	Tally	Frequency
90–94 cm	ⅲ	5
95–99 cm	ⅲ ‖‖‖	9
100–104 cm	ⅲ ⅲ ⅲ ‖	17
105–109 cm	ⅲ ⅲ ⅲ ⅲ ⅲ ‖‖	28
110–114 cm	ⅲ ⅲ ⅲ ⅲ ‖	21
115–119 cm	ⅲ ⅲ	10

Total: 90

When you make a frequency table from a set of raw data, work down the columns, making a tally mark for each value in the tally column next to the appropriate group. Do *not* go through the data looking for values that fit into the first group and the second group and so on.

BAR CHARTS

We saw in Book 1 that a frequency table can be illustrated by a bar chart.

The following bar chart illustrates the frequency table above:

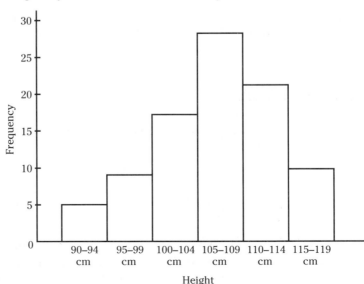

Notice that each group covers the same span of 5 cm so we make each bar the same width.

Exercise 28a

1. Fifty Junior School children joined the school's computer club. Their ages were recorded:

10	8	9	10	7	8	8	11	10	9
7	8	9	9	10	11	11	10	9	8
8	7	9	7	10	7	10	8	9	11
10	11	8	10	9	8	9	7	11	10
9	10	10	11	10	11	7	11	10	9

Make a frequency table showing the number of children of each age and illustrate this information with a bar chart

2. The local ice-cream parlour had 56 customers one Saturday evening. They spent the following amounts, in cents:

270	110	45	96	250	490	325	45
382	136	125	450	420	380	150	250
85	250	320	525	218	210	216	120
155	430	250	40	510	150	510	245
320	120	316	150	260	45	180	310
273	280	85	280	318	45	210	282
462	316	218	316	325	45	560	315

Use groups 0–99 c, 100–199 c, 200–299 c, 300–399 c, 400–499 c, 500–599 c, to make a frequency table and illustrate the data with a bar chart.

3. The weights, to the nearest gram, of 30 bags of popcorn sold at a fête are given below:

69	83	75	65	68	68	73	70	80	79
70	76	63	86	69	65	66	74	66	68
70	60	67	74	65	65	67	88	81	63

Choose your own groups and make a frequency table. Illustrate the data with a bar chart. Compare and discuss your bar chart with those of other members of your class.

HISTOGRAMS

Consider the following frequency table, which was compiled from the weights (in kilograms) of 100 people:

Weights (kg)	50–59	60–69	70–79	80–89	90–99	100–109	
Frequency	15	30	35	15	3	2	Total = 100

A frequency table tells us the number of items in each group. In this example, there are 15 people with weights between 50 kg and 59 kg, 30 people with weights between 60 kg and 69 kg, and so on. The bar chart illustrates this frequency table:

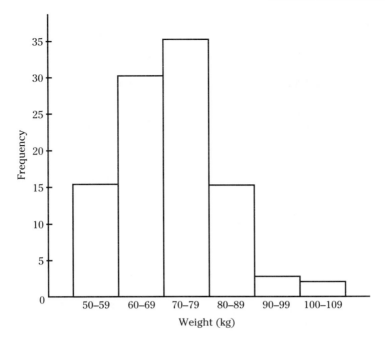

It is the *area* of a bar that gives the impression of the number of items in a group.

When a bar chart is constructed so that the *area* of each bar is proportional to the number of items in each group it is called a *histogram*.

The diagram above is also a histogram: each group covers the same span so each bar has the same width. Hence the area of each bar is proportional to its height. In this case, therefore, the height of each bar is proportional to the number of items in the group.

Most bar charts showing frequencies are histograms but some are not. Consider the bar chart below. It shows the number of cans of fizzy drink sold by a manufacturer for each of the years 1994, 1995 and 1996:

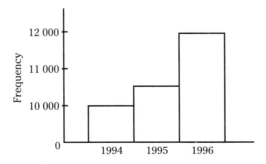

Each bar is the same width, but because the frequency scale does not start at zero the heights, and therefore the areas, of the bars are not proportional to the frequencies of sales each year.

Hence this bar chart is *not* a histogram.

Exercise 28b

Draw a histogram to represent the frequency tables in questions 1 to 3.

1. The table shows the distribution of ages of 100 people attending a school concert.

Age (years)	0–19	20–39	40–59	60–79	80–99
Frequency	43	24	17	10	6

2. The table shows the results of a survey on the weekly earnings of 100 sixteen-year-olds.

Weekly earnings ($)	20–29	30–39	40–49	50–59	60–69	70–79
Frequency	45	10	11	21	10	3

3. The table shows the distribution of the average marks of 40 children in the end-of-year examinations.

Average mark	1–20	21–40	41–60	61–80	81–100
Frequency	2	4	19	12	3

4. The histogram shows the distribution of the times taken by 50 children to get to school.

   Construct a frequency table from this histogram.

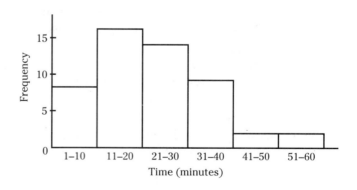

5. The histogram is based on the number of hours that 30 children spent watching television on a particular Saturday.

   Construct a frequency table from this histogram.

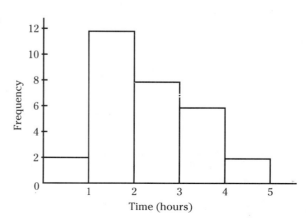

VARYING WIDTH BARS

Consider the following frequency table which shows the results of a survey on the annual pay of 100 women:

Pay ($)	0–1999	2000–3999	4000–5999	6000-9999	10 000–19 999
Frequency	20	36	25	14	5

The spans of the groups are *not* equal.
    the first three groups each cover a span of $2000
    the fourth group spans $4000, twice the span of the first three
    the fifth group spans $10 000, five times the span of the first three.

To illustrate this distribution on a histogram, we must make
    the width of the first three bars equal
    the width of the fourth bar twice that of the first three
    the width of the fifth bar five times that of the first three.

Now consider the 14 incomes in the group $6000–$9999. If we suppose that these incomes are evenly spread throughout this group then there are

    seven women with incomes in the group $6000–$7999 and
    seven women with incomes in the group $8000–$9999.

The fourth bar is therefore seven units high for the whole group. Because the width of this bar is twice that of the others used, its *area* is proportional to the frequency of the group.

We can see from this example that if we have a bar twice as wide as the others used, the height of that bar is *half* the number of items in the group.

If we assume that the incomes in the fifth group are evenly spread throughout the group then there is one woman with an income in each of the subgroups spanning $2000. The fifth bar is therefore one unit high for the whole group. Again, because the width of this bar is five times that of the first three bars, its area is proportional to the frequency of the group.

Note that we do not use 'frequency' to label the vertical axis because it is the area of the bar that represents the frequency and not the height.

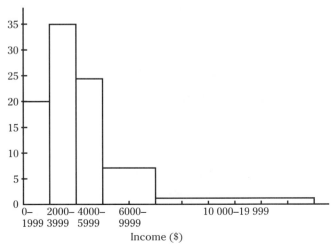

Exercise 28c

Draw a histogram to illustrate the following frequency table which shows the distribution of the ages of 300 people attending a school concert:

Age (years)	0–19	20–29	30–39	40–49	50–59	60–99
Frequency	20	40	100	110	10	20

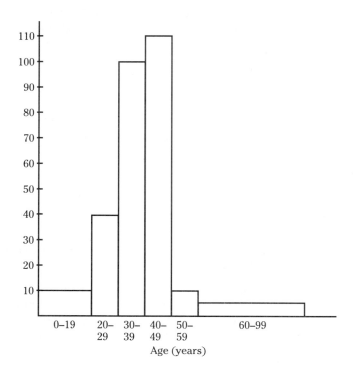

(The width of the first group is twice that of the middle groups, so its height is half of its frequency, i.e. $\frac{1}{2}$ of 20. The last group is four times the width of the first group, so the height of the bar is $\frac{1}{4}$ of 20 on the vertical scale.)

Draw a histogram to illustrate the frequency tables in questions 1 to 6.

1. The table gives the distribution of marks of 30 children in a test:

Mark	0–39	40–59	60–79	80–99
Frequency	8	8	10	4

2. The table gives the distribution of lengths (to the nearest mm) of 50 blades of grass:

Length (mm)	40–49	50–59	60–69	70–79	80–109
Frequency	6	8	12	12	12

3. The table shows the distribution of times (in seconds) taken for 40 children to complete an obstacle race:

Time (seconds)	1–40	41–50	51–60	61–70
Frequency	8	15	7	10

4. The table shows the distribution of weights of 30 bags of crisps from a shop:

Weight (grams)	1–50	51–60	61–70	71–80
Frequency	4	8	14	4

5. The table gives the distribution of marks of 100 children in an end-of-term mathematics examination:

Mark	0–29	30–39	40–49	50–59	60–99
Frequency	10	15	25	34	16

6. The table shows the distribution of weights (in kilograms) of 60 ten-year-old boys:

Weight (kg)	31–36	37–39	40–42	43–45	46–54
Frequency	8	10	18	12	12

7. The table shows the distribution of times taken (in minutes) for 50 five-year-old children to eat their school dinners:

Time (minutes)	4–5	6–7	8–9	10–11	12–15	16–19	20–29
Frequency	5	4	10	9	6	6	10

Make a frequency table from the histogram below which shows the distribution of the ages of people boarding buses at the bus station between 0830 and 0900 one morning.

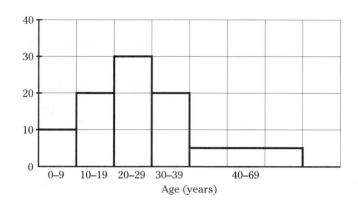

Age (years)	0–9	10–19	20–29	30–39	40–69
Frequency	10	20	30	20	15

(The width of the last bar is three times that of the other bars, so the frequency in this group is three times the height of the bar.)

In questions 8 to 11, make a frequency table from the histograms:

8.

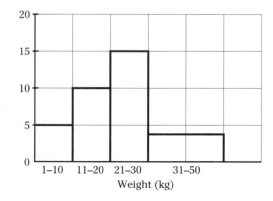

9.

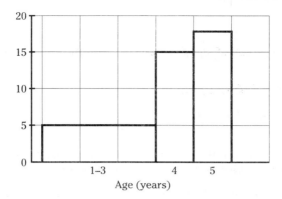

10.

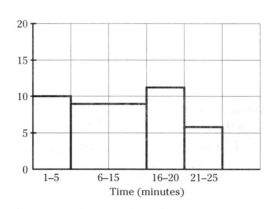

11.

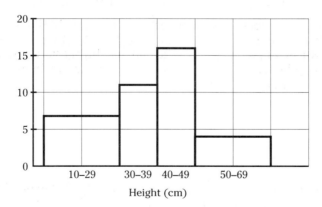

MEAN, MODE AND MEDIAN

In Book 2, we saw that, when we have a set of numbers there are three different measures we can use that attempt to give a 'typical member' that is representative of the set.

MEAN

The *mean* (arithmetic average) of a set of n numbers is the sum of the numbers divided by n.

The mean of the set 2, 6, 8, 8, 10, 10, 12, is

$$\frac{2 + 6 + 8 + 8 + 10 + 10 + 12}{7} = \frac{56}{7} = 8$$

The mean value of a set of numbers is the most frequently used form of average, so much so that the word 'average' is often used for 'mean value'.

For example, if you were asked for your average mark in a set of examinations, you would total the marks and divide by the number of examinations, i.e. you would find the mean mark.

MODE

In a set of numbers, the mode is the number that occurs most often. For example, for the set 2, 2, 4, 4, 4, 5, 6, 6, the mode is 4 as no other number occurs more than twice.

The mode is easier to find if the numbers are arranged in order of size.

If the numbers in a set are all different, there is no mode. For example, the set 1, 2, 3, 5, 8, 10, has no mode.

If there are two (or more) numbers which equally occur most often, there are two (or more) modes. For example, in the set 1, 2, 2, 3, 5, 5, 8, both 2 and 5 are modes.

The mode of a set of numbers is sometimes more useful than the mean and it is much easier to find. For example, if a shoe manufacturer records the size of each pair of shoes that is sold in different areas, it would be the mode of those sizes that he would be interested in (i.e. which size is the most common), because he would have to supply most of that size.

MEDIAN

If we arrange a set of numbers in order of size, the median is the number in the middle. For example, for the seven numbers in the set 2, 4, 5, ⑦, 7, 8, 9, the median is 7.

When there is an even number of numbers in the set, the median is the mean of the two middle numbers. For example, for the eight numbers in the set 2, 3, 4, 4, 5, 6, 7, 7, the median is the mean of 4 and 5, i.e. 4.5.

The median is sometimes a better representative number to use than the mean. Suppose, for example, that a pupil got the following marks for end-of-term examinations: 5,   52,   58,   59,   66

The mean mark is 48 which is lower than all but one of these marks. This is because one very low mark has affected the mean and in this case the mean mark does not give a fair impression of performance. It would be better to use the median mark, which is 58, as representative of the set.

For a small set of numbers, say 15, it is easy to find the median and we can see that it is the $\dfrac{15+1}{2}$ th value, i.e. the 8th value. From examples such as this we deduce that, for n numbers arranged in order of size, the median is the $\left(\dfrac{n+1}{2}\right)$ th number.

For example, for 59 numbers, the median is the $\left(\dfrac{59+1}{2}\right)$ th number, i.e. the 30th number.

For 60 numbers, the median is the $\left(\dfrac{60+1}{2}\right)$ th number, i.e. the $\left(30\tfrac{1}{2}\right)$ th number. This means the average of the 30th and 31st numbers.

Exercise 28d

A page from a novel by George Lamming was chosen at random and the number of letters in each of the first twenty words on that page was recorded:

3, 4, 5, 3, 7, 8, 3, 3, 6, 2, 4, 6, 4, 6, 3, 13, 4, 3, 3, 2

Find the mean, modal and median number of letters per word.

Arranging the numbers in size order:

2, 2, 3, 3, 3, 3, 3, 3, 3, 4, 4, 4, 4, 5, 6, 6, 6, 7, 8, 13

10th   11th

The mean is $\dfrac{92}{20} = 4.6$

The mode is 3

The median is the value of the $\left(\dfrac{20+1}{2}\right)$ th number,

i.e. the $\left(10\tfrac{1}{2}\right)$ th number, which is the average of the 10th and 11th numbers

∴ the median is 4

Find the mean, mode and median of the sets of numbers in questions 1 to 8. Remember to arrange them in order of size first. Give answers correct to three significant figures where necessary:

1. 3, 6, 2, 5, 9, 2, 4

2. 10, 8, 10, 16, 7, 9, 10, 8, 9

3. 13, 16, 12, 14, 19, 12, 14, 13

4. 1.6, 2.4, 3.9, 1.7, 1.6, 0.2, 1.3, 2.0

5. 4, 3, 4, 5, 2, 5, 4, 3

6. 5, 7, 9, 12, 10, 8, 7, 9, 7, 8, 12, 7

7. 0.8, 0.7, 0.6, 0.7, 0.8, 0.8, 0.9, 0.5

8. 1.3, 1.8, 1.7, 1.9, 1.4, 1.5, 1.3, 1.8, 1.2

9. Ten music students took a Grade 3 piano examination. They obtained the following marks: 106, 125, 132, 140, 108, 102, 75, 135, 146, 123. Find the mean and median marks. Which of these two representative measures would be most useful to the teacher who entered the students? (Give *brief* reasons, do not write an essay on the subject.)

10. A small firm employs ten people. The salaries of the employees are as follows: $30 000, $8000, $5000, $5000, $5000, $5000, $4000, $3000, $1500. Find the mean, mode and median salary. Which of these three figures is a trade union official likely to be interested in, and why?

11. Thirty 15-year-olds were asked how much pocket money they received each week and the following amounts (in cents) were recorded: 0, 0, 0, 50, 50, 50, 100, 100, 100, 100, 100, 100, 100, 150, 150, 200, 200, 200, 200, 200, 200, 200, 200, 200, 250, 250, 250, 500, 1000.
Find the mean, mode and median amount.

If you were presenting your parents with an argument for an increase in pocket money, which of the three representative measures would you use and why?

12. The first eight customers at a supermarket one Saturday spent the following amounts: $25.10, $3.80, $20.50, $15.70, $38.40, $9.60, $46.20, $10.50. Find the mean and median amount spent.

FINDING THE MODE FROM A FREQUENCY TABLE

The frequency table shows the number of houses in a village that are occupied by different numbers of people:

Number of people living in one house	0	1	2	3	4	5	6
Frequency	2	10	8	15	25	12	4

It is clear that there are more houses with four people living in them than any other number, i.e. the mode is 4.

This frequency table was made from information about the weights (in kg) of 90 eleven-year-olds:

Weight (in kg)	35–39	40–44	45–49	50–54	55–59	60–64
Frequency	4	10	30	28	10	8

Because the weights have been placed into groups, we have lost some of the detail; we do not know how many children have a weight of 46 kg or any other particular weight. It is possible that more children have a weight of 52 kg than any other weight, but, as we just do not know, we cannot give the mode as a single figure.

However, we *can* say that more children have a weight in the group 45–49 kg than in any other group. We call this the *modal group*.

Exercise 28e

Write down the mode or modal group for each of the following frequency tables or bar charts:

1.

Length of time of a telephone call (minutes)	1–5	6–10	11–15	16–20
Frequency	20	30	10	5

2.

Number of tickets bought per person for a football match	1	2	3	4	5	6	7
Frequency	250	200	100	50	10	3	1

3.

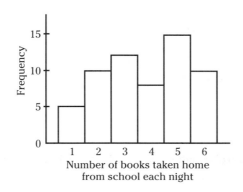

4. Give the modal group for each of the questions in Exercise 28b.

FINDING THE MEAN FROM A FREQUENCY TABLE

The pupils in class 3G were asked to state the number of children in their own family and the following frequency table was made:

Number of children per family	1	2	3	4	5
Frequency	7	15	5	2	1

Total no. of families = 30

This information has not been grouped: all the numbers are here so we can total this set. We have seven families with one child giving seven children, fifteen with two children giving thirty children and so on, giving the total number of children as

$$(7 \times 1) + (15 \times 2) + (5 \times 3) + (2 \times 4) + (1 \times 5) = 65$$

There are 30 numbers in the set, so the mean is

$$\frac{65}{30} = 2.2 \quad \text{(to 1 d.p.)}$$

i.e. there are, on average, 2.2 children per family.

To avoid unnecessary errors, this kind of calculation needs to be done systematically and it helps if the frequency table is written vertically.

We can then add a column for the number of children in each group and sum the numbers in this column for the total number of children.

Number of children per family x	Frequency f	fx
1	7	7
2	15	30
3	5	15
4	2	8
5	1	5
	No. of families = 30	No. of children = 65

$$\therefore \text{ mean} = \frac{65}{30} = 2.2 \quad \text{(to 1 d.p.)}$$

Exercise 28f

1. This table shows the results of counting the number of prickles per leaf on 50 rose trees.

Number of prickles	1	2	3	4	5	6
Frequency	4	2	8	7	20	9

Find the mean number of prickles per leaf.

2. A six-sided dice was thrown 50 times. The table gives the number of times each score was obtained.

Score	1	2	3	4	5	6
Frequency	7	8	10	8	5	12

Find the mean score per throw.

3. Three coins were tossed together 30 times and the number of heads per throw was recorded.

Number of heads	0	1	2	3
Frequency	3	12	10	5

Find the mean number of heads per throw.

4. The table shows the result of noting the number of people per car in cars passing the school entrance between 9 and 9.30.

Number of people	1	2	3	4	5	6
Frequency	50	38	15	6	4	7

How many cars passed the school between 9 and 9.30? Find the mean number of people per car.

FINDING THE MEAN FROM A GROUPED FREQUENCY TABLE

The pupils in one class were asked to count the number of items in their pockets and the following frequency table was drawn up:

Number of items	0–4	5–9	10–14	15–19	20–24
Frequency	6	11	6	4	3

We can see that six pupils had between 0 and 4 items. We do not know the exact number of items that each of these pupils had, so we cannot find the exact total number of items that all six pupils had in their pockets.

However, if we *assume* that the average number of items in that group is halfway between 0 and 4, i.e. 2, then we can find an approximate total, i.e. $6 \times 2 = 12$ items.

Using the halfway value in the same way for the other groups, we can find (approximately) the total number of items in the pockets of all 30 pupils:

Number of items	Frequency f	Halfway values x	fx
0–4	6	2	12
5–9	11	7	77
10–14	6	12	72
15–19	4	17	68
20–24	3	22	66
Total: 30			Total: 295

Therefore, the mean number of items is $\frac{295}{30} = 9.8$ 9 to 1 d.p.)

Remember that this calculation is based on the assumption that the average of each group is the halfway value of that group.

Exercise 28g

1. Fifty boxes of peaches were examined and the number of bad peaches in each box was recorded with the following result:

No. of bad peaches per box	0–4	5–9	10–14	15–19
Frequency	34	11	4	1

Find the mean number of bad peaches per box.

2. Twenty tomato seeds were planted in a seed tray. Four weeks later the heights of the resulting plants were measured and the following frequency table was made:

Height (in cm to the nearest cm)	1–3	4–6	7–9	10–12
Frequency	2	5	10	3

Find the mean height of the seedlings.

3. The table shows the result of a survey amongst 100 pupils on the amount of money each of them spent in the school canteen on one particular day:

Amount (cents)	0–24	25–49	50–74	75–99
Frequency	26	15	38	21

Find the mean amount of money.

4. The histogram shows the result of an examination of 20 boxes of screws:

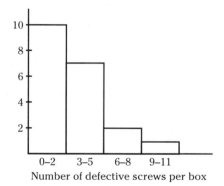

Number of defective screws per box

Make a frequency table and find the mean number of defective screws per box.

5. The table shows the distribution of heights of 50 adult females, measured to the nearest cm:

Height (cm)	145–149	150–154	155–159	160–164	165–169	170–174
Frequency	1	3	21	18	5	2

Find the mean height.

6. Ninety pupils in one year sat a mathematics examination and the following frequency table was drawn up from the results:

Mark	0–14	15–29	30–44	45–59	60–74	75–89	90–100
Frequency	7	5	6	34	22	12	4

Find the mean mark.

7. The table shows the results of a survey amongst 70 pupils on the amount of money that each of them brought to school on a particular morning:

Amount (cents)	0–49	50–99	100–149	150–199
Frequency	11	35	15	9

Find the mean amount of money.

8. Find the mean of the frequency distribution given in question 1 of Exercise 28b.

9. Find the mean of the frequency distribution given in question 1 of Exercise 28c.

10. Use the list of numbers on the first page this chapter to find the exact mean height of the 90 five-year-olds used in that example. Then find the mean using the frequency table drawn up for those heights (page 451). Compare your answers.

11. Use the information gathered from a project of your own to find the mean (a) from the raw data (b) from a grouped frequency distribution made from the raw data.
Suggestions for projects follow in the next exercise.

PROJECTS

Exercise 28h

From a chosen project, collect the information (raw data), decide on the groups it can be divided into and make a frequency table. Illustrate your results with a histogram and find the mean value from the frequency table.

Suggestions for class projects

1. Heights of pupils in the class.

2. Weights of pupils in the class.

3. Costs of journeys to school this morning.

4. Times of journeys to school (in minutes).

5. Numbers of brothers and sisters per pupil.

6. Numbers of items in school bags.

7. Ages of pupils (in months).

8. Results of an experiment in science (where every pupil did the same experiment).

9. The prices of a 500 g packet of cornflakes (or any other item) from as many shops as possible.

Suggestions for individual projects

10. Choose a page of text from a book and record the number of letters per word (about 100 words is enough).

11. Use the same page of text and record the number of words per sentence.

12. Choose a completely different type of book from that used in question 10 and repeat questions 10 and 11.

13. Count the number of people per car passing a particular place in the evening rush hour.

14. Repeat question 13 at a different time of day.

15. From as many brochures as possible, find the cost of a two-week holiday in August to a particular place, say Miami.

16. Use either a daily newspaper, or your school weather station if you have one, to record the daily temperature in your area for a period of 30 days.

17. Use the class register to find the number of absences for each pupil in your class last term.

RANGE AND QUARTILES

One measure of the spread of data is the *range*. The range is the difference between the largest and the smallest value observed. Thus for the heights of the five-year-olds from one infant school, given on page 450, the range is $(118 - 92)\,\text{cm} = 26\,\text{cm}$. Note that the range would be unchanged even if one pupil were 92 cm tall, one 118 cm tall and all the others 100 cm tall. Therefore the range gives us very limited information.

Other indicators of the spread, or *dispersion*, of the observations may be found using a technique similar to that used for finding the median. Recall that half of the observed values are greater than the median and half are less.

If we can find a value that is greater than one-quarter of the observed values and a value that is less than one-quarter of the observed values, then we shall have a useful indication of the dispersion. These values are called *quartiles*. One-quarter of the observed values are less than the *lower quartile* and one-quarter of the observed values are greater than the *upper quartile*. The measure of the spread is called the *interquartile range*, which is the difference between the upper quartile and the lower quartile.

Taken together, the median, the quartiles and the interquartile range give us more detailed information about the frequency distribution than the median alone.

Exercise 28i

The following frequency distribution shows the heights of students in Form 3 of a school:

Height (cm)	Number of students
145	4
147	2
150	1
152	5
155	2
157	7
160	3
162	2
165	2
167	4

Total: 32

Find the range, median, lower quartile and upper quartile.

$$\text{Range} = (167 - 145)\,\text{cm} = 22\,\text{cm}$$
$$\text{Median} = 156\,\text{cm}$$
$$\text{Lower quartile} = 152\,\text{cm}$$
$$\text{Upper quartile} = 160\,\text{cm}$$
$$\text{Interquartile range} = \quad 8\,\text{cm}$$

1. Find the range, lower quartile, upper quartile, median and interquartile range for the following data:

   (a) 14, 14, 15, 15, 16, 16, 17, 17, 18, 19, 22, 24
   (b) 48, 49, 50, 55, 60, 62, 62, 62, 47
   (c) 14, 15, 15, 15, 17, 17, 27, 29

2. Twenty-seven pupils obtained the following marks in a mathematics test:

   44, 46, 44, 48, 40, 46, 42, 38, 34,
   46, 44, 40, 44, 40, 46, 50, 46, 42,
   42, 44, 48, 46, 44, 46, 42, 44, 42

   Find the upper and lower quartiles and the interquartile range.

3. Eighty-seven third-year pupils in a school were late during the term as shown in the distribution below:

No. of times late	0	1	2	3	4	5	6	7	8	9	10
No. of pupils	18	15	15	11	9	5	6	2	3	2	1

Find the upper quartile, lower quartile, and interquartile range for the distribution.

STANDARD DEVIATION

Another measure which gives a good indication of the dispersion of data is the *standard deviation*. The standard deviation is considered to be the most useful of the measures of dispersion.

At this stage we shall learn how to calculate the standard deviation, so as to be able to give results for our data in the form commonly used by statisticians and scientists.

Exercise 28j

Five dogs were found to have the following weights:

13 kg, 18 kg, 26 kg, 31 kg, 42 kg

Calculate the standard deviation.

Step 1 Calculate the mean, $\bar{x}$.

$$\bar{x} = \frac{13 + 18 + 26 + 31 + 42}{5}$$

$$= \frac{130}{5} = 26$$

Step 2 Find the *deviation* of each weight from the mean, i.e. the difference between each weight and the mean.

$$26-13, \quad 26-18, \quad 26-26, \quad 26-31, \quad 26-42$$

i.e.   13,   8,   0, -5, -16

Step 3 Square each deviation.

$$169, \quad 64, \quad 0, \quad 25, \quad 256$$

Step 4 Find the sum of the squared deviations.

$$169 + 64 + 0 + 25 + 256 = 514$$

Step 5 Find the mean of the squared deviations.

$$\frac{514}{5} = 102.8$$

Step 6 Find the standard deviation.

$$\sqrt{102.8} = 10.1$$

For the sake of convenience, the information for calculating the standard deviation is usually set out in tabular form as shown in the following example:

Calculate the mean and standard deviation of the scores obtained by ten students in a test:

75, 62, 52, 45, 43, 43, 42, 40, 40, 40

Scores, x	Frequency, f	fx	$x - \bar{x}$	$(x - \bar{x})^2$	$(x - \bar{x})^2 f$
75	1	75	26.8	718.24	718.24
62	1	62	13.8	190.44	190.44
52	1	52	3.8	14.44	14.44
45	1	45	−3.2	10.24	10.24
43	2	86	−5.2	27.04	54.08
42	1	42	−6.2	38.44	38.44
40	3	120	−8.2	67.24	201.72
Total	10	482			1227.60

$$\text{Mean, } \bar{x} = \frac{482}{10}$$
$$= 48.2$$

$$\text{Standard deviation, } s = \sqrt{\frac{1227.60}{10}}$$
$$= \sqrt{122.76}$$
$$= 11.1$$

When the data are grouped, the standard deviation may be calculated in the following way:

Consider the frequency table, given on page 452, for the weights of 100 people. Calculate the mean and standard deviation.

Weights, (kg)	Frequency, f	x	fx	$(x - \bar{x})^2$	$(x - \bar{x})^2 f$
50–59	15	54.5	817.5	278.89	4183.35
60–69	30	64.5	1935	44.89	1346.7
70–79	35	74.5	2607.5	10.89	381.15
80–89	15	84.5	1267.5	176.89	2653.35
90–99	3	94.5	283.5	542.89	1628.67
100–109	2	104.5	209	1108.89	2217.78
Totals:	100		7120		12411

$$\text{Mean, } \bar{x} = \frac{7120}{100}$$

$$= 71.2$$

$$\text{Standard deviation, } s = \sqrt{\frac{12\,411}{100}}$$

$$= \sqrt{124.11}$$

$$= 11.1$$

Calculate the standard deviation for the frequency distributions given in questions 1, 2, 3, 5, 6 and 7 of Exercise 28g, pages 466–7.

PROBABILITY

MUTUALLY EXCLUSIVE EVENTS

In Book 2 we calculated probabilities by considering possibility spaces.

When we calculated the probabilities for the events formed by several outcomes, we used a very important idea – the idea of *mutually exclusive events*. That is, if one of the events occurs, the others cannot occur. For example, if we toss two coins the outcome of a head on the first and a tail on the second excludes any other outcomes. In this case, we may calculate the probability of (H, T) and (T, H) separately and then find the probability of a head and a tail, in either order, by adding the two probabilities.

Consider the event of obtaining a 1 or a 2 from the roll of an ordinary six-faced die. The possible outcomes are 1, 2, 3, 4, 5, 6. Of these six outcomes, two are favourable – 1 or 2 on the die. Therefore the probability for the event is

$$\frac{2}{6} = \frac{1}{3}$$

Now the probability of 1 on the die is $\frac{1}{6}$, and the probability of 2 on the die is $\frac{1}{6}$.

We have

$$\frac{1}{6} + \frac{1}{6} = \frac{1}{3}$$

Therefore, the probability of obtaining 1 or 2 is equal to the *sum* of the probability of obtaining 2 alone and the probability of obtaining 1 alone.

We may find the probability of several events by adding the probabilities of the individual events *only* when the individual events are mutually exclusive.

What is the probability that a roll of two ordinary six-faced dice will give a total of 5, 7 or 9?

$$\text{The total number of outcomes} = 36$$

$$\text{The probability of a total of } 5 = \frac{4}{36}$$

$$\text{The probability of a total of } 7 = \frac{6}{36}$$

$$\text{The probability of a total of } 9 = \frac{4}{36}$$

These events are mutually exclusive, therefore the probability of 5, 7 or 9 is

$$\frac{4}{36} + \frac{6}{36} + \frac{4}{36} = \frac{14}{36} \qquad = \frac{7}{18}$$

INDEPENDENT EVENTS

An example of two *independent events* would be a head from the toss of a cent and a head from the toss of a quarter.

Let us consider one experiment, the toss of a cent resulting in a head, h; and a second experiment, the toss of a quarter resulting in a head, H.

For the toss of a cent we have two outcomes; head, h and tail, t. For the toss of a quarter we have two outcomes: head, H and tail, T.

If both coins are tossed simultaneously we have four outcomes:

hH, hT, tH, tT

From these results we see that for the toss of a cent, the probability of h is $\frac{1}{2}$; for the toss of a quarter, the probability of H is $\frac{1}{2}$.

When both coins are tossed simultaneously, the probability of hH is $\frac{1}{4}$.

In this case, the probability of two single events *both* occurring together is the *product* of each of the individual events.

In general, the probability of all of several events considered as one compound event is the product of the probability of each of the individual events, if the events are independent.

Exercise 28k

If a coin is tossed and an ordinary six-faced die is rolled, what is the probability of obtaining a head and a 3?

The two events are independent since they can occur separately.

The probability of a 3 in the roll of a die $= \dfrac{1}{6}$

The probability of a head in the toss of a coin $= \dfrac{1}{2}$

$\therefore$ the probability of a head and a 3 $= \dfrac{1}{2} \times \dfrac{1}{6}$

$= \dfrac{1}{12}$

1. A coin is tossed and a four-faced die is rolled:

   (a) What is the probability that a head and a number greater than 2 will occur?

   (b) What is the probability that a tail and a number less than or equal to 2 will occur?

   (c) What is the sum of these two probabilities?

   of what event, if any, is this result the probability?

2. A builder finds that 10% of the bolts he buys are too large and 5% are too small. What is the probability that a bolt selected at random will be either too large or too small?

3. An ordinary six-faced die is thrown twice. What is the probability that the sum of the faces that appears will be at least 3? If E_1 represents the event 'The sum of the faces that appear is greater than 8.', and E_2 represents the event 'The sum of the faces that appear is an even number greater than 6.', prove that E_1 and E_2 are independent events.

4. A machine produces nails. Of the nails produced at any time only 0.2 will be defective. It is known that the outcomes for successive nails are independent; what is the probability that two nails in a row are not defective?

5. Two brothers are in a group of eight people waiting to cross a river by boat which can only take two people at a time. If the boatman chooses first one, then another person at random, what is the probability that both brothers will be selected?

6. The failure rate in mathematics in a school is 20% and in science, 15%. The failure rate in both subjects is, however 10%. Are the events of failure in mathematics and in science independent? Justify your answer.

ARE GAMES ALWAYS FAIR?

Definition: A game is **fair** if each player has a fifty-fifty chance of winning, or if the probability of winning is $\frac{1}{2}$.

Try the following games:

Version 1
This is played by two people.
One person is called 'Even' and the other is called 'Odd'.
Each person writes down a number from 0 through 9, and hides the number.
Next show the numbers. If the sum of the two numbers is even, then Even wins. If the sum is odd, then Odd wins.
Play the game several times, and record wins by tally marks in the chart.
Is the game fair?
Argue your case

		Total wins
Even		
Odd		

Version 2
Repeat the game above, using the numbers 1 through 9 this time.
Is this version fair?
Who has the advantage?

Definition: The probability of winning is the number of favourable outcomes divided by the total number of possible outcomes.

Use the table on the right to find the **probability** that Odd will win.

From the table we have 81 possible outcomes.
How many of these have an odd sum?
What is the probability that Odd will win?

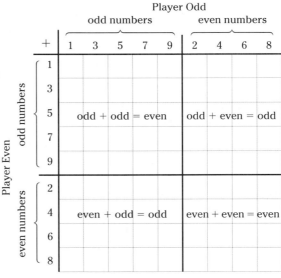

ADDITION TABLE

NUMBER BASES

At the end of the chapter you should be able to:

1. Use markers to represent groups of fives or powers of fives for a given number.
2. Write in figures the numbers represented by markers under the headings of five and powers of five.
3. Write, in headed columns, numbers to a given base.
4. Write, in base ten, numbers given in other bases.
5. Write a number given in base ten as a number to another given base.
6. Perform operations of addition, subtraction and multiplication in bases other than ten.
7. Determine the base in which given calculations have been done.

DENARY SYSTEM (BASE TEN)

We have ten fingers. This is probably why we started to count in tens and developed a system based on ten for recording large numbers. For example

$$3125 = 3 \text{ thousands} + 1 \text{ hundred} + 2 \text{ tens} + 5 \text{ units}$$
$$= \quad 3 \times 10^3 \quad + \quad 1 \times 10^2 \quad + 2 \times 10 + 5$$

Each column is ten times the value of its right-hand neighbour. The base of this number system is ten and it is called the *denary system*.

BASE FIVE

If man had started to count using just one hand, we would probably have a system based on five.

Suppose we had eleven stones. Using one hand to count with, we could arrange them like this:

i.e.   two handfuls + one
or   2   fives   + 1

The next logical step is to use a single marker to represent each group of five. We also need to place these markers so that they are not confused with the marker representing the one unit. We do this by having separate columns for the fives and the units, with the column for the fives to the left of the units.

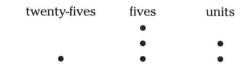

We can write this number as 21_5 and we call it 'two one to the base five'. We do *not* call it 'twenty-one to the base five', because the word 'twenty' means 'two tens'.

To cope with larger numbers, we can extend this system by adding further columns to the left such that each column is five times the value of its right-hand neighbour. Thus, in the column to the left of the fives column, each marker is worth twenty-five, or 5^2.

	twenty-fives	fives	units
		●	
For example		●	●
	●	●	●

The markers here represent 132_5 and it means

$$(1 \times 5^2) + (3 \times 5) + 2$$

Exercise 29a

Write in figures the numbers represented by the markers:

5^3	5^2	5	Units
	●		
	●		●
●	●		●

The number is 1302_5

(The '5' column is empty, so we write zero in this column.)

Write in figures the numbers represented by the markers in questions 1–4:

	5^4	5^3	5^2	5	Units
1.			●		●
			●	●	●
			●		●
2.					●
					●
		●			●
		●		●	●

5^4	5^3	5^2	5	Units
3. • • • •	•	• •	• • • •	
4. • • •		• •		•

Write 120_5 in headed columns.

5^2	5	Units
1	2	0

Write the following numbers in headed columns.

5. 31_5 **7.** 410_5 **9.** 34_5 **11.** 204_5

6. 42_5 **8.** 231_5 **10.** 10_5 **12.** 400_5

Write 203_5 as a number to the base 10

$$203_5 = (2 \times 5^2) + (0 \times 5) + 3$$
$$= 50_{10} \qquad + \qquad 3_{10}$$
$$= 53_{10}$$

(Although we do not normally write fifty-three as 53_{10}, it is sensible to do so when dealing with other bases as well.)

Write the following numbers as denary numbers, i.e. to base 10:

13. 31_5 **16.** 121_5 **19.** 32_5 **22.** 400_5

14. 24_5 **17.** 204_5 **20.** 20_5 **23.** 240_5

15. 40_5 **18.** 43_5 **21.** 4_5 **24.** 300_5

Write 38_{10} as a number to the base 5

(To write a number to the base 5 we have to find how many ... 125s, 25s, 5s and units the number contains.)

Method 1 (Starting with the highest value column.)
38 contains no 125s.

$$38 \div 25 = 1 \text{ remainder } 13 \quad \text{i.e. } 38 = 1 \times 5^2 + 13$$

$$13 \div 5 = 2 \text{ remainder } 3 \quad \text{i.e. } 13 = 2 \times 5 + 3$$

$$\therefore \quad 38 = 1 \times 5^2 + 2 \times 5 + 3$$

$$= 123_5$$

Method 2 (Starting with the units.)

$$
\begin{array}{r}
5\,)\,\underline{38} \\
5\,)\,\underline{\ 7} \\
5\,)\,\underline{\ 1} \\
0
\end{array}
$$

5) 38
5) 7   remainder 3 (units)
5) 1   remainder 2 (fives)
   0   remainder 1 (twenty-fives)

$$\therefore \qquad\qquad 38 = 123_5$$

Write the following numbers in base 5:

25. 8_{10} **28.** 39_{10} **31.** 7_{10} **34.** 128_{10}

26. 13_{10} **29.** 43_{10} **32.** 21_{10} **35.** 82_{10}

27. 10_{10} **30.** 150_{10} **33.** 30_{10} **36.** 100_{10}

OTHER BASES

Any number can be used as a base for a number system.

If the base is 6, we write the number in columns such that each column is 6 times the value of its right-hand neighbour. For example, writing 253_6 in headed columns gives

6^2	6	Units
2	5	3

We see that 253_6 means $(2 \times 6^2) + (5 \times 6) + 3$

Similarly 1011_2 means $(1 \times 2^3) + (0 \times 2^2) + (1 \times 2) + 1$

Exercise 29b

Write 425_7 in headed columns and then write it as a denary number.

7^2	7	Units
4	2	5

$$\therefore \quad 425_7 = (4 \times 7^2) + (2 \times 7) + 5$$
$$= 196_{10} + 14_{10} + 5_{10}$$
$$= 215_{10}$$

Write the following numbers

(a) in headed columns

(b) as denary numbers

1. 23_4 **5.** 57_8 **9.** 21_3 **13.** 303_4

2. 15_7 **6.** 204_5 **10.** 18_9 **14.** 1001_2

3. 131_4 **7.** 210_3 **11.** 24_6 **15.** 1211_3

4. 101_2 **8.** 574_9 **12.** 175_8 **16.** 1000_6

Write 29_{10} as a number

(a) to the base 9

(b) to the base 2

(a)
```
9)29
9) 3   r.   2 (units)
   0   r.   3 (nines)
```
$\therefore \quad 29_{10} = 32_9$

(b)
```
2)29
2)14   r.   1 (unit)
2) 7   r.   0 (twos)
2) 3   r.   1 (2²)
2) 1   r.   1 (2³)
   0   r.   1 (2⁴)
```
$\therefore \quad 29_{10} = 11101_2$

Write the following denary numbers to the base indicated in brackets:

17. 9 (4)   **21.** 13 (5)   **25.** 8 (3)

18. 12 (5)   **22.** 32 (6)   **26.** 15 (6)

19. 24 (7)   **23.** 53 (8)   **27.** 34 (9)

20. 7 (2)   **24.** 49 (7)   **28.** 28 (3)

29. 56 (7)   **33.** 163 (8)   **37.** 43 (6)

30. 89 (9)   **34.** 640 (4)   **38.** 55 (5)

31. 45 (2)   **35.** 142 (2)   **39.** 99 (2)

32. 333 (3)   **36.** 158 (6)   **40.** 394 (7)

Express each of the following numbers as a number to the base indicated in brackets:

41. 45_6 (4)   **44.** 432_5 (3)   **47.** 11011_2 (8)

42. 23_4 (6)   **45.** 562_8 (4)   **48.** 378_9 (3)

43. 17_8 (2)   **46.** 2120_3 (5)   **49.** 3020_4 (8)

ADDITION, SUBTRACTION AND MULTIPLICATION

Numbers with a base other than 10 do not need to be converted to base 10; provided that they have the same base they can be added, subtracted and multiplied in the usual way, as long as we remember which base we are working with.

For example, to find $132_5 + 44_5$ we work in fives, not tens. To aid memory, the numbers can be written in headed columns:

Twenty-fives	Fives	Units	
1	3	2	
⑦	4 ⑦	4	+
2	3	1	
	⑧	⑥	

Adding the units gives 6 units:

$$6 \text{ (units)} = 1 \text{ (five)} + 1 \text{ (unit)}$$

We put 1 in the units column and carry the single five to the fives column.

Adding the fives gives 8 fives

$$8\,(\text{fives}) = 5\,(\text{fives}) \qquad + 3\,(\text{fives})$$
$$= 1\,(\text{twenty-five}) \quad + 3\,(\text{fives})$$

We put 3 in the fives column and carry the 1 to the next column.

Adding the numbers in the last column gives 2,

i.e. $\qquad 132_5 + 44_5 = 231_5$

If the numbers are not to the same base we cannot add them in this way.

For example, 432_7 and 621_8 cannot be added directly.

Exercise 29c

Find $174_8 + 654_8$

8^3	8^2	8	Units	
	1	7	4	
①	6 ①	5 ①	4	+
1	0	5	0	
	⑧	⑬	⑧	

$\therefore \qquad 174_8 + 654_8 = 1050_8$

Find:

1. $12_5 + 31_5$

2. $11_3 + 2_3$

3. $11_4 + 13_4$

4. $10_2 + 1_2$

5. $24_6 + 35_6$

6. $21_3 + 11_3$

7. $43_8 + 52_8$

8. $101_2 + 11_2$

9. $43_5 + 24_5$

10. $132_4 + 201_4$

11. $345_6 + 402_6$

12. $1101_2 + 111_2$

13. $122_3 + 101_3$

14. $231_4 + 103_4$

15. $635_7 + 62_7$

16. $10\,010_2 + 1111_2$

Find $132_4 - 13_4$

(There are two methods of doing subtraction and we show both of them here.)

First method

4^2	4	Unit	
1	$\overset{②}{\cancel{3}}$	$\overset{⑥}{\cancel{2}}$	
	1	3	—
1	1	3	

(We cannot take 3 from 2 so we take one 4 from the fours' column, change it to 4 units and add it to the 2 units.)

Second method
If you use the 'pay back' method of subtraction, the calculation looks like this:

4^2	4	Unit
1	3	$2^{⑥}$
	$1_{⑦}$	3
1	1	3

In either case $132_4 - 13_4 = 113_4$

Find:

17. $153_6 - 24_6$ **21.** $210_3 - 1_3$ **25.** $231_4 - 32_4$ **29.** $144_6 - 53_6$

18. $110_3 - 2_3$ **22.** $305_5 - 14_5$ **26.** $153_7 - 64_7$ **30.** $1010_2 - 101_2$

19. $32_4 - 23_4$ **23.** $253_8 - 25_8$ **27.** $205_6 - 132_6$ **31.** $724_8 - 56_8$

20. $52_7 - 14_7$ **24.** $10_2 - 1_2$ **28.** $100_2 - 10_2$ **32.** $120_3 - 12_3$

Find $352_6 \times 4_6$

6^3	6^2	6	Units
	3	5	2
			4
②	③	①	
2	3	3	2
	⑮	㉑	⑧

$\therefore$ $352_6 \times 4_6 = 2332_6$

Find:

33. $4_5 \times 3_5$ **37.** $5_6 \times 4_6$ **41.** $132_4 \times 2_4$

34. $2_4 \times 3_4$ **38.** $13_5 \times 2_5$ **42.** $501_6 \times 5_6$

35. $12_3 \times 2_3$ **39.** $24_7 \times 3_7$ **43.** $202_3 \times 2_3$

36. $20_4 \times 3_4$ **40.** $56_9 \times 3_9$ **44.** $241_5 \times 2_5$

Find:

45. $261_7 + 123_7$

46. $32_4 \times 2_4$

47. $434_5 - 142_5$

48. $36_7 \times 2_7$

49. $451_6 + 124_6$

50. $232_4 - 103_4$

51. $22_5 \times 4_5$

52. $365_8 + 173_8$

53. $121_3 - 112_3$

54. $34_8 \times 5_8$

HARDER EXAMPLES

Exercise 29d

Find:

1. $123_4 \times 23_4$

2. $413_5 \times 24_5$

3. $1001_2 \times 1101_2$

4. $73_8 \times 26_8$

5. $2120_3 \times 212_3$

6. $46_8 \times 35_8$

7. $234_5 \times 423_5$

8. $452_7 \times 324_7$

9. (a) Find $64_8 \times 27_8$ as a number to the base 8.

(b) Express 64_8 and 27_8 as denary numbers.

(c) Multiply together your two answers for (b).

(d) Change your answer to (c) into a number to the base 8. Does this answer agree with your answer to (a)?

10. (a) Find $476_9 \times 57_9$ as a number to the base 9.

(b) Express 476_9 and 57_9 as denary numbers.

(c) Multiply together your two answers for (b).

(d) Change your answer to (c) into a number to the base 9. Does this answer agree with your answer to (a)?

11. Find $55_8 \times 43_8$ and use the process described in questions 9 and 10 as a check on your working.

12. Choose a base and make up a long multiplication question of your own. Check your calculation using the process above.

BINARY NUMBERS

Numbers with a base of two are called *binary numbers*. We have singled binary numbers out for special attention because of the wide application that they have, especially in the world of computers.

Exercise 29e

1. (a) Convert 7_{10}, 5_{10}, 10_{10}, 16_{10}, 19_{10}, 24_{10}, into binary numbers.

   (b) How many symbols are needed to represent all binary numbers?

   (c) Write each of the denary numbers 1 to 20 as binary numbers.

   (d) How can you see when a binary number is even?

   (e) How can you see when a binary number is odd?

2. If you have access to a microcomputer and have done some programming using machine code, or have copied program listings from magazines, you will have seen instructions such as

   BIN 1101, 1011, 11001, 100, 1100, 11101

   'BIN' means 'binary'.
   Convert the binary numbers given above to denary numbers.

3. Basically, computers are very simple; their fundamental computing parts can only be off (0) or on (1), i.e. computers count in binary numbers.

   (a) Complete the following addition table for binary numbers.

+	0	1
0		
1		

   (b) Find $1011011_2 + 110101_2$.

4. (a) Subtract 23_{10} as many times as you can from 138_{10}. Hence write down the value of $138_{10} \div 23_{10}$.

   (b) Subtract 11_2 from 1111_2 as many times as you can.
   Hence find $1111_2 \div 11_2$.

5. Complete the following multiplication table for binary numbers.

+	0	1
0		
1		

MIXED PROBLEMS

Exercise 29f

1. Convert the following denary numbers to base 3 numbers:

   (a) 5   (c) 12
   (b) 8   (d) 31

2. How many different symbols are needed to represent all numbers in base three?

3. Make up a multiplication table for base three numbers.

4. Use repeated subtraction to find the value of $1111_3 \div 101_3$.

5. Convert the following denary numbers to base 5 numbers:

   (a) 27   (b) 18   (c) 153

6. What do you think 31.2_5 could mean?

7. If a number to the base 10 ends in 0, what does the same number to the base 5 end in?

8. Is it possible to write a number in base one?

9. How many digits are there in 5^3 written in base 5?

10. How many digits are there in 3^7 written in base 3?

11. (a) Convert $10_2, 10_3, 10_4, 10_5, 10_6, 10_7, 10_8$ into denary numbers.
    (b) Find (i) $1101_2 \times 10_2$ (ii) $121_3 \times 10_3$ (iii) $175_8 \times 10_8$
    (c) What is the effect of multiplying a number by the base number?

Find the base in which the following calculation has been done: $13 + 5 = 22$

$$
\begin{array}{r}
13 \\
\textcircled{\scriptsize 7}\ 5\ + \\
\hline
22 \\
\hline
\textcircled{\scriptsize 8}
\end{array}
$$

From the addition, $5 + 3 = 8$. To leave 2 in the units column, 6 units have been carried to the next column. The total in the next column is 2, so the 6 units have been carried as 1 to the next column.

∴ the base is 6

Find the bases in which the following calculations have been done.

12. $15 + 23 = 42$

13. $12 + 13 = 31$

14. $110 + 121 = 1001$

15. $134 + 213 = 350$

16. $13 - 4 = 4$

17. $21 - 2 = 17$

18. $13 \times 2 = 31$

19. $21 \times 3 = 103$

20. Is the following statement true or false?
    A number written to any base is even if it ends in zero.

MIXED EXERCISE

Exercise 29g

1. Write the following numbers as denary numbers

   (a) 12_4 (b) 101_2 (c) 403_6

2. Write the denary number 20 as a number to the base

   (a) 5   (b) 3   (c) 8

3. Find:

(a) $204_5 + 132_5$

(b) $110_3 - 2_3$

(c) $212_8 \times 3_8$

4. There are four possible answers given below to the calculation $213_4 \times 2_4$. Only one answer is correct. Which one is it?

(a) 426_4　　　　(c) 1032_4

(b) 2130_4　　　(d) 221_4

MATHS IS OUT THERE

The JIBARO Indians of the Amazon rain forest express the number 'five' by the phrase 'wehe amukei', meaning 'I have finished one hand', and the number 'ten' by 'mai wehe amukei' meaning 'I have finished both hands'.

'mai wehe amukei'

30 ▶ EARTH GEOMETRY

At the end of the chapter you should be able to:

1. Define great circles and parallels of latitude for the Earth.
2. Identify a parallel of latitude given its latitude north or south of the Equator.
3. Identify meridians given their longitude west or east of the prime meridian.
4. Locate a point on the Earth, given its latitude and longitude.
5. Define a nautical mile in terms of arc length of a great circle and angle subtended at the centre of the Earth.
6. Calculate, in nautical miles, the distance between two points on the same meridian.
7. Calculate the radius of a circle of given latitude.
8. Calculate the distance between two points neither on the Equator nor on the same meridian, but on the same circle of latitude.

We will consider the Earth to be a sphere.

TERMINOLOGY

The Earth rotates about a diameter, called its *axis*, whose end points are the *North Pole* and the *South Pole*.

Any plane intersects the Earth's surface in a circle. Any plane through the centre of the Earth intersects the Earth in a *great circle*. The *Equator* is the great circle halfway between the poles.

A great circle through the poles is called a *meridian* or *line of longitude*. Circles parallel to the Equator are called *parallels of latitude*. A meridian of longitude is the path of a ship travelling due north or south and a parallel of latitude is the path of a ship travelling due east or west.

The terms above are illustrated in the following diagram. N and S are the North and South Poles, AB is the Equator, O is the centre of the Earth, NES is a meridian circle, and CD is a parallel of latitude.

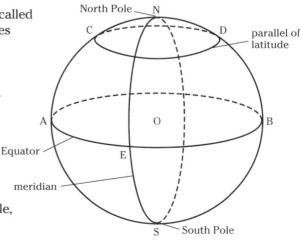

LATITUDE OF A POINT

In the diagram, Q is a point on the surface of the Earth, R is a point where the meridian circle through Q meets the Equator, and O is the centre of the Earth. The angle QOR is called the *latitude* of Q. The angle TOR, where T is another point on the same meridian circle, is called the latitude of T.

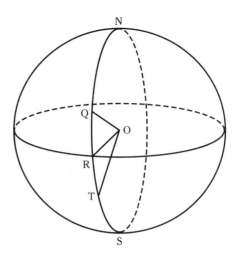

We distinguish between Q and T by giving their positions as north or south of the Equator. If the angles QOR and TOR each measure 30°, we say that the latitude of Q is 30° *north* and the latitude of T is 30° *south*.

The latitude of the North Pole is 90° north, and the latitude of the South Pole is 90° south.

LONGITUDE OF A POINT

The North and South Poles divide each meridian circle into two parts called *meridians*. The meridian passing through Greenwich, England, is used as a reference for measuring longitude, and is called the *prime meridian*.

Consider the point A in the figure. The parallel of latitude through A meets the prime meridian in some point B. If the centre of this parallel of latitude is C, then ACB is called the *longitude* of A. Any other point, A′, on the same meridian as A would have the same longitude as A, since

$$A'\widehat{C}'B' = A\widehat{C}B$$

To distinguish positions west of the prime meridian from those east of the meridian, the former are said to have *west longitude* and the latter *east longitude*. The angle of longitude must not exceed 180°. For example, if in the figure $A\widehat{C}B$ and $B\widehat{C}D$ are each 60°, we say that the longitude of A is 60° *west* and that of D is 60° *east*.

Each point on the Earth's surface therefore has a latitude and a longitude. The point can be located when both its latitude and longitude are given. For example, there is a place in St Lucia which has a latitude of 14° north and longitude 61° west.

NAUTICAL MILE

The fundamental unit of distance used in navigation is the *nautical mile*. It is the length of an arc of a great circle which subtends an angle of 1 minute at the centre of the Earth.

A ship travelling $3°$ along the Equator covers 180 nautical miles, since $3° = 180$ minutes ($1° = 60$ minutes). As a ship moves along a meridian its latitude changes. Hence, the number of nautical miles travelled in moving along a meridian is equal to the number of minutes by which the latitude has changed.

Two places A and B have north latitude $30°$ and $35°$, respectively, and lie on the same meridian. How many nautical miles will a ship travel in going from A to B along the meridian?

Change in latitude in travelling from A to B $= 5°$

∴   Number of nautical miles travelled $= 5 \times 60$

$\qquad\qquad\qquad\qquad\qquad\qquad = 300$ nautical miles

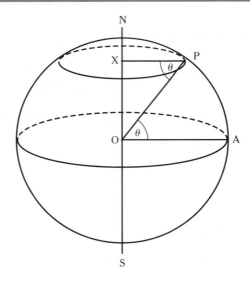

RADIUS OF A CIRCLE OF LATITUDE

Consider a point P on a circle of latitude θ as shown in the diagram above. Let O be the centre of the Earth and OA a radius of the Equator.

If X is the centre of the parallel of latitude on which P lies, then XP is parallel to OA and

$\qquad X\hat{P}O = P\hat{O}A = \theta$

From the triangle XPO

$$\frac{XP}{OP} = \cos \theta$$

$\therefore$ $\qquad$ $XP = OP \cos \theta$

$$= R \cos \theta$$

where R is the radius of the Earth.

Thus, if r is the radius of a circle of latitude, then

$$r = R \cos \theta$$

In an earlier section we calculated, in nautical miles, the distance between two places which were on the same meridian. We will now consider two places which are neither on the same meridian nor on the Equator but are, however, on the same circle of latitude.

By definition, 1 nautical mile is the length of an arc of a great circle which subtends an angle of 1 minute at the centre of the Earth. Let R be the radius of the Earth. Then the length of an arc of a circle of radius R which subtends an angle of 1 minute, or $\frac{1^\circ}{60}$, is given by

$$\frac{2\pi R}{360} \times \frac{1}{60} = 1 \text{ nautical mile}$$

To find the distance d, in nautical miles, between two places on a circle of latitude θ°, whose difference in longitude is m minutes:

$$m \text{ minutes} = \frac{m}{60} \text{ degrees}$$

The radius r of a circle of latitude θ° is given by

$$r = R \cos \theta$$

As $\qquad$ $d = \dfrac{2\pi r}{360} \times \dfrac{m}{60}$

$$= \frac{2\pi R \cos \theta}{360} \times \frac{m}{60}$$

$$= \frac{2\pi R}{360} \times \frac{1}{60} \times m \cos \theta$$

But $\qquad$ $1 \text{ nautical mile} = \dfrac{2\pi R}{360} \times \dfrac{1}{60}$

$\therefore$ $\qquad\qquad\qquad$ $d = m \cos \theta \text{ nautical miles}$

Exercise 30a

A ship sets out from a place which has latitude 42° north and longitude 71° west, and sails due east to a place with latitude 42° north and longitude 68° west.

Calculate the distance travelled by the ship in (a) nautical miles (b) kilometres. (Take the radius of the Earth to be 6380 km.)

The ship travels along the circle of latitude 42° north through a difference of longitude of

$$71° - 68° = 3° \quad \text{(or 180 minutes)}$$

(a) $$d = m \cos \theta$$

$$\therefore \qquad \text{Distance in nautical miles} = 180 \cos 42°$$
$$= 180 \times 0.7431$$
$$= 133.8 \text{ nautical miles}$$

(b) If r is the radius of circle of latitude 42°

$$r = R \cos 42°$$
$$= 6380 \cos 42°$$

The distance travelled (km) is the length of arc of the circle of latitude 42° which subtends an angle of 3° centre of circle:

$$\text{Distance in kilometres} = 2\pi r \times \frac{3}{360}$$
$$= 2\pi\, 6380 \cos 42° \times \frac{3}{360} \text{ km}$$
$$= \frac{6380\pi \cos 42°}{60} \text{ km}$$
$$= 248 \text{ km}$$

1. How many nautical miles separate two points on the meridian of 70° west, whose latitude differ by 15°?

2. Calculate the distance in nautical miles between P, with latitude 60° north longitude 75° east, and Q, with latitude 60° north and longitude 80° east.

3. A ship travels 240 nautical miles due south from a point with latitude 40° north, longitude 60° east. Find its new position.

4. (a) An aircraft flies from a point P (65°N, 30°W) directly to the North Pole, N. Calculate the distance PN in nautical miles.

   (b) The aircraft flies from N to Q where NQ = 2PN. Find the latitude and longitude of Q.

   (c) A second aircraft flies due east from P to a point R (65°N, 20°E). Calculate in nautical miles the distance it travels.

5. Taking the radius of the Earth as 6400 km and π as 3.14, calculate

   (a) the circumference of the parallel of latitude 75° north

   (b) the shortest distance from the North Pole to a place with latitude 65° north.

6. Calculate the longitude of a point B which is 660 nautical miles due east of a point A (30°N, 10°E).

7. Calculate the distance between two places with positions (15°N, 120°W) and (15°N, 60°W) measured.

   (a) in nautical miles along a parallel of latitude

   (b) in kilometres along the great circle route through the North Pole.

   Take π to be 3.14 and the radius of the Earth to be 6400 km.

8. Two aeroplanes set out from a place whose position is 10°N, 50°W.
   One flies due north for 450 nautical miles, then turns due west and flies a distance of 450 nautical miles.
   The other flies due west for 450 nautical miles, and then turns due north and flies for 450 nautical miles.
   Find the final position of each aeroplane.

REVIEW TEST 3: CHAPTERS 23–30

In questions 1–10 choose the letter for the correct answer.

1. 442 acres of a plantation include 120 acres of vegetables. The rest is divided between citrus and bananas in the ratio $5:2$. How many acres are planted with bananas?

   (A) 48   (B) 60   (C) 92   (D) 161

2. Which of the three sets of numbers are measures of the sides of a right angled triangle?

   (i) $\{6, 8, 10\}$ (ii) $\{5, 12, 13\}$ (iii) $\{2, 3, 4\}$

   (A) i and ii only   (B) ii and iii only   (C) i and iii only   (D) i, ii and iii

3. Which of the following cannot be the value of the sine of an angle?

   (i) 0.235   (ii) -0.156 (iii) 1.32

   (A) ii only   (B) iii only   (C) i and ii only   (D) ii and iii only

4. From the top of a building 20 metres high the angle of depression of a point is 50 degrees. The distance of the point from the foot of the building is

   (A) $\dfrac{20}{\tan 50°}$ (B) $20\tan 50°$ (C) $20\cos 50°$ (D) $\dfrac{20}{\cos 50°}$

5. From a deck of 52 cards one card is drawn. What is the probability that the card is either a queen or a six?

   (A) $\frac{4}{52}$ (B) $\frac{6}{52}$ (C) $\frac{8}{52}$ (D) $\frac{12}{52}$

6.

Scores	40	50	60	70	80	90
Frequency	6	5	5	10	3	2

   In the above distribution the median score is

   (A) 60   (B) 65   (C) 70   (D) 80

7. The binary number 1101 is equivalent to the decimal number

   (A) 3   (B) 5   (C) 13   (D) 26

8. What is the distance in nautical miles, between two places at $(30°\,N, 40°\,W)$ and $(30°\,N, 45°\,W)$ measured along a parallel of latitude?

   (A) 5 cos 30°   (B) 85 cos 30°   (C) 85 cos 60°   (D) 300 cos 30°

9. The third quartile is also called the 75th percentile. For a set of scores, 60 is the score for the 75th percentile. Which statement is true?

   (A) Sixty scores are at or below 75
   (B) Seventy-five scores are at or below 60
   (C) Seventy-five per cent of the scores are at or below 60
   (D) Sixty per cent of the scores are at or below 75

10. The bearing of P from Q is 30°. What is the bearing of Q from P?

    (A) 60°   (B) 150°   (C) 210°   (D) 330°

11. A ship starts from X in latitude $50.6°\,N$ and sails due North for 1740 kilometres to Y. Taking π to be 3.142 and the radius of the Earth to be 6400 kilometres, calculate the latitude of Y.

12. ABC is a triangle whose base $BC = 17.5\,cm$. The point X on BC is such that $BX = 10.5\,cm$, $AX = 8\,cm$ and $A\hat{X}B = 60°$. Calculate   (i) AB   (ii) AC   (iii) $B\hat{A}C$

13.

Runs scored	Frequency
1–10	4
11–20	11
21–30	6
31–40	5
41–50	2

   The table above shows the distribution of runs scored by a batsman in 28 innings.

   (a) Draw a histogram for the data.
   (b) Calculate the mean score.
   (c) Which interval contains the median?
   (d) If one of the innings is chosen at random, what is the probability that the score is greater than the mean?

14. (a) John, James and Mary invest $2000, $2500 and $3500 respectively in a business. If the year's profits of $16 000 are divided proportionally, how much does each receive?

    (b) In 1992 a house was rated at $800 and the rate was $0.90 in the dollar. How much was paid in rates?

       In 1993 the rating was increased by 5 per cent and the rate per dollar reduced by 6 per cent. Calculate the change in the amount paid in rates, to the nearest cent.

15. (a) Evaluate, giving your answer in binary form, $1101_2 + 111_2$
    (b) MINT is a rectangle in which $TM = 6\,cm$, $TN = 14\,cm$. Points K and P are on TN and MI such that TKPM is a square. Calculate PN.

MATHS IS OUT THERE

Having completed this series you are now on your way to becoming involved in more advanced mathematics. You may even become a computer expert. Here are some ways to spot a computer expert:

1. They talk a lot about 'hardware' without being able to tell the difference between a gasket and a hexagonal lug nut.

2. The person claims to know several 'languages'.

3. He or she often uses the expression 'garbage in garbage out', even when not eating in the cafeteria.

4. When playing cards he or she becomes very nervous whenever anyone says 'shuffle the deck'.

5. He or she spells 'cat' and 'square root' as 'KAT' and 'SQRT'.

6. If you tell him or her that you ruptured a 'disk', he or she will ask 'what was stored on it?'.

ST(P) CARIBBEAN MATHEMATICS 3
Answers

ANSWERS

CHAPTER 1

Exercise 1a   page 1
1. 2, 3, 5, 7
2. 2, 3, 5, 7
3. 11, 13, 17, 19
4. 2, 3, 5, 7
5. 5, 7, 11, 13
6. 13, 17
7. 23
8. no

Exercise 1b   page 2
1. (a) yes   (c) yes   (e) yes
   (b) no   (d) no
2. If a number is even then 2 is a factor
3. (a) no   (c) yes   (e) no
   (b) yes   (d) yes   (f) yes
4. If a number ends in 0 or 5 then 5 is a factor
5. (a) 8, 16, 40, 206   (b) 40, 35, 515
6. (a) yes   (c) no   (e) no
   (b) yes   (d) yes
7. 6, yes
8. (a) 12, yes   (b) 3, yes

Exercise 1c   page 2
1. 1, 2, 3, 6
2. 1, 2, 4, 8
3. 1, 2, 5, 10
4. 1, 2, 4
5. 1, 3, 9
6. 1, 2, 3, 6, 9, 18
7. 1, 3, 5, 15
8. 1, 2, 4, 8, 16
9. 1, 3, 7, 21
10. 1, 2, 13, 26
11. 1, 3, 17, 51
12. 1, 19

Exercise 1d   page 3
1. 2×5
2. 3×7
3. 5×7
4. $2 \times 2 \times 3$
5. $2 \times 2 \times 2$
6. $2 \times 2 \times 7$
7. $2 \times 2 \times 3 \times 5$
8. $2 \times 5 \times 5$
9. $2 \times 2 \times 3 \times 3$
10. $2 \times 3 \times 11$
11. $2 \times 3 \times 3 \times 7$
12. $2 \times 2 \times 3 \times 3 \times 3$

Exercise 1e   page 4
1. (a) 2, 6, 8, 10, 12, 14, 16, 18, 20
   (b) 3, 6, 12, 15, 18
   (c) 8, 12, 16, 20
   (d) 5, 10, 15, 20
   (e) 6, 12, 18
   (f) 8, 16
2. (a) 7, 14, 21, 28   (d) 10, 20, 30, 40
   (b) 5, 10, 15, 20   (e) 12, 24, 36, 48
   (c) 8, 16, 24, 32   (f) 15, 30, 45, 60
3. 54, 63, 72, 81, 90, 99
4. 14, 21, 28, 35, 42, 49
5. 11, 22, 33, 44, 55, 66, 77, 88, 99

Exercise 1f   page 4
1. 4, 9
2. 16, 25, 36, 49, 64, 81, 100

3. 4, 16
4. 4, 16, 64
5. 9, 81
6. $6 = 2 \times 3$; $8 = 2 \times 2 \times 2$; $25 = 5 \times 5$;
   $64 = 2 \times 2 \times 2 \times 2 \times 2 \times 2$; $81 = 3 \times 3 \times 3 \times 3$;
   $125 = 5 \times 5 \times 5$. 8, 64, 125

Exercise 1g   page 5
1. 24
2. 30
3. 40
4. 28
5. 30
6. 60
7. 36
8. 42
9. 60
10. 96
11. 105
12. 120

Exercise 1h   page 5
1. 4
2. 6
3. 6
4. 11
5. 13
6. 7
7. 1
8. 12
9. 10
10. 10
11. 13
12. 1
13. 5
14. 16
15. 6
16. 5
17. 8
18. 9
19. 4
20. 9
21. 8
22. 7
23. 17
24. 13

Exercise 1i   page 6
1. (a) 2, 5, 41   (d) 2, 12, 18, 36
   (b) 1, 5, 9, 21, 39, 41   (e) 9, 12, 18, 21, 36, 39
   (c) 2, 12, 18, 36   (f) 1, 2, 9, 12, 18, 36
2. (a) 2   (b) 5   (c) 4
3. (a) 6   (b) 20   (c) 12
4. (a) 24   (b) 14   (c) 11
5. (a) 6   (b) 11   (c) 5
6. (a) 6   (b) 3, 5   (c) 72   (d) 72
7. (a) 12   (b) 3, 5   (c) 180   (d) 180

Exercise 1j   page 6
1. (a) 5, 15, 21, 23, 27, 29
   (b) 5, 15, 20
   (c) 4, 5, 8, 20
   (d) 5, 23, 29
   (e) 4, 6, 8, 12, 20
   (f) 4, 8, 12, 20
2. (a) 48   (b) 8   (c) 8
3. (a) 2   (b) 5   (c) 72

Exercise 1k   page 6
1. C   2. D   3. A   4. A   5. B

CHAPTER 2

Exercise 2a   page 9
1. 21
2. 18
3. 40
4. 12
5. 6
6. 20
7. 12
8. 60
9. 42
10. 18
11. 24
12. 72
13. $1\frac{13}{24}$
14. $\frac{9}{10}$
15. $1\frac{29}{40}$

16. 1
17. $1\frac{17}{48}$
18. $1\frac{11}{12}$
19. $\frac{8}{9}$
20. $1\frac{3}{4}$
21. $2\frac{1}{5}$
22. $\frac{71}{126}$
23. $1\frac{13}{24}$

24. $1\frac{23}{42}$
25. $\frac{13}{36}$
26. $\frac{1}{36}$
27. $\frac{7}{30}$
28. $\frac{1}{20}$
29. $\frac{1}{40}$
30. $\frac{5}{18}$
31. $3\frac{29}{40}$

32. $\frac{7}{18}$
33. $-\frac{9}{40}$
34. $3\frac{11}{12}$
35. $4\frac{7}{8}$
36. $\frac{17}{20}$
37. $4\frac{2}{15}$
38. $\frac{1}{8}$
39. $1\frac{1}{12}$

Exercise 2b   page 11
1. $\frac{5}{9}$
2. $1\frac{1}{3}$
3. $1\frac{1}{2}$
4. $\frac{1}{10}$
5. $\frac{10}{21}$
6. $\frac{3}{10}$
7. $\frac{4}{7}$
8. 6
9. $\frac{7}{22}$
10. 2
11. 3
12. 3
13. $\frac{3}{2}$
14. $\frac{4}{3}$
15. $\frac{8}{7}$

Exercise 2c   page 12
1. $\frac{1}{4}$
2. 2
3. $\frac{5}{2}$
4. $\frac{1}{10}$
5. 8
6. $\frac{11}{3}$
7. $\frac{1}{100}$
8. $\frac{9}{2}$
9. $\frac{4}{15}$
10. $1\frac{1}{3}$
11. 2
12. $\frac{5}{8}$
13. $6\frac{1}{4}$
14. $\frac{14}{81}$
15. $\frac{2}{3}$
16. $\frac{12}{49}$
17. $\frac{1}{18}$
18. $4\frac{1}{2}$
19. $\frac{13}{30}$
20. $\frac{69}{112}$
21. $\frac{8}{25}$
22. $2\frac{1}{18}$
23. $5\frac{3}{10}$
24. $\frac{57}{110}$
25. $4\frac{23}{42}$
26. $\frac{7}{20}$
27. $-\frac{1}{2}$
28. $3\frac{7}{12}$
29. $3\frac{3}{140}$
30. $\frac{2}{5}$
31. $\frac{22}{63}$
32. 14
33. 7
34. $\frac{9}{50}$
35. $1\frac{2}{25}$
36. $\frac{1}{14}$
37. $\frac{21}{68}$
38. $1\frac{1}{4}$
39. 2

Exercise 2d   page 14
1. $\frac{7}{20}$
2. $\frac{27}{125}$
3. $\frac{51}{250}$
4. $1\frac{9}{25}$
5. $\frac{3}{100}$
6. $\frac{3}{250}$
7. $\frac{1}{200}$
8. $1\frac{1}{100}$
9. $\frac{11}{100}$
10. $2\frac{1}{20}$
11. $1\frac{13}{125}$
12. $\frac{1}{10\,000}$
13. 0.15
14. 0.125
15. 0.6
16. 0.24
17. 0.0625
18. 0.54
19. 1.75
20. 0.156 25
21. 0.16
22. 0.3125
23. 2.375
24. 0.002

Exercise 2e   page 15
1. $0.\dot{3}$
2. $0.\dot{2}$
3. $0.8\dot{3}$
4. $0.0\dot{6}$
5. $0.\dot{1}42857\dot{7}$
6. $0.08\dot{3}$
7. $0.0\dot{9}$
8. 0.05
9. $0.41\dot{6}$
10. $0.0\dot{7}1428\dot{5}$
11. $0.2\dot{3}$
12. $0.\dot{0}7692\dot{3}$

Exercise 2f   page 16
1. 5.01
2. 19.1
3. 6.17
4. 8.8
5. 1.82
6. 26.36
7. 4.832
8. 1.106
9. 0.002 02
10. 3.2
11. 3.3
12. 0.08
13. 1.21
14. 0.49
15. 23.02

16. 0.361
17. 1.83
18. 0.0068
19. 0.96
20. 0.042
21. 0.008
22. 0.01
23. 0.25
24. 0.360 72
25. 3.36
26. 3.355 11
27. 0.000 384
28. 7
29. 0.3
30. 2.7
31. 0.008
32. 0.015
33. 5.9
34. 1
35. 0.02
36. 0.001
37. 0.6
38. 7.8
39. 0.5
40. 129
41. 11.882
42. 3.094
43. 1
44. 2
45. 1.69
46. 0.2
47. 0.4
48. 8.95

Exercise 2g   page 17
1. <
2. >
3. <
4. <
5. >
6. >
7. >
8. >
9. >
10. $0.6, \frac{2}{3}, \frac{4}{5}$
11. $0.79, \frac{4}{5}, 0.85$
12. $\frac{1}{5}, \frac{2}{7}, 0.3$
13. $\frac{5}{7}, 0.75, \frac{7}{9}, 0.875$
14. $\frac{3}{20}, 0.16, 0.2, \frac{6}{25}$
15. $1\frac{1}{8}, 1\frac{1}{5}, 1.24, 1.3$

Exercise 2h   page 18
1. 25
2. 81
3. 32
4. 125
5. 64
6. 144
7. 1600
8. 864
9. 2048
10. 27 783
11. 325
12. 8010
13. 720
14. 1102
15. 1 100 000
16. 2^7
17. 3^7
18. Not possible
19. 5^4
20. 2^5
21. 7^7
22. 4^9
23. a^5
24. Not possible
25. 2^2
26. 7
27. Not possible
28. 4^3
29. Not possible
30. 3^4
31. 3^3
32. a^4
33. Not possible

Exercise 2i   page 20
1. $\frac{1}{2}$
2. $\frac{1}{10}$
3. $\frac{1}{5}$
4. $\frac{1}{7}$
5. $\frac{1}{8}$
6. $\frac{1}{4}$
7. $\frac{1}{a}$
8. $\frac{1}{x}$
9. 3
10. $1\frac{1}{2}$
11. 4
12. $1\frac{1}{3}$
13. 5
14. $1\frac{1}{4}$
15. a
16. $\frac{y}{x}$
17. $\frac{1}{8}$
18. $\frac{1}{25}$
19. $\frac{1}{1000}$
20. $\frac{1}{36}$
21. $\frac{1}{32}$
22. $\frac{1}{10\,000}$
23. $\frac{1}{100}$
24. $\frac{1}{64}$
25. 125
26. 16
27. 32
28. 81
29. 512
30. 10 000
31. 8
32. 36
33. $1\frac{7}{9}$
34. $3\frac{3}{8}$
35. $5\frac{1}{16}$
36. $12\frac{1}{4}$
37. $5\frac{1}{16}$
38. $2\frac{7}{9}$
39. $123\frac{37}{81}$
40. $2\frac{14}{25}$

Exercise 2j   page 21
1. 8
2. $6\frac{1}{4}$
3. $\frac{1}{16}$
4. 64
5. 1
6. 1
7. 125
8. $\frac{1}{9}$
9. 16
10. 1
11. $2\frac{10}{27}$
12. $3\frac{1}{2}$
13. 1
14. $2\frac{314}{343}$
15. $\frac{1}{4}$
16. $\frac{64}{125}$
17. $\frac{1}{12}$
18. 729
19. 64
20. 1

Exercise 2k   page 22
1. 345
2. 1200
3. 0.0501
4. 0.0047
5. 280
6. 0.73
7. 902 000
8. 0.000 637
9. 8 720 000

10. 2.65×10^2 **16.** 8.5×10^{-4} **22.** 7×10^{-6}

11. 1.8×10^{-1} **17.** 7×10^3 **23.** 8×10^{-1}

12. 3.02×10^3 **18.** 4×10^{-3} **24.** 5.6×10^{-4}

13. 1.9×10^{-2} **19.** 5.87×10^4 **25.** 2.4×10^4

14. 7.67×10^4 **20.** 2.6×10^3 **26.** 3.9×10^7

15. 3.9×10^5 **21.** 4.5×10^5 **27.** 8×10^{-11}

28. (a) 6.25×10^{10} (c) 6.4×10^{-9}
(b) 6.6049×10^8 (d) 4.9×10^{-11}

Exercise 2l   page 23

1. (a) 2.785 (b) 2.78
2. (a) 0.157 (b) 0.157
3. (a) 3.209 (b) 3.21
4. (a) 0.073 (b) 0.0733
5. (a) 0.151 (b) 0.151
6. (a) 0.020 (b) 0.0204
7. (a) 0.780 (b) 0.780
8. (a) 3.299 (b) 3.30
9. (a) 254.163 (b) 254
10. (a) 0.001 (b) 0.000 926
11. (a) 7.820 (b) 7.82
12. (a) 0.010 (b) 0.009 64
13. 0.04; 0.0384 **23.** 5; 4.58
14. 60 000; 47 500 **24.** 6; 5.38
15. 0.05; 0.0447 **25.** 60; 56.0
16. 80; 69.8 **26.** 0.04; 0.0390
17. 0.2; 0.216 **27.** 80; 69.3
18. 500 000; 665 000 **28.** 0.03; 0.0328
19. 2; 2.17 **29.** 2; 1.74
20. 0.2; 0.217 **30.** 0.06; 0.0403
21. 9; 8.89 **31.** 0.1; 0.105
22. 0.08; 0.0688

Exercise 2m   page 24

1. (a) 30 (b) 42

2. (a) $\frac{4}{3}$ (b) $\frac{y}{x}$

3. (a) $\frac{3}{2}$ (b) $\frac{4}{9}$

4. $2\frac{3}{10}$

5. (a) 3.36 (b) 0.2943 (c) 109
6. (a) 16 (b) 1 (c) $\frac{1}{16}$
7. (a) 5^2 (b) 5^{12}

8. (a) 2.56×10^3 (b) 2.56×10^{-4}
9. $1.45\,\text{mm} \leqslant$ diameter $< 1.55\,\text{mm}$
10. $65 \leqslant$ number of children $\leqslant 74$ (whole numbers)

Exercise 2n   page 25

1. (a) 24 (b) 30
2. (a) 5 (b) $\frac{2}{3}$
3. (a) $\frac{3}{4}$ (b) $1\frac{17}{20}$
4. (a) $3\frac{1}{12}$
5. (a) 1.45 (b) 2.625 (c) 0.42
6. (a) $\frac{1}{4}$ (b) 1 (c) 4
7. (a) 5.7×10^5 (b) 5.7×10^{-2}
8. $445 \leqslant$ number of tacks $\leqslant 454$ (whole numbers)
9. $0.745\,\text{m} \leqslant$ diameter $< 0.755\,\text{m}$

Chapter 3

Exercise 3a   page 27

1. $4 > 2$ **5.** $2 > -1$ **9.** $5 > -5$
2. $3 < 5$ **6.** $-4 < 3$ **10.** $4 > -2$
3. $-1 > -4$ **7.** $-5 > -6$ **11.** $-3 < 0$
4. $-5 < -2$ **8.** $0 > -4$ **12.** $0 < 6$

Exercise 3b   page 28

1. -5 **10.** 7 **19.** 4 **28.** 2
2. -2 **11.** -10 **20.** -3 **29.** 11
3. -6 **12.** 6 **21.** -12 **30.** 7
4. -2 **13.** -5 **22.** -6 **31.** 0
5. 1 **14.** 6 **23.** -5 **32.** -2
6. 8 **15.** -5 **24.** 4 **33.** -1
7. -9 **16.** -3 **25.** 5 **34.** 7
8. 6 **17.** 3 **26.** 4 **35.** -1
9. -6 **18.** -2 **27.** -5 **36.** 1

Exercise 3c   page 29

1. -6 **7.** -12 **13.** 2 **19.** 3
2. 12 **8.** 14 **14.** -2 **20.** 5
3. 56 **9.** 4 **15.** -2 **21.** 2
4. 27 **10.** -15 **16.** 2 **22.** -3
5. -8 **11.** 9 **17.** -2 **23.** -1
6. 30 **12.** -18 **18.** -5 **24.** -3

Exercise 3d   page 30

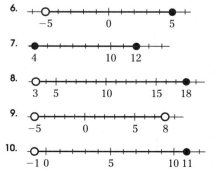

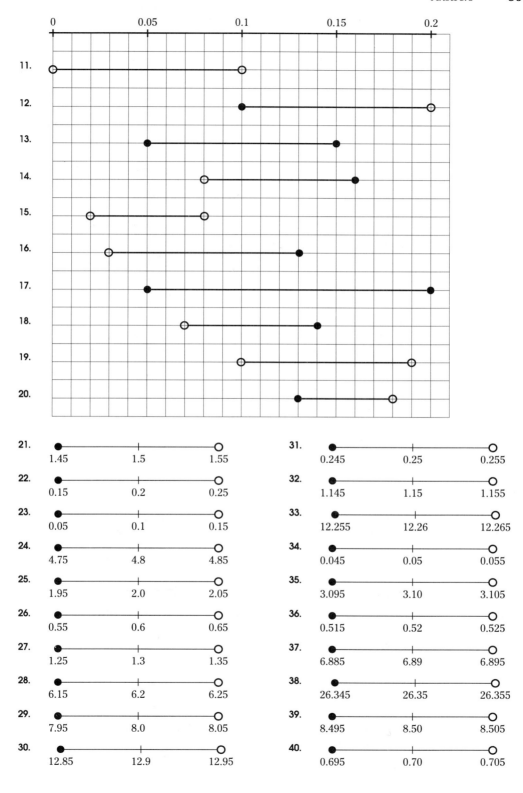

Exercise 3e   page 32
1. $5.55 \leqslant w < 5.65$
2. $2450 \leqslant x < 2550$
3. $2.75 \leqslant x \leqslant 2.85$
4. $12.45 \leqslant x < 12.55$
5. $6500 \leqslant x < 7400$
6. $1.245 \leqslant d < 1.255$
7. 65 people
8. \$254
9. $252.5 \leqslant \text{length} < 257.5$
10. 97.5 m

Exercise 3f   page 33
1. 3
2. -12
3. 25
4. 2
5. 3
6. -12
7. 5
8. 36
9. 13
10. -30
11. -4
12. 3
13. -3
14. -28
15. 81
16. -4
17. 2
18. 20
19. -2
20. 0
21. 1
22. -5
23. -14
24. 7
25. 1.45 mm, 1.54 mm
26. 65, 74
27. 445, 454
28. 0.745 m, 0.745 m

Chapter 4

Exercise 4a   page 34
1. Not possible
2. $2a$
3. Not possible
4. $7v$
5. $2x$
6. $p + q$
7. $4x - 2y$
8. $5u$
9. $3b - a$
10. $4c + 2d$

Exercise 4b   page 35
1. xy
2. a^2
3. $6s^2$
4. $12x^2$
5. $\dfrac{u}{v}$
6. $\dfrac{-a}{b}$
7. 1
8. $\dfrac{3b}{c}$
9. Not possible
10. Not possible
11. $-mn$
12. Not possible
13. $-2a$
14. $4p^3$
15. $\dfrac{2u}{w}$
16. Not possible
17. $6st$
18. $2p^2$
19. $-4q$
20. $r + 4s$
21. $\dfrac{4p}{q}$
22. $6st$
23. $-2b^2$
24. $\dfrac{x}{y}$
25. $3b - 2a$
26. $a^2 - a$
27. $3a - 3b$
28. $6a - 4c - 2b$
29. $2z - y$
30. $6x + 4y + 2z$
31. $p + 3q - 2r$
32. $x - y$

33. $5q - p$
34. $a^2 + ab - 2a + 2b$
35. $x^2 + y^2 - 2xy$
36. $2b - 6c$
37. $2p - 2q$
38. $w^2 + x^2$
39. $8n - 2m$
40. $2b - 8c$

Exercise 4c   page 37
1. $p = -\frac{2}{3}$
2. $s = \frac{1}{2}$
3. $x = 3\frac{1}{2}$
4. $a = \frac{1}{5}$
5. $x = 1$
6. $y = 1$
7. $x = 2$
8. $a = 4$
9. $x = \frac{1}{2}$
10. $x = 2$
11. $x = -\frac{1}{2}$
12. $x = -5$
13. $x = -\frac{1}{7}$
14. $y = 3\frac{1}{3}$
15. $x = 2\frac{4}{7}$
16. $x = 3\frac{2}{3}$
17. $a = -11$
18. $p = 0$
19. $w = 2$
20. $x = 5$
21. $x = 6\frac{1}{2}$
22. $x = -\frac{1}{6}$
23. $x = 2\frac{1}{2}$
24. $x = 1\frac{3}{4}$
25. $x = \frac{3}{14}$
26. $b = 19$
27. $x = \frac{5}{6}$
28. $x = -1$
29. $x = 2$
30. $x = \frac{1}{2}$

Exercise 4d   page 38

1. 7
2. 4
3. -2
4. 0
5. -2
6. $\frac{1}{2}$
7. 5
8. 0
9. 1.5

10. (a) 2, 3, 4, 6, 7
    (b) 2, 5, 7, 8, 9
    (c) 2, 3, 7, 9
    (d) 2, 3, 4, 6, 7
    (e) 2, 3, 4, 7, 9
12. (a) $5 > 3$; Yes
    (b) $1 > -1$; Yes
    (c) $-2 > -4$; Yes
    (d) $7 > 5$; Yes
13. (a) $0 > -1$; Yes
    (b) $-4 > -5$; Yes
    (c) $-7 > -8$; Yes
    (d) $2 > 1$; Yes
14. (a) $1 < b$; Yes
    (b) $-3 < 2$; Yes
    (c) $-6 < -1$; Yes
    (d) $3 < 8$; Yes

Exercise 4e   page 39
1. $x < 12$ 12
2. $x < 2$ 2
3. $x > 5$ 5
4. $x > 2$ 2
5. $x < -2$ -2
6. $x < 3$ 3
7. $x < -3$ -3
8. $x < -7$ -7
9. $x < -5$ -5
10. $x < -2$ -2
11. $x > -1$ -1

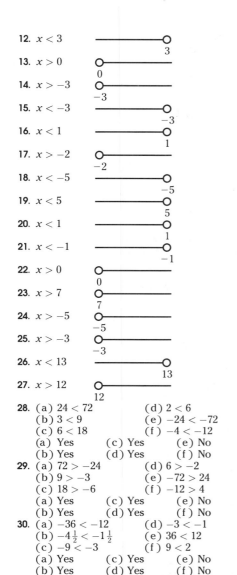

12. $x < 3$ — $\underset{3}{\circ}$
13. $x > 0$ $\underset{0}{\circ}$ —
14. $x > -3$ $\underset{-3}{\circ}$ —
15. $x < -3$ — $\underset{-3}{\circ}$
16. $x < 1$ — $\underset{1}{\circ}$
17. $x > -2$ $\underset{-2}{\circ}$ —
18. $x < -5$ — $\underset{-5}{\circ}$
19. $x < 5$ — $\underset{5}{\circ}$
20. $x < 1$ — $\underset{1}{\circ}$
21. $x < -1$ — $\underset{-1}{\circ}$
22. $x > 0$ $\underset{0}{\circ}$ —
23. $x > 7$ $\underset{7}{\circ}$ —
24. $x > -5$ $\underset{-5}{\circ}$ —
25. $x > -3$ $\underset{-3}{\circ}$ —
26. $x < 13$ — $\underset{13}{\circ}$
27. $x > 12$ $\underset{12}{\circ}$ —

28. (a) $24 < 72$ (d) $2 < 6$
    (b) $3 < 9$ (e) $-24 < -72$
    (c) $6 < 18$ (f) $-4 < -12$
    (a) Yes (c) Yes (e) No
    (b) Yes (d) Yes (f) No

29. (a) $72 > -24$ (d) $6 > -2$
    (b) $9 > -3$ (e) $-72 > 24$
    (c) $18 > -6$ (f) $-12 > 4$
    (a) Yes (c) Yes (e) No
    (b) Yes (d) Yes (f) No

30. (a) $-36 < -12$ (d) $-3 < -1$
    (b) $-4\frac{1}{2} < -1\frac{1}{2}$ (e) $36 < 12$
    (c) $-9 < -3$ (f) $9 < 2$
    (a) Yes (c) Yes (e) No
    (b) Yes (d) Yes (f) No

32. Only when you are multiplying by a positive number.

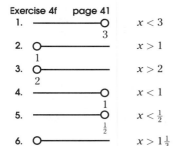

Exercise 4f   page 41
1. — $\underset{3}{\circ}$ $x < 3$
2. $\underset{1}{\circ}$ — $x > 1$
3. $\underset{2}{\circ}$ — $x > 2$
4. — $\underset{1}{\circ}$ $x < 1$
5. — $\underset{\frac{1}{2}}{\circ}$ $x < \frac{1}{2}$
6. $\underset{1\frac{1}{3}}{\circ}$ — $x > 1\frac{1}{3}$

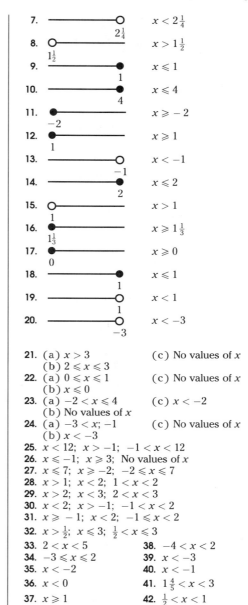

7. — $\underset{2\frac{1}{4}}{\circ}$ $x < 2\frac{1}{4}$
8. $\underset{1\frac{1}{2}}{\circ}$ — $x > 1\frac{1}{2}$
9. — $\underset{1}{\bullet}$ $x \leqslant 1$
10. — $\underset{4}{\bullet}$ $x \leqslant 4$
11. $\underset{-2}{\bullet}$ — $x \geqslant -2$
12. $\underset{1}{\bullet}$ — $x \geqslant 1$
13. — $\underset{-1}{\circ}$ $x < -1$
14. — $\underset{2}{\bullet}$ $x \leqslant 2$
15. $\underset{1}{\circ}$ — $x > 1$
16. $\underset{1\frac{1}{3}}{\bullet}$ — $x \geqslant 1\frac{1}{3}$
17. $\underset{0}{\bullet}$ — $x \geqslant 0$
18. — $\underset{1}{\bullet}$ $x \leqslant 1$
19. — $\underset{1}{\circ}$ $x < 1$
20. — $\underset{-3}{\circ}$ $x < -3$

21. (a) $x > 3$ (c) No values of x
    (b) $2 \leqslant x \leqslant 3$
22. (a) $0 \leqslant x \leqslant 1$ (c) No values of x
    (b) $x \leqslant 0$
23. (a) $-2 < x \leqslant 4$ (c) $x < -2$
    (b) No values of x
24. (a) $-3 < x; -1$ (c) No values of x
    (b) $x < -3$
25. $x < 12; \ x > -1; \ -1 < x < 12$
26. $x \leqslant -1; \ x \geqslant 3; \ $ No values of x
27. $x \leqslant 7; \ x \geqslant -2; \ -2 \leqslant x \leqslant 7$
28. $x > 1; \ x < 2; \ 1 < x < 2$
29. $x > 2; \ x < 3; \ 2 < x < 3$
30. $x < 2; \ x > -1; \ -1 < x < 2$
31. $x \geqslant -1; \ x < 2; \ -1 \leqslant x < 2$
32. $x > \frac{1}{2}; \ x \leqslant 3; \ \frac{1}{2} < x \leqslant 3$
33. $2 < x < 5$ 38. $-4 < x < 2$
34. $-3 \leqslant x \leqslant 2$ 39. $x < -3$
35. $x < -2$ 40. $x < -1$
36. $x < 0$ 41. $1\frac{4}{5} < x < 3$
37. $x \geqslant 1$ 42. $\frac{1}{2} < x < 1$

Exercise 4g   page 44
1. $a = b + c$ 9. $k = 2u + 3v$
2. $m = 2(n + p)$ 10. $x = 2y - z$
3. $z = xy$ 11. $n = p + p^2$
4. $a = 2bc$ 12. $v = u + at$
5. $v = n^2$ 13. $R = Np$
6. $d = e - f$ 14. $y = nx$
7. $x = \dfrac{y}{2}$ 15. $X = xy$
8. $a = \dfrac{b}{2c}$ 16. $N = y + z$

17. $P = \dfrac{x+y}{50}$

18. $b = \dfrac{ac}{1000}$

19. $n = 1 + 2m$

20. $R = \dfrac{x}{10} + \dfrac{y}{5}$

Exercise 4h   page 45

1. $p = 8$

2. $v = 2$

3. $z = \frac{3}{4}$

4. $a = 2$

5. $x = 25$

6. $C = 30$

7. $x = 24$

8. $p = 6$

9. $s = 10$

10. $v = -5$

11. $p = 4$

12. $a = 9$

13. $r = 2\frac{2}{3}$

14. $n = \frac{1}{2}$

15. $a = 2$

16. $V = 32$

17. $p = 21$

18. $a = 6$

Exercise 4i   page 46

1. $s = p - r$

2. $y = x - 3$

3. $b = a + c$

4. $Y = X + Z$

5. $s = r - 2t$

6. $m = k - l$

7. $v = u + 5$

8. $y = z - x$

9. $P = N + Q$

10. $u = v - 10t$

11. $y = \dfrac{x}{2}$

12. $t = 2v$

13. $b = \dfrac{a}{c}$

14. $u = 3t$

15. $m = kl$

16. $b = \dfrac{a}{3}$

17. $N = 10X$

18. $u = \dfrac{v}{t}$

19. $w = 100z$

20. $p = qn$

21. $s = \dfrac{P - r}{2}$

22. $t = \dfrac{u - v}{3}$

23. $c = \dfrac{b - a}{4}$

24. $v = \dfrac{V - 3u}{2}$

25. $w = \dfrac{x + y}{2}$

26. $t = \dfrac{l - k}{4}$

27. $y = \dfrac{x - w}{6}$

28. $s = \dfrac{lt - N}{2}$

29. $y = \dfrac{4x}{3}$

30. $t = \dfrac{u - v}{5}$

31. $I = 10(A - P)$

32. $y = 3(x - z)$

33. $R = \dfrac{IV}{2}$

34. $r = \dfrac{p + w}{2}$

35. $c = 2(a - b)$

36. $r = 5(q - p)$

37. $u = v - at; u = 140$

38. $B = A - \dfrac{C}{100}; B = 17.5$

39. $C = NP; C = 40$

40. $x = 2(z + 3t); x = -10$

41. (a) $a = b + 2c$
(b) $a = 4$
(c) $b = a - 2c$

42. (a) $x = 2yz$
(b) $x = 12$
(c) $y = \dfrac{x}{2y}$

43. (a) $d = e^2 + 2f$
(b) $f = \dfrac{d - e^2}{2}$
(c) $f = \frac{1}{2}$

44. (a) $R = \dfrac{3xn}{25}$
(b) $R = 4.8$

Exercise 4j   page 47

1. (a) -4 (b) -1 (c) -2

2. (a) $4x$ (b) $6b$ (c) $-3x^3$

3. (a) $a + b$ (b) $a + 5b$

4. (a) $x = 1\frac{1}{4}$ (b) $x = 4\frac{2}{3}$

5. (a) $x > 2$ (b) $x \leqslant 6$ (c) $-2 < x < 1\frac{1}{2}$

6. (a) $r = \dfrac{v - u}{4}$ (b) $r = \dfrac{ps}{5}$

7. (a) $P = 37\frac{1}{2}$ (b) 40

Exercise 4k   page 47

1. (a) 13 (b) 2 (c) 4

2. (a) $10a - 3b$ (b) $4x + x^2$ (c) $12ab$

3. (a) $3y - 2x$ (b) $2y - 6x$

4. (a) $a = -1$ (b) $x = \frac{7}{8}$

5. (a) $x > 1$ (b) $x > -1$ (c) $-1 < x < 1$

6. (a) $d = \dfrac{C}{\pi}$ (b) $d = \dfrac{a + s}{7}$

7. (a) $u = 56$ (b) $u = -86$

Chapter 5

Exercise 5a   page 50

	Fraction	Percentage	Decimal
1.	$\frac{3}{5}$	60%	0.6
2.	$\frac{2}{5}$	40%	0.4
3.	$\frac{11}{20}$	55%	0.55
4.	$\frac{17}{20}$	85%	0.85
5.	$\frac{27}{50}$	54%	0.54
6.	$\frac{6}{25}$	24%	0.24
7.	$\frac{23}{25}$	92%	0.92
8.	$\frac{21}{25}$	84%	0.84
9.	$\frac{37}{40}$	$92\frac{1}{2}\%$	0.925
10.	$\frac{2}{3}$	$66\frac{2}{3}\%$	0.6

11. 24%

12. 64%

13. 20%

14. 40%

15. 25%

16. 34%

17. 5%

18. 2.5%

19. 2%

20. 27%

21. 40%

22. 225%

23. 75

24. 92 c

25. 0.61 cm

26. 0.54 km

27. 189 g

28. 42 m²

29. 2.5%

30. 2%

31. 1.5%

32. 2.5%

33. 2.4%

34. 60%

35. 30%

36. 89.6%

37. 949

38. 1007

39. 627

40. 381

41. 49.28

42. 348

43. 31.59

44. 172

45. 64.68

46. 294

47. 5.74

48. 59.4 kg

49. \$19 350

50. 51

Exercise 5b   page 53

1. 25%

2. 30%

3. 25%

4. 10%

5. 20%

6. 20%

7. 15%

8. 24%

9. \$56

10. \$72

11. \$60.90

12. \$18

13. \$27

14. \$80

15. \$8

16. \$14.40

17. \$12

18. \$16.20

19. \$14

20. (b) by \$8

21. (b) by 70 c

---

22. the same
23. $138
24. $368
25. $96.60
26. $174.80
27. $2760
28. $9.20
29. $23.92
30. $17.25

Exercise 5c page 55
1. $1500 **9.** $4000 **17.** $368
2. $2400 **10.** $7680 **18.** $51.20
3. $1950 **11.** $5400 **19.** $232
4. $3750 **12.** $3300 **20.** $134.40
5. $1935 **13.** $10 620 **21.** $38.25
6. $2478 **14.** $6336 **22.** $16.15
7. $3300 **15.** $12 810 **23.** $14.30
8. $2240 **16.** $84 **24.** $32.25
25. (a) $12.20 (b) $14.80

Exercise 5d page 58
1. $70 **11.** $40 **21.** $240
2. $40 **12.** $80 **22.** $250
3. $16 **13.** $200 **23.** $520
4. $6 **14.** $18 **24.** $184
5. $2.70 **15.** $13.60 **25.** $184
6. $32 **16.** $50 **26.** $72
7. $800 **17.** $160 **27.** $1950
8. $900 **18.** $17 **28.** $320
9. $800 **19.** $160 **29.** $850 cm^3
10. $20 **20.** $2000 **30.** 25 cm

Exercise 5e page 60
1. $127 680
2. $41.07
3. $33\frac{1}{3}$%
4. 40%
5. $1200
6. $112.50
7. 212.5 cm^3
8. $3440
9. 15 km/h
10. 44 275
11. (a) $14.40 (b) $13.20
12. $840

Exercise 5f page 61
1. $32 **6.** $126 **11.** $440
2. $112 **7.** $201.60 **12.** 7 years
3. $284.70 **8.** $375.30 **13.** 6.5%
4. $118.72 **9.** $500 **14.** $300
5. $162.50 **10.** $168.80 **15.** 4%
16. (a) $170.40 (b) $392 (c) $816.20
17. (a) $200 (b) $170 (c) $360
18. (a) 3 years (b) 5 years (c) 4 years

Exercise 5g page 63
1. $42 **4.** $191.77 **7.** $252.68 **10.** $4374
2. $76.32 **5.** $143.99 **8.** $96 800 **11.** $12 800
3. $103.88 **6.** $206.72 **9.** $76

Chapter 6

Exercise 6a page 67
1. 70° **3.** 60° **5.** 45° **7.** 125°
2. 110° **4.** 70° **6.** 55° **8.** 66°

Exercise 6b page 70
1. Yes **6.** No
2. No **7.** Yes
3. Yes **8.** No
4. No **9.** Yes
5. Yes **10.** Yes

Exercise 6c page 72
1. Reflection in *x*-axis; Yes
2. Rotation of 90° anticlockwise about 0; Yes
3. Enlargement, scale factor 2, centre $(0,0)$; No
4. Translation $\begin{pmatrix} -3 \\ -2 \end{pmatrix}$; Yes
5. Reflection in *y*-axis; Yes
6. Enlargement, scale factor $\frac{1}{2}$, centre $(-4,0)$; No
7. Rotation of 90° clockwise about (5, 2); Yes
8. Translation $\begin{pmatrix} -3 \\ -2 \end{pmatrix}$; Yes

Exercise 6d page 74
1. $B\hat{A}C = 38.7°$, $A\hat{B}C = 51.3°$, $A\hat{C}B = 90°$; Yes
2. No
3. $B\hat{A}C = 106°$, $A\hat{B}C = 39.9°$, $A\hat{C}B = 34.1°$; Yes
4. No
5. The length of one side

Exercise 6e page 75
1. Yes; SSS **6.** Yes; SSS
2. No **7.** Yes
3. No **8.** $\triangle$ ABC and $\triangle$ ADC
4. No **9.** Yes
5. No **10.** Yes

Exercise 6f page 77
5. Two are: $\triangle$ ABC and $\triangle$ LMN
6. Two

Exercise 6g page 78
1. Yes; AAS **6.** Yes; AAS
2. No; similar **7.** Yes; AAS
3. Yes; AAS **8.** No
4. Yes; AAS **9.** Yes
5. No **10.** Yes

Exercise 6h page 80
1. Yes; AC = 4.4 cm, $\hat{A} = 34.3°$, $\hat{C} = 115.7°$
2. No
3. Yes; PR = 7.2 cm, $\hat{R} = 46°$, $\hat{P} = 74°$
4. No
5. Yes; DF = 7.8 cm, $\hat{D} = 50°$, $\hat{F} = 40°$

Exercise 6i page 81
1. Yes
2. No; there are two possibilities
3. Yes
4. No; there are two possibilities
5. Yes
6. Yes
7. In questions 1, 3 and 5 we can calculate the length of the third side.

Exercise 6j   page 81

1. Yes; SAS
2. Not necessarily
3. Yes; SHR
4. Yes; SAS
5. Yes; SAS
6. Not necessarily
7. Yes; SHR
8. Not necessarily
9. Yes; SHR
10. Yes

Exercise 6k   page 84

1. No
2. Yes; AAS
3. Yes; SSS
4. Yes; AAS
5. No
6. Yes; SAS
7. No; similar
8. Yes; ASS
9. Yes; SHR
10. Yes; SSS
11. Yes; ASS
12. Yes; SAS
13. No
14. No; similar
15. Yes; SHR

Exercise 6l   page 87

9. $\triangle$ BDF and $\triangle$ CDE

Exercise 6m   page 89

Only for the most able children.

Exercise 6n   page 94

1. AC bisects both angles; Yes
2. Both are right angles
3. No
4. They are equal
5. Yes; No; Yes, of AC; they are all right angles
6. No
7. They are equal

Exercise 6p   page 97

1. 5 cm
2. 5 cm
3. 60°
5. 8 cm
6. 5 cm
7. 9.5 cm
8. 6 cm
9. 5.7 cm

Chapter 7

Exercise 7a   page 101

1. 3, 2
2. 2, 4
3. 3, 5
4. 1, 7
5. 4, −3
6. 2, 5
7. −2, 1
8. 5, 1
9. 3, $1\frac{1}{2}$
10. 6, 0
11. −1, −2
12. 0, 9

Exercise 7b   page 102

1. 3, 1
2. 4, 2
3. 3, 4
4. 3, −1
5. 3, $\frac{1}{2}$
6. 9, 1
7. 4, −2
8. 1, 0
9. 0, 6
10. 2, 3
11. 2, 3
12. 4, −1
13. 6, 2
14. 5, $1\frac{1}{2}$
15. 4, 3
16. $\frac{1}{2}$, 4
17. 4, −2
18. −3, 1
19. 2, $\frac{1}{3}$
20. 3, −2
21. 3, 2
22. 4, 5
23. 3, 0
24. $1\frac{1}{2}$, 2
25. −3, 2
26. 4, −2
27. 6, 2
28. 4, 3
29. −1, 4
30. −1, −2
31. 5, 4
32. 2, −4

Exercise 7c   page 105

1. 3, 1
2. 1, 2
3. $\frac{1}{3}$, 1
4. −12, 27
5. 0, 1
6. 4, 3
7. 1, 2
8. 2, 1
9. 3, −1
10. 0, 3
11. 1, −1
12. 3, $\frac{1}{2}$

Exercise 7d   page 106

1. 3, 2
2. 1, 5
3. 3, 1
4. $1\frac{1}{2}$, 0
5. 0, 6
6. 3, −1
7. 1, 4
8. 1, 1
9. 2, 2
10. 3, −1
11. 4, 2
12. −3, 0

13. 2, $\frac{2}{3}$
14. −1, 2
15. 3, −2
16. 2, −2
17. 0, 4
18. −1, −2
19. 1, 1
20. 3, 1
21. 2, −1
22. 8, 4
23. −3, 4
24. 3, −3$\frac{1}{2}$
25. 3, 4
26. 2, 5
27. 3, 2
28. −1, −3

Exercise 7e   page 108

1. 1, 4
2. −1, 5
3. 3, −2
4. 6, 28
5. 2, 3
6. −1, −1
7. 3$\frac{1}{2}$, 2$\frac{1}{2}$
8. 1, −2
9. 5, 0
10. 0, 4
11. −1, −1
12. −4, −5

Exercise 7f   page 108

1. 2, 4
2. 5, 3
3. 1, 1
4. −2, 7
5. 4, 6
6. 1, 1
7. 1, 10
8. 2$\frac{1}{3}$, −$\frac{2}{3}$
9. 1, 5
10. −12, −4
11. 2, 6
12. 4$\frac{1}{2}$, 7$\frac{1}{2}$

Exercise 7h   page 110

1. 12, 8
2. 11, 5
3. 8, 2
4. 10, 3
5. 10, 6
6. 11, 5
7. 3 choc ices, 7 orange ices
8. 54, 36
9. cup $1.35, saucer $1.80
10. Petties $1.40 each, Roti $2.10 each
11. Harry 32, Adam 10, Sam 20
12. 3, 5
13. AB = 9$\frac{1}{2}$ cm, BC = 6 cm
14. $m = 2$, $c = 4$, $y = 2x + 4$

Exercise 7i   page 112

1. 1$\frac{1}{2}$, 4$\frac{1}{2}$
2. 1$\frac{1}{3}$, 3$\frac{2}{3}$
3. 1$\frac{1}{2}$, 5$\frac{1}{2}$
4. −$\frac{1}{2}$, 1$\frac{1}{2}$
5. $\frac{1}{2}$, 2
6. 1$\frac{1}{2}$, 3$\frac{1}{2}$
7. 2$\frac{2}{5}$, 1$\frac{4}{5}$
8. −$\frac{2}{5}$, 1$\frac{3}{5}$
9. 2$\frac{2}{5}$, 1$\frac{1}{5}$
10. $\frac{1}{3}$, 1$\frac{2}{3}$

Chapter 8

Exercise 8a   page 115

1. 2×2
2. 2×3
3. 2×1
4. 1×3
5. 1×1
6. 3×2
7. (a) 6   (b) 8   (c) 2   (d) 7
8. 3 1 7; 7 (a) 7   (b) 6   (c) 4

9. $\begin{pmatrix} 0 & 0 & 0 \\ 1 & 1 & 1 \\ 2 & 2 & 2 \end{pmatrix}$
10. $\begin{pmatrix} 3 & 1 \\ 3 & 1 \\ 3 & 1 \end{pmatrix}$

Exercise 8b   page 116

1. $\begin{pmatrix} 12 \\ 15 \end{pmatrix}$
2. $\begin{pmatrix} 15 & 4 \\ 7 & 1 \end{pmatrix}$
3. Not possible
4. (9, 5)

5. $\begin{pmatrix} 11 & 2 & 2 \\ 6 & 7 & 7 \end{pmatrix}$

15. $\begin{pmatrix} -3 \\ -3 \\ 6 \end{pmatrix}$

9. $\begin{pmatrix} 8 \\ 9 \\ 3 \end{pmatrix}$

11. Not possible

6. $\begin{pmatrix} 11 & 11 \\ 11 & 5 \end{pmatrix}$

16. Not possible

10. $\begin{pmatrix} 24 & 8 & -4 \\ 16 & 12 & 16 \end{pmatrix}$

12. $\begin{pmatrix} 8 & -2 & -2 \\ 1 & 4 & 4 \end{pmatrix}$

7. $(5 \ 3 \ 5)$

17. $\begin{pmatrix} 2 & 10 \\ 5 & -3 \end{pmatrix}$

8. Not possible

18. $\begin{pmatrix} 5 & -5 \\ 3 & 0 \end{pmatrix}$

Exercise 8e   page 120
1. B 2×1, **C** 2×2, **D** 2×2, **E** 1×3, **F** 1×2,
   G 2×3

9. $\begin{pmatrix} 6 & 8 \\ 7 & 7 \\ 7 & 7 \end{pmatrix}$

19. $\begin{pmatrix} 0 & 8 \\ 8 & -2 \end{pmatrix}$

2. $\begin{pmatrix} 9 & 4 & 4 \\ 7 & 1 & 7 \end{pmatrix}$

8. Not possible

10. $(10 \ \ 8)$

20. Not possible

3. Not possible

9. $\begin{pmatrix} 1 & -2 & 2 \\ 5 & -3 & 1 \end{pmatrix}$

11. $\begin{pmatrix} 1 & 8 \\ -4 & 7 \end{pmatrix}$

21. Not possible

4. $\begin{pmatrix} 4 & -1 \\ 0 & 6 \end{pmatrix}$

10. $\begin{pmatrix} 24 \\ 6 \end{pmatrix}$

12. $\begin{pmatrix} -2 \\ 2 \end{pmatrix}$

22. $(1 \ \ 6 \ \ -3)$

5. $\begin{pmatrix} 12 & 9 & 3 \\ 3 & 6 & 9 \end{pmatrix}$

11. $\begin{pmatrix} 4\frac{1}{2} & 1\frac{1}{2} \\ \frac{3}{4} & 3 \end{pmatrix}$

13. $\begin{pmatrix} -2 & 7 \\ -5 & 3 \end{pmatrix}$

23. $\begin{pmatrix} 2 & 3 & 4 \\ 5 & 0 & -12 \end{pmatrix}$

6. Not possible
7. $(1\frac{1}{2} \ \ 1)$

12. Not possible
13. Not possible

14. $(4 \ \ 6)$

Exercise 8c   page 118

1. $\begin{pmatrix} 3 \\ 6 \\ 12 \end{pmatrix}$

7. $\begin{pmatrix} 2 & -2 \\ 1 & 3 \end{pmatrix}$

Exercise 8f   page 121

1. $\begin{pmatrix} 29 \\ 27 \end{pmatrix}$

6. $\begin{pmatrix} 18 \\ 14 \end{pmatrix}$

2. $\begin{pmatrix} 2 & 8 & 0 \\ 4 & -2 & 6 \end{pmatrix}$

8. Not possible

2. $\begin{pmatrix} 14 \\ 11 \end{pmatrix}$

7. $\begin{pmatrix} 26 \\ 10 \end{pmatrix}$

3. $\begin{pmatrix} 1 & 2 \\ \frac{1}{2} & 3 \\ 1\frac{1}{2} & 4 \end{pmatrix}$

9. $\begin{pmatrix} -3 \\ 3 \\ 0 \end{pmatrix}$

3. $\begin{pmatrix} 5 \\ 7 \end{pmatrix}$

8. $\begin{pmatrix} 58 \\ 19 \end{pmatrix}$

4. $\begin{pmatrix} 9 \\ 2 \end{pmatrix}$

9. $\begin{pmatrix} 56 \\ 49 \end{pmatrix}$

4. $\begin{pmatrix} 6 & 24 \\ 18 & -12 \end{pmatrix}$

10. $\begin{pmatrix} 2 & 4 & 2 \\ -3 & -3 & -1 \end{pmatrix}$

5. $\begin{pmatrix} 9 \\ 5 \end{pmatrix}$

10. $\begin{pmatrix} 26 \\ 10 \end{pmatrix}$

5. $\begin{pmatrix} -6 & -30 \\ 6 & 12 \end{pmatrix}$

11. Not possible

Exercise 8g   page 123

6. $\begin{pmatrix} 4 & 0 \\ \frac{2}{3} & 1\frac{1}{3} \\ 2 & 3\frac{1}{3} \end{pmatrix}$

12. $\begin{pmatrix} -3 & -1 & 2 \\ 9 & 5 & 4 \\ 1 & 11 & 5 \end{pmatrix}$

1. $\begin{pmatrix} 7 \\ 10 \end{pmatrix}$

8. $\begin{pmatrix} 17 & 19 \\ 5 \end{pmatrix}$

2. $\begin{pmatrix} 14 \\ 22 \end{pmatrix}$

9. $\begin{pmatrix} 22 & 52 \\ 10 & 22 \end{pmatrix}$

Exercise 8d   page 119

1. $\begin{pmatrix} -1 & 8 \\ 6 & 1 \end{pmatrix}$

5. $\begin{pmatrix} 1\frac{1}{3} \\ 1\frac{2}{3} \\ -\frac{1}{3} \end{pmatrix}$

3. $\begin{pmatrix} 37 \\ 2 \end{pmatrix}$

10. $\begin{pmatrix} 44 & 32 \\ 8 & 7 \end{pmatrix}$

4. $\begin{pmatrix} 23 & 16 \end{pmatrix}$

11. $\begin{pmatrix} 16 & 14 \\ 11 & 14 \end{pmatrix}$

2. $\begin{pmatrix} 3 & 0 \\ 0 & 3 \end{pmatrix}$

6. $\begin{pmatrix} -3 \\ -3 \\ -3 \end{pmatrix}$

5. $\begin{pmatrix} 19 \\ 22 \end{pmatrix}$

12. $\begin{pmatrix} 8 & 18 \\ 18 & 36 \end{pmatrix}$

3. Not possible

7. $\begin{pmatrix} 2 & 8 \\ 6 & 4 \end{pmatrix}$

6. $\begin{pmatrix} 16 \\ 12 \end{pmatrix}$

13. $\begin{pmatrix} 44 & 40 \\ 18 & 31 \end{pmatrix}$

4. $\begin{pmatrix} 7 & -1 \\ 5 & -1 \end{pmatrix}$

8. $\begin{pmatrix} -1 & 2 \\ 1\frac{1}{2} & -\frac{1}{2} \end{pmatrix}$

7. $\begin{pmatrix} 12 \\ 3 \end{pmatrix}$

14. $\begin{pmatrix} 21 & 7 \\ 17 & 9 \end{pmatrix}$

15. $\begin{pmatrix} 0 & 14 \\ 10 & 8 \end{pmatrix}$ **18.** $\begin{pmatrix} -24 & -17 \\ -10 & -9 \end{pmatrix}$

16. $\begin{pmatrix} 15 & 20 \\ 5 & 0 \end{pmatrix}$ **19.** $\begin{pmatrix} 21 & 11 \\ 9 & 2 \end{pmatrix}$

17. $\begin{pmatrix} 3 & -4 \\ 13 & 6 \end{pmatrix}$ **20.** $\begin{pmatrix} -16 & 1 \\ -6 & -1 \end{pmatrix}$

Exercise 8h   page 124

1. $\begin{pmatrix} 20 & 13 \\ 8 & 5 \end{pmatrix}$ **7.** $\begin{pmatrix} 15 & 17 \\ 31 & 35 \end{pmatrix}$

2. $\begin{pmatrix} 10 & 7 \\ 22 & 15 \end{pmatrix}$ **8.** $\begin{pmatrix} 46 & 31 \\ 6 & 4 \end{pmatrix}$

3. $\begin{pmatrix} 31 & 35 \\ 15 & 17 \end{pmatrix}$ **9.** $\begin{pmatrix} 4 & 2 \\ 8 & 6 \end{pmatrix}$

4. $\begin{pmatrix} 44 & 29 \\ 6 & 4 \end{pmatrix}$ **10.** $\begin{pmatrix} 4 & 2 \\ 8 & 6 \end{pmatrix}$

5. $\begin{pmatrix} 8 & 6 \\ 4 & 2 \end{pmatrix}$ **11.** $\begin{pmatrix} 14 & 16 \\ 2 & 2 \end{pmatrix}$

6. $\begin{pmatrix} 8 & 6 \\ 4 & 2 \end{pmatrix}$ **12.** $\begin{pmatrix} 14 & 16 \\ 2 & 2 \end{pmatrix}$

13. One of the two matrices was **D**

Exercise 8i   page 125

1. $\begin{pmatrix} 7 \\ 10 \end{pmatrix}$ **6.** $\begin{pmatrix} 24 \\ 33 \\ 42 \end{pmatrix}$

2. $\begin{pmatrix} 13 \\ 32 \end{pmatrix}$ **7.** $(13 \quad 31 \quad 27)$

3. (10) **8.** $\begin{pmatrix} 10 & 11 \\ 36 & 30 \\ 31 & 28 \end{pmatrix}$

4. $\begin{pmatrix} 20 & 10 \\ 70 & 23 \end{pmatrix}$ **9.** $\begin{pmatrix} 21 & 39 & 8 \\ 17 & 26 & 7 \end{pmatrix}$

5. $\begin{pmatrix} 32 & 26 & 16 \\ 20 & 19 & 11 \end{pmatrix}$ **10.** (15)

Exercise 8j   page 127

1. $2 \times \boxed{2 \quad 2} \times 1 = 2 \times 1$; $\begin{pmatrix} 7 \\ 6 \end{pmatrix}$

2. $2 \times \boxed{3 \quad 3} \times 1 = 2 \times 1$; $\begin{pmatrix} 22 \\ 12 \end{pmatrix}$

3. $1 \times \boxed{2 \quad 2} \times 1 = 1 \times 1$; (10)

4. $2 \times \boxed{3 \quad 3} \times 2 = 2 \times 2$; $\begin{pmatrix} 20 & 10 \\ 70 & 23 \end{pmatrix}$

5. $2 \times \boxed{2 \quad 2} \times 2 = 2 \times 2$; $\begin{pmatrix} 11 & 20 \\ 24 & 43 \end{pmatrix}$

6. $2 \times \boxed{1 \quad 1} \times 2 = 2 \times 2$; $\begin{pmatrix} 3 & 4 \\ 6 & 8 \end{pmatrix}$

7. $1 \times \boxed{2 \quad 2} \times 2 = 1 \times 2$; $(21 \quad 36)$

8. $3 \times \boxed{1 \quad 1} \times 3 = 3 \times 3$; $\begin{pmatrix} 4 & 5 & 6 \\ 8 & 10 & 12 \\ 12 & 15 & 18 \end{pmatrix}$

9. $\begin{pmatrix} 16 \\ 6 \end{pmatrix}$ **14.** Not possible

10. Not possible   **15.** (30)

11. $\begin{pmatrix} 11 & 20 \\ 24 & 43 \end{pmatrix}$ **16.** Not possible

12. Not possible   **17.** $(3 \quad 24)$

13. $\begin{pmatrix} 15 & 4 & 3 \\ 48 & 13 & 12 \end{pmatrix}$ **18.** $\begin{pmatrix} 6 & 12 & 15 \\ 8 & 16 & 20 \\ 2 & 4 & 5 \end{pmatrix}$

Exercise 8k   page 128

1. $\begin{pmatrix} 6 \\ 5 \end{pmatrix}$ **6.** $(-38 \quad 12)$

2. $\begin{pmatrix} 10 \\ -19 \end{pmatrix}$ **7.** (-26)

3. $(-2 \quad -6)$ **8.** $\begin{pmatrix} -24 & -4 & 12 \\ 6 & 1 & -3 \\ 6 & 1 & -3 \end{pmatrix}$

4. $\begin{pmatrix} 1 \\ 1 \\ -22 \end{pmatrix}$ **9.** $\begin{pmatrix} 7 & 18 & -1 \\ -7 & -18 & 1 \end{pmatrix}$

5. $\begin{pmatrix} 8 & -26 \\ -16 & -17 \end{pmatrix}$ **10.** $\begin{pmatrix} 12 & 18 \\ 8 & 12 \\ -6 & -9 \end{pmatrix}$

Exercise 8l   page 129

1. $\begin{pmatrix} 13 & -8 \\ 7 & -2 \end{pmatrix}$ **6.** Not possible

2. $\begin{pmatrix} 2 & -1 \\ 12 & 9 \end{pmatrix}$ **7.** Not possible

3. $\begin{pmatrix} 10 \\ 5 \end{pmatrix}$ **8.** Not possible

4. Not possible   **9.** Not possible

5. $\begin{pmatrix} 3 & 4 \\ 6 & 8 \end{pmatrix}$ **10.** (11)

11. $(14 \quad 6)$
12. Not possible
13. Not possible
14. $(9 \quad 12)$
15. Not possible

16. $\mathbf{AA} = \begin{pmatrix} 19 & 18 \\ 6 & 7 \end{pmatrix}$ $\mathbf{DH} = \begin{pmatrix} 3 \\ 6 \end{pmatrix}$

$\mathbf{AC} = \begin{pmatrix} 21 & 8 \\ 4 & 2 \end{pmatrix}$ $\mathbf{EA} = (16 \quad 17)$

$\mathbf{BB} = \begin{pmatrix} -5 & -2 \\ 3 & -6 \end{pmatrix}$ $\mathbf{EB} = (15 \quad -6)$

$\mathbf{BC} = \begin{pmatrix} 8 & 2 \\ 18 & 6 \end{pmatrix}$ $\mathbf{FE} = \begin{pmatrix} 18 & 24 \\ 3 & 4 \\ -12 & -16 \end{pmatrix}$

$\mathbf{BD} = \begin{pmatrix} -3 \\ 3 \end{pmatrix}$ $\mathbf{FH} = \begin{pmatrix} 18 \\ 3 \\ -12 \end{pmatrix}$

$\mathbf{CA} = \begin{pmatrix} 26 & 22 \\ -4 & -3 \end{pmatrix}$ $\mathbf{GF} = \begin{pmatrix} -4 \\ 15 \\ 5 \end{pmatrix}$

$\mathbf{CB} = \begin{pmatrix} 12 & -12 \\ -1 & 2 \end{pmatrix}$ $\mathbf{GG} = \begin{pmatrix} 18 & -2 & 17 \\ -13 & 35 & 11 \\ 23 & 4 & 27 \end{pmatrix}$

$\mathbf{CC} = \begin{pmatrix} 34 & 12 \\ -6 & -2 \end{pmatrix}$ $\mathbf{HH} = (9)$

$\mathbf{CD} = \begin{pmatrix} 10 \\ -1 \end{pmatrix}$

Exercise 8m   page 129

1. $\begin{pmatrix} 8 & 2 \\ -21 & -8 \end{pmatrix}$ 7. $(-2 \quad -3)$

2. $\begin{pmatrix} 7 & 4 \\ -3 & 3 \end{pmatrix}$ 8. $\begin{pmatrix} -2 & 1 \\ 8 & 12 \end{pmatrix}$

3. $\begin{pmatrix} -5 & 0 \\ -5 & 3 \end{pmatrix}$ 9. $\begin{pmatrix} 5 & 3 & 3 \\ 11 & 5 & 9 \\ 2 & 2 & 0 \end{pmatrix}$

4. $\begin{pmatrix} 5 & 0 \\ 5 & -3 \end{pmatrix}$ 10. Not possible

5. Not possible   11. Not possible

6. Not possible   12. $(4 \quad 2)$

Exercise 8n   page 130

1. $\begin{pmatrix} 12 & 10 \\ -2 & 13 \end{pmatrix}$ 7. $\begin{pmatrix} 78 & 8 \\ 31 & 28 \end{pmatrix}$

2. $\begin{pmatrix} 78 & -10 \\ 31 & -13 \end{pmatrix}$ 8. $\begin{pmatrix} 50 & 27 \\ 32 & 56 \end{pmatrix}$

3. $\begin{pmatrix} 13 & -6 \\ 18 & 1 \end{pmatrix}$ 9. $\begin{pmatrix} 55 & -11 \\ 66 & -22 \end{pmatrix}$

4. $\begin{pmatrix} 68 & 16 \\ 61 & 4 \end{pmatrix}$ 10. $\begin{pmatrix} -16 & 56 \\ -56 & 20 \end{pmatrix}$

5. $\begin{pmatrix} 48 & 40 \\ 38 & 17 \end{pmatrix}$ 11. $\begin{pmatrix} -64 & 0 \\ 0 & -64 \end{pmatrix}$

6. $\begin{pmatrix} 34 & -25 \\ 75 & -16 \end{pmatrix}$ 12. $\begin{pmatrix} 68 & -12 \\ 61 & -7 \end{pmatrix}$

Exercise 8p   page 130

1. 2×2 and 2×1
2. Yes
3. **A, C** are compatible but not **C, A**
4. $\begin{pmatrix} 23 & -11 \\ 19 & -13 \end{pmatrix}$
5. $\mathbf{A}^2 = \begin{pmatrix} 27 & 18 \\ 9 & 18 \end{pmatrix}$. It is not possible to find $\mathbf{C}^2$
6. Not possible
7. $\begin{pmatrix} 9 & -3 \\ 12 & -9 \end{pmatrix}$ 9. 4
8. $\begin{pmatrix} 13 & 3 \\ 6 & 5 \end{pmatrix}$ 10. **BC**

Exercise 8q   page 131

1. $\begin{pmatrix} 4 & 2 & -2 \\ 8 & 6 & 2 \end{pmatrix}$ 5. No
2. Not possible   6. 3
3. Not possible   7. 1
4. 2×3 and 2×2 8. **QP**
9. $\begin{pmatrix} 17 \\ 13 \end{pmatrix}$
10. $\mathbf{P}^2$ is not possible to find. $\mathbf{Q}^2 = \begin{pmatrix} 7 & 14 \\ -7 & 14 \end{pmatrix}$

Chapter 9

Exercise 9a   page 133

1. Yes, 3×3 3. Yes, 2×2 5. Yes, 2×2
2. No   4. No   6. Yes, 3×3

Exercise 9b   page 134

1. $\begin{pmatrix} 4 & 7 \\ 7 & 11 \end{pmatrix}$ 7. $\begin{pmatrix} 11 & 7 \\ 7 & 4 \end{pmatrix}$

2. $(7 \quad -6)$ 8. Not possible

3. $\begin{pmatrix} 7 & 10 & 1 \\ 15 & 26 & 1 \end{pmatrix}$ 9. $\begin{pmatrix} 4 & 28 & 4 \\ 3 & 18 & 3 \\ 2 & 12 & 2 \end{pmatrix}$

4. Not possible   10. (24)

5. Not possible   11. $\begin{pmatrix} 1 \\ -1 \end{pmatrix}$

6. $\begin{pmatrix} 26 & 13 \\ -4 & -2 \end{pmatrix}$ 12. $(34 \quad 6)$

Exercise 9c   page 135

1. $\begin{pmatrix} 4 & 2 \\ 3 & 4 \end{pmatrix}$ 4. $\begin{pmatrix} 0 & 0 \\ 0 & 0 \end{pmatrix}$

2. $\begin{pmatrix} 4 \\ 5 \end{pmatrix}$ 5. $(3 \quad 2)$

3. $(0 \quad 0)$ 6. $\begin{pmatrix} 3 & 2 & -1 \\ 4 & 3 & -1 \end{pmatrix}$

Exercise 9d   page 135

1. $\begin{pmatrix} 1 & 0 \\ 0 & 1 \end{pmatrix}$

2. $\begin{pmatrix} 5 & 0 \\ 0 & 5 \end{pmatrix}$

3. $\begin{pmatrix} 5 & 0 \\ 0 & 5 \end{pmatrix}$

4. $\begin{pmatrix} 2 & 0 \\ 0 & 2 \end{pmatrix}$

5. $\begin{pmatrix} 3 & 0 \\ 0 & 3 \end{pmatrix}$

6. $\begin{pmatrix} 3 & 0 \\ 0 & 3 \end{pmatrix}$

7. $\begin{pmatrix} -1 & 0 \\ 0 & -1 \end{pmatrix}$

8. $\begin{pmatrix} 1 & 0 \\ 0 & 1 \end{pmatrix}$

10. $\begin{pmatrix} 6 & -2 \\ -8 & 3 \end{pmatrix}$

11. $\begin{pmatrix} 3 & -1 \\ -2 & 2 \end{pmatrix}$

12. $\begin{pmatrix} 3 & 1 \\ 20 & 6 \end{pmatrix}$

13. $\begin{pmatrix} 5 & 3 \\ -1 & 1 \end{pmatrix}$

14. $\begin{pmatrix} 4 & -7 \\ -3 & 5 \end{pmatrix}$

15. $\begin{pmatrix} 6 & -3 \\ -9 & 5 \end{pmatrix}$

16. $\begin{pmatrix} 8 & -4 \\ -9 & 5 \end{pmatrix}$

17. $\begin{pmatrix} 4 & -2 \\ -14 & 6 \end{pmatrix}$

18. $\begin{pmatrix} 1 & -2 \\ -2 & 1 \end{pmatrix}$

19. $\begin{pmatrix} -2 & 3 \\ -3 & 4 \end{pmatrix}$

Exercise 9e   page 000

1. $\begin{pmatrix} 2 & -1 \\ -7 & 4 \end{pmatrix}$

2. $\begin{pmatrix} 2 & -3 \\ -7 & 11 \end{pmatrix}$

3. $\begin{pmatrix} -2 & 3 \\ -7 & 10 \end{pmatrix}$

4. $\begin{pmatrix} 7 & -5 \\ -4 & 3 \end{pmatrix}$

5. $\begin{pmatrix} 7 & -4 \\ -12 & 7 \end{pmatrix}$

6. $\begin{pmatrix} 2 & -1 \\ -1 & 1 \end{pmatrix}$

Exercise 9f   page 138

1. $\begin{pmatrix} 1\frac{1}{2} & -1 \\ -4 & 3 \end{pmatrix}$

2. $\begin{pmatrix} \frac{1}{3} & -\frac{2}{3} \\ -1 & 3 \end{pmatrix}$

3. $\begin{pmatrix} 1\frac{1}{2} & -\frac{1}{2} \\ -2\frac{1}{2} & 1 \end{pmatrix}$

4. $\begin{pmatrix} \frac{1}{3} & \frac{2}{3} \\ -\frac{1}{3} & \frac{1}{3} \end{pmatrix}$

5. $\begin{pmatrix} \frac{1}{2} & 0 \\ 0 & \frac{1}{3} \end{pmatrix}$

6. $\begin{pmatrix} 4 & -1 \\ -5\frac{1}{2} & 1\frac{1}{2} \end{pmatrix}$

7. $\begin{pmatrix} 4 & 3 \\ 5 & 4 \end{pmatrix}$

8. $\begin{pmatrix} 4 & -3 \\ -5 & 4 \end{pmatrix}$

9. $\begin{pmatrix} 1 & 1 \\ \frac{1}{2} & \frac{3}{4} \end{pmatrix}$

10. $\begin{pmatrix} -1 & 1 \\ 3\frac{1}{2} & -3 \end{pmatrix}$

11. $\begin{pmatrix} -1 & 2 \\ 2\frac{1}{2} & -4\frac{1}{2} \end{pmatrix}$

12. $\begin{pmatrix} -\frac{1}{5} & \frac{1}{5} \\ \frac{1}{5} & \frac{4}{5} \end{pmatrix}$

13. $\begin{pmatrix} -1 & 1 \\ 2 & -1\frac{1}{2} \end{pmatrix}$

14. $\begin{pmatrix} -1 & -1\frac{1}{3} \\ -1 & -1 \end{pmatrix}$

15. $\begin{pmatrix} -3 & 2 \\ 4 & -2\frac{1}{2} \end{pmatrix}$

16. (a) Yes   (b) No   (c) Yes
17. (a) Yes   (b) Yes   (c) Yes

18. $\begin{pmatrix} 1 & -1 \\ -1 & 1\frac{1}{5} \end{pmatrix}$

19. No inverse

20. $\begin{pmatrix} \frac{1}{5} & 0 \\ 0 & \frac{1}{5} \end{pmatrix}$

21. $\begin{pmatrix} -4 & 7 \\ 3 & -5 \end{pmatrix}$

22. $\begin{pmatrix} 2 & -1 \\ -3 & 1\frac{2}{3} \end{pmatrix}$

23. No inverse

Exercise 9g   page 139

1. 1, $\begin{pmatrix} 2 & -3 \\ -3 & 5 \end{pmatrix}$

2. 2, $\begin{pmatrix} 1\frac{1}{2} & -1 \\ -1 & 1 \end{pmatrix}$

3. I

4. $\begin{pmatrix} 16 & 19 \\ 10 & 12 \end{pmatrix}$

5. $\begin{pmatrix} 6 & -9\frac{1}{2} \\ -5 & 8 \end{pmatrix}$

6. $\begin{pmatrix} 6 & -5 \\ -9\frac{1}{2} & 8 \end{pmatrix}$

7. $\begin{pmatrix} 6 & -9\frac{1}{2} \\ -5 & 8 \end{pmatrix}$

8. $\begin{pmatrix} 34 & 21 \\ 21 & 13 \end{pmatrix}$

9. $\begin{pmatrix} 13 & -21 \\ -21 & 34 \end{pmatrix}$

10. $\begin{pmatrix} 13 & -21 \\ -21 & 34 \end{pmatrix}$

11. $\begin{pmatrix} 2 & 1 \\ -3\frac{1}{2} & -1\frac{1}{2} \end{pmatrix}$

12. $\begin{pmatrix} -2\frac{1}{2} & 4 \\ -2 & 3 \end{pmatrix}$

Exercise 9h   page 141

1. 9
2. 17
3. 0
4. 19
5. −14
6. 10
7. −1
8. −8
9. 9
10. 5
11. 5
12. −9

Exercise 9i   page 142

1. $x + 2y = 3$
   $3x + 2y = 5$
2. $4x + 2y = 12$
   $5x + 3y = 15$
3. $9x + 2y = 24$
   $4x + y = 11$
4. $6p - q = -8$
   $2p + q = 0$

5. $\begin{pmatrix} 3 & 2 \\ 1 & 1 \end{pmatrix} \begin{pmatrix} x \\ y \end{pmatrix} = \begin{pmatrix} 8 \\ 3 \end{pmatrix}$

6. $\begin{pmatrix} 4 & -3 \\ 2 & 1 \end{pmatrix} \begin{pmatrix} x \\ y \end{pmatrix} = \begin{pmatrix} 1 \\ 3 \end{pmatrix}$

7. $\begin{pmatrix} 4 & 3 \\ 5 & 4 \end{pmatrix} \begin{pmatrix} x \\ y \end{pmatrix} = \begin{pmatrix} 5 \\ 6 \end{pmatrix}$

8. $\begin{pmatrix} 3 & -2 \\ 1 & -1 \end{pmatrix} \begin{pmatrix} x \\ y \end{pmatrix} = \begin{pmatrix} 1 \\ 0 \end{pmatrix}$

9. $\begin{pmatrix} 7 & -2 \\ 3 & 4 \end{pmatrix} \begin{pmatrix} x \\ y \end{pmatrix} = \begin{pmatrix} 3 \\ 11 \end{pmatrix}$

10. $\begin{pmatrix} 5 & 1 \\ 4 & -3 \end{pmatrix} \begin{pmatrix} x \\ y \end{pmatrix} = \begin{pmatrix} -8 \\ -14 \end{pmatrix}$

Exercise 9j   page 143

1. $x = 1$, $y = 2$
2. $x = 2$, $y = 3$
3. $x = 1$, $y = -1$
4. $x = 2$, $y = -1$
5. $a = 3$, $b = 0$
6. $x = 1$, $y = 2$
7. $x = 4$, $y = 2$
8. $x = 1$, $y = -2$
9. $x = 4$, $y = 2$
10. $p = 1$, $q = 1$
11. $s = -2$, $t = 3$

12. $\begin{pmatrix} 1 & 1 \\ 1 & 2 \end{pmatrix}\begin{pmatrix} x \\ y \end{pmatrix} = \begin{pmatrix} 2 \\ 3 \end{pmatrix}$; $\quad x = 1, \quad y = 1$

13. $\begin{pmatrix} 4 & -1 \\ 1 & 1 \end{pmatrix}\begin{pmatrix} x \\ y \end{pmatrix} = \begin{pmatrix} 5 \\ 5 \end{pmatrix}$; $\quad x = 2, \quad y = 3$

14. $\begin{pmatrix} 5 & 4 \\ 1 & 1 \end{pmatrix}\begin{pmatrix} x \\ y \end{pmatrix} = \begin{pmatrix} 1 \\ 0 \end{pmatrix}$; $\quad x = 1, \quad y = -1$

15. $\begin{pmatrix} 2 & 3 \\ 3 & 5 \end{pmatrix}\begin{pmatrix} x \\ y \end{pmatrix} = \begin{pmatrix} 15 \\ 23 \end{pmatrix}$; $\quad x = 6, \quad y = 1$

16. $\begin{pmatrix} 9 & 2 \\ 3 & 1 \end{pmatrix}\begin{pmatrix} x \\ y \end{pmatrix} = \begin{pmatrix} 11 \\ 5 \end{pmatrix}$; $\quad x = \frac{1}{3}, \quad y = 4$

17. $\begin{pmatrix} 2 & 3 \\ 3 & 2 \end{pmatrix}\begin{pmatrix} x \\ y \end{pmatrix} = \begin{pmatrix} 7 \\ 8 \end{pmatrix}$; $\quad x = 2, \quad y = 1$

18. $\begin{pmatrix} 5 & 2 \\ 3 & -1 \end{pmatrix}\begin{pmatrix} x \\ y \end{pmatrix} = \begin{pmatrix} 16 \\ 3 \end{pmatrix}$; $\quad x = 2, \quad y = 3$

19. $\begin{pmatrix} 1 & 4 \\ 2 & 3 \end{pmatrix}\begin{pmatrix} x \\ y \end{pmatrix} = \begin{pmatrix} 11 \\ 7 \end{pmatrix}$; $\quad x = -1, \quad y = 3$

20. Determinant is zero so there is no inverse.
21. Determinant is zero so there is no inverse.

Exercise 9k   page 144

1. $\begin{pmatrix} 5 & 6 \\ -3 & 0 \end{pmatrix}$ **5.** $\begin{pmatrix} 2 & 1\frac{1}{2} \\ 1 & \frac{1}{2} \end{pmatrix}$

2. $\begin{pmatrix} 7 & 2 \\ -3 & 2 \end{pmatrix}$ **6.** $\begin{pmatrix} 3 & -6 \\ 0 & 3 \end{pmatrix}$

3. $\begin{pmatrix} 15 & 19 \\ 9 & 9 \end{pmatrix}$ **7.** $\begin{pmatrix} 3 & -1 \\ -5 & 1 \end{pmatrix}$

4. $\begin{pmatrix} -5 & -6 \\ 3 & 0 \end{pmatrix}$ **8.** $\begin{pmatrix} -\frac{1}{2} & 1\frac{1}{2} \\ 1 & -2 \end{pmatrix}$

Exercise 9l   page 144

1. $\begin{pmatrix} 5 & 4 & 3 \\ 10 & -8 & 4 \end{pmatrix}$ **4.** $\begin{pmatrix} \frac{4}{7} & -\frac{3}{7} \\ -\frac{3}{7} & \frac{4}{7} \end{pmatrix}$

2. $\begin{pmatrix} 1 & 3\frac{1}{2} \\ 1\frac{1}{2} & -\frac{1}{2} \end{pmatrix}$ **5.** (-9)

3. 24   **6.** $\begin{pmatrix} 13 & 33 \\ 6 & 22 \end{pmatrix}$

Exercise 9m   page 145

1. $\begin{pmatrix} 5 & 3 \\ -1 & 4 \end{pmatrix}$ **4.** $\begin{pmatrix} 3 \\ -1 \end{pmatrix}$

2. 2   **5.** $(6 \quad 10)$

3. $\begin{pmatrix} 1 & 1 \\ 2 & 3 \end{pmatrix}$ **6.** $(3 \quad -1\frac{1}{2})$

Chapter 10

Exercise 10a   page 147
  1. $x = 4$ **3.** $y = -3$
  2. $y = 5$ **4.** $x = -2$

5.

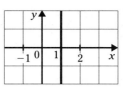

6.

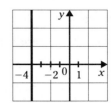

7.

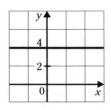

8.

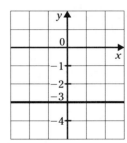

Exercise 10b   page 149

1.

x	-2	0	4
y	2	4	8

2.

x	-2	0	3
y	-3	1	7

3.

x	-3	0	3
y	7	4	1

4.

x	-1	0	3
y	5	2	-4

13. (a) $1\frac{1}{2}$ (b) 0.4   (c) -1.6
14. (a) 0   (b) -0.8 (c) -3.4
15. (a) -2.6 (b) -1.8 (c) 1.2
16. (a) 3.6   (b) 0.6   (c) 1.2
17. (a) $-2\frac{1}{2}$ (b) 4.4   (c) 2.4
18. (a) 4.8   (b) 1.2   (c) -11.2
19. (a) -1.4 (b) 1.4   (c) 3.5
20. (a) 8.6   (b) 2.8   (c) 3

Exercise 10c   page 152
1. Yes, No   3. No, No   5. Yes, Yes
2. Yes, No   4. No, Yes   6. No, Yes

Exercise 10d   page 153
1. Lines are parallel; coefficient of x is 2 in each equation
2. Lines are parallel; coefficient of x is -3 in each equation
3. Lines are parallel; coefficient of x is $\frac{1}{2}$ in each equation
4. Lines are parallel; coefficient of x is 1 in each equation
5. Lines (a) and (c) are parallel
6. Lines are parallel; coefficient of x is -1 in each equation

Exercise 10e   page 156
1. 4   3. 1   5. $-\frac{9}{5}$
2. -2 4. $-\frac{3}{4}$ 6. $\frac{2}{3}$
7. 0
8. y-axis. You find yourself dividing by zero
9. (a) parallel to the y-axis
   (b) zero gradient
   (c) zero gradient
   (d) parallel to the y-axis

Exercise 10f   page 157
1. 2   3. 2   5. 4
2. 1   4. -2

6. (a) 4   (b) -3 (c) 1   (d) $\frac{1}{2}$

7. (a)

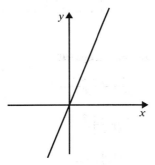

(b)

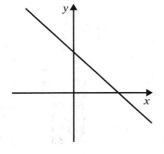

8. (a)

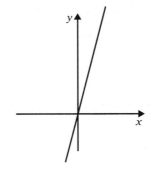

(b)

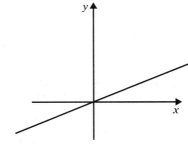

9. (a)

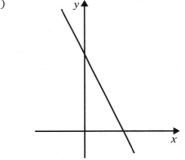

(b)

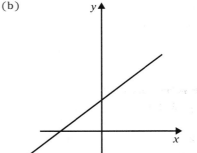

Exercise 10g   page 159
1. 2, 4   5. $-2, 3$ 9. $-\frac{1}{3}, 4$ 13. $-0.4, 9$
2. 5, 3   6. $-4, 2$ 10. 3, -7 14. 5, 4
3. 3, -4 7. 5, 2   11. $-3, 7$ 15. $2, 2\frac{1}{2}$
4. 1, -6 8. $\frac{1}{2}, -1$ 12. $\frac{1}{3}, 7$ 16. $\frac{1}{3}, -2$

17. $\frac{2}{5}, 1$

18. $-\frac{3}{4}, 2$

19. $y = 2x + 7$

20. $y = 3x + 1$

21. $y = x + 3$

22. $y = 2x - 5$

23. $y = \frac{1}{2}x + 6$

24. $y = -2x + 1$

25. $y = x - 2$

26. $y = -\frac{1}{2}x + 4$

Exercise 10h   page 161

1. $y = 3x + 1$, $y = 5 + 3x$, $y = 3x - 4$

2. $y = 2 - x$, $y = 4 - x$, $2y = 3 - 2x$, $y = -x + 1$, $y = -x$

3. $3y = x$, $y = \frac{1}{3}x + 2$, $y = \frac{1}{3} + \frac{1}{3}x$, $y = \frac{1}{3}x - 4$

4. $y = \frac{1}{2}x + 2$ and $y = \frac{1}{2}x - 1$; $y = 2 - \frac{1}{2}x$ and $2y = 3 - x$

5. 2; $y = 2x + 3$

6. -3; $y = -3x + 1$

7. $y = 4x$

8. e.g. $y = 6 - x$, $y = -x$, $y = -2 - x$

9. (a) $y = 4x + 4$ (c) $y = \frac{1}{2}x + 4$
   (b) $y = -3x + 4$

10. (a) $y = \frac{1}{3}x + 6$ (c) $y = \frac{1}{3}x - 3$
    (b) $y = \frac{1}{3}x$

11. (a) $y = 2x + 2$ (c) $y = 2x - 4$
    (b) $y = 2x + 10$

12. $y = 3 + 2x$ and $y = 2x - 3$

13. $-3, 4$; $4, -3$; $y = -3x - 3$

14. (a) $y = -4x$ (b) $y = -4x - 7$

Exercise 10i   page 162

1. $-\frac{3}{5}$ 4. -1 7. $\frac{1}{3}$

2. $-\frac{1}{3}$ 5. -2 8. 2

3. $\frac{1}{4}$ 6. $-\frac{1}{3}$ 9. -1 in each case

Exercise 10j   page 163

1. $-\frac{3}{4}$ 3. $\frac{1}{2}$ 5. 2

2. $-\frac{3}{5}$ 4. -2 6. $\frac{3}{4}$

7. (a) $(2, 0)$, $(0, 4)$ (b) $(12, 0)$, $(0, -9)$

8. (a) $\frac{x}{6} + \frac{y}{5} = 1$ (b) $\frac{x}{4} - \frac{y}{3} = 1$

9. $-\frac{1}{3}$

Exercise 10k   page 164

1. $-\frac{3}{5}, 3$ 8. $-\frac{3}{5}, 3$ 15. $-2, 4$

2. $-\frac{1}{3}, 2$ 9. $\frac{1}{2}, -2$ 16. $-\frac{2}{5}, 3$

3. $\frac{1}{4}, -2$ 10. $-3, 6$ 17. $-\frac{1}{2}, 5$

4. $\frac{1}{3}, -2$ 11. $-\frac{4}{3}, 4$ 18. $2, \frac{5}{2}$

5. $3, 6$ 12. $\frac{4}{3}, -4$ 19. $2, -4$

6. $-\frac{1}{3}, 2$ 13. $4, 2$ 20. $-1, -3$

7. $-\frac{3}{4}, 3$ 14. $-1, 4$ 21. $-\frac{3}{4}, 3$

Exercise 10l   page 166

1. $-\frac{4}{3}, 4$; $y = -\frac{4}{3}x + 4$ 7. $\frac{1}{6}, 1$; $y = \frac{1}{6}x + 1$

2. $-2, 7$; $y = -2x + 7$ 8. $\frac{4}{5}, -3$; $y = \frac{4}{5}x - 3$

3. $\frac{3}{5}, 1$; $y = \frac{3}{5}x + 1$ 9. $\frac{5}{3}, -4$; $y = \frac{5}{3}x - 4$

4. $-\frac{4}{3}, 2$; $y = -\frac{4}{3}x + 2$ 10. $-1, -5$; $y = -x - 5$

5. $\frac{7}{2}, -4$; $y = \frac{7}{2}x - 4$ 11. $2, 12$; $y = 2x + 12$

6. $\frac{1}{3}, -1$; $y = \frac{1}{3}x - 1$ 12. $\frac{5}{6}, 6$; $y = \frac{5}{6}x + 6$

13. AB, $5y = 2x + 20$;   AC, $5x + 3y = 12$

14. $3, y = 3x - 11$ 19. $-1, y = -x + 3$

15. $-3, y = -3x + 7$ 20. $-1, y = -x + 1$

16. $\frac{5}{2}, y = \frac{5}{2}x - \frac{1}{2}$ 21. $2, y = 2x - 11$

17. $2, y = 2x + 7$ 22. $\frac{1}{5}, y = \frac{1}{5}x - \frac{6}{5}$

18. $5, y = 5x - 21$ 23. $-\frac{5}{2}, y = -\frac{5}{2}x + \frac{19}{2}$

24. $-\frac{5}{4}, \dfrac{x}{4} + \dfrac{y}{5} = 1$ or $y = -\frac{5}{4}x + 5$

25. $-\frac{2}{3}, \dfrac{x}{3} + \dfrac{y}{2} = 1$ or $y = -\frac{2}{3}x + 2$

26. $\frac{2}{3}, \dfrac{x}{3} - \dfrac{y}{2} = 1$ or $y = \frac{2}{3}x - 2$

27. $-3, \dfrac{x}{2} + \dfrac{y}{6} = 1$ or $y = -3x + 6$

28. $3, y = 3x - 10$ 30. $-\frac{7}{2}, y = -\frac{7}{2}x - 6$

29. $-1, y = -x + 4$ 31. $-1, y = -x + 3$

32. $\frac{5}{2}, -\dfrac{x}{2} + \dfrac{y}{5} = 1$ or $y = \frac{5}{2}x + 5$

33. $\frac{2}{11}, y = \frac{2}{11}x + \frac{21}{11}$ 35. $-\frac{1}{4}, y = -\frac{1}{4}x + \frac{11}{4}$

34. $1, y = x - 1$

Exercise 10m   page 168

1. $y = 3x - 16$

2. Square

3. Rhombus

4. $(\frac{1}{2}, 3)$

5. Midpoint is $(5, 3)$; $y = -2x + 13$

6. $y = -x + 4$

7. Square

Exercise 10n   page 168

1. 2 5. $y = 5x$

2. $(0, 4)$ 6. $(12, 0)$

3. $(4, 0)$ 7. Yes

4. 12 8. $\frac{3}{5}$

Exercise 10p   page 169

1. -3 5. $(0, 6)$, $(6, 0)$

2. No   6. $-\frac{3}{2}$

3. $y = -4x$ 7. $y = \frac{1}{2}x$

4. $(0, 4)$ 8. $(2, 0)$, $(0, 3)$

Chapter 11

Exercise 11a   page 172
1. (a) $200t$ — (b) 3.16 cm
2. (a) \$168.9 — (b) 7.27 years
3. (a) 3.6 — (b) 2.3
4. (a) 3 cm — (b) 67 cm^2
5. (a) 16.5 cm — (b) 2.21

Exercise 11b   page 174
1. (a) 59.5 m — (b) 4.47 s
2. (a) 4.8 — (b) 7.5
3. (a) 1.67 — (b) 1.09
4. 2.65, 5.29
5. (a) 3.33 — (b) -1.43

Exercise 11c   page 176
1. The graph passes through the origin O, which is also the lowest value for y.
2. (a) 1.73 or -1.73 — (b) No
3. (a) 2 and -2 — (b) 1 and -1, Yes
4. They all have the same shape.
   They all have the same shape but cross the y-axis at different points.
5. (a) When $x = 0$ and $x = 3$
   (b) -0.79 and 3.79
6. (a) When $x = 0$ and 1.5
   (b) $-1\frac{1}{8}$ when $x = \frac{3}{4}$
7. (a) -2 when $x = -1$ — (c) 0 and -2
   (b) 10.5
8. (a) -4 when $x = 1$
   (b) (i) -1.24 and 3.24 — (ii) -2.46 and 4.46
9. (a) 6.25 when $x = 0.5$
   (b) (i) -2.37 and 3.37 — (ii) -1 and 2

Review test 1   page 180
1. A   3. C   5. C   7. C   9. A
2. D   4. B   6. A   8. B   10. A
11. (a) $-12/1$ — (b) 2
12. (a) $3\frac{1}{2}\%$ — (b) \$40 500
13. (a) 5.9
    (b) $v = 60°$, triangles PST and TRQ
14. (a) 11 — (b) $-\frac{7}{2} < x < \frac{5}{3}$
15. (a) $\begin{pmatrix} 2 & 3 \\ 3 & -1 \end{pmatrix} \begin{pmatrix} x \\ y \end{pmatrix} = \begin{pmatrix} 7 \\ 5 \end{pmatrix}$ $x = 2, y = 1$
    (b) $y = 4x - 22$

Chapter 12

Exercise 12a   page 183
1. 40 cm^2
2. 10 cm^2
3. 17 cm^2
4. 19.35 cm^2
5. 12 sq. units
6. 30 sq. units
7. 12 sq. units
8. 16 sq. units
9. $24\frac{1}{2}$ sq. units
10. 4 cm
11. 450 mm^2
12. 5 cm
13. 5 m, 25 m^2
14. 4 cm
15. (a) 17.5 cm^2 — (b) 5.83 cm
16. (a) 12 cm^2 — (b) 3.43 cm
17. (a) 40 cm^2 — (b) 6.67 cm
18. (a) 7 cm^2 — (b) 2 cm

Exercise 12b   page 185
1. 60 cm^2
2. 40 cm^2
3. 30 cm^2
4. 45 cm^2
5. 135 cm^2
6. 27.75 cm^2

Exercise 12c   page 187
1. 42 cm^2
2. 94.5 cm^2
3. 21 cm^2
4. 8.75 cm^2
5. 30 sq. units
6. 33 sq. units
7. 56 sq. units
8. 16 sq. units
9. 84 sq. units
10. 47 sq. units

Exercise 12d   page 188
1. Area of each parallelogram is 35 cm^2
2. Area of each triangle is 28 cm^2
3. Each parallelogram has a base of length 4 units and height of 3 units. The areas are each equal to 12 sq. units.
4. Each base is 6 units long. Each height is 3 units. The areas are each equal to 9 sq. units.
8. Ratio of heights is $4 : 5 : 7 : 9$. Ratio of areas is $4 : 5 : 7 : 9$. The ratio of areas is equal to the ratio of heights.
9. The y coordinate of D is 9 (or -7 if drawn below the x-axis)
10. The y coordinate of E is 3 (or -1 if drawn below the x-axis)
11. (a) $4 : 5 : 3 : 9$ — (b) $4 : 5 : 3 : 9$
    The triangles have equal heights and the ratio of their areas is equal to the ratio of their bases

Exercise 12e   page 191
7. 12 cm
8. $2 : 1$
9. 14 cm
10. 8 cm
11. 30°
12. $\triangle$ BEC $= 27$ cm^2
    $\triangle$ DEC $= 12$ cm^2
13. 132°
14. 6 cm
15. 36 cm^2

Chapter 13

Exercise 13a   page 195
1. 46
2. 40
3. 20
4. 41.4
5. (a) 255 — (b) 51
6. (a) 366 — (b) 61
7. 765, 153
8. 558
9. 29°
10. 52 c
11. \$5.75
12. 80 cl
13. 8800 t
14. (a) \$602.50 — (b) \$794.40 — (c) \$191.90
15. (a) 130 — (b) 192 — (c) 62
16. (a) 225 — (b) 25
17. 17 y 5 m, 43 y 9 m
18. 42.5 kg
19. 66.4 kg
20. 2

Exercise 13b   page 199

1. 60 km/h
2. 30 km/h
3. 36 km/h
4. 90 km/h
5. 18 km/h
6. $262\frac{1}{2}$ km/h
7. 50 mph
8. 8 mph
9. 45 mph
10. 54 mph
11. 260 km
12. 80 miles
13. 155 km
14. 81 miles
15. 3 hours
16. 5 hours
17. 20 min
18. 45 min

Exercise 13c   page 200

1. 22.5 km//h
2. 100 km/h
3. 140 km/h
4. 9 km/h
5. 90 km/h
6. 55 km/h
7. 80 km/h
8. (c)

Chapter 14

Exercise 14a   page 203

1. $2x + 2$
2. $3x - 3$
3. $4x + 12$
4. $5a + 20$
5. $3b + 21$
6. $3 - 3a$
7. $5 - 5b$
8. $6a - 2$
9. $8 + 12b$
10. $5ab - 5ac$
11. $4ab - 8ac$
12. $6a^2 + 3ab$
13. $15xy + 5xz$
14. $16xy + 12yz$
15. $6np - 10nq$
16. $16rt - 8rs$
17. $3ab - 15ac$
18. $12xy + 8xz$

Exercise 14b   page 214

1. $ac + ad + bc + bd$
2. $ps + pt + qs + qt$
3. $2ac + 4ad + bc + 2bd$
4. $5xz + 15x + 2yz + 6y$
5. $xz - 4x + yz - 4y$
6. $ac + ad - bc - bd$
7. $xy + xz + y^2 + yz$
8. $6ac + 2ad + 3bc + bd$
9. $5xz + 10x + 4yz + 8y$
10. $15x - 3xz - 10y + 2yz$
11. $2ps - 3pt + 2qs - 3qt$
12. $ac - ad - 2bc + 2bd$
13. $6uw - 30ur - 5vw + 25vr$
14. $6ac - 9ad + 8bc - 12bd$
15. $9xz + 6x + 6yz + 4y$
16. $12pr - 9ps - 4qr + 3qs$
17. $9ac + 12ad - 12bc - 16bd$
18. $21x - 14xz - 6y + 4yz$
19. $10ac - 4a + 5bc - 2b$
20. $15a - 10ad - 12b + 8bd$

Exercise 14c   page 205

1. $x^2 + 7x + 12$
2. $x^2 + 6x + 8$
3. $x^2 + 7x + 6$
4. $x^2 + 7x + 10$
5. $x^2 + 11x + 24$
6. $a^2 + 9a + 20$
7. $b^2 + 9b + 14$
8. $c^2 + 10c + 24$
9. $p^2 + 15p + 36$
10. $q^2 + 17q + 70$
11. $x^2 - 5x + 6$
12. $x^2 - 12x + 35$
13. $a^2 - 10a + 16$
14. $x^2 - 13x + 30$
15. $b^2 - 10b + 25$
16. $x^2 - 7x + 12$
17. $x^2 - 12x + 32$
18. $b^2 - 6b + 8$
19. $a^2 - 8a + 16$
20. $p^2 - 15p + 56$
21. $x^2 + x - 6$
22. $x^2 + x - 20$

23. $x^2 - 3x - 28$
24. $a^2 - 7a - 30$
25. $p^2 - 25$
26. $x^2 + 5x - 14$
27. $x^2 + x - 30$
28. $x^2 + 9x - 10$
29. $b^2 - 15b + 56$
30. $z^2 - 13z + 12$

Exercise 14d   page 207

1. $x^2 + 9x + 20$
2. $a^2 + 7a + 10$
3. $x^2 - 9x + 20$
4. $a^2 - 7a + 10$
5. $x^2 + 14x + 48$
6. $a^2 + 17a + 70$
7. $x^2 - 14x + 48$
8. $a^2 - 17a + 70$
9. $a^2 - 3a - 10$
10. $y^2 - 3y - 18$
11. $z^2 - 6z - 40$
12. $p^2 - 3p - 40$
13. $a^2 - 3a - 70$
14. $y^2 + 8y - 20$
15. $z^2 - 11z - 12$
16. $p^2 - 11p - 26$
17. $x^2 - 6x + 5$
18. $b^2 + 16b + 63$
19. $a^2 - 16$
20. $r^2 - 12r - 28$
21. $p^2 + 14p + 24$
22. $t^2 - 7t - 60$
23. $c^2 + 3c - 40$
24. $x^2 - 25$

Exercise 14e   page 207

1. $2x^2 + 3x + 1$
2. $5x^2 + 12x + 4$
3. $5x^2 + 17x + 6$
4. $3x^2 + 19x + 20$
5. $3x^2 + 5x + 2$
6. $3x^2 + 11x + 6$
7. $4x^2 + 7x + 3$
8. $7x^2 + 23x + 6$
9. $6x^2 + 13x + 6$
10. $12x^2 - 25x + 12$
11. $10x^2 - 3x - 18$
12. $21a^2 - 58a + 21$
13. $10x^2 + 31x + 15$
14. $21x^2 - 20x + 4$
15. $12x^2 - 5x - 2$
16. $6b^2 - 5b - 25$
17. $4a^2 - 9$
18. $9b^2 - 49$
19. $49y^2 - 25$
20. $20a^2 + a - 12$
21. $16x^2 - 9$
22. $25y^2 - 4$
23. $9x^2 - 1$
24. $16x^2 - 8x - 35$
25. $6x^2 + 5x + 1$
26. $-5x^2 + 8x + 4$
27. $-6x^2 + 19x - 3$
28. $-35a^2 + 29a - 6$
29. $8 + 10x - 3x^2$
30. $4x^2 + 7x - 15$
31. $15x^2 + 26x + 8$
32. $-14x^2 + 13x + 12$
33. $-20x^2 + 27x - 9$
34. $12 - p - p^2$
35. $x^2 - 3x - 10$
36. $4x^2 + 9x - 9$

Exercise 14f   page 209

1. $x^2 + 2x + 1$
2. $x^2 + 4x + 4$
3. $a^2 + 6a + 9$
4. $b^2 + 8b + 16$
5. $t^2 + 20t + 100$
6. $x^2 + 24x + 144$
7. $x^2 + 16x + 64$
8. $p^2 + 14p + 49$
9. $x^2 + 2xy + y^2$
10. $y^2 + 2yz + z^2$
11. $c^2 + 2cd + d^2$
12. $m^2 + 2mn + n^2$
13. $p^2 + 2pq + q^2$
14. $a^2 + 2ab + b^2$
15. $e^2 + 2ef + f^2$
16. $u^2 + 2uv + v^2$
17. $4x^2 + 4x + 1$
18. $16b^2 + 8b + 1$
19. $25x^2 + 20x + 4$
20. $36c^2 + 12c + 1$
21. $9a^2 + 6a + 1$
22. $4x^2 + 20x + 25$
23. $9a^2 + 24a + 16$
24. $16y^2 + 24y + 9$
25. $x^2 + 4xy + 4y^2$
26. $9x^2 + 6xy + y^2$
27. $4x^2 + 20xy + 25y^2$
28. $9a^2 + 12ab + 4b^2$
29. $9a^2 + 6ab + b^2$
30. $p^2 + 8pq + 16q^2$
31. $49x^2 + 28xy + 4y^2$
32. $9s^2 + 24st + 16t^2$
33. $x^2 - 4x + 4$
34. $x^2 - 12x + 36$
35. $a^2 - 20a + 100$
36. $x^2 - 2xy + y^2$
37. $x^2 - 6x + 9$
38. $x^2 - 14x + 49$
39. $a^2 - 2ab + b^2$
40. $u^2 - 2uv + v^2$
41. $9x^2 - 6x + 1$
42. $25z^2 - 10z + 1$

43. $100a^2 - 180a + 81$
44. $16x^2 - 24x + 9$
45. $4a^2 - 4a + 1$
46. $16y^2 - 8y + 1$
47. $49b^2 - 28b + 4$
48. $25x^2 - 30x + 9$
49. $4y^2 - 4yx + x^2$

50. $25x^2 - 10xy + y^2$
51. $9m^2 - 12mn + 4n^2$
52. $49x^2 - 42xy + 9y^2$
53. $a^2 - 6ab + 9b^2$
54. $m^2 - 16mn + 64n^2$
55. $25a^2 - 20ab + 4b^2$
56. $9p^2 - 30pq + 25q^2$

Exercise 14g   page 211

1. $x^2 - 16$
2. $b^2 - 36$
3. $c^2 - 9$
4. $x^2 - 144$
5. $x^2 - 25$
6. $a^2 - 49$
7. $q^2 - 100$
8. $x^2 - 64$
9. $4x^2 - 1$
10. $9x^2 - 1$
11. $49a^2 - 4$
12. $25a^2 - 16$
13. $25x^2 - 1$

14. $4a^2 - 9$
15. $100\,m^2 - 1$
16. $36a^2 - 25$
17. $9x^2 - 16y^2$
18. $4a^2 - 25b^2$
19. $1 - 4a^2$
20. $49y^2 - 9z^2$
21. $100a^2 - 81b^2$
22. $25a^2 - 16b^2$
23. $1 - 9x^2$
24. $9 - 25x^2$
25. $25m^2 - 64n^2$
26. $36p^2 - 49q^2$

Exercise 14h   page 212

1. $2x^2 + 9x + 12$
2. $2x^2 + 9x + 2$
3. $x^2 + 15x + 32$
4. $a^2 - 9a + 36$
5. $2a^2 - 10a - 3$
6. $x^2 + 13x + 25$
7. $x^2 - 2x - 21$
8. $x^2 - 2x - 23$
9. $16x^2 + 6x - 10$
10. $12x^2 + 8x - 20$

11. $x^2y^2 - 6xy + 9$
12. $25 - 10yz + y^2z^2$
13. $x^2y^2 + 8xy + 16$
14. $9p^2q^2 + 48pq + 64$
15. $a^2 - 2abc + b^2c^2$
16. $a^2b^2 - 4ab + 4$
17. $36 - 12pq + p^2q^2$
18. $m^2n^2 + 6mn + 9$
19. $u^2v^2 - 4uvw + 4w^2$

Exercise 14i   page 000

1. $5x + 10$
2. $24pq - 16pr$
3. $6a^2 - 13ab - 5b^2$
4. $12x^2 - 17x - 5$
5. $x^2 + 16x + 60$

6. $x^2 - 20x + 96$
7. $16y^2 - 16y - 21$
8. $16y^2 - 81$
9. $25x^2 - 70a + 49$
10. $4a^2 - 28ab + 49b^2$

Exercise 14j   page 214

1. $8 - 20x$
2. $16a - 24a^2$
3. $12a^2 - 35a - 33$
4. $x^2 + 2x - 99$
5. $-20x^2 - 48x + 5$

6. $y^2 + 4yz + 4z^2$
7. $36y^2 + 24yz - 5z^2$
8. $16a^2 + 8a + 1$
9. $25a^2 - 70a + 49$
10. $36z^2 - 156zy + 169y^2$

Exercise 14k   page 214

1. $6 - 3a$
2. $8ab + 4ac$
3. $10ac + 25ad + 4bc + 10bd$
4. $x^2 - 19x + 84$
5. $a^2 + 16a + 63$
6. $a^2 - a - 20$
7. $6x^2 + 11x + 3$
8. $25x^2 - 4$
9. $9x^2 - 42x + 49$
10. $25x^2 - 4y^2$

Exercise 14l   page 215

1. $15 - 5x$
2. $36x^2 - 24x$
3. $6xy - 15xz$
4. $ac + ad - bc - bd$
5. $x^2 + 3x - 28$

6. $x^2 - 11x + 18$
7. $12x^2 + 11x + 2$
8. $x^2 - 8xy + 16y^2$
9. $4x^2 + 28xz + 49z^2$
10. $1 - 25a^2$

Chapter 15

Exercise 15a   page 216

1. $4(x + 1)$
2. $3(4x - 1)$
3. $2(3a + 1)$
4. $5(a - 2b)$
5. $3(t - 3)$
6. $5(2a - 1)$
7. $4(3a + 1)$
8. $2(a + 2b)$
9. $7(2x - 1)$
10. $x(x + 2)$
11. $x(x - 7)$
12. $a(a + 6)$
13. $x(2x + 1)$
14. $2t(2 - t)$
15. $x(x + 5)$
16. $x(x - 4)$
17. $b(b + 4)$
18. $a(4a - 1)$
19. $2x(x - 3)$
20. $2z(z^2 + 2)$
21. $5a(5a - 1)$
22. $4x(3x + 4)$
23. $5b(a - 2c)$
24. $3y(y + 9)$
25. $2a(a - 6)$

26. $2p(3p + 1)$

27. $3y(3y - 2)$
28. $2(x^2 + 2x + 3)$
29. $5(2a^2 - a + 4)$
30. $b(a + 4c - 3d)$

31. $4(2x - y + 3z)$

32. $3a(3b - 2c - d)$
33. $3(x^2 - 2x + 3)$

34. $4(a^2 + 2a - 1)$
35. $x(5y + 4z + 3)$

36. $5b(a + 2c + d)$
37. $2y(x - 2z + 4w)$
38. $x^2(x + 1)$
39. $x^2(1 - x)$
40. $5a^2(4 - a)$
41. $4x^2(3x - 4)$
42. $4x^2(x^2 + 3)$
43. $a^2(1 + a)$
44. $b^2(b - 1)$
45. $2x^2(2x - 1)$
46. $9a^2(3 - 2a)$
47. $5x^2(2 - 3x^2)$
48. $4(3x + 2)$
49. $4x(2x + 3)$
50. $3(3x^2 - 2x + 4)$
51. $5x(x^2 - 2)$
52. $4q(2p + r)$
53. $x(x - 8)$
54. $3(4 + 3y^2)$
55. $4x(3y + 4z + 2)$
56. $2x(2x^2 + 3)$
57. $4bc(3a - 2d)$
58. $\frac{1}{2}h(a + b)$
59. $m(g - a)$
60. $\frac{1}{2}m(v^2 + u^2)$

61. $p\left(1 + \dfrac{RT}{100}\right)$

62. $\pi r(2r + h)$
63. $\pi(R^2 + r^2)$
64. $2g(h_1 - h_2)$
65. $m(\frac{1}{2}v^2 - gh)$

66. $\dfrac{\pi r^2}{3}(4r - h)$

67. $\pi r(3r + 2h)$
68. $\frac{1}{2}mu(u + 1)$
69. $\frac{1}{4}c(2b - a)$

Exercise 15b   page 219

1. $(x + 3)(y + 3)$
2. $(a + 2b)(1 + b)$
3. $(a + b)(a + c)$
4. $(x - 3)(y + 2)$
5. $(x + 1)(y + z)$
6. $(x + 2)(y + 4)$
7. $(a + b)(c + 4)$
8. $(x + 4)(y - 2)$
9. $(p + q)(r + s)$
10. $(y + 4)(x - 3)$
11. $(x + 2)(y - 5)$
12. $(p + q)(r - s)$

13. $(a + 2)(b - 3)$
14. $(p - q)(r + s)$
15. $(p + 4)(q + 2)$
16. $(2 + a)(3 + b)$
17. $(p - q)(r - s)$
18. $(3a - b)(3 - b)$
19. $(2a - b)(1 - b)$
20. $(a - 2)(a + 2b)$
21. $(2 - x)(3 - y)$
22. $(a - 2)(4a - b)$
23. $(3a - b)(2a - 3)$
24. $(2m - 3n)(1 - n)$

25. $(t+r)(t+s)$
26. $(x-1)(x+y)$
27. $2(1-a)(2a+b)$
28. $(x+y)(1-y)$
29. $(2a+3b)(2-3a)$
30. $(a+b)(2a+c)$
31. $2(2x+y)(1-y)$
32. $(x+y)(y+z)$
33. $(x-2)(5-y)$
34. $(a+4)(b-3)$
35. $(x+3)(y-z)$
36. $(p-4)(2-q)$
37. $(a-2)(b-3)$
38. $(a-4)(3-b)$

39. $(m+n)(m+1)$
40. $(a+1)(a-b)$
41. $(2p+1)(p-2q)$
42. $(x+1)(1-y)$
43. $(a+b)(a+1)$
44. $(a-b)(a+1)$
45. $(x+y)(x-1)$
46. $(a-1)(2a+b)$
47. $(x+2y)(5x-1)$
48. $(n-1)(m-1)$
49. $(x-1)(3x+y)$
50. $(2p-1)(p+2q)$
51. $(1-a)(3a+b)$
52. $(1-z)(2x+y)$

Exercise 15c   page 222
1. $(x+1)(x+2)$
2. $(x+1)(x+5)$
3. $(x+3)(x+4)$
4. $(x+3)(x+5)$
5. $(x+1)(x+20)$
6. $(x+1)(x+7)$
7. $(x+6)(x+2)$
8. $(x+1)(x+12)$
9. $(x+1)(x+15)$
10. $(x+2)(x+10)$

11. $(x+4)(x+4)$
12. $(x+3)(x+12)$
13. $(x+1)(x+18)$
14. $(x+2)(x+20)$
15. $(x+1)(x+8)$
16. $(x+3)(x+3)$
17. $(x+2)(x+18)$
18. $(x+3)(x+6)$
19. $(x+5)(x+6)$
20. $(x+4)(x+10)$

Exercise 15d   page 223
1. $(x-1)(x-8)$
2. $(x-3)(x-4)$
3. $(x-2)(x-15)$
4. $(x-4)(x-7)$
5. $(x-6)(x-7)$

6. $(x-2)(x-3)$
7. $(x-1)(x-15)$
8. $(x-3)(x-3)$
9. $(x-2)(x-16)$
10. $(x-7)(x-9)$

Exercise 15e   page 223
1. $(x+2)(x-3)$
2. $(x+5)(x-4)$
3. $(x-4)(x+3)$
4. $(x-4)(x+7)$
5. $(x+5)(x-3)$

6. $(x-6)(x+4)$
7. $(x-3)(x+9)$
8. $(x-11)(x+2)$
9. $(x-7)(x+5)$
10. $(x-10)(x+2)$

Exercise 15f   page 224
1. $(x+2)(x+7)$
2. $(x-3)(x-7)$
3. $(x+7)(x-2)$
4. $(x+6)(x-5)$
5. $(x+1)(x+8)$
6. $(x-5)(x-5)$
7. $(x+9)(x-1)$
8. $(x-13)(x-2)$
9. $(x+8)(x-7)$
10. $(x+2)(x+30)$
11. $(x+3)(x-9)$
12. $(x+20)(x-4)$

13. $(x+1)(x+13)$
14. $(x-2)(x+14)$
15. $(x+10)(x-8)$
16. $(x-5)(x-6)$
17. $(x-4)(x+12)$
18. $(x+6)(x+12)$
19. $(x+4)(x+13)$
20. $(x+2)(x-14)$
21. $(x+3)(x+8)$
22. $(x+3)(x-14)$
23. $(x-2)(x-16)$
24. $(x+12)(x-5)$

Exercise 15g   page 225
1. $(x+1)(x+8)$
2. $(x-3)(x-3)$
3. $(x+4)(x+7)$
4. $(4-x)(5+x)$

5. $(x+3)(x+3)$
6. $(x-1)(x-8)$
7. $(x+2)(x+15)$
8. $(9+x)(3-x)$

9. $(x+2)(x+11)$
10. $(x-13)(x+2)$
11. $(x-1)(x-7)$
12. $(x-6)(x+7)$
13. $(x-8)(x+3)$
14. $(x-2)(x-7)$
15. $(x+1)(x+27)$
16. $(x-7)(x+9)$

17. $(x+5)^2$
18. $(x-5)^2$
19. $(x+2)^2$
20. $(x-7)^2$
21. $(x+6)^2$
22. $(x-6)^2$
23. $(x-2)^2$
24. $(x+8)^2$

Exercise 15h   page 225
1. $(2+x)(1+x)$
2. $(3-x)(2+x)$
3. $(1-x)(4+x)$
4. $(4-x)(2+x)$
5. $(3+x)(2-x)$
6. $(2-x)(1+x)$
7. $(4+x)(2-x)$
8. $(5+x)(1-x)$

9. $(5+x)(2-x)$
10. $(6-x)(2+x)$
11. $(5-x)(1+x)$
12. $(7+x)(2-x)$
13. $(6-x)(1+x)$
14. $(5+x)(4-x)$
15. $(5+x)(3-x)$
16. $(4-x)(3+x)$

Exercise 15i   page 226
1. $(x+5)(x-5)$
2. $(x+2)(x-2)$
3. $(x+10)(x-10)$
4. $(x+1)(x-1)$
5. $(x+8)(x-8)$
6. $(x+4)(x-4)$
7. $(x+6)(x-6)$
8. $(x+9)(x-9)$
9. $(x+7)(x-7)$

10. $(3+x)(3-x)$
11. $(6+x)(6-x)$
12. $(10+x)(10-x)$
13. $(a+b)(a-b)$
14. $(3y+z)(3y-z)$
15. $(4+x)(4-x)$
16. $(5+x)(5-x)$
17. $(9+x)(9-x)$
18. $(x+y)(x-y)$

Exercise 15j   page 227
1. $3(x+4)$
2. $5x(5x+2)$
3. $4(3x^2-2)$
4. $7(2x+3)$
5. $2(2x^2+1)$
6. $7(3x-1)$
7. $9x(x-2)$
8. $4(5x+3)$
9. $2(2x-7)$
10. $4x(2x-1)$

11. $2(x+3)(x+4)$
12. $3(x-1)(x-8)$
13. $7(x+1)^2$
14. $4(x+3)(x-4)$
15. $5(x+1)(x+7)$
16. $3(x+2)(x+6)$
17. $4(x-3)^2$
18. $5(x+2)(x-3)$
19. $2(x+2)(x-11)$
20. $3(x-5)(x+8)$

Exercise 15k   page 228
1. $(2x+1)(x+1)$
2. $(3x-2)(x-1)$
3. $(4x+3)(x+1)$
4. $(2x-1)(x-3)$
5. $(3x+1)(x+4)$
6. $(3x-2)(x-2)$
7. $(2x+1)(x+4)$
8. $(5x-2)(x-3)$
9. $(2x+3)(x+4)$
10. $(7x-1)(x-4)$

11. $(2x+1)(x-2)$
12. $(3x+4)(x-1)$
13. $(5x+2)(x-3)$
14. $(x+2)(4x-3)$
15. $(3x-2)(x+4)$
16. $(7x+2)(x-3)$
17. $(6x+5)(x-2)$
18. $(5x-4)(x-3)$
19. $(3x+4)(x-5)$
20. $(4x-3)(x+5)$

Exercise 15l   page 228
1. $(3x+2)(2x+1)$
2. $(2x+3)(3x+5)$
3. $(3x+1)(5x+2)$
4. $(2x+3)(6x+5)$
5. $(7x+2)(5x+2)$

6. $(3x-1)(2x-3)$
7. $(3x-2)(3x-4)$
8. $(2x-1)(8x-1)$
9. $(5x-3)(3x-7)$
10. $(5x-2)(4x-3)$

11. $(4x+1)(2x-3)$
12. $(5x-2)(3x+1)$
13. $(3x+2)(7x-4)$
14. $(10x+3)(8x-3)$
15. $(3x+4)(8x-5)$
16. $(3a-5)(2a+3)$
17. $(3t-2)(2t+1)$
18. $(3b-2)^2$
19. $(x-2y)(5x+3y)$
20. $(x-2)(4x-3)$

Exercise 15m   page 229
1. $(2x+5)(2x-5)$
2. $(3x+2)(3x-2)$
3. $(6a+1)(6a-1)$
4. $(4a+b)(4a-b)$
5. $(3x+5)(3x-5)$
6. $(2a+1)(2a-1)$
7. $(4a+3b)(4a-3b)$
8. $(5s+3t)(5s-3t)$
9. $(10x+7y)(10x-7y)$
10. $(3y+4z)(3y-4z)$
11. $(2x+7y)(2x-7y)$
12. $(9x+10y)(9x-10y)$
13. $(3a+2b)(3a-2b)$
14. $(8p+9q)(8p-9q)$
15. $3(a+3b)(a-3b)$
16. $2(3t+5s)(3t-5s)$
17. $3(3x+y)(3x-y)$
18. $5(3x+2)(3x-2)$
19. $5(a+2)(a-2)$
20. $5(3+b)(3-b)$
21. $\frac{1}{2}(a+2b)(a-2b)$

22. $\left(\dfrac{a}{2}+\dfrac{b}{3}\right)\left(\dfrac{a}{2}-\dfrac{b}{3}\right)$ or $\frac{1}{36}(3a+2b)(3a-2b)$

23. $\frac{1}{3}(9x+y)(9x-y)$

24. $\left(\dfrac{x}{4}+\dfrac{y}{5}\right)\left(\dfrac{x}{4}-\dfrac{y}{5}\right)$ or $\frac{1}{400}(5x+4y)(5x-4y)$

Exercise 15n   page 230
1. 7.5
2. 18.5
3. 17.7
4. 35.04
5. 31.2
6. 20.4
7. 12.9
8. 178.97
9. 1000
10. 336
11. 53.2
12. 5.336
13. 8
14. 140
15. 75.8
16. 0.526

Exercise 15p   page 230
1. $5(x+1)(3x+2)$
2. $2(x-2)(2x+1)$
3. $3(x+1)(2x+1)$
4. $3(x-2)(6x+5)$
5. $2(x+5)(4x-3)$
6. $2(x+1)(4x+3)$
7. $5(x-3)(5x+2)$
8. $3(x-1)(3x+4)$
9. $2(x+4)(3x+1)$
10. $5(x+4)(3x-2)$
11. $2(3x-2)(3x-4)$
12. $3(2x-1)(8x-1)$
13. $2(2x+1)(3x+2)$
14. $5(4x-3)(5x-2)$
15. $4(2x+1)(3x-2)$
16. $7(x+4)(3x-2)$
17. $(4+3x)(1-2x)$
18. $(4-3x)(3+4x)$
19. $(7-x)(3+4x)$
20. $2(2-x)(6-x)$
21. $2(4+x)(2-3x)$
22. $(9-x)(1+x)$
23. $(12+x)(1-x)$
24. $2(2+3x)^2$
25. $5(3-x)^2$
26. $5(2+x)(2+3x)$

Exercise 15q   page 231
1. $(x+5)(x+8)$
2. $(3x+1)(2x+1)$
3. $(x+6)(x-6)$

4. Does not factorise
5. $(x-2)(x-6)$
6. $(2x-3)(x+5)$
7. $(x+7)(x-1)$
8. $(5x-2)(x+1)$
9. $(x-3)(x-8)$
10. $(3x+2)(x+3)$
11. $(x+15)(x-1)$
12. $(4x-1)(3x-1)$
13. $(x+2)(x+6)$
14. $(4x+1)(2x-1)$
15. $(x+7)(x-7)$
16. Does not factorise
17. $(3x+2)(2x-5)$
18. $(x+6)(x+7)$
19. $(2x+3y)(2x-3y)$
20. $(5x-4)(3x-2)$
21. $(2x-3)(3x+2)$
22. $(x+13)(x-2)$
23. $2(3x+1)(5x-2)$
24. $(4+x)(7-x)$
25. $(2x-1)(3x+4)$
26. $5(2x+1)(3x+2)$
27. $(x+2)(x+9)$
28. $(x-4)(x-6)$
29. $4(x+2y)(x-2y)$
30. Does not factorise
31. $2(3x+2)(2x-5)$
32. $(x-2)(x+15)$
33. $(2-x)(14+x)$
34. $(a-7)(a-9)$
35. $2(3-2x)(1-2x)$
36. $(1+2x)(1+4x^2)$
37. $(x+17)(x-4)$
38. $(2x-1)(x^3+2)$
39. $3(2x+1)(x-2)$
40. $(p+1)(p^2+1)$
41. $(a+b+c)(a+b-c)$
42. $(29x+1)(4x-1)$
43. $(a+16)(a+7)$
44. $(x^2+y+1)(x^2-y-1)$
45. $(a-8)(3a-7)$
46. $2(x+7)(x-11)$
47. $(2x+y-z)(2x-y+z)$
48. $(ab+18)(ab-19)$

Exercise 15r   page 232
1. (a) $7a+21$
   (b) $3x-6y$
2. (a) $x^2+14x+40$
   (b) $6x^2-19x+15$
3. (a) $25+10x+x^2$
   (b) $25-10x+x^2$
   (c) $25-x^2$
4. (a) $10(a+2)$
   (b) $5p(3p-2)$
5. (a) $(a+1)(a^2+1)$
   (b) $(k+l)(2m-n)$
6. (a) $(x-3)(x+9)$
   (b) $(x-7)(5x-7)$
   (c) $\left(a+\dfrac{b}{2}\right)\left(a-\dfrac{b}{2}\right)$
7. (a) $(5x+2)(2x-3)$
   (b) $(10a+9b)(10a-9b)$

Exercise 15s   page 233
1. (a) $5a^2 + 15a$ (b) $12x^2 - 8xy$
2. (a) $y^2 - 9y + 20$ (b) $15x^2 - 14xy - 8y^2$
3. (a) $4p^2 + 12pq + 9q^2$ (c) $4p^2 - 9q^2$
   (b) $4p^2 - 12pq + 9q^2$
4. (a) $4z^2(2z - 1)$ (b) $5y(x - 4z)$
5. (a) $(m + 1)(2 + 3n)$
   (b) $(a + 2b)(c - 2d)$
6. (a) $(x + 3)(x - 9)$
   (b) $(4x - 1)(x + 7)$
   (c) $(2m + 9n)(2m - 9n)$
7. (a) $3(x - 3)(5x - 3)$
   (b) Does not factorise or $5(3 + 5x - 4x^2)$

Exercise 15t   page 233
1. (a) $4a + 28$ (b) $6x^2 - 9xy$
2. (a) $x^2 + 12x + 27$ (b) $15x^2 - x - 2$
3. (a) $25x^2 + 20x + 4$ (c) $25x^2 - 4$
   (b) $25x^2 - 20x + 4$
4. (a) $6z(2z - 1)$ (b) $4y(2x - 3z)$
5. (a) $(z + 2)(z^2 + 1)$ (b) $(3a + b)(c + 2)$
6. (a) $(x - 6)(x + 4)$
   (b) $(2a + 5)(2a - 3)$
   (c) $\left(3m + \dfrac{n}{3}\right)\left(3m - \dfrac{n}{3}\right)$
7. (a) $(5x - 3)(3x + 2)$
   (b) $(3 + 5x)(2 - 3x)$
8. (a) Hint: rewrite $100a + 10b + c$ as
       $98a + 2a + 2b + 7b + b + c$
   (b) Hint: rewrite $100a + 10b + c$ as
       $91a + 9a + 9b + b + c$

Chapter 16

Exercise 16a   page 235
1. (a) 8   (b) 0   (c) 0
2. (a) 0   (b) 5   (c) 0
3. (a) 0   (b) 7   (c) 0
4. (a) 0   (b) 0   (c) 3
5. (a) 20   (b) 0   (c) 6
6. (a) 33   (b) 0   (c) 0
7. (a) -24 (b) 0   (c) 0
8. (a) 70   (b) 0   (c) 0
9. (a) 0   (b) 0   (c) 20
10. (a) -9 (b) 0   (c) 0

Exercise 16b   page 236
1. 0
2. 0
3. 0
4. any value
5. 4
6. 1
7. 0
8. 2
9. 0
10. 7
11. any value
12. 0
13. (a) 0 (b) 0
14. (a) 0 (b) 0
15. (a) 0 (b) 0
16. (a) 0 (b) any value
17. $a = 0$ or $b = 1$
18. $a = 0$ or $b = 5$
19. $a = 0$ or $b = 2$
20. $a = 3$ or $b = 0$
21. $a = 9$ or $b = 0$
22. $a = 0$ or $b = 4$
23. $a = 0$ or $b = 10$
24. $a = 1$ or $b = 0$
25. $a = 7$ or $b = 0$
26. $a = 12$ or $b = 0$

Exercise 16c   page 238
1. 0 or 3
2. 0 or 5
3. 0 or 3
4. 0 or -4
5. 0 or -5
6. 0 or 6
7. 0 or 10
8. 0 or 7
9. 0 or -7
10. 0 or -9
11. 1, 2
12. 5 or 9
13. 7 or 10
14. 4 or 7
15. 1 or 6
16. 8 or -11
17. 3 or -5
18. -7 or 2
19. -2 or -3
20. -4 or -9
21. -1 or -8
22. p or q
23. $-a$ or -6
24. 4 or -1
25. -9 or 8
26. -6 or -7
27. -10 or -11
28. a or b
29. $-a$ or 6
30. c or $-d$

Exercise 16d   page 239
1. 1 or $2\frac{1}{2}$
2. 4 or $\frac{2}{3}$
3. $\frac{4}{5}$ or $\frac{3}{4}$
4. 0 or $1\frac{1}{4}$
5. 0 or $\frac{3}{10}$
6. $-\frac{2}{5}$ or 7
7. $-\frac{5}{6}$ or $\frac{2}{3}$
8. $\frac{3}{8}$ or $-2\frac{1}{2}$
9. $1\frac{1}{7}$ or $-3\frac{3}{4}$
10. $-\frac{3}{4}$ or $-1\frac{1}{2}$
11. $2\frac{1}{3}$ or 2
12. $1\frac{2}{3}$ or $\frac{1}{2}$
13. 0 or $\frac{1}{3}$
14. 0 or $\frac{3}{7}$
15. $-1\frac{1}{2}$ or 3
16. $-\frac{3}{4}$ or $2\frac{1}{2}$
17. $-\frac{9}{10}$ or $\frac{4}{5}$
18. $\frac{2}{3}$ or $-2\frac{1}{4}$
19. $2\frac{2}{5}$ or $-3\frac{1}{2}$
20. $-1\frac{3}{5}$ or $-\frac{3}{4}$

Exercise 16e   page 239
1. 1 or 2
2. 1 or 7
3. 2 or 3
4. 2 or 5
5. 3 or 4
6. 1 or 5
7. 1 or 11
8. 2 or 4
9. 2 or 6
10. 1 or 12
11. 1 or -7
12. 4 or -2
13. 3 or -4
14. 5 or -3
15. 2 or -9
16. -1 or 13
17. 2 or -3
18. -2 or 6
19. 4 or -5
20. -3 or 8
21. -1 or -2
22. -1 or -7
23. -3 or -5
24. -2 or -6
25. -2 or -9
26. -1 or -6
27. -2 or -5
28. -1 or -13
29. -1 or -15
30. -3 or -6
31. ± 1
32. ± 3
33. ± 4
34. ± 9
35. ± 13
36. ± 2
37. ± 5
38. ± 10
39. ± 12
40. ± 6

Exercise 16f   page 241
1. 0 or 2
2. 0 or 10
3. 0 or -8
4. 0 or $\frac{1}{2}$
5. 0 or $\frac{5}{4}$
6. 0 or 5
7. 0 or -3
8. 0 or -1
9. 0 or $\frac{5}{3}$
10. 0 or $\frac{7}{5}$
11. 0 or $-\frac{3}{2}$
12. 0 or $-\frac{5}{8}$
13. 0 or 7
14. 0 or $-\frac{5}{3}$

15. 0 or $\frac{12}{7}$

16. 0 or $-\frac{7}{6}$

17. 0 or $-\frac{7}{12}$

18. 0 or -4

19. 0 or $\frac{2}{7}$

20. 0 or $-\frac{3}{14}$

Exercise 16g   page 242

1. 1 (twice)
2. 5 (twice)
3. 10 (twice)
4. -4 (twice)
5. -3 (twice)
6. 3 (twice)
7. 4 (twice)
8. 9 (twice)
9. -1 (twice)
10. -10 (twice)

11. -9 (twice)
12. 7 (twice)
13. 11 (twice)
14. -6 (twice)
15. $\frac{1}{2}$ (twice)
16. -5 (twice)
17. 6 (twice)
18. 20 (twice)
19. 8 (twice)
20. $-\frac{2}{3}$ (twice)

Exercise 16h   page 243

1. $\frac{1}{2}$ and 2
2. $1\frac{1}{2}$ and 4
3. $2\frac{1}{2}$ and 4
4. -1 and $-\frac{2}{3}$
5. -7 and $2\frac{1}{2}$
6. $\frac{2}{3}$ and 3
7. $\frac{1}{3}$ and 2
8. $1\frac{1}{2}$ and -4
9. $-\frac{2}{3}$ and -3
10. $-\frac{2}{5}$ and -5
11. $-\frac{1}{2}$ and $\frac{2}{3}$
12. $\frac{2}{5}$ and $-1\frac{1}{3}$
13. $\frac{1}{3}$ and $\frac{1}{4}$
14. $-\frac{1}{3}$ and $2\frac{1}{2}$
15. $-\frac{1}{5}$ and $-\frac{3}{4}$

16. $\frac{3}{4}$ and $1\frac{1}{2}$
17. $-\frac{5}{6}$ and $2\frac{1}{2}$
18. $-\frac{1}{2}$ and $-1\frac{1}{2}$
19. $-\frac{2}{3}$ and $-\frac{3}{4}$
20. $3\frac{1}{2}$ and $-\frac{3}{5}$
21. $\pm\frac{5}{4}$
22. $\pm\frac{9}{10}$
23. $\pm\frac{5}{2}$
24. $\pm\frac{4}{3}$
25. $\pm\frac{12}{5}$
26. $\pm\frac{2}{3}$
27. $\pm\frac{5}{9}$
28. $\pm\frac{2}{5}$
29. $\pm\frac{5}{6}$
30. $\pm\frac{9}{2}$

Exercise 16i   page 244

1. -5 and 6
2. -2 and 8
3. 3 and -12
4. $\frac{2}{3}$ and -2
5. 3 and -2
6. 1 and -7
7. $\frac{1}{2}$ and -3
8. 3 and $-\frac{3}{5}$
9. 3 or -1
10. -4 and 6
11. 5 and 7
12. $-\frac{1}{5}$ and $1\frac{1}{2}$
13. -2 and 5
14. 2 and 4
15. $\frac{1}{2}$ and $-\frac{1}{3}$
16. $\frac{1}{3}$ and 4
17. 2 and 5

18. 1 and 7
19. 2 and 4
20. 3 and 7
21. 2 and 6
22. 4 and 5
23. 5 and 7
24. 3 and 5
25. 0 and $\frac{1}{2}$
26. 2 and 3
27. 2 and 6
28. -1 and $-\frac{2}{3}$
29. $\frac{1}{2}$ and -3
30. 0 and 3
31. 1 and 2
32. -1 and -2
33. $\frac{1}{3}$ and 2
34. $-\frac{1}{5}$ and $1\frac{1}{2}$

Exercise 16j   page 246

1. -4 and 5
2. 2 (twice)
3. $\pm\frac{1}{3}$
4. 0 and $-3\frac{1}{2}$
5. -1 and -12
6. $\pm\frac{1}{4}$
7. 0 and 6
8. -5 and 7
9. 2 and $-3\frac{1}{2}$
10. -3 (twice)
11. 1 and -7
12. $\pm\frac{2}{5}$
13. $\pm 2\frac{1}{2}$
14. -2 and -9
15. $\frac{1}{2}$ and $-\frac{2}{3}$
16. 0 and $2\frac{1}{2}$
17. 2 and $-\frac{1}{3}$
18. $-\frac{1}{2}$ and $-1\frac{1}{3}$
19. 0 and $1\frac{3}{4}$
20. $\frac{1}{3}$ and $\frac{1}{4}$
21. $\frac{1}{3}$ and $-2\frac{1}{2}$
22. $-\frac{1}{3}$ and 2
23. $-\frac{1}{2}$ and $-1\frac{1}{2}$
24. $\pm\frac{1}{2}$
25. 3 and -4

26. 3 and -1
27. $\frac{1}{2}$ and $-\frac{1}{3}$
28. 1 and 4
29. -3 and 8
30. 5 and 7
31. -2 and $\frac{2}{3}$
32. $-\frac{1}{3}$ and 2
33. 5 and -10
34. -11 and 8
35. 5 and -9
36. -2 and 7
37. 7 and -4
38. 5 and -11
39. -4 and -5
40. -4 and -5
41. 0, 1 and 2
42. 0, 3 and -4
43. 0, 2 and $2\frac{1}{2}$
44. 0, 1 and 1
45. 0, $-\frac{1}{2}$ and -4
46. 0, 6 and 7
47. 0, -2 and 5
48. 0, 5 and $-2\frac{1}{3}$
49. 0, $\frac{3}{2}$ and $-\frac{3}{2}$
50. 0, 2 and 4

Exercise 16k   page 248

1. -2 or 8
2. -2 or 7
3. -7 or 6
4. $x + (x^2 - 6) = 66$; $x = -9$ or 8; 8 marbles
5. $x + x^2 = 56$; $x = -8$ or 7; Ahmed is 7 and his father is 49
6. $x + (x^2 + 2) = 44$; $x = -7$ or 6; Kathryn is 6 and her mother is 38
7. $x(x + 5) = 84$; $x = 7$ or -12; Peter is 7
8. $x(x - 4) = 140$; $x = 14$ or -10; Ann is 10
9. $x(x + 3) = 28$; $x = 4$ or -7; 4 cm by 7 cm
10. $x(x + 5) = 66$; $x = -11$ or 6; 6 cm by 11 cm
11. $\frac{1}{2}x \times \frac{1}{2}x = 25$; $x = \pm 10$; 5 cm
12. (a) $A = 20x\,\text{m}^2$, $B = x^2\,\text{m}^2$, $C = 30x\,\text{m}^2$
   (b) $x^2 + 50x = 104$; $x = 2$ or -52; path is 2 m wide

Exercise 16l   page 250

1. $0.225, -2.22$
2. $0.839, -0.239$
3. $2.50, 1.50$
4. $-10.5, -0.191$

5. $3.58, 0.419$
6. $2.47, -0.135$
7. $-4.14, -0.363$
8. $7.90, -1.90$

Exercise 16m   page 252

1. $x = 0$, $y = 5$; $x = -4$, $y = -3$
2. $x = -\frac{2}{5}$, $y = -\frac{11}{5}$; $x = 2$, $y = -1$
3. $x = \frac{2}{11}$, $y = \frac{19}{11}$; $x = -2$, $y = 1$

4. $x = \frac{27}{11}$, $y = \frac{29}{11}$; $x = 3$, $y = 1$
5. $x = 2$, $y = 5$; $x = -1$, $y = -4$
6. $x = 3$, $y = 6$
7. $x = \frac{17}{3}$, $y = -\frac{7}{3}$; $x = 3$, $y = -1$
8. $x = 2$, $y = 4$
9. $x = -\frac{4}{3}$, $y = -\frac{3}{2}$; $x = 2$, $y = 1$
10. $x = 3$, $y = -2$; $x = -15$, $y = -14$
11. $x = 2$, $y = -12$; $x = 12$, $y = 2$
12. $x = \frac{3}{2}$, $y = 6$; $x = 2$, $y = -1$

Exercise 16n   page 253
1. Minimum $= -13$
2. Minimum $= -\frac{49}{4}$
3. Minimum $= -14$
4. Minimum $= -\frac{19}{2}$
5. Minimum $= -\frac{13}{8}$
6. Minimum $= \frac{37}{8}$
7. (a) 5625 m^2 (b) 75 m, 75 m
8. 9, 9
9. 37.5 m, 75 m
10. 12 500 m, 50 s

Exercise 16p   page 254
1. $\{x : -1 < x < 6\}$ 6. $\{x : -3 < x < -1\}$
2. $\{x : -8 \leqslant x \leqslant 5\}^1$ 7. $\{x : -\frac{5}{3} < x < 1\}$
3. $\{x : -3 \leqslant x \leqslant -2\}^1$ 8. $\{x : x > -1\}$
4. $\{x : 3 < x < 4\}$ 9. $\{x : -3 < x < \frac{1}{3}\}$
5. $\{x : 0 < x < 3\}$ 10. $\{x : -\frac{3}{2} \leqslant x \leqslant \frac{1}{2}\}$

Exercise 16q   page 255
1. (a) -10 (b) 0   (c) 8
2. (a) 0 or -7 (b) 0 or $\frac{1}{2}$
3. (a) 3 and 8   (b) 2 and $-\frac{3}{5}$
4. (a) 7 and -5 (b) 5 and 8
5. (a) $\frac{1}{2}$ and $\frac{4}{5}$ (c) $\pm\frac{2}{3}$
   (b) $\frac{2}{5}$ and $-\frac{1}{3}$
6. (a) 0 and 2   (b) 0 and $\frac{3}{4}$
7. (a) $-\frac{1}{3}$ and $\frac{2}{3}$ (b) $\frac{1}{2}$ and $2\frac{1}{3}$
8. (a) 5 and -9 (b) 5 and -6
9. (a) 0.4 and -1.4 (b) 3.5 and -1.5

Exercise 16r   page 256
1. (a) -2 (c) 12
   (b) 0   (d) 0
2. (a) 0 and 2   (b) 0 and $-\frac{3}{7}$
3. (a) 2 and -5 (c) $-1\frac{1}{2}$ and $1\frac{1}{2}$
   (b) -2 and $1\frac{1}{3}$
4. (a) -3 and 2   (b) -5 and -6
5. (a) $\frac{1}{5}$ and $-\frac{3}{4}$ (b) $-\frac{2}{5}$ and $-2\frac{1}{3}$
6. (a) 0 and $-\frac{2}{3}$ (b) 0 and $-\frac{3}{7}$
7. (a) 5 and $-\frac{3}{4}$ (b) $-\frac{1}{2}$ and $2\frac{1}{3}$
8. (a) -4 and 8   (b) -2 and 4
9. (a) $\frac{2}{3}$ and $-\frac{1}{2}$ (b) $\frac{3}{4}$ and -1

Exercise 16s   page 257
1. (a) -11 (c) 0
   (b) 0
2. (a) 0, -7 (b) 0, $\frac{3}{4}$
3. (a) $-4, 5$
   (b) $1\frac{3}{4}, -3$
   (c) $\frac{3}{5}, -\frac{3}{5}$
4. (a) 5, -3 (b) $-4, -8$
5. (a) $-\frac{1}{5}, -\frac{3}{4}$ (b) $-\frac{2}{7}, \frac{1}{4}$
6. (a) 0, $-1\frac{1}{3}$ (b) 0, $-1\frac{2}{3}$
7. (a) $\frac{2}{7}, -1$ (b) $-\frac{1}{2}, 1\frac{2}{3}$
8. (a) $-5, 2$ (b) $-10, 3$
9. (a) $\{x : x < -3, x > 3\}$
   (b) $\{x : x - 1 \leqslant x \leqslant \frac{2}{3}\}$
   (c) $\{x : x < \frac{2}{3}, x > 1\}$

Chapter 17

Exercise 17a   page 260
1.
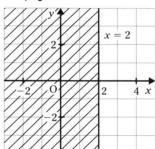

2.
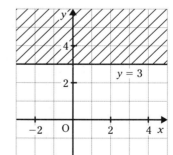

3.
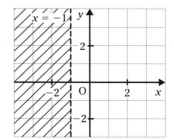

4.
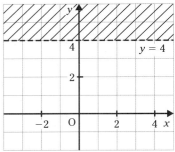

5.
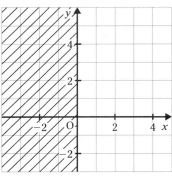

6.

7.
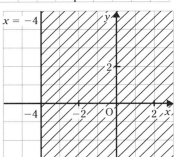

8.
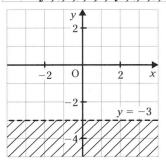

9.
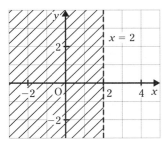

10.
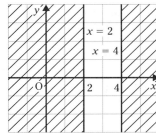

11.
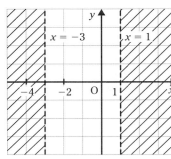

12.
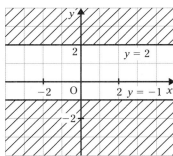

13.
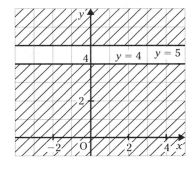

14.

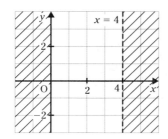

15.

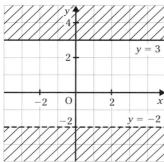

16.

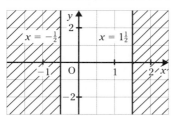

17.

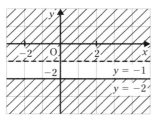

18.

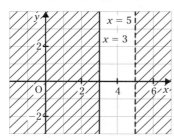

19. 10: No   11: No   12: No
20. $x \leqslant 2$ **22.** $x < -1$ **24.** $-1 \leqslant x < 2$
21. $y < 3$ **23.** $-2 \leqslant y \leqslant 2$ **25.** $-\frac{1}{2} < y < 2\frac{1}{2}$
26. 20: Yes 21: Yes 22: No 23: Yes 24: No 25: No
27. $-3 \leqslant x \leqslant 1$ **29.** $2 \leqslant y < 3$
28. $-4 < y < -1$ **30.** $3 \leqslant x \leqslant 6$
31. 27: Yes 28: No 29: Yes 32: No

Exercise 17b   page 263
1.

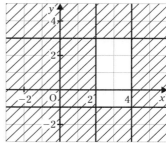

2.

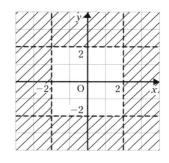

3.

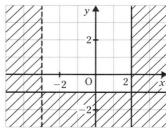

4.

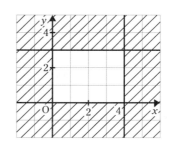

5.

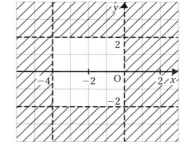

6.

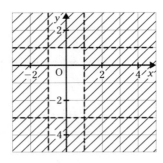

7.

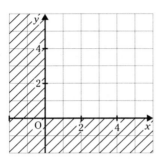

8.

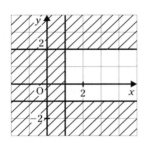

9. $-2 \leqslant x \leqslant 3, \quad -1 \leqslant y \leqslant 2$
10. $-2 < x \leqslant 2, \quad -2 \leqslant y \leqslant 1$
11. 9: Yes 10: Yes
12. $-2 \leqslant x \leqslant 1, \quad y \geqslant -1$
13. $x < 0, \quad y > 0$
14. $-2 < x < 2, \quad -2 < y < 2$
15. $1 < x < 3, \quad 1 < y < 3$
16. $x \geqslant -2, \quad y \leqslant -1$
17. $x < 1, \quad -2 < y < 2$
18. 16: Yes 17: No

Exercise 17c   page 266

1.

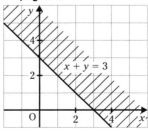

2.

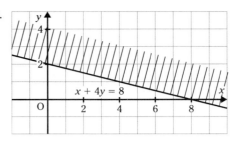

3.

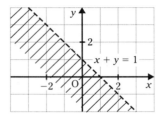

4.

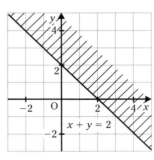

5.

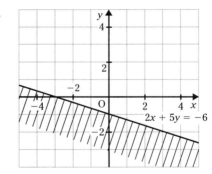

6.

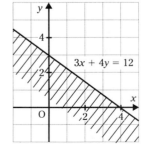

7.

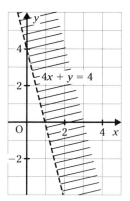

$4x + y = 4$

8.

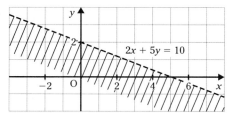

$2x + 5y = 10$

9.

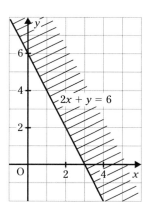

$2x + y = 6$

10.

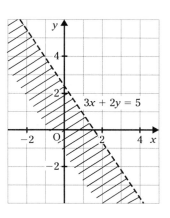

$3x + 2y = 5$

11.

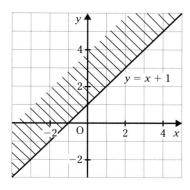

$y = x + 1$

12.

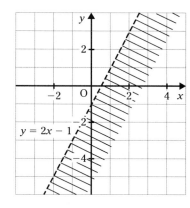

$y = 2x - 1$

13.

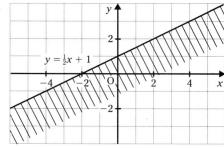

$y = \frac{1}{2}x + 1$

14.

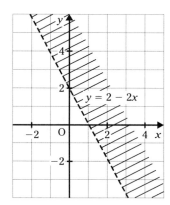

$y = 2 - 2x$

15.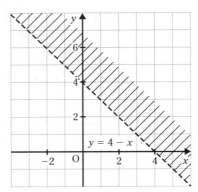

16.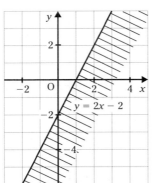

17.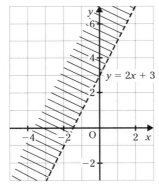

18.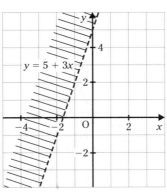

19.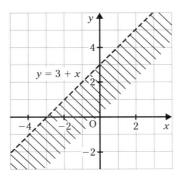

20.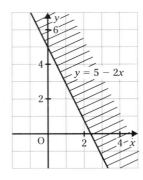

21.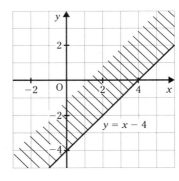

22.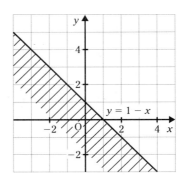

Exercise 17d   page 268

1. $x + y \leqslant 3$
2. $2x + y \geqslant 2$
3. $x + 2y < 2$
4. $x + y < 2$
5. $3x - y \leqslant 3$
6. $2y - 3x \leqslant 6$
7. $y \leqslant x + 1$
8. $y > -2x - 4$
9. $y \geqslant \frac{1}{2}x + 2$
10. $y > -x + 2$ or $x + y > 2$
11. $y \geqslant 2x - 2$
12. $y < -\frac{1}{2}x + 2$ or $x + 2y < 4$
13. $y \leqslant 2x + 2$

Exercise 17e   page 271

1.

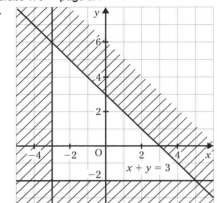

2.

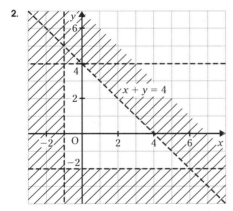

3.

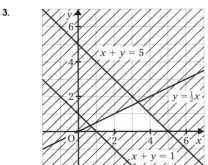

4.

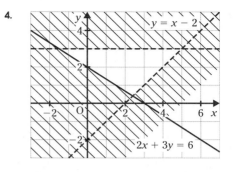

5.

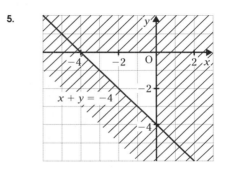

6.

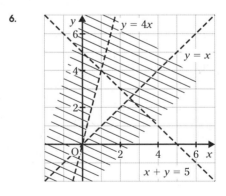

7.

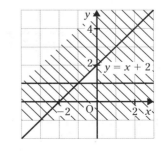

8.

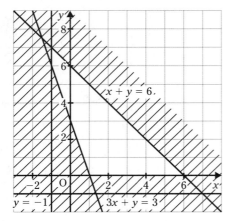

9.

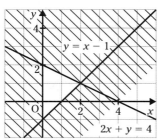

10.

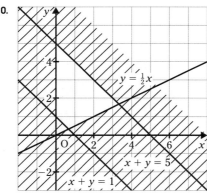

11.

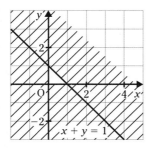

12. It does not exist
13. (a) Region consists of 1 point (1, 2)
(b) Region does not exist

Exercise 17f   page 273

1.

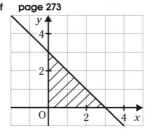

2.

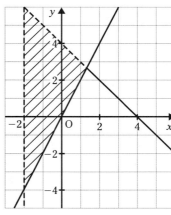

3.

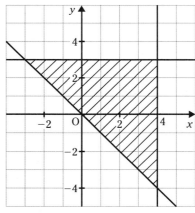

4.

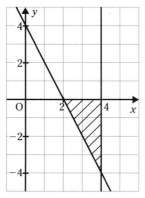

5.

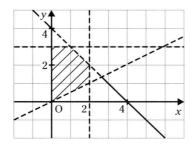

6.

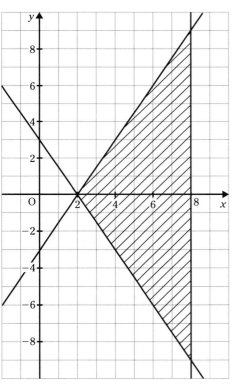

7.

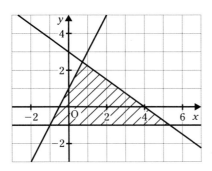

8.

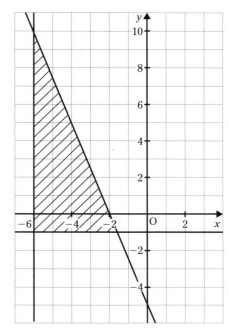

9.

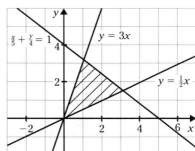

10.

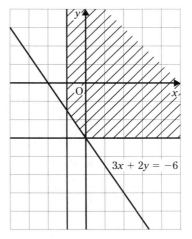

Exercise 17g   page 274
1. $x \geqslant -1$, $y \geqslant -2$, $x + y \leqslant 3$
2. $y \geqslant 0$, $2y \leqslant x + 2$, $x + y \leqslant 4$
3. $y \leqslant x - 3$, $2y \geqslant x - 6$
4. $x \leqslant 1$, $y \leqslant x + 1$, $3x + y > -3$
5. $y > -1$, $x + y < 3$, $y \leqslant 2x + 2$
6. $y \geqslant 0$, $x \geqslant -1$, $y \leqslant x + 2$
7. $y < 3x + 3$, $y > 3x - 3$
8. $y \leqslant \frac{1}{3}x + 1$, $y \geqslant -\frac{1}{3}x - 1$, $y \geqslant \frac{5}{3}x - 7$
9. (a) $x + y \leqslant 3$, $4y \geqslant x$, $y \leqslant x + 3$
   (b) $4y \leqslant x$, $x + y \geqslant 3$
   (c) $y \leqslant x + 3$, $x + y \geqslant 3$, $4y \geqslant x$
   (d) $4y \leqslant x$, $x + y \leqslant 3$, $y \leqslant x + 3$
   (e) $y \geqslant x + 3$, $x + y \geqslant 3$
   (f) $x + y \leqslant 3$, $4y \geqslant x$, $y \geqslant x + 3$
10. (a) $x + y \geqslant 1$, $y \leqslant 2x + 4$
   (b) $y \leqslant 2$, $x + y \geqslant 1$
   (c) $y \geqslant 2$, $y \leqslant 2x + 4$
   (d) $y \geqslant 2x + 4$, $x + y \geqslant 1$
   (e) $x + y \leqslant 1$, $y \geqslant 2x + 4$
   (f) $y \leqslant 2$, $y \leqslant 2x + 4$
11. (a) C   (b) A   (c) B

Exercise 17h   page 277
1. $(2, 2)$, $(-2, 4)$, $(-2, -2)$
2. $(2, 3)$, $(-1, 0)$, $(0, -2)$
3. $(1, -2)$, $(1, 1.5)$, $(6, -2)$
4. $(1, 1)$, $(7, 3)$, $(4, 6)$, $(-4, 6)$
5.

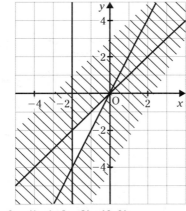

$(-2, -4)$, $(-2, -2)$, $(0, 0)$

6.

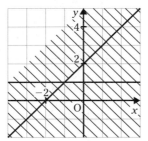

$(0, 1)$, $(0, 2)$ and $(-1, 1)$

7. 1. 19 points $(-2, -2)$, $(-2, -1)$, $(-2, 0)$,
                   $(-2, 1)$, $(-2, 2)$, $(-2, 3)$,
                   $(-2, 4)$, $(-1, -1)$, $(-1, 0)$,
                   $(-1, 1)$, $(-1, 2)$, $(-1, 3)$,
                   $(0, 0)$, $(0, 1)$, $(0, 2)$, $(0, 3)$,
                   $(1, 1)$, $(1, 2)$, $(2, 2)$
   2.   4 points $(0, 0)$, $(1, 1)$, $(0, -1)$, $(0, -2)$
   3. 20 points $(-6, -2)$, $(-5, -2)$, $(-4, -2)$,
                   $(-4, -1)$, $(-3, -2)$, $(-3, -1)$,
                   $(-2, -2)$, $(-2, -1)$, $(-2, 0)$,
                   $(-1, -2)$, $(-1, -1)$, $(-1, -0)$,
                   $(0, -2)$, $(0, -1)$, $(0, 0)$, $(0, 1)$,
                   $(1, -2)$, $(1, -1)$, $(1, 0)$, $(1, 1)$
8. 13 points $(-1, -0)$, $(-1, 1)$, $(-1, 2)$,
               $(-1, 3)$, $(0, -1)$, $(0, 0)$, $(0, 1)$,
               $(0, 2)$, $(0, 3)$, $(1, 0)$, $(1, 1)$,
               $(1, 2)$, $(2, 1)$
9. 3 points $(1, 1)$, $(2, 1)$, $(1, 2)$
10. 9 points $(2, -1)$, $(2, 0)$, $(2, 1)$, $(2, 2)$,
               $(3, 1)$, $(4, 0)$, $(5, -1)$, $(4, -1)$,
               $(3, -1)$

Exercise 17i   page 280
1. $5, 2, -4$
2. $4, -3, 7$
3. $11, -14, 0$
4. $5, 22$; At $(2, -8)$
5. $10, -1$; At $(3, 8)$
6. (a) $(-2, -1)$, $(3, -1)$, $(3, 3)$, $(0, 3)$
   (b) $(3, 3)$
   (c) $(-2, -1)$
   (d) 20
   (e) No
7. (a) $(6, 0)$, $(0, 3)$, $(-2, -3)$
   (b) $(6, 0)$
8. (a) $(4, 1)$, $(-2, 2)$, $(-2, 5)$
   (b) (i) $(4, 1)$ (ii) $(-2, 5)$
   (c) $(-2, 3)$, $(-2, 4)$, $(-1, 2)$, $(-1, 3)$,
       $(-1, 4)$, $(0, 2)$, $(0, 3)$, $(1, 2)$, $(1, 3)$,
       $(2, 2)$; 10 points
   (d) No
9. (b) $(5, -3)$, $(-2, 4)$, $(-2, -3)$
   (c) 33 points
   (d) greatest at $(5, -3)$, least at $(-2, 4)$

Exercise 17j   page 282
1. $(1, 2)$
2. $(2, -2)$
3. $(2, -1)$
4. $(0, 4)$, $(1, 2)$, $(2, 0)$, $(3, -2)$
5. $(0, 3)$
6. $(0, 3)$; No
7. $3000
8. 10 type B
9. $1 \leqslant x \leqslant 5$; $7 \leqslant y \leqslant 10$; $x + y \leqslant 12$
10. $2x + y \geqslant 8$; $x + 9y \geqslant 18$; $x + 3y \geqslant 12$

Chapter 18

Exercise 18a   page 285
1. $\dfrac{x}{4}$ 3. $\dfrac{p}{q}$ 5. $\dfrac{x}{y}$

2. $\dfrac{a}{2}$ 4. $\dfrac{a}{b}$ 6. $\dfrac{1}{2a}$

7. $\dfrac{a}{2c}$ **11.** $\dfrac{a}{2}$ **15.** $\dfrac{q}{2}$

8. $\dfrac{2}{q}$ **12.** $\dfrac{z}{2}$ **16.** $\dfrac{2}{3y}$

9. $\dfrac{pq}{2}$ **13.** $\dfrac{b}{d}$ **17.** $\dfrac{m}{k}$

10. $\dfrac{a}{c}$ **14.** $\dfrac{1}{3x}$ **18.** $\dfrac{s}{4t}$

7. $\dfrac{x-y}{3x-2y}$ **14.** $\dfrac{-1}{1+a}$

8. $\dfrac{2-x}{y}$ **15.** $a+b$

9. $-a$ **16.** $\dfrac{-(x+5)}{(x+1)}$

10. $\dfrac{y+3}{2y+1}$ **17.** $\dfrac{2(2x-1)}{x-3}$

11. $\dfrac{x-3y}{x}$ **18.** $\dfrac{x-2y}{y}$

12. $\dfrac{4x+1}{4x}$ **19.** $\dfrac{1-x}{3(x+2)}$

13. $\dfrac{2x-3}{x-5}$ **20.** $\dfrac{1+y}{x+y}$

Exercise 18b   page 287

1. $\dfrac{1}{x}$ **7.** $p-q$ **13.** $\dfrac{2a}{3(a-b)}$

2. $\dfrac{t}{s-t}$ **8.** $\dfrac{1}{(4-a)}$ **14.** $\dfrac{2(x-y)}{3xy}$

3. not possible **9.** not possible **15.** not possible

4. not possible **10.** $\dfrac{1}{v}$ **16.** $u-v$

5. $\dfrac{x}{2(x-y)}$ **11.** $\dfrac{y}{x+y}$ **17.** not possible

6. $\dfrac{(a+b)}{2ab}$ **12.** $\frac{1}{2}$ **18.** $\dfrac{1}{(s-6)}$

Exercise 18e   page 290

1. $\dfrac{ac}{bd}$ **19.** $\dfrac{a}{4b}$

2. $\dfrac{ad}{bc}$ **20.** $\dfrac{a^3}{b^3}$

3. $\dfrac{5(x-y)}{2x}$ **21.** $\dfrac{1}{4(b-2)}$

4. $\dfrac{x(x-y)}{10}$ **22.** $2(x-2)$

5. $\dfrac{a}{bc}$ **23.** $2(a+3)$

6. $\dfrac{ac}{b}$ **24.** 6

7. $\dfrac{3(a-b)}{4(a+b)}$ **25.** $x-3$

8. $\dfrac{(x-2)(x+3)}{3}$ **26.** $x-3$

9. $\dfrac{x-2}{3(x+3)}$ **27.** $\dfrac{1}{x-2}$

10. $\dfrac{pr}{q}$ **28.** $\dfrac{2}{x+4}$

11. $\dfrac{6b}{a}$ **29.** $\dfrac{3(x-2)}{5(x+6)}$

12. $\dfrac{q}{2p}$ **30.** $\dfrac{2(2x-3)}{9}$

13. $\dfrac{12y}{x}$ **31.** $\dfrac{3}{3x+2}$

14. $\dfrac{2b^2}{5}$ **32.** $\dfrac{2x-3}{2}$

15. $\dfrac{pq}{6}$ **33.** $\dfrac{2x-1}{6x+1}$

16. $\dfrac{x}{2y}$ **34.** a

17. $\dfrac{1}{2b}$ **35.** $\dfrac{-c(a+b)}{b}$

18. $\dfrac{2}{3p}$ **36.** $(x-4)(x-2)$

Exercise 18c   page 288

1. $\dfrac{2a}{4a-b}$ **12.** $\dfrac{p+q}{5}$ **23.** $\dfrac{3}{x+3}$

2. $\dfrac{2q}{p-q}$ **13.** $\dfrac{1}{3}$ **24.** $\dfrac{9}{y+2}$

3. $\dfrac{1}{a}$ **14.** $\dfrac{3+a}{4b}$ **25.** $\dfrac{y}{x-2}$

4. $\dfrac{3}{5}$ **15.** $\dfrac{2-y}{x}$ **26.** $\dfrac{q}{p+2}$

5. $\dfrac{2-x}{3y}$ **16.** $\dfrac{1}{3y}$ **27.** $\dfrac{t}{s-7}$

6. $\dfrac{a}{3-b}$ **17.** a **28.** $\dfrac{1}{p+3}$

7. $\dfrac{1}{3a}$ **18.** $\dfrac{p}{2}$ **29.** $\dfrac{1}{x+6}$

8. s **19.** $\dfrac{1}{a-2}$ **30.** $\dfrac{2}{x-4}$

9. $\dfrac{3}{a}$ **20.** $\dfrac{1}{x-4}$ **31.** $\dfrac{3}{x-4}$

10. $\dfrac{2x}{3x-y}$ **21.** $\dfrac{1}{y+2}$ **32.** $\dfrac{v}{u+6}$

11. $\dfrac{3a}{a+b}$ **22.** $\dfrac{2}{a+3}$ **33.** $\dfrac{y}{x-2}$

Exercise 18d   page 289

1. $\dfrac{x+3}{2x-1}$ **4.** $\dfrac{1}{2-x}$

2. $\dfrac{4}{x+2}$ **5.** $\dfrac{a+b}{a-b}$

3. $\dfrac{2x-1}{x-2}$ **6.** $\dfrac{a+b}{2a+b}$

Exercise 18f   **page 293**

1. pq
2. rst
3. 30
4. abc
5. $wxyz$
6. ad
7. uvw
8. 168
9. pqr
10. xy
11. $2x^2$
12. $3pq$
13. $2x^2y$
14. abc
15. st
16. $3p^2$
17. $5ab$
18. $3pq^2$
19. $6x$
20. $8x$
21. $18a$
22. 60
23. a^2b
24. $30x$
25. $12x$
26. $15y$
27. $12x$

Exercise 18g   **page 294**

1. $\dfrac{x+y}{xy}$
2. $\dfrac{3q+2p}{pq}$
3. $\dfrac{2t-s}{st}$
4. $\dfrac{6b+a}{2ab}$
5. $\dfrac{5y-6x}{15xy}$
6. $\dfrac{2b+5a}{2ab}$
7. $\dfrac{2y-3x}{xy}$
8. $\dfrac{4q+6p}{3pq}$
9. $\dfrac{3y-2x}{xy}$
10. $\dfrac{20b+21a}{28ab}$
11. $\dfrac{5}{6x}$
12. $-\dfrac{1}{35x}$
13. $\dfrac{5}{4y}$
14. $\dfrac{1}{8p}$
15. $\dfrac{13}{8a}$
16. $\dfrac{4}{21x}$
17. $\dfrac{6}{35x}$
18. $\dfrac{1}{3y}$

19. $\dfrac{3a+2b}{4ab}$
20. $\dfrac{ab-2a^2}{2b^2}$
21. $\dfrac{3y-4}{xy}$
22. $\dfrac{4-3p}{2p^2}$
23. $\dfrac{9a^2+2b^2}{12ab}$
24. $\dfrac{10q-3p}{4pq}$
25. $\dfrac{2s+ts^2}{2t^2}$
26. $\dfrac{15b+4}{6ab}$
27. $\dfrac{3+2x}{3x^2}$
28. $\dfrac{4y^2-9x^2}{6xy}$
29. $\dfrac{5y+4x}{8xy}$
30. $\dfrac{pq+3p^2}{3q^2}$
31. $\dfrac{10y-3}{14xy}$
32. $\dfrac{18b-3a}{2a^2b}$
33. $\dfrac{3x^2-3y^2}{2xy}$
34. $\dfrac{14q-15p}{18pq}$
35. $\dfrac{5a^2+4ab}{5b^2}$
36. $\dfrac{21+8p}{15pq}$

Exercise 18h   **page 296**

1. $\dfrac{9x+3}{20}$
2. $\dfrac{5-x}{12}$
3. $\dfrac{13x+1}{15}$
4. $\dfrac{4x+13}{12}$

5. $\dfrac{1-2x}{35}$
6. $\dfrac{7x+3}{10}$
7. $\dfrac{3x+9}{35}$
8. $\dfrac{5x-3}{42}$
9. $\dfrac{5-22x}{21}$
10. $\dfrac{7x+9}{12}$
11. $\dfrac{22-13x}{6}$
12. $\dfrac{11-7x}{12}$
13. $\dfrac{20-17x}{24}$
14. $\dfrac{22-7x}{20}$
15. $\dfrac{10-5x}{6}$
16. $\dfrac{31x-6}{24}$
17. $\dfrac{11-7x}{10}$
18. $\dfrac{2-11x}{18}$
19. $\dfrac{26x+34}{15}$

20. $\dfrac{17x-1}{12}$
21. $\dfrac{5x-19}{21}$
22. $\dfrac{42x-49}{10}$
23. $\dfrac{27x+3}{14}$
24. $\dfrac{19x-73}{9}$
25. $\dfrac{26x-18}{15}$
26. $\dfrac{-17x+104}{30}$
27. $\dfrac{3a+6}{a(a+3)}$
28. $\dfrac{6x+4}{x(x+2)}$
29. $\dfrac{7x-4}{2x(x-4)}$
30. $\dfrac{2x-3}{4x(2x+1)}$
31. $\dfrac{5a+12}{a(a+4)}$
32. $\dfrac{7x-4}{x(x-1)}$
33. $\dfrac{11x+1}{3x(2x+1)}$
34. $\dfrac{21x-6}{5x(2x+3)}$

Exercise 18i   **page 298**

1. $\dfrac{2c-ab}{ac}$
2. $\dfrac{qr^2}{p}$
3. $\dfrac{7x-14}{12}$
4. $\dfrac{a}{a-b}$
5. $\dfrac{1}{12x}$
6. $\dfrac{1}{x+2}$
7. $\dfrac{-p}{p+q}$
8. $\dfrac{12-2x}{3x^2}$
9. $\dfrac{1-2x}{x(x+1)}$
10. $\dfrac{ab}{c}$
11. $\dfrac{8}{15}$
12. $\dfrac{23}{20x}$
13. $\dfrac{3}{10x^2}$
14. $\dfrac{4x+7}{10}$
15. $\dfrac{(x+4)(2x-1)}{50}$
16. $\dfrac{25}{12x}$
17. $\dfrac{25}{24x^2}$
18. $\dfrac{3}{2}$

19. $\dfrac{19x - 1}{3x(x - 1)}$ **22.** $\dfrac{3}{a - 1}$

20. $\dfrac{2}{x(x - 1)}$ **23.** $\dfrac{3}{y}$

21. $\dfrac{-a - 3}{2a(a - 1)}$ **24.** -1

Exercise 18j page 299

1. 8	15. 21	29. 1, 1
2. -5	16. $\frac{4}{9}$	30. $\frac{2}{3}$, 1
3. 6	17. $-2\frac{1}{2}$	31. 2, $-\frac{2}{3}$
4. $1\frac{1}{3}$	18. -17	32. -2, 1
5. 10	19. 2	33. $4\frac{1}{2}$
6. 5	20. 4	34. $\frac{2}{5}$
7. $9\frac{3}{5}$	21. 1	35. 2, 1
8. $5\frac{1}{4}$	22. $-2\frac{1}{19}$	36. $-2\frac{4}{5}$
9. -1	23. -2, -1	37. -40
10. $8\frac{3}{4}$	24. 3, 2	38. $\frac{2}{5}$
11. 2	25. -2, -2	39. 0, 4
12. -18	26. -3, -3	40. 3
13. 3	27. 1, -4	41. $\frac{1}{2}$, $-\frac{1}{2}$
14. -1	28. -3, -3	42. 3

Exercise 18k page 302

1. (a) $\dfrac{b}{2}$ (b) a (c) $a - b$

2. (a) $\dfrac{4}{3x}$ (b) $\dfrac{1}{3x^2}$ (c) 3

3. (a) -13 (b) 3, -1

4. (a) $\dfrac{5x - 7}{6}$ (b) $1\frac{7}{10}$

Exercise 18l page 302

1. (a) $\dfrac{2x}{y}$ (b) $\dfrac{x - y}{2x}$ (c) $x + 3$

2. (a) $\dfrac{1}{6p}$ (b) $x - 2$ (c) $\dfrac{3y}{2x}$

3. (a) $\frac{8}{9}$ (b) 7, -2

4. (a) $\dfrac{x^2 - 2x + 12}{4x}$ (b) $6\frac{1}{2}$

Exercise 18m page 302

1. (a) $\dfrac{v}{uw}$ (b) $\dfrac{1}{2a - b}$ (c) $\dfrac{x}{3 - x}$

2. (a) $18s^2$ (b) $2(x - 2)$ (c) $\dfrac{2 - 5x}{x(4x - 1)}$

3. (a) 4   (b) 1, 2

4. (a) $\dfrac{x}{6}$ (b) 30

5. (a) $x = 40$ (b) $x = 21$ (c) $x = 66$
 x equals the LCM

6. $x = ab$

Chapter 19

Exercise 19a page 305

1. $\begin{pmatrix} 4 \\ 5 \end{pmatrix}$ **5.** $\begin{pmatrix} 5 \\ 3 \end{pmatrix}$ **9.** $(-2, -4)$

2. $\begin{pmatrix} 3 \\ -2 \end{pmatrix}$ **6.** $\begin{pmatrix} -5 \\ 2 \end{pmatrix}$ **10.** $(2, -3)$

3. $\begin{pmatrix} -7 \\ 5 \end{pmatrix}$ **7.** $(5, 2)$ **11.** $(-6, 2)$

4. $\begin{pmatrix} -3 \\ -5 \end{pmatrix}$ **8.** $(1, -3)$ **12.** $(2, -6)$

Exercise 19b page 305

1. $\begin{pmatrix} 2 \\ -5 \end{pmatrix}$ **3.** $\begin{pmatrix} -4 \\ 2 \end{pmatrix}$ **5.** $\begin{pmatrix} 3 \\ 5 \end{pmatrix}$

2. $\begin{pmatrix} -4 \\ -3 \end{pmatrix}$ **4.** $\begin{pmatrix} 5 \\ 3 \end{pmatrix}$ **6.** $\begin{pmatrix} 4 \\ 2 \end{pmatrix}$

Exercise 19c page 307

1. $\begin{pmatrix} 5 \\ 11 \end{pmatrix}$ **3.** $\begin{pmatrix} 4 \\ 1 \end{pmatrix}$ **5.** $\begin{pmatrix} 5 \\ 4 \end{pmatrix}$

2. $\begin{pmatrix} 9 \\ 6 \end{pmatrix}$ **4.** $\begin{pmatrix} -2 \\ -5 \end{pmatrix}$ **6.** $\begin{pmatrix} -1 \\ -1 \end{pmatrix}$

7. $A'(-1, 1)$, $B'(-3, 2)$
8. $A'(-1, -1)$, $B'(2, 4)$
9. $A'(10, 3)$, $B'(-5, -2)$
10. $A'(3, 3)$, $B'(-6, 0)$
11. $A'(-3, 2)$, $B'(3, -7)$
12. $A'(7, 4)$, $B'(1, -8)$

Exercise 19d page 310

1. $A'(-2, -1)$, $B'(2, -1)$, $C'(3, -2)$,
 $D'(-1, -2)$; Reflection in x-axis
2. $A'(1, 1)$, $B'(1, 4)$, $C'(2, 4)$; Reflection in line
 $y = x$
3. $A'(-2, -3)$, $B'(-5, -3)$, $C'(-3, 2)$; Reflection
 in y-axis
4. $A'(-1, -4)$, $B'(-3, -3)$, $C'(0, -2)$; Reflection
 in line $y = -x$
5. $A'(1, 1)$, $B'(1, 3)$, $C'(2, 3)$, $D'(2, 1)$; Reflection
 in line $y = x$
6. $A'(0, 2)$, $B'(0, 4)$, $C'(2, 4)$, $D'(2, 2)$; Reflection
 in line $y = x$
7. $A'(-1, -1)$, $B'(-1, -2)$, $C'(-2, -2)$,
 $D'(-2, -1)$; Reflection in line $y = -x$
8. $A'(-1, 0)$, $B'(-4, 0)$, $C'(-4, 2)$; Reflection in
 y-axis
9. $A'(2, -1)$, $B'(3, -1)$, $C'(3, -4)$, $D'(2, -4)$;
 Reflection in x-axis
10. $A'(1, 1)$, $B'(1, 3)$, $C'(3, 4)$, $D'(3, 3)$; Reflection
 in line $y = x$
11. $A'(-2, 4)$, $B'(-4, 5)$, $C'(-3, 2)$; Reflection in
 y-axis

Exercise 19e   page 312

1. A$'$(1, −1), B$'$(1, −4), C$'$(3, −4), D$'$(3, −1); Rotation of 90° clockwise about O
2. A$'$(−1, −1),   B$'$(−4, −1),   C$'$(−4, −2), D$'$(−1, −2); Rotation of 180° about O
3. A$'$(0, 1), B$'$(0, 3), C$'$(−4, 4); Rotation of 90° anticlockwise about O
4. A$'$(1, −1), B$'$(1, −4), C$'$(4, −4); Rotation of 90° clockwise about O
5. A$'$(−3, −2), B$'$(−4, −3), C$'$(−1, −4); Rotation of 180° about O

Exercise 19f   page 313

1. A$'$(2, 0), B$'$(6, 0), C$'$(6, 6); Enlargement centre O, scale factor 2
2. A$'$(0, 3),   B$'$(−6, 3),   C$'$(−6, 0),   O$'$(0, 0); Enlargement centre O, scale factor 3
3. A$'$(3, 3),   B$'$(3, 6),   C$'$(6, 6),   D$'$(6, 3); Enlargement centre O, scale factor $1\frac{1}{2}$
4. A$'$(10, 5),   B$'$(10, 10),   C$'$(−10, 10); Enlargement centre O, scale factor $2\frac{1}{2}$
5. O$'$(0, 0),   A$'$(0, −2),   B$'$(2, −2),   C$'$(+2, 0); Enlargement centre O, scale factor −2
6. A$'$(0, −2), B$'$(−3, −2), C$'$(−3, −5), D$'$(0, −5); Enlargement centre O, scale factor −1

Exercise 19g   page 315

1. A$'$(3, 0), B$'$(9, 0), C$'$(9, 2), D$'$(3, 2); Stretch parallel to x-axis, scale factor 3
2. A$'$(1, 0), B$'$(3, 0), C$'$(3, 4), D$'$(1, 4); Stretch parallel to y-axis, scale factor 2
3. A$'$($1\frac{1}{2}$, 1),   B$'$(6, 1),   C$'$(6, 2),   D$'$($1\frac{1}{2}$, 2); Stretch parallel to x-axis, scale factor $1\frac{1}{2}$
4. A$'$(−2, 3), B$'$(1, 3), C$'$(1, 6), D$'$(1, 6); Stretch parallel to y-axis, scale factor 3

Exercise 19h   page 316

1. A$'$(−2, 0), B$'$(2, 0), C$'$(4, 2), D$'$(0, 2); Shear, invariant line the x-axis, (2, 2) → (4, 2)
2. A$'$(0, 1), B$'$(2, 5), C$'$(2, 6), D$'$(0, 2); Shear, invariant line the y-axis, (2, 2) → (2, 6)
3. A$'$(1, 0), B$'$(3, 0), C$'$(6, 2); Shear, invariant line the x-axis, (2, 2) → (6, 2)
4. A$'$(−2, 0),   B$'$(2, 0),   C$'$(−2, 2),   D$'$(−6, 2); Shear,   invariant   line   the   x-axis, (2, 2) → (−2, 2)
5. A$'$(0, 1), B$'$(3, 4), C$'$(3, 5), D$'$(0, 2); Shear, invariant line the y-axis, (3, 2) → (3, 5)
6. A$'$(−1, 2),   B$'$(2, −1),   C$'$(2, 2),   D$'$(−1, 5); Shear, invariant line the y-axis, (2, 4) → (2, 2)
7. A$'$(−2, −1),   B$'$(1, −1),   C$'$(2, 2);   Shear, invariant line the x-axis, (0, 2) → (2, 2)
9. A$'$(−2, 1),   B$'$(2, 1),   C$'$(−1, 4),   D$'$(−5, 4); Shear, invariant line the x-axis, (3, 1) → (2, 1)
10. A$'$(−1, 1), B$'$(1, 1), C$'$(5, 3), D$'$(3, 3); Shear, invariant line the x-axis, (−3, 1) → (−1, 1)
11. A$'$(−1, −3),   B$'$(−1, 0),   C$'$(−3, −4), D$'$(−3, −5); Shear, invariant line the y-axis, (−1, −1) → (−1, −3)
12. A$'$(−4, 2), B$'$(−1, 2), C$'$(−5, 4), D$'$(−8, 4); Shear,   invariant   line   the   y-axis, (0, 2) → (−4, 2)

Exercise 19i   page 319

1. A$'$(−1, −3), B$'$(1, 3), C$'$(5, 5), D$'$(3, −1); (Parallelogram)
2. A$'$(−1, 3), B$'$(1, −3), C$'$(−3, −1), D$'$(−5, 5); (Parallelogram)
3. A$'$(−4, −3), B$'$(2, −3), C$'$(2, 6), D$'$(−4, 6); (Rectangle)
4. A$'$(−8, −4), B$'$(−2, −1), C$'$(6, 3), D$'$(0, 0); (Straight line)
5. A$'$(1, −2), B$'$(−3, 6), C$'$(−1, 2), D$'$(3, −6); (Straight line)
6. All points → the origin

Exercise 19j   page 320

1. O$'$(0, 0),   A$'$(2, 0),   B$'$(2, −1),   C$'$(0, −1); Reflection in x-axis
2. O$'$(0, 0), A$'$(2, 0), B$'$($3\frac{1}{2}$, 1), C$'$($1\frac{1}{2}$, 1); Shear, invariant line the x-axis, (2, 1) → ($3\frac{1}{2}$, 1)
3. O$'$(0, 0), A$'$(0, −2), B$'$(−1, −2), C$'$(−1, 0); Reflection in line $y = -x$
4. O$'$(0, 0), A$'$(−6, 0), B$'$(−6, 3), C$'$(0, 3)
5. O$'$(0, 0), A$'$(4, 6), B$'$(1, 8), C$'$(−3, 2)
6. O$'$(0, 0), A$'$(4, 0), B$'$(4, 1), C$'$(0, 1); Stretch parallel to the x-axis, scale factor 2
7. O$'$(0, 0),   A$'$(8, 0),   B$'$(8, 4),   C$'$(0, 4); Enlargement centre O, scale factor 4
8. O$'$(0, 0), A$'$(2, 2), B$'$(4, 6), C$'$(2, 4)
9. O$'$(0, 0), A$'$(2, 0), B$'$(2, 3), C$'$(0, 3); Stretch parallel to the y-axis, scale factor 3
10. O$'$(0, 0),   A$'$(1, 0),   B$'$(1, $\frac{1}{2}$),   C$'$(0, $\frac{1}{2}$); Enlargement centre O, scale factor $\frac{1}{2}$
11. O$'$(0, 0), A$'$(4, 2), B$'$(6, 5), C$'$(2, 3)
12. O$'$(0, 0), A$'$(2, 4), B$'$(2, 5), C$'$(0, 1); Shear, invariant line the y-axis, (2, 1) → (2, 5)
13. The unit square OABC; A(1, 0), B(1, 1), C(0, 1); or the unit triangle OAB
14.

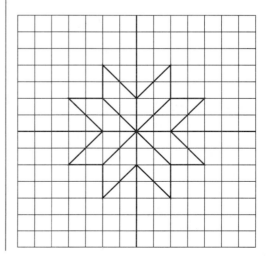

15. The image is the same as the object in each case
16. (a) A′(1,0), B′(0,−1)
    (b) A′(2,0), B′(0,2)
    (c) A′(1,0), B′(2,1)
    (d) A′(2,4), B′(5,−1)
    The columns of the matrices give the position vectors of A′ and B′

Exercise 19k   page 322
1. Rotation of 90° anticlockwise about the origin
2. Enlargement centre O and scale factor $\frac{1}{3}$
3. Reflection in the *x*-axis
4. Rotation of 45° clockwise about the origin

Exercise 19l   page 323
1. (a) A′(0,1), B′(0,3), C′(−3,3)
   (b) Rotation of 90° anticlockwise about the origin
   (c) $\begin{pmatrix} 0 & 1 \\ -1 & 0 \end{pmatrix}$
   (d) The image is ABC
   (e) Rotation of −90° clockwise about design
2. (a) A′(3,3), B′(6,3), C′(6,6), D′(3,6)
   (b) Enlargement centre O, with scale factor 3
   (c) $\begin{pmatrix} \frac{1}{3} & 0 \\ 0 & \frac{1}{3} \end{pmatrix}$
   (d) The image is ABCD
   (e) Rotation of 90° clockwise about the origin
3. (a) A′(0,−1), B′(1,−3), C′(2,−3), D′(1,−1)
   (b) Rotation of 90° clockwise about the origin
   (c) $\begin{pmatrix} 0 & -1 \\ 1 & 0 \end{pmatrix}$
   (d) The image is ABCD
   (e) Rotation of 90° anticlockwise about the origin. Yes
4. (a) A′(3,1), B′(9,3), C′(7,3)
   (b) Shear, invariant line the *x*-axis, (1,1) → (3,1)
   (c) $\begin{pmatrix} 1 & -2 \\ 0 & 1 \end{pmatrix}$
   (d) The image is ABC
   (e) Shear, invariant line the *x*-axis, (3,1) → (1,1); Yes
5. (a) A′(1,3), B′(3,9), C′(5,13), D′(3,7)
   (b) $\begin{pmatrix} -2 & 1 \\ 3 & -1 \end{pmatrix}$
   (c) A′B′C′D′ → ABCD
6. (a) O′(0,0), A′(2,1), B′(10,5), C′(8,4); Image is a straight line
   (b) No inverse
   (c) Transformation has no inverse either

Exercise 19m   page 325
1. O′(0,0), A′(2,0), B′(6,2), C′(4,2); O and A
2. O′(0,0), A′(4,0), B′(4,4), C′(0,4); O
3. O′(0,0), A′(2,0), B′(2,−2), C′(0,−2); O and A
4. O′(0,0), A′(4,2), B′(6,6), C′(2,4); O
5. The origin; Yes

Exercise 19n   page 326
1. Translation defined by the vector $\begin{pmatrix} 5 \\ 1 \end{pmatrix}$
2. Translation defined by the vector $\begin{pmatrix} -5 \\ 1 \end{pmatrix}$
3. Translation defined by the vector $\begin{pmatrix} 3 \\ -4 \end{pmatrix}$
4. Translation defined by the vector $\begin{pmatrix} -4 \\ 0 \end{pmatrix}$
5. O′(3,1), A′(4,1), B′(4,3), C′(3,3)
6. A′(−1,−2), B′(−1,0), C′(−2,0)
7. A′(1,−1), B′(2,−1), C′(2,1)
8. A′(0,1), B′(1,1), C′(1,3), D′(0,3)
9. Translation defined by the vectors:
   1. $\begin{pmatrix} -5 \\ -1 \end{pmatrix}$ 5. $\begin{pmatrix} -3 \\ -1 \end{pmatrix}$
   2. $\begin{pmatrix} 5 \\ -1 \end{pmatrix}$ 6. $\begin{pmatrix} 3 \\ 3 \end{pmatrix}$
   3. $\begin{pmatrix} -3 \\ 4 \end{pmatrix}$ 7. $\begin{pmatrix} -4 \\ 2 \end{pmatrix}$
   4. $\begin{pmatrix} 4 \\ 0 \end{pmatrix}$ 8. $\begin{pmatrix} 1 \\ -1 \end{pmatrix}$

Chapter 20

Exercise 20a   page 329
1. No, angles not equal
2. Yes
3. No, sides not equal
4. No, $\begin{cases} \text{sides not equal} \\ \text{angles not equal} \end{cases}$
5. No, $\begin{cases} \text{sides not equal} \\ \text{angles not equal} \end{cases}$
6. No, $\begin{cases} \text{sides not equal} \\ \text{angles not equal} \end{cases}$
7. Yes
8. No, not bounded by straight lines

Exercise 20b   page 331
1. 180°
2. 360°
3. (a) $p = 100°$, $r = 135°$, $x = 55°$, $q = 125°$
   (b) 360°
4. (a) $w = 120°$, $x = 60°$, $y = 120°$, $z = 60°$
   (b) 360°
5. (a) 180°   (b) 540°   (c) 180°   (d) 360°
6. 360°
7. (a) equilateral   (d) 60°
   (b) 60°   (e) 360°
   (c) 120°

Exercise 20c   page 333
1. 60°   6. 90°   11. $x = 50°$
2. 90°   7. 95°   12. $x = 30°$
3. 50°   8. 55°   13. $x = 24°$
4. 50°   9. 30°   14. (a) 5
5. 60°   10. 125°   (b) 8

Exercise 20d   page 336
1. 36°
2. 45°
3. 30°
4. 60°
5. 24°
6. 20°
7. 40°
8. 22.5°
9. 18°

Exercise 20e   page 337
1. 720°
2. 540°
3. 1440°
4. 360°
5. 900°
6. 1800°
7. 2880°
8. 1260°
9. 2340°

Exercise 20f   page 338
1. (a) 3240°   (b) 2520°   (c) 1620°
2. 80°
3. 120°
4. 110°
5. 105°
6. 85°
7. 110°
8. 108°
9. 120°
10. 135°
11. 144°
12. 150°
13. 162°
14. (a) 18   (b) 24
15. (a) 12   (b) 20
16. (a) yes, 12   (d) yes, 6
    (b) yes, 9   (e) no
    (c) no   (f) yes, 4
17. (a) yes, 4   (d) yes, 72
    (b) yes, 6   (e) yes, 36
    (c) no   (f) yes, 8

Exercise 20g   page 340
1. 54°
2. 45°
3. 150°
4. 72°
5. 60°
6. 50°
7. 80°
8. 135°
9. 100°
10. 60°
11. 72°
12. 45°
13. 60°
14. 36°
15. (a) 36°   (b) 36°
16. (a) 128.6°   (b) 25.7°
17. 77.1°
18. (a) 22.5°   (b) 22.5°
19. 22.5°
20. 45°

Exercise 20h   page 345
1. (a) The interior angles (135°) do not divide
       exactly into 360°
   (b) A square
2. (a) No
   (b) A regular ten-sided polygon
4. Square, equilateral triangle

Chapter 21

Exercise 21a   page 348
1. AB, AC, AD, BC, BD, CD. Yes, AC.
2.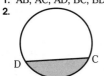
3.

4. 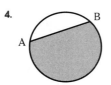   5.

Exercise 21b   page 350
1. Minor arc DC
2. Minor arc BC
3. A$\widehat{C}$B, A$\widehat{D}$B
4. B$\widehat{A}$C, B$\widehat{D}$C
5. DA
6. AB
7. Minor arc BE
8. Minor arc CD
9. CE
10. DB
11. (a) A$\widehat{C}$B, A$\widehat{E}$B
    (b) B$\widehat{A}$C, B$\widehat{E}$C
12. (a) A$\widehat{B}$E, A$\widehat{C}$E, A$\widehat{D}$E
    (b) C$\widehat{D}$E, C$\widehat{A}$E, C$\widehat{B}$E

Exercise 21c   page 351
Answers depend on pupils' drawings but in each
question the angles should be equal

Exercise 21d   page 351
1. $h = 38°$
2. $i = 39°, j = 46°$
3. $x = 33° = y$
4. $p = 72°, q = 57°$
5. $l = 100°$
6. $x = 108°, y = 26°$
7. $w = 57°, x = 123°$
8. $c = 144°$

Exercise 21e   page 353
Answers depend on pupils' drawings but in each
question $y = 2x$

Exercise 21f   page 354
1. $d = 80°$
2. $e = 64°$
3. $f = 114°$
4. $i = 38°$
5. $g = 98°$
6. $h = 32°$
7. $l = 132°$
8. $m = 102°$

Exercise 21g   page 356
Answers depend on pupils' drawings but in each
question $p + q = 180°$

Exercise 21h   page 357
1. $d = 108°$
2. $e = 84°$
3. $f = 103°$
4. $k = 115°$
5. $l = 131°$
6. $m = 87°, n = 112°$
7. $g = 121°, h = 68°$
8. $i = 110°, j = 50°$

Exercise 21i   page 359
Answers depend on pupils' drawings but the
conclusions should be:
1. $p = q$
2. $v = u$
3. $s = r$
4. $x = w$
5. $y = 100°$
6. $z = 109°$
7. $p = 54°, q = 76°$
8. $r = 126°, s = 83°$

Exercise 21j   page 360
1. $d = 75°$, $e = 65°$, $f = 140°$
2. $p = 60°$, $q = 60°$, $r = 120°$, $s = 60°$
3. $k = 30°$, $l = 30°$, $m = 30°$, $n = 60°$
4. $g = 24°$, $h = 156°$, $i = 74°$
5. $w = 73°$, $x = 34°$, $y = 34°$, $z = 73°$
6. $d = 64°$, $e = 64°$, $f = 116°$, $g = 116°$, $b = 64°$
7. $a = 44°$
8. $c = 60°$, $d = 46°$
9. $g = 116°$
10. $b = 78°$
11. $e = 34°$, $f = 52°$
12. $h = 72°$
13. $l = 154°$, $m = 40°$, $n = 37°$
14. $r = 110°$, $s = 122°$
15. $x = 30°$, $y = 58°$, $z = 88°$
16. $c = 25°$, $d = 25°$, $e = 50°$
17. $h = 116°$, $i = 32°$
18. $l = 126°$, $m = 63°$, $n = 117°$
19. $u = 34°$, $v = 68°$, $w = 56°$, $x = 56°$
20. $k = 62°$, $l = 56°$, $m = 124°$, $n = 16°$

Exercise 21k   page 362
1. $d = 90° = e$
2. $f = 90° = g$
3. $h = 90° = i$

Exercise 21l   page 363
1. $d = 90°$, $e = 53°$
2. $f = 90°$, $g = 45°$
3. $h = 90°$, $i = 26°$
4. $l = 90°$, $m = 61°$
5. $j = 90°$, $k = 55°$
6. $p = 90°$, $q = 38°$
7. $r = 90°$, $s = 52°$, $t = 90°$, $u = 43°$
8. $d = 90°$, $e = 45°$, $f = 90°$, $g = 18°$
9. $c = 90°$, $d = 58°$, $e = 32°$
10. $v = 90°$, $w = 47°$, $x = 90°$, $y = 51°$
11. $j = 90°$, $k = 33°$, $l = 33°$, $m = 57°$
12. $f = 45°$, $g = 58°$, $h = 45°$, $i = 32°$

Exercise 21m   page 366
2. 5.83 cm
3. (a) 10.9 cm   (b) 6.3 cm
4. O is the midpoint of AB
   $\widehat{ACB} = 90°$ since it is in a semicircle
5. (a) They all pass through one point
   (b) It is outside the triangle
6. Yes. It passes through D.
   Because the trapezium is symmetrical about the perpendicular bisector of AB
   No

Exercise 21n   page 367
1. $d = 106°$
2. $e = f = 38°$
3. $d = 34°$, $e = 68°$
4. $x = 75°$, $y = 15°$, $z = 132°$
5. $p = 36° = q$, $r = 39°$
6. $x = 112°$, $y = 68°$, $z = 112°$
7. $g = 54°$, $h = 120°$
8. $d = 37°$, $e = 53°$, $f = 57°$, $g = 33°$

Chapter 22

Exercise 22a   page 370
1. 3.49 cm
2. 2.09 cm
3. 20 cm
4. 2.09 rad
5. 9.81 cm^2
6. 62.8 cm
7. 2.5π
8. (a) 0.96 rad   (b) 55°
9. 5 cm
10. (a) 270°   (b) $\frac{10}{3}\pi$ (c) 5.5π

Review test 2   page 373
1. B   3. B   5. A   7. B   9. A
2. C   4. D   6. B   8. C   10. B
11. Average speed $= 60\frac{2}{3}$ km/h
12. (a) 130 cm^2, 46 cm
    (b) (i)   30°
        (ii) 60°
        (iii) 75°
13. (a) (i) $2x(x - 6y)(x + 6y)$
        (ii) $(a - 2b)(a + c)$
        (iii) $(3x - 4)(2x + 1)$
    (b) -0.15, -3.35
14. (a) $\begin{pmatrix} 0 & -2 \\ 2 & 0 \end{pmatrix}$ (b) $\begin{pmatrix} 5 & 0 \\ 0 & 5 \end{pmatrix}$
    $x = \frac{11}{5}$, $y = -\frac{19}{5}$
15. $(10, 20)$

Chapter 23

Exercise 23a   page 375
1. $2 : 3$
2. $1 : 2 : 3$
3. $7 : 5$
4. $2 : 3$
5. $18 : 8 : 9$
6. $2 : 3 : 1$
7. $4 : 9$
8. $3 : 5 : 4$
9. $2 : 3 : 1$
10. $6 : 11$
11. $15 : 4$
12. $31 : 4$
13. $5 : 16$
14. $1.5 : 1$
15. $2.4 : 1$
16. $0.857 : 1$
17. $2.73 : 1$
18. $0.6 : 1$
19. $2.63 : 1$
20. $1.33 : 1$
21. $0.75 : 1$
22. $1.43 : 1$

Exercise 23b   page 375
1. $9 : 2$
2. $2 : 5$
3. $17 : 60$
4. $2 : 125$
5. $9 : 20$
6. $50 : 3$
7. $20 : 19$
8. $36 : 35$
9. $27 : 25$
10. $9 : 10$
11. $25 : 24$
12. (a) $3 : 2$ (b) $2 : 3$ (c) $3 : 5$
13. (a) $2 : 3$ (c) $21 : 23$
    (b) $9 : 5$ (d) $6 : 5$
14. $18 : 25$
15. (a) $1 : 1$ (d) $1 : 1$
    (b) $1 : 2$ (e) $1 : 3$
    (c) $1 : 8$ (f) $1 : 8$
16. (a) $1 : 9$ (b) $1 : 4$ (c) $4 : 9$

Exercise 23c   page 379
1. $1\frac{1}{9}$ or 1.11
2. $\frac{3}{7}$ or 0.429
3. $7\frac{1}{2}$ or 7.5
4. $1\frac{3}{7}$ or 1 : 43
5. 24
6. $22\frac{1}{2}$
7. $9\frac{1}{3}$ or 9.33
8. $2\frac{8}{11}$ or 2.73
9. $1\frac{1}{5}$ or 1.2
10. $7\frac{1}{5}$ or 7.2
11. $3\frac{1}{3}$ or 3.33
12. $8\frac{4}{7}$ or 8.57
13. 12 grandsons; 3 : 7
14. 152
15. 10.1 cm
16. 264

Exercise 23d   page 380
1. $20, $25
2. 54 m, 42 m
3. 0.625 kg, 1.25 kg, 3.125 kg
4. $\frac{1}{2}$ h, $2\frac{1}{2}$ h, 4 h
5. 18 boys, 14 girls
6. 60°, 50°, 70°
7. 9, 12, 9
8. 66 hits, 24 misses

Exercise 23e   page 381
1. 9 : 7
2. 30 m, 42 m
3. $5\frac{1}{4}$
4. $2\frac{2}{9}$ or 2.22
5. 27.5 cm
6. 5 : 3
7. 500 : 53
8. 4 : 3
9. 3 : 4
10. $\frac{2}{3}$

Exercise 23f   page 381
1. (a) $1.80   (b) $7.20
2. (a) 6 units   (b) $\frac{3}{4}$ unit
3. (a) 72 km   (b) 118.8 km
4. (a) 35 rows   (b) 42 rows
5. (a) 1.12\frac{1}{2}$ (b) $5.40

Exercise 23g   page 382
1. $1.20
2. 15.5 km
3. $4\frac{1}{3}$ or 4.33 km
4. 65 c
5. $7.70
6. $4.20
7. $8.30
8. 1.5 c
9. 1.5 m
10. 5.5 m²

Exercise 23h   page 383
1. 3.2 litres
2. 3 hours
3. $12\frac{1}{2}$ units
4. 3.6 hours
5. (a) $30 (b) 35 km
6. $96
7. 700
8. $2.64
9. 66 rows
10. 20.25 cm
11. $168
12. 392
13. 65.6 km
14. (a) 2.25×10^7
    (b) 8.1×10^6
    (c) 1.35×10^5
15. 15 V
16. 24.7 joules
17. $2.032, $2.03
18. $42.15

Exercise 23i   page 386
1. $5\frac{1}{2}$ hours
2. 12
3. 203
4. 8 days
5. 25 cm
6. 20
7. 16 cm
8. 44
9. 49

Exercise 23j   page 387
1. (a) TT$15
   (b) 2100 yen
2. $195.70
3. $3\frac{1}{2}$ hours
4. No answer
5. 4.46 cm
6. 49
7. 24
8. 34
9. 1.44 m
10. 6 weeks
11. No answer
12. 1.5 amps

Exercise 23k   page 388
1. 3 : 1
2. $3\frac{3}{5}$ or 3.6
3. 8 m, 16 m, 32 m
4. 114 km (3 s.f.)
5. 6 hours 40 mins
6. 6 : 2 : 1
7. 9
8. $\frac{6}{5}$: 1 or 1.2 : 1

Exercise 23l   page 388
1. 4 : 3
2. 12, 8, 20
3. $6\frac{3}{5}$ or 6.6
4. 8 : 7
5. 0.6 : 1
6. £7.50
7. 1 : 3
8. $112.50

Chapter 24

Exercise 24a   page 389
1. 38.44
2. 187.69
3. 58 564
4. 7 728 400
5. 0.5041
6. 0.003 481
7. 0.000 002 89
8. 97 344
9. 9.7344
10. 0.000 973 44
11. 84.64
12. 8464
13. 27 140 000
14. 2714
15. 0.2714
16. 0.002 714
17. 3.142
18. 4.461
19. 11.14
20. 311.1
21. 0.2195
22. 0.069 43
23. 9.798
24. 17.92
25. 1.619
26. 0.2490
27. 0.027 93
28. 0.7071
29. 0.6790
30. 2.147
31. 21.47
32. 0.021 47

Exercise 24b   page 391
1. 10.3 m
2. 15.3 m
3. 3.22 m
4. 136 cm
5. 23.0 cm
6. 102 cm
7. 12.6 cm
8. 7.97 cm
9. 2.31 cm
10. 5.31 cm
11. 0.8 cm
12. 73.3 cm
13. 50 cm
14. 26 cm
15. 4.4 cm
16. 100 cm
17. 2.4 cm
18. 20 cm

Exercise 24c   page 394
1. Yes
2. Yes
3. No
4. No
5. Yes
6. No

Exercise 24d   page 395
1. 18.9 cm
2.. 6.52 cm
3. 2.02 cm
4. 0.0265 cm
5. 20.5 cm
6. 4.16 cm
7. 0.05 cm
8. 13.0 cm
9. 3.58 cm
10. 64.5 cm
11. Yes
12. 3.13 cm
13. 26.2 cm
14. Yes, $\widehat{M} = 90°$

Exercise 24e   page 396

1. 8.94 units
2. 38.8 n.m.
3. 5.52 m, 35.4°
4. 0.589 cm
5. 21.2 cm
6. (a) 39.4 cm   (b) 47.9°
7. (a) 2.4 cm
   (b) 4.64 cm   No. $AC^2 \neq AB^2 + BC^2$
8. (c) AC = 7.07 cm, AD = 8.66 cm, AE = 10 cm
9. Use 7 cm and 4 cm or 8 cm and 1 cm.
   $\sqrt{65} = 8.06$

Exercise 24f   page 398

1. (a) EA = FB = GC = HD; AB = EF = HG = DC;
   BC = FG = EH = AD; 24 right angles
   (b) EB = 5 cm, $E\hat{B}A = 36.9°$
   (c) FC = 12.4 cm, $F\hat{C}B = 14.0°$
2. (a) AC = 12.6 cm
   (b) $E\hat{A}C = 90°$, EC = 13 cm, $E\hat{C}A = 13.3°$
3. (a) FC = 8.25 cm
   (b) AF = 5.39 cm, $F\hat{A}B = 21.8°$
   (c) EG = 9.43 cm, 32.0°

Exercise 24g   page 399

1. (a) 14.4 cm   (b) 15.3 cm   (c) 19.1°
2. (a) 3.61 cm   (b) 33.7°   (c) 6.71 cm
3. (a) 10 cm   (b) 15.6 cm   (c) 39.8°
4 (a) 14.9 cm   (c) 19.1 cm   (e) 47.7°
   (b) 19.1 cm   (d) 47.5°
5. 24.7 cm
6. (a) 15 cm   (b) 16.6 cm   (c) 25.0°
7. (a) 7.07 cm   (b) 7.07 cm   (c) 600 cm²
8. (a) 33.7°   (b) 56.3°   (c) 31.4°
9. (a) 7.07 cm   (b) 336 cm²

Exercise 24h   page 401

1. (a) AB = DC = FE, BC = AD, EC = FD,
   14 right angles
   (b) $E\hat{B}C = 33.7°$, BE = 7.21 cm
   (c) AC = 11.7 cm, $C\hat{A}B = 31.0°$, Yes
   (d) AE = 12.3 cm, AE = FB
2. (a) 3.00 cm   (c) 10.9 cm
   (b) 7.42 cm   (d) 15.4°
3. (a) 27.5 m   (d) 49.5 m
   (b) 48.5 m   (e) 11.6 m
   (c) 29.2 m   (f) 53.8°
4. (a) 24.4°   (b) 13.9°
5. (a) 2.62 cm   (b) 3.98 cm   (c) 5.76 cm

Exercise 24i   page 402

1. (a) $A\hat{B}C$, $B\hat{C}D$, $C\hat{D}A$, $D\hat{A}B$, $A\hat{F}B$, $B\hat{F}C$, $C\hat{F}D$,
   $D\hat{F}A$, $B\hat{F}E$, $C\hat{F}E$, $D\hat{F}E$, $A\hat{F}E$. (12).
   AE = BE = CE = DE
   (b) AC = 2.83 cm, AF = 1.41 cm
   (c) EF = 5.83 cm, $E\hat{C}F = 76.4°$
2. (a) AC = 5.66 cm, AF = 2.83 cm
   (b) AE = 5.74 cm, $E\hat{A}F = 60.5°$
   (c) EG = 5.39 cm, $E\hat{G}F = 68.2°$
3. (a) $E\hat{B}A = 36.9°$, $E\hat{D}A = 45°$
   (b) 5 cm
   (c) 5.83 cm
4. (a) PR = 8.54 cm   (c) 54.5°
   (b) PY = 4.27 cm   (d) 7.37 cm

Exercise 24j   page 403

1. (a) 7.28 m
   (b) 31.2°
   (c) 23.3 m, 17.3°
2. (a) AC = CD′ = AD′ = 5.66 cm.
       Equilateral triangle
   (b) Rectangle;
       AC′ = A′C = BD′ = DB′ = 6.93 cm
3. (a) BD = 8.49 m, BE = 4.24 m
   (b) EF = 4.24 m. Height = 8.49 m
   (c) 45°
4. (a) 7.07 cm   (c) 4.85 cm
5. (a) BD = 8.94 cm
   (b) $D\hat{B}A = 26.6°$
   (c) 11.3 cm
   (d) DC = BD = 8.94 cm
   (e) $D\hat{C}A = D\hat{B}A = 26.6°$

Chapter 25

Exercise 25a   page 406

7. $\frac{5}{12}$, 0.4167   10. $\frac{3}{4}$, 0.75
8. $\frac{8}{15}$, 0.5333   11. $\frac{12}{5}$, 2.4
9. $\frac{3}{4}$, 0.75   12. $\frac{35}{12}$, 2.917

Exercise 25b   page 408

1. 1.8807   7. 4.8716   13. 10.1°   19. 42.7°
2. 0.2493   8. 1   14. 19.6°   20. 38.7°
3. 0.5890   9. 0.5774   15. 55.0°   21. 17.8°
4. 0.3019   10. 1.1184   16. 23.4°   22. 69.6°
5. 0.0805   11. 0.0524   17. 53.7°   23. 42.7°
6. 3.0777   12. 0.5635   18. 32.3°   24. 0.1°

Exercise 25c   page 409

1. 32.0°   4. 35.8°   7. 31.0°   10. 47.7°
2. 63.4°   5. 51.3°   8. 51.3°   11. 34.2°
3. 23.2°   6. 60.9°   9. 48.4°

Exercise 25d   page 410

1. 2.44 cm   11. 3.60 cm
2. 5.40 cm   12. 11.4 cm
3. 2.56 cm   13. 2.42 cm
4. 6.12 cm   14. 1.76 cm
5. 17.0 cm   15. 46.6 cm
6. 81.8 cm   16. 10.4 cm
7. 5.62 cm   17. 4.69 cm
8. 22.2 cm   18. 366 cm
9. 2.82 cm   19. 0.976 cm
10. 7.54 cm   20. 69.5 cm

Exercise 25e   page 413

1. 0.8862   8. 0.5   15. 31.6°
2. 0.9397   9. 0.9903   16. 65.4°
3. 0.2470   10. 0.4664   17. 41.8°
4. 0.1564   11. 0.2723   18. 21.8°
5. 0.2622   12. 0.9988   19. 37.9°
6. 0.6088   13. 15.7°   20. 46.7°
7. 0.8625   14. 26.2°   21. 7.1°

Exercise 25f   page 413

1. 30°
2. 17.5°
3. 48.6°
4. 44.4°
5. 14.5°
6. 62.7°
7. 44.4°
8. 41.8°
9. 23.6°
10. 19.5°
11. 4.38 cm
12. 10.6 cm
13. 1.46 cm
14. 4.57 cm
15. 11.7 cm
16. 23.2 cm
17. 6.31 cm
18. 21.9 m
19. 3.34 cm
20. 45.7 cm

Exercise 25g   page 416

1. 0.8480
2. 0.7455
3. 0.1392
4. 0.6717
5. 0.5
6. 0.9632
7. 0.6143
8. 0.6561
9. 0.3040
10. 69.7°
11. 20.6°
12. 44.0°
13. 69.6°
14. 51.1°
15. 71.6°
16. 30.1°
17. 89.2°
18. 85.8°

Exercise 25h   page 416

1. 34.9°
2. 36.9°
3. 45.6°
4. 48.2°
5. 48.2°
6. 53.1°
7. 50.2°
8. 66.4°
9. 81.4°
10. 25.8°
11. 34.0°
12. 3.50 cm
13. 26.9 m
14. 1.96 cm
15. 11.6 cm
16. 38.2 cm
17. 2.90 cm
18. 17.1 cm
19. 2.23 cm
20. 4.12 cm
21. 13.5 cm

Exercise 25i   page 419

1. 40.0°
2. 33.6°
3. 51.3°
4. 42.8°
5. 35.5°
6. 33.7°
7. 39.8°
8. 33.7°
9. 37.7°
10. 53.1°
11. 68.5°
12. 14.5°
13. 56.9°
14. 37.8°
15. 39.3°
16. 55.6°
17. 42.1°
18. 66.2°
19 6.69 cm
20. 19.3 cm
21. 8.03 cm
22. 4.86 cm
23. 4.48 cm
24. 80.5 cm
25. 6.04 cm
26. 3.50 cm
27. 13.7 cm
28. 3.08 cm
29. 113 cm
30. 2.59 cm
31. 9.99 cm
32. 7.45 cm
33. 14.5 cm
34. 21.4 cm
35. 74.5 cm
36. 60.6 cm

Exercise 25j   page 421

1. 4.13 cm
2. 8.72 cm
3. 23.3 cm
4. 4.67 cm
5. 14.9 cm
6. 17.0 cm
7. 4.40 cm
8. 14.9 cm
9. 33.1 cm
10. 42.6 cm

Exercise 25k   page 423

1. 8.99 cm
2. 47.7 m
3. 143 m
4. 39.8°
5. 61.6°
6. 56.3°
7. 48.2°
8. 11.3°
9. (b) 5.30 cm   (c) 6.25 cm
10. (a) 5.20 cm   (b) 15.6 cm^2
11. 4.66 m
12. (a) $A\widehat{O}B = 72°$, $O\widehat{A}B = 54°$
    (b) 6.88 cm
    (c) 34.4 cm^2, 172 cm^2

Exercise 25l   page 426

1. $a = 6$
2. $c = 36$
3. $b = 8.49$ cm
4. $a = 7.42$, $c = 11.4$
5. $\sin B = 0.25$
6. 1.41
7. $B = 66.9°$

Exercise 25m   page 427

1. $c = 5.52$
2. $b = 17.9$
3. $c = 13.9$
4. $b = 11.0$, $\widehat{A} = 46.6°$, $\widehat{C} = 90.4°$
5. $c = 7.4$, $\widehat{B} = 40.6°$, $\widehat{A} = 102.4°$
6. $\widehat{C} = 117.3°$
7. $\widehat{A} = 41.4°$
8. 18 nautical miles
9. 36 m

Chapter 26

Exercise 26a   page 430
Revises three figure bearings.

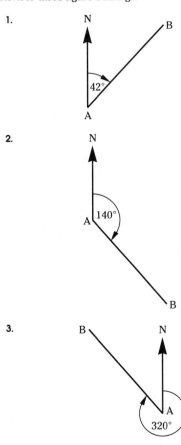

1.

2.

3.

4.

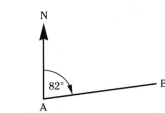

5.

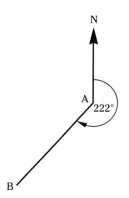

6.

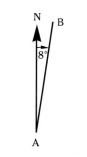

7.

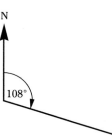

8.

9.

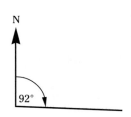

10. 062°   **12.** 328°   **14.** 249°   **16.** 154°
11. 098°   **13.** 262°   **15.** 254°   **17.** 050°

18.

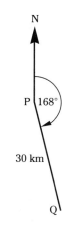

19.

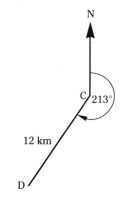

20.

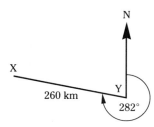

21.

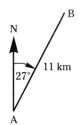

22.

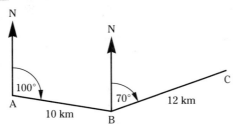

23.

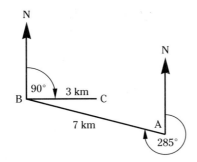

24.

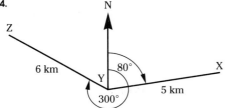

25.

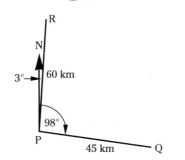

26.

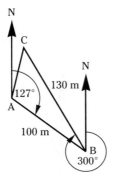

27.

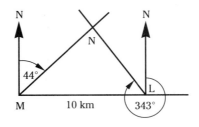

Exercise 26b   **page 433**
1. 240°   3. 342°   5. 172°
2. 112°   4. 032°   6. 305°

Exercise 26c   **page 433**

1.

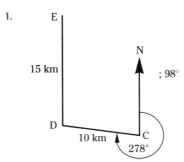

; 98°

2.

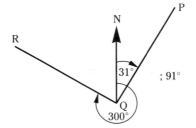

; 91°

3.

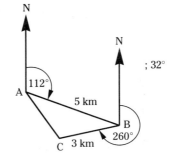

; 32°

4.

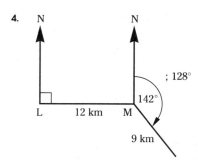

; 128°

5.

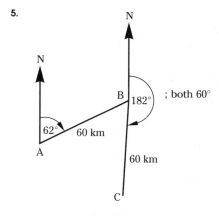

; both 60°

6.

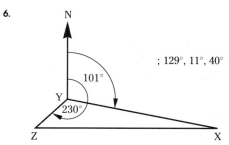

; 129°, 11°, 40°

7.

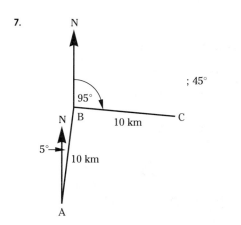

; 45°

8.

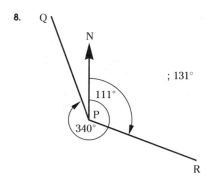

; 131°

Exercise 26d   page 434

1.

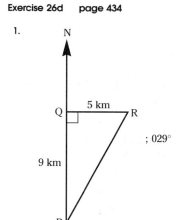

; 029°

2.

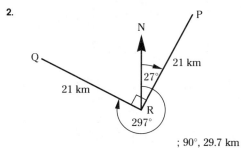

; 90°, 29.7 km

3.

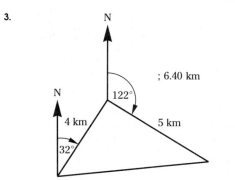

; 6.40 km

4. (a) 5.81 km   (b) 144°

5.

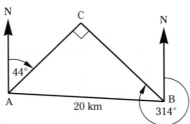

(a) 46°, 44°, 90°   (b) 14.4 km

6.

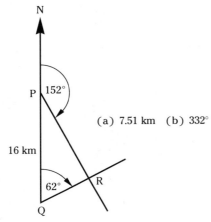

(a) 7.51 km   (b) 332°

7.

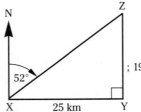

; 19.5 km, 31.7 km

8.

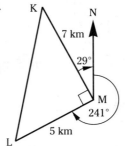

(a) 54.5°
(b) 186.5°
(c) 007°

Chapter 27

Exercise 27a   page 436
1. 223   **2.** 282   **3.** 474   **4.** 1257   **5.** 455
6. 842, 476, 353, 1136
7. 738, 301, 174, 806
8. 29 041, 29 387, 302, 30 704

9. 34 802, 35 161, 826, 36 930
10. $57.80   **13.** $83.58
11. $264.87   **14.** $119.82
12. $98.22   **15.** $78.09

Exercise 27b   page 439
1. 375   **13.** £170
2. 209   **14.** £79
3. 2115   **15.** £371.15, 371
4. 2868   **16.** £192.38, 192
5. 404, 184, 203, 396   **17.** £483.43, 483
6. 17 000   **18.** £56.49, 56
7. 26 400   **19.** £101.84, 102
8. 62 400   **20.** $331.18
9. 320.9   **21.** $344.65
10. 470.8   **22.** Credit by £9
11. 667.7   **23.** Credit by £10
12. £40   **24.** Credit by £3.40

Exercise 27c   page 444
1. $14 000   **14.** 75 c
2. $76 000   **15.** 134 c
3. $345 000   **16.** $100
4. $150 000   **17.** $350
5. $16 250   **18.** $720
6. $73 470   **19.** $295.16
7. $3 200 000   **20.** $564.40
8. $1 564 000   **21.** $438.90
9. $80 080 000   **22.** $382.50
10. $7 242 000   **23.** $196
11. $592 400   **24.** $458.64
12. $3 747 000   **25.** $433.44
13. 80 c

Exercise 27d   page 447
1. 90 c   **4.** 94 c   **7.** $300   **10.** $820
2. 120 c   **5.** 158 c   **8.** $250   **11.** $564
3. 130 c   **6.** 163 c   **9.** $450   **12.** $356

Exercise 27e   page 448
1. $75 500   **5.** $395.67
2. $2 088 000   **6.** 84 c
3. $344 500   **7.** $384
4. 77 c

Exercise 27f   page 448
1. $215, $236.50
2. $390.60, $476.28
3. $526.40
4. 93 c, $273.42, $327.36
5. $652.32
6. $347.71
7. $11.10, $213.12
8. $340.56

Exercise 27g   page 449
1. $99.20   **4.** $622.08
2. 393, $148.78   **5.** $5 372 000
3. $110.36

Chapter 28

Exercise 28a   page 452

1. | Age (yrs) | 7 | 8 | 9 | 10 | 11 |
   |---|---|---|---|---|---|
   | Frequency | 7 | 9 | 11 | 14 | 9 |

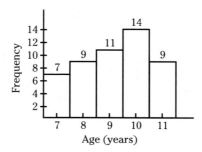

2. | Cents | 0–99 | 100–199 | 200–299 | 300–399 | 400–499 | 500–599 |
   |---|---|---|---|---|---|---|
   | Frequency | 9 | 10 | 16 | 12 | 5 | 4 |

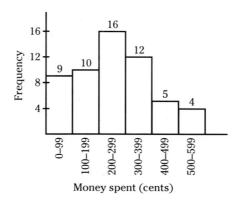

3. | Weight (g) | 60–64 | 65–69 | 70–74 | 75–79 | 80–84 | 85—89 |
   |---|---|---|---|---|---|---|
   | Frequency | 3 | 13 | 6 | 3 | 3 | 2 |

(suggested groups)

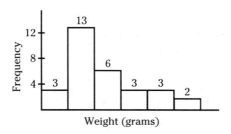

Exercise 28b   page 454

1.

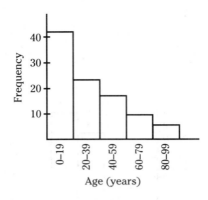

2.

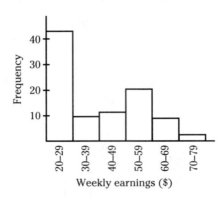

3.

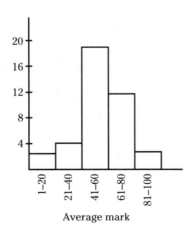

4. Time taken (minutes)	1–10	11–20	21–30	31–40	41–50	51–60
Frequency	8	16	13	9	2	2

5. No. of hours spent watching T.V.	up to 1	1 up to 2	2 up to 3	3 up to 4	4 up to 5
Frequency	2	12	8	6	2

Exercise 28c   page 456

1.

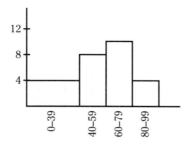

Mark

2.

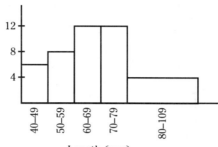

Length (mm)

3.

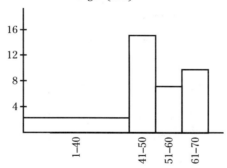

Time (seconds)

4.

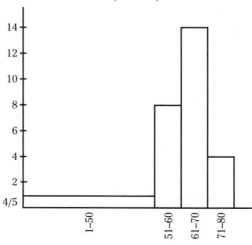

Weight (grams)

5.

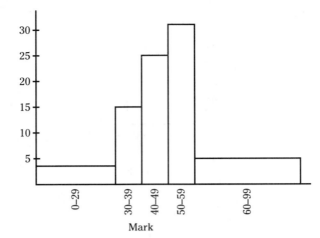

Mark

6.

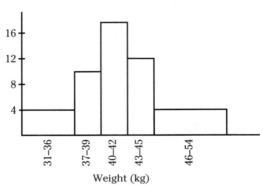

Weight (kg)

7.

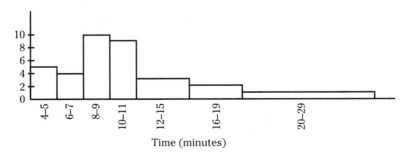

Time (minutes)

8.

Weight (kg)	1–10	11–20	21–30	31–50
Frequency	5	10	15	8

9.

Age (yrs)	1–3	4	5
Frequency	15	15	18

10.

Time (mins)	1–5	6–15	16–20	21–25
Frequency	10	18	11	6

11.

Height (cm)	10–29	30–39	40–49	50–69
Frequency	14	11	16	8

Exercise 28d   page 461

	Mean	*Mode*	*Median*
1.	4.43	2	4
2.	9.67	10	9
3.	14.1	12, 13, 14	13.5
4.	1.84	1.6	1.65
5.	3.75	4	4
6.	8.42	7	8
7.	0.725	0.8	0.75
8.	1.54	1.3, 1.8	1.5

9. mean 119.2, median 124
10. mean \$7150, mode \$5000, median \$5000
11. mean 180 c, mode 200 c, median 175 c
12. mean \$21.23, median \$18.10

Exercise 28e   page 463
1. Modal group: 6–10 minutes
2. Mode: 1 ticket per person
3. Mode: 5 books
4. 0–19 yrs, \$0–\$9, 41–60 marks, 11–20 minutes, 1–2 hours

Exercise 28f   page 464
1. 4.28
2. 3.64
3. 1.57
4. 120, 2.14

Exercise 28g   page 466
1. 4.2
2. 7.1 cm
3. $50\frac{1}{2}$ c

4.
Number of defective screws per box	0–2	3–5	6–8	9–11
Frequency	10	7	2	1

, 3.1

5. 160 cm
6. 55.4
7. 90.2 c
8. 31.9
9. 53.5
10. 106.7, 106.5

Exercise 28i   page 469
1. (a) Range = 10, $Q_1 = 15$, $Q_3 = 18.5$, median = 16, interquartile range = 3.5
   (b) Range = 15, $Q_1 = 48.5$, $Q_3 = 62$, median = 5.5, interquartile range = 13.5
   (c) Range = 15, $Q_1 = 15$, $Q_3 = 22$, median = 16, interquartile range = 17
2. $Q_3 = 46$, $Q_1 = 42$, $Q_3 - Q_1 = 4$
3. $Q_3 = 4$, $Q_1 = 1$, $Q_3 - Q_1 = 3$

Exercise 28j   page 470
1. 3.63
2. 2.53
3. 27.3
4. 2.53
5. 2.66
6. 21.6
7. 44.4

Exercise 28k   page 474
1. (a) $\frac{1}{4}$ (b) $\frac{1}{4}$ (c) $\frac{1}{2}$
   The probability that a head and a number greater than 2, or a tail and a number less than or equal to 2 will occur
2. $\frac{3}{20}$
3. $\frac{35}{36}$ E_1 and E_2 are not independent

4. 0.64
5. $\frac{1}{56}$
6. P (maths) $\odot$ P (science) $\neq$ P (maths and science)
   $\therefore$ not independent

Chapter 29

Exercise 29a   page 477
1. 213_5 2. 2014_5 3. 41240_5 4. 30201_5

	5^3	5^2	5	unit
5.			3	1
6.			4	2
7.		4	1	0
8.		2	3	1
9.			3	4
10.			1	0
11.		2	0	4
12.		4	0	0

13. 16_{10}
14. 14_{10}
15. 20_{10}
16. 36_{10}
17. 54_{10}
18. 23_{10}
19. 17_{10}
20. 10_{10}
21. 4_{10}
22. 100_{10}
23. 70_{10}
24. 75_{10}
25. 13_5
26. 23_5
27. 20_5
28. 124_5
29. 133_5
30. 1100_5
31. 12_5
32. 41_5
33. 110_5
34. 1003_5
35. 312_5
36. 400_5

Exercise 29b   page 480
1. (a)
4	1
2	3
   (b) 11_{10}

2. (a)
7	1
1	5
   (b) 12_{10}

3. (a)
4^2	4	1
1	3	1
   (b) 29_{10}

4. (a)
2^2	2	1
1	0	1
   (b) 5_{10}

5. (a)
8	1
5	7
   (b) 47_{10}

6. (a)
5^2	5	1
2	0	4
   (b) 29_{10}

7. (a)
3^2	3	1
2	1	0
   (b) 12_{10}

8. (a)
9^2	9	1
5	7	4
   (b) 472_{10}

9. (a)
3	1
2	1
   (b) 7_{10}

10. (a)

9	1
1	8

   (b) 17_{10}

11. (a)

6	1
2	4

   (b) 16_{10}

12. (a)

8^2	8	1
1	7	5

   (b) 125_{10}

13. (a)

4^2	4	1
3	0	3

   (b) 67_{10}

14. (a)

2^3	2^2	2	1
1	0	0	1

   (b) 9_{10}

15. (a)

3^3	3^2	3	1
1	2	1	1

   (b) 49_{10}

16. (a)

6^3	6^2	6	1
1	0	0	0

   (b) 216_{10}

17. 21_4
18. 22_5
19. 33_7
20. 111_2
21. 23_5
22. 52_6
23. 65_8
24. 100_7
25. 22_3
26. 23_6
27. 37_9

28. 1001_3
29. 110_7
30. 108_9
31. 101101_2
32. 110100_3
33. 243_8
34. 22000_4
35. 10001110_2
36. 422_6
37. 111_6
38. 210_5

39. 1100011_2
40. 1102_7
41. 131_4
42. 15_6
43. 1111_2
44. 11100_3
45. 11302_4
46. 234_5
47. 33_8
48. 102122_3
49. 310_8

Exercise 29c **page 482**
1. 43_5
2. 20_3
3. 30_4
4. 11_2
5. 103_6
6. 102_3
7. 115_8
8. 1000_2
9. 122_5
10. 333_4
11. 1151_6
12. 10100_2
13. 1000_3
14 1000_4
15. 1030_7
16. 100001_2
17. 125_6
18. 101_3

19. 3_4
20. 35_7
21. 202_3
22. 11_5
23. 226_8
24. 1_2
25. 133_4
26. 56_7
27. 33_6
28. 10_2
29. 51_6
30. 101_2
31. 646_8
32. 101_3
33. 22_5
34. 12_4
35. 101_3
36. 120_4

37. 32_6
38. 31_5
39. 105_7
40. 180_9
41. 330_4
42. 4105_6
43. 1111_3
44. 1032_5
45. 414_7
46. 130_4
47. 242_5
48. 105_7
49. 1015_6
50. 123_4
51. 143_5
52. 560_8
53. 2_3
54. 214_8

Exercise 29d **page 484**
1. 10221_4
2. 22022_5
3. 1110101_2
4. 2422_8
5. 2011210_3
6. 2116_8
7. 222142_5
8. 2200041_7
9. (a) 2254_8
   (b) 52, 23
   (c) 1196_{10}
   (d) 2254_8
10. (a) 31026_9
   (b) 393, 52
   (c) 20436
   (d) 31026_9
11. 3047_8

Exercise 29e **page 485**
1. (a) 111_2, 101_2, 1010_2, 10000_2, 10011_2, 11000_2
   (b) two
   (c) 1, 10, 11, 100, 101, 110, 111, 1000, 1001, 1010, 1011, 1100, 1101, 1110, 1111, 10000, 10001, 10010, 10011, 10100
   (d) when it ends in zero
   (e) when it ends in one
2. 13, 11, 25, 4, 12, 29
3. (a)

+	0	1
0	0	1
1	1	10

   (b) 10010000_2
4. (a) 6   (b) 101_2
5.

×	0	1
0	0	0
1	0	1

Exercise 29f **page 485**
1. (a) 12_3 (c) 110_3
   (b) 22_3 (d) 1011_3
2. Three
3.

×	0	1	2
0	0	0	0
1	0	1	2
2	0	2	11

4. 11_3
5. (a) 102_5 (b) 33_5 (c) 1103_5
6. $31_5 + \frac{2}{5}$ or 16.4_{10}
7. 0
8. No
9. Four, $5^3 = 1000_5$
10. Eight, $3^7 = 10000000_3$
11. (a) 2, 3, 4, 5, 6, 7, 8
   (b) (i) 11010_2 (ii) 1210_3 (iii) 1750_8
   (c) The figures move one column to the left; i.e. the effect is the same as multiplying a denary number by ten.
12. 6   15. 7   18. 5
13. 4   16. 5   19. 6
14. 3   17. 9   20. False

Exercise 29g **page 486**
1. (a) 6   (b) 5   (c) 147
2. (a) 40_5 (b) 202_3 (c) 24_8
3. (a) 341_5 (b) 101_3 (c) 636_8
4. part (c)